2015

Year B - I

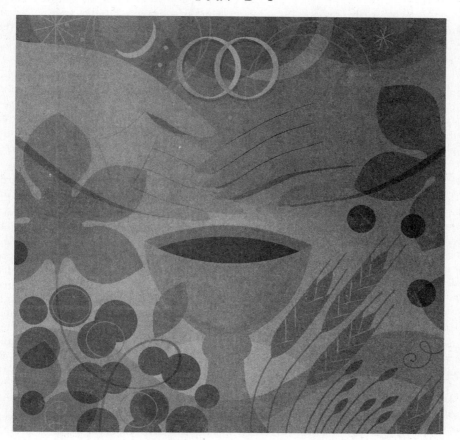

THE ALMANAC FOR PASTORAL LITURGY

SOURCEBOOK

FOR SUNDAYS, SEASONS, AND WEEKDAYS

Charles A. Bobertz

Mary A. Ehle

Claire M. Gilligan

Joseph DeGrocco

Genevieve Glen, OSB

Julie M. Krakora

Graziano Marcheschi

Biagio Mazza

Jo-Ann Metzdorff

Mary M. McGlone, CSJ

Jill Maria Murdy

Michael R. Prendergast

Jakob K. Rinderknecht

Paul Turner

D. Todd Williamson

Trish Sullivan Vanni

LTP

LITURGY
TRAINING
PUBLICATIONS

Nihil Obstat
Very Reverend Daniel A. Smilanic, JCD
Vicar for Canonical Services
Archdiocese of Chicago
December 18, 2013

Imprimatur
Most Reverend Francis J. Kane, DD
Vicar General
Archdiocese of Chicago
December 18, 2013

The *Nihil Obstat* and *Imprimatur* are declarations that the material is free from doctrinal or moral error, and thus is granted permission to publish in accordance with c. 827. No legal responsibility is assumed by the grant of this permission. No implication is contained herein that those who have granted the *Nihil Obstat* and *Imprimatur* agree with the content, opinions, or statements expressed.

CONTENTS

INTRODUCTION

Overview of *Sourcebook*

SOURCEBOOK *for Sundays, Seasons, and Week-days 2015: The Almanac for Pastoral Liturgy* provides guidance regarding the various liturgical elements (music, environment, prayers, readings, etc.) so that communities can prepare liturgies rooted in the vision of the Second Vatican Council.

Sourcebook is organized to help you follow liturgical time in sequence. It begins with Advent, which is the start of the liturgical year, and it continues with Christmas Time. Next begins Ordinary Time, so-named because the Sundays are designated by their ordinal (counted) numbers. *Sourcebook* tags the Sundays in Ordinary Time after Christmas Time and up until Lent as "Ordinary Time (during Winter)." This is not an official description or designation, but merely a chapter heading *Sourcebook* uses to differentiate between the two parts of Ordinary Time.

Next you will find Lent, followed by the Sacred Paschal Triduum, and then Easter Time. After the Solemnity of Pentecost, Ordinary Time resumes. *Sourcebook* refers to this longer stretch as "Ordinary Time (during Summer and Fall)." When Ordinary Time concludes, the next liturgical year begins, so this chapter takes us right up to the end of the liturgical year. A supplemental liturgical music preparation sheet and a checklist for those who serve during the Triduum are available online at www.ltp.org/t-resources.aspx. These sheets may be reproduced and distributed to your ministers for free.

Within each of the chapters of *Sourcebook*, you will find two sections: "The Liturgical Time" and "The Calendar." "The Liturgical Time" is organized into several parts:

- *The Meaning*: the theological meaning and history of the liturgical time or season

- *The Saints*: how the living witness of the saints can deepen and enrich liturgical time

- *The Liturgical Books*: what the *Lectionary for Mass, The Roman Missal,* and other ritual texts tell us about liturgical time; information particular to the third edition of *The Roman Missal* is under this same category

- *The Liturgical Environment*: ideas for the appearance of worship spaces

- *The Liturgical Music*: the musical expression of liturgical time and how to enhance it

- *Devotions and Sacramentals*: ideas to foster the parish's devotional life while emphasizing the primacy of the liturgy

- *Liturgical Ministers*: tips and formational notes for all liturgical ministers

- *Children's Liturgy of the Word*: how to prepare the Sunday children's Liturgy of the Word

- *The Parish and the Home*: how to carry liturgical time from the parish to the domestic Church (at home)

- *Mass Texts*: original prayers for the Order of Mass (where options are permitted)

"The Calendar" is a straightforward almanac for each day of the liturgical year. You can look up any day of the year and find basic liturgical information as well as ideas for how to celebrate it. The primary purpose of *Sourcebook*, however, is to help you celebrate Sundays, solemnities, feasts, and all of liturgical time. For this reason, you will find most of the material in "The Calendar" devoted to Sundays, solemnities, and feasts, which include the following three sections:

◆ *Lectionary for Mass*: an explanation of how the Scriptures of the day relate to what is being celebrated

◆ *The Roman Missal*: insights into the prayers and suggestions about options; particular notes are provided for the third edition of the Missal

◆ *Other Ideas*: Additional ideas for parishes, families, or liturgies

Other days include additional sections:

◆ *"About this . . ."*: what the Church is celebrating on this day and why

◆ *Today's Saint*: Biographies of the saints celebrated on that day

About the Authors

◆ Rev. Mr. Charles A. Bobertz received his BA from St. John's University in 1980 (history and German) and his master of theological studies degree (Scripture) from Harvard University in 1983. He received MA, THM and PHD degrees (New Testament and early Christianity) from Yale University in 1988. He was ordained to the diaconate for the diocese of St. Cloud in 1997. He is professor of New Testament and patristics at St. John's School of Theology*Seminary (MN). Charles provided the Overview of the Gospel According to Mark in this Pastoral Introduction.

◆ Mary A. Ehle holds a doctorate in religious studies from Marquette University in Milwaukee, Wisconsin, as well as degrees from St. John's University in Collegeville, Minnesota, and St. Norbert College in De Pere, Wisconsin. She is an experienced liturgist, pastoral musician, and director of faith formation. Mary provided the Lectionary commentary for Ordinary Time in Winter.

◆ Claire M. Gilligan holds a BA in catechetics from the Franciscan University of Steubenville and an MA in liturgical studies from the Liturgical Institute in Mundelein, Illinois. Claire provided the seasonal overviews for "The Saints," "The Pastoral Care of the Sick," "The Liturgy of the Hours," "The Rite of Christian Initiation of

Adults," "Liturgical Ministers," "Sacramentals and Devotions," and "The Rite of Marriage."

◆ Msgr. Joseph DeGrocco, pastor of Our Lady of Perpetual Help Church, Lindenhurst, New York, and former professor of liturgy and director of liturgical formation at the Seminary of the Immaculate Conception in Huntington, New York, holds an MA in theology (liturgical studies) from the University of Notre Dame and a doctor of ministry degree from the Seminary of the Immaculate Conception. A widely published author, he has provided the seasonal overviews on *The Roman Missal* and the daily Missal commentaries for Ordinary Time (during the Winter), Lent, Triduum, Easter Time, and Ordinary Time (during Summer and Fall).

◆ Genevieve Glen, osb, is a Benedictine nun of the contemplative Abbey of St. Walburga in Virginia Dale, Colorado. She holds master's degrees in systematic theology from Saint John's University, Collegeville, Minnesota, and in spirituality from the Catholic University of America in Washington, DC, where she also did extensive doctoral studies in liturgy. Sr. Genevieve contributed the Lectionary commentaries for Lent.

◆ Julie M. Krakora received her BA in theology from Marquette University and her MA in pastoral studies from Loyola University in Chicago. She has been in professional lay ministry for the past sixteen years through her roles in high school and college campus ministry, as well as a parish youth ministry where she once again currently serves as director. Julie loves to be involved in her own parish choirs and to write anything that will bring people closer in relationship with God. She is the author of many LTP pastoral resources. She has provided "The Parish and the Home" section.

◆ Graziano Marcheschi speaks nationally on liturgy and the arts, Scripture, and lay ministry. He is the executive director of University Ministry at Saint Xavier University, Chicago, and formerly served as director of lay ministry formation for the Archdiocese of Chicago. He holds an MA in drama from the University of Minnesota, an MDiv from Loyola University Chicago, and a DMIN from the University of St. Mary of the Lake. Graz contributed the Lectionary commentaries for Advent and Christmas Time.

◆ Biagio Mazza is pastoral associate at St. Sabina Parish in Belton, Missouri, coordinating and facilitating adult faith formation. Biagio was a staff member of the Center for Pastoral Life and Ministry in the Diocese of Kansas City-St. Joseph for over seventeen years where he did ministry formation. He has a master's degree in theology from Fordham University, Bronx, New York, with postgraduate work at Maryknoll School of Theology, Maryknoll, New York. Biagio provided the Lectionary commentary for Easter Time.

◆ JO-ANN METZDORFF, DMIN, director of religious education and RCIA at the parish of St. Agnes Cathedral in Rockville Centre, New York, holds a bachelor's degree in art education from St. John's University, New York, a master's in elementary education from Adelphi University and a master's in theology from the Seminary of the Immaculate Conception, New York, and the University of Notre Dame. Her doctor of ministry degree is from the Seminary of the Immaculate Conception. Ms. Metzdorff provided the sectionary on Children's Liturgy of the Word in each seasonal overview.

◆ MARY M. McGLONE is a Sister of St. Joseph of Carondelet with a PHD in historical theology. In addition to her scholarly work she has ministered extensively in Latin America and various parts of the United States. She is a member of Most Precious Blood Parish in Denver, Colorado. Mary provided the Lectionary commentary for May 25 through August 29.

◆ JILL MARIA MURDY serves as director of music for a Catholic parish. Her background includes monastic liturgy, small rural parishes, and very large urban parishes. Murdy holds a BA in music from Dickinson State University and an MA in theology from the University of Notre Dame. Jill has provided the "Mass Texts" and "Other Ideas."

◆ MICHAEL R. PRENDERGAST is coordinator of liturgy at St. Andrew Church in Portland, Oregon; an instructor in the Lay Ministry Formation program for the Archdiocese of Portland; and an instructor in the theology department at the University of Portland. Michael has provided the daily commentaries on "The Roman Missal" for Advent and Christmas Time as well as the seasonal overviews for "The Order of Christian Funerals," "The Rite of Penance," and "The Liturgical Music."

◆ JAKOB KARL RINDERKNECHT is a doctoral candidate in systematic theology at Marquette University. He has been involved with parish liturgical ministry across the country and coordinated liturgical environment for the 2011 Southwest Liturgical Conference. His research interests include sacramental and ecumenical theology and their expression in the life of the local Church. Jakob provided the reflections on the "Liturgical Environment."

◆ PAUL TURNER is pastor of St. Anthony Parish in Kansas City, Missouri. A priest of the Diocese of Kansas City-St. Joseph, he holds a doctorate in sacred theology from Sant'Anselmo in Rome. He has published many pastoral resources. Paul provided the Lectionary overviews for the Sacred Paschal Triduum.

◆ D. TODD WILLIAMSON, MTS, is the director of the Office for Divine Worship in the Archdiocese of Chicago. In addition to writing, Todd is a teacher and national speaker in the areas of liturgy and the sacraments. He provided the reflections on the "Book of Blessings."

◆ TRISH SULLIVAN VANNI earned an interdisciplinary doctoral degree in ecclesiology and organizational leadership at the Graduate Theological Union, Berkeley, California. She also holds degrees from St. John's University in Collegeville, Minnesota, and Georgetown University in Washington, DC. Trish has provided the Ordinary Time Scripture commentaries for September 1 through the last Saturday in Ordinary Time.

The Gospel According to Mark

THE primary evangelist for Year B is Mark. As with our other Gospel accounts, the earliest extant manuscripts of the Gospel according to Mark are anonymous and date from the fourth century after Christ. The earliest Christian legend that a Christian named Mark (see Colossians 4:10; Acts of the Apostles 12:12) wrote Mark's Gospel account comes to us from a second century bishop of Hierapolis in Asia Minor, Papias, who tells us Mark was the interpreter of Peter. Scholars disagree on what Papias might have meant by "interpreter" and therefore disagree on how closely the Gospel stories in Mark are related to Peter's teaching. In addition, it is reasonable to conclude that

Mark did have other written sources. He may well have had a written account of the Passion as well as originally independent groups of stories, such as the five controversy stories that run from 2:1 to 3:6. Recent scholarship suggests it is not possible to determine how much Mark edited these earlier sources to fit his own purpose in writing his Gospel.

The original audience for Mark was probably living outside of the Holy Land in a place that was largely populated by non-Jews. We know this because Mark, in some places, appears to be confused about the geography of Palestine (see 5:1 and 7:31) and indicates that his audience would not be familiar with Jewish customs (7:4). He also at times translates Aramaic terms into Greek for his Greek speaking audience (5:41; 15:34).

The date of the Gospel according to Mark depends largely on how one understands Jesus's prediction of the fall of the Jerusalem Temple to the Romans in 70 AD. Those who believe this prediction was created by Mark and not actually spoken by Jesus understand this verse to refer to the actual destruction of the Temple in 70 AD. Thus the Gospel must have been after that date yet early enough to have become a primary source for the other two synoptic Gospel accounts, Matthew and Luke, written some time in the two decades following Mark. Scholars who argue that it is not unlikely that Jesus himself would have made such a prediction about the fall of the Temple often date the Gospel according to Mark to around 60 – 70 AD and even more precisely to the probable time of Peter's death in Rome under the Emperor Nero (c. 64 AD).

It is best to understand Mark not as giving us information about the life of Jesus or as a source of Peter's teaching but rather as a Gospel created by an independent and fascinating theologian who crafted the story of Jesus to communicate deep theological insight about Christian life in Christ. How Mark does this is to take us deep into an understanding of the two primary sacraments of the earliest Christian Churches: the immersion in water known as Baptism and the sacred meal known as the Lord's Supper. This is the vantage point from which the remainder of this introduction will be presented.

The Gospel accounts of Matthew and Luke begin with separate stories about the birth of Jesus in Bethlehem and the early years of the Holy Family. Mark, on the other hand, begins with the baptism of Jesus who is, presumably, already a young adult. And he immediately ties the story of the baptism to the story of the Cross at the end of the Gospel: Jesus is proclaimed Son of God in the first verse and at the foot of the Cross (1:1; 15:39); John the Baptist appears in the guise of the prophet Elijah who is called for by Jesus's detractors at the Cross (1:6; 15:36); the Baptism of the Spirit predicted at 1:8 happens at the Death of Jesus in 15:37; the heavens are torn open at the Baptism (1:10) and the Temple curtain is torn when Jesus dies (15:38). Moreover, Jesus himself within the Gospel according to Mark understands baptism to be associated with his death (10:38 — 39). What this means is that Mark's account from its very first verse invites the reader to consider what it means to be baptized into the Death of Jesus.

In the earliest Christian Churches the practice of admitting uncircumcised Gentiles into the Lord's Supper to eat with the Jews was highly controversial. Paul in his letter to the Galatians describes vividly one encounter in Antioch when he confronted Peter and Barnabas for withdrawing from eating this meal with Gentiles (2:11 — 14). Mark appears to address this same issue in his Gospel account and presents an understanding of Baptism into the death of Christ as the primary means by which non-Jews (Gentiles) are brought into the Christian community with full participation at the Lord's Supper. Mark has Jesus state at 10:45 that his death is a "ransom for the many" which, in the context of the Gospel to this point, refers to the influx of Gentiles into the Christian community.

Gentiles who were baptized as Christians were isolated in ancient society. They could no longer participate in the myriad of pagan rituals that filled the life of the ancient cities (see 1 Corinthians 10:14–23) and, without circumcision, were not considered to be Jews by Jewish Synagogues. This led to both the official and unofficial persecution described vividly in Mark 13:11–13. For Mark such suffering, entered into at Baptism, was participation in the Death of Christ. Yet just as Jesus's suffering and Death, begun at his baptism, led to his glorification, so also would suffering and death entered into at Baptism bring glorification to his disciples (8:35; 10:38–39).

It is however Mark's response to the issue of Gentiles and Jews eating the Lord's Supper together that binds the narrative of Mark into a timeless and powerful theological message of inclusivity. The first eight chapters of Mark depict Jesus himself as beginning the mission to the

Gentiles, a mission which is both misunderstood and resisted by both his Jewish opponents and his earliest Jewish disciples. In chapter two, for example, Jesus heals a paralytic lowered through the roof into his house by "four men," an inclusive number in the ancient world (four winds, four corners of the earth), and commends their faith (2:5). In chapter three Jesus's Jewish family wants him to withdraw from the house (3:32) but Jesus responds by saying that his family is "whoever does the will of God" (3:31), undoubtedly a reference to the Gentiles who have gathered in the house with Jesus.

In Mark, Jesus also commissions the disciples for the Gentile mission. Peter and his brother Andrew are called by Jesus and told that they will become "fishers of men" (1:17). Later upon the completion of the disciples' mission culminating in the first feeding narrative the disciples discover they have, surprisingly, five loaves and two fish for the meal (6:38). The total (five + two) indicates the restoration of the Genesis creation in the Christian meal. Jesus commands the disciples to feed bread to the crowd of Jews and Gentiles and then Jesus himself gives the two fish to everyone gathered. Upon completion of the meal Mark tells us that "everyone ate and was satisfied" and that they took up twelve baskets (an allusion to the twelve tribes of Israel) of bread pieces (6:41 — 43). Immediately after this meal, when Jesus walks upon the water (an allusion to Baptism and Resurrection), the disciples are "surprised because they did not understand about the loaves" (6:52): they did not understand that on the basis of their baptismal death the Gentiles were to be part of the meal experiencing the Resurrection.

The first feeding narrative locates Jesus, his disciples and the crowd somewhere in Jewish Galilee. The second feeding narrative (8:1–11) finds Jesus and the gathering outside of Jewish Galilee and in the Gentile area of the Decapolis (ten Greek cities, 7:31). The disciples' question at 8:4, "how can one feed these people with loaves here in the Wilderness" is a reference to the Gentiles who have gathered at the meal to eat with the Jewish disciples. Here, though, the venue has changed (we are on Gentile soil) and so have the numbers: the disciples come up with seven loaves (again creation restored) and some fish (the number seven is preserved). Again the disciples are commanded to feed the Gentile crowd and everyone eats (8:6–8). In the first feeding narrative Mark described 5,000 males being fed (five is indicative of the five books

of Moses) and twelve baskets of bread pieces being gathered (twelve is indicative of the twelve tribes of Israel). Here, however, Mark states that 4,000 people were fed and seven baskets of bread pieces were gathered. Mark not only refers inclusively to the Gentiles but quite specifically to women as well.

Immediately following this, and in the course of another water and boat episode, the Jewish disciples fail to understand what has just happened. At 8:14 Mark tells us enigmatically that the disciples had forgotten to bring "loaves" but had one "loaf" with them on the boat. The ensuing conversation about being aware of the leaven of the Pharisees and of Herod leads Jesus to ask the disciples about the number of baskets of bread pieces they had taken up in the first and second feeding narrative (twelve and seven respectively): Jesus then asks his disciples what they do not understand about the one loaf they did have with them on the boat (8:21). Thus Mark has Jesus teach his Jewish disciples that the twelve (Jewish) and seven (Gentiles and women) baskets of bread pieces are all part of the one loaf of the Eucharist.

The next time in Mark that we encounter this one loaf is at the Last Supper immediately prior to the Passion and Death of Jesus (14:22–26). Here Jesus takes up the "one loaf" which the reader of Mark now knows constitutes Jews, Gentiles, men and women and declares the one loaf to be his body. This is the body that will suffer and die only to be restored in the new creation which is the Resurrection of Christ. This is also all Christians, then and now, who have become part of the suffering and Death of Christ through Baptism and so joined with him in the new creation of Resurrection celebrated in the meal of the Resurrection.

Writing in a poor Greek style, Mark has created a brilliant theological narrative whose message is as relevant today as it was then: our Baptism unites all of us to Christ and joins us together at the Eucharistic meal to experience a new life and new creation united with God.

—Charles A. Bobertz, PhD

The Gospel According to John

We hear the Gospel according to John proclaimed almost fifty times over the course of the three-year Lectionary cycle of readings. In this Year B, we hear from John on select Sundays in Ordinary Time. John's account was written between 80 and 110 AD in Ephesus, most likely during the latter part of that time period. The Gospel stands as a testimony to the developing Christian community's understanding and lived experience of its faith. Similar to the other Gospel accounts, the writing of John went through stages. Its two endings, one in Jerusalem and one in Galilee, provide evidence of this. The same person who is responsible for the Gospel's main ideas, may, in fact, not be the person responsible for putting the ideas down in writing. The "disciple whom Jesus loved" (John 20:2), the Beloved Disciple, perhaps is the source of the Gospel's ideas and unity. His followers are more than likely responsible for composing the written Gospel and editing it.

We know that at the time John was written, the community of followers faced internal challenges from other Christians who denied the fullness of Jesus's divinity and external challenges from the Jewish leadership who were expelling those who believed in Jesus from the synagogues. These followers wanted to find a way to bring the story of Jesus to bear on the life of their community and the world.

The Gospel writer shows knowledge of the synoptic Gospel accounts. He probably used Mark and Luke more than Matthew, and depended on Mark the most. John's similarity to Mark is seen in the stories of feeding the multitudes, Jesus's walking on water, Peter's confession, and the Passion, among others. There are also sayings in John about Jesus as the Son of Man that parallel sayings in Mark.

Yet even though John had knowledge of one or more of the synoptics, the differences between his account and the other three shows that it also developed independently within the emergent Christian community. In John, Jesus speaks in lengthy discourses, engages in extensive conversations, and uses symbolic language. He does not teach with parables, speak in proverbs, or preach about the kingdom of God. The Gospel writer has Jesus communicate in this manner to convey and explain the truth and meaning of Jesus's unique relationship to the Father. This is crucial for John because he intensely desires that all know the possibility of eternal life that believing in Jesus affords: sharing in the divine life in union with the Father, Son, and Spirit.

While Jesus performs many healings in the synoptic accounts, John's account centers on seven signs or miracle stories: 1) the changing of water into wine at Cana; 2) the cure of the royal official's son; 3) the cure of the paralytic at the pool; 4) the multiplication of loaves; 5) walking on water; 6) the healing of the man born blind; and 7) the raising of Lazarus. John derived these miraculous signs from a "Sign Source."

Whereas the synoptics used a source that contained Jesus's sayings, John almost certainly used a different source for Jesus's lengthy discourses. Most likely, he drew on an earlier account of the Passion and traditions about Jesus's post-Resurrection appearances. The well-known Prologue comes from an early hymn. An editor inserted it and the comments on John the Baptist after the completion of the rest of the Gospel.

One of the noteworthy differences between John and the synoptic accounts is that John does not include a narrative of the institution of the Eucharist in his Last Supper account. Rather, as we know from the liturgy on Holy Thursday, John's account of this meal focuses on Jesus's example of service and humility. John narrates Jesus's actions of washing his disciples' feet and his instructions to the disciples to do the same. John's account of the Last Supper includes lengthy discourses in which Jesus converses with his disciples about grief and loss, his departure and return, and the coming of the Advocate (the Spirit) preparing them for how to live and love as his disciples before he comes again in glory.

John's account is often referred to as the Hellenistic (Greek) Gospel because of what appear to be Greek philosophical influences from Platonism, Stoicism, and Gnosticism on his thought. Based on the contrasts between above / below, spirit / flesh, natural world / eternal world, light / dark, truth / falsehood, and the use of *Logos* (Word), it makes sense to see Greek philosophical influences on John's account. John wrote his Gospel in a particular cultural milieu colored by these philosophies. The Gospel writer's use of these philosophies serves his purpose of proclaiming the truth of Jesus as the Messiah, the Son of God.

John presumes those who hear the Gospel are familiar with the story of Jesus and John the Baptist. His audience was primarily Christians who would recognize titles for Jesus such as Son of God and Son of Man. They would have understood the references to Baptism, the Lord's supper, and the Advocate (the Spirit). Though John primarily addressed his account to Christians, he also has in mind those who do not yet believe and desires their conversion.

Prophetic sayings and major themes of the Old Testament would resonant with John's audience. When John speaks of the Word becoming flesh, he knows his hearers versed in Judaism would hearken back to the divine Word in Genesis. John assumes they know Jewish feasts such as Passover and the leadership institutions of Judaism.

John identifies the purpose of his Gospel as helping to lead people to faith in Jesus (see John 20:30–31). The themes of his Gospel serve this purpose. The contrast between belief and unbelief is continuous throughout the Gospel. Belief in Jesus brings life and salvation. Unbelief is the source of darkness and death. Belief means acceptance of Jesus. Unbelief is rejection of the Son of God. Belief itself is a gift the Father gives. Those who are Jesus's adversaries lack faith and do not receive eternal life.

John's account is full of Christological themes. Primary among them is his portrayal of Jesus as the Son of God who has a special, unique relationship with the Father. Jesus reveals the Father to those who believe. How does Jesus reveal the Father? Jesus is the preexistent, creative *Logos* / Word related to divine Wisdom of the Old Testament whom the Father sends "from above." He is the Son of Man who descends to earth, becomes flesh to be one with us and among us, and who ascends and returns to the Father when he completes his earthly mission. Jesus reveals the Father's glory in his triumph on the Cross.

Other themes in John include how he understands the end of the world and the Second Coming of Jesus (eschatology), the Church (ecclesiology), and the sacraments (sacramentalism). When people believe in Jesus, the Messiah gifts them with eternal life. They do not need to wait until the end of time to receive this wondrous gift. They already hold inside themselves the glory of the end times. This gift allows us now to live out of his glory for the benefit of the world, so that others might come to believe and live as God's beloved children.

In John's account it is easy to see the importance of individual belief in Jesus, but those who believe also serve together as Jesus's disciples. The Church is a community of close-knit disciples who dearly love God, love Jesus, and love one another in the Spirit. They know their mission in the world will not be without struggle, even persecution, so they must remain intent on staying together as a community. This community takes as its model Jesus's own humility and service.

John focuses on the meaning of the Sacraments of Baptism and Eucharist within the Christian community. Although he provides few details, he understands that, in Baptism, God calls us to be God's children and God pours forth the Spirit on us. The waters of Baptism are waters of eternal life born of Jesus's own Death and Resurrection. The Eucharist is the Bread of Life. John's inclusion of lengthy Bread of Life discourses underscores the importance of this sacrament. Jesus is food for us now and Jesus is eternally food for us; he is water and food that forever quenches our thirst and satiates our hunger.

John used the phrase "the Jews" as a functional device to develop his theme of belief and unbelief. "The Jews" were antagonizing characters to Jesus and set in opposition to those who believed in him. Most often, the term related to Jewish leadership, not the entire Jewish people as a particular ethnic or religious people. In either case, it is necessary to remember the historical context of John's time when Christians faced expulsion from synagogues and not to extend this situation to our present context to justify anti-Semitism.

The early Church Father Clement of Alexandria called John's account the "spiritual Gospel." We must not think of his Gospel as "spiritual" in the sense of being unconcerned with the world. His is a Gospel entirely grounded in reality because Jesus is the Son of God made flesh—affords us the opportunity to reflect on the central questions "Who is Jesus for us?" and "Who are his disciples?" in light of our world today, a world always and everywhere longing for the life and food only Jesus the Messiah can give.

—Mary A. Ehle, PHD

ADVENT

The Liturgical Time

The Meaning / The Lectionary for Mass

ADVENT is always fraught with tension between what it "wants" to be and what it "needs" to be. But complaining against the commercialism that overshadows the religious observance of Advent is futile at best. It may be better to let the culture do what it wants to do, even if that means Christmas decorations in stores the day after Thanksgiving, and let us Christians do what we need to do: recognize the fullness of this complex season and celebrate that fullness amidst the colored lights and reindeer, music and the parties, and Christmas wishes.

That may sound like rationalization, but it's actually a call for fervent, consistent, and uncompromising expression of all we believe this holy season to be. And that is best done not by lamenting how the culture is missing the boat, but by being fully focused on hitting the mark. And the mark, of course, is Christ. Christ who came among us as a child born in the humblest of circumstances and who will come again as the King.

Because God came among us and transformed human life, the vulgar and mundane can't silence God's voice nor veil his splendor. Nothing we do can change God or lessen his love for us or his desire to claim our hearts. But what can be affected by what we do is our ability to hear and see, to listen and respond. That is why Advent has two equally important foci.

The first calls us to celebrate God present among us, here and now. The Incarnation is both a historical and an ongoing event: Christ is still taking on flesh and he is continually present through his body, the Church. Living in the now is essential because the present is the only place we can encounter God. But Christianity reminds us that in Christ we also have a future, Advent's second focus. Just as Christ came at Bethlehem and now lives in us, he will come again in the fullness of time when he will judge the living and the dead.

That message could inspire fear, but only if we divorce what will happen in the future from what happened in the past. When we recall the humility of God made flesh in the humble circumstances of Bethlehem, we can trust it will be a God of love and mercy before whom we stand on Judgment Day.

The Church relies on the prophet Isaiah for the substance of some of the season's main themes. From his pen and through his poetry we hear of repentance for sin, inner conversion, and the salvation God offers not only to Israel but to the nations. Advent also calls us to assume a posture of waiting; tutored by Israel's example, we long for the savior's appearance. It invites us to prepare ourselves for the celebration of Jesus's birth and for the day we stand before him in judgment. The Northern Hemisphere's shortening days and lengthening nights underscore Advent's theme of light—for a light has come into the world that dispels all darkness.

◆ SUNDAYS: Throughout Advent, most of the Old Testament readings come from the book of the prophet Isaiah. In the Year B cycle of Sunday readings, we will hear from Isaiah three times and once from 2 Samuel. These readings follow a progression from the urgent cry, "Rend the heavens and come down" (Isaiah 63:19), to a word of comfort for God's people, the promise that God's Chosen One will care for all the poor, and, finally, God's promise to raise up a Savior from the house of David. Each of these readings contributed in its own way to sustain Israel's hope for salvation and the coming of the Messiah.

The psalms of Advent correspond beautifully with the messages of the First Readings. In Psalm 80 on the First Sunday of Advent, after crying,

"Rouse your power, / and come!" (80:3), we beg to see the saving face of the Lord. Responding to Isaiah's words of comfort on the Second Sunday of Advent, we announce the nearness of salvation. On the Third Sunday, we sing with Mary that Isaiah's promises have been fulfilled. Finally, on the last Sunday before Christmas, we proclaim God's kindness and that the throne of his Son will last forever. At the same time, these psalms look forward to the Gospel messages of hoping for Christ's presence and watching for his return.

Advent's Second Readings are chosen from four different letters and underscore the themes of each of the Sundays. What unites them is their unwavering focus on God's promises. From 1 Corinthians, we hear of God's faithfulness. The Second Letter of Peter reminds us that God has promised new heavens and earth. On the Third Sunday, we are told to rejoice because God can bring us to holiness. Finally, Paul calls us to give glory to the God whose mystery we have seen revealed.

In this liturgical year, we will hear the Year B cycle of readings, mainly focusing on the Gospel according to Mark. During Advent, however, we will hear from Mark on the first two Sundays, from John on the third, and from Luke on the fourth. The reason for this, as we shall see throughout this year, is that Mark's account of the Gospel is significantly more compact than the others. Mark says less than the others about John the Baptist and has no infancy narrative at all.

The progression of these Gospel readings seemingly reverses our understanding of chronological order. We begin with a focus on Christ's coming at the end of time. After that, we have two presentations of John the Baptist's witness to Jesus, the one who will come after him. Finally, we hear the narrative of the Annunciation in which Mary speaks the words that summarize her life: "May it be done to me according to your word" (Luke 1:38). From beginning to end, the message is clear: the Christ who came will return, and his kingdom will have no end.

During the earlier weeks of Advent, the Lectionary draws heavily from Isaiah following the progression of the book through its most important passages, even reprising those most significant texts that are also read on Sundays. Isaiah paints images of Edenic peace and of a king who will rule with justice. The daily Gospel selection is related to the First Reading, but by Thursday of the second week the Gospel pericopes begin to focus on John the Baptist.

For the last week of the season, Matthew and Luke are used to narrate the events that led to the Incarnation. At this point, the First Reading is chosen specifically to correspond with the Gospel and is drawn from various Old Testament books that contain messianic prophecies.

◆ WEEKDAYS: Within the two series of weekday readings (early Advent and the last week of Advent) we can discern three separate movements. First are the Isaiah texts read consecutively during fourteen of the first seventeen weekdays of Advent. The second movement—occurring during weeks two and three—brings John the Baptist to the fore. Of this great figure we hear that none greater than he was born, that the people rejected him and the Son of Man, that in him Elijah came but was not recognized, that he baptized, that sinners believed in him, and that John was a "messenger" and a "burning and shining lamp." The third movement during Advent's final week recounts the details we most associate with the Christmas story: Jesus's genealogy, the prophetic dreams of Joseph, the announcements of the births of John and Jesus, Mary's hurried visit to her cousin Elizabeth and her remarkable *Magificat*, the birth and naming of John, and the Benedictus—Zechariah's hymn of gratitude and blessing.

Advent's final days also provide an opportunity to reflect, in the form of the O Antiphons, on the various titles the Old Testament writers gave to the longed-for Messiah: O Wisdom . . . O Adonai . . . O Root of Jesse . . . O Key of David . . . O Rising Sun (Dayspring) . . . O King of the Nations . . . O Emmanuel. The titles speak of our own longing to be embraced by the Wisdom of ages; by the God of unspeakable name who summoned Moses from the burning bush; by the root of Jesse and the key of David who rules nations and liberates prisoners; by the morning star, the eternal sun of righteousness; by the king of nations who comes to save; and by Emmanuel, God with us and in us who works for us and through us.

Such are the longings of Advent. Such are the prayers of God's people expressed in all of Advent's liturgies. An interesting feature of the antiphons makes them a worthy conduit of Advent's spirituality. In Latin, and ordered from last to first, the initial letters of the seven antiphons form an acrostic that spells the Latin words *ero cras* which means, "Tomorrow, I will come." Individually, the antiphons express the Church's Advent longing for the coming of the Lord; collectively, they spell out for us his reassuring response.

The Roman Missal

ADVENT texts in *The Roman Missal* are found as the first segment of the Proper of Time. Every day has its own Mass—a proper Entrance Antiphon, Collect, Prayer over the Offerings, Communion Antiphon, and Prayer after Communion are provided. Formularies begin with the First Sunday of Advent and end with the Morning Mass for December 24. Starting with December 17, date-specific Mass formularies are given, and must be used, for the corresponding day, that is, December 17, December 18, December 19, and so on. Consequently, use of the non-date specific weekdays of Advent (for example, Monday of the First Week of Advent, Wednesday of the Second Week of Advent, etc.) is discontinued and the date-specific Mass formularies are used, except for the Fourth Sunday of Advent, when that Mass replaces whatever date it falls on.

The Collects reflect the overall sense of joyful expectation and this thematic movement from the Second Coming to the Nativity. Images and phrases such as the Christian people having "the resolve to run forth to meet your Christ / with righteous deeds at his coming" (First Sunday of Advent), to the request for their being found to be "worthy of the banquet of eternal life" (Wednesday of the First Week of Advent), and of their hastening, "alert and with lighted lamps, to meet him when he comes" all give expression to the theme of the Second Coming, while, as of the Third Sunday of Advent, the Collects shift to speak of "faithfully await[ing] the feast of the Lord's Nativity" and go on to refer specifically to the Virgin Mary (for example, December 19 and 20) and the Incarnation (for example, Fourth Sunday of Advent, and December 20 and 22).

Communities may wish to consider marking the liturgical time by consistent use of selected texts. For example, if one form of the greeting is usually used, priest celebrants might consider switching to another form during Advent. Although for the Penitential Act any invocations may be used for the third form (#6 in the Order of Mass), Option I as found in the Sample Invocations for the Penitential Act in Appendix VI at the back of the Missal might be most appropriate, as those invocations highlight past, present, and future comings of Christ. Option II, using phrases such as "mighty God and Prince of peace," "Son of Mary," and "Word made flesh" might also be a good choice, although this set of invocations might also be better left for Christmas Time.

The first or second acclamations for "The Mystery of Faith," insofar as they both refer to Christ's coming again, might be preferable over the third option for this liturgical time.

The Gloria is omitted during Advent, except for the Solemnity of the Immaculate Conception and the Feast of Our Lady of Guadalupe. The Creed, usually omitted on weekdays, is said on the Solemnity of the Immaculate Conception.

There are two seasonal Prefaces, the first two in a series of Prefaces found in the Order of Mass as part of the Eucharistic Prayer. Preface I of Advent, which speaks of the two comings of Christ, is used from the First Sunday of Advent to December 16 and in other Masses during Advent that do not have their own proper Preface. And Preface II of Advent, which describes the expectation of Christ's coming and specifically mentions the Nativity, is used in Masses of Advent from December 17 to December 24. These Prefaces may still be used even if Eucharistic Prayer for Reconciliation II is used.

There is an option to use a Solemn Blessing over the people that is specific to Advent; priest celebrants should give due consideration to using this three-part blessing, at least on Sundays. It can be found in the section "Blessings at the end of Mass and Prayers Over the People" which immediately follows the Order of Mass in the Missal. There is also the possibility of selecting one of the twenty-six choices for a Prayer over the People.

Children's Liturgy of the Word

DURING Advent we wait in joy and hope. It is similar to the joy that parents experience waiting for a child to be born. Children can relate to this comparison well, and the image of the pregnant Mary waiting for the birth of Jesus is familiar and endearing for the children. The fact that Advent comes at a time of year in the Northern Hemisphere when the days are at their shortest, and in some areas days are dark and bleak, is also a fitting image for this season. This darkness is a great way to connect to the truth of Christ's coming into the world to dispel the darkness and to offer the hope of salvation. The images of light are prevalent during this season and it is worthwhile to emphasize this in some way with the children. Connect it with decorating their homes with lights as a way to await the birth of Christ, the Light of the World.

◆ ADVENT READINGS: During Advent, however, we will only hear Mark's account on the First and Second Sundays of Advent. Mark does not include an Infancy Narrative or stories leading to the birth of Jesus in his Gospel account, but begins with John the Baptist proclaiming the coming of Christ. John the Baptist is a prominent figure in the Advent readings as is the concept of watching and waiting for the coming Messiah. For Mark, it is not an infant Christ-child that we are preparing for, but for the Second Coming of Christ at the end of time. This is what the Gospel accounts from the weeks previous to Advent have been leading up to. The third week, John's account of the Gospel leads us deeper into the concept of preparing through the testimony of John the Baptist pointing out Jesus as the one who is to come. The Gospel for the Fourth Sunday of Advent is from Luke's account and presents the familiar story of the Annunciation that serves as a segue into Christmas Time.

The First and Second readings during Advent speak of the promise of a Messiah and of how we are to prepare, especially through the prophecies of Isaiah. Children can understand the sense of waiting anxiously and also of being good in preparation for Christmas. Yet it needs to be emphasized that we are preparing for Jesus and that being good prepares us for his coming more than for expecting presents.

◆ ADVENT ENVIRONMENT: Each season of the year has a character that is reflected in the worship space. Advent is a season of joyful anticipation. The color for Advent is violet. Violet is a color associated with penitence and as such we use it also during Lent. Advent does have a penitential character to it but it is not a mini-Lent. The color reminds us that we are called to prepare ourselves for the Lord's coming by opening up our hearts to him, seeking forgiveness as we await his coming. Violet is also the color of royalty and the use of it in ancient times indicated wealth and power. We are reminded that during this season we are awaiting the birth of the king of heaven and earth. For Advent some parishes make use of deep bluish violet. This color also reminds us of the color of the clear dark winter sky filled with stars, a popular image used in many Advent and Christmas carols. Don't forget that the Third Sunday of Advent is Gaudete Sunday. *Gaudete* is Latin for "Rejoice," which is the first word of the Entrance Antiphon for this Sunday. We make use of the liturgical color rose as a sign of our approaching joy.

An Advent wreath prominently but not overbearingly displayed in the children's space and lit at the beginning of the session again connects the children to what happens in the larger assembly. Avoid using any Christmas decorations in the worship space until Christmas.

◆ Music: Advent is such a short season and it is unfortunate that we do not have an extended opportunity to sing the many beautiful Advent hymns and carols. There are a good number of Advent hymns that are very appropriate for young children and some specifically written for them. Ask your parish music director to help you in choosing music or to offer assistance in leading the children in song. Helping the children learn and sing these Advent hymns keeps our musical tradition alive for future generations instead of being lost. Just as with our Christmas hymns and carols, Advent hymns should become ones that we welcome and look forward to singing each Advent. You can have a hymn sung as the children enter the space or close your session with the same one that the main assembly is singing as the children return to their parents.

The Saints

THE preeminent feast of Advent, especially in the United States, is the Immaculate Conception of the Blessed Virgin Mary. Why do we let this solemnity of Our Lady temporarily overshadow our Advent preparations for the coming of Our Lord? The simplest answer is that we celebrate the Nativity of Mary nine months later, but this response does little to illumine the timing of the solemnity, although it does furnish us with the interesting report of the widespread historical

precedent for celebrating her birth on or around September 8. Still, important though historicity is, historical accuracy cannot be the only reason for retaining such a solemnity in a Church with as rich a sacramental economy as ours.

There is a sort of thematic connection between the Immaculate Conception and Christmas: on a natural level, the conception of the one makes possible the birth of the other. Indeed, his birth explains her Immaculate Conception — not so much the fact that she was conceived as that, at the very same moment, she was preserved from original sin.

Precisely because she did not bear with her the marks of original sin, Our Lady was able to consent perfectly to God's will, and to prepare herself for his coming. In the season of Advent, when we are all focused on Christ's coming in our own lives, perhaps the Church has given us the Immaculate Conception to inspire us to be as virtuous, as obedient, as faithful as she, in the face of this newborn Child upon whom depends so much.

The Liturgy of the Hours

AH, the Divine Office in Advent! This is one of the places where the prayer of the Church really shines. Not only does the Office show clearly a sense of liturgical time, but the famous "O Antiphons" come originally from Vespers during the nine days preceding Christmas: rooting us all in a sort of official novena leading up to the coming of Our Lord.

As you may have seen elsewhere, if one lines up the O Antiphons as in an acrostic and reads their first letters backward from December 23 back through December 17 the letters spell *ero cras* — "I will come tomorrow." But it is not merely the beauty of the O Antiphons that moves me; it's the vitality given to Vespers by their presence. Now that the O Antiphons have been copied into the Lectionary as each day's Gospel acclamation verse, more Catholics are exposed to them in a liturgical setting. The importance the O Antiphons have continued to hold in the life of the Church gives us some insight into the importance of Vespers, and especially into the primacy of each day's *Magnificat* antiphon. This single prayer sets the tone for the entire liturgical day, even though it might not be first prayed until the evening hours.

Evening is a time of vigil, and in these last days of Advent, the Liturgy of the Hours remind us that we are truly keeping vigil for Our Lord.

The Rite of Christian Initiation of Adults

IT takes energy to catechize and lovingly challenge members of the parish staff, Catholic school teachers, catechists, parishioners, and, yes, even sometimes our pastors to keep the season of Advent with "devout and expectant delight" (*Universal Norms on the Liturgical Year and the General Roman Calendar* [UNLY], 39). Preparing the seasonal environment, music, liturgy, domestic Church celebrations, devotions and sacramentals (for example, Advent wreath, *Las Posadas*, *Simbang Gabi*) and the special days of the season (St. Nicholas, the Immaculate Conception, St. Juan Diego, Our Lady of Guadalupe, and St. Lucy), and the communal celebration of the Sacrament Reconciliation already places high demands on the parish staff during these short four or so weeks. All of these celebrations and sounds of the season are opportunities for the formation of catechumens and candidates which should be "gradual and complete in its coverage, accommodated to the liturgical year, and solidly supported by the celebrations of the word" (*Rite of Christian Initiation of Adults* [RCIA], 75.1).

Celebrating the richness of the season of Advent requires that our time and energy be spent counter culturally and fully embracing the mystery of these days and fully living in the tension of the "already but not yet." Since the "Advent plate" is so full one should look at another time in the liturgical year for celebrating the Rite of Acceptance. The Rite of Christian Initiation of Adults tells us "the rite of acceptance into the order of catechumens is to take place when the time is right" (RCIA, 28). In further exploring the ritual we also discover that during the period of the catechumenate the catechumen should have "sufficient time to conceive an initial faith and to show the first signs of conversion" (RCIA, 18). This right time can hardly be "scheduled" for the First Sunday of Advent.

The first period of the RCIA is evangelization and pre-catechumenate (see RCIA, 36 – 40), also known as the period of inquiry. During this period, teaching is given to people who are interested in learning more about the Catholic faith. The sessions cover basic information about the faith and fundamentally communicate the Gospel of Jesus Christ. The Church is offering here an invitation to initial conversion. There is no obligation involved in attending these meetings—they are intended to help a person decide whether they want to continue learning about the faith. Attendees at this stage are known as inquirers.

Catechumens are dismissed from the liturgical assembly after the Homily. They are called to reflect on the rich and powerful images of the Advent cycle of readings. For catechumens, candidates and inquirers, Advent is a season to cultivate the seeds of faith that have been planted in the hearts and minds of these seekers.

The Sacraments of Initiation

At their November meeting in 2013, the United States Bishops approved the new translation of the *Rite of Confirmation.* At the time of this printing, the revised text is still pending the *recognitio* from the Holy See.

THE Rites of Baptism for Children, Confirmation, and first Holy Communion may be scheduled during the season of Advent. Because the main focus is Advent with its prayers and readings, it may not be the most opportune time to celebrate these sacraments during Sunday Mass.

Ritual Masses are prohibited on Sundays of Advent. This means that the readings and prayers of the sacramental rite cannot be used, though the sacrament itself could be celebrated.

The Rite of Penance

ADVENT is not considered a penitential season but rather a period of "devout and expectant delight" (UNLY, 39). Celebrating the Sacrament of Penance should be part of one's preparation for the season of the Incarnation.

Extend an invitation to members of the faith community to participate in celebrations of the *Rite of Penance* (RP), Form I. Be sure to schedule additional opportunities for people to celebrate the sacrament, especially during the days preceding the celebration of Christmas. Take advantage of the parish's website to promote the celebrations of the sacrament and reach out to those who have been estranged from the Church or the community and invite them back.

The penitential celebrations found in Appendix II in the *Rite of Penance* are golden opportunities for various groups in the parish to prepare for "a more fruitful celebration of the sacrament of penance" (see RP, Appendix II, 1). These celebrations which do not include sacramental confession and absolution may be celebrated during the season leading up to the parish's communal penance service using Form II or preparing for the celebration of the sacrament using Form I. These celebrations may be led by a lay leader of prayer, a catechist, or a deacon. Appendix II of the *Rite of Penance* includes celebrations for Advent, children, young people, and the sick.

Communal penance services using Form II of the *Rite of Penance* are popular in many faith communities during Advent. Encourage penitents to stay after individual confession and remain with the entire community in prayer until the service has officially ended.

Perhaps a small candle could be given to each penitent by the confessor, which in turn could be lit from the Advent wreath and then placed in a bowl of sand. The light from these candles can prepare us for the light of the Incarnation that is soon to be upon us. Be sure to provide a prayer card or a small booklet of prayers or Scripture for the community to use as a reflection while others are celebrating the sacrament. After all have celebrated the sacrament the rite calls for the "Proclamation of Praise for God's Mercy" (RP, 56). While any psalm, hymn, or litany may be sung in acknowledging God's power and mercy, the ritual book suggests the "Canticle of Mary" followed by a concluding prayer, blessing, and dismissal.

When celebrating communal penance services during Advent, consider scheduling them at various times during the day and evening. Not all parishioners are able to come out for celebrations that are scheduled only during the evening hours. Plan to invite as many priests as possible from the local area to serve as ministers of the sacrament. The ritual book includes several options for readings or the readings from Advent, especially those that use the imagery of light and darkness and the call to conversion as found in the story of John the Baptist.

Consider obtaining several copies of LTP's *Preparing for Confession: Receiving God's Mercy* by Paul Turner. This small booklet is a marvelous aid for preparing one to celebrate the sacrament and opens up the richness and power of the sacrament. Place these booklets on tables near the entrances to the church, the reconciliation chapel, and in the confessionals. This booklet is also available in Spanish.

The Rite of Marriage

At their November meeting in 2013, the United States Bishops approved the new translation of the *Rite of Marriage* (their approved text uses the title, *Order of Celebrating Matrimony*). At the time of this printing, the revised text is still pending the *recognitio* from the Holy See.

ADVENT is not exactly prime wedding season. Behind the scenes in most American churches, there seems to be a mixture of busyness and idleness. Busy because everyone is executing preparations for the Christmas liturgies, decorating the church, and planning celebratory parties. Yet at the same time idle because everyone else is so busy, all you can really do is your own independent work.

This down time can be a perfect opportunity to closely examine wedding policies, volunteer liturgical minister rosters and training sessions, and any other preparation work that goes on to ensure that the marriages celebrated throughout the year can be more smoothly carried out, more fruitfully prayed, and less stressful on everyone.

In all things, Advent is a time of preparation and waiting. Those involved in ministry to couples to be married, even if only on the day of the wedding itself, can take advantage of this brief break from the ministry to meditate on Mary and Joseph's path to marriage, and to pray for engaged couples, newlyweds, and their coming children. Would that they each might keep "all these things, reflecting on them in [their] heart" (Luke 2:19).

The Pastoral Care of the Sick

ADVENT seems to be the time of year when many people most remember their brothers and sisters in nursing homes. Christmas parties, Christmas presents, Christmas caroling—the season of giving extends to those who might otherwise be forgotten, and everyone seems to remember their infirm elders all at once.

But, as anyone involved in bringing Communion to the sick knows, nursing homes are but the tip of the iceberg. What about the homebound? Unless visited quite frequently by their families, many homebound people's only source for the holiday spirit is television and the radio! Now, their circumstances preclude the kind of large group celebration that's possible and even common in nursing homes, but even the weekly (or daily) delivery of the Blessed Sacrament to such a Christian should be festive as well.

Imagine the joy, the reminder of Advent, the extended presence of the community, if the priest, deacon, or extraordinary minister bringing Communion to homebound parishioners carried an Advent wreath with him or her and lighted it while singing an Advent hymn at the beginning of the Communion service? He (or she) ought to realize before each visit that he brings to this homebound sister or brother in Christ not only the Most Blessed Sacrament, but also the whole Church community, in a way that is only more profound during this sacred season of preparation.

Another idea might be to send each extraordinary minister with cards from the priest(s) offering their willingness to come to the parishioner's house at a time to be scheduled in order to celebrate the Sacrament of Penance for them and their family members or caretakers. This sacrament of healing, often as part of the continuous rite of Anointing of the Sick, is especially appropriate as a way of preparing for Christ's threefold coming—in history, at the end of time, and in our hearts—and again serves to bring the Church community to the parishioner who seems so far from it.

Uniting the sick with the whole parish community is a difficult task, especially for those parishioners who live alone or with only a caretaker, but with the spirit of Advent for a guide, many parochial graces can yet be shared, in the name of him who is to come so very soon.

The Order of Christian Funerals

As with all of our sacramental celebrations, ongoing catechesis is essential. Authentic catechesis on the *Order of Christian Funerals* (OCF) helps us realize the ultimate meaning of our faith journey begun at Baptism and fulfilled in our belief that death is not the end. The *Order of Christian Funerals* presumes full and fruitful use of *Pastoral Care of the Sick* (PCS). The OCF picks up both ritually and contextually where the PCS leaves off. The OCF is primarily about the ministry of consolation, offering comfort in time of grief or distress. Christians who minister consolation to the bereaved do so in the context of their own faith and those who console must be at home with an understanding of death that is rooted in the Paschal Mystery of Christ.

The OCF encourages the priest to be sensitive "to the possible needs for reconciliation" and calls for the minister to aid in the "process of reconciliation when needed" (OCF, 13). Ritual Masses for the dead are not allowed on the Sundays of Advent and on the Solemnity of the Immaculate Conception. The funeral Mass may be celebrated on any other day during Advent. The color of vestments for the funeral liturgy may be white, violet, or black. Psalm 25, the seasonal or common psalm for Advent, is a good choice for funerals. Many of the suggested readings in the *Order of Christian Funerals* include themes of hope and waiting such as Job (#1), Isaiah (#4), and Daniel (#6) and from the New Testament Romans (#5 and #6), 1 Corinthians (#8), Thessalonians (#13), and Revelation (#19). These readings look toward the Second Coming of Christ and would be appropriate choices for the funeral liturgy. Appropriate Gospel passages include Luke's account of the wise and foolish virgins (#3), Matthews's parable of the last judgment (#4), and the description of the resurrection of the dead by John (#11). *The Roman Missal* contains six prefaces for the dead which can be used at funeral Masses.

The Book of Blessings

THE *Book of Blessings* provides a wonderful way for the community to develop and deepen the liturgical life of the parish. For many of the orders of blessings found in the *Book of Blessings*, there is the option of celebrating them outside of Mass or within Mass. Some blessings can only be celebrated within Mass. Exploring these blessings with the parish can extend the praise and thanksgiving that is at the heart of the Sunday celebration of the Eucharist in a profound way. At the same time it can be a solid way to "round out" the parish's liturgical life.

The Blessing of the Advent Wreath

The primary order of blessing for Advent is the Blessing of the Advent Wreath (chapter 47). Although it originated as a home devotion, the Advent wreath has become a seasonal staple in just about every parish church. As a means of helping to mark the passing of the season, it is a symbol of the hopeful expectation of Advent. It is quite fitting then that the community should gather at the beginning of the season to bless the wreath. Context for the blessing

The Order of Blessing the Advent Wreath can be celebrated either within the first Mass of Advent, within a separate Liturgy of the Word, or the celebration of Evening Prayer.

Most parishes will bless the wreath within the celebration of Mass. In this case, the blessing takes place *after the Universal Praye*r (Prayer of the Faithful)—the prayer of blessing serves as the concluding prayer to the Universal Prayer. The *Book of Blessings* includes intercessions that can be used or adapted for the specific needs of the parish. Consider using these intercessions because the imagery of the texts beautifully incorporates the themes of Advent. After the prayer of blessing, the first violet candle on the wreath is lit and the Mass continues with the Preparation of the Altar and Gifts. (Note that white candles may also be used.)

The *Book of Blessings* clearly presumes that the wreath is blessed only once, either before or at the first Mass of the season. It is not appropriate to repeat the blessing at each Mass. In fact, for every Mass that follows, the candle(s) of the wreath are lit before Mass begins or immediately before the Collect and no further rites or prayers are used. If the wreath is blessed within a celebration of a Liturgy of the Word or Evening Prayer (Vespers), the order of blessing presumes that the celebration takes place before the first Mass of Advent. If there is no Saturday evening Vigil Mass, for example, then blessing the wreath within either of these liturgies would be very appropriate.

If the wreath is blessed within a separate service of a Liturgy of the Word, the order of service includes the following elements:

- ◆ Hymn
- ◆ Greeting
- ◆ Introductory Comments
- ◆ Reading
- ◆ Psalm
- ◆ Intercessions
- ◆ Lord's Prayer
- ◆ Prayer of Blessing of the Wreath
- ◆ Concluding Rite

The *Book of Blessings* provides options for the readings and the psalm.

If the wreath is being blessed within the celebration of Evening Prayer (Vespers), the order of service includes the following elements:

- ◆ Introductory Verse
- ◆ Hymn
- ◆ Psalmody (two psalms and a New Testament canticle)
- ◆ Reading
- ◆ Responsory
- ◆ Gospel Canticle
- ◆ Intercessions (may be taken from the Order of Blessing)
- ◆ Lord's Prayer
- ◆ Prayer of Blessing of the Wreath
- ◆ Dismissal

Ministries

The ordinary minister of blessing is a bishop, priest, or deacon. However, the *Book of Blessings* does allow for trained lay persons to preside when the ritual is within a Liturgy of the Word or Evening Prayer. The order of blessing carefully details the words, gestures, and postures assumed by the lay presider.

Time for the Celebration

As noted, most parishes will bless the Advent wreath within the first Mass of Advent, and for the majority of parishes in the United States this is the Saturday evening vigil Mass. If there is no

Saturday evening Mass or other liturgical celebration the blessing takes place during the first Mass on Sunday morning.

The Liturgical Environment

IN the dark of December, wakefulness can be difficult. Our bodies want to slow down, to be quiet in the longer nights and colder days. The liturgical environment should both reflect the quiet and the dark in which we wait and encourage our ongoing vigil for the coming Lord. The traditional symbols do both of these things—if we don't clutter them up or relegate them to second-place behind a bright, noisy, commercial Christmas Time. The color of the season is violet, ideally a different violet than that used for Lent. Advent's violets should be more at the blue end of the spectrum, reminiscent of the night sky just before the dawn. Different, complementary violets can be combined to add to the sense that the dawn is at hand, although as in all fabric choices for church, it is important that they enhance the action of the liturgy without drawing undue attention away from the central actions of Word and Eucharist. At the Third Week of Advent, the Church traditionally breaks with the violet of the season and may use rose in response to the Introit and the readings for that week which proclaim joy in the coming Lord. Rose in Advent further underscores the dawn imagery of the season, and ideally draws from those colors of the pre-morning sky, instead of being a pure, shocking, pink.

Light imagery is replete throughout the texts we hear, and invites creative use of light in this season. Central to this motif is the Advent wreath, a devotional practice that has found a home in many liturgical spaces. Many churches have Advent wreaths on stands that sit in the sanctuary, while others suspend a wreath from the ceiling. Wherever it is, it should not block the sight lines to the ambo or altar. The wreath should be of a size proportional to the space in which it is displayed, beautiful, and well-made. Ideally, a parish should have one wreath, rather than many smaller wreaths scattered through offices, classrooms, and the church. It need not be in the sanctuary; it may be better in some parishes to place a wreath in a central space where it will be seen more regularly. In this case, the assembly could process to the wreath on the First Sunday of Advent for the blessing.

Wreaths are usually constructed out of live greenery. Misting the boughs with water daily will help preserve them throughout the season. Oftentimes, reasonably fresh greenery can be procured without cost from sellers of Christmas trees. They usually trim the bottom branches for each buyer, and are often willing to let parishes take these trimmed-off boughs for free. Attach branches to the wreath's frame with florist's wire. Different types of branches, if mixed, will add subtle visual interest to the wreath. Other items can be added to the wreath for color and interest. Traditional choices include pomegranates, sticks of cinnamon, dried lavender, oranges, and pinecones. Other items from your region would certainly be appropriate.

The wreath should have four lights. Typically, these are candles, colored with the colors of the four weeks of Advent: violet (week I), violet (week II), rose (week III), and violet (week IV). All violet or all white may also be used. Candles are not the only option for lighting an Advent wreath. Seven-day candles can be safely left burning all week, and can add to the sense that the wreath is part of the community's keeping watch. Oil lamps figure prominently in the readings of Advent, and would be an appropriate source of light for the wreath. White or unbleached candles can be differentiated with a simple ribbon tied around their base, or on the greenery near each candle. Because there is quite a bit of room for local adaptation and creativity, creating the Advent wreath is a good activity to involve a variety of people. Children might be invited to help assemble the wreath or different parish groups might be invited to make the wreath each year.

Light can also be used well apart from the wreath. Additional oil-lamps or candles might be added to the nave and the sanctuary. If your parish celebrates Evening Prayer in this season, it can be quite effective to dim the lights and focus attention with spots on the areas of liturgical action. Whatever is done, the liturgical space should not be cluttered. The quiet of winter and of pre-dawn which Advent assumes can be drowned out if there is too much visual clutter. The anticipatory nature of the season would make it entirely appropriate for the sanctuary to start very simple, with additions throughout the season.

The Liturgical Music

SING *to the Lord: Music in Divine Worship* (STL) suggests that during Advent "musical instruments should be used with moderation and should not anticipate the full joy of the Nativity of the Lord" (114). The music during the season of Advent therefore takes on a sense of watching and waiting, a certain starkness and anticipation. The choice of the music for the entrance rites can shape the prayer tone of the season.

Consider any of the following pieces to use for the Introductory Rites during this holy season: "Come, O Come, Emmanuel / O Antiphons" by Gary Daigel (GIA); "Advent Litany and Gathering Rite" by Michael R. Prendergast and Rick Modlin (OCP); or "Litany of the Word" by Bernadette Farrell (OCP). If your community is bilingual, consider "*Letania de Advento* / Advent Litany" by Jamie Cortez (OCP).

The common psalms for Advent are Psalms 25 and 85. A plethora of settings are available including those by Gelineau (GIA), Alstott (OCP), Guimont (GIA), Schiavone (OCP), Haugen (GIA), Hurd (OCP), Joncas (OCP), Peña (GIA), Willcock (OCP), and Soper (OCP). For bilingual and Spanish language psalms consider the settings in ¡*Aclama, Tierra Entera*! / Sing All You Lands! (WLP); and *Cantaré Eternamente* / For Ever I Will Sing, Volume 1 (OCP). The following Gospel Acclamations work well to welcome the proclamation of the Good News: "Advent / Christmas Gospel Acclamation" by David Haas (GIA); "Advent Gospel Acclamation" by Andrew Wright (OCP); "Advent Gospel Acclamation" by Michael R. Prendergast and Joseph Sullivan (OCP); "Advent Gospel Acclamation" by Paul French (WLP); and "Psalm and Gospel Acclamation for Advent" by Stephen Pishner (GIA). For a Mass setting for Advent, consider the "*Missa Emmanuel*" by Richard Proulx (GIA). Using the same Mass setting from year to year will alert the assembly to this new season.

Communion processionals should be well known and generally include a short refrain for the people such as "O Come, O Come Emmanuel."

Mary holds a prominent position in Advent: Immaculate Conception is on December 8 and Our Lady of Guadalupe is on December 12. Mary is also a central figure of the Gospel on the Fourth Sunday of Advent. Every community should have a setting of the *Magnificat* that the assembly can easily sing from memory.

Celebrations of communal reconciliation are frequent during Advent. Consider the penitential litany, "Lead Us to Act Justly" by Michael Prendergast and Joseph Sullivan (OCP). The refrain is based on Micah 6:8 and the verses are directly from the *Rite of Penance*.

Advent Lessons and Carols are popular in many parishes; one can find the traditional outline and text for the traditional nine lessons and carols at the King's College Chapel website: www.kings.cam.ac.uk/events/chapel-services/nine-lessons.html. Consider Jim Hansen's "Advent of Our God" (OCP) which includes the proclamation of the birth legends from Scripture interspersed with Advent carols.

The Liturgical Ministers

SCHEDULING ministers will admittedly be difficult, as everyone's month is full of holiday parties and even preemptive Christmas parties (sadly, often in Catholic schools or religious ed programs). But, though the month of December is in reality a time of hustle and bustle, the season of Advent is, theogically and spiritually, a time of expectant waiting . . . and looking to the future. The gifts of Christmas are reflections of the gift of the Incarnation!

After a few months of Ordinary Time during busy autumn, we all need a few moments to collect ourselves and recall first that we are looking forward to something (really, someone)—Christ himself. Perhaps send Advent e-mails to the liturgical ministers: a brief meditation on each day's Collect, a walk through salvation history via the Jesse Tree, a sentence or two of locally composed prayers, a new image each day of artistic masterpieces depicting the Nativity.

Devotions and Sacramentals

WHILE the wider world is concerned with decking the halls and buying presents and spreading holiday cheer, the Church focuses on the threefold coming of her Christ: in history, at the end of time, and in our hearts. Two of the many Advent devotions really drive home that sense of expectant waiting: the Advent wreath and the Jesse Tree.

What cradle Catholic didn't make an Advent wreath as a child? So many parishes and schools host events wherein the participants start with a cheap ring wreath, wrap it in (fake) greenery, and put in three violet tapers and one pink. The idea, of course, is always to take it home and pray with it as a family. Before the family dinner seems to be an optimal time. After lighting the appropriate number of candles, the family can sing a hymn, read Scripture, or even discuss the coming of the Lord, as desired. Even on days when the family is "too busy" to spend five extra minutes in prayer, how much is gained by taking a few seconds to quietly light the appropriate candles before the meal!

The tradition of the Jesse Tree is far less known, but even more profound. Rather than immediately decorating the tree with Christmas ornaments, a special set of Advent ornaments are made — even if only out of construction paper — and one is hung on each day of Advent, as a corresponding story from the Old Testament is read. This is easily done in a home or a school, and has the advantage of renewing in the minds of children especially the wonders God has done for his people through the many centuries during which he has cared for us.

The Parish and the Home

THE countdown to Christmas comes with great joy and anticipation for children within the secular anticipation for Santa Claus and the opening of presents; the parameters of time for the new liturgical year are ripe with beautiful rituals of prayer and times for new traditions.

The family is the domestic Church. After attending Mass together, pick a night of the week to have intentional family time and create a prayer service where each person of the family is in charge of some part of the prayer. On the First Sunday of Advent discuss the purpose of using things we know and see in nature, such as the green of the pine tree, and the circle it creates for the Advent wreath. Then invite each family member to share what they need in order to feel connected and be valued as a member of the family. Share how the community, either at church or in the family, are the true "candle holders" for Advent as each person is meant to be light for the world. Young or old alike, discover the beautiful story, *The Christmas Candle*, by Richard Paul Evans, and read the story out loud.

The weeks of Advent can be described as "peace," "hope," "joy," and "love." Each week choose one of these words to focus upon as the gift of your heart to be offered at Christmas. Or, maybe choose a new word or Scripture verse to intentionally live out each week through acts of service or times of prayer. On the first Sunday consider looking up the story of *The Sparkle Box* and create one of your own. Each week of Advent, invite your family to choose something to do, individually and as a family, to purposefully create more room for Jesus to come into your hearts. This could be the way you live out your chosen Scripture verse or the family-prayer word and how it is enacted. Incorporate these gifts into a family prayer service each week around the crèche; as you move figures in closer proximity to the manger know your hearts move closer to the Christ child. Make sure each person places their intentional gifts into the box each week. Then, when Christmas Day comes, Jesus's birthday present will be ready under the Christmas tree, or in front of your crèche.

There are also some wonderful solemnities, feasts, memorials and other traditions to celebrate as part of Advent. Continue or create your own tradition for the role of St. Nicholas (December 6), a good-natured man who cared for the poor. Look up the origin of the candy cane. As some cultures leave shoes outside to receive small gifts, leave a candy cane with a love note for each person. Teach how simple treats can teach the deep love and life of Jesus. If you haven't done so already, pick a name or a family in need from your parish giving tree and make sure each person works toward and helps to choose gifts for that family. Give a special ornament that represents the gifts or talents of that family member which can then go on the tree. Or, create ornaments which hold the names of many people who have affected your lives and whom you love and want to pray for through Christmas Time by placing them on your tree.

Mary is essential to our prayer lives and the Christmas story. Without the humble submission of Mary, God would not have come into our world as a human being. God needed someone who willingly chose to say "yes." Aside from going to Mass to honor Mary's Immaculate Conception on December 8, choose a day to say (or teach) the Rosary. This can be done as part of your weekly family prayer service or on a different day. After you pray at least one decade of the Rosary, ponder how hard it is to say "yes" to something you aren't sure of—and in understanding this, you uncover the beauty of Mary's soul and her love which guides our lives. On December 12, the Feast of Our Lady of Guadalupe, buy some roses and share the story of St. Juan Diego and Mary's "proof of love" in his own robe full of roses. Mary comes in many ways because she wants us to understand how to love God through her son.

Advent is all about waiting to receive the light of Christ into our world. The tradition associated with St. Lucy (December 13) is for girls to wear a crown around their head with candles. While Advent candles are used each week, on this day talk about St. Lucy and the concept of "light for the world." As the world outside grows darker with each day, may the light of your life continue to burn bright and strong.

Mass Texts

◆ DISMISSAL FOR CHILDREN'S
LITURGY OF THE WORD

My dear children,
throughout this season of Advent,
we await the birth of Jesus in our hearts and in our
    world.
As you leave here today,
take the Word of God with you,
and listen to it and carry it in your heart
as Mary carried Jesus in her womb.
May you always pray
"Come, Lord Jesus, Come."
Go forth in peace.

◆ DISMISSAL OF THE CATECHUMENS
Dear catechumens,
Advent is a time of darkness and waiting,
but also a season of great hope.
As you continue your studies
and journey toward initiation,
may your body, mind, and soul
be filled with hope,

as you prepare for Jesus
to be born in you anew.
Go forth in peace.

◆ INTRODUCTION TO THE MASS

Advent is a time of new beginnings, and now we begin Year B of the Sunday Lectionary which is mainly from the Gospel according to Mark. We may think of Advent as a time of dormancy, or waiting, but each week the gospel calls us to action: "Watch," "Prepare the Way," "Make straight the path," "Conceive, believe, trust." Being Catholic, being Christian, never means being complacent. God continually calls us to grow and to listen to his Word as it unfolds.

◆ UNIVERSAL PRAYER OR PRAYER OF THE FAITHFUL

Introduction

"You, LORD, are our father of our redeemer you are named forever;" and so we have the courage to bring our prayers before God, who knows and hears our needs.

Intercessions

1. For our Holy Father, Pope Francis, and all Church leaders, that they may continue to be inspired by the words of action found in our Advent Gospel readings, we pray to the Lord: Lord, hear our prayer.

2. For our nation's leaders, that they may respond to the needs of their people with mercy, love, and compassion, we pray to the Lord: Lord, hear our prayer.

3. For all who are hungry, lonely, tired, and poor, that God may comfort his people, and speak tenderly to their hearts and renew their spirits, we pray to the Lord: Lord, hear our prayer.

4. For those who are exploring their vocations to priesthood and religious life, married or single life, that they may listen and respond with as much passion as Mary or John the Baptist, we pray to the Lord: Lord, hear our prayer.

5. For all people, that they may celebrate Advent with anticipation, as they await the birth of Jesus in their hearts and for his coming at the end of time, we pray to the Lord; Lord, hear our prayer.

Conclusion

God our Father
you have heard our prayers this day,
and in your infinite love and wisdom
answer them as you will.
Through Christ our Lord.
Amen.

November
Month of All Souls

(#2, LM)   violet

30 First Sunday of Advent

The Lectionary for Mass

The daily Scripture commentaries for Advent were written by Graziano Marcheschi. The Sunday Scripture commentaries for Advent are adaptations of material by Denise Simeone © LTP.

◆ FIRST READING: Isaiah admonishes the Israelites to remember that God had saved them in the past and would do so again. In return, they must be faithful, crying out to God to lead them to salvation. By confessing their guilt and putting themselves into God's hands, they will know God's presence among them again.

◆ RESPONSORIAL PSALM 80: We hear in the psalm how we are to return to God. We ask God to show compassion to us, be kind to us, protect us, and save us. God, as the guiding shepherd, reminds us that we are not abandoned, but saved. He has saved his people in the past and he will do so again.

◆ SECOND READING: The letter from Paul assures us of God's faithful initiative and action. Paul's words are assuring to us, too, as we await God's revelation in our lives this Advent. Paul reminds us how we are to treat one another.

A community that acts with love for others is a reflection and a sign to the world of God's love. Such a community is a true witness to Jesus Christ.

◆ GOSPEL: No one knows when the Messiah will come; therefore, Jesus is clear in his warnings to disciples to watch, stay awake, and be alert. Jesus does not want disciples to miss the opportunity; he does not want distractions to get in the way of our seeing the presence of God in our midst. Seeing God and knowing that he is present despite perils or hardships gives us hope that God's saving power can be found clearly among his people.

The Roman Missal

Consider using the second form of the Penitential Act throughout Advent. The Gloria is omitted in Advent except for the Solemnity of the Immaculate Conception and the Feast of Our Lady of Guadalupe.

The Collect for the First Sunday of Advent begins by acknowledging God's relationship with his faithful ones. Our journey through life is described as running ahead to meet Christ. On this journey we accomplish honorable deeds by the grace of God. As we run forth to this encounter, Christ is coming to meet us. The Trinity is giver of gifts, and we in turn give ourselves over to God.

The Prayer Over the Offerings tells how the Lord gives life to all things and with human nurturing brings forth the grain and the grape from the earth. What we offer we share in Holy Communion and share with our neighbor in their need. In this holy exchange and by our devout celebration of the liturgy we gain eternal redemption.

On this Sunday, Preface I of Advent is used. The Preface speaks of the two comings of Christ; the "first coming" refers to the fulfillment of God's design, opening for us the way to eternal salvation. The "second coming" proclaims that everything will be made manifest in Christ and the Church will inherit God's promise.

Other Ideas

Prepare an Advent Calendar for your congregation as a bulletin insert or website feature. Include prayers for an Advent wreath, instructions and explanations of the Jesse Tree, and your complete Advent and Christmas schedule (especially noting times of reconciliation, communal penance services, Advent days/evenings of prayer, and rehearsal times for Christmas liturgies or other forthcoming events).

December
Month of the Divine Infancy

MON 1 (#175)   violet
Advent Weekday

The Lectionary for Mass

◆ FIRST READING: Isaiah paints two dramatic images: the first imagines the world streaming to God's holy mountain seeking instruction in God's ways. The second image is of weapons of war being turned into farming implements. Tools of destruction will no longer tear at human flesh but will tear open the earth instead to draw forth sustenance for a people who will live in God's peace. These images fuel a desire to walk only by the light of the Lord!

◆ RESPONSORIAL PSALM 122: God's temple was the manifestation of God's presence among his people; for only among them did God make a home. The privilege then of going on pilgrimage "to the house of the Lord" built in the city of David brought great joy and awakened the responsibility to pray for peace over this city that had known devastation.

◆ GOSPEL: The universality of God's offer of salvation is made manifest here in Jesus's pronouncement that "many . . . from the east and the west" will join the Patriarchs in God's kingdom. The Centurion manifests exemplary faith because from his experience he understands that when one has authority it flows as it should unimpeded. What distinguishes his faith is the confidence he has in Jesus's authority. While many of Jesus's own people doubted or questioned the source of his power, this man has no doubts. Just say the word, he asks, just say the word.

The Roman Missal

The entrance antiphon for today's liturgy is based on Jeremiah 31:10; and Isaiah 35:4. The nations of the world hear the word of God and watch for the Savior. Today's Collect calls the Church to "keep us alert" and be "watchful in prayer" as we "await the advent" of Christ. The Prayer over the Offerings and the Prayer after Communion are the same as those used on the First Sunday of Advent. The Communion Antiphon is based on Psalm 106 (105):4–5 and Isaiah 38:3. The Church waits for the Lord who will "visit us in peace." Preface I of Advent is used until December 16.

T U E 2 (#176) violet
Advent Weekday

The Lectionary for Mass

◆ FIRST READING: "His delight shall be the fear of the LORD." In the center of this glorious text that presents an idealized portrait of God's messianic servant we find this central attribute that encompasses piety, reverence and awe, hatred of sin, and faithful adherence to God's will. Moses, Solomon, Peter, and Paul all agree with the psalmist that "fear of the LORD is the beginning of wisdom." It is this attribute, when it becomes a leaven

among the people, that helps usher in the time when knowledge of the Lord creates a pervasive peace that covers the earth like the sea.

◆ RESPONSORIAL PSALM 72: The reign of the messianic king will be like no other's reign, for justice and peace shall flourish. His sovereignty will be marked by care of the poor and neglected whose plight will not go unnoticed. And from the heart of God's people God's mercy and justice will reach the ends of the earth where even the tribes who know him not will find blessing and respond with joy.

◆ GOSPEL: The ideal king of today's text from Isaiah is actualized in Jesus whose oneness with the Father incarnates in his very person what the prophets of old only longed to see and hear. It is not the wise and learned who apprehend the great truth of who Jesus is. From them it has been kept hidden. But to the simple and lowly, to the open and childlike this revelation has been made apparent. The challenge of perceiving "who the Son is" is beyond the grasp of anyone but those to whom he wishes to reveal it. "Blessed are the eyes that see."

The Roman Missal

The orations for today's liturgy remind the Church of God's great compassion and mercy.

W E D 3 (#177) white
Memorial of St. Francis Xavier, Priest

◆ FIRST READING: These heartening words even inspired the seer of the Book of Revelation. The future God's promises will be utterly unlike our past. Tears of sorrow will be wiped away, darkness will be dispelled, the web of sin that binds us will be broken, and death, the ultimate enemy, will be vanquished. The day will come, indeed it draws near, when we will no longer await the salvation of God

but will declare it accomplished by the mighty hand of our loving God.

◆ RESPONSORIAL PSALM 23: Because human life won't last without nourishment, God's provident care is often conveyed through metaphors of food and drink. The psalmist imagines a table not only laden with food but set in the "sight of my foes." Israel expressed notions of redemption in images of "restful waters" and healing oil similar to the way sacramental rites express God's saving action through signs and symbols. The confidence of the psalmist is perhaps his best gift to us.

◆ GOSPEL: This seminal story tells of God's abundance, not our generosity. No matter what we contribute to the kingdom, we will come up short if God does not provide what we simply do not have to give. First Jesus heals the mute, the lame, the blind, and the deformed. Then he shows that God alone can satisfy all the hungers that afflict us. Only God can do the impossible and turn the little we can offer into an abundance that satisfies and overwhelms and leaves behind more than that with which we started.

The Roman Missal

The prayers for today's memorial are found in the Proper of the Saints or the prayers for the Common of Pastors; For Missionaries may also be used. Consider using the Collect for Wednesday of the First Week of Advent as the conclusion to the Universal Prayer. The orations speak of the missionary zeal that the entire Church is called to embrace.

Today's Saint

St. Francis Xavier (1506–1552), a native Spaniard, was one of the founding members of the Society of Jesus (the Jesuits). Francis Xavier felt called to be a "spiritual soldier" through missionary endeavors to Christianize foreign lands and convert the hearts of unbelievers. One of the many honors Francis received in his life was his appointment by the pope as *apostolic nuncio* (an ambassador of the Church) to the East. He traveled to many places, including India, the Philippines, and Japan. In his travels, Francis tended to the needs of the sick and infirm, revitalized the liturgical and sacramental life of already existing Christian populations, and drew people to faith in Jesus Christ.

THU 4 (#178) violet
Advent Weekday

Optional Memorial of St. John Damascene, Priest and Doctor of the Church / white

The Lectionary for Mass

◆ FIRST READING: The reversals of God's kingdom are heralded here as they are in the *Magnificat* Mary proclaims after the angel's startling announcement. God humbles the haughty and tears down the proud, but the lowly God exalts, allowing them to trample the "lofty city" underfoot. Again, Isaiah is anticipating a future time when the nation will be safe, delivered from its time of destruction and humiliation. But at this time, the nation will stand faithful and just, animated by its firm trust in the Lord.

◆ RESPONSORIAL PSALM 118: Redolent of thanksgiving, this psalm praises God's goodness and mercy that surpass that of any earthly leader. The second verse speaks of the safety afforded by the gates of the city, gates only the just may enter. The concluding verse asks God to "grant salvation," (the Hebrew of this plea is rendered in English as "hosanna") and lauds the one who comes in God's name bringing his "light."

◆ GOSPEL: The First Reading declared "the LORD is an eternal Rock." Jesus tells us to build upon that rock if we want a house that

can withstand the buffets of wind and flood. When it comes time for judgment, it will be those who heard God's Word and kept it who will be admitted into the kingdom. It is not enough to simply know the Lord; what's needed is the willingness to hear and obey. Those who do are "wise," but those who pay lip service are but fools who build in vain.

The Roman Missal

The Collect echoes Psalm 80:3 and is full of urgency. Our sins may hold us back, but God's mercy can overcome these obstacles and speed us on our way.

This resource does not include commentary about optional memorials throughout the various seasons. You always have the option to celebrate these days! Always refer first to the Proper of Saints to explore options for the orations.

Today's Saint

Monk, Doctor of the Church, theologian, scholar, poet, hymnologist, liturgist—these are just a few of the roles St. John (657–749) fulfilled as a faithful son of the Church. Most notably, he is remembered for his avid defense of the use of sacred art in churches, monasteries, and homes. Born only five years after the death of Muhammad, John was thrust into conflict, particularly regarding the heresy iconoclasm. The iconoclastic heresy, which sought to destroy all images of devotion, resulted from the misinterpretation on the part of the emperor and many others that Christians were using sacred art as a means of idol worship. St. John composed three treatises with the goal of lifting up images of Christ, the saints, and Mary as a doorway to the mystery of God's saving work.

FRI 5 (#179) violet
Advent Weekday

The Lectionary for Mass

◆ FIRST READING: Isaiah keeps us focused on "that day" when the mercy of God will flow like a river transforming parched land into orchards and liberating the afflicted from every malady. At that time tyranny will end and justice will prevail; the weak will no longer be exploited and all will be instructed and achieve understanding. Only faith can make such words credible; but with faith there is no choice but to stand in awe before the God of Israel.

◆ RESPONSORIAL PSALM 27: As we contemplate Christ's eventual return we encounter a verse of supreme comfort: since the Lord is our light and salvation, whom should we fear? That is not the chutzpah of a schoolyard bully, but the confident refrain of those who know the true source of their security. In the second verse, the psalmist announces his one desire—to live forever within God's house. But the psalm ends with conviction that God's goodness will be experienced even in this life; we need but wait with patience and courage.

◆ GOSPEL: Two blind men ask Jesus for healing and Jesus asks them if they truly believe. Jesus asks despite the fact that the men followed him both on the road and into the house he entered. Having affirmed the importance of their faith, he then speaks his fiat that their request be granted "according to [their] faith." After the healing, how can these men possibly heed Jesus's command to keep their mouths closed when he has just miraculously opened their eyes?

The Roman Missal

The orations focus on the Christ who will come and rescue his people.

S A T **6** (#180) violet
Advent Weekday

Optional Memorial of St. Nicholas, Bishop / white

The Lectionary for Mass

◆ FIRST READING: With God we have to take the long view. God's mercy and salvation unfold over time and what may look like chastisement today becomes jubilant deliverance tomorrow. Isaiah reminds the people that their tears will come to an end and the Lord who seemed hidden will again reveal himself. God will teach, guide, and protect his people and bring abundance from the earth for people and livestock. And on "that day" when towers of pride collapse and destruction falls upon evildoers, the wounds of God's people will be healed and all signs of their chastisement erased.

◆ RESPONSORIAL PSALM 147: The refrain proclaims that the right attitudes with which to stand before the Lord are patience and trust. Again, we need the long view, for God "rebuilds" what he destroys and "gathers" what he scatters. He heals the chastised and broken. With infinite vision, power, and wisdom, God dwells in an eternal now, not the confines of the moment. This great but merciful God never loses sight of the lowly and snatches them from the hands of the wicked.

◆ GOSPEL: Jesus is moved to pity by the plight of this shepherdless flock. Whether it was an individual widow or a large crowd, Jesus never failed to respond to need. Here his response is a truly pastoral plan for evangelization in both word and deed. Lamenting the dearth of laborers for God's abundant harvest, he commissions the twelve to preach and to heal body and spirit. And they are to give as freely as they received.

The Roman Missal

The Collect stresses that it is Christ who frees us from the bondage (enslavement) of sin. The Prayer over the Offerings recognizes that our worship unites us with the sacrifice of Christ. The Prayer after Communion implores for the mercy of Christ and for him to cleanse us from sin.

Today's Saint

Little is known about Nicholas, the "wonderworker," other than the fact that he lived sometime during the fourth century and was bishop of the city of Myra in Asia Minor. There is some evidence that he was imprisoned during the Diocletian persecutions, and later condemned Arianism, a heresy that denied the Son was co-eternal with the Father. Many stories exist about St. Nicholas, but the best known is the one about a poor man who could not feed or clothe his three daughters. Upon hearing of this man's dire situation, St. Nicholas tossed three bags of gold through his window one evening so the man could tend to his daughters' needs. Modern folklore about Santa Claus, Kris Kringle, and Father Christmas are based on the stories of St. Nicholas and his great love for and generosity toward children.

7 (#5) violet
Second Sunday of Advent

The Lectionary for Mass

◆ FIRST READING: Isaiah, speaking to Israel during her exile, announces in beautifully poetic language that God has forgiven her. He also gives instructions. God's people are to build a highway for God, leveling all the bumps, ruts, and hills that are in the way. They are to walk along the road, proclaiming the Good News of God's salvation, announcing it to all, crying out in a loud voice. We can rejoice because God has forgiven Israel for her sins! Those who were exiled can return home. But in return, they must do their part to fulfill their covenant with God.

◆ RESPONSORIAL PSALM 85: The images in the verses are signs of hope for the restoration of the covenant relationship with God. God's presence can be seen when faithful virtues like justice, kindness, and peace (shalom) are practiced. Those who practice this love give abundant expression to the way of God and prepare the way so the entire world can see God.

◆ SECOND READING: The epistle reminds listeners that God does not perceive time in the same way that human beings do. Written with the Second Coming of the Messiah in mind, it gives appropriate instructions for us as we prepare ourselves during our Advent journey. We do not know God's ways, but we can hold fast to the belief that this time is a gift from God for us to repent and learn to live holy lives, be ready, and prepare for the day of the Lord's coming.

◆ GOSPEL: Many people were coming to John and acknowledging their sins as they were baptized. This is the mission that disciples are invited to follow. Many of the men and women need to be reminded that they are called to follow Jesus Christ and to preach the Gospel to the entire world. Mark reminds us about one who was not afraid, who did not abandon his role as herald; instead, by his words and actions, he invited other believers to do the same. John the Baptist calls out to us as we continue on our Advent journey, inviting our faithful response to prepare the way of God.

The Roman Missal

Consider the second form for the Penitential Act. The Gloria is omitted in Advent.

The Collect for the Second Sunday of Advent represents our response to Christ's request to join his company. Again this week's prayer is about hastening to meet Christ. In accepting the Wisdom of God we conduct our earthly activities in a way that does not impede our single-minded quest of Christ and his companions.

The Prayer over the Offerings suggests that our prayer and our offering however insufficient are accepted through the abundant mercy of God.

On this Sunday Preface I of Advent is used. The idea of the two comings of Christ (see week one) has its roots in 1 Corinthians 16:22, which contains the Aramaic word *Maranatha* which can mean "the Lord has come" or "come O Lord."

The Prayer after Communion speaks of the Communion we have just shared which is called both

food and spiritual nourishment. To dine of the Eucharistic food and drink is to share in the mystery of Christ's Body and Blood, and we do so as a community, itself the Body of Christ, the Church.

A Solemn Blessing for Advent may be used.

Other Ideas

In many dioceses, the collection for the Retirement Fund for Religious is taken on the Second Sunday of Advent. Will there be a speaker? Include this need in the Universal Prayer. There are many helpful resources at http://www.retiredreligious.org.

(#689) white

Solemnity of the Immaculate Conception of the Blessed Virgin Mary, Patronal Feastday of the United States of America

MON 8

About this Solemnity

Today we celebrate Mary's Immaculate Conception, that is, her total freedom from original sin from the moment of her conception. This freedom from the sin of Adam and Eve is shown in today's Gospel. In Mary's response to the angel, she shows her willingness to place herself fully in God's hands, even when it promises to be difficult and requires great faith and trust.

Please note that the obligation to attend Mass today has been lifted.

The Lectionary for Mass

◆ FIRST READING: The serpent gets the brunt of divine reproach in this passage where God sets up a cosmic and enduring struggle between the tempter and "the woman" and her "offspring," who will strike at the tempter's head. That key verse (verse 15), known as the *protoevangelium*, is the first biblical assurance of God's intent to deliver humanity from the consequences of sin. Clearly chosen to present Mary as the new Eve

who, in Christ, became the new "mother of all the living," the text also contrasts the disobedience of our first parents with Mary's total surrender to God's will.

◆ RESPONSORIAL PSALM 98: On this day, Mary is the cause of great rejoicing for in her person we see the saving hand of God making "his salvation known." God works through the created order to manifest his goodness. All the hopes of centuries and all the joys of the nation meet in the humble person of Mary who becomes the incarnation of God's remembered kindness and faithfulness toward the house of Israel. It is no accident that she is made a central figure of Advent.

◆ SECOND READING: All that the Church asserts of Mary, Paul ascribes to every believer. We, too, he insists, were chosen before the creation of the world to be "holy and without blemish." This exalted destiny is, in Christ, extended to all who believe in him. As Mary was chosen, we were chosen; and we share in her destiny to exist for the praise of God's glory.

◆ GOSPEL: The Annunciation might be called "the great disruption." God barges into Mary's life and makes a life-altering request. But though Mary is frightened, her quick assent suggests that God was no stranger to her. Even before her fiat, Mary was already living with God. The angel's words that "nothing will be impossible" rang true in her heart because she had long before invited God to be her lord. Mary could give herself so completely only to one who was not a stranger. And her response proves it: "Behold, I am the handmaid of the Lord."

The Roman Missal

In both the Collect and the Prayer over the Offerings of today's celebration the title of this observance is named as "Immaculate Conception of the Blessed Virgin." The phrase "prevenient grace," is used in the Prayer over the Offerings. This Christian theological concept that is rooted in Augustinian theology and means divine grace that precedes human decision is used in the Prayer over the Offerings. Since this word will be foreign to many, the presiding minister may want to break open this concept for the gathered Church in the Homily. All of the orations from today's liturgy point to the teaching of the Church that Mary "was kept sinless."

T U E 9 (#182) violet
Advent Weekday

Optional Memorial of St. Juan Diego Cuauhtlatoatzin / white

The Lectionary for Mass

◆ FIRST READING: While Luke (3:4) quotes Isaiah as calling for conversion from the desert, we see here that Isaiah actually calls for conversion in the desert. This is more than a small point of interest only to Scripture scholars. Isaiah's diction suggests that away from God we are all in the desert and it is there, in our personal wilderness, that we must hear the prophetic call to conversion and begin patting down the mountain of resistance in our lives and filling in the valleys of apathy and neglect that impede the kingdom of God from claiming us fully.

◆ RESPONSORIAL PSALM 96: This joyous psalm celebrates the coming of the Lord and calls for an active response of joyful singing and, more importantly, of announcing to the nations God's marvelous deeds!

◆ GOSPEL: God's benevolent will is underscored by Jesus's parable. God will go to ridiculous lengths to recover lost sheep . . . even to the point of sending his son to die for them. God's proactive posture is

personified by the shepherd as surely as by the father of the prodigal son.

The Roman Missal

If you are celebrating the optional memorial, catechesis will be needed to unpack the word *Cuauhtlatoatzin* which is pronounced "Coo-a-oo-tlaa-tot-sing." *Cuauthloatzin* is the proper indigenous last name of Juan Diego and means "the talking eagle."

Today's Saint

St. Juan Diego Cuauhtlatoatzin (1474–1548) was a native Mexican, a farmer, and a laborer. On December 9, 1531, on his way to attend Mass, he heard a woman call out from Tepeyac Hill. She was the Virgin Mary, and she asked Juan Diego to tell the bishop to build a chapel on the site. Juan Diego went to the bishop with the request, but the bishop scoffed at him. He returned with his cloak, or tilma, filled with roses, and when he unfurled it before the bishop, the woman's image was imprinted on the inside. The bishop believed, and the church was built. The image on Juan Diego's tilma is venerated as that of Our Lady of Guadalupe.

W E D 10 (#183) violet
Advent Weekday

The Lectionary for Mass

◆ FIRST READING: Human determination and endurance fail, sometimes when we need them most. Friends can desert us or be too preoccupied with their own needs to really notice ours. But God remains constant, all-powerful, and caring in every season and through every trial. But with God, it doesn't end there: those who trust in him will find themselves renewed and reinvigorated. They will soar to lofty heights of insight and wisdom; they will run the good race and not lose heart.

◆ RESPONSORIAL PSALM 103: Goodness for the good is not

remarkable. Even pagans do that, Jesus said. But when goodness is extended to sinner, to those who knowingly wrong us, that's goodness indeed. The psalm not only extols God's mercy, it points out that God is fully aware of our iniquities and knows the number of all our sins. But God's way is not one of retribution but of forgiveness and healing.

◆ GOSPEL: Anyone who has tried to live a holy life knows that it's not "easy" and it can, at times, feel burdensome. Was Jesus misleading when he claimed his yoke was easy? Not when you compare the yoke of Christ to the ones we place upon ourselves. Those truly are burdens. The anger and resentments we hold on to, the fears under which we labor, the addictions that accumulate like the wax from a spent candle weigh much more upon us than the yoke he offers. The only burden Jesus puts upon us is love. And in comparison with the weight of sin, that burden is lighter than air.

The Roman Missal

The Collect for today's liturgy uses the imagery of "infirmity" and calls on the "presence of our heavenly physician" to come to the aid of the Church. The Entrance Antiphon based on Hebrews 2:3 and 1 Corinthians 4:5 speaks of the illumination of Christ who will "reveal himself to all the nations." The Communion Antiphon is based on Isaiah 40:10; 35:5 which speaks of the Lord coming with power and providing clarity to "the eyes of his servants."

T H U 11 (#184) violet
Advent Weekday

Optional Memorial of St. Damasus I, Pope / white

The Lectionary for Mass

◆ FIRST READING: Divine frustration is amply evident in God's characterization of Israel as "worm" and "maggot." In both Testaments, God's constant message to his creation is "fear not." Fear is the opposite of faith and faith is the chief attribute of a disciple; all else comes after. But though God is weary of their timidity and insecurity, he nonetheless reassures them and pledges mighty deeds of wonder on their behalf. During these Advent days as we anticipate the celebration of the Incarnation it's not difficult to believe God can transform even the desert and wasteland.

◆ RESPONSORIAL PSALM 145: The psalm reinforces what we witnessed in the First Reading. Though God tires of our lukewarm faith and fearfulness, he nonetheless remains faithful and true to his merciful nature. Over and over we sin and God does not strike us down. Instead, God sends an abundance of grace into our lives giving us ample reason to give thanks.

◆ GOSPEL: Powerful, unparalleled words spoken of the Baptist! John's favored status derives from the privilege of announcing that the kingdom was near. But Jesus surprises with the assertion that membership in that kingdom is so great a benefit that anyone who has it is "greater" than John. The kingdom has enemies who wish to prevent others from entering it and who violently try to snatch it from those who have perceived it. Adding to the remarkable role in which John is cast, Jesus further announces that in John the return of Elijah is accomplished.

The Roman Missal

See the commentary for the Second Sunday of Advent for the Prayer over the Offerings and the Prayer after Communion. The Collect asks God to stir up our hearts so that we may be ready to serve him.

Today's Saint

Two significant historical events formed the backdrop of St. Damasus' life: the witness of courageous martyrs during the Diocletian persecutions and the granting of religious freedom to Christians by Emperor Constantine. St. Damasus I reigned as pope for twenty-four years. He is remembered for revitalizing devotion to the relics of martyrs by adorning catacombs, building churches, making shrines more accessible, and marking the resting places of the martyrs with unique inscriptions and epigrams.

FRI 12 Feast of Our Lady of Guadalupe
(#690A, 707–712) white

About this Feast

Behind the miraculous appearance and icon that define Our Lady of Guadalupe is a story of persistence and courage. When Our Lady appeared to Juan Diego, she sent him to the bishop to request that a church be built. Juan Diego, an indigenous peasant farmer, had no status, power, or influence with which to impress the bishop, yet he followed Our Lady's request. Risking rejection or even ridicule, he returned twice with his amazing story of the vision. With the blooming flowers packed in his tilma (poncho), and the miraculous icon that emerged beneath them, Our Lady helped Juan Diego make his point. The story teaches us trust and the certainty that, when God calls us to proclaim his kingdom, we are surrounded by the grace we need to see our mission through. May we persist in sharing the Good News, even in the face of great challenges.

The Lectionary for Mass

◆ FIRST READING: Zechariah foresees nations joining themselves to the Lord on the day the Lord joins himself with "daughter Zion." Mary is the new Zion, and, through her appearance among the indigenous peoples of America, great multitudes came to embrace faith in her son. The "woman" of Revelation can more easily be aligned with Mary. What's significant about the text is not the celestial sweep of moon and stars, but the salvation that's birthed amid wailing and cosmic chaos as the "dragon" senses (and dreads!) the coming of God's "Anointed."

◆ CANTICLE: The response for this feast is taken from the Book of Judith. The antiphon extols a woman whose singular courage and whose trust in God led to routing the enemies of Israel. Judith scorned her countrymen for their lack of trust in God; Mary is extolled as the one who trusted that God's promises to her would be fulfilled. Scripture constantly reminds us that before anything else the disciple is a person of faith.

◆ GOSPEL: As with the First Reading, we have two options for the Gospel. Each option is taken from Luke. One narrates the Annunciation and the second Mary's visitation with her cousin Elizabeth. Both are "joyful mysteries" dealing with the unfolding of God's plan of salvation and Mary's unique role in it. The graceful words first uttered about Judith are more than aptly applied to Mary whose singular role in salvation history indeed makes her "the highest honor of our race." Her courageous "yes" to God and her unflinching faith, despite whatever scorn she may have tasted for being an "unwed mother," turn into a joyous song of praise for God her savior.

The Roman Missal

The Gloria is said or chanted on this day. Our Lady of Guadalupe appeared to Juan Diego and in today's Collect she is seen as one who leads the "peoples in the ways of justice and of peace." The Prayer over the Offerings says that we may live as "children of the Virgin Mary." Preface II for the Blessed Virgin Mary is the best option for today's celebration since it echoes Mary's *Magnificat*.

(#186)   red

S A T
13 Memorial of St. Lucy, Virgin and Martyr

The Lectionary for Mass

◆ FIRST READING: Echoing the Gospel readings of the Second and Third Sundays of Advent, today's readings focus on John the Baptist as the fulfillment of the prophecy that announced the return of the great prophet Elijah. The singular ministry of Elijah is recounted in this text from Sirach. A fierce critic of Israel for her idolatry, Elijah tangled with Jezebel and King Ahab and incurred their wrath. Elijah unmasks the false prophets of Baal and eventually his remarkable ministry comes to an end when he is taken up within a whirlwind in a fiery chariot. The return of Elijah was expected before the advent of the Messiah.

◆ RESPONSORIAL PSALM 80: The Lord is characterized as both the "shepherd of Israel" and the "LORD of hosts" in this psalm that calls on God to shelter Israel, which God himself has planted, from all that would harm her or impede her growth. But the poetry goes even further asking God for "new life," that is, a conversion of heart, so that the people can be fully devoted to the Lord and rely solely on his mercy.

◆ GOSPEL: With authority, Jesus declares that in John the Baptist the prophecy of Elijah's return was fulfilled, though John himself denied he was Elijah. But though John fulfilled the office of Elijah, he was not recognized as such by his enemies who eventually murdered him. That John would minister in "the spirit and power of Elijah" (Luke 1:17) was prophesied by the angel to John's father Zechariah before John's birth. Jesus uses the Apostles' inquiry about Elijah to draw a parallel between John's death and his own coming passion.

The Roman Missal

The Collect is found in the Proper of the Saints and the additional orations may be chosen from the Common of Martyrs: For a Virgin Martyr or from the Common of Virgins: For One Virgin. Consider using the Collect for Saturday of the Second Week of Advent as the conclusion to the Universal Prayer.

Today's Saint

Even from a young age, St. Lucy (c. † 304) had a burning desire to serve God and an infinite love for the poor. Living in Syracuse, a city in Sicily, she fell prey to the Diocletian persecutions, which eventually resulted in her martyrdom. She resisted a man, believed to be a Roman soldier, who tried to rape her. He, in turn, denounced her as a Christian and had her tortured and killed. Numerous legends revolve around her death. One well-known legend is that she tore out her eyes to resist her attacker. Her name comes from the Latin, *lux/Lucia*, meaning *light*; therefore, many northern countries honor her at this time of year when darkness is pervasive. Sweden celebrates the virginity and martyrdom of St. Lucy during a festival of light with a sacred procession of young girls clothed in white dresses with red sashes, and crowned with lit candles.

(#8)   violet/rose

14 Third Sunday of Advent

The Lectionary for Mass

◆ FIRST READING: The people of Israel had returned from exile to find that Jerusalem had been ruined. Yet it was there in this awful time of pain and loss that the Israelites felt the presence of God. They had been liberated, freed by God, and Isaiah reminds them that they have reason to rejoice at that sign of God's action in their lives. They have not been abandoned.

◆ CANTICLE: Mary joyfully proclaims it in response to Elizabeth's greeting to her as the Mother of the Lord. Mary's canticle speaks especially of God's regard for the lowly (also known as the *anawim*). It is to these who are most in need that God has given favor and mercy. It is an invitation for us to add our joyful praise and witness to God in this Advent hymn on what is traditionally referred to as Gaudete Sunday (*gaudete* being the Latin word for *rejoice*).

◆ SECOND READING: Paul gives clear images of a person who is faithful to God. The faithful have been given the Good News by Jesus Christ, and now it is up to disciples to live a worthy life. They must rejoice, pray, give thanks. They must live holy lives and allow the Holy Spirit to be manifested and to test that it is truly from God. If it builds up the community and if it witnesses to Christ, then it is to be retained. If their aim is toward God, the Thessalonians will give joyous witness. If we give witness and live lives such as Paul describes, we, too, will be joyful signs of the light that has come among us in the Messiah's Incarnation.

◆ GOSPEL: The image of John the Baptist in John's account of the Gospel is different from the one we heard from Mark on the First Sunday of Advent. Mark and Luke identify John's baptism of sinners as a baptism of repentance for the forgiveness of sin. The baptist in John points clearly to the coming Baptism by Christ that will purify disciples.

The Roman Missal

Consider the second form of the Penitential Act. The Gloria is omitted. The Collect for the Third Sunday of Advent shifts our attention toward the coming Solemnity of the Nativity of the Lord. In this prayer we see that God is looking at us, which gives us the occasion to look forward to Christmas as we enter into "solemn worship and glad rejoicing."

The Prayer over the Offerings uses the phrase "sacrifice of our worship," evoking the rising of incense as found in Psalm 141:2, Malachi 1:11 and Hebrews 13:15. Eucharist is described as holy and pure "sacrifice of praise" (see *Catechism of the Catholic Church*, 1330).

On this Sunday, Preface I of Advent is used. The two comings of Jesus (see the First Sunday of Advent) suggest the fact that the kingdom is here but not yet. The Church is caught in the eschatological advent of the two comings.

The Prayer after Communion speaks of our sharing in the "divine sustenance," recalling our communion in the Body and Blood of Christ and our chewing on the Word of God. As we prepare for the approaching feasts by being cleansed of our faults we look for

the occasion to celebrate the Sacrament of Penance in preparation for Christmas.

A Solemn Blessing for Advent may be used.

Other Ideas

The days leading up to Christmas are filled with much activity. At this time, many are praying the Christmas novena which takes many forms. Latino cultures may be celebrating *Las Posadas* and the Filipino pray the *Simbang Gabi.* The "O Antiphons" are included in Evening Prayer. Prepare a handout for the congregation on each of the antiphons, or offer a brief daily reflection before Mass each day beginning on the 17th or prepare written text to post on the parish website, blog, or social media site. The antiphons are such powerful fodder for prayer, and many are not familiar with them other than the hymn text for "O Come, Emmanuel."

MON 15 (#187) violet
Advent Weekday

The Lectionary for Mass

◆ FIRST READING: Balaam is no exemplary figure; in fact he is covetous and scheming. Yet, God uses him to bless Israel, thwarting the purposes of the king who had sent him to curse the Israelites. Here, he announces the rising of the star that will signal the coming of the Messiah. The paean to his credibility is likely compensating for the fact he did God's bidding in spite of himself. But what is said of Balaam is a fitting description of all God's prophets. They are not individuals who "see the future" but who are gifted to see what God sees and to know what God knows. The prophet's oneness with God sets them apart and makes them a gift to the people.

◆ RESPONSORIAL PSALM 25: The psalmist asks God for the attributes of a prophet: to understand God's

ways and grasp his truth. To help us see as God sees is the surest way for God to set us on the right path. Because the right path leads away from destruction and toward the shores of salvation, God's mercy is manifest in showing "sinners the way." Without God's help we would not find the way of justice.

◆ GOSPEL: The religious leaders want Jesus to justify himself. But he'll give these hypocrites nothing unless he gets something first, so he asks them about John. They don't even seem to care about the truth, just about protecting their own interests, so they feign ignorance. Jesus is not fooled or intimidated. Today, some reduce Jesus to a warm-and-fuzzy, always-kind and always-smiling character. That's not the real Jesus. As we see here, Jesus was a man of strength who never was afraid to call things as he saw them.

The Roman Missal

The Entrance Antiphon based on Jeremiah 31:10 and Isaiah 35:4 echoes the familiar Advent call to "Hear the word of the Lord, O nations." The Communion Antiphon based on Psalm 106 (105):4–5 and Isaiah 38:3 pick up on the familiar Advent theme of "peace."

TUE 16 (#188) violet
Advent Weekday

The Lectionary for Mass

◆ FIRST READING: The remnant—the anawim—are the poor and lowly ones who recognize their dependence on God and realize all they have has come from God's goodness and generosity. They are the opposite of those who reside in "the tyrannical city" (Jerusalem) whom God will rise to accuse on "that day." These "proud braggarts" and their lying tongues will be eliminated in God's kingdom. But a faithful remnant will remain, comprised of the humble and those who speak God's truth.

◆ RESPONSORIAL PSALM 34: Ultimate vindication rests with God, and those who most can rely on it are the lowly, the forsaken, the poor. Therefore, praise belongs on our lips "at all times," not only when all is well but even in the time of trial, if we have faith like the psalmist. Evildoers who seem to thrive in this life will receive their due from the Lord because God "is close" to their brokenhearted victims. With faith in God, it is possible to believe along with Julian of Norwich that "all will be well."

◆ GOSPEL: Can Jesus's frequent exhortations to the chief priests and elders have been meant solely for that select, historical population? Do we not find traces of self-righteousness within ourselves? Having found a formula for right living, an approach to spirituality that's comfortable, is it not difficult to be pried out of that comfort zone by those whose prophetic voices urge or nag us? It is not ignorance but hard-heartedness to ignore evidence of goodness and divine presence that's right before us. Jesus did not spare the hypocrites. How can we avoid taking their path?

The Roman Missal

The Entrance Antiphon based on Zechariah 14:5, 7 focuses our attention on the familiar Advent theme of the Lord's coming, "a great light." The Communion Antiphon based on 2 Timothy 4:8 looks to the second coming of Christ when "those who eagerly await his coming" will be crowned with "righteousness."

W
E 17 (#193) violet
D **Advent Weekday**

The Lectionary for Mass

◆ FIRST READING: Today's Gospel presents the genealogy of Jesus that dates back to Jacob, his father, Isaac, and his father's father, Abraham. On his deathbed, Jacob assigns primacy to his son Judah who, though he was not the eldest, had assumed a role of leadership among his brothers. This deathbed blessing by Jacob of his son Judah in the presence of his brothers confirms his special role. But it is the final sentence that is most important for this Advent. Christianity has traditionally understood the assertion that the scepter would never depart from Judah to indicate that Judah's descendants would rule Israel until the coming of the messiah. Jesus is linked to this lineage through his stepfather, Joseph.

◆ RESPONSORIAL PSALM 72: This royal psalm is a prayer for the king that also expresses longing for the ideal king who will be Israel's messiah. This leader will rule with the insight and wisdom of God and his reign will be characterized by justice, and thus he will bring a "profound peace" to his people. In Jesus, the Prince of Peace, the Church sees this longing of Israel finally and fully realized.

◆ GOSPEL: This listing of forty-two generations is much more than the enumeration of many names. Manifested here is the history of Israel and, more importantly, the saving love of God revealed in the lives and stories of the men (and several women) who populate this list. God's plan of salvation unfolded in the lives represented here. Each person, whether noble or dishonorable, bears witness to God's involvement in human history and particularly in the life of Israel. Through Joseph, Jesus is made a kin to these men of the promise, and a descendant of the royal house of David.

The Roman Missal

We begin the final days of Advent, and the orations and antiphons for today's liturgy are found in *The Roman Missal* in the section of Advent: From December 17 to 24. Preface II of Advent is used beginning today.

T
H 18 (#194) violet
U **Advent Weekday**

The Lectionary for Mass

◆ FIRST READING: Being chosen certainly did not ensure an easy life for Israel. Jeremiah asserts that a day will come when people no longer say, "God delivered us from slavery in Egypt," but will proclaim instead, "God brought us home from exile among the nations." In both instances, God's mercy follows a period of great trial. But as a newborn child quickly dims a mother's memory of childbirth's pain, so the mercy of the Lord, especially when incarnated in the "shoot [of] David," quickly supplants memories of pain and abandonment with hope of new life in the land of promise.

◆ RESPONSORIAL PSALM 72: Perennial hope echoes in the words of the prophet who longs for justice to be incarnated in Israel, especially among the poor. Only in the ideal king, the Messiah, will this hope be fully realized. But the kingdom he establishes will be an eternal kingdom where justice and peace will flourish forever.

◆ GOSPEL: The days before Christmas narrate the events surrounding the birth of Jesus as related by Matthew and Luke. Today's pericope highlights both the fulfillment of prophecy and the courage and generosity of Joseph who overcame the shock of seeming betrayal by the one he loved. He risked shame and ridicule by taking into his home a woman seemingly pregnant by another man. It took the angel's word to assure Joseph he had not been betrayed, but such was his love that even before that knowledge he planned to spare Mary any shame and embarrassment. His heart was wide to God's word and God's will.

The Roman Missal

Today's Collect lifts the Church from the "yoke of sin" as it awaits the Nativity of our Lord. The Incarnation is central to our understanding of the great Paschal Mystery of Christ. The Entrance Antiphon uses imagery of Christ as King, the "Lamb foretold by John." The Communion Antiphon based on Matthew 1:23 uses the familiar Advent imagery of Emmanuel, "God-with-us."

FRI 19 (#195) violet
Advent Weekday

The Lectionary for Mass

◆ FIRST READING: The Lectionary sees the circumstances surrounding the conception of Samson as foreshadowing what will happen many generations later will happen to Elizabeth. In each instance, the longing and longsuffering of women blighted with barrenness is transformed, at God's initiative, into a great blessing not only for the woman and her family but for the nation. As we will see in the angel's words to Zechariah, and then later to Mary, the destiny of each child is clearly prophesied, emphasizing that the child will be God's instrument for the salvation of his people.

◆ RESPONSORISAL PSALM 71: With great confidence, the psalm asserts that God's plan for us began unfolding from our time in the womb. Our current relationship with the Lord is but a point on a continuum that initiated at our conception and that will perdure into eternity.

◆ GOSPEL: The mother of Samson calls the angel who spoke to her "terrible indeed" (see the First Reading), and, under similar circumstances, Zechariah is troubled and filled with fear. The inbreaking

of grace can be unsettling and even terrifying because we suddenly are confronted with the reality that we are not the masters of our destiny. Even when prayers are answered, we realize God's intervention will alter our lives forever, something for which we might not be ready despite the prayers we prayed. Zechariah's feeble faith is also highlighted here. He's a priest of the Lord who doubts God's miraculous intervention. True discipleship requires ready and resilient faith.

The Roman Missal

The Collect for today's liturgy calls on the Church to "venerate with integrity of faith" the wondrous mystery of the Incarnation. The Prayer over the Offerings and The Prayer after Communion call on the Church to be "sanctified" and "made pure." The Entrance Antiphon again takes up the call for the Lord to come without delay (see Hebrews 10:37) and the Communion Antiphon takes up the familiar Advent theme of God's "peace" (see Luke 1:78–79).

SAT 20 (#196) violet
Advent Weekday

The Lectionary for Mass

◆ FIRST READING: The duplicitous Ahaz feigns piety. He has already made his plans and military alliances and thinks he has no need of God's help. So he claims to be unworthy to ask any special "sign" of God's favor. Because he's dissembling, God speaks a word of warning through Isaiah. "Listen, he says, your lack of faith wears down everyone else; will you also wear down God?!? Want it or not God will give you a sign" (author's paraphrase). For Ahaz this was a prophecy of the birth of his own son who would be a great king of Judah, but Christianity hears in these lines an announcement of the

coming of the savior who will be Emmanuel, God with us.

◆ RESPONSORIAL PSALM 24: Great, powerful, and terrifying is the Lord, no one to be toyed with. And yet, who can dare to ascend to "the mountain of the LORD?" Not the mighty nor the rich, but only those whose hands and hearts are clean. Ahaz was among the mighty, yet he was not worthy of the Lord. But the lowliest and simplest whose hands are not blotted with sin can stand tall and without fear in the awesome presence of God.

◆ GOSPEL: Like Zechariah, Mary responds with fear to the sudden advent of the angel. And immediately she begins to ponder. The announcement to Mary includes who her son will be and what he will accomplish, communicated with familiar words — "the throne of David his father," "the house of Jacob" — that surely quickened Mary's heart. Why is she not struck dumb like Zechariah? Perhaps because she was a young girl and not a priest of the Lord; or perhaps because she was simply asking "how" things would unfold, not doubting that they would. Her pondering leads to praise as she speaks her faith-filled fiat.

The Roman Missal

The Entrance Antiphon (see Isaiah 11:1; 40:5 and Luke 3:6) tells of the branch sprouting "from the root of Jesse" and of how the splendor of the Lord will permeate the entire earth. The Communion Antiphon (Luke 1:31) recalls the Annunciation of the Angel to the Blessed Virgin Mary with the news that she will "conceive and bear a son" whose name will be Jesus. The Collect also echoes the visitation of the Angel to the "immaculate Virgin." In the Prayer after Communion the Church delights in the sacred mysteries that will give her "the joy of true peace."

21 (#11) violet
Fourth Sunday of Advent

The Lectionary for Mass

◆ FIRST READING: David wants to build a house for God, but instead God responds that he will build the house. God promises David that this house and kingdom will be firm forever. The house of David also means the household, family, or relations of David. David's salvation does not come alone as an individual or even as a king. Rather, it comes in community, among people who are in relationship with one another.

◆ RESPONSORIAL PSALM 89: Psalm 89 laments over the suffering of the king, possibly because of his defeat and disgrace in battle. Yet in the verses we hear on this Advent Sunday, we hear no laments, but only praise for the God of the covenant. The opening line announces the theme of God's faithfulness over all time. Seen in light of a possible military loss, it is certain that despite defeat, God's love for David does not change.

◆ SECOND READING: Found at the end of Paul's epistle, these verses are a doxology or a benediction, a hymn of praise and glory to God. This reading echoes connections to the other readings in images of the endless mystery of God to be proclaimed to all nations. In proclaiming this gracious and generous message of covenantal relationship and compassion to all,

it will become known to the world that God is indeed faithful.

◆ GOSPEL: In telling Mary's story on this last Sunday, the Church highlights her response to the overwhelming power of God's Spirit. In her acceptance and trust of God's promise, Mary responded as a faithful servant of the line of David. There had been no kings in the Davidic line for over five centuries since the Babylonian exile, yet God is faithful and has found a way to allow the Son of the Most High to inherit David's throne. Mary has responded as a faithful disciple and, because of her willingness to allow God to enter into her very self, God's salvation will be seen upon the earth.

The Roman Missal

Consider the second form for the Penitential Act. The Gloria is omitted. The Collect preserves a basic insight that the entire mystery of Christ—from his Incarnation, Passion, Death, Resurrection, and his constant presence in his Body the Church—is one central mystery. The Prayer over the Offerings speaks of the Spirit who is always the active transforming agent at work in the liturgy changing bread and wine along with people into the Body and Blood of Christ. We prepare to celebrate the birth of Christ with this reference to the Incarnation: the Annunciation of the Angel to the Virgin Mary when she conceived our Savior.

On this Sunday Preface II of Advent is used. This Preface is used from December 17 to December 24 when the O Antiphons accompany the *Magnificat* at Evening Prayer. A Solemn Blessing for Advent may be used.

Other Ideas

Announce all times for Christmas liturgies, final music rehearsals, and times of reconciliation. Make sure this information is front and center

on church and office doors, on the parish website and social media sites, the parish bulletin, outgoing phone message, and anyplace else it may be prominently posted. Consider promotional ads on the local radio station, newspaper, and online media. Create a flyer with Mass times and maps to the church for local hotels as an added form of hospitality. Confirm all ministers are scheduled and prepared in advance.

MON 22 (#198) violet
Advent Weekday

The Lectionary for Mass

◆ FIRST READING: Hannah, another of Scripture's barren women whose prayers to bear a child are finally answered, returns with the son who was her prayer's fulfillment to offer him to the Lord's service. Filled with joy and gratitude, Hannah praises God and announces the vindication of the just, the punishment of the wicked, and she expresses her conviction that God has had mercy upon her and blessed her mightily.

◆ CANTICLE: Hannah's song of praise comprises today's response and, like Mary's *Magnificat*, it speaks of much more than the favor God bestowed on her personally; rather, it sings of God's mercy and of the justice that will be visited upon the land through God's mighty hand. Her prayer celebrates the great reversals of the kingdom—the mighty are taken down and the lowly raised up. God is sovereign and his will is accomplished, thus the lowly will be exalted and the rich humbled.

◆ GOSPEL: In response to Elizabeth's words of blessing, Mary sings a song that captures the longing and the long-suffering of all Israel's faithful children. It is not only Mary who receives God's mercy and whose lowliness God redeems.

In her is actualized the mercy God extended "in every generation" to all who trusted in him. Like Hannah in today's responsorial, Mary rejoices in the upheavals that characterize the kingdom: rulers fall from their thrones and the lowly are lifted up; the hungry are filled and the rich go away empty. Because of her lowliness, Mary is blessed and a blessing for all ages.

The Roman Missal

The Entrance Antiphon calls the Church to lift up its heads, to open the "ancient doors" so that the "king of glory" may enter in. The Communion Antiphon echoes the *Magnificat* (see Luke 1:46, 49). The Collect again speaks of the Incarnation of God's only Begotten Son and that as a Church we "may merit his company as [our] Redeemer." The Prayer After Communion assures us that through sacramental Communion we too will "merit the rewards of the blessed."

TUE 23 (#199) violet
Advent Weekday

Optional Memorial of St. John of Kanty, Priest

The Lectionary for Mass

◆ FIRST READING: Expect mercy, take the long view, and await fulfillment are the messages of this text. "Lest I come and strike / the land with doom" is the merciful motivation for sending a messenger to prepare the way. God would have ample reason to bring judgment upon the land, but God stays his hand to provide time to repent and turn from evil. Unless we take the long view, we will lose hope and not see the working of grace in the world. But with God fulfillment does come, though often when we least expect and in a different form than we anticipated.

◆ RESPONSORIAL PSALM 25: The verses echo a constant scriptural theme: "teach me your paths." The frequency with which we encounter this petition in Scripture might suggest God is a poor teacher, but minimal awareness of human nature suggests the problem is with us. Either we learn slowly or we forget quickly. The refrain announces the great reality that has grown palpably manifest: redemption is near at hand.

◆ GOSPEL: The clear intervention of God can be so overwhelming that it inspires fear among those who have not learned to trust in the Lord. The birth of John becomes a time of rejoicing and confusion for the neighbors of Elizabeth and Zechariah. Oddly, they are less awed by her giving birth at an advanced age than by the convergence of name selection by the mother and father. What they sense clearly is God's hand on the family and especially on the special child with which God has gifted them.

The Roman Missal

To retain the continuity of the season, use the prayers for December 23 in the Proper of Time.

Today's Saint

St. John empowered people to bridge the ponderings of the mind with the feelings of the heart. He followed the simple, austere practices of the desert fathers — never clinging to material goods, fasting whenever possible, and living in contemplative awareness.

WED 24 (#200) violet
Advent Weekday (Morning Mass)

The Lectionary for Mass

◆ FIRST READING: Nathan advises David to follow his instincts and do for God what he intends. When Nathan listens to the Lord, he receives a very different message and must return to David both to correct and to encourage. With mild reproach God reminds David of who's done what for whom. If any building is to be done, it will be God who does it. And not only will God build a "house" for David and establish a throne that will stand firm forever, but God will also raise up an heir to David, whom God himself will father.

◆ RESPONSORIAL PSALM 89: The psalmist proclaims God's goodness and God repeats his promise to sustain David's lineage and keep firm his royal throne.

◆ GOSPEL: In Zachariah's great canticle we hear echoes of the hopes of many generations. What is remarkable about this priest of the Lord is that he recognizes the time of fulfillment has arrived. Only faith could grant such understanding, for the eyes of his body would have seen only a newborn child. Yet he recognizes instead a prophet of God Most High who will prepare the way for the redemption God is about to visit upon his people. Zechariah is "filled with the Holy Spirit," a strong Lucan theme throughout this Gospel, and the child grows "strong in the spirit" (see v. 80) to ready him for his bold mission.

The Roman Missal

We now come to the final day of the Advent Season and we rejoice that "God sent his Son into the world" (See Entrance Antiphon: Galatians 4:4). The fervent prayer of the Church is clearly stated in the Collect: "come quickly, we pray, Lord Jesus, and do not delay." The gift of the Eucharist has now made ready the Church as she prepares to "celebrate in adoration the festivities" of the Nativity of the Lord (see Prayer after Communion).

CHRISTMAS TIME

The Liturgical Time

The Meaning / The Lectionary for Mass

THE conviction with which some people assert their understanding of the meaning of Christmas is remarkable: "It's all about the children," they say. But, of course, it's not. Even to say it's about the "child" misses the mark if by that one reduces the holyday to the birthday — celebrated with an exchange of gifts in the midst of festive lights and ornaments — of a child born two thousand years ago in a humble stable who spent his first night in a manger. Making Christmas "all about the children" misses the earth-shattering event we call the Incarnation. That well-intentioned formula recognizes that there is something special about this time of year. It understands that we become a little kinder and more attentive to the needs of others. But it misses the reason why. As wonderful as it feels to focus on the simplicity and innocence of children and to desire to extend that goodness, for a day or for a season, to the wider culture, those well-intentioned motives rob us of something much grander and much richer.

A virgin conceived. God became human. A promise was fulfilled. The world changed forever. Given that, perhaps in one sense Christmas can be "all about the children" because children believe in miracles and are open to wonder. If they are taught the true meaning of Christmas, children embrace it because they can embrace a God who is greater even than their imaginations. That is our task at Christmas Time: to be overwhelmed by the awesome goodness of God who emptied himself to become one of us, and who did so that humanity might understand more clearly the calculus that governs the world: God became human that we might become more like God. That is our ultimate destiny, and the festivity that surrounds this holyday, distracting as it might be, can be a reminder to celebrate that conviction. Perhaps the most complete way to announce the true meaning of Christmas is to remind ourselves and others that God came and remains among us that we might all be divinized!

From our elder siblings in Judaism we have learned to extend the liturgical celebrations of our major holydays. Other than the annual observance of the Lord's Passion, Death, and Resurrection, the Church holds nothing more central than the observance of Christ's birth and his initial manifestations. Within the contours of this season we honor the Christ-like first martyr Stephen; John, the beloved disciple; the Holy Innocents whose blood was shed in place of the Christ child's; and Mary, the Mother of Jesus and of the Church; but we never lose sight of the season's primary purpose — to memorialize the Lord's birth and celebrate his manifestation to Israel and to the nations.

The Scriptures of Christmas Time invite us to contemplate and surrender to mystery. The Incarnation can't really be explained nor can its wonder be exhausted. Within the eternal Godhead, in the divine community we call the Trinity, there now participates in full and everlasting communion, a human being we know as Jesus Christ. He was born of a woman. He nursed and wet his diapers. He enjoyed food, laughter, and the company of his friends. He calmed the sea and healed the skin of lepers, and now he reigns forever as King of the Universe.

Because of the four different Masses that can be celebrated on Christmas — the Vigil, and the Masses during the Night, at Dawn, and during the Day — this is the only liturgical day on which we proclaim four different sets of Scripture readings. The first three Masses recount various aspects of Jesus's birth drawn from Matthew and Luke, but the Prologue of the Gospel according to John is proclaimed at the Mass for Christmas Day.

The readings of the Vigil Mass illustrate God's fidelity to the covenant and announce radical transformation as the Lord calls us into a relationship that is as intimate and passionate as that between a bridegroom and his bride.

Liberation is the dominant note sounding in the readings of the Mass at Midnight. Isaiah announces freedom from darkness and the oppressive weight of our own rebellion. Paul further spiritualizes the freedom God dispenses and hails liberation from "godless ways and worldly desires." Being freed from our unmanageable desires and unruly wills may be the greatest freedom of all.

At the Mass at Dawn the readings announce the salvation that has come into the world. Isaiah heralds "your savior comes!" and Paul recognizes that our salvation results not from any merit of ours but from God's abundant mercy.

The Mass during the Day rejoices in the good news that is proclaimed in our midst. Isaiah realizes that the news of our salvation even renders the messenger who bears it beautiful in our sight. Paul revels that what others more worthy than we longed for centuries to hear has now been spoken in our midst, and that word is God's own son!

St. Stephen, the Church's first martyr is given the distinction of greatest proximity to the celebration of Christ's birth. From the readings of the day we are made mindful of the risks of discipleship. While we continue to revel in the joy of the Incarnation we also realize allegiance to the son of God puts us at risk, sometimes even from those closest to us. But the day reminds us that suffering for Christ is not a burden to be feared but a badge to be worn with honor.

As we celebrate St. John, the friend and follower of Jesus, we hear of both the privilege and the pain of discipleship. John had the privilege of seeing, hearing, and touching the living Lord during his years of ministry; he also endured the pain of seeing him crucified and laid in a tomb. Beloved of Christ, John points to the great truth that each of us is also God's beloved.

On the Feast of the Holy Innocents we remember the world's hostility to the light of Christ. The moment he was born, his light was seen as a threat by those who preferred darkness; innocent children's lives were taken in a vain attempt to snuff that light. While in many places still "Rachel weep[s] for her children" whose lives are too soon taken because of selfishness and hatreds, we cling to the word of John who assures us that "God is light, and in him there is no darkness."

The Feast of the Holy Family presents Abraham as a role model of faith. Perhaps the message to us is that the family is the primary locus of faith, with parents passing on their faith to their children in word and especially in deed. Simeon and Anna also bear witness to faith in God's word. If the home is the place where such faith is taught, it will become a womb where the goodness of God can flourish and from which it change the world.

On the Octave of Christmas, the Solemnity of Mary, the Holy Mother of God, celebrated on the first day of the new year, the unique role of the Israelite woman Mary in God's plan of salvation is spotlighted. Through Mary God brought into the world Israel's greatest blessing. The blessing God taught to Moses took on flesh in the person of Jesus whose holy name becomes the name of blessing in the new covenant.

The Solemnity of the Epiphany uses the convention of light to celebrate the universal salvation made available through Christ. Isaiah's splendid poetry and the Magi who followed a star provide apt and joyous images of the truth that was kept hidden in former times but now is boldly proclaimed by Paul: "Gentiles are coheirs . . . [and] copartners" in God's promise of salvation in Christ. The manifestation of Christ is not for some, but for all.

The theme of manifestation characterizes all of Christmas Time. The readings focus on the childhood manifestation of Jesus to Simeon and Anna and to the Magi. The first days of the new year bring John the Baptist to the fore with four consecutive days of witnessing to the Lord whose sandals John is not worthy to unfasten. During the week between the Solemnity of the Epiphany of the Lord and the Feast of the Baptism of the Lord, the Gospel texts illustrate the manifestations of the Lord during his early ministry — at Cana, preaching in Galilee, feeding the multitude, walking on water, and preaching to, but being rejected by, his own neighbors. The First Readings continue to come from the First Letter of John who speaks with poetic intimacy of the consequences of uniting our lives to God in Christ and addresses some of the specific problems and dangers that confront the nascent Church.

Christmas Time concludes with the Feast of the Baptism of the Lord that narrates the baptism of Jesus at the hands of his cousin, John. All three readings of the day emphasize the singular identity and role of Jesus, culminating in the voice from heaven that announces unique, divine favor upon this "beloved Son." As one of the three major "epiphanies" of the Lord, this day culminates the season that has been all about manifestation. A light cannot be hidden under a bushel basket and Jesus is the Light of the World who must be made known and recognized. He is the fulfillment of the longing of ages, the rabbi who teaches, the savior who heals, the miracle worker who has authority over heaven and earth. He came in power and compassion to comfort and unsettle just like the prophets of old. Those of us who minister in his name will do the same if we announce the good news of his kingdom with equal vigor to the powerful and to the lowly.

The Roman Missal

THE texts for the days of Christmas Time are located in two different places in the Missal. A segment for Christmas Time follows the Advent segment in the Proper of Time section at the front of the Missal. Here can be found Mass formularies for the four Masses for the Nativity — the Vigil Mass, the Mass during the Night, the Mass at Dawn, and the Mass during the Day; for the Sunday within the Octave of the Nativity, which is the Feast of the Holy Family of Jesus, Mary, and Joseph; for the Sixth and Seventh Days within the Octave; the Solemnity of Mary, the Holy Mother of God; for two Masses for the Epiphany of the Lord — a Vigil Mass and a Mass during the Day; and for the weekdays of Christmas Time. Finally, Mass formularies are also given for the Sunday after the Epiphany, which is the Feast of the Baptism of the Lord.

Other texts for Christmas Time are found in the Proper of Saints. In that section can be found the obligatory feasts of St. Stephen, St. John the Apostle and Evangelist, and the Holy Innocents. Other texts found in this section are those for the obligatory memorials of Sts. Basil the Great and Gregory Nazianzen and Elizabeth Ann Seton, and optional memorials for St. Thomas Becket, St. Sylvester, the Most Holy Name of Jesus, St. André Bessette and St. Raymond of Penyafort.

If a particular form of the greeting was used all during Advent, priest celebrants might consider switching to another form during Christmas Time and using that one consistently. For the Penitential Act, although any invocations may be used for the third form (#6 in the Order of Mass), Option II in the section of sample invocations for the Penitential Act found in Appendix VI of the Missal, with phrases such as "mighty God and Prince of peace," "Son of Mary," and "Word made flesh," would seem to be a very appropriate choice, as they echo Christmas themes. Option I might be considered another appropriate choice insofar as those invocations highlight past, present, and future comings of Christ: "you came to gather the nations into the peace of God's kingdom; you come in word and sacrament to strengthen us in holiness; you will come again in glory with salvation for your people."

Eucharistic Prayer I, the Roman Canon, has proper inserts that should be used when this prayer is prayed at Masses on the Nativity of the Lord and throughout its Octave and on the Epiphany of the Lord. The first or second acclamations for "The Mystery of Faith," insofar as they both refer to Christ's coming again, might be preferable over the third option, although that option does use the word "Savior," which would echo the notion of the Savior who is born for us.

The Gloria returns at the celebration of the Nativity and is sung or said every day throughout the Octave.

There are three Prefaces for the Nativity of the Lord, any of which might be equally appropriate on the solemnity itself, during its Octave, and on the other weekdays of Christmas Time, even if that day might otherwise have its own proper Preface (except, according to the rubrics, in "Masses that have a proper Preface concerning the divine mysteries or divine Persons"). Preface I of the Nativity of the Lord focuses on Christ as the Light of the World and as the visible image of the invisible God. Preface II highlights the mystery of the Incarnation; while this Preface also speaks about the invisible divinity being made visible in Christ, it goes on to focus on the "awe-filled mystery" of the One who was "begotten before all ages." In that mystery of the Incarnation, all that was cast down is raised up, all unity is restored to creation and humanity is called back to the heavenly kingdom. Preface III highlights the "holy exchange that restores our life" as human nature is assumed by the Word. Additionally, there is a Preface of the Epiphany of the Lord that is used in the Masses of the Solemnity of the Epiphany and

may also be used in Masses after the Epiphany up to the Saturday preceding the Feast of the Baptism of the Lord. The Preface for the Baptism of the Lord is found in the Proper of Time section with the other formularies for that Mass.

Several special three-part Solemn Blessings specific to this liturgical season are given in the section for "Blessings at the End of Mass and Prayers over the People." There is one for the Nativity of the Lord (#2), one for the beginning of the year (#3), and one for the Epiphany of the Lord. As always, one of the choices of the Prayers over the People may also be used.

Children's Liturgy of the Word

CHILDREN love Christmas, but it is often a challenge to channel the excitement that is usually associated with secular festivities into our experience of worship. It is one of the times of year when a great number of families come to Mass who do not come regularly. This makes it especially important to prepare the children's Liturgy of the Word well and to be ready for a larger number of children who may not be familiar with what is occurring when the children are dismissed.

On Christmas day especially, it may be necessary to get the assistance of additional adults to keep order in the children's prayer space. Many parishes suspend the children's Liturgy of the Word on Christmas Day because of the large numbers who attend. Parishes may have one Mass on Christmas Eve dedicated to families with young children. It would be beneficial to work with the liturgy committee and the presider when preparing this liturgy in order to try to achieve some form of continuity for those who regularly attend the children's Liturgy of the Word.

◆ READINGS: On Christmas it is important to note that there are different readings for the liturgies of the solemnity of Christmas depending on the time of day the Mass is celebrated. At the first Masses on Christmas Eve the beginning of the Gospel according to Matthew is proclaimed. This Gospel focuses of the genealogy of Jesus and it is a difficult Gospel to preach to children, but it can be done with proper preparation and a bit of imagination. The Lectionary however also gives the option to use any one of the readings assigned to the other Christmas Masses. Many presiders choose the reading from Luke from the Mass during the Night since that is the one people are most fond of hearing. Whichever Gospel is chosen, be sure the reflections focus on the birth of Jesus and his continued birth in their hearts each day. It is important to note that on Christmas the readings from the *Lectionary for Masses with Children* can be used only at a *separate* children's Liturgy of the Word. If you are not dismissing the children on Christmas the regular Lectionary must be used.

The readings we hear on the Feast of the Holy Family and the Solemnity of Mary, the Holy Mother of God, are from Luke, chapter two. On the Solemnity of the Epiphany we hear the familiar story of the Magi from Matthew, and the Feast of the Baptism of the Lord brings us back to Mark. All these readings are filled with wonderful images that can be explored in reflections with the children and continue the Christmas theme throughout the entire season.

◆ ENVIRONMENT: The children's worship space should reflect the beauty and splendor of the main worship space, yet not go so overboard that the environment overshadows the children's ability to focus on the readings, the reflection, their participation, and responses. Remember the central symbol of the children's Liturgy of the Word is the proclamation of the readings. Highlight in some way the place where the readings are proclaimed. Making use of additional candles during the proclamation of the Gospel is one way to do this, always remembering to make safety a priority. The liturgical color for Christmas is white, although gold is also appropriate. Avoid using red and green except in plants used as decoration. If using a Christmas tree in the space, it should be decorated modestly, perhaps with just lights and simple balls or bows. Avoid non-religious ornaments as they detract from the focus on the birth of Christ. It is quite appropriate that a nativity scene be visible throughout the season. If banners are used to lead the dismissal of the children, consider one made of long wide ribbons with bells attached on the bottom. This makes for a festive alternative to a simple cloth banner. These banners can also be used as part of the entrance procession and recessional at Mass throughout Christmas Time.

◆ MUSIC is always an important part of Christmas liturgies. During Christmas Time we should help fully engage the children in singing from our rich tradition of Christmas hymns and carols. Christmas carols can be sung as the children enter the worship space, and, if there is time, sing a verse or two of a carol before leading the children back to the main assembly. Coordinate with the music director so that the children are singing the hymn or carol the main assembly is singing for the Preparation of the Gifts. Another idea is to have a few children with hand bells accompany the procession of the children from and back into the main worship space.

The Saints

WHEN I first came to understand the concept of an Octave—a feast so important that we celebrate it for eight days, just like the feasts God demanded of our Hebrew forebears—I was pretty excited. We Catholics really do know how to party! The Octave of Easter immediately made sense to me: it's Easter Day every day of that week, culminating in the Second Sunday of Easter. Each day of the octave is so important that any lesser feast on that day is either ignored or moved.

But, curiously, Christmas doesn't follow those rules. One day for the Nativity of the Lord, and then Stephen, John, and the Holy Innocents! Why are these martyrs getting in the way of the extended celebration of Christmas?!

Well, it took a few years, but a Scripture scholar finally enlightened me: Christmas is, among many other things, about the fulfillment of God's covenant to David—about the promised Messiah, the King from David's line, who would bring God's blessings to all the people of the earth. And a king goes nowhere alone! He's always surrounded by his royal court, the most important people in his kingdom, who are in some way representative of his whole kingdom.

So, immediately after the Feast of our Lord begins, we celebrate the First Martyr, Steven, who stands for all the martyrs (and, by extension, all the saints). Next up we have John, who is an apostle and evangelist—and, tradition has it, virgin. That covers wide swaths of the rest of the saints in some way or other. After him come the Holy Innocents who stand for youth and innocence, and represent the sorrows that we all suffer throughout our lives. Then, on the Octave Day, the day that's just barely second to the Feast itself, we celebrate Mary, the Holy Mother of God. Who better to finish up the royal train than the Queen Mother?

The Liturgy of the Hours

ON the one hand, Christmas Time seems so short: Barely three weeks for the season with the greatest volume of beautiful music, not to mention so many lovely devotions and traditional practices. On the other hand, Christmas seems so long, probably because the secular "holiday" season begins the moment the Halloween displays are taken down.

But the Liturgy of the Hours is oblivious to our emotions. It is as if it expects us to be wrapped up in amazement at the Incarnation, absorbed in this divine babe as a mother is with her newborn child, with wonder and joy and nothing else of consequence.

After all the preparations of the holidays, the bustle is over, and Christ is here. The Office, even more so than the Mass, spends these days simply lingering over the mystery of the Incarnation. May we each have the grace of contemplating them as did Our Lady, who "kept all these things, reflecting on them in her heart" (Luke 2:19).

The Rite of Christian Initiation of Adults

CATECHUMENS continue to be dismissed from the Sunday assembly following the Homily. The rich images of the Incarnation are like facets of the diamond that shine in the hearts of the Church. Jesus Christ, the word of God who became flesh, is the light burning brightly dispelling the darkness of winter (in the Northern Hemisphere). The feasts, solemnities, and memorials of this short season, including the solemnities of Mary, the Holy Mother of God, and the Epiphany of the Lord; the feasts of the Holy Family of Jesus, Mary, and Joseph, the Baptism of the Lord, St. Stephen, St. John, and the Holy Innocents; and the memorials

of Sts. Basil the Great and Gregory Nazianzen, St. Elizabeth Anne Seaton, and St. John Neumann, all shed light on the mystery of the Incarnation.

Unfortunately in many places "ritual music" for the RCIA is simply seen as an add-on or an afterthought. The USCCB document *Sing to the Lord: Music in Divine Worship* states, "it is important to choose sung responses, acclamations, antiphons, Psalms, and other songs that will enable the whole community to participate at the appropriate times" (202). The document reminds us that "the initiation of adults is the responsibility of all the baptized" ("General Introduction," *Christian Initiation*, 9). Pastoral musicians are then charged to find ritual music that can be sung robustly by the gathered faith community so both they and those coming for the Easter sacraments know that the community is standing together on the journey.

The Sacraments of Initiation

OF those people who realize that Christmas does not end on December 25, most think it ends on Epiphany. In reality, however, Christmas Time continues for another week, ending on the frequently overshadowed Feast of the Baptism of the Lord.

The Baptism of the Lord is dedicated to that very action of Christ which precedes and inspires our own first acceptance into his divine life. It is very easy to take our own Baptism for granted, especially for those of us who can't remember the moment. It is so easy to forget the importance of being adopted by God, not only as children but also heirs, of receiving full membership in his Church, his very Body on earth!

How appropriate it would be to celebrate this first sacrament on the liturgical feast of its inception! Even in places where the custom is to baptize only in private ceremonies on Saturdays and Sunday afternoons, perhaps just one or two Baptisms could be scheduled at the principal Sunday Mass, to remind all present of the great gift our Lord has given us in this sacrament.

Our own practice of Baptism is rooted in Jesus's example. Being without sin, he submitted to John's baptism of repentance for our sake, thereby sanctifying the waters of Baptism for us. At the very moment of his baptism came the theophany, that manifestation of the Holy Trinity — again, for our benefit. Though we do not see the divine presence so clearly in the average infant's Baptism, there is nonetheless a natural understanding of the goodness and purity of this child, who is welcomed by the community into the family of God.

Is it possible to celebrate this feast without celebrating sacramental Baptism, too? Of course. Is it possible to transition from Christmas Time to Ordinary Time without lingering over this great gift our Lord left us from just before beginning his public ministry? People do it all the time. But such beautiful opportunities for grace are here for the taking, if we would only take advantage of them.

The Rite of Penance

MANY people in the liturgical assembly on Christmas or liturgies during Christmas Time have often been estranged or alienated from the Church or the community. Make an extra effort to reach out and welcome these people. Good hospitality and good preaching are essential in healing those who have been wounded. There is no place for laying on guilt or chiding those who have been away. This will only lead to further alienation and distance, rather than leading people to embrace the light of Christ. Include an invitation in the parish bulletin or on the parish website inviting those who have been estranged from the Church to come back by celebrating the Sacrament of Reconciliation. Take your lead from Pope Francis who continues to reach out with an embrace and welcome for all.

The Rite of Marriage

CHRISTMAS Time is not a popular time for weddings, at least not in the northeast. Perhaps this is mostly practical, because of the danger of snow and its potential to cancel plans for traveling guests. The few Christmas weddings seem nearly always to be of teachers, whose only guaranteed vacation before the hot summer months is that solitary week between Christmas and the New Year.

Yet a couple's work schedule (or perhaps even aesthetic designs) ought not to overwhelm pious devotion! Whatever the reason for a couple's Christmas Time nuptials, the inherent symbolism of the season is no less striking. Christmas is a time of gift, of the Father's gift to us of his Only Begotten Son — of the Son's gift to us of himself! What else is the married couple's commitment but to love each other, to give themselves to each other even at the expense of their own comforts?

We live in a time and place that is dominated by commercial industries, and here are the intersection of two of the biggest: the holiday industry and the wedding industry. Yet both miss the point of the sacrament entirely. Both Christmas and matrimony are about self-sacrificial love undertaken for the good of the other. What a wonderful reflection to keep in the minds of all involved in such a beautiful double celebration!

The Pastoral Care of the Sick

FOR far too many Catholics, Christmas ends on December 25. When one is in control of his own life and surroundings, one can choose not to trim the tree until Gaudete Sunday, for instance, or not to take it down until Epiphany (or Feast of the Baptism of the Lord!).

But after December 25, the Christmas visits and celebrations in most nursing homes, assisted care facilities, and hospitals are abruptly finished.

But why let this interfere with the joy of the season? Things are a bit quieter at the parish, likewise, a bit quieter at institutions that care for the sick and elderly, and even in the lives of most families. What better opportunity, then, to practice that important spiritual work of mercy of visiting the sick?

In response to God's gift to us of himself in human flesh, how can we do better than to give of ourselves, our time, to those who cannot pay us back? "Blessed indeed will you be because of their inability to repay you. For you will be repaid at the resurrection of the righteous" (Luke 14:14).

Who can reach old age without experiencing suffering and pain? The holidays are often painful reminders of lost loved ones, and who has lost more than our elders? Then, as if to add insult to injury, age and/or ill health have robbed these people, often longtime parishioners, of the liberty to be physically part of the parish community.

All the more, then, is it appropriate to be the healing love of Christ to his people. This is done in a more intense way through the sacraments, of course, but pastoral care of the sick requires so much more than the delivery of a sacrament, no matter how efficacious. It requires sacrifice, it requires relationship, it requires love.

And some days, what it requires is sitting there and listening to stories of Christmases long past, perhaps punctuated by the singing of a beloved Christmas hymn or two.

The Order of Christian Funerals

WHEN a member of Christ's body dies, all the faithful are called to enter into the ministry of consolation. The Church calls each member of Christ's Body — priest, deacon, lay ecclesial ministers and all the baptized, members of the faith community, health care professionals, funeral directors, friends, and relatives — to participate in the ministry of consolation; "to care for the dying, to pray for the dead and to comfort those who mourn" (OCF, 8). The preparation of the funerals rites is important, and family and friends as well as the person who is dying (if circumstances allow) should have input into the funeral preparations. The Christian way of life does not deny death, and death is not the end of Christian life; for Christ's Resurrection promises each of us our own resurrection.

Christmas Time is a difficult time to experience the death of a loved one or friend. Death at this time of the year changes the meaning of the season forever for mourners. Funerals may not be celebrated on the Solemnity of the Nativity of the Lord; the Feast of the Holy Family; the Solemnity of Mary, the Holy Mother of God; the Solemnity of the Epiphany of the Lord; or the Feast of the Baptism of the Lord. If staff is on vacation after Christmas, make sure parishioners are available to be present to meet with families at the time of death. The Paschal Mystery is revealed in the story of the Holy Innocents; this would be a most appropriate day to celebrate a funeral in the Christmas season. Since the church may already be

decorated with poinsettias and evergreens, additional flowers may not be needed. Homilists may want to make the connection between the wood of the manger and the wood of the Cross that link Jesus's life. Christmas carols and seasonal music are certainly appropriate for funerals held during the Christmas season, especially "Good Christian Friends, Rejoice," "Once in Royal David's City," and "Hark the Herald Angels Sing."

The Book of Blessings

IN most parishes, the dominating elements of the environment will include the nativity scene and the Christmas tree. The *Book of Blessings* includes an order for blessing both the crèche and the tree. Including these blessings in the life of the parish helps to deepen an understanding of and appreciation for Catholic rites and rituals.

Because most parishes experience a very hectic schedule for Christmas Eve and Christmas Day, careful and creative preparation allows for these blessings to be part of the observance and yet not overload the Masses of Christmas. For example, the Order for the Blessing of the Nativity Scene (BB, chapter 48) may take place outside the celebration of Mass, "at another suitable time" (BB, 1542). Similarly, blessing the Christmas tree before Mass makes a very suitable preparation of the people to enter the celebration of Christmas.

For example, many parishes precede Christmas Masses with a service of carols. This would be an appropriate opportunity to bless the nativity scene, the Christmas tree, or both. Note that the Order of Blessing a Christmas Tree (BB, chapter 49) directs that the lights of the tree be turned on during the prayer of blessing. Not only would these blessings help prepare people for the celebration of Mass which will follow, but they will also help prepare the environment!

Though your parish may not have the custom of celebrating the Liturgy of the Hours on Christmas, the *Book of Blessings* does allow for the blessing of the Christmas tree during Morning or Evening Prayer. In this case, the prayer of blessing takes place after the Gospel canticle. The intercessions and concluding prayer are then taken from the order of blessing rather than from the Liturgy of the Hours. Other orders of blessing that might well be appropriate for the Christmas season include:

- Blessing of Homes During the Christmas Season (chapter 50): Parishioners might be encouraged to use this blessing on Christmas Day, perhaps right before Christmas dinner or during the time when the family would gather.
- Blessing of Religious Articles and Rosaries (chapters 44 and 45): this would be particularly suitable when these articles are received as Christmas gifts.
- Blessing Before and After Meals (chapter 30): this could be made available for parishioners to use at home during the festive meals of the season.

The Liturgical Environment

ONE of the more difficult aspects of living out the liturgical calendar for contemporary Catholics is maintaining the differentiation between the seasons of Advent and Christmas Time. There is tremendous pressure to fill the quiet space of Advent with the noise and the color of Christmas Time. If the parish is intentional about making a strong differentiation, it will support the efforts of parishioners in their home lives to practice Advent. Similarly, celebrating the whole of Christmas Time until the Feast of the Baptism of the Lord requires Catholics to be intentionally counter-cultural as the Christmas lights have been taken down elsewhere and the trees that were put up in November have already been taken to the curb.

The Solemnity of the Nativity of the Lord begins with the vigil Mass on December 24. This year it falls in the middle of the week, allowing some time after the Fourth Sunday of Advent for the sanctuary to be prepared for the season. Nevertheless, the daily Masses and the Liturgy of the Hours in the Fourth Week of Advent should not have to be celebrated in the environment of a season which has not yet arrived. With some preparation, the Christmas environment can be set up just before the first Masses of Christmas, which will protect the integrity of both Advent and Christmas Time and give the new environment more impact as it is experienced fully for the first time at the Masses of the Nativity.

Like Advent, Christmas Time falls at the depths of winter, which is the darkest time of the Northern Hemisphere. It is also the coldest time

of the year in many places. Light and warmth are therefore chief symbols of the season and are emphasized in much of our Christmas music, in the liturgical prayers, and in our piety. They should be carefully considered in constructing the worship environment and, if well used, will add to the celebration of the liturgy without drawing undue attention to themselves. Consider augmenting the light sources used during Advent. Candles and lamps can have a particular impact, providing the warm glow of light which we associate with the season. With added flames, however, comes added risk of fire. Be attentive to the risk in setting up the space, keeping flammable items (like greenery and fabric) well away from flames. Using lamps or candles with glass chimneys can help mitigate the risk.

Christmas Time has as its color white or gold, evoking the risen sun after the long pre-dawn twilight of Advent. These colors are also associated with joy in Christian liturgy and with the Lord. Ideally, a parish would have at least two sets of white or gold vestments and paraments ("paraments" is the collective noun for the cloth dressings of the altar, ambo, and so on). One set would be fairly simple and might be used for the feasts of non-martyr saints. The other would be more ornate and reserved for the high feasts of Christmas Time and Easter Time. Another way of differentiating these kinds of festivals is to have one set which can be used in multiple ways. A well-made, simple white altar cloth might be used for all the white feasts, with an added gold hanging for the higher feasts. Similar things could be done at the ambo; it is more difficult to construct vestments which can be worn in different ways, but a set might be made to coordinate with each. It would also be wise to procure a cope in the more ornate set, as it is more likely that the parish will celebrate liturgies at which it would be appropriate during the festal seasons. In designing or choosing these vestments, remember that more ornate does not always mean more festive. Something that is well made of beautiful, simple fabric can underline the importance of an event where the more ornate might detract. The architectural choices which have already been made in your parish will also affect what environmental choices will work. Be attentive to the situation of your parish, and regularly ask if the choices you have historically made are still working.

Plants will likely be an important part of the Christmas environment. Certainly people expect to see greenery in the form of boughs, garland, and trees. Consider using living plants for some of this greenery, which can then be planted in the spring. Live trees can provide greenery throughout the winter and with some care will last much longer than cut. Generally, plants which are brought indoors for Christmas must be kept indoors until the spring to avoid shocking them by repeated temperature changes. Check with a knowledgeable arborist in your area about the specific species you are using and their care in your climate. Poinsettias are also traditional for Christmas in the United States. If properly cared for, they will grow into sizeable bushes over several years and can be reused for several Christmases. Because they are so associated with Christmas Time, however, they are not likely to be used for the environment during other seasons and would require significant space for eleven months a year. Committees, therefore, might consider using plants which could be used throughout the year for at least a significant portion of plants, with perhaps a few poinsettias mixed in each year.

Most parishes have one major set-piece in their Christmas environment: the crèche. This tradition, often credited to St. Francis of Assisi, is important in many Catholic traditions. It can provide a focus for telling the Christmas story and often bears cultural meaning in addition to its theological import. Like all items of the liturgical environment, it should be an expression of the careful preparation which worship receives: made of quality materials, carefully displayed, and incorporated into the worship life of the parish. Care should be taken in placing the crèche, especially with larger sets. It should not dwarf or distract from the primary liturgical actions centered on the proclamation of the Word and the celebration of the Eucharist. Like the Advent wreath, this is a devotional item, which, while it can strengthen the parish's worship life, can also be a distraction. A location outside of the worship space may be desirable, especially in parishes with narrow aisles and little extra space. As the crèche may serve as a particular draw to children, setting it where they can see it clearly, and possibly interact with it, should be considered.

The Liturgical Music

WHILE many parishes have choirs or a variety of musical ensembles, it is very important to choose several traditional carols so that all who gather can participate in "singing the liturgy." Likewise, the responses, acclamations, and ritual dialogues should be familiar to all who have gathered so they may also "sing the liturgy." Consider using "A Christmas Mass" by Paul Gibson (OCP). This Mass setting is based on three Christmas carols: "Angels We Have Heard on High," "God Rest Ye Merry Gentlemen," and *Divinum Mysterium*.

In many communities, Mass during the Night may be preceded by some form of lessons and carols and conclude with the chanting of "The Nativity of our Lord Jesus Christ" (from the *Roman Martyrology*) found in Appendix I of *The Roman Missal* or the "Christmas Martyrology" by J. Michael Thompson (WLP). Consider singing it by candlelight near the crèche followed by the congregational "O Come All Ye Faithful" while all the lights in the Church are turned on.

Based on the French carol GLORIA, both "A Christmas Gloria" by Paul Gibson (OCP) and "Christmas Gloria" by Daniel Laginya (GIA) are favorites of pastoral musicians and the assembly which gathers during the Christmas season. Provide bells for children and members of the assembly to ring during the singing of the Gloria.

For a festive Gospel procession consider one of the "Six Alleluia Canons" for Christmas Time by David Hurd (GIA), the "Christmas Season Gospel Acclamation" based on the Sussex Carol by Barbara Bridge (OCP), or "Christmastime Alleluia" based on ADESTE FIDELES by James Chepponis (GIA).

It is best to stick to familiar Christmas carols for the season. A few arrangements work well as Communion processionals such as "Rise Up, Shepherd" arranged by Rob Glover (GIA).

The "Announcement of Easter and the Moveable Feasts" dates from a time when calendars were not available. The Epiphany proclamation still has value as a reminder of the centrality of the Resurrection of the Lord in the liturgical year and of the importance of the great mysteries of faith which are celebrated each year. A setting of the proclamation is found in Appendix I of *The Roman Missal*.

Several quodlibets have been put together in the past few years and they have become very popular with both choirs and members of the assembly. The two most familiar are "Night of Silence" paired with "Silent Night" (STILLE NACHT) by Daniel Kantor (GIA) and "Child of the Poor" paired with "What Child Is This" (GREENSLEEVES) by Kevin Keil (OCP). For two newer settings look at "In a Manger Lowly" (MUELLER), one of the tunes associated with Luther's "Cradle Song," paired with "Infant Lowly" (WZLOBIE LEZY), the traditional Polish carol, and "Star of Wonder," which pairs KINGS OF ORIENT and GREENSLEEVES, both by Kevin Keil (OCP).

Liturgical Ministers

IN some parts of this country, the observance of Christmas ends at bedtime on December 25. In other places, lawn decorations may stay up until the New Year, or even the Epiphany, or the Baptism of the Lord. While Christmas Time truly lasts until the Feast of the Baptism of the Lord, few but liturgical ministers and catechists (including parishioners who served in these roles previously) are aware of this. But because liturgical ministries often require a closer engagement with the liturgical texts, ministers are more readily aware of the additional demands the liturgy makes upon their spiritual lives.

Everybody throws Christmas parties these days (excepting those who throw other December holiday parties instead). But aside from Christmas in early December being "liturgically incorrect," think of how much more relaxed everyone would be—both those hosting and those attending—if a parish were to thank its liturgical ministers with an "Epiphany Party" instead?

Rather than giving everyone a small Christmas tree ornament (or something similar), schedule a Mass and offer intentions for all liturgical ministers. A simple dinner might be provided, both to express thanksgiving for their service and to build community within the parish and within each ministry. Let's not stop at keeping Christ in Christmas—let's keep the Mass, too, throughout the season.

Devotions and Sacramentals

EVERY Catholic American has a Christmas tree. But how many think to have that tree blessed? The *Book of Blessings* even offers a prayer that any layperson can lead, making it possible for a family's Christmas Eve or Christmas morning traditions to include Mom or Dad leading the family in asking that "this tree, arrayed in splendor, / remind us of the life-giving cross of Christ, / that we may always rejoice / in the new life that shines in our hearts" (BB, 1587).

What about the Epiphany house blessing? More common in some cultures than others, this devotion is a wonderful way to consecrate the new year to the Lord, in a way that remains visible due to the chalked blessing on the lintel. At the same time, it serves as an opportunity to invite the parish priest not only to visit but perhaps to dinner with the family, a mutually beneficial situation in which he can grow closer to his parish community, while the domestic Church grows in love and understanding of the universal Church.

While many Christmas Time devotions are centered around family life, here, as elsewhere, the Church offers additional opportunities for grace that are freely available to Christians in all walks of life. On the vigil of the Solemnity of Mary, the Holy Mother of God—that is, the very last day of the calendar year—the Church offers a plenary indulgence to any group that publicly recites the *Te Deum*, that ancient prayer of praise, "in thanksgiving to God for the favors received in the course of the entire year" (Apostolic Penitentiary, *Enchiridion Indulgentiarum*, 4th ed., 1999, no. 26 §1, 1°). The next day, the first of the new civic year, she offers the same reward for the recitation in word or song of the *Veni, Creator Spiritus*, as if to consecrate the new year to God by requesting an outpouring of the Holy Spirit.

The Parish and the Home

THE gift of Christmas is also the gift of our faith, our belief system which holds, forms, and transforms our lives. Christian doctrine is hidden in the song "The Twelve Days of Christmas." Look up the history of the song and then spend the twelve days of Christmas "un-wrapping" the gifts given from our faith. Once you uncover the secrets, see how those twelve aspects of faith are incorporated in our lives.

Since Christmas has only just begun for those in Catholic families, be creative in offering those you love with the gift of time. As the Christ-child is swaddled close, intentionally spend extra time with those who need the gift of your life surrounding them. On the Feast of the Holy Family, make sure to go to Mass together. Whether you are a family of husband and wife, a couple with children, single, divorced, or widowed, the Feast of the Holy Family is vital to who we each are in learning how to give and receive love, from the example set forth in our Christmas gift.

As the days of December come to a close and the New Year's Eve parties take over in preparation, find time to stay close to the tree, the crèche, and pray in thanksgiving for the gift of time and life we are given because of our faith in God. Resolutions are wonderful personal gifts of inner growth. Consider writing a letter to God talking about the past year, your hopes, and your dreams for the future. Write the prayer of your heart and maybe choose to verbalize some of these thoughts with those near. On New Year's Day, start off the year by eating right (partaking in the Eucharist,) and being healthy (honoring relationships which are important), specifically our spiritual Mother, Mary. The Solemnity of Mary, the Holy Mother of God, is a beautiful way to weave together the special moments of Christmas Time. This is Mary's special day. She wants our time spent in prayer learning from her devotion to honor God's will in her life and for us to continue adoring her Son Jesus.

Epiphany is a grand event which deserves special attention. To most, an "epiphany" is a fabulous idea that comes right when we need it. Jesus comes each moment—each day of our lives. Continue to give Jesus the attention he deserves. Continue to celebrate Christmas by paying homage to the Christ-child, falling to your knees at the crèche at your Church and offering the gifts hidden quietly in your heart. Wear red to Church and celebrate the season's full festivity for we still "need a little Christmas" long after the world has stopped celebrating. Be filled with the awe and wonder which captivated and possessed the three wise ones to give up all they had to search for Jesus and give him the greatest gifts, ones which honored his reign as King and prepared him for what was yet to come, death. Pray with this question: what are you called to give up in your lives daily to search for and then gift back to Christ? Offer your response to God in a way most fitting of your life.

Christmas Time ends quietly with the Baptism of our Lord. Decorations can come down this day and all your special memories and prayers are packed away as precious gifts in boxes, but also within your hearts. As Jesus was presented back to his Father, we each are called to claim our baptismal call to know our true identity. Honor that call. Speak to those in your family of their giftedness. Christmas now lives in you and the actions you give to the world.

Mass Texts

◆ DISMISSAL FOR CHILDREN'S
LITURGY OF THE WORD

My dear children,
during Christmas Time we celebrate the wonder
    and the joy of Jesus's birth.
As you listen to the Word of God this day,
know that it is more than the story
of a babe wrapped in swaddling clothes;
for Jesus's birth always leads
to Jesus's Death on the Cross.
That is the true miracle of Christmas Time.
Go now, and hear the Word of God,
that you may gain eternal life.

◆ DISMISSAL OF THE CATECHUMENS

As we call forth the catechumens
let us continue to pray for them,
as they seek a fuller relationship
with Holy Mother Church.
May the harsh reality of cradle and Cross
only deepen their awareness of God,
and his overwhelming love,
in sending us Jesus, his only begotten Son.

◆ INTRODUCTION TO THE MASS

Christmas is a time of great joy, as we celebrate the birth of our Savior, Jesus Christ. For many, it may be a time of great stress as well, as they struggle with financial pressures, family dynamics, or the loss of loved ones. Let us remember that Jesus was conceived, born, lived, died, and rose from the dead for us all. Let us then put aside those other concerns, as we rejoice in God's amazing love for us.

◆ Universal Prayer or Prayer of the Faithful

Introduction

"Joy to the World, the Lord is come!" And because of this we can bring our prayers and praise before the God who loves us.

Intercessions

1. For our Holy Father, Pope Francis, that he may help us all keep the birth of Christ alive in our hearts, we pray to the Lord: Lord, hear our prayer.

2. For world leaders, that they may grant their people the freedom to worship, we pray to the Lord: Lord, hear our prayer.

3. For our society, that we may break free from the commercialism of Christmas and recall the birth of Christ as we proclaim, "Every nation on earth will adore you Lord," we pray to the Lord: Lord hear our prayer.

4. For those who are alone this holiday season, or struggling with the loss of a loved one, or depression, that they may find warmth and joy in Jesus, we pray to the Lord: Lord, hear our prayer.

5. For those who struggle with their sinfulness in this holy time, that they may experience the Sacrament of Reconciliation and the healing love of Jesus, our Savior, we pray to the Lord: Lord, hear our prayer.

6. For those gathered here today, that they may experience the mystery of Christ's birth, Death, and Resurrection in this liturgy and throughout their lives, we pray to the Lord: Lord, hear our prayer.

Conclusion

"The Word was made flesh and dwelt among us."
O God, because you have dwelt among us,
you understand our joys, our pains, our sorrows,
     and our failings.
You know the prayers we bring before you
and those that lie deep within.
In your loving mercy,
answer them as you will,
and draw us ever closer to you
and to the glory of the Father.
Through Christ our Lord.
Amen.

December
Month of the Divine Infancy

WED 24 (#13) white **Vigil of the Solemnity of the Nativity of the Lord**

About this Solemnity

The events surrounding Jesus's birth are found only in Matthew's and Luke's accounts. In John's account, which was written later than the others, there is a totally different presentation of Jesus coming into the world, as "the Word became flesh" (John 1:14). The other Gospel accounts stress the humanity of Jesus while John's prologue stresses the divinity. The essence of the prologue that is important to proclaim is that God took on human flesh. God became incarnate in Jesus.

The Lectionary for Mass: At the Vigil Mass

The daily Scripture commentaries were written by Graziano Marcheschi. The Sunday Scripture commentaries were adapted from writings by Denise Simeone © LTP.

◆ FIRST READING: God's own voice announces the great joy that will accompany the coming of the Messiah. Waiting has been long and wearisome, hope has worn thin, and several more centuries would unfold before this vision is actually realized, yet Isaiah calls the people to dream a glorious, joyful dream of fulfillment and deliverance. His images of wedding feast and coronation remain compelling, for they communicate both the yearning and completion that characterized the history of Israel. God's mercy will be manifest in the changing of Israel's name (and therefore her identity) from "Forsaken" to "My Delight."

◆ RESPONSORIAL PSALM 89: The First Reading spoke a word of hope to people still suffering in exile. The psalm takes up this theme assuring Israel that God has not forgotten the covenant promise made to David. God allows us to endure the consequences of our own decisions and actions, but God never forgets his promises. Therefore, those who trust in the Lord can shout joyfully in God's presence and God's servant will acknowledge the Lord as "father, "rock," and "savior."

◆ SECOND READING: Paul evangelizes the Jews of Antioch by reminding them of God's promises to David and asserting that Jesus is both David's descendant and the one to whom John pointed and whose superiority he readily acknowledged. The early witness to Jesus always asserts that he is not acting on his own nor in discontinuity with the old law; rather, Jesus is the fulfillment of what the law and the prophets announced for centuries.

◆ GOSPEL: There is a special grace in the rhythmic recitation of the ancestry of Jesus that powerfully reinforces the perception of Jesus as the flowering of an ancient promise. The familiar details of Jesus's birth are compelling because they show the difficult human dynamics that Mary's "yes" brought into her life and Joseph's. Eager to spare her embarrassment, despite his own pain over what looked like betrayal, Joseph receives a graced revelation about God's hand at work in his and Mary's lives and he has the courage and humility to believe and act upon that revelation.

The Roman Missal: At the Vigil Mass

The Gloria is said or sung and the Creed is said (or sung) and all kneel at the words "and by the Holy Spirit was incarnate."

At the Vigil Mass and at Mass during the Night, Preface I, II, or III of the Nativity of the Lord may

be used. These prefaces are used throughout Christmas Time except for the Solemnities of Mary and the Epiphany of the Lord. When the Roman Canon is used, the *Communicantes* ("In communion with those") is said. Preface I seeks out to announce the significance of new light. This light can only be seen through the eyes of faith. "In the mystery of the Word made flesh" we encounter God who is made visible and this encounter transforms us. Preface II is inspired by Sermon 22.2 of Pope Leo the Great. In this Preface we are acknowledging the importance of the Incarnation in salvation history. As we celebrate the Nativity of the Lord we see that Christ brings humanity into the heart of the Blessed Trinity. Preface III shows the mystery of the Incarnation as a wonderful exchange between the divine and the human. This great and holy exchange transforms and restores our humanity which is made eternal. The Solemn Blessing may be used at all the Masses of Christmas.

The Prayer Over the Offerings looks ahead to the manifestations of the Lord so that we may serve him "all the more eagerly" as we participate in this great solemnity (see the notes above about the Christmas Prefaces). In the Prayer after Communion the Church celebrates the "heavenly mystery" of eating and drinking the Body and Blood of Christ so that she may "draw new vigor" in service of the Lord.

THU 25 (#14, #15, #16) white **Solemnity of the Nativity of the Lord**

The Lectionary for Mass: At the Mass during the Night

◆ FIRST READING: Isaiah was speaking hope to a people who had experienced the devastation of military invasion, destruction, and exile. This hymn-like text was intended for a royal liturgy that would crown Israel's ultimate King, her Messiah, whose reign would banish "darkness" and bring new "light" of hope and redemption. On this special night, Christians find unique fulfillment of these words in the life and ministry of Jesus. Jesus came to be the light in the darkness of our sinfulness and his light shines forever despite our tendency to prefer darkness. The joy his birth ushers in is compared to the rejoicing of harvest festivals and battlefield victory. But his greatest gift is endless peace.

◆ RESPONSORIAL PSALM 96: A new era has dawned and it calls for a "new song" to celebrate the grace and blessing it brings. So great is the transformation that is visited on the earth that all of nature senses and responds to it. No one and no thing can be unaware that God has ushered in a new age that is characterized by "justice" and is meted out by God's own hands and "with his constancy."

◆ SECOND READING: Paul alludes the Christ's birth ("The grace of God has appeared"), his act of self-sacrifice ("who gave himself for us") and his eventual return in glory ("we await the . . . appearance . . . of our great God), all themes of Advent just ended. No feast ever focuses on one aspect of the mystery of salvation to the exclusion of the others. Thus Christmas never forgets that the wood of the manger will become the wood of the Cross nor that the babe in the stable will return upon the clouds in glory.

◆ GOSPEL: Luke's beloved narrative contrasts the humble birth of a baby with the powerful political figures who dominate the world into which he's born. Contrasted, too, is the humble village of Nazareth with Bethlehem of Judea, the source of the Davidic dynasty from which this child springs. Yet there was no room for him in the inn and those to whom the announcement of his birth is made are but simple shepherds. To them is spoken a familiar refrain — "Do not be afraid" — that typically signals the announcement of God's saving action in the world.

The Roman Missal: At the Mass during the Night

The Collect is filled with images of the radiance of this holy night when the Church basks in the "mysteries of his light on earth." The light of Christ breaks into the darkness of this night and promises the Church "delight in his gladness in heaven." The Prayer over the Offerings calls the Church to be "found in the likeness of Christ" through the "most holy exchange." Christ comes and takes on human form and we share in his divine nature (see notes on the Preface above). The Prayer after Communion acknowledges that today we are "gladdened" in our sharing in the celebration of Lord's Nativity and though our "honorable way of life" we grow to be worthy of coming together with Christ (see notes on the Preface above).

The Nativity of our Lord Jesus Christ from the Roman Martyrology

The text for this proclamation can be found as the last item in Appendix I of the Missal. The proclamation, coming from the Roman Martyrology, declares in a formal way the birth of Christ, using references from Sacred Scripture. The text is either sung (preferably) or recited. The Missal specifies that at Mass it is to be done before the beginning of Christmas Mass during the Night, although it may also be done on December 24 during the celebration of the Liturgy of the Hours. The proclamation is done before Mass begins and the Introductory Rites (indeed, the rest of the Mass) occur as usual. Since the rubrics do not specify any particular minister to proclaim the announcement, it may be done, depending on circumstances, by a deacon, cantor, reader, or, if necessary, even the priest himself. It is arguable whether or not the ambo is an appropriate place from which to sing or recite the proclamation, although it would appear to be allowable to do so based on the precedent that, according to the rubrics, The Announcement of Easter and the Moveable Feasts announced on the Epiphany of the Lord is to be done from the ambo.

The Lectionary for Mass: At the Mass at Dawn

◆ FIRST READING: Isaiah's poetic words announce the arrival of salvation, and in his vision, salvation is a person who comes bringing his "reward with him." To capture the joy of this Christmas morning the Church employs this text that originally celebrated the end of Israel's captivity in Babylon and looked to the restoration of the Jerusalem temple that had been utterly destroyed. Everything is made new: Israel's punishment is at an end, renewal is on the horizon, and the mercy of God has turned Israel from one forsaken into one sought out. Today, we rejoice with Israel that we are "the redeemed of the LORD."

◆ RESPONSORIAL PSALM 97: The first verse announces the joy that God brought upon the world. And nature responds to the goodness of our sovereign Lord for shedding pure light upon us. The second verse announces who recognizes and rejoices in the Lord who "is born for us" — the "just" and righteous. Of course, Christ was born for all, but to be aware of God's mercy requires a righteous heart, a heart that can hear nature's song of praise and enter it joyfully.

◆ SECOND READING: The Trinity—Father, Son, and Spirit—is at work in every divine act. Hence, even as we celebrate the birth of Jesus, we hear of the mercy of God pouring out on us, through Jesus, the gift of the Holy Spirit. No Person of the Trinity acts in isolation from the others; so God saves us through the waters of Baptism and "renewal by the Holy Spirit." And note, it is God who saves, not we who save ourselves through any supposed acts of righteousness.

◆ GOSPEL: Like Mary, the shepherds trusted the word that the Lord communicated to them. So they rush to see its fulfillment in the person of a child lying in a manger. Remarkably, they but "see" and believe and then instantly become evangelists making known what the angels had told them of the child. In the midst of the shepherds' excitement, Mary remains centered and focused, and she not only treasures the extraordinary words of the shepherds but she ponders those words and the meaning they will have in her life and in the life of her remarkable child.

The Roman Missal: At the Mass at Dawn

The Collect proclaims that we are united to Christ and we share in his divinity. The Prayer over the Offerings tells of the mystery of the Incarnation, and the simple gift we bring to the Eucharistic banquet confers "on us what is divine." Faith is a constant theme in today's Prayer after Communion and as we celebrate the thrill of the Nativity we enter into "the hidden depth of this mystery."

The Lectionary for Mass: At the Mass during the Day

◆ FIRST READING: God is always drawing us into the web of his mercy and drawing us out of the mire of our sinfulness into the joy of his redemption. That effort is visible only to eyes of faith, but when the full glory of what God has readied for us is seen, there can only be joy and singing. The messenger bears joy within him to such a degree that everything about him is made beautiful. Most important is the news that God comes not only to liberate and restore but to dwell among his people. God does not watch from a distance, but walks alongside his people forever.

◆ RESPONSORIAL PSALM 98: Two strong themes emerge from this psalm. First is the joy expressed in song that characterized today's text from Isaiah. All creation is invited to join the chorus. The second significant notion is how God makes manifest his saving action. "The ends of the earth" have seen God's salvation. God makes his salvation known to anyone who has eyes to see. Perhaps there is encouragement there for us to make God's wondrous deeds manifest to our world.

◆ SECOND READING: The author of Hebrews addresses the identity of the one whose birth we celebrate: he is God's "very imprint" because he is God's own "Son." God no longer settles for speaking to us through intermediaries like the prophets. In the fullness of time, God sent his son to be God's full communication with us. His status is greater even than the Angels' who were created, not "begotten" by God. As the Angels in heaven are called to worship him so are we who—wonderful to declare!—share his flesh.

◆ GOSPEL: The exalted poetry of John's prologue recounts the history of God's self-revelation and has it culminate in Christ. This joyful hymn exalts that the one through whom all of Israel's longing was fulfilled has come into the world. The mention of John the Baptist only serves to underscore Christ's supremacy and unites our calling to John's—that through our witness others might come to know Jesus. He struggled against darkness and prevailed, so now he is the light of the world that came to be through him. Though rejected by his own, he grants to those who embrace him the power to become God's own children.

The Roman Missal: At the Mass during the Day

Today's Collect reminds us of God "who wonderfully created the dignity of human nature and still more wonderfully restored it." Since Christ shared in our humanity, the humble servant raises the human race to share in his divinity. The Prayer over the Offerings continues with a theme of reconciliation and "makes us wholly pleasing" in God's eyes (see notes on the Preface above). In the Prayer after Communion we pray that Christ, "the author of divine generation" for the Church, will also grant her "immortality."

Other Ideas

The *Book of Blessings* includes a special prayer for the blessing of a crèche (BB, 1544). Make sure that clergy, liturgical environment team members, and worship commission members are aware of when and where this may take place, (for example, at the end of the prelude or during the Liturgy of the Hours). The crèche and the altar should not be competing with each other as a primary symbol.

The liturgies themselves are so full and rich, be sure to thank all the visible and invisible people who made them take place. Be sure to order many extra bulletins for this weekend, and have extra hospitality people on hand. Invite people to participate in the whole Octave of Christmas.

FRI 26 (#696) red
Feast of St. Stephen, the First Martyr

The Lectionary for Mass

◆ FIRST READING: As Christianity's first martyr who, in dying, so admirably imitated the Lord, Stephen has the distinction of being honored on the day after the commemoration of the Savior's birth. He ministered with "grace and power" and when the religious leaders found themselves bested by his wisdom they reacted with deadly menace — the frequent recourse of those who live in darkness when confronted by the light. The young Saul stands by collecting cloaks. Soon he will imitate these leaders by grinding his own teeth at the fledgling Church of Christ.

◆ RESPONSORIAL PSALM 31: Cognizant that Stephen surrendered himself to death even praying for his executioners as Jesus did, the Church adorns his festal liturgy with a recitation of the words Jesus prayed as he hung on the Cross. The psalm is full of confident hope in the face of opposition and danger. Every believer facing trial, whether physical, spiritual, or psychological can pray these words committing their fate to the mercy of God.

◆ GOSPEL: So soon after the celebration of Jesus's birth, we begin to hear of the cost of discipleship. Jesus's prophetic words were too soon realized in the life of Stephen and today they are realized on an almost daily basis as thousands of Christians are martyred each year throughout the world. Jesus's words call for wariness because the world will not be a friend of the Gospel. But when believers are handed over, wisdom from on high will issue from their mouths. And while he warns that they will be hated, he also promises that endurance brings salvation.

The Roman Missal

The Gloria is said or chanted throughout the Octave of Christmas. The texts from *The Roman Missal* are proper for this day. The Collect salutes the first martyr, Stephen, who is lifted up as a model as we are called to follow his example in loving our enemies. As the Collect reminds us, Stephen "knew how to pray even for his persecutors," and we are called to do the same. The Prayer over the Offerings calls on God to accept our gifts that we present on this feast. The Prayer after Communion mentions the Nativity of the Lord and notes that we are saved by this mystery as we commemorate with delight the "celebration of the blessed Martyr Stephen."

One of the three Prefaces of the Nativity is used today. Since we are within the Octave of the Nativity, be sure to use the proper form of the *Communicantes* if Eucharistic Prayer I is used.

Today's Saint

St. Stephen (c. † 34) is the protomartyr, the first martyr. When the Apostles chose deacons to help in their ministry, he was among the first seven. Stephen was arrested and tried by the Sanhedrin for blasphemy. His fate was sealed when he had a vision during his trial and cried out, "I see the heavens opened and the Son of Man standing at the right hand of God" (Acts of the Apostles 7:56). He was taken out to be stoned to death by a mob, which included Saul of Tarsus. Stephen is shown in art with three stones and a martyr's palm, sometimes wearing a dalmatic, a deacon's vestment.

SAT 27 (#697) white
Feast of St. John, Apostle and Evangelist

The Lectionary for Mass

◆ FIRST READING: The author of First John makes it clear he is not referring to metaphors when he speaks of the "Word of life" that was "made visble" among the first disciples. He emphasizes that they heard and saw and touched the reality they now proclaim. Unlike us who share a faith that was handed on to us, they testify and pass on their experience of the one who gave them "fellowship . . . with the Father." Note, too, that the one who "was made visible to us" preexisted with the Father for all eternity.

◆ RESPONSORIAL PSALM 97: The Lord is majestic and mysterious. So awesome is the Lord that clouds veil his glory and the earth melts before his grandeur. It is the mighty Lord in whom we are told to rejoice and the reason is that the Lord is just. From those who emulate God's justice, the Lord does not hide his glory and they will rejoice in his light.

◆ GOSPEL: The "disciple whom Jesus loved" is often identified with John the apostle/evangelist, though much scholarly debate still simmers on that point. On this his feast day, we are reminded of John's prominence among the band of apostles for he is the first among them to hear of and reach the empty tomb, though he lets Peter be the first to enter. It was also to John that Jesus entrusted his mother, Mary. But we remember him not because he was especially beloved by Jesus but because, like the other apostles, he answered the call to follow Christ.

The Roman Missal

Preface I, II, or III of the Nativity of the Lord may be used and the Gloria is said or sung throughout the Octave of Christmas. The texts for today's feast are found in the Proper of the Saints. The orations and prayers from today's liturgy all contain Johannine themes, including the Word of God brought to the Church from the Apostle John which has "so marvelously [been] brought to our ears" (see the Collect); the "hidden wisdom of the eternal word" revealed through John (see the Prayer over the Offerings); and the image of the "Word made flesh" in the Prayer after Communion.

Today's Saint

St. John (first century), Apostle and fourth Evangelist, is called the "beloved disciple" because of his close relationship with Jesus. Throughout his account of the Gospel, St. John, named as the son of Zebedee and brother of St. James the Greater, makes an appearance at significant moments in Jesus's life, specifically, at the Last Supper, the Garden of Gethsemane, the foot of the Cross, and the upper room. These appearances point to the intimate relationship he had with our Lord. His account of the Gospel is quite different from the synoptic accounts (Matthew, Mark, and Luke) due to his high Christology (divine emphasis), which is proclaimed through symbolic language and poetic form. The eagle is the chosen symbol for John's account, ultimately representing the depth and height to which the human spirit must soar in order to grasp the meaning of John's text. Among his many important contributions to the Church, other scriptural writings are attributed to his name, including three epistles and the Book of Revelation.

(#17)   white

28 Feast of the Holy Family of Jesus, Mary, and Joseph

About this Feast

This liturgical feast has been on the Church calendar for about one hundred years, often on different dates. It is a "devotional" or "idea" feast that was inaugurated by Holy Family associations. Everything we know about the Holy Family, which is not much, comes from the Gospel accounts read over the three years. It celebrates the unity and love so evident in the family of Joseph, Mary, and Jesus.

The Lectionary for Mass: Year B

◆ FIRST READING: The readings for this Feast of the Holy Family take us back to Jesus's roots in the family of Israel. We hear of the "first" Jewish parents, Abraham and Sarah, who received their son (Isaac) as the child promised to them in their old age, the reward for their fidelity to God. From them, countless descendants as numerous as the stars have come forth.

◆ RESPONSORIAL PSALM 105: God remembers his covenant forever. So it was when he remembered his promise to Abraham (third and fourth stanzas) and Jacob, Abraham's grandson, with whom God renewed the covenant. The psalm is one of thanksgiving, not only in the house of Israel, but among the nations (Gentiles) as well.

◆ SECOND READING: Once again, our focus is on Abraham and Sarah, this time from the Letter to the Hebrews' account of their fidelity and trust in God. We also hear of Abraham's total obedience and complete trust in God even to the point of offering his son Isaac in sacrifice, the very one on whom the fulfilment of God's promises depended.

◆ GOSPEL: Mary and Joseph are righteous Jews, faithful in their observance of the law. We see them here in the Temple in Jerusalem for the dedication of the child and the ritual purification of his mother in accord with the law of the Lord. We meet also the righteous Simeon and Anna the prophetess who encounter the child and his parents in the temple. Note Simeon's reference to the child as a light for revelation to the Gentiles and the glory of Israel. Simeon also recognizes the opposition the child will encounter and the sorrow his mother will bear. Anna speaks a prophetic word about the child to all who awaited the redemption of Israel.

The Lectionary for Mass: Year A

The Year A readings may be used for the First or Second Reading.

◆ FIRST READING: This passage from Sirach speaks about the honor and respect that children are to give to their parents and lays out clear actions that one can do. It can be thought of as a practical explanation of how to follow the Fourth Commandment: "Honor your father and your mother, that you may have a long life in the land which the Lord, your God, is giving you" (Exodus 20:12). Its instructions teach how children are to act with love toward their parents.

◆ SECOND READING: This passage from Colossians is part of a longer section that tells how a Christian is to live ethically in the world

(Colossians 3:1 — 4:6). It begins with a list of virtues and continues with a code of how members of a household are to act toward one another. Paul wrote in a patriarchal society. In that society, protecting the authority and responsibility of the patriarch was important for order and societal integration. In maintaining right relationships, Paul's lasting contribution is his emphasis that Christian relationships are to be guided by what God has done for all through Jesus Christ. God's love has saved us, forgiven us our sins, and given us peace. We are to put on that same kind of love in our families and in our relationships with all God's people.

The Roman Missal

Preface I, II, or III of the Nativity of the Lord may be used and the Gloria is said or sung throughout the Octave of Christmas. Consider using Preface II since it declares Christ restoring unity to all creation and calling humanity back to himself, a theme to be embraced by all families. The Collect holds in great esteem the Holy Family as a shining example to model our lives after and thus perform the "virtues of family life [and the] bonds of charity." The Prayer over the Offerings also looks to the Virgin Mary and St. Joseph to intercede for all families to live "firmly in [God's] grace and [his] peace." Again, the Prayer after Communion calls on the Church "to imitate constantly the example of the Holy Family."

Other Ideas

Offer a blessing of families found in the *Book of Blessings* (BB, 66), and include prayers for families in the intercessions. While the Church surely endorses a traditional family, there are many variations on that with blended families today, so make sure your choices reflect that. In 2012 the USCCB approved a "Blessing of a Child within a

Womb" and several other prayers. You could pray this within the liturgy, or by inviting expectant families to come near the font after Mass. Balancing the liturgy so it doesn't get too heavy is important.

Remind the congregation of times for Masses on New Year's Day and remind them that the Solemnity of the Blessed Virgin Mary, Mother of God, is indeed a Holyday of Obligation.

(#202) white

29 MON
Fifth Day within the Octave of the Nativity of the Lord

Optional Memorial of St. Thomas Becket, Bishop and Martyr / white

The Lectionary for Mass

◆ FIRST READING: It is surprising how often the New Testament equates love and/or knowledge of Christ with keeping the Commandments. The First Letter of John makes no apologies for asserting that anyone who does not keep the Commandments is both a liar and ignorant of Christ. Christ's advent ushered in a new age in the history of humanity; it is an age of light that dispels the darkness. But those who fail to love are still clinging to the darkness of the former age. Whether one belongs to Christ and walks in his light is easy to discern — they walk as Christ walked and love their neighbor.

◆ RESPONSORIAL PSALM 96: As we move through the Octave of Christmas, the theme of rejoicing claims our hearts. We sing God a new song because God has created a new reality in which we live. In Christ all is made new and the grateful heart seeks to announce that good news to all the earth. The third verse is a clear and simple statement of facts: God is creator of all things; he is splendid and awesome; praise fills the sanctuary, because it flows endlessly from grateful hearts.

◆ GOSPEL: It is fitting that Simeon is immortalized in the Church's Liturgy of the Hours in which we daily recite his song that begins, "Let your servant go in peace . . . ." Luke's witness to the holiness of this Spirit-filled man is remarkable. Like Mary, he trusted that God's Word to him would be fulfilled, and he is graced both with the fulfillment of God's promise and the ability to recognize God's anointed though he discovers him as a mere babe in arms. Simeon sees clearly with Spirit-blessed eyes what the eyes of his body could not have discerned. A heart so attuned to the promptings of God's Spirit is an ideal we all must seek to emulate.

The Roman Missal

Preface I, II, or III of the Nativity of the Lord may be used and the Gloria is said or sung throughout the Octave of Christmas. The prayers for the Octave Mass are found in the Proper of Time.

Note that the Missal commentary throughout does not include optional memorials. You always have the option to use these texts. Refer first to the Proper of Saints for options.

Today's Saint

Saint Thomas Becket (1118–1170) was born in London as the son of Norman parents (he was not a Saxon, as in the play, *Becket*). He received a good education at Merton Abbey, and later in Paris. When he left school, he became a secretary, a position of some prestige in a society with limited literacy. Eventually, he became assistant to Theobald, archbishop of Canterbury. Recognizing his talent, Theobald sent him to the court of King Henry II, and eventually Thomas was named Lord Chancellor of England. In 1162, hoping to gain control over the Church, Henry had him installed as archbishop of Canterbury, but Thomas had a conversion, resigned as Chancellor, and thus began a conflict between King and archbishop. When Thomas returned from exile in France and excommunicated Henry's followers, Henry said in a rage, "Will no one rid me of this meddlesome priest?" Four knights took this as a command and killed Thomas as he went to join the monks for vespers in the abbey church. The story is retold in T. S. Eliot's play *Murder in the Cathedral* and Jean Anouilh's play, *Becket*.

(#203)   white

TUE 30 Sixth Day within the Octave of the Nativity of the Lord

The Lectionary for Mass

◆ First Reading: The poetic lines that open this text remind us of what we already know and of what has been accomplished for us in Christ: our sins are forgiven; we know Christ and the Father; and the hold of the evil one over us is broken. The balance of the reading might be used to accuse Christians of being too other-worldly and not prizing life and the joys of this world. But that would be to misunderstand the author's intent who means by "the world" all those things that are hostile to God. Instead, he calls us to live the new life we've received eschewing excessive physical desires, greed, and pretentiousness.

◆ Responsorial Psalm 96: continues to give us a glimpse of our heavenly destiny where we will naturally desire to praise and worship the Lord because God's goodness will so overwhelm us that praise will overflow our hearts. On this side of paradise, we need reminding, expressed here in imperative verbs: "Give to the Lord . . . Bring gifts . . . Say among the nations . . . ." We stand trembling before the Lord not out of fear but because even a glimpse

of the goodness of God causes us to quake with joy.

◆ Gospel: Probably sixty-plus years a widow, Anna inhabited the temple precincts because she was a prophetess for whom living with the Lord had become a way of life. Like Simeon, she had dedicated her life to the Lord and had mastered the art of listening to God. No doubt some considered her eccentric (and more!), but she immediately perceived the epiphany God placed in her path and her evangelistic response was instant, confident, and full of gratitude. How often does God place revelations in our path that we fail to recognize? Mary and Joseph's response to the outpourings of prayer and praise for their child is to bring him home to live a hidden life as he grows in wisdom and God's favor.

The Roman Missal

Preface I, II, or III of the Nativity of the Lord may be used and the Gloria is said or chanted throughout the Octave of Christmas. In the Collect we again recall the Nativity of the Lord, wherein the Only-Begotten Son of God will set us free "beneath the yolk of sin." The Prayer over the Offerings recalls the Church's profession of "devotion and faith." When we receive the Eucharist, the sacrament has the power to transform our lives. The Prayer after Communion acknowledges the "effects of its power in our hearts."

(#204)   white

WED 31 Seventh Day within the Octave of the Nativity of the Lord

Optional Memorial of St. Sylvester, Pope / white

The Lectionary for Mass

◆ First Reading: Anticipating the imminent return of Christ, the First Letter of John labels the time between Christ's Resurrection and Ascension and his return in glory as "the last hour." Already

the Christian community was experiencing difficulties and crises, especially the disheartening experience of seeing members of the community abandon the faith. Those perceived to be enemies or opponents of Christ were seen as "antichrists" and those who committed apostasy proved themselves to be void of true faith. As light and darkness represent opposing sides in the fight for the human soul, so truth and lies represent what, and who, does and does not belong to Christ.

◆ Responsorial Psalm 96: Despite the marvel of the Incarnation and the world-shattering victory of the Resurrection, the Christian heart longs for the return of Christ and the fullness of the kingdom. The psalm presciently sings of the coming of the Lord to rule over the earth and all of creation. The promise of "justice" and "constancy" will, of course, be fulfilled only in the new kingdom that the prophets and the psalmist could only intuit and see as a distant vision. In Christ, that vision is already partially realized. May our longing and just living speed its coming in fullness.

◆ Gospel: The majestic prologue to John's account of the Gospel sings of the preexistent Christ through whom all things came to be and through whom light and life were given to the human race. The text moves seamlessly from Christ to his precursor, John, whose humble witness continues to challenge all followers of Christ to imitate his willingness to diminish in order that Christ might increase. "And the Word became flesh . . . among us" is the New Testament's most sublime announcement of the Incarnation. Note the contrast of Moses and Christ who are vehicles of very different divine gifts to the human community. The oneness of Christ and the Father is perhaps the most notable aspect of this Gospel text.

The Roman Missal

Preface I, II or III of the Nativity of the Lord may be used and the Gloria is said or sung throughout the Octave of Christmas. Select from the prayers provided in the Proper of Time.

Today's Saint

Very little is known about St. Sylvester I. He was pope from 314 to 335 during the era of Constantine, when the Church was able to come out of hiding after years of persecution. During his pontificate some of the great churches in Rome were built, such as the Lateran Basilica and the original St. Peter's Basilica on the Vatican Hill (the present St. Peter's Basilica was constructed between 1506 and 1626). The First Council of Nicaea in 325, at which the Nicene Creed was adopted, occurred during his papacy. Sylvester did not attend, but he sent two legates.

January
Month of the Holy Name

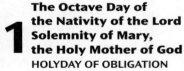

(#18)   white

The Octave Day of the Nativity of the Lord Solemnity of Mary, the Holy Mother of God
HOLYDAY OF OBLIGATION

THU 1

About this Solemnity

We are still in the midst of Christmas Time, and today the Church celebrates the Solemnity of Mary, the Holy Mother of God. One of the most outstanding characteristics of Mary is her willingness to know and do God's will. While we would like to follow her example, we wonder how she was so sure of it. Today's Gospel gives a clue. She reflected on events that happened and were happening. She meditated. In our busy lives today, we often overlook meditation as a prayer.

Lectionary for Mass

◆ FIRST READING: The blessing formula of this ancient prayer invokes the name of God three times, an unintended but nonetheless remarkable foreshadowing of the Christian Trinitarian formula. By speaking God's name, a blessing invokes God's presence among those blessed. The first invocation is a prayer for shelter and sustenance; the second asks that the light of God's face shine upon us; and the final asks God to look upon us and give us genuine shalom, a peace the world can't render.

◆ RESPONSORIAL PSALM 67: The psalm borrows words from the Numbers text of the First Reading to ask God's blessing upon us. The prayer doesn't ask a transcendent and distant God to send down a blessing upon us; it speaks to an immanent God asking him to look full-face upon us so that his face will shine on us. The God of Scripture is like a parent smiling at a child and beaming rays of purest love upon it. The last verse twice exhorts people to praise God and once to "fear him" — a much out-of-fashion term that we would do well to better understand.

◆ SECOND READING: This rich text provides several potential focal points: we might consider the significance of Jesus's birth through "a woman" (Mary) or of his birth "under the law," which we see demonstrated through the Holy Family's participation in the circumcision ritual retold in today's Gospel. But the chief point of this text is Paul's assertion regarding our "adoption." The mystery of the Incarnation proclaims that great truth: Christ was born through Mary that we might shed our status as slaves and put on the cloak of adoption as God's sons and daughters.

◆ GOSPEL: The shepherds register amazement and go off announcing the wonder they have witnessed. But Mary sits peacefully at the center of the reading pondering and treasuring the events that have forever transformed her life and our world. Her calm does not flow from blissful ignorance but from a deep conviction that the God who caused this child to take root in her womb will also guide her destiny and his. The circumcision of Jesus initiates him into the community of Israel and places on him the mark of the covenant of which he is the ultimate fulfillment. The name given him before his conception reminds us God saves not from afar but by becoming Emmanuel, God among us.

The Roman Missal

Preface I of the Blessed Virgin Mary is used today. When the Roman Canon is used, the prayer form of the *Communicantes* ("In communion with those") is said. The Gloria is said or sung and the Creed is said and all kneel at the words "and by the Holy Spirit was incarnate." The Solemn Blessing for "The Nativity of the Lord," "The Blessed Virgin Mary" or even "Ordinary Time I" (since the blessing of Aaron is heard in the First Reading) may be used.

This solemnity is celebrated as the Church concludes the Octave of Christmas. Today the Missal emphasizes Mary's "fruitful virginity" and recognizes the intercessory role that Mary plays as the woman "through whom we were found worthy, to receive the author of life, our Lord Jesus Christ, your Son."

The Collect acknowledges the virginity of Mary who through God bestows on the human race "the author of life." The Prayer over the Offerings gives witness to the joy of this solemnity by which we revel in God's grace. We will one day "rejoice in its completion." The Prayer after Communion refers to Holy Mary as both "Mother of your Son" and "Mother of the Church."

Other Ideas

This day is many things to many people: The Octave of Christmas, a Marian solemnity, New Year's Day, and the World Day of Peace. Incorporate aspects of these elements through your prelude musical selections and the Universal Prayer. Despite its jumble of ideas, the day is first and foremost a Marian day during the Christmas season, and the music for the Mass should be reflective of this observance.

(#205) white

FRI 2 — Memorial of Sts. Basil the Great and Gregory Nazianzen, Bishops and Doctors of the Church

The Lectionary for Mass

◆ First Reading: The blunt tone and admonitions of this text arise from two realities: one, the conviction that Christ's return in glory was imminent and, two, the assertion by some gnostic groups that the human Jesus was not the Christ, the Son of God. John's audience had been taught the truth about Jesus as the anointed one sent by God for the salvation of all peoples. Now they are exhorted to cling to that belief and not to be misled by the lies of false teachers who do not know God and serve the purposes of evil. Trust in the testimony of the apostolic witnesses is the best assurance that one remains close to Christ rather than ingesting the poison of the "antichrist."

◆ Responsorial Psalm 98: The Good News of Christ gives us much over which to rejoice. Our task as Christians is to cling to that Good News, realizing that many will conspire to take it from us. Even our own natures will work overtime to persuade us that what we believe is folly and that our hope is in vain. But the practice of praise is our best defense against such attacks. When we are rooted in gratitude and raise our voices in praise we draw close to the source of our joy and announce our faith to the nations.

◆ Gospel: The longing for the Messiah in Jesus's day was so great that the people were eager to identify the one whom God would send. John seems to fit the bill primarily, we must assume, because he spoke with authority and gained a large, admiring following. But John won't allow any confusion: "I am not the Christ," he asserts. But their conviction that something special drives this man makes them ask further, so he tells them plainly that he's but a herald of one whose sandal he is not worthy to untie. Cleverly, John makes them curious about the one who will come after him but is already among them. The one who will baptize with more than water.

The Roman Missal

Since we are out of the Octave of Christmas the Gloria is no longer used on weekdays. Preface I, II, or III of the Nativity of the Lord may be used. The propers for the day are found in the Proper of the Saints. The Collect invites the Church to adhere to the teaching and pattern of these holy bishops. The Prayer over the Offerings assures the Church that this holy sacrifice is "a means to our eternal salvation."

Today's Saints

Saints Basil and Gregory became close friends as students in Athens. Together they fought against the Arian heresy, which denied the full divinity of Christ. Their writings also aided the Church's understanding of the Holy Spirit and the Trinity. With Basil's brothers, Gregory of Nyssa and Peter of Sebaste, they are among the Capadocian Fathers. Gregory is known as "the Theologian" by the Eastern Churches. Basil is known as the father of Eastern monasticism and had a great influence on the development of liturgy, East and West.

SAT 3 (#206) white — Christmas Weekday

Optional Memorial of the Most Holy Name of Jesus / white

Today's Optional Memorial

The name of Jesus is important. It means "God saves." His family does not choose the name of Jesus; rather, God gives it to him before his birth: "You are to name him Jesus," the angel tells Joseph in a dream, "because he will save his people from their sins" (Matthew 1:21). Jesus's name is both his identity and his mission. Jesus's name is powerful: "Whatever you ask in my name, I will do," he tells his disciples (John 14:13). In the letter to the Philippians, St. Paul sings a hymn to the power of Jesus's name: "God greatly exalted him and bestowed on him the name that is above every name, / that at the name of Jesus every knee should bend, of those in heaven and on earth and under the earth, / and every tongue confess that Jesus Christ is Lord, to the glory of God the Father" (Philippians 2:9–11).

The Lectionary for Mass

◆ First Reading: Our relationship with Christ makes us, like him, true children of God. This relationship initiated now will perdure throughout eternity, where we will come to know God "as he is." The best way to prepare for that eternal destiny is to grow in our likeness to Christ by living lives of obedience and self-giving as he did. Sin, of course, distorts our likeness from that of Christ; it is a work of "lawlessness," that is, of the antichrist whose goal is to make us as hostile to God's will as he is. While Christians are not immune to sin, we must realize that sin alienates us from the one who has called us into filial relationship.

◆ Responsorial Psalm 98: Only one new verse is added to yesterday's selection from Psalm 98 whose theme is again summarized with "the ends of the earth have seen the saving power of God." As we continue to celebrate the Christmas mysteries we are filled with awareness of God's intrusion into human history. No absent or distant God, the Lord is both a savior and a loving parent. The ends of the earth have seen the wonders of God's victory over the enemies of his people, but they have also seen the marvel of a vulnerable child who is Emmanuel, and who is raised up as "Prince of Peace" (Isaiah 9:5)

◆ GOSPEL: Twice John confesses "I did not know him," but there is no guilt in being unable to recognize one who is hidden, who has not unmasked his true identity. But when the spirit speaks in the heart or when the mask is removed so that the truth is fully and visibly manifest, then only intentional closing of the eyes or heart will leave one steeped in ignorance. For John, it was God's word that allowed him to recognize the one on whom the Spirit descended. It was Jesus's authoritative teaching and his many signs and wonders that should have led the crowds and religious leaders to say with John: "Now I have seen and testified." How privileged we are to see as clearly as John did.

The Roman Missal

Preface I, II, or III of the Nativity of the Lord may be used. If you are using the texts from the Proper of Time for Tuesday of the Weekday of Christmas be sure to use the first Collect, "Before the Solemnity of the Epiphany," since two options are provided.

☀ **4** (#20) white
Solemnity of the Epiphany of the Lord

About this Solemnity

The Solemnity of the Epiphany of the Lord has several themes. First, we have the wise men being guided through darkness by the light of the star. Second, we have the star as a sign that leads the wise men to Jesus. Third, we have the manifestation of God to Gentiles, not just Jews, pointing to the reality that Jesus came for all people. Fourth, we have the mystery that God does reveal his very self in human flesh. Young children relate better to the themes of signs and being a sign of Jesus to others. It is important to keep repeating those themes throughout the year.

The Lectionary for Mass

◆ FIRST READING: In Isaiah's splendid poetry, Israel heard a promise of the exiles' return from Babylonian captivity and a prophesy that Gentiles would one day come to honor the city. Light and darkness are the images he uses to suggest the difference that will be manifest when God's strong arm demonstrates divine power over the earth. To Christian ears Isaiah's words announce the coming of the light of Christ who dispels the "darkness" of sin and fills us with radiant light. Note: it is from this text, not Matthew's account of the Gospel, that we derive the details of kings and camels that we generally associate with the magi.

◆ RESPONSORIAL PSALM 72: The psalm extols the virtues of Israel's ideal king and prophesies, as does today's First Reading from Isaiah, the coming of foreign kings to brings gifts and pay homage to the Lord's servant. The verses offer a blend of praise for and promise of a reign of justice and concern for the poor. God's anointed does not simply enjoy the privileges of royalty, instead he extends himself on behalf of the people, ensuring them peace built on justice and genuine concern for the poor and afflicted.

◆ SECOND READING: Unique among the band of Apostles, Paul gained knowledge of the mysteries of salvation by direct revelation from Christ himself without ever having known him in the flesh. The special charge entrusted to Paul was to evangelize the Gentiles, and such was his success that his efforts could only have been fueled by divine grace. The revelation Paul asserts here was a disquieting one among the early Christians: Gentiles are made coheirs with the Jews. The mercy and generosity of God goes far beyond our own; Jews cannot claim exclusive right to Christ. In Christ, Jews and Gentiles are made members of one body and both are sharers in the promises of Christ.

◆ GOSPEL: The arrival of the "magi" and their inquiry regarding the child born to be "king of the Jews" strikes fear in the heart of Herod and all his minions. Immediately, he seeks information about the prophesied birth of the Messiah, so Herod fears not some future human usurper, but the divine will itself that will place a true and eternal king upon the throne of David. The sad details of the story tell of this tragic king's futile efforts to thwart the will of God through schemes and subterfuge. But we're left with a hopeful image of a child in his mother's lap plied with gifts that dimly foreshadow his destiny as King and Savior.

The Roman Missal: At the Vigil Mass

There are two different Masses for this solemnity, one for the Vigil on the day before the solemnity, and one for the Mass during the Day; be sure to use the correct formularies.

The Gloria is sung or said today. The Creed is said or sung.

Light, splendor, brightness, shining, appearance: these are the themes that are conveyed in the three orations for this Mass. The Preface used is the Preface of the Epiphany of the Lord, which is found after the third Preface of the Nativity. There is no mention that the proper form of the *Communicantes* for the Epiphany of the Lord is to be used if Eucharistic Prayer I, the Roman Canon, is prayed. This is because the Vigil Mass is a distinct Mass with its own set of texts and, as it were, its own focus. The proper form of the *Communicantes* for the Epiphany of the Lord only refers to "the most sacred day" whereas the form for the Nativity of the Lord, for example, has the option of using either "night" or "day." Thus, the insert should not be used at the Vigil Mass. Aside from that, there is a certain validity to using Eucharistic Prayer III at this Mass, with an echo of Baruch in the line "from the rising of the sun to its setting."

The same principle would apply for *The Announcement of Easter and the Moveable Feasts* (the "Epiphany Proclamation"—see below, "At the Mass during the Day"). Since no mention is made of it here but it is mentioned at the Mass during the Day, it is something that is envisioned to be done only on the day itself, not at the Vigil.

Be sure to use the Solemn Blessing at the end of Mass, the one for The Epiphany of the Lord (#4).

The Roman Missal: At the Mass during the Day

The Gloria is sung or said today. The Creed is said or sung.

The famed star of Scripture and of song is mentioned in the Collect, as the prayer asks that just as the star was the guide for the revelation of God's only begotten Son to the nations, so may we too "be brought to behold the beauty of your sublime glory."

A rubric for the Mass during the Day suggests announcing the moveable feasts of the upcoming year. This proclamation can be found as the next-to-last item in Appendix I of the Missal, just before the Nativity Proclamation. It is sung or said from the ambo by a deacon or a cantor immediately after the Gospel. Although optional, this is a wonderful practice to include as it brings to the forefront the importance that the rhythm of liturgical time should hold in every Catholic's life; it can serve as a springboard for a catechesis on the liturgical year. As the Epiphany is all about the manifestation of the coming of God in the flesh, so too do we acknowledge how the Paschal Mystery is manifested in the various feasts and times throughout our year.

The Prayer over the Offerings makes a beautiful connection between the gifts of gold, frankincense, and myrrh once offered by the Magi and the gifts we offer today at this sacrifice, namely, the gift of "he who by them is proclaimed, / sacrificed and received, Jesus Christ."

The Preface assigned for today is the Preface of the Epiphany of the Lord, which can be found after Preface III of the Nativity of the Lord.

The Prayer after Communion uses the motif of light to ask that we might better understand and dwell in "the mystery in which you have willed us to participate."

For the Final Blessing, be sure to use the Solemn Blessing for the Epiphany of the Lord (#4).

Other Ideas

The traditional New Year's Blessing of Homes may be done today. It's not included in the *Book of Blessings* but is of considerable antiquity. The blessing is associated with the Magi—whose names, according to tradition, are Caspar, Melchior, and Balthazar. After the prayer of blessing, the family moves in procession through the home. Walking from room to room, they inscribe over each door the numbers of the new year and the initials of the Magi: 20 + C + M + B + 15, invoking the intercession of these holy men for the family during the coming new year.

MON 5 (#212) white
Memorial of St. John Neumann, Bishop

The Lectionary for Mass

◆ FIRST READING: When we surrender our will to God's embracing love of neighbor and faith in Christ, then we are assured of abiding in God's love. But the Christian walk is also fraught with danger because those who align themselves with Christ will encounter the enemies of Christ. Those who are hostile to God and who refuse to embrace Christ have embraced the lawlessness of the antichrist, which already has made a home in the world. And if by antichrist one understands the powers of darkness, John offers consolation: "the one who is in you (Christ) is greater than the one who is in the world." That word is as true and comforting today as when John wrote it.

◆ RESPONSORIAL PSALM 2: Yesterday's Gospel account told of the fear that gripped Herod and all Jerusalem at the news of the star that heralded the coming of Israel's new king. Today's psalm gives earthly rulers good reason for concern and exhorts them to let fear grip their hearts. Rulers must take "warning" and rejoice before the Lord, but with "trembling." The reason for this is that the Lord has promised all the nations of the earth to "my Son." Earthly power will melt like wax before the Lord's anointed, so all who wield power had better do so in great humility and abundant fear.

◆ GOSPEL: In prudently distancing himself from Nazareth after the death of John, Jesus fulfills Isaiah's prophecy regarding light breaking out in the midst of darkness. And the brilliance of his light is manifest in his many healings and deliverances and in the way he ends pain and paralysis and proclaims the good news of God's mercy. And those who saw believed and followed him.

The Roman Missal

Preface I, II, or III of the Nativity of the Lord or the Epiphany may be used. The Collect announces the charity and pastoral service of the shepherd to the people of America who fostered Christian education of youth and witnessed love to the family under his care. Today the Church prays that we will follow his example.

In the Prayer over the Offerings we pray that our lives, too, might "reflect the image of Christ." Like St. John Neumann, we are called to imitate what we celebrate. Again, we call on the example of St. John Neumann that as we receive the sacrament, we will continue to participate in the Paschal Mystery of Christ.

Today's Saint

With an intellectual capacity far surpassing his peers and a special talent for languages, Saint John Neumann (1811–1868) came to the United States from what is now called the Czech Republic with the dream of being a priest and missionary. Received with open arms by the bishop of New York, Saint

John was ordained and immediately asked to help build churches and schools for German immigrants and Native Americans. Needing spiritual support and companionship, he eventually entered a religious order, the Redemptorists, where he was made novice-master and eventually vicar of all the Redemptorists in the United States. The larger Church recognized his holiness and affinity for leadership by appointing him bishop of Philadelphia, the largest diocese at the time. While bishop, he was an avid supporter of the work of religious orders, a proponent of Catholic education, and an advocate for the needs of immigrants.

T U E 6 (#213)   white
Christmas Weekday

Optional Memorial of St. André Bessette, Religious / white

The Lectionary for Mass

◆ FIRST READING: God sets the bar for what love is, because God is love. All we know of love we know first from God. Friends and lovers make great sacrifices for each other; but as exemplary and noble as that may be it does not approach the love of God who, while we were still sinners, "sent his Son as expiation for our sins." God had nothing to gain in loving us that much; God gave only for our benefit. Our lives, then, must manifest love if we hope to speak of God, for anyone who does not know love — intimately, from the inside out, in a selfless way that seeks the good of the other more than the good of the self — does not know God. Those who love are one with the heart of God.

◆ RESPONSORIAL PSALM 72: The love John calls for in the First Reading and the love Jesus demonstrates in the Gospel is celebrated in the Psalm. Judgment and justice, peace and care of the afflicted with which we ask God to "endow the king" are but manifestations of

God's enduring love. The care that God's chosen one will show toward God's people is a sacrament of that divine love that stretches from sea to sea. When we pray for our leaders, civic and ecclesial, we are asking God to endow them with justice and judgment that is born of God's own love.

◆ GOSPEL: All four Gospel accounts relate this story of how God's abundance overwhelms our scarcity. Giving what we have, no matter how much it may be, will never be sufficient to feed the hungers of the world. Were this a story of a miracle of sharing it would recount something that happened once and long ago. But the universal agreement that this story points to and anticipates the eucharist compels us to see God at work supplying a bounty no amount of human sharing could accomplish. The eucharist is not something we pull out of our pockets or picnic baskets to share with those who have less; it is a divine self-giving that depends only on our willingness to receive and be nourished.

The Roman Missal

Preface I, II, or III of the Nativity of the Lord or the Epiphany may be used. For the remaining prayers, refer to *The Roman Missal* for the days "after Epiphany."

Today's Saint

St. André Bessette (1845 – 1937) modeled his life on that of St. Joseph, to whom he had a great devotion. As a brother of the Congregation of the Holy Cross in Montreal, he was given the post of doorkeeper at Notre Dame College, a post he kept for forty years. A simple, holy man, André had a special gift of praying over the sick. His prayers were answered, sometimes in miraculous ways, and people began to come to him in large numbers. He gave all the credit to St. Joseph, and he dreamed of a shrine to St. Joseph on Mount Royal. He lived to see the building of the magnificent Oratory of St. Joseph begun. By the time of his death he was receiving some 80,000 letters per year from people begging for his prayers. When he died, a million people filed in procession past his coffin. Today, the Oratory of St. Joseph at Mount Royal receives two million pilgrims each year. André Bessette was beatified by Pope John Paul II in 1982 and canonized by Pope Benedict XVI on October 17, 2010.

W E D 7 (#214) white
Christmas Weekday

Optional Memorial of St. Raymond Penyafort, Priest / white

The Lectionary for Mass

◆ FIRST READING: The invisible God is made visible within the circle we create when we imitate God and love one another. Christ promised to remain with us always and the seal he set upon that promise is the Holy Spirit who empowers us to know and believe in God's great love for us. And a hallmark of that love is the absence of fear; in fact God's love repels fear as oil repels water. Lack of fear and trust in God's abundant mercy, in fact, are nearly infallible signs of genuine growth into mature faith.

◆ RESPONSORIAL PSALM 72: The psalm throws focus upon the Davidic king asking God to mark his reign with justice. The Christian consciousness cannot fail to understand these words in reference to Christ, the Messiah, who came to establish a kingdom of everlasting justice and peace. This savior who was born in the humblest of circumstances will not be deaf to the need and the cries of the poor. He will be the hope of the afflicted and the savior of the lowly and the poor. But we mustn't forget that, in this

life, he can't accomplish it without our arms and hands.

◆ GOSPEL: Having satisfied the hungers of the multitude with his teaching and with the abundance he created from a few loaves and fish, Jesus withdraws for solitary prayer. Refreshed and nourished on prayer, Jesus returns to find the disciples buffeted by the sea. His walking on the water manifests his divinity as does his self-identification, "it is I" that echoes the response of God to Moses at the burning bush (Exodus 3:14). Despite their being tossed about, Jesus has no intent to stop; only when they call out—in reaction to his appearance, not the winds and choppy sea—does Jesus identify himself and enter the boat. Remarkably, they had failed to understand the "sign" of the loaves and also miss the meaning of this extraordinary moment. The reason Mark offers is the same he assigned to those who plotted Jesus's death: "their hearts were hardened."

The Roman Missal

Preface I, II, or III of the Nativity of the Lord or the Epiphany may be used. For the remaining prayers, refer to *The Roman Missal* for the days "after Epiphany."

Today's Saint

As a Dominican priest and scholar, St. Raymond traveled far and wide to convert non-believers, change the hearts of heretics, and infuse the great universities of Europe with solid theological instruction, resulting in a presence of the Dominicans at the universities of Oxford and Cambridge. Recognized as a visionary leader, St. Raymond was elected third master general of the Dominican order, following in the footsteps of Blessed Jordan of Saxony. His spiritual aptitude and theological literacy reached beyond the walls of the Dominicans to other areas: He served as spiritual director to the pope, Archbishop of

Tarragona, and compiler and reviser of Church laws (canon law).

T H U 8 (#215) white
Christmas Weekday

The Lectionary for Mass

◆ FIRST READING: Pope Francis has reminded us of the simplicity of the Christian message. Stripped of its intellectual accretions, the Christian formula is very uncomplicated: I love God because he first loved me. And because God loves me, I must love my neighbor. And anyone who claims to love God without loving their neighbor is a liar! Simple. The way we show that love is by keeping God's Commandments. The world deems the Commandments burdensome, but faith enables us to see that God's law is but an invitation to love, a broad broom that sweeps obstacles to love from our path so we can walk in the ways of the Lord.

◆ RESPONSORIAL PSALM 72: The Lord is our strong arm, our defense against those who would defraud us, raise arms against us, and shed our blood. Such threats take many forms in this and every age and danger ever lurks about us. But does God really care whether we are cheated and deceived? Does God mourn our losses and hold precious the blood we shed? The psalmist believes so and calls upon all the nations to proclaim it.

◆ GOSPEL: After the travail of the desert, Jesus returns to the comfort of his boyhood home and in the synagogue selects the passage on which to focus his neighbors. His choice from Isaiah casts him in the role of the biblical prophet anointed for God's service. The selection also underscores Jesus's concern for the poor and disadvantaged, a theme that recurs throughout Luke's account. The final lines of today's portion are the calm before the storm that will erupt in the following verses where Jesus's rejection by his neighbors will foreshadow his rejection by Israel. But in today's text, Jesus announces that the hopes of their ancestors have found fulfillment, and Luke will make Jesus the locus of that fulfillment, played out in his ministry and in his Death and Resurrection.

The Roman Missal

Preface I, II, or III of the Nativity of the Lord or the Epiphany may be used. We now come to the final three days of Christmas Time, and the orations are found in *The Roman Missal* in the weekdays of Christmas Time before the Feast of the Baptism of the Lord. The Collect (the option for after the Solemnity of Epiphany), acknowledges the eternal light to the nations and "the full splendor of their Redeemer, that bathed ever more in his radiance, they may reach everlasting glory." Walking in the light of Christ, the Church looks forward to the coming of Christ at the end of time. The Prayer over the Offerings again references the "glorious exchange." The short Prayer after Communion assures the Church that its life will be continuously sustained by "the power of these holy mysteries."

FRI 9 (#216) white
Christmas Weekday

The Lectionary for Mass

◆ FIRST READING: In the struggle between the followers of Christ and the forces opposed to him and his kingdom, victory goes to the one who surrenders to Christ in faith, embracing him as the true Son of God. The witnesses that affirm Christ's identity are the Spirit (present at his baptism), the water of the Jordan where he was baptized and where God pronounced him his beloved son, and the blood he shed on the wood of the Cross. The message proclaimed by these witnesses

is clear and life-changing: salvation that leads to eternal life comes only through Christ. But belonging to Christ is not primarily about adhering to a creed or a value system; first and foremost, it is the embrace of a person: Jesus the Christ.

◆ RESPONSORIAL PSALM 147: In light of the First Reading, the words of the psalm remind us that God fortifies his people with knowledge of his son; the "bars of [our] gates" are strengthened because we have God's testimony that Jesus is the source of life. God's word "swiftly runs" and is proclaimed to Israel and Jacob, but not to all the nations. Such privilege is cause of great rejoicing for the "word" God has proclaimed is not a doctrine of a set of laws, but God's own son.

◆ GOSPEL: The man full of leprosy sensed that Jesus needed only to will his healing and the leprosy would disappear. Jesus first speaks his desire to heal the man then stretches out his arm to accomplish it. But his affirmative response is spoken not only to the leper but to all who wonder if they are within the orbit of God's love and concern: "Lord, do you know me?" "I do." "Lord, do you love me?" "Of course" (author's paraphrase). Though Jesus orders the leper to keep silent, the command is futile; who could keep silent about an encounter with the Lord of life?

The Roman Missal

Continue to use the prayers for after Epiphany.

SAT 10 (#217) white
Christmas Weekday

The Lectionary for Mass
◆ FIRST READING: The Christian can pray with confidence because we have a rock-solid relationship with Christ who, like a parent or dear friend, will grant anything we ask that is "according to his will."

The love we receive we also extend to others, especially sinners who are in need of our intercession. The "deadly" sin for which we may but are not ordered to pray probably refers to some form of apostasy. Disciples and the allies of the evil one are like magnets with opposite poles repelling each other. But those who belong to Christ know the one true God and therefore are not led astray by false idols that would usurp God's rightful place in our lives.

◆ RESPONSORIAL PSALM 149: Exuberant joy dominates the verses of today's psalm. The people of Israel, named the "children of Zion," rejoice in God's goodness. The Lord not only loves his people, he is especially mindful of the lowly and clothes them in "victory." Whenever we pause to be mindful of the graces that daily flow into our lives, when we remember the privilege of knowing the Lord and of understanding his ordinances, are we not moved to exultation and to singing the praises of our God?

◆ GOSPEL: The famous words of John about Christ's ascendency and his own diminishment lead us toward the end of Christmas Time. John's disciples are annoyed that Jesus and his disciples have invaded their turf, but John refuses to get dragged into an intramural squabble about baptism. He immediately reiterates his clear assertion about his identity: he is the "best man," not the "bridegroom." In Jewish custom it was the best man, in light of his close relationship with the groom, who made the wedding arrangements. Their deep friendship would not permit a hint of rivalry or competition. John's joy — and his mission — are complete in seeing Jesus assume his rightful role.

The Roman Missal

Preface I, II, or III of the Nativity of the Lord or the Epiphany may be used. The Collect used for today's Mass is the one for After the Solemnity of Epiphany. Since God's Only Begotten Son is a new creation of God, we too are "found in the likeness of him, in whom our nature is united." The Prayer over the Offerings calls on our prayer to be one of peace so that the Church may "do fitting homage to your divine majesty" as she partakes of the sacred mystery. The Prayer after Communion refers to the grace of the sacrament that sustains the Church now and in the future. The Eucharist is referred to as a remedy for the "things that pass away."

(#21)   white

☀ 11 Feast of the Baptism of the Lord

About this Feast

The Feast of the Baptism of the Lord proclaims a theophany, a revelation or manifestation of the divine Sonship of Jesus by his anointing and appointing to his messianic office. It is the feast that proclaims the Baptism that elevates believers to the status of sons and daughters of God.

The Lectionary for Mass

◆ FIRST READING: No doubt the invitation to "come to the water" prompted the selection of this beautiful text of Isaiah for today's First Reading. In the water, life is to be found. Note the themes of repentance and turning to the Lord, of metanoia in the second part of the reading. We think of

the word (Word) in the last lines of the reading not only as Torah (Law), but also, in Christmas Time, of Jesus, the Word made flesh, who will do God's will and accomplish the purpose for which he was sent.

◆ CANTICLE: Today's response is actually a hymn taken from the prophet Isaiah. Our antiphon, from the hymn, associates water with salvation. The stanzas are a confident and joyful hymn of praise to the Lord who is and has been experienced as Savior.

◆ SECOND READING: The language of "begotten" points to parental relationship: both Jesus's and ours with the heavenly Father. Our new birth comes through belief in Jesus. The testimony of the Father and the Spirit is evident at Jesus's baptism. The testimony of blood will come in the gift of his life on the Cross, his mission completed.

◆ GOSPEL: Jesus comes forward as one of the many people who heard John, as one just like any other person. John knows that the one to come is at the same time different from all other people. Jesus's baptism was a moment of intense revelation: he saw the Spirit descend upon him; he heard the voice of the Father say: "You are my beloved Son . . . ." (Mark 1:11). He will show us the way to the Father by walking it himself.

The First or Second Readings from Year A may be used.

◆ YEAR A, FIRST READING: The actions of God are commanding: he calls, grasps, forms, and sets the servant as a light for the nations. God called and sent the servant. God filled the servant with his spirit who then teaches and brings justice to the earth, fulfill the command to be light, give sight to the blind, release prisoners, and free those who are in darkness. Christians see the servant fulfilled in the person of Jesus Christ.

◆ YEAR A, SECOND READING: Peter emphasizes that all that God has created is good, not profane or wicked. God has created Jews and Gentiles alike and made them coheirs. God indeed shows no partiality.

The Roman Missal

Two options for the Collect are offered in the Missal. The first Collect contains three important components of Christ's baptism: water, the Holy Spirit, and the declaration that he is the "beloved Son." The Collect shows God's great love for all of his beloved sons and daughters. The alternative Collect focuses on the title "Son" and on Christ's humanity: he "appeared in our very flesh."

The Prayer over the Offerings calls to our attention that the Holy Spirit is always the active transforming agent at work in the Church, changing bread and wine and people into the Body and Blood of Christ. Again, this oration calls us to faithful listening, not just to what we have heard in the Mass, but to what we will do in the world.

The Prayer after Communion reminds us that, having been nourished with the sacred gifts, we must be God's children "in name and in truth" by "faithfully listening to your Only Begotten Son."

Other Ideas

While the world has moved well past Christmas, the Church still celebrates it today. One must combine the Feast of the Baptism of the Lord with a farewell for Christmas in this liturgy. The addition of a "John the Baptist" song will take us full circle back to Advent. It is a wonderful day for parish Baptisms as well as the addition of the sprinkling rite. If help is needed transforming the church back to Ordinary Time, or if the parish is giving away Christmas florals, be sure to annouce it at all the Massses today.

ORDINARY TIME (DURING WINTER)

The Meaning / The Lectionary for Mass

BETWEEN the Feast of the Baptism of the Lord and Ash Wednesday, we celebrate the weekdays and Sundays of Ordinary Time. Deep into winter in the Northern Hemisphere, many of us experience respite from the hustle and bustle of the holidays. We return to the routine marked by school and work schedules, as well as family activities. This year, the period of time between the end of Christmas Time and the beginning of Lent is relatively brief.

Five Sundays, the Second through the Sixth Sundays in Ordinary Time, and five weeks and the beginning of a sixth, provide us with an interim period during which we can reflect on the origins of our call to be a follower of Christ and what accepting that call means for the way we live in the world. No different than other times of the year, we give pause to consider what God is doing in Christ, what God is doing in us, and through our partners in discipleship in the Church and in the world.

The First Readings from the weekday Lectionary for the initial four weeks come from the Letter to the Hebrews. Written primarily for Jewish Christians, one of the author's primary tasks is to defend the full divinity of Jesus Christ in light of those who believed that Jesus was less than God because of his humanity. The passages selected for proclamation provide us the opportunity to internalize the meaning of Jesus's divinity and his high priesthood for our faith lives. Over and over, we hear in different ways how Jesus's high priesthood and sacrifice differ from that of previous high priests. Jesus offered a once and for all sacrifice. This sacrifice does not need to be repeated and it marks him as the eternal high priest. He is the high priest we follow in life and the One whom we praise every time we gather for worship. There will never be another.

After four weeks proclaiming the First Reading from the Letter to the Hebrews, the daily Lectionary shifts to the Book of Genesis for the Fifth Week in Ordinary Time and the two days prior to Ash Wednesday. In Genesis, we begin where it is only fitting, with the first account of God's creation. From there we hear from the second account of creation as well as about the fall of humanity in the garden and our loss of innocence. The tragic story of Cain murdering his brother Abel and the hopeful story of the protection of Noah and other living creatures from the great flood become occasions on which we once again discover God's mercy. We hear the call to acknowledge our sinfulness and rest in divine forgiveness and compassion—to recognize in all humility that God created us and we are not God.

The Responsorial Psalms provide us with ways to respond to the living word proclaimed in the First Readings. Frequently during these weeks, the words of the psalms help us to sing praise and glory to God, the author of creation and the giver of the covenant fulfilled in Jesus Christ. Some of the psalms, such as Psalm 95, call us to listen to God rather than closing our hearts. The psalms during this time also lead us to acknowledge our own offenses and not only accept, but rejoice in the mercy God graciously extends to us. In the midst of daily life, when we are aware of God's presence in and around us, we are also aware of our limitations and how much we need the grace of God's forgiveness.

Beginning with Monday of the first week in Ordinary Time, we start a continuous reading of the Gospel according to Mark. During the five and a half weeks prior to Lent, the Gospel readings progress from chapter 1 of Mark through chapter 8. For Mark, from the beginning of the Gospel, Jesus is always the Son of God, the Messiah. When Jesus calls his disciples and they follow, they embark on a journey to learn what Jesus's messiahship means. They embrace, though not always willingly, the ups and downs of walking with him. Jesus sends the Twelve out on their own to preach and teach and heal. Courageously, they go and we go with them.

On the weekdays of Ordinary Time, we travel with Jesus and the disciples as the Messiah exorcises demons, heals illnesses, experiences rejection, engages the Pharisees' intentional attacks on him, teaches in parables, calms fears, and feeds the multitudes. All the while, we hear the message that "the Kingdom of God is at hand." We sense the newness that has taken place in Jesus. We wonder if we will be able to follow the instructions the Gospel writer often has Jesus give—to not tell anyone what they witnessed. The Gospel, the day before Ash Wednesday, leaves us to ponder whether we will be able to remain faithful disciples or whether we will succumb to the evil leaven of the Pharisees. For our ongoing discernment in this matter, the journey of Lent awaits.

The First Readings for the Second through the Sixth Sundays in Ordinary Time come from a variety of books of the Old Testament. On the Second Sunday in Ordinary Time, the Lectionary pairs the narrative of the call of Samuel from the first book of Samuel with the Gospel reading of John's account of the call of the first disciples. On the Third Sunday, the passage from the prophet Jonah, which recounts Nineveh's change of heart and God's merciful response, coincides with Mark's account of the call of the first disciples. For Mark, the initial step in discipleship is repentance; turning one's heart away from evil and toward God marks one's faith that the kingdom of God is at hand in Jesus.

The First Reading for the Fourth Sunday gives us Moses's words to the people predicting the Lord will raise up a prophet from among them who will speak God's words. The Gospel reading for this Sunday shows us that Jesus is the complete fulfillment of Moses's words. Jesus's words, spoken with divine authority, even expel unclean spirits.

Our amazement mirrors that of the people in the synagogue!

We are familiar with Job's reflection on life's drudgery that we hear proclaimed on the Fifth Sunday. Though the reading seems to end pessimistically, Job never completely loses faith. So many people express their faith in Jesus as they seek him out to perform miracles in the Gospel coupled with the Job reading. From Mark, on this Sunday, we experience how Jesus's ministry grows exponentially.

The Sixth Sunday of Ordinary Time also brings us a familiar First Reading and Gospel. The passage from Leviticus reminds us how the community considered a person with leprosy to be unclean and an outsider until ritually cleansed. Jesus's compassionate words and actions in the Gospel recall the truth for us that in the kingdom there are no outsiders. A life of faith affords healing to all. We cannot help but announce to the world this Good News even when it conflicts with past customs.

We enter more deeply into the First Readings with the Responsorial Psalms, intentionally chosen to reflect themes in the reading and to facilitate our response to them. The psalmody for this period of Ordinary Time focuses on our response to God's call (Psalm 40), our willingness to ask God to teach us his ways (Psalm 25), our ability to listen to God's voice rather than closing our hearts to God (Psalm 95), our praise for God who heals (Psalm 147), and the joy of salvation that we experience when we turn to God with our sin and at other times of need (Psalm 32).

The Second Readings for this period of Ordinary Time are from chapters 6 to 10 of Paul's First Letter to the Corinthians. In the midst of conflict, struggle, and division in the early Christian community at Corinth, Paul teaches believers about how they are to live in the interim before the Second Coming of Christ, the Parousia. The commonly held belief was that the Parousia was imminent. Thus, Paul focused his teaching to the Corinthians on practical matters, such as moral living, a lack of attachment to the world, reducing anxiety in one's present state of life, and being mindful of one's brothers and sisters in the community.

Paul consistently preached that everything we do we do for the glory of God, not for our own glory. The readings for these Sundays call us to proclaim the Gospel so that we might experience its grace in Christ Jesus, and to be imitators of Christ, the Messiah in whom the Gospel lived.

While the Sunday Lectionary readings are the same every three years, and the weekday readings the same every two years, we change, our lives change, and our relationships grow, some withering and dying. Yet we remain followers, disciples of Jesus. God continues to call us to know more profoundly who Jesus the Messiah is, for us and for the world. May these weeks of Ordinary Time during winter provide us with the opportunity to see how God in Christ is present in our lives this year, calling us into newness and into mission for the sake of the world. May we allow God's grace to buoy us for any rough roads on the journey, and may we always rejoice in the joy of salvation!

The Roman Missal

THE Mass formularies for this segment of Ordinary Time are found in the "Ordinary Time" section that follows the "Easter Time" section in the Missal. Each Sunday has its own proper Collect, Prayer over the Offerings, and Prayer after Communion, as well as Entrance and Communion Antiphons. There are no formularies for ferial weekdays. Customarily, priests will repeat the prayers from the previous Sunday, although there is no hard-and-fast rule about this; in fact, orations from any Sunday in Ordinary Time may be used on any ferial weekday. Note that there are no formularies for the "First Sunday in Ordinary Time," since the Sunday that begins the First Week in Ordinary Time is always either the Feast of the Baptism of the Lord or the Solemnity of the Epiphany of the Lord (in some years, the Feast of the Baptism of the Lord is celebrated on the Monday after Epiphany); thus, orations used for weekday Masses during the First Week in Ordinary Time should come from the page titled accordingly.

Children's Liturgy of the Word

READINGS: The readings during this portion of Ordinary Time reflect growth in the ministry of Jesus as he chooses his disciples and celebrates his first miracles. We begin on the Second Sunday with John's account of the Gospel and the calling of Simon Peter and Andrew as the first disciples. It is important to articulate to the children that Jesus did not command the disciples to follow him but offered them the invitation to "come, and you will see." He offers us the same invitation. His call is gentle. Here we also see introduced the title "Lamb of God." You may want to point out to the children the different times we use that title during the Mass.

The call of the Apostles continues with the Third Sunday as we return to Mark's account of the Gospel and his version of the call of Peter, Andrew, James, and John, calling them from their fishing boats to become "fishers of men" (1:17). We also are introduced to a theme that will be an important aspect of Jesus's ministry, the call to repentance and belief in the Good News of Jesus. The Old Testament readings during these weeks also speak of God calling those who will speak his word to the people: Samuel, Moses, and Jonah.

The remaining three weeks' Gospel readings focus on the healing miracles of Jesus. For Mark, healing the sick and the possessed was integral to Jesus's ministry but predominantly as a way to show his authority and power. The Old Testament readings proclaimed during these Sundays also speak about healing. As a rule, the First Reading usually relates in some way to the Gospel connecting both Testaments.

The Second Readings during these winter Sundays of Ordinary Time are taken from St. Paul's First Letter to the Corinthians. This beautiful letter addresses moral issues that plagued the people of Corinth and still plague the world today. In this letter Paul shows his great love and concern for the Corinthians, encouraging them not to turn away from all he has taught them about Jesus and following the way of God.

◆ ENVIRONMENT: With any change of liturgical season the change in the liturgical environment should be noticeable. The liturgical color for Ordinary Time is green. Green is the color of growth and of hope. Plants and flowers could be used to emphasize this. Green cloths and banners can be used throughout the space. If the space and the furnishings in the room allow for it, rearranging the seating area or the place where the reflection will take place gives the sense that we are entering a new time in the liturgical year.

On the Sixth Sunday of Ordinary Time, the Sunday before Lent begins, it might be appropriate to display a banner with the word *Alleluia* written on it. This Sunday will be the last time we will sing Alleluia until Easter. After the Gospel, the banner could be ritually folded or processed out and put away.

If you have a prayer table set up in the space, consider using icons that fit with the season. These do not have to be purchased. Parishioners may be willing to lend an icon or other image to decorate the space, or a creative parishioner could create an icon from a downloaded picture or write an icon for the children's Liturgy of the Word. This not only decorates the space but introduced the children to religious art.

◆ MUSIC: It is always important to discuss music with the parish music director, and a change in season is an opportune time to do this. Using a seasonal psalm with the children helps them to fully participate in singing the psalm response. If you are not using a seasonal psalm, make sure that the psalm and response is simple enough for the children to remember and sing. Remember that music does not have to be childish in order for children to be able to sing. Many parishes are able to use the same psalm tones with the children that are being used in the larger worship space. The use of good liturgical music helps to form children as members of the liturgical assembly. Inviting older children to minister as psalmists and cantors helps encourage them to perhaps enter this ministry one day, but it is important that whoever is singing the psalm is able to engage the children and has pronunciation that is clear enough for the children to understand the words being sung. Consult the parish music director or consider the musical suggestions in *Children's Liturgy of the Word: A Weekly Resource* from LTP.

The Saints

W E tend to think of the annual festivals of the saints as separate from the cycle of Christ's Passion, Death, Resurrection, and Ascension, but this is not so. The saints demonstrate for us the intersection of the life of Christ with the secular world, giving us concrete examples of how his mysteries can be lived out in our own time.

Our favorite saints are easy: Mary, Joseph, Patrick, Thérèse, Francis . . . every Catholic who goes to church more than twice a year—or even merely grew up in a Catholic environment—knows them. But what about the lesser-known ones? Another missionary martyr, another religious foundress, another pope, another virgin martyr: How can each of these revitalize the parish community?

Maria Goretti's commitment to purity may not seem relevant to every parishioner's life, but her concern for the soul of her attacker challenges each one of us to truly love our enemies. Stanislaus is important not only to those with Polish heritage, but to any who might fear a political backlash for speaking the truth. Hilary is relevant not just to bishops, academics, and heretics, but to all of us whose daily interactions provide opportunities to defend Christ's divinity.

The challenge facing us today is to look deeply into a saint's life and find not only piety but inspiration, a reflection of Christ's life and a model for our own. The liturgical texts offered for each saint provide us with an entry point, so that we never have to stop at learning about a saint, but are always prepared to take that essential next step: not only to pray to each day's saint, but to let their very lives draw us to Christ.

The Liturgy of the Hours

TIME is a creature. This sounds funny because we're used to "creatures" being strange, mutated animals in fictional stories. But the word really means simply "something that was created by God." We are all creatures; God, the Creator.

Time is a creature. This is part of why we are obliged to give him back at least one hour of that time each week, but it's so much more than that. In contemporary American society, what causes us more stress than time? It marches inexorably on, moving quickly when we want it to be leisurely, and slowly when we want it to be speedy.

Time is a creature. In many ways, this is the central logic behind the Liturgy of the Hours. By stopping our ordinary work during the course of the day—even if only for five minutes at a time—we consecrate the day; we give time itself back to God. And time, like any other creature in

the same situation, acts just a tiny bit differently after it has been consecrated to the Creator.

Time is a creature. As such, it is fulfilling its eternal purpose, its highest possible end, when it is drawing us to the Father.

The Rite of Christian Initiation of Adults

THE assembly should continue to be catechized about the RCIA. Whenever you have inquirers who are ready to become catechumens celebrate the Rite of Acceptance with them, on any given Sunday throughout the liturgical year, when the time seems right. Look in your RCIA ritual book and open it to the very back. Look for the section that is titled "Appendix III: National Statutes for the Catechumenate" (NSC). Then find paragraph 6, and underline the last sentence: "Ordinarily [the period of the catechumenate] should go from at least the Easter season of one year until the next; preferably it should begin before Lent in one year and extend until Easter of the following year" (NSC, 6).

This suggests that one of the "right times" to celebrate the Rite of Acceptance is on one of the Sundays between Epiphany and Ash Wednesday. This way you can have a little over a year for the process of the catechumenal journey and can begin to move away from the nine month school model. The prayers in the ritual provide us with an insight into what catechumens need to do to "follow God's light" (RCIA, 52 A) "in our company" (RCIA, 52 B) , "to become his disciples and members of his Church" (RCIA, 52 C). Since catechesis echoes the Gospel, catechumens should be afforded at least a year or more for the process of accepting the teachings of Christ. Little of this can be accomplished in a few short weeks between the seasons of Advent and Lent. By embracing a year-round model for initiating and celebrating the rites at the "right times," the parish community will move closer to an understanding that "the initiation of adults [and children] is the responsibility of all the baptized" (RCIA, 9).

As they enter into the period of the catechumenate these seekers must have in mind someone who would be willing to sponsor them. The sponsors are usually practicing Catholics that the catechumens know. The duties of a sponsor are to go with them through the various rites and provide individual instruction about matters of faith. From this point until their Baptism, catechumens are dismissed after the Liturgy of the Word when they attend Mass at the parish at which they had the Rite of Acceptance. This is to make the process feel more like it was in the early Church, when Christian converts were dismissed before Communion prior to their Baptism, which often took years to prepare for, largely to make the Communion more secret and more meaningful.

The Rite of Welcoming the Candidates (RCIA, 411–415) is celebrated when inquirers, who have already been validly baptized in another non-Catholic ecclesial community or baptized Catholic but not confirmed as a child, are welcomed to this next stage via the Rite of Welcoming the Candidates. They enter this rite as candidates, and they are known by this title from now on. Their Rite of Welcome often does not take place at the same time as the catechumen's Rite of Acceptance. The candidates' rite can take place at any time. Generally, candidates are not dismissed from the Sunday assembly since they are already baptized.

Paragraph 75 is the heart of the RCIA. The suitable pastoral formation and guidance, aimed at training catechumens in the Christian life, include celebrations of the Word of God. During this period these catechumens learn to: "turn more readily to God in prayer"; "bear witness to the faith"; "keep their hopes set on Christ"; "follow supernatural inspiration in their deeds"; and "practice love of neighbor, even at the cost of self-renunciation" (RCIA, 75). Through all of this they are gaining knowledge and practicing with others to spread the Gospel. During the period of the catechumenate the catechumens: continue to build community, get more engaged in parish activities, learn about the rudimentary teachings and beliefs of the Catholic Church, and delve into important and foundational Scripture passages. More importantly, it is a time for continuing to look into the presence of God in their lives — past and present — to develop a life of prayer, to enter into communal worship with the parish community, to foster conversion, and to develop and improve their relationship with God.

The Sacraments of Initiation

THE Eucharist is tricky, in comparison with the other Sacraments of Initiation, because not only is it the last, the culmination of the Sacraments of Initiation — even if pastoral practice often makes this less than obvious — it is also the only Sacrament of Initiation that can be repeated.

With the other two sacraments, the focus is on a unique, one-time gift, a particular unrepeatable sharing in the life of the Holy Trinity. But the Eucharist is different. Like Baptism and Confirmation, it gives us a particular sharing in the life of the Holy Trinity. But this sharing is more complete: in the Eucharist we receive all of Christ himself, Body, Blood, soul, and divinity, and we can receive him again and again, as many times as we want.

In a way, the Eucharist is like Ordinary Time: there's so much of it, it's easy to forget how special it really is.

Although this brief period of Ordinary Time is not a popular time for the celebration of First Communion, it is, nonetheless, appropriate now to pause and consider the role that the Eucharist has as a Sacrament of Initiation, even in our continuing reception of it.

The Eucharist is "the food of eternal life" (CCC, 1212). Just as in the natural life a child's first solid food is a significant occasion, so is one's first Holy Communion in the spiritual life. But the analogy continues. Just as at major life events — weddings, funerals, graduations, even birthdays — food is always served to the guests at the party, so does the Church offer a festive celebration of the Eucharist to her people at every major occasion; yet at the same time, the sacrament is there day in and day out, just as our bodies need daily nourishment to survive.

But again like the natural order of things, a special event is not necessary in order to have special food. Someone might cook a delicious favorite recipe for no apparent reason except the love of a spouse or child who appreciates it. Another time, she might spring for that intriguing new restaurant just because it fits in the budget. Or he might even order takeout at work, despite having brought leftovers, because his co-workers are ordering from his favorite lunch spot.

Likewise, Mass does not need to be on a particular feast, or at an especially beautiful church, or with a memorably inspiring preacher, in order to offer us a chance at deepening our relationship with the Lord. He will always be present for us in the Eucharist, "initiating" us further into his divine life, and we can always make our own special occasion merely by better disposing ourselves to receive him.

The Rite of Penance

ANY time of the year is appropriate for catechesis on the *Rite of Penance*. It is unfortunate that forty-plus years later after the post-Conciliar reforms, priests, deacons, catechists, and members of the lay faithful are still not familiar with the many options and the rich theology found in the ritual. The rite emphasizes the importance of inner conversion. This conversion is expressed through four major actions: contrition, confession, penance, and absolution (see RP, 6). Contrition, for example, happens before we come to the sacrament. Rooted in God's love for us, contrition allows us to see how our actions may have violated this love relationship with God. The story of the prodigal son (Luke 15:11–32) is the perfect example. Catechesis for the sacrament should lead people to come to know, believe and experience this love of God. The *Catechism of the Catholic Church*, part 2, chapter 2, article 4 and following, is an excellent place to find catechesis on the Sacrament of Reconciliation.

Celebrating the penitential celebration for children or young people, found in Appendix 2 of the *Rite of Penance*, would be appropriate during Catholic Schools Week (begins the last Sunday in January). Children and young people need to be taught about the communal nature of sin. Perhaps an anti-bullying campaign could be introduced in the school and parish to help illustrate one example of the communal nature of sin. Begin promoting the times for the celebration of the sacrament that will be held during the upcoming season of Lent.

The Rite of Marriage

CONSIDER how the parish catechizes and advises the couples who come seeking the Sacrament of Matrimony. Most couples do not get much catechesis about the sacrament and truly do not understand that they, "as ministers of Christ's grace mutually confer upon each other the sacrament of Matrimony" (*Catechism of the Catholic Church*, 1623). Many parishes offer the couple a chance to choose the scripture readings and music, but they might also be invited to consider the configuration of the Entrance procession. The procession truly says something about the festivity or solemnity of a liturgy and, at a wedding, gives the couple a chance to express something about themselves. The *Rite of Marriage* (19 – 20) encourages us to offer various ways to form the procession at a wedding and encourages all ministers to be part of the procession. This includes the groom since he and the bride are the ministers of this sacrament. Including the groom in the procession also avoids the troublesome notion that the bride is more important than the groom, as well as the image of the father "giving away" the bride to the groom. Of course, young people are so accustomed to that model of procession they don't think to question what the action symbolizes or ask how their procession should reflect what they believe about themselves.

The Pastoral Care of the Sick

SICKNESS and death have no off-season. But, since most of the rest of life's busying influences are quiet now, what better time to address the sacrament of the sick in Homilies and bulletin articles? Too many Catholics still think that caring for the sick only means giving "Last Rites"—privately, quietly, and not until the recipient is really on his deathbed. But the sacrament of the sick, like all the sacraments, really, is designed to incorporate the recipient into the life of the Church—which, on the local scale, means the life of the parish.

This is a two-way street: Christ and the Christian community must be brought to the sick, and the sick must be brought to the parish community. These few quiet weeks between Christmas Time and Lent might be all the time that's needed to accomplish this feat.

A parish information session could be held about the Sacrament of Anointing: where it comes from, who is eligible to receive the sacrament, how the family of the sick person can be involved. A corner of the bulletin that might ordinarily carry seasonal meditations could, for this short time, anticipate common misconceptions about the sacrament and explain its reality. A special "ministry drive/fair" could be held specifically to recruit extraordinary ministers to the sick—especially since the same emotional connections that make this ministry so fruitful for some make it too taxing for others.

The Order of Christian Funerals

BETWEEN the time of death and the funeral liturgy the Church offers witness of faith to the bereaved in special moments of group prayer. The ritual book provides prayers for after death (see OCF, 101–108). These prayers are celebrated in the home, hospital, and so on. The priest should not be expected to lead these prayers since every Christian can lead prayer and every Christian can invite others to pray. Therefore, every funeral home, nursing home, hospital, care center, and pastoral minister should have a copy of the ritual book that contains the vigil and its related rites.

At the time of death someone should meet with the family as soon as possible. Pastoral care is always required at the time of death. Be sensitive to the person's ethnic background and traditions, the family of one who died by suicide, alienated Catholics, or non-traditional families. The ministry of consolation calls caregivers to a ministry of presence with the bereaved and accompanies them in their sorrow and loneliness. How the family and friends of the deceased are treated in the days preceding the funeral liturgy leaves a lasting impression. Take your lead from Pope Francis who has encouraged us to welcome all who come to the house of the Church.

The *Order of Christian Funerals* envisions three primary times for prayer—vigil, funeral liturgy, and committal. The vigil (see OCF, 54–81) is the time when the community keeps watch with the family in prayer and is the first major ritual moment in the funeral process and may be adapted based on pastoral circumstances (see OCF, 55). Vigils can be celebrated in the home, the funeral home, or the church, with the church as the preferred setting. The time of the vigil is rather flexible however; it must be celebrated at a time not attached to the time of the funeral liturgy (see OCF, 55). The choice of the presiding minister is not limited to a priest or deacon—a lay leader of prayer can lead the vigil for the deceased.

The vigil may be celebrated in the context of Evening Prayer and the Office of the Dead (see OCF, 348–395). The Rosary is a common form of the vigil service in many parishes. It is not mentioned in the OCF perhaps because the Rosary is a private devotion rather than part of the Church's official liturgy. In areas where tradition is long established, it might seem most appropriate for the practice to continue. However, in these cases it would be better to incorporate the Rosary or parts of it into the Church's prescribed pattern of prayer. There is also the matter of being sensitive to non-Catholics who are gathered to grieve, and whose primary experience of prayer is to gather and reflect on the proclamation of God's Word.

The funeral liturgy is the central celebration of the Christian community for the deceased, celebrated with the Eucharist or outside of Mass (OCF, 128). At the funeral liturgy the community gathers with the family and friends of the deceased to give praise and thanks to God for Christ's victory over sin and death, to commend the deceased to God's tender mercy and compassion, and to seek strength in the proclamation of the Paschal Mystery (see OCF, 129). There are no restrictions for celebrating a Funeral Mass in the evening (see OCF, 158). This would accommodate more people who might be able to participate, and the body could stay in the church overnight.

The final stage of the OCF is the Rite of Committal, which includes Scripture, prayers, intercessions, concluding prayers, and prayers over the people (see OCF, 216–223). The Church encourages the lowering of the body into the grave as part of this rite.

Other military honors or other ceremonies should be conducted before the Rite of Committal since the Church should always have the final word. The committal may be lead by a deacon or lay leader of prayer. In places where the ground is frozen the Rite of Committal may need to be delayed to a later date.

The Book of Blessings

MANY of the orders of blessing found in the *Book of Blessings* are "extra-seasonal." That is, they can be celebrated at any time of the liturgical year. These are blessings that might have to do with the ebb and the flow of our human lives. We all have cycles that flow throughout the life of our families, the life of our communities, or the life of our countries. There are cycles of illness and cycles of health, cycles of birth and cycles of death, cycles of feasting and cycles of fasting.

By punctuating these cycles and events with orders of blessing, we proclaim our belief that the Father, through Christ and in the Spirit is never far from anything of our experience! Moreover, flowing from the praise and thanksgiving that we offer in the parish's Sunday celebration of the Eucharist, these blessings help us to lead truly Eucharistic lives, acknowledging that it is "truly right and just, our duty and salvation, always and everywhere" to give God thanks and praise.

For example, chapter 1 of the *Book of Blessings* offers a whole variety of blessings connected to family events (birth, sickness, anniversaries, adoption, birthdays) and to family members (infants, children, those who are married, the elderly). There is a general Blessing of Families in Their Homes (chapter 1.II) and a blessing of Parents before or after Childbirth (chapter 1.VII and VIII).

Other blessings may surround events in our lives that happen throughout or within any of the seasons in our liturgical calendar. We may move to a new home at any point during the year, in which case the Blessing of a New Home (chapter 11) would be suitable. Parishes register new members and bid farewell to other members throughout the whole year. The Orders of Blessing New and Departing Parishioners (chapters 66 and 67) could be celebrated a couple of times during the year.

During this portion of Ordinary Time during the winter, some blessings that might be pertinent to the season would be:

- Blessing Throats on the Feast of Saint Blaise on February 3 (chapter 51)
- Blessing of the Sick on February 11, World Day of the Sick and optional Memorial for Our Lady of Lourdes

- Blessing of Students and Teachers during Catholic Schools Week
- Blessing of Catechumens, which might be encouraged during these final weeks as the Church comes to final discernment of those who will be sent for Election in Lent

The Liturgical Environment

THERE is no need for the environment of Ordinary Time to be highly ornate. After the four weeks of Advent anticipation and the usual explosion of light at Christmas, Ordinary Time can provide a chance to return to the winter's quiet. There is little reason to add extra ministers or those responsible for keeping up the liturgical spaces between Christmas and Lent, both of which usually bring sharp increases in workload.

One thing which should happen, however, is that the Christmas environment be removed neither too early or too late. Ordinary Time deserves its own rightful place, but Christmas should be allowed all the time it has on the liturgical calendar. Packing away the Christmas decorations, including the crèche, the greenery, and other season-specific decoration, signals the end of Christmas Time, an end which our culture trains us to anticipate, usually by several weeks.

The left-over, usually dry greenery is very flammable. In many countries, there is a tradition of making a bonfire from the trees and garlands as a celebration of Epiphany during the long winter night. If you do so, be careful to observe local fire code and prepare to control and completely extinguish your fire.

Ordinary Time has green as its liturgical color, one of the most difficult colors to use well. Green fabrics and paints often look flat and uninviting, in part because they are usually a single hue. This is not how green appears in nature. Picture a vibrant field in your mind. We are used to seeing green in plants which often grow mixed with other kinds of plants, and move in the wind, causing variations of sun and shade. As a result, the shades of green we see are usually variegated and mixed with other tones. Single expanses of green cannot live up to this, and end up looking flat and dated. In choosing greens for the liturgical environment, therefore, it can be beneficial to look for fabrics that have some variation of tone or texture. Such fabrics can be found from simple slubbed weaves (common in cottons, linens, and silks), to highly-ornate, tapestry-woven designs. If you have different sets of vestments and paraments for Ordinary Time, you might consider using a set that is either darker or more muted, mimicking the greens that continue to be found in the Northern Hemisphere in winter: evergreen trees and dormant grasses and grains.

One thing which should be discussed is the use of banners. It is tempting to fill the space during Ordinary Time with ideas and concepts sewn on pieces of cloth, if only to provide something for the eye to rest on. Generally, I would discourage the use of banners because they often provide a single idea to the viewer, instead of the more multifaceted symbolic representation which is more native to the liturgy. This is especially true of banners which make use of text. Colors, plants, processions, art, sacraments, sacramentals, all of these are the "stuff" out of which the liturgy is made, and none of them provides a singular meaning to the assembly. Once viewed, a banner has done its work. A worthy piece of liturgical art can be returned to again and again, striking those who see it with new aspects on repeated viewings. Even simple things, like the use of color, do not serve up a single meaning, but provide a background against which the liturgical actions play out their symbolic mediations of divine revelation.

If you have potted plants that are usually in your church, keeping them in the church for this season can add some much-needed life to the otherwise cold landscape. Having an attractive but simple baseline to which the church returns during Ordinary Time can also help highlight the differences of the seasons. It can also provide a sense of homecoming after the often hectic holidays. As nice as it is to visit family for the holidays, returning to our own space and our normal lives can be a welcome relief. A simple environment which can be easily maintained can provide a similar experience to the worshiping community.

This season contains a number of feast days which can be celebrated within the Ordinary Time environment, perhaps with a simple addition, such as a statue or other item. Chief among these is the Feast of the Presentation of the Lord (February 2) at which the candles for the year are traditionally blessed. A very effective environment is to place baskets and piles of different kinds of candles in the church on this day, including those that will be used for the blessing of the throats on the following day (St. Blaise). Other days which might receive a special environment include St. Anthony, Abbot (January 17), Sts. Timothy and Titus (January 26), St. Thomas Aquinas (January 28), St. Agatha (February 5), St. Scholastica (February 10), and Sts. Cyril and Methodius (February 14). For these feasts and memorials, the color will change to white or red, which can provide enough of a change. If your parish has a well-sized statue or icon of one of these saints, placing this out on their feast day is appropriate and easily done. It might be given emphasis with a plant, or placed on a pedestal if that would make it fit the space better.

The Liturgical Music

PASTORAL musicians take a special leadership role in building up the Church, the "sacrament of unity" (SC, 26). One way in which we do this is by creating a common repertoire of music so the assembly may enter fully into the liturgy. *Sing to the Lord: Music in Divine Worship* encourages "[f]amiliarity with a stable repertoire of liturgical songs rich in theological content [that] can deepen the faith of the community through repetition and memorization" (STL, 27).

Ordinary Time is a perfect opportunity to begin to evaluate the repertoire of the faith community you serve and to teach the assembly a new Gloria or a new set of Eucharistic acclamations. Find settings that can be easily sung by the community. When teaching a new Mass setting during this time of the year make sure that the songs, psalms, and hymns are familiar to the assembly so they are not overwhelmed by learning too much new music. Since the introduction of the new translation of *The Roman Missal* over fifty new Mass settings along with dozens of revised settings have been published.

Before the busy seasons of Lent, Triduum, and Easter Time roll along, this is an appropriate time to evaluate the music and worship resources used in the parish. Does the parish need a new hymnal or is it time to change worship resources? Perhaps the community is becoming more and more bilingual and discovering a need to consider an English-Spanish hymnal or resource. Take time to clean out your file cabinets and choir rooms.

Are you missing choir books or octavos, and will the budget support their replacement?

Communion is probably the most difficult time to get people to sing at the liturgy, yet it is one of the most important times for the assembly to sing. The *General Instruction of the Roman Missal* reminds us that "the Communion chant begins while the priest is receiving the Sacrament" (GIRM 86). Although this rubric is clear, in so many parishes we find this pause awkward while the other ministers and even the musicians receive Communion before the assembly. This is not what the rite envisions; rather the Communion song should begin as soon as the priest receives Communion. *Sing to the Lord: Music in Divine Worship* reinforces what the GIRM says when it tells us "the singing begins immediately . . . because the Communion Chant expresses the unity of those processing and receiving the Holy Sacrament, communal singing is commendable. The singing of the people should be preeminent" (STL, 189).

Even though Communion is a difficult time to get the assembly to sing, pastoral musicians must provide ongoing catechesis about the purpose of the Communion Rite and the role of the Communion song. Instrumental music, singing of metrical hymns, solos, and anthems by the choir are not appropriate during the time of Holy Communion. What is appropriate and called for by the rite is a Communion chant or song or responsorial music, similar to what we sing between the Scripture readings. In fact, the two most ancient Communion chants of the Roman Rite are "Psalm 23: The Lord is My Shepherd" and "Psalm 34: Taste and See the Goodness of the Lord." Every community should have two or three settings of these psalms and use them often throughout the year as Communion chants. You probably already have a favorite setting or two of each of these psalms. Communion is to always follow this pattern: first the instrumentalist plays through the antiphon or refrain one time; it is then sung by the cantor or choir; then the assembly sings the refrain together with the musicians. Plan to repeat the refrain twice between each verse. When the musicians begin with the refrain and go right into a verse it signals to the assembly that they are not needed. Keep in mind that one of our roles as musicians is to support the song of the assembly not usurp it.

Liturgical Ministers

EVERYBODY thinks of Lent as the time for retreats. Confirmation retreats, school or youth group retreats, men's and women's group retreats . . . so perhaps the two and a half weeks before Lent begins, what was once known as Pre-Lent or *Septuagesima*,* could be a very beneficial time for a liturgical minister formation retreat.

In most circumstances, this time in late January or February is down time: winter sports are winding down or finished, but little league hasn't yet begun. Apart from Martin Luther King Jr. Day, Valentine's Day, and Presidents' Day, there are no major holidays to interfere with scheduling. And these months are not popular for weddings, first Holy Communions, Confirmations, Ordinations, graduations, etc. In short: If one doesn't take advantage of this quiet time after Christmas, quiet won't come again until things switch to the summer schedule in June or July!

So: retreats! A retreat for liturgical ministers doesn't need to be anything complicated, but it ought to be hearty: an evening of prayer in front of the Blessed Sacrament with confessions, music, and silence; instruction on how to pray the Scriptures using *lectio divina*; guided reflections on an individual's relationship with God; a guest speaker from a nearby religious community.

If the liturgical ministers—really, all the parish volunteers—are cared for as an extension of the parish staff, who are themselves an extension of the parish priests, how much will our parishes benefit from their formation! How fruitful can Ordinary Time be for refreshing our ministers before the busy liturgies that are so soon to come.

* Literally "seventy days," as it began thirty days before Lent, which in Latin is *Quadragesima* ("forty days").

Devotions and Sacramentals

IT is well known that "the Lord's Day—as Sunday was called from Apostolic times—recalls the day of Christ's Resurrection. It is Easter which returns week by week, celebrating Christ's victory over sin and death" (*Dies Domini*, 1). After the primacy of Sunday, the weekdays tend to pale in comparison, but Monday recalls the Holy Spirit and the souls in purgatory; Tuesday, the Guardian Angels; and Wednesday, St. Joseph.

Thursdays recall the institution of the Holy Eucharist, and consequently many pray especially for priests on this day. To this end, many parishes that are not able to expose the Blessed Sacrament all week have a long-standing tradition of having adoration on Thursdays.

Fridays, of course, recall the Crucifixion and are days of penitence throughout the year. First Friday and First Saturday devotions, focused on the Sacred and Immaculate Hearts, respectively, tie in with Sunday's Easter theme and keep the Paschal Mystery close to the heart.

The last day of the week is likewise no stranger to Christian devotions. Each Saturday is a remembrance of the maternal example and discipleship of the Blessed Virgin Mary who, strengthened by faith and hope, on that great Saturday on which Our Lord lay in the tomb, was the only one of the disciples to hold vigil in expectation of the Lord's Resurrection; it is a prelude and introduction to the celebration of Sunday, the weekly memorial of the Resurrection of Christ; it is a sign that the Virgin Mary is continuously present and operative in the life of the Church.

Whether or not a given parish has a Marian Society or Rosary Sodality, it's almost guaranteed that either before or after Saturday's Mass, people will assemble to pray the Rosary, one of the most popular and widespread devotions in the history of the Church.

The Parish and the Home

THIS is a time to focus on the ministry of Christ, his parables shared to teach us all, and the wisdom imparted meant to inspire us to live bolder lives of peace and justice.

The foundation to a stronger relationship with Jesus comes from listening and spending time in gentle silence unencumbered with great feasts. This quietness allows for the light of Christ to shine down and help us to continue to grow and change, to say yes to the path of service and

faithful witness required of us. Our call to discipleship comes during Ordinary Time when we are each called by name. What does this interlude of time between Christmas and Lent mean for you?

With the Advent ritual far in the distance, go back to the essence of what prepared you to receive Jesus — *Logos*, the Word become flesh. Each week as you hear Scripture proclaimed, listen deeply for the word or phrase which speaks directly to your heart. Maybe it is a song at Mass that tugs at your soul which answers an unspoken need. Allow the little nudges of God to become sustenance for your journey of learning to become a better version of yourself. Hold onto this word, Scripture phrase, or song lyric as your mantra to live and grow during the week. Come back each week to receive new instructions to continue to be the vessel who births Christ into the world — to your home, family, workplace, and community.

On February 2 we celebrate the Presentation of the Lord, which is also known by some as Candlemas Day. On this day Jesus is received by the elders, Simeon and Anna, and recognized and affirmed for his true identity. He is made known to all. Celebrated mid-season during "winter" Ordinary Time, make this day special and celebrate others for their unique role in your life. Simeon prayed: "for my eyes have seen your salvation, / which you prepared in sight of all the peoples: / a light for revelation to the Gentiles, / and glory for your people Israel" (Luke 2:30–32). Who are the people who allow you to know yourself and your gifts, who offer the light of Christ to you so you can pass the flame to another? With Christmas gift-giving forty days past, surprise those special spiritual companions who see you for the giftedness you are and call you forth to always be that person. Offer them some symbol of your gratefulness for being known on the journey and similarly recognize them for their light.

During these colder and quieter months, spend some time reading. Look up some good books in biblical or Christian fiction, spiritual readings of the saints, or even brush up on catechetical learning such as the meaning of our essential beliefs found in the Apostles' and Nicene Creed. Intellectually learn what your heart professes to believe each week. Words can add depth to life or became dull to our hearts. Listen and learn from your own life. When you pray the Our Father, what does it mean to you? Be conscious of your attitude and how you are "programmed" to pray. Do you just say rote prayers because that is what you were taught? Break patterns during this Ordinary Time and open space in your life to become a new person ready to be transformed.

Mass Texts

◆ **Dismissal for Children's Liturgy of the Word**

Beloved children of God,
as you go forth to listen to the Sacred Scriptures
you may be amazed at all the stories of what Jesus says and does.
He asks his people to do many different things.
When people do as he requests,
great miracles can happen.
Perhaps he is asking something special of you this day.
Pray that God may open your ears to hear his Word in a new and special way.
Go in peace.

◆ **Dismissal of the Catechumens**

My dear catechumens,
as we send you forth to reflect on the Word of God,
be mindful of the the many ways that he may be working in your lives,
and in the lives of those around you.
As the Scriptures unfold,
you will see that God appears to ordinary people,
in ordinary situations,
and that he teaches us using examples found in nature and our daily lives.
Incline the ear of your heart to God speaking to you this day.
Go in peace.

◆ **Introduction to the Mass**

The Church is now entering into what we call "Ordinary Time," but, in truth, these are extraordinary times indeed. Over the next few weeks, we will be experiencing the beginning of Jesus's ministry, from his baptism, to calling his disciples, and early healing miracles. God also asks extraordinary things of ordinary people. As you pray today, listen to what God may be asking of you!

◆ **Universal Prayer or Prayer of the Faithful**

Introduction

Jesus came on earth and was a human like us. He knows our joys and our burdens, and so we have the courage to bring our prayers now before God.

Intercessions

1. For Pope Francis, that he may always be awake and attuned to the voice of God speaking in his life, we pray to the Lord: Lord, hear our prayer.

2. For all government officials, that they may always listen to the needs of their people, and make efforts to heal, educate, and nurture all, we pray to the Lord: Lord, hear our prayer.

3. For those called to single life, for those called to married life, and for those called to priesthood or religious life, that we may always respond with joy, "Here am I, Lord; I come to do your will," we pray to the Lord: Lord, hear our prayer.

4. For those who struggle with demons of physical and emotional illness, addiction, and sin, that they may do as Christ says and trust in Jesus to heal them, we pray to the Lord: Lord, hear our prayer.

5. For those who serve the Lord in healing professions, helping all those who are ill in body, mind, and spirit, that they may be inspired by Christ in their work, we pray to the Lord: Lord, hear our prayer.

6. For those gathered here today, that we may be open to the ways of the Lord working in our lives, we pray to the Lord: Lord, hear our prayer.

Conclusion

O Jesus, Lamb of God, you are all that we seek.
You know our weakness and our frailty,
and our desire to love and serve you.
Hear the prayers we offer to God the Father,
and with your Holy Spirit
teach us to follow you ever more closely.
You live and reign forever.
Amen.

January
Month of the Holy Name

Except for the days of the First and Thirty-Fourth Weeks in Ordinary Time, The Roman Missal does not provide prayer texts for the week-days in Ordinary Time. Instead, priest celebrants and those who prepare the liturgy may select from among the prayers provided for the Sundays in Ordinary Time. Your diocesan Ordo will provide suggestions. The Missal commentaries below do not include reflections for optional memorials. However, on days celebrated as optional memorials, prayers may be from the Sundays of Ordinary Time, the Proper of Saints, or the Commons. Always refer first to the Proper of Saints to become familiar with proper and optional texts. On all Saturdays during Ordinary Time that do not have an obligatory memorial, a memorial to the Blessed Virgin Mary may be celebrated. The prayers may be selected from the Common of the Blessed Virgin Mary. Commentary below is only provided for Sundays, solemnities, feasts, and obligatory memorials.

MON 12 (#305) green
Weekday (First Week in Ordinary Time)

The Lectionary for Mass

◆ First Reading: The introduction to Hebrews focuses on Jesus as the revelation of God and the personification of Wisdom. In verses that probably come from an ancient liturgical hymn, Hebrews understands Jesus is the reflection of divine glory who purified us from sin and now sits at God's right hand. The assertion that Jesus is superior to the angels was important for the author of Hebrews to make in order to address misconceptions about the fullness of Jesus's divinity. Quoting the Old Testament, Hebrews recognizes Jesus's sonship as God's firstborn and, thus, his superiority to the angels.

◆ Responsorial Psalm 97 is an enthronement psalm that acclaims the Lord who comes from heaven to earth as king. The psalm follows well on the First Reading's acclamation of Jesus's superiority. Having just concluded Christmas Time, this psalm serves to help us remember what we recently celebrated. For us, Jesus is the Lord who rules over all the earth. Neither clouds, nor darkness, nor enemies can destroy him, for the underpinnings of his throne are justice and righteousness. The foundation of our life is to be the same.

◆ Gospel: Jesus's ministry follows the conclusion of John the Baptist's. The Gospel Jesus proclaims is clear from the beginning of this short passage: the kingdom of God is here—repent, and believe. In Mark, after Jesus's proclamation of the Gospel, he immediately calls the first disciples. As he passes by the Sea of Galilee, Jesus offers the invitation to come after him to two brothers, Simon and Andrew. They accept, leaving their boat and nets behind. Jesus also calls the sons of Zebedee who leave not only their boat and nets behind, but also their father. The proclamation of the Gospel and the call go hand in hand. Will you accept the call?

The Roman Missal

Because *The Roman Missal* does not include prayer texts for the week-days of Ordinary Time, there will be no Missal commentary for ferial weekdays. Instead, please refer to your local *Ordo* for suggestions.

TUE 13 (#306) green
Weekday (First Week in Ordinary Time)
Optional Memorial of St. Hilary, Bishop and Doctor of the Church / white

The Lectionary for Mass

◆ First Reading: The author of Hebrews is unconcerned about the source for the quotation from Psalm 8 in today's First Reading. Rather, his concern is the content of the psalmist's testimony. For him, Jesus is the son of man whom God made lower than the angels and crowned with glory. In Jesus's suffering and death, exaltation came through abasement. We share in God's grace which perfected Jesus through suffering, for God is our common origin. For God's work in Jesus leading us to salvation, we proclaim and praise his name in our worshipping assemblies.

◆ Responsorial Psalm 8 is a song of praise to God, the Creator. The psalm reflects on the wonder of God's creation, both the heavens and the earth. This reflection leads to the question about the significance of humans, which the psalmist answers with the recognition that, even though God made humans less than a god, still God crowned them with glory. All things that God has created are subject to humans. And, with the application of the psalm's reference to the "son of man" to Jesus in the reading from Hebrews, Jesus is seen as our Lord, Son of God and Son of Man.

◆ Gospel: The newly called disciples Andrew, Simon, James, and John follow Jesus as he begins his healing ministry. Notice that the cure of the man possessed with a demon occurs on a Sabbath and in a synagogue. Jesus's teaching contrasts with that of others whom the people have previously heard teach. Jesus teaches with authority. Neither the source of this authority nor the content of Jesus's teaching is specified. What we do know is the man with the unclean spirit attempted to cancel out Jesus's power by correctly identifying him as the Holy One of God. He thought his knowledge of Jesus's identity would show the spirit within him to be superior. The man's strategy did not work. Jesus drove the unclean spirit out, leaving the crowds amazed and wondering who Jesus is. We confess Jesus as God's Son, and his authority over life and death still amazes us!

The Roman Missal

Sourcebook does not include reflections on the Missal texts for optional memorials. You always have the option of celebrating these days. Always refer first to the Proper of Saints. It is here you will discover which prayers are proper and from which Common to use for other prayers.

Today's Saint

St. Hilary was the Bishop of Poitiers, France, during the era of the Arian heresy, and he fought for the correct understanding and expression of the divinity of Christ. He was known as the "hammer against Arianism" and the "Athanasius of the West," after the Bishop of Alexandria who fought the heresy in the East. The Christian world was so divided by Arianism that Hilary was exiled twice. His great contribution was the successful expression in Latin of the theology about Christ, or Christology, that had been developed in Greek.

WED 14 (#307) green
Weekday

The Lectionary for Mass

◆ FIRST READING: The primary theme of Hebrews is the high priesthood of Jesus. In Hebrews 2:14, this theme emerges for the first time. Following yesterday's First Reading, which emphasized Jesus's exaltation in glory through his death, today's passage defines why Jesus is exalted in death. Through death, Jesus brings the forgiveness of sins. He had to experience death on a Cross so he could free those

of us, descendants of Abraham, enslaved by sin. In his Resurrection, he destroyed the power of death. Jesus is, therefore, the Exalted One; evil and death no longer reign.

◆ RESPONSORIAL PSALM: The opening verses of Psalm 105 may have originally served as a call to worship. Charging God's people to give thanks and praise for God's wondrous deeds, the verses of the psalm then remember God's reign over the earth and the covenant made with Abraham. The psalm finds a connection with the First Reading in its reference to Abraham. For Christians, God fulfills the covenant in Jesus. In his wondrous deeds culminating in his Death and Resurrection, he is the fulfillment of the covenant.

◆ GOSPEL: Jesus's ministry of healing continues in today's Gospel reading. The ministry is personal as he heals Simon's mother-in-law who was sick with a fever. Having been healed by Jesus in the presence of his fledgling disciples, she serves them. The text informs us that, as evening came, the disciples led Jesus to others who were ill or possessed by demons. Indeed, the entire town came to the door of the house, evidence of how quickly Jesus's reputation was spreading. We also hear that Jesus performs many healings and exorcised many demons. Before dawn, still under the cover of partial darkness, Jesus left to recharge himself through prayer and quiet time away. But his disciples followed because people apparently inquired of them where Jesus was. Jesus heard the people's needs and went on to their towns to preach and heal.

THU 15 (#308) green
Weekday

The Lectionary for Mass

◆ FIRST READING: Citing Psalm 95, the author of Hebrews warns

Christians to not let their hearts be hardened. Like Moses who remained faithful to God, and unlike the Israelites whose hearts did harden in the desert, we are to encourage each other each day to remain faithful. Jesus, the high priest, was faithful to death. In him is the source of our hope. It is God's voice of new life over sin and death that we are called to hear.

◆ RESPONSORIAL PSALM: The opening verses of the response call us to worship God and remind us that we are God's people. This is the encouragement we need to remain faithful. Despite our best efforts, "contention" and "testing," the meaning of Meribah and Massah, often get the best of us in difficult situations, like they did with the Israelites. Our faithfulness to God who triumphed in Jesus goes astray. The antiphon of today's psalm reminds us to not harden our hearts when we hear God's voice and provides a direct connection with the First Reading.

◆ GOSPEL: In today's Gospel, a leper kneels before Jesus desiring that Jesus cure him. The man does not demand Jesus heal him, but rather leaves the decision to cure him entirely up to Jesus by saying "If you wish . . ." Jesus chooses to cure him and performs the healing with care and compassion. This healing is personal as are Jesus's others. As part of Mark's unfolding of Jesus's messianic identity, the Gospel account writer has Jesus instruct the healed man not to tell anyone what happened. He should simply show himself to the priest and be declared clean so he might be welcomed into the community again (see Leviticus 13–14). The man, however, did not follow Jesus's instructions. He made the matter public, and who wouldn't?

FRI 16 (#309) green
Weekday

The Lectionary for Mass

◆ FIRST READING: Yesterday's First Reading concluded with the mention of God's rest. In relation to the Israelites' journey through the desert, this rest referred to the Promised Land. With respect to the new covenant in Jesus, this rest references the life of God into which Jesus draws believers. The promise to abide with God is good news for Christians. Dwelling with God is participation with God in the Sabbath rest of the seventh day. Our faithfulness leads us to this land of plenty.

◆ RESPONSORIAL PSALM 78: Today's psalm recounts the history of Israel from the exodus to the beginnings of the monarchy. The verses we proclaim recall the Lord's mighty deeds performed on behalf of Israel. The psalmist tells us that we must remember this story, the story of God working for his people, and tell it to our children and our children's children. The proclamation of the people's history will help them to remain faithful to God and not fall victim to the infidelity of their ancestors who forgot all that God did for them.

◆ GOSPEL: Today's Gospel text is not only about Jesus healing the paralytic because of his faith and that of his friends who lowered him through the roof, it also marks the beginning of the conflict between Jesus and his opponents: in this text, the scribes. The growth of the conflict will eventually lead to the plot to put Jesus to death. That Jesus told the paralytic his sins were forgiven leads the scribes to question his authority, since only God can forgive sins. It would have been much easier for Jesus to only forgive the man's sins, but he goes on to command him to rise and go

home, an amazing miracle for many and disconcerting for others.

SAT 17 (#310) white
Memorial of St. Anthony, Abbot

◆ FIRST READING: There are two main parts to today's First Reading. The first describes the challenge and judgment of the word of God. God will receive us into divine rest based on our faithfulness to his word. The second half of the reading returns to the subject of Jesus's high priesthood. Christians often use these verses to talk about the difference between Jesus's humanity and ours. Jesus is like us in all things except our sin. That is why he is able to lead us, despite our sins, to the throne of God's grace.

◆ RESPONSORIAL PSALM: Verses 8–10 of Psalm 19 are from the section of the psalm that is a wisdom hymn. These verses speak of the wisdom of God's word of the Torah and identify it with the synonyms "law," "decree," "precepts," and "command." The antiphon attests that God's word brings everlasting life. Verse 15 of the psalm is the conclusion to the psalmist's prayer for forgiveness for his failures. Our prayer today meets with this prayer as we confess the Lord as our Redeemer.

◆ GOSPEL: Levi, whom the other lists of disciples name Matthew, was a tax collector who was sitting at his customs post collecting not only the tariffs rightly owed, but probably monies above those. This money he could keep as profit. Surprisingly, Jesus calls him with the two simple words: "Follow me." Perhaps even more astonishingly, Levi follows and the next we know, Jesus is sharing a meal at table in Levi's house with many other tax collectors and sinners. Not unexpectedly, the smug Pharisees question Jesus about this, but he responds plainly: he calls sinners,

not the righteous — or those who think they are already righteous.

The Roman Missal

The Mass texts are proper for today and can be found in the Proper of Saints at January 17. The orations all echo the virtues of St. Anthony's life: his "wondrous way of life in the desert" and the need for self-denial in order to love God above all things (Collect); being free from "earthly attachments" so that "we may have our riches in you alone" (Prayer over the Offerings); and the saint's "glorious victories / over the powers of darkness" (Prayer after Communion). Although no particular Preface is indicated in the rubrics for today, certainly one should be chosen from among the two Prefaces of Saints or the Preface of Holy Virgins and Religious.

Today's Saint

Early in his life, St. Anthony of Egypt (251–356) discovered the importance of solitude in knowing oneself in relationship to God. Solitude provides the vehicle through which one battles demons and removes worldly distractions that distance the heart from the will of God. St. Anthony journeyed in the desert for nearly thirty years where he lived a life of solitary prayer and self-discipline — a life of utter dependence on God. After his time in the desert, he emerged as a man of balance, ready to share all he learned regarding the human thirst for God. Realizing that the spiritual life takes root within a community of believers, he founded a group of monks. While serving as abbot, a spiritual father, to the monks, St. Anthony mentored them in the ways of contemplative prayer and helped them overcome illusory thinking. His dynamic personality continued to attract individuals. As a result, he counseled a steady stream of pilgrims and laid the foundation for many monasteries.

18 (#65) green
Second Sunday in Ordinary Time

The Lectionary for Mass

◆ FIRST READING: Samuel responded to Eli two times instead of knowing that it was the Lord who was calling. Samuel's eventual response to the Lord is the response we strive to have when the Lord calls us. How will we open ourselves and respond to the Lord's call, even when we know the call comes with challenges, both known and unknown?

◆ RESPONSORIAL PSALM: The part of Psalm 40 for this Sunday is an individual's thanksgiving hymn to the Lord. The psalmist recounts patiently waiting for the Lord and then the fact that the Lord did come near and hear the psalmist's cry. Not wanting sacrifice, but only open ears, the Lord receives just that from the psalmist who goes forth to proclaim the Lord's justice.

◆ SECOND READING: The Holy Spirit resides in the bodies of each and every one of us. In today's passage, Paul instructs the Corinthians to avoid immorality because their bodies are members of Christ, temples of the Holy Spirit. Paul's instructions are necessary guidance for us today as well. We ponder how we can glorify God in our bodies, reverencing each other's God-given humanity.

◆ GOSPEL: In all three years of the Lectionary cycle of readings, the Gospel on the Second Sunday of Ordinary Time comes from John. On the basis of John the Baptist's identification of Jesus as the Lamb of God, Andrew and Simon Peter followed Jesus. They told Jesus they were looking for the Rabbi or Teacher. In response, Jesus invites them to come and see. Jesus invites us, like Andrew and Simon Peter, to come and stay with him so that we too, might say, "We have found the Messiah."

The Roman Missal

The Mass texts for today are found in the "Ordinary Time" section of the Proper of Time. The Gloria is sung or said today. The Creed is said or sung.

The Collect acknowledges God as the one who governs "all things," and so asks him to "bestow [his] peace on our times." The Prayer over the Offerings reiterates how "whenever the memorial of this sacrifice is celebrated / the work of our redemption is accomplished." The Prayer after Communion highlights the unity of the faithful that is a constitutive element in the meaning of the Eucharist. It asks God to pour the Spirit of love on us so that those who have been nourished by the "one heavenly Bread" may become "one in mind and heart."

Any one of the eight Prefaces of the Sundays in Ordinary Time may be selected for today.

Other Ideas

Today's First Reading is about God calling Samuel in the temple. This would be an ideal day to bless parish servers or have an "altar server recognition day" for all those involved in this ministry. It is also the Week of Prayer for Christian Unity (this week begins on January 18 and concludes on January 25). Your parish may wish to engage in ecumenical activities with area churches. Taizé prayer is a natural format for this type of service. But it could also be something fun like a volleyball game followed by a potluck dinner! For more information and ideas see the Greymoor Ecumenical and Interreligious Institute at http://www.geei.org or the World Council of Churches at http://www.oikoumene.org/en/resources/week-of-prayer.

Thursday is a Day of Penance for Violations to the Dignity of the Human Person and Prayer for the Dignity of Life. Make sure the congregation is aware of any Holy Hour for Life, life chain, or layette for life programs that have been scheduled. While there are many graphic images available that show the horrors of abortion or the growth stages of a fetus, avoid using the "shock value" approach of posters in the narthex or images on projection screens. White or violet vestments may be used. Use the "Mass for Peace and Justice #22" under the Masses for Various Needs and Occasions.

19 (#311) green
MON Weekday

◆ FIRST READING: As a high priest like other high priests, Jesus was called by God to this role. Able to deal with people compassionately, he has both empathy for a person's situation and is able to deal fairly with them. By mentioning that weakness plagues the high priest like it does those to whom he ministers, the author of Hebrews is not saying that Jesus sinned, but rather that he dealt with temptation. Jesus's high priesthood differs from the high priests in the order of Melchizedek, the king of Jerusalem who blessed Abraham in Genesis 14 and also performed high priestly functions, in that it doesn't end with death. Through his Death and Resurrection Jesus draws us to eternal salvation.

◆ RESPONSORIAL PSALM: A fitting choice for today's liturgy, Psalm 110 echoes its quotation in the First Reading. The psalm was traditionally sung at a king's coronation. Christians see Jesus as the fulfillment of the office and ministry of the high priest. As a result of his ascension to the throne, there will never be a need for another high priest to reign over our enemies.

◆ GOSPEL: Disciples of John the Baptist and the Pharisees come together to question Jesus about why his disciples do not fast. Their question signals the developing controversy between Jesus and his opponents. In response to the question, Jesus identifies himself as the bridegroom, an allusion to his messianic identity, and hints at his own Death, the day when the bridegroom will be taken away. Ultimately, Jesus's response to the question of fasting teaches us to look at what God is doing new in him for us. As Jesus's disciples, we just might need to change our old ways of doing things as we follow him.

T U E 20 (#312) green
Weekday

Optional Memorials of St. Fabian, Pope and Martyr / red; St. Sebastian, Martyr / red

The Lectionary for Mass

◆ FIRST READING: At the conclusion of Hebrews 5, we learn that the author of Hebrews concerns himself with Christians who have become sluggish and forgetful of the truths of their faith (verses 11–12). By now, they should have been teachers of the faith, but since they are not capable of this, the author tasks himself with explaining the fundamentals in depth. Following the example of Abraham and others faithful to God's word in the Old Testament, we are to trust in the immutable or unchanging nature of God's promise to anchor our hope.

◆ RESPONSORIAL PSALM: A hymn of praise, Psalm 111 begins with a single individual extolling the Lord. The singer's words provide the opening for this joyful, communal psalm which, as many of our psalms during the weeks of Ordinary Time do, tells us the Lord's wondrous deeds. The psalm makes specific mention of the food the Lord provided to the Israelites in the desert

as a sign of faithfulness to the covenant. God's faithfulness, as the First Reading also declares, is undeniable and lasts forever. Our praise of God carries on forever as well.

◆ GOSPEL: The last in a series of confrontations in Mark 2 is today's Gospel text. Stylistically following the same outline as the text from Mark 2:18–22 proclaimed yesterday, today's text presents the Pharisees' question to Jesus about why his disciples are working on the Sabbath. Jesus's response references the Old Testament example from 1 Samuel 21:2–7 when David approached Ahimelech, the priest of Nob and father of Abiathar, to provide food for his hungry men. In doing so, Ahimelech made an exception to the regulations found in Leviticus 24:9. The words of Jesus show his authority over the Sabbath as Son of Man. His followers never go hungry; even on the Sabbath, he provides.

Today's Saints

The Church celebrates the lives of two holy men today, Sts. Fabian († 250) and Sebastian († 288), both of whom were martyred for their faith. Very little is known about each of these martyrs, yet they continue to capture the hearts of Catholic Christians everywhere. St. Fabian was elected pope in 236, even though he was not a priest. During his pontificate, Emperor Decius came into power and began persecuting Christians who would not return to pagan worship. St. Fabian was the first among many killed under this emperor's violent reign. While serving as a soldier, St. Sebastian was persecuted at the hands of Diocletian. According to legend, he was pierced with arrows so that he would die a slow and painful death, but this attempt on his life was unsuccessful due to his athletic stamina. He eventually became well enough to confront the emperor regarding the way

Christians were being treated. This led to his execution.

W E D 21 (#313) red
Memorial of St. Agnes, Virgin and Martyr

The Lectionary for Mass

◆ FIRST READING: Hebrews 7 explains in detail how Melchizedek serves as a type of Christ. A "type" is a person or figure who represents, foreshadows, or symbolizes another. Our reading today begins with the presentation of Melchizedek's importance beginning with his meeting with Abraham, followed by the meaning of his name, and the acknowledgement that he has no known human lineage, a Jewish tradition that developed because Genesis 14 provides no details about his ancestry. The reading concludes with the comparison: like Melchizedek's priestly call, Christ's is from God and will last forever.

◆ RESPONSORIAL PSALM: Today's response is the same from this past Monday. See the comments for that day.

◆ GOSPEL: This Gospel reading marks the beginning of Chapter 3 in Mark, but it comes immediately after yesterday's passage. It is still the Sabbath and Jesus enters the synagogue where he encounters a man with a withered hand. In full view of the Pharisees, Jesus invites the man to come forward and, upon his doing so, Jesus questions the Pharisees about the legitimacy of doing good and saving life on the Sabbath, rather than doing evil and destroying life. As legalists, the Pharisees have no answer to this question. Jesus heals the man and this act of saving life compels the Pharisees to draw up their plot to put Jesus, the One who gives salvation, to death with a sense of urgency.

The Roman Missal

The Collect is the only oration proper for today, and it is found at January 21 under the Proper of Saints. The prayer has Pauline echoes in its assertion that God chooses "what is weak in the world to confound the strong." The other orations are taken either from the Common of Martyrs: for a Virgin Martyr, or from the Common of Virgins: For One Virgin. Although no particular Preface is indicated in the rubrics for today, certainly one of the two Prefaces of Holy Martyrs should be considered as likely choices, although the Preface of Holy Virgins and Religious could be another candidate.

Today's Saint

St. Agnes (291–304) lived a very short life, but each and every moment was filled with inestimable worth. She felt called to consecrate her virginity to Christ in a culture that lived according to the flesh rather than the spirit. When St. Agnes refused numerous marriage proposals because of her espousal to Christ, she was tried and beheaded. Two words embody the whole of her life: faithfulness and purity. No human being or earthly promise could shatter St. Agnes's commitment to her beloved God, nor could any hatred or vengeance taint her virginal heart. Devotion to St. Agnes gained popularity in the Middle Ages, along with other virginal saints like Ursula, Dorothy, and Barbara. In religious art, she is often depicted with a lamb, symbolizing the spotless (pure) sacrifice she made for the Lord.

THU 22 (#314) green
Weekday

Day of Prayer for the Legal Protection of Unborn Children (U.S.A.) / white or violet

About this Day of Prayer

On this day, the Church gives us prayers rooted in hope as the United States mourns the loss of millions of lives by abortion. In the Mass for Peace and Justice, we pray that all governments, especially our own, seek a truly just society, one in which the common good of all people, including the most vulnerable, is sought. In a very real way, we pray for the end of this genocide, the victims of which we remember with our violet vestments and mournful hymns. This Mass celebrates their brief lives, reminding us also of the beauty and sacredness of the lives around us, who have not yet been lost. We remember, we intercede, we hope — and the Church leads us in all three.

On this sensitive day, we should remember that there may be members of our parish who are still in the process of reconciling with God and the Church because they have had an abortion. If able, provide counselors to support those who have participated in an abortion. Using this day to condemn rather than to show mercy causes unecessary pain. We are called to show compassion and God's mercy as we restore all and renew all in Christ's love and life. You might also host a Rosary for life.

The Lectionary for Mass

◆ First Reading: The conclusion of today's text identifies Jesus as the mediator of a new covenant. Tomorrow's passage compares and contrasts the two covenants. Through his unique high priesthood, Jesus mediates a covenant based on his sacrifice of death. His is a once-for-all sacrifice in which he offered himself. No need will ever exist to repeat his sacrifice. Jesus's sacrifice differentiates him from the Jewish high priests who needed to offer multiple sacrifices. This is why he now sits at God's right hand, where from the heavenly sanctuary he intercedes for us now and forever.

◆ Responsorial Psalm: Verses 7–10 of the psalm are part of a thanksgiving hymn. Verse 17, the concluding verse of the psalm, is from a prayer of lament. The psalm reminds us that God no longer wants sacrifices and offerings; God only desires obedience to God's will. For Christians, Jesus is the realization par excellence of God's desires. We, too, endeavor to open our ears and hearts to God's will, and since we long for help in doing so, we always praise and glorify God.

◆ Gospel: In this summary and transitional passage, Mark communicates the optimistic response to Jesus's ministry of healing and exorcism. Throngs of people from various places and regions came to Jesus. His request to have his disciples procure a boat is simply pragmatic; he does not want to be crushed by the masses. Similar to Mark 1:24–25, even the unclean spirits recognize Jesus's identity as the Son of God. Theirs is not a confession, but still Jesus warns the demons not to let on. The journey to the Cross will eventually reveal the fullness of his person and mission.

The Roman Missal

The prayers for the ferial weekday are taken from the Masses and Prayers for Various Needs and Occasions, from one of two formularies: either the Mass "For Giving Thanks to God for the Gift of Human Life" (#48/1), in which case white vestments are worn, or the Mass "For the Preservation of Peace and Justice" (#30), in which case violet vestments are worn.

For the Day of Prayer for the Legal Protection of Unborn Children, use the Mass "For Giving Thanks to God for the Gift of Human Life." It has two different sets of orations from which to choose. All the prayers, though, express the Church's concern for the dignity of life and the need to both reverence and give witness to that dignity.

FRI 23 (#315) green
Weekday

Optional Memorial of St. Vincent, Deacon and Martyr / red; Optional Memorial of St. Marianne Cope, Virgin / white

The Lectionary for Mass

◆ FIRST READING: The opening verse of today's First Reading repeats the closing verse of yesterday's reading. Hebrews cites Jeremiah in the body of our passage in order to substantiate why the old covenant needed to be followed by a new covenant. The new covenant in Jesus the high priest is written on people's hearts. In his sacrifice, Jesus forgives sins and Christians know him as Lord. In Christ, the old covenant is not "close to disappearing" as the author of Hebrews suggests. Both the author and we know that in Christ it has indeed been fulfilled.

◆ RESPONSORIAL PSALM 85: This psalm is a national lament. The psalmist prays for the people to experience once again God's love and mercy. Beautiful imagery of love and truth, and justice and peace meeting describes the arrival of God's salvation. In the closing verses, confidence abounds that God's love will yield prosperity for the people. Our hope in Christ as the mediator of the new covenant mirrors this confidence.

◆ GOSPEL: The solemn moment of Jesus appointing the Twelve to be his followers and to be sent forth to preach, heal, and drive out demons as he did is our Gospel reading for today. Jesus's mission as the Messiah extends to his disciples and specifically to the Twelve whom he also called apostles, which comes from the Greek word *apostolos* meaning "one who is sent." Prepared or not, the Twelve, led by Simon whose name Jesus changed to Peter, will imbue themselves with Jesus's teaching and his life of compassion, experience rejection, and journey to the cross with him. They, and we today, are the chosen ones to carry on Jesus's mission for the sake of the world.

Today's Saints

St. Vincent was from Saragossa in third-century Spain. He is also known as Vincent the deacon and served under St. Valerius, bishop of Saragossa. He was martyred in 304 during the persecution by the emperor Diocletian. Just before he was killed on a gridiron or grill, he was offered his freedom if he would throw a copy of the Scriptures on the fire that was prepared for him, but he refused. After witnessing Vincent's faith and heroism, his executioner converted to Christianity.

St. Marianne Cope (1838–1918) was born in West Germany, but a year after her birth the Cope family emigrated to the United States of America to seek work and educational opportunities. From a young age, she felt the call to enter religious life, which led to her decision to enter the Sisters of St. Francis in Syracuse, New York. She had a deep affection for the suffering and sick. Marianne was instrumental in the establishment of two of the first hospitals in the central New York area—hospitals that were open to all people regardless of ethnicity, religion, or race. While serving as superior general of her religious community, she accepted an invitation to care for the sick, especially those afflicted with leprosy, in Hawaii. Marianne joined the mission to Hawaii where she helped establish homes for leprosy patients and cared for St. Damien De Veuster of Moloka'i who contracted leprosy because of his ministry to the sick. Following the death of St. Damien, Marianne continued his compassionate ministry of care for leprosy patients. Marianne lived the Franciscan call to serve the "crucified," the most vulnerable, in society. The inclusion of her "feast day" as an optional memorial for the dioceses of the United States was approved by the Vatican in early 2013.

SAT 24 (#316) white
Memorial of St. Francis de Sales, Bishop and Doctor of the Church

The Lectionary for Mass

◆ FIRST READING: Christ abides in the sanctuary of heaven, a sanctuary not made of human hands. He mediates the new covenant through his own Blood, which cleanses us from sin. The author of Hebrews uses the phrase "once for all" that occurs eleven times in his work to describe Christ's entry into the heavenly sanctuary. His entry into the sanctuary not made by human hands will not have to occur again for the good of our salvation he has accomplished.

◆ RESPONSORIAL PSALM 47: Our psalm for today is the same psalm used on the Solemnity of the Ascension of the Lord. Filled with imagery of the Lord mounting the throne, the psalm exudes praise and worship for the Lord who rules over peoples and nations. The Lord's kingship indeed extends to the entire earth. Christians readily apply this psalm to Christ, who reigns from heaven. Joy at Christ's triumph exudes from the psalm's words.

◆ GOSPEL: Our very brief Gospel reading has Jesus returning home to Nazareth where his relatives still lived. Crowds followed him in such numbers making it impossible for Jesus and the Twelve to eat. Into this home setting, Mark inserted text in which the scribes once again intend to demean Jesus. Today's passage ends with some of Jesus's relatives even questioning his state of mind, increasing our awareness as to the source of Jesus's opposition. Even family members do not believe. The narrative continues next Monday.

The Roman Missal

The orations are proper for today and are found in the Proper of Saints at January 24. The prayers include mention of St. Francis de Sales by way of his gentleness, his meekness, his charity, and his being inflamed with the Holy Spirit. Although no particular Preface is indicated in the rubrics for today, the Preface of Holy Pastors would make sense, since St. Francis was a bishop.

Today's Saint

St. Francis de Sales (1567–1622), bishop of Geneva, contributed immensely to the development of spirituality through the publication of his book, *An Introduction to the Devout Life.* Living at a time when manuals on spirituality were written primarily for clerics and members of religious orders, St. Francis's book provided a practical path to holiness for people from all states of life. He challenged the prevailing belief that only a select few could obtain sanctity. Along with his accomplishments in the area of an everyday, or lay, spirituality, he cofounded with St. Jane Frances de Chantal the Order of the Visitation of Holy Mary, a religious community of nuns that would move beyond traditional enclosure to a healthy blend of prayer and service to the poor. Together, Sts. Francis and Jane, with their close friends Sts. Vincent de Paul and Louise de Marillac, transformed the face of the Church in France. St. Francis has been named a Doctor of the Church.

☀ **25** (#68) green
Third Sunday in Ordinary Time

The Lectionary for Mass

◆ FIRST READING: This is the only Sunday in all three years of the Lectionary cycle of readings that we hear a passage from the book of Jonah proclaimed. God's mercy abounds! This is the message of the reading which recounts Jonah's journey to Nineveh with the prophetic message of repentance and change. The people of Nineveh heard the possibility of destruction and turned away from evil. God, in turn, responded choosing life over destruction.

◆ RESPONSORIAL PSALM 25: The antiphon for today's psalm would be a good mantra to begin each day: "Teach me your ways, O Lord." As the psalmist recognizes, learning the Lord's ways is something we cannot do on our own. Rather, working in concert with the Lord, God will guide us and direct us with compassion even when we err.

◆ SECOND READING: Paul and the early Christians believed that Christ's second coming at the Parousia was imminent. Thus, Paul's main concern in this brief passage is that the Corinthians not be overly attached to the world. The present is passing away; what is good in it can lead us to Christ, but the allure of its evil we must not allow to deceive us. We must always be prepared for Christ's glorious coming.

◆ GOSPEL: Leave your job and family. Follow Jesus, not alone, but with others. Repent. Accept and live the message that the kingdom of God is at hand. These are summary statements of the call to discipleship found in Mark. We, like the first disciples, come after Jesus, believing that in him God's kingdom is present. This is the kingdom we proclaim to the world by virtue of our Baptism and our repentance.

The Roman Missal

The Mass texts for this Sunday are found in the "Ordinary Time" section of the Proper of Time. The Gloria is sung or said today. The Creed is said or sung.

The Collect asks that God may direct our actions so that "in the name of your beloved Son / we may abound in good works." In the Prayer over the Offerings we are asking God to accept our offerings so that, in sanctifying them, "they may profit us for salvation." The Prayer after Communion asks that, as a result of receiving the grace of being brought to new life (for example, in the Eucharist), "we may always glory in your gift."

Any one of the eight Prefaces of the Sundays in Ordinary Time may be selected for today.

The deacon's or priest's use of the third option for the dismissal formula, "Go in peace, glorifying the Lord by your life," would make a nice connection with the Prayer after Communion.

Other Ideas

Today concludes the Week of Prayer for Christian Unity, so be sure to recall this in the intercessions. Today is also the Collection for the Church in Latin America (CLA) which supports many projects in the Latino Church in the Northern Hemisphere. The USCCB website is chock full of good resources for this day.

Sometimes in a parish, there are so many fund raisers and activities going on that it can be overwhelming, and people feel that the Church is always asking for more money. If that is the case, then perhaps you need to pick and choose how much emphasis you give some of these special needs projects — simply by providing continued information about the organization (provide links to prayer and financial support), you are helping them already.

MON 26
(#520; Gospel #317)   white

Memorial of Sts. Timothy and Titus, Bishops

The Lectionary for Mass

◆ FIRST READING: Two options are given for this memorial honoring two prominent assistants to Saint Paul: Timothy and Titus. Both texts are taken from the beginning of the letters which, according to tradition, the Apostle wrote to them. Notice Paul's self-identification in each letter, presenting his ministry as a vocation from God. Note also that both Timothy and Titus are addressed as "my . . . child" (2 Timothy 1:2; Titus 1:4), thus pointing to Paul's role in enlivening and nurturing their faith. The text to Timothy stresses Paul's gratitude and prayer for him. The reference to Timothy's mother and grandmother and their role in Timothy's faith makes them models for our own day. Timothy is encouraged not to take for granted the grace received through Paul's laying hands on him—a gesture evoking the sacraments as we celebrate them today, and good advice for us as well. He is encouraged to fidelity despite the hardships involved, knowing that strength will be given him from God. Titus's mission is to complete the work Paul had begun and to appoint presbyters or local leaders of the Church in every town.

◆ RESPONSORIAL PSALM 96: The antiphon is most appropriate for today's memorial, given the ministry of Timothy and Titus. The reference to the nations points to the universal outreach (to Gentiles) of their mission. God's marvelous deed in sending his Son Jesus has truly brought salvation to all.

◆ GOSPEL: Today's Gospel reading continues immediately where last Saturday's left off. New opponents, the scribes who had come from Jerusalem, make their first appearance. They level a double accusation against Jesus reproaching him for being possessed by an unclean spirit and for driving out demons. Jesus's response points to the unreasonableness of their accusations. He uses a parable to show unequivocally he is not possessed by Satan and a solemn teaching introduced by an "Amen" to reveal his authority to drive out demons comes not from Satan, but from the Holy Spirit.

The Roman Missal

The prayers are found in the Proper of Saints.

Appropriately on this memorial, the Collect echoes the words of Saint Paul's letter to Timothy (2:12). We pray that we may live "justly and devoutly in this present age" and so come to our "heavenly homeland." In the Prayer over the Offerings, we ask for "sincerity of heart," that we may be acceptable to God. We pray that the sacrament we receive may nourish us in the faith which was taught and "kept safe" by Sts. Timothy and Titus (Prayer after Communion). The Preface of Pastors is used.

Today's Saints

Sts. Timothy and Titus, first century bishops and martyrs, are celebrated together because of their joint association with St. Paul. Timothy is first mentioned in Acts of the Apostles 16:1–2, when Paul visits Lystra, in what is now Turkey. Timothy's mother was Jewish; Paul circumcised him so he would be accepted by the Jewish Christians. Timothy accompanied Paul on some of his journeys, and he is the one addressed in the Letters to Timothy in the New Testament. Tradition says that Paul made him bishop of Ephesus in 65. He was martyred by stoning in either the year 65 or 80 for preaching against the worship of idols.

St. Titus was also a disciple and companion of St. Paul. He was probably a Gentile, and Paul refused to have him circumcised because the Gospel freed Gentiles from the Law of Moses. Although he is not mentioned in the Acts of the Apostles, he is mentioned several times in Paul's letters and was probably commissioned to preach to the Gentiles. According to Paul, Titus was with Paul and Timothy at Ephesus and was sent to Macedonia to collect alms for the Christians in Jerusalem. He also spent time in Macedonia, Crete, and Dalmatia in modern-day Croatia. Tradition says that he was a bishop in Crete and died in the year 107.

TUE 27
(#318)   green

Weekday

Optional Memorial of St. Angela Merici, Virgin / white

The Lectionary for Mass

◆ FIRST READING: The author of Hebrews places verses from Psalm 40 on Jesus's lips at his Incarnation. He has come to do God's will. After the sacrifice of Jesus's own life, other sacrifices such as those performed on the annual Day of Atonement are no longer necessary. Christ took away the need for other sacrifices through the offering of his own body. The totality of his obedient self-sacrifice consecrates us to God and unites us with him in holiness.

◆ RESPONSORIAL PSALM 40: An individual thanksgiving for the new song God puts in our mouth, this psalm reflects God's preference for obedience over sacrifice. Cited in today's First Reading from Hebrews, the psalm stresses the delight of doing God's will made perfect in Christ. Written on our heart, God's law leads us to see the newness God has done in Christ. For this covenant Christ mediates, the first stanza tells us, generations waited.

◆ GOSPEL: Jesus's mother and brothers were not present when Jesus first arrived at home in the Gospel reading from last Saturday. Now, the crowd informs Jesus, they are outside the house and would like to see him. Taking advantage of the opportunity, Jesus rhetorically queries the crowd about who really are his mother and brothers. His question leads us to ask if he would include us as his family members since he teaches that those who do God's will rather than genetic ties constitute relationships in his family.

Today's Saint

Several miraculous occurrences, including restoration of sight and visions, surrounded the life of St. Angela Merici (1474–1540), a native of Desenzano in northern Italy. She was profoundly impacted by one vision in which she saw a great company of virgins and saints singing and playing instruments while descending from a staircase in the heavens. Based upon this vision, St. Angela founded a group of consecrated women known as the Ursulines, dedicated to the education of young women, especially the poor. They were named after the fourth-century martyr and protector of women, St. Ursula, to whom St. Angela had a special devotion from an early age. Unlike

the traditional customs practiced by those in religious orders, the members of this community did not wear habits, take vows, or live behind an enclosure. The women often resided with their own families, but met for instruction. St. Angela was gravely concerned that customary practices or rules not hinder the women from freely serving those in need.

(#319) white
Memorial of St. Thomas Aquinas, Priest and Doctor of the Church
WED 28

The Lectionary for Mass

◆ FIRST READING: Citations from Psalm 110 and Jeremiah 31 form the basis of today's First Reading. The passage declares once again that the difference between the sacrifices performed by the Levitical priesthood and the one sacrifice offered by Christ lies in the fact that the forgiveness given in the latter lasts forever. The forgiveness given in the new covenant replaces the need for forgiveness to be given multiple times through multiple sacrifices. The repetition of these main themes in Hebrews during these weeks of Ordinary Time gives us pause to reflect on how we appropriate our belief in the new wonders God has done in Christ as we live in the interim before his enemies are made subject to him again at his Second Coming.

◆ RESPONSORIAL PSALM: For the third time in ten days, this psalm is our response. See the commentary on Monday, January 19, 2015, for background. The First Reading cites the psalm's reference to the king's enemies becoming his footstool. In antiquity, triumphant kings actually did put their feet on their enemies' bodies using them as footrests.

◆ GOSPEL: The Twelve understand the mystery of the kingdom of God, but for those who do not, Jesus must speak in parables.

Today's Gospel reading is comprised of the well known parable of the sower and its explanation. People respond in different ways to the in-breaking of the kingdom of God in the world. The parable affords us the opportunity to consider how we have responded to the kingdom at various points in our life and how we are responding today, at this moment. At times, we might be like the privileged Twelve who understand the kingdom's mystery, but most often we are in need of Jesus sowing the kingdom's seed in our hearts and expanding our minds to comprehend its challenges and possibilities.

The Roman Missal

The Collect is proper for today and is to be found in the Proper of Saints at January 28. The first part of the oration recognizes St. Thomas Aquinas's zeal for holiness and study of sacred doctrine; the second part asks God to grant "that we may understand what he taught / and imitate what he accomplished." The other prayers are taken either from the Common of Doctors of the Church or from the Common of Pastors: For One Pastor. The Preface to use is either the Preface of Holy Pastors or one of the two Prefaces of Saints.

Today's Saint

St. Thomas Aquinas (1225–1274), a Doctor of the Church, felt drawn to the charism of the Dominicans, even though his parents wanted him to become a Benedictine monk. As a young Dominican, his reserved demeanor led his classmates to believe he was unintelligent; therefore, they called him the "dumb ox." Little did they know St. Thomas was a brilliant man who would write the *Summa Theologica* — a theological masterpiece that explicates the truths of the Catholic faith by demonstrating the intimate relationship between reason and revelation. His intellectual genius and method of theological inquiry was greatly influenced by his mentor and teacher St. Albert the Great. The person once thought to be a "dumb ox" became known as the "angelic doctor" due to his profound impact on theological thought, as far reaching as the Second Vatican Council and contemporary theologians like Karl Rahner.

THU 29 (#320) green
Weekday

The Lectionary for Mass

◆ FIRST READING: This passage focuses on our responsibility in light of Christ's sacrifice. Confidence, a sincere heart, absolute trust, and an unwavering confession in relation to the new covenant all can belong to us as a result of Christ's obedience to God's will. Yet we must not simply take these to ourselves through a selfish act, we must use them to support one in another in our Christian life together, a life of love and good works.

◆ RESPONSORIAL PSALM: A hymn of praise recognizing the Lord created the earth and all that is within it, this psalm also rhetorically questions who is able to ascend the Lord's mountain to the holy and heavenly throne. Those who can make this procession and enter the divine court have clean hands and pure hearts. Their sins are forgiven. Christ gives us access to the heavenly sanctuary because of his atoning sacrifice. We receive blessing and, in turn, respond in love.

◆ GOSPEL: Jesus's call to those with ears to hear comes in between the familiar parables of the lamp and the measure. The mystery of the kingdom of God will be brought to light. It will not be hidden to those who desire to hear it. In the concluding verse, Jesus applies a saying about people's economic livelihoods at the time to various degrees of spiritual understanding about the kingdom. The more we understand about the kingdom, the more Jesus will make available for us to learn.

FRI 30 (#321) green
Weekday

The Lectionary for Mass

◆ FIRST READING: The journey is long. Confidence and endurance must remain with us. The text from Hebrews reminds us of the times in the past when Christians faced persecution and endured a tremendous amount of suffering. They knew public humiliation and experienced imprisonment. All this occurred after they had been "enlightened," a reference to their Baptism, and accepted the new covenant in Christ. We must not retreat from our faith journey, the passage warns us, but must constantly seek after God's will. If we do, life, not death, will be ours.

◆ RESPONSORIAL PSALM 37: This psalm echoes the theme of endurance found in the First Reading. God's people are to trust, delight, commit, and live with integrity. God gifts those who live in such a manner with the fulfillment of the promise of salvation. Should we need help persevering in a life of faith and turning away from evil—and we all will—God will help us. Our salvation is in God.

◆ GOSPEL: Today's Gospel reading immediately follows yesterday's and contains two parables. In the first which describes how a seed grows, Jesus illustrates how the kingdom of God is already present but will grow into its fullness as the end times approach. The second is the familiar nature parable about the mustard seed. In this nature parable Jesus teaches us about the universal reach of God's kingdom, noting how the smallest of seeds yields the largest of plants.

SAT 31 (#322) white
Memorial of St. John Bosco, Priest

The Lectionary for Mass

Our First Reading begins with an eloquent statement about faith that underscores its relational nature and its content. The main part of the reading attests to Abraham's faithfulness. Faith made it possible for Abraham to obey God and journey to an unknown land. Faith enabled him to trust in God's promise of a child. Faith allowed him to give up his only son, Isaac, and to receive him back. By faith we now believe God raised Christ from the dead. This is the hope we live in each day.

◆ CANTICLE: Today's response comes not from a psalm, but from the Gospel according to Luke. The Canticle of Zechariah, also used in Morning Prayer, is Zechariah's hymn of praise for the birth of John the Baptist. We find the connection to the First Reading in the canticle's mention of God's oath sworn to Abraham.

◆ GOSPEL: The faith Abraham had is the faith the disciples lack in today's Gospel. For many of us Jesus's calming of the storm at sea provides an example of how faith can quiet fear. When the violent storm arises, the disciples immediately think of the worst case scenario: they will die. After the disciples woke him, Jesus calms the storm with words only. He calls the disciples to faith and they pause to question who this man is that they are following.

The Roman Missal

The Collect for St. John Bosco is proper. The remaining prayers may be taken from the Common of Pastors: For One Pastor, or from the Common of Holy Men and Women: For Educators.

Today's Saint

God gifted St. John Bosco (1815–1888) with the ability to read and interpret the signs of the times. Living during rapid industrialization and growing anti-clericalism, he became very concerned about the emotional and spiritual livelihood of people, especially the plight of the young. St. John worked to provide positive and affirming environments, including orphanages and oratories, where the young could learn and recognize their infinite potential. In the spirit of his favorite hero, St. Francis de Sales, he founded the Salesians, a religious congregation devoted to works of charity, with an emphasis on empowering young people to become strong pillars of faith in a culture of instability. His work among young men living in the slums proved to be a worthy endeavor. Whether he was presiding at Mass or playing games with children or carrying the sick to hospitals, it was obvious he lived until his "last breath . . . day and night, morning and evening" for the neglected and abandoned (as quoted in *Butler's Lives of the Saints: January, New Full Edition*, p. 229).

February
Month of the Passion of Our Lord

 1 (#71)   green
Fourth Sunday in Ordinary Time

The Lectionary for Mass

◆ FIRST READING: Moses, the first among the prophets for the Israelites, speaks about another prophet that the Lord will raise up. The Lord's words will come from the mouth of this prophet. A true prophet speaks the words of the Lord; those who speak what the Lord has not commanded will perish. Christians see God's promise delivered by Moses to raise up another prophet fulfilled in Jesus.

◆ RESPONSORIAL PSALM 95: The psalm's antiphon encourages us to respond to God's voice when we hear it, not to harden our hearts. With thanksgiving and joy, the psalm calls us to sing God's praise. God is our Creator and God is our Savior who shepherds us and guides us. Psalm 95 also served as the psalm for Thursday, January 15, 2015.

◆ SECOND READING: Today's Second Reading continues immediately from last Sunday's. With belief in the imminent return of Christ in the background, Paul responds to practical questions about the issues of marriage and virginity.

Paul's main point is not to uphold the unmarried life as better than the married life, but rather to encourage people to remain in their present state of life as they prepare themselves for the Lord's coming. To change one's state of life would, for Paul, create more anxiety in preparation for the end times.

◆ GOSPEL: The newly called disciples follow Jesus to Capernaum, where they begin to witness firsthand who he is. Jesus enters the synagogue and teaches with an authority different from that of the scribes. He exorcises an unclean spirit from a man possessed. It was the man with an unclean spirit who, even before Jesus cast out the demon, proclaimed him as the Holy One of God.

The Roman Missal

The simple Collect echoes the words of Christ to the scribe who asked him which Commandment was most important: we are to "honor [God] with all our mind, / and love everyone in truth of heart." In the Prayer over the Offerings, we ask God to transform the "offerings of our service" and make them "the Sacrament of our redemption." In the Prayer after Communion, we pray that the "redeeming gifts" we receive may help the faith to spread. The sacrifice is offered not just for our own salvation, but for that of the whole world.

Other Ideas

Monday is the celebration of the Presentation of the Lord—this day is traditionally known as Candlemas Day. Invite the congregation to bring their candles to be blessed, and use the glorious solemn procession opening if you are able. Getting a large stack of all the candles used in the church throughout the year can be a wonderful symbol of the prayer that does take place here. This is a wonderful liturgy to celebrate with school children.

Tuesday is the optional Memorial of St. Blaise with the traditional blessing of throats (chapter 51, *Book of Blessings*). This blessing may take place after the Universal Prayer. While one can purchase the entwined Blaise candle sticks, simply cross two candles and secure with string or a large rubber band, and wrap the joint with a red bow. You can create as many sets as needed for the liturgy. While you could have people do this at all Communion stations, it is really good if all can receive the blessing from the priest or deacon if that will work pastorally.

(#524) white

M O N 2 Feast of the Presentation of the Lord

About this Feast

The Feast of the Presentation of the Lord is rooted in everyday life. In faithful observance of the law of Moses, Mary and Joseph present Jesus in the Temple to consecrate him to the Lord. There they met the righteous Simeon and the prophet Anna, for whom Temple worship was part of everyday life. God rewarded their fidelity by allowing them to see the one who was Savior and to hold him in their arms. When the ceremony of presentation was completed, Mary and Joseph and Jesus returned to their hometown. There, they created a home and a family life. There, Jesus grew up, becoming strong and wise, and the grace of God was upon him.

The Feast of the Presentation of the Lord, on February 2, is also called Candlemas Day. According to Luke's account of the Gospel, Simeon recognized Jesus as the Messiah in the Temple and declared him "a light for revelation to the Gentiles, and glory for your people Israel" (Luke 2:32). This sparked the tradition of blessing enough candles to last an entire year. This led to candle processions in churches and in the streets, which became known as "Candlemas."

The Lectionary for Mass

◆ FIRST READING: The book of the prophet Malachi is three short chapters. Written by the prophet who named himself "Malachi," meaning "My Messenger," to disguise his identity so the priests and rulers he criticized would not locate him, the prophet's goal is to call God's people back to faith. Our First Reading speaks about the messenger who will be sent to God's Temple to refine and purify the people like gold and silver so that they may once again offer acceptable sacrifices to the God. Matthew and Mark apply this passage to John the Baptist, but our celebration of the feast of the Presentation recognizes Jesus as the one who purifies us and leads us back to God.

◆ RESPONSORIAL PSALM: We proclaimed the opening stanzas of Psalm 24 during the previous Thursday's liturgy. Originally a processional hymn, this psalm was sung as the Ark of the Covenant made its way into the Temple. The stanzas used today celebrate the return of God as our victorious king.

◆ SECOND READING: On today's feast we return to an early chapter of Hebrews for the Second Reading. The proclamation of this passage occurred previously on Wednesday of the first week in Ordinary Time. In the context of today's feast, we focus on Jesus as the high priest who shares in our humanity and knows the reality of suffering. In contrast to the unfaithful priests and rulers Malachi addresses, Hebrews acknowledges Jesus as the "merciful and faithful" high priest.

◆ GOSPEL: The Gospel reading narrates the faithfulness of Mary and Joseph to the Mosaic law. Simeon's proclamation of Jesus as the bringer of salvation, the light to the Gentiles, and the glory for Israel, reveals how he will fulfill not only God's promise to Simeon, but to Israel as well. The longer form of today's Gospel includes the narration of Anna's thanksgiving to God and her testimony about redemption in Jesus.

The Roman Missal

Everything is proper to today's feast, so all texts and rubrics are found at February 2 in the Proper of Saints.

The Blessing of Candles and the Procession

The Missal calls for this Mass to begin with the blessing of candles and a procession, in one form or another. Two possibilities are given in the Missal: "The Procession" and "The Solemn Entrance."

First Form: The Procession

All should gather in a place apart from the worship space where the procession will go to—for example, a smaller church, or perhaps a space in the parish hall, or perhaps even the gathering space of the church. The gathered faithful are to be already holding candles, so either the people bring candles with them or candles are handed to them as they gather. The priest, wearing white Mass vestments (although he may wear a cope at this point instead of a chasuble), and the ministers enter. There is no mention of a procession or of any singing, so the priest and the ministers just informally take their places. First, light everyone's candles and while this is done the antiphon suggested in the Missal (*Ecce Dominus noster* — "Behold, our Lord will come with power, to enlighten the eyes of his servants, alleluia" — or some other appropriate song is sung. If another song or chant is used, the words should speak of the imagery of light.

After the candles are lit and the singing is concluded, the priest begins with the Sign of the Cross and one of the usual forms of the Greeting for Mass. Then he gives an introductory address; he may use the exact words as provided in the Missal at #4 for the Feast of the Presentation of the Lord, or he may use similar words. The address as given in the Missal notes the passing of forty days since the celebration of the Nativity and recalls how "Today is the blessed day / when Jesus was presented in the Temple by Mary and Joseph." It goes on to speak of the meaning of this feast as Jesus "coming to meet his believing people" and how Simeon and Anna, enlightened by the Holy Spirit, recognized him. It ends with the exhortation that we should "proceed to the house of God to encounter Christ," particularly as we shall recognize him in the breaking of bread until he comes again. Whether the priest uses the exact words in the Missal or similar words, the point of the address is to encourage the faithful "to celebrate the rite of this feast day actively and consciously."

After the address, the priest extends his hands and blesses the candles using the exact words of one of the two prayers of blessing given at #5 in the Missal (Feast of the Presentation of the Lord). In the first prayer, which specifically recalls Simeon and which refers to "the Light for revelation to the Gentiles," the priest makes the gesture of blessing with the Sign of the Cross where indicated; there is no such gesture in the second prayer,

which speaks more generally about light and God's glory.

Next, the priest sprinkles the candles with holy water without saying anything. Then he puts incense into the thurible for the procession, receives his lighted candle from the deacon or another minister, and the procession begins with the words of invitation from the Missal, given by the deacon, or, if there is no deacon, by the priest himself.

With everyone carrying lighted candles, the procession, in the usual order (that is, thurifer, crossbearer, candlebearers, and so on), moves into the worship space while an appropriate antiphon or song is sung. This Missal offers two suggestions for antiphons: "A light for revelation to the Gentiles and the glory of your people Israel" or "For my eyes have seen your salvation, which you have prepared in the sign of all the peoples." The Latin text for the first option is provided in the Missal.

When the priest arrives at the altar in the church, he venerates it and incenses it, if incense is being used. He then goes to the chair where he changes from the cope into the chasuble, if he wore a cope for the procession. The Gloria is then sung, after which the priest prays the Collect, and Mass continues as usual.

Second Form: The Solemn Entrance

When the procession as described above is not going to take place, then the assembly gathers in the church as they usually do, holding candles. The priest, along with the ministers and a representative group of the faithful, goes to a place in the church that is visible to the rest of the assembly. They can be at the doors of the church or even somewhere inside the church itself. Notice that it is presumed that more than just the priest and ministers will gather and move in procession; a certain number of the faithful are

expected to participate in this. The priest wears white Mass vestments; no mention is made of using a cope in this form of the entrance.

The priest and the others arrive at the place for the blessing of candles, without any music or formal procession. Once they are in place, everyone's candles are lit, with an antiphon or song being sung, as described above (this may take a little bit of thinking-through ahead of time, so that it is not done haphazardly; ushers can be of assistance here). Once everyone's candles are lit, the priest begins in the same way as in the first form above, with the Sign of the Cross, Greeting, introductory address, and blessing of candles and sprinkling, followed by the procession, accompanied by singing; he uses the same texts as designated for the first form of procession. As in the first form, the priest incenses the altar when arriving there, if incense is being used, and then he goes to the chair, at which point the Gloria is sung and Mass continues in the usual manner.

At the Mass

The Collect makes a connection between Christ's being presented "on this day in the Temple / in the substance of our flesh" and the request that, by God's grace, "we may be presented to you with minds made pure."

The Prayer over the Offerings draws a parallel between the offering of the Son, offered as the Lamb without blemish for the life of the world, and the offering we make now with exultation, asking that our offering here and now be pleasing to God, as was the offering of the Son.

The Preface, found right along with the other texts for this Mass in the Proper of Saints, is a brief one, succinctly stating that the "co-eternal Son was presented on this day in the Temple / and revealed by the Spirit / as the glory of Israel and the Light of the nations." Because of this, "we, too, go forth, rejoicing to encounter your Salvation." This going forth to encounter salvation occurs on many levels: certainly in the journey of our life, but also as we continue forth with the offering of this sacrifice, where we will encounter Christ in the salvific power of the Paschal Mystery made present in the Church's anamnesis of the Eucharistic Prayer and in Christ's Real Presence in the Eucharist. This would be a good occasion to chant the introductory dialogue and Preface, in order to highlight the festivity of this liturgy.

Simeon is mentioned again, this time in the Prayer after Communion, as we pray that just as his expectation was fulfilled "that he would not see death / until he had been privileged to welcome the Christ," so too may we meet the Lord in the gift of eternal life.

T U E 3 (#324) green Weekday

Optional Memorials of St. Blaise, Bishop and Martyr / red; St. Ansgar, Bishop / white

The Lectionary for Mass

◆ FIRST READING: Today marks the beginning of the final five days in which the First Reading comes from Hebrews. We hear how Jesus's endurance when he faced opposition encourages us in our struggles, particularly those against our own shortcomings. Most of us have not had to resist to the extent of physically sacrificing ourselves. We are to look to our ancestors in faith from the Old Testament to garner strength to live out our faith, but our greatest support comes from Jesus.

◆ RESPONSORIAL PSALM: Today's psalm, an individual lament, also serves as the psalm for Palm Sunday. On that occasion, the stanzas come from the earlier portion of the psalm. The response today comes

from the latter half of the psalm, in which the psalmist calls us to praise God and enjoy life with God forever. Our praise is fitting for all that God has done for us in Jesus on the cross as the First Reading attests. People from all time periods — the past, present, and future — will give homage to him as the final stanzas of the psalm declare.

◆ GOSPEL: Two miracle stories compose today's Gospel reading. The Gospel opens by setting the scene for the cure of a synagogue official's daughter. Into the narrative of Jairus's dying daughter, the Gospel writer inserted the story of the woman who had been hemorrhaging for twelve years. After Jesus cures her, the story of the healing of the twelve-year-old girl resumes. Through both miracles, we learn it is faith — Jairus's and the woman's with a hemorrhage — that saves.

Blessing of Throats

The optional Memorial of St. Blaise is the traditional day for the blessing of throats. Although the Missal is silent on it, the *Book of Blessings* states that throats may be blessed at Mass, following the Homily and the Universal Prayer. For pastoral reasons, it may take the place of the final blessing of the Mass. The formula of blessing is: "Through the intercession of St. Blaise, bishop and martyr, may God deliver you from every disease of the throat and from every other illness: In the name of the Father, and of the Son, and of the Holy Spirit. Amen."

Today's Saints

Although St. Blaise († 316) and St. Ansgar (801–865) were separated by time, they both wanted to care for souls. While serving as Bishop of Sebastea, in Armenia, St. Blaise was a visible witness of the Gospel, which eventually led to his martyrdom during the persecutions of Diocletian. His feast day is commemorated with a blessing of

throats because legend says that he cured a young boy choking on a fish bone. St. Ansgar, born in France, was a monk with a missionary spirit. He longed to travel to distant lands to draw more and more souls to the saving message of Christ. His missionary endeavors were directed toward Scandinavian territory, thus earning him the title Patron of Denmark. He is credited with organizing missions to Denmark, Sweden, and Norway and building the first Christian church in Sweden. Due to his excellent leadership and preaching skills, St. Ansgar was appointed Archbishop of Hamburg.

W E D 4 (#325) green Weekday

The Lectionary for Mass

◆ FIRST READING: Our First Reading begins by reiterating the closing verse of yesterday's reading to remind us that our struggle with sin has yet to entail all that Jesus did. Then, quoting from Proverbs, the text shows us that the God's discipline goes hand in hand with God's love for us. Parents know this truth; children have a difficult time accepting it. The reading concludes encouraging us to care for one another, seeking peace and living in holiness in order that we might experience God's grace.

◆ RESPONSORIAL PSALM 103: The connection to the First Reading lies in the psalm's comparison of the Lord's compassion to a father's for his children. The Lord's kindness lasts forever; our descendants will know the Lord's faithfulness to the covenant. In Christ, we know divine kindness as the gift of eternal life. For this gift of salvation, our entire being blesses the Lord!

◆ GOSPEL: Faith is the issue, and Jesus found little of it in his hometown synagogue. The Gospel writer communicates to us once again people's wonderment at Jesus's words.

The people ask a series of questions obviously intended to question Jesus's authority because, the text tells us, of the offense the people took at Jesus. Jesus's response relates his own rejection to the rejection that the Old Testament prophets experienced. The rejection he faces serves as a prelude to his Passion and Death, and also prepares us to accept the negativity we'll encounter as his disciples.

T H U **5** (#326) red
Memorial of St. Agatha, Virgin and Martyr

The Lectionary for Mass

◆ First Reading: The First Reading paints a picture of two distinct assemblies. The first assembly is the Israelites gathered at Mount Sinai to receive the Mosaic law and seal the covenant. The second is of those who follow Jesus, the mediator of the new covenant, assembled at Mount Zion, the heavenly Jerusalem. According to the text, the second covenant speaks "more eloquently" because Jesus's sacrifice provides a way for all to access the joy of the heavenly court.

◆ Responsorial Psalm 48: This psalm depicts our journey to the heavenly sanctuary where we hope to reside forever with the Lord. The psalm opens with words of praise for the Lord who resides in Jerusalem, historically recognized as the city of God. We desire to be among those who assemble on the holy mountain of the heavenly Jerusalem and so we, too, praise God as we look forward to participating in this eternal gathering.

◆ Gospel: Jesus called them, gave them authority, and now, on the heels of his own hometown rejection, he sends them out on a mission. One has to wonder what the Twelve must have been thinking. Yet they went out without any provisions except sticks to aid their walking and preached, healed, exorcised demons, and anointed and cured the sick. Presumably they followed Jesus's instruction to simply move on when they faced rejection, neither wallowing in self-pity nor confronting those who rejected their message of repentance. Their journey had to continue and so does ours.

The Roman Missal

The Mass text that is proper for today is the Collect, and it is found in the Proper of Saints at February 5. The prayer highlights St. Agatha's courage in martyrdom and her chastity. The Prayer over the Offerings and the Prayer after Communion will come either from the Common of Martyrs: For a Virgin Martyr, or from the Common of Virgins: For One Virgin. For the Preface, one of the two Prefaces of Holy Martyrs would be a good choice.

Today's Saint

Agatha was born in Sicily, probably around the year 231, and is one of the women mentioned by name in Eucharistic Prayer I. According to legend, she was the daughter of a prominent family and was very beautiful. The Roman senator Quintianus wished to marry her, but when Agatha spurned him, he had her put in a brothel. In spite of this, Agatha held to her Christian faith. Quintianus then had her tortured by having her breasts cut off. She eventually died in prison in 253. St. Agatha is the patron of the city of her martyrdom, Catania, and is invoked against the fire, earthquakes, and eruptions of Mount Etna. In recent years, because her breasts were cut off as part of her torture, she is considered the patron saint of breast cancer patients.

F R I **6** (#327) red
Memorial of St. Paul Miki and Companions, Martyrs

The Lectionary for Mass

◆ First Reading: We read from the final chapter in Hebrews today and tomorrow. A series of practical instructions for living together in community with allusions to the Old Testament begins today's First Reading. Although community leaders who preached God's word have died, the author of Hebrews exhorts Christians to remember their example. We have all known influential faith leaders whose witness helped us to stay the course, but who now live with God. Jesus the high priest will remain our leader forever.

◆ Responsorial Psalm 27: Trust and confidence color the opening lines of this psalm alluded to in the First Reading. The tone then shifts to one of longing as the individual deeply desires to see the face of the saving God. We have confidence in God, for, as the passage from Hebrews tells us, Jesus is the same throughout all time.

◆ Gospel: Discipleship has a cost to it and that cost sometimes is death. This is the point Mark wanted to illustrate when he chose to insert the account of the death of John the Baptist in between the sending forth and the return of the Twelve. The Gospel reading begins with the various opinions about Jesus's identity. Herod, who probably is as perplexed as anyone, chooses to believe Jesus is really John the Baptist raised from the dead. Of significant note are the similarities between the account of John's death and Jesus's passion, especially the parallels between Herod and Pilate, who both chose self-preservation over integrity and truth, modeling well the characteristics of a non-disciple.

The Roman Missal

The Collect, which is proper for today, is found in the Proper of Saints at February 6. The prayer refers to God as "the strength of all the Saints," and asks that through the intercession of St. Paul Miki and companions, "we may hold with courage even until death / to the faith that we profess," just as they did. The Prayer over the Offerings and the Prayer after Communion are taken from the Common of Martyrs: For Several Martyrs. For the Preface, use one of the two Prefaces of Holy Martyrs.

Today's Saints

St. Paul Miki († 1597), a Jesuit priest, was one of the twenty-six martyrs of Japan. Feeling threatened by the growing influence of the Jesuits, the local governor had members of the Christian community arrested and thrown in jail. They were forced to walk 600 miles from Kyoto to Nagasaki as a deterrent to other Christians, but they sang the *Te Deum* as they went. At Nagasaki they were crucified. When Christian missionaries returned to Japan in the nineteenth century, they found that a secret Christian community had survived by transmitting their beliefs and prayers from generation to generation.

S A T **7** **(#328)** green
Weekday

Optional Memorial of the Blessed Virgin Mary / white

The Lectionary for Mass

◆ FIRST READING: After providing some final practical suggestions, the author of Hebrews concludes his work with a blessing that ties together major themes. Christ serves as our great shepherd whom God has raised from the dead. His death sealed the new and everlasting covenant, through which he offers to us a share in divine goodness. May we

be open ourselves to the fulfillment of God's will in us through Jesus Christ.

◆ RESPONSORIAL PSALM 23: Hebrews' acknowledgment of Christ as the great shepherd is the obvious reason for the choice of today's psalm. Beloved by many, this psalm begins with the personal confession that "The Lord is my shepherd." Whether in green pastures, by safe waters, right paths, or dark valleys, the Lord takes care of each one of us. We will lack nothing with Jesus Christ as our shepherd for our dwelling will be with him.

◆ GOSPEL: We pick up our continuous reading of Mark 6 with the return of the Twelve from their mission. As if giving an internship report, the Twelve provide the details of their experience to Jesus. He recognizes their need for solitude and rest, but once more as so often happens in our own lives, people follow us. There is no sense that either Jesus or the Twelve experienced frustration or disappointment; the text communicates only Jesus's compassion and his immediate response to teach the people. May Jesus's example of shepherding teach us how to respond when people hasten after us after long and intense days of physical, mental, and emotional exertion.

8 **(#74)** green
Fifth Sunday in Ordinary Time

The Lectionary for Mass

◆ FIRST READING: Job's story of restlessness, sleeplessness, and sadness is the story of many people. His reflections on life's drudgery, however, are not his entire story. While he never answers the question why God seems to permit suffering, his experience teaches us that God is faithful. What God asks of him and of us is to be faithful in the midst of suffering, because as humans, all of us will encounter suffering in one form or another.

◆ RESPONSORIAL PSALM 147: Today's psalm is a psalm of praise to the Lord. Knowing the reality of human suffering, we sing praise to the Lord who heals the brokenhearted. God's goodness and graciousness are signs of his faithfulness to us as we live out our lives. God's might and power is as personal as his knowing how many stars there are and calling each star by name.

◆ SECOND READING: Paul preaches the Gospel without want of any reward. His desire is only that all, whether weak or strong, might hear the freedom the Gospel offers. Our mission is nothing less than Paul's mission: the proclamation of God's grace in Christ Jesus through the Gospel. We carry this mission out with the confidence of Paul that we, too, will share in the Gospel's grace.

◆ Gospel: At the conclusion of last Sunday's Gospel, we heard of the rapid expansion of Jesus's reputation based on his healing of the man with an unclean spirit. Today's Gospel is another passage about healing which begins with the individual healing of Simon's mother-in-law and then narrates the healing of many in the entire town. After doing this work, Jesus prays alone in a deserted place, yet Simon and others follow him, telling him that everyone is looking for him. Jesus knows he must continue to preach and heal, and so he goes forth from his short-lived place of solitude.

The Roman Missal

The Mass texts for today are found in the "Ordinary Time" section of the Proper of Time. The Gloria is sung or said today. The Creed is said or sung.

The Collect asks that the Lord will keep us safe as we rely "solely on the help of heavenly grace." The Prayer over the Offerings prays for the transformation of the created realities we offer, that is, bread and wine, so that just as they are material sustenance for us, so too may they become "the Sacrament of eternal life." The Prayer after Communion highlights the unity of the faithful that is to be the result of their participation in the Eucharist. Being united in the one Body of Christ through "the one Bread and the one Chalice" (a presumption that the chalice is offered to the assembly at all Masses?) is the way that we "joyfully bear fruit / for the salvation of the world."

Any one of the eight Prefaces of the Sundays in Ordinary Time may be selected for today.

Other Ideas

Remind your congregation to return old palms that are to be burned before the beginning of Lent and begin announcing times for Ash Wednesday services and any other Lenten activities taking place within the parish.

February is also Black History Month — include this need in the Universal Prayer. February 11 is the World Day of the Sick. Also include the ill and all their caretakers in the Unviersal Prayer. Consider having a special blessing or thanksgiving for these ministers today. The Conference of Catholic Chaplains provides a number of resources (www.nacc.org/resources/wds/). A simple internet search of "World Day of Sick / Vatican" will provide you with links of the pope's message for this day. (At time of printing, no resources for 2015 were yet available.)

February 14 is Valentine's Day. Include an intercession for engaged and married couples as well as for the sanctity of marriage in the Universal Prayer. You might also include a note about World Wide Marriage Encounter, "date night," or any other parish marriage programs in the parish bulletin.

Today is also "Boy Scout Sunday" so be prepared to work with the boyscouts, assigning them liturgical ministries, and allowing for a blessing within the Mass.

MON 9 (#329) green Weekday

The Lectionary for Mass

◆ First Reading: For the next eight weekdays before Ash Wednesday, we read from the Book of Genesis. We begin with the first half of the first account of creation. Creation began with the heavens and the earth; they come out of nothing but chaos. Then, God speaks and out of his word light and water come forth, vegetation arises, the sun and moon appear. Everything is good, God says. The sun rises and sets each day as it has for billions of years.

◆ Responsorial Psalm 104: This psalm is a hymn of praise that also occurs as the response to the creation reading at the Easter Vigil, though with a few added stanzas. The stanzas begin, as the story of creation does, by praising God for the creation of the heavens and earth, and then move on to mention the waters and springs that provide drink to the earth's creatures. Praise be to God who created good order out of chaos!

◆ Gospel: In our reading of Mark 6, we skip over the miracle of the multiplication of the loaves and the episode of Jesus walking on water to today's brief passage. Jesus and the disciples started out en route to Bethsaida, but perhaps the wind caused them to veer from their course and land in Gennesaret. As the Gospel writer often does, he portrays the people as scurrying about to locate the sick and bring them to Jesus. They know Jesus heals, and his healing power indeed manifests itself merely with the touch of his cloak's tassel.

TUE 10 (#330) white Memorial of St. Scholastica, Virgin

The Lectionary for Mass

◆ First Reading: God's word gives us, living creatures, the gift of our humanity which mirrors the divine image and likeness. Created out of God's word with the responsibility to serve as stewards of creation, we have the task of preserving, honoring, and using well the good that comes forth from the divine Word. The seventh day is God's day of rest; God speaks no words. The day is holy, and forever to be a Sabbath. Today we praise God on the Sabbath for the goodness of the divine word.

◆ Responsorial Psalm 8, like yesterday's response to the first half of the creation story, is a hymn of praise to God the Creator. Our stanzas show the psalmist wondering in amazement at the heavens, the moon, and the stars. The psalmist's wonder leads to a reflection on the significance of humanity and then to the affirmation of the dignity with which God endows us — for God chose us — no one and nothing else — for the sacred responsibility of tending creation.

◆ GOSPEL: The behavior of the disciples leads the Pharisees and scribes to question Jesus about why they are not following the tradition of the elders with respect to ritual purification practices. Quoting the prophet Isaiah, Jesus uses a source familiar to the Pharisees to criticize their legalistic ways. God's commandment, Jesus says, should never be put aside for human traditions. Aligning our hearts with God in love is the moral imperative of the divine commandment.

The Roman Missal

The Mass text that is proper for today is the Collect, found in the Proper of Saints at February 10. The Prayer over the Offerings and the Prayer after Communion are taken either from the Common of Virgins: For One Virgin, or from the Common of Holy Men and Women: For a Nun. For the Preface, choose either the Preface of Holy Virgins and Religious or one of the Prefaces of Saints.

Today's Saint

Information regarding the life of St. Scholastica (480–547) is rather meager, but her legacy continues to live on. She was the twin sister of St. Benedict, the father of Western Monasticism. From a young age, she expressed a deep desire to dedicate her life to God through the monastic vows: obedience, conversion of life (poverty and chastity), and stability. She founded and supervised a monastery of nuns near her brother's monastery

at Monte Casino. Once a year St. Scholastica and St. Benedict would meet somewhere between their two monasteries to pray and discuss spiritual matters. Just prior to her death she met with her brother one more time. As the time came for him to leave, she prayed that somehow his visit would be extended. All of a sudden, a violent thunderstorm broke forth from the heavens, preventing St. Benedict from departing. Her prayers were answered — they spent the entire night pondering the deeper mysteries of life.

WED 11 (#331) green
Weekday

Optional Memorial of Our Lady of Lourdes / white

The Lectionary for Mass

◆ FIRST READING: The second creation story is ours to hear this day. Into the clay of the earth, God's very breath gave life and being to man. After creating man, God plants a garden in the middle of which arose the tree of life, for Christians a symbol of eternal life that comes through the Cross. The tree of knowledge of good and bad, the forbidden fruit, also grows in the garden.

◆ RESPONSORIAL PSALM 104: Today's psalm also was the selection for Monday's liturgy, though with different stanzas. The stanzas used today come from the latter part of the psalm and focus on the breath of God (the spirit) as the source of human life. Without breath, we are nothing. Without God, we lack life. For the gift of life, we praise God!

◆ GOSPEL: A short saying in which Jesus seems to be breaking away from the strict observance of some purification laws occurs at the beginning of today's Gospel. Jesus and his disciples then return home where Jesus queries his disciples — and us — as to whether or not we understand the point he is

making. Nothing external to us that we chose to take in is unclean. Only that which is in our heart can be the source of evil. So, the question we're left to ponder is: what resides in our heart, the organ which gives rhythm to our life?

Today's Optional Memorial

Today we commemorate the Virgin Mary's appearances in 1858 to Bernadette Soubirous, a 14-year-old peasant girl. This created an uproar in the small town, and Bernadette was repeatedly questioned and pressured by the local officials to recant her story. The parish priest told her to ask the lady's name. Bernadette returned and said, "I am the Immaculate Conception," a title for Mary of which Bernadette would have known nothing. One of the lady's requests was that a chapel be built on the site of her appearance. Eventually a large church was built there (Lourdes, France), which is now a popular pilgrimage site (visit their website: http://fr.lourdes-france. org). Today would be an appropriate day for a communal celebration of the Anointing of the Sick (or on the predecing Sunday in anticipation of this day). The prayers for this Mass are from the Proper of Saints (Collect) or from the Common of the Blessed Virgin Mary.

THU 12 (332) green
Weekday

The Lectionary for Mass

◆ FIRST READING: Companionship is necessary for human beings to thrive. The Lord God knew this from the very beginning. Having instructed the man from which trees he should eat, God creates animals and birds to provide the man company. God gives the man the responsibility of naming the creatures. But the Lord God deemed human partnership essential.

◆ RESPONSORIAL PSALM: Today's psalm is a happy psalm indeed!

Recognized as a wisdom psalm, Psalm 128 speaks of those who fear the Lord and the reward gained for their labor. The blessings for an adult male will be a wife and children. Yet the psalm speaks in general terms as well: all who fear the Lord will be blessed.

◆ GOSPEL: Jesus and his disciples move on to Gentile territory. In today's Gospel account, Jesus expels a demon from a Syrophoenician woman's daughter. At the outset of his conversation with the woman, it appears as if Jesus attests to the exclusivity of his mission, but this is not the case. The woman's rejoinder, however, makes clear her faith in the availability of God's saving power to all. On the basis of her statement, Jesus relays to her that the demon no longer resides within her daughter.

F R I 13 (#333) green Weekday

The Lectionary for Mass

The First Reading for today and tomorrow is the narrative of the fall of humanity. Today's passage includes the acts of disobedience on the part of both the woman and man. They gave into the temptation to eat of the forbidden fruit and succumbed to the human desire to know everything as God knows. The reading concludes today with their recognition that God is present in the garden breeze, and their choice to try and hide from God.

◆ RESPONSORIAL PSALM 32: This psalm contains characteristics of both wisdom and thanksgiving psalms. When seen in light of the First Reading, this psalm poses quite a contrast. Whereas both the man and woman attempted to hide from God after their acts of disobedience, the individual in the psalm confesses his sin to God. God, in turn, removes the guilt caused by the sin. The sinner can once again

be truly happy because of God's forgiveness. Hiding from God is wholly unnecessary.

◆ GOSPEL: Jesus moves on from the district of Tyre to Decapolis, also a Gentile region, where he once again encounters a crowd. The people bring Jesus a deaf man with a speech impediment and ask him to heal the man. The miracle Jesus performs is personal and apparently private as he takes the man away from the crowd. However, the crowd clearly knows what occurs because in Mark's traditional style, Jesus warns them not to tell anyone what they witnessed. Yet once again in the Gospel account writer's narrative, they couldn't help but proclaim the Good News.

S A T 14 (#334) white Memorial of Sts. Cyril, Monk, and Methodius, Bishop

The Lectionary for Mass

◆ FIRST READING: We read today from the second part of the narrative from Genesis that describes humanity's loss of innocence. God finds the man who tried to hide in shame and the blame-game begins. The man blames the woman, and, in turn, the woman blames the serpent. Each faces consequences for their actions, but God fashions new garments for the man and woman, a sign that God continues to care for them in their humanity.

◆ RESPONSORIAL PSALM 90: The connection between today's psalm, a communal lament, and the First Reading lies in the recollection of creation and the fall. Mortality is the mark of human life. Sin besets us. Like those who originally sang the psalm, we ask God to bestow on us the heart's wisdom and to have compassion on us.

◆ GOSPEL: This is the second account of the multiplication of the loaves in Mark and the first

proclaimed in the weekday cycle. (For the first, see Mark 6:34–44.) The details of the two accounts differ, but the similarity lies in the abundance of Jesus's compassionate care for the people. Notice that in today's passage, the disciples have seven loaves of bread and, after distributing the bread Jesus blessed and broke, they filled the same number of baskets, seven, with the fragments leftover. The number seven often refers to the mission of the early Church to the Gentiles. Jesus's mission extends beyond the twelve tribes of Israel to the Gentiles. Jesus is food for all peoples.

The Roman Missal

All the texts for this Mass text are proper for this day, and they are found in the Proper of Saints at February 14.

The Collect makes explicit reference to Sts. Cyril's and Methodius's mission to the Slavic peoples. The Prayer over the Offerings speaks of the transformation that we pray will occur as a result of entering into the Sacrifice. It's a reminder that at the heart of all Christian missionary work is the belief that the sharing in the life of Christ makes all things new, and that one of the fruits of living in Christ's love is reconciliation. The Prayer after Communion refers to the universality of the Eucharist: God is the "Father of all nations," the one who makes us "sharers in the one Bread and the one Spirit." As a result of our sharing in the Eucharist, we pray that "the multitude of your children, / persevering in the same faith, / may be united in building up the Kingdom of justice and peace."

No rubric assigns a particular Preface for this Mass; since the two saints are honored together and one is a monk while the other one is a bishop, one of the two general Prefaces of Saints would probably be the best choice.

Today's Saints

Sts. Cyril (827–869) and Methodius (815–884) were brothers bound not only by biology, but by their longing to evangelize the unenlightened heart. Their missionary zeal led them to Slavic territories where the seeds of Western Christendom had yet to be planted. At the time, the Western Church only recognized the Hebrew, Greek, and Latin languages; therefore, they were charged with the task of translating the Bible and liturgical texts into Slavonic. Because Slavonic did not have a written language, the brothers had to develop a script, which later became known as the Cyrillic alphabet, named after St. Cyril. Shortly after his brother died, St. Methodius was consecrated a bishop. Because Sts. Cyril and Methodius are venerated in both the East and West, they are considered the patrons of ecumenism.

☀ **15** (#77) green
Sixth Sunday in Ordinary Time

The Lectionary for Mass

The First Reading comes from a section of Leviticus that describes the purity codes relating to unclean animals, childbirth, leprosy, and bodily cleanliness. A priest is to declare a person who bears the sores of leprosy "unclean." Today's reading, however, does not provide for the healing of lepers as the ritual codes in the next chapter of Leviticus do.

The Lord wants people to be healed. The link with today's First Reading and Gospel is Jesus's healing of the leper. No one's home will be outside and away from God. Once healed, all will dwell with God.

◆ RESPONSORIAL PSALM 32: A hymn of thanksgiving, this psalm praises the Lord for the joy that is ours through God's forgiveness of sin. Following upon the First Reading it is easy to connect sin with illness and disease. Today, we know that sin causes neither. Whatever the sin, God asks us to confess it. We rejoice in the Lord for the healing of our relationships made necessary by sin and for our wholeness restored.

◆ SECOND READING: Paul's advice in this brief reading is to keep everyone else in mind when we act. Selfishness does not lead to God's glory, imitating Christ's unselfish ways does. Letting God's glory be foremost in our minds and hearts, Paul calls us to imitate him just as he imitates Christ.

◆ GOSPEL: Healed by Jesus, the leper is no longer unclean, nor is he an outsider in Jesus's world. He, too, like those without leprosy, dwells with God in Jesus. We do not know whether or not the leper followed Jesus's instructions to show himself to the priest as required by the purity laws. We do know that he disobeyed Jesus's command to not tell anyone about how he was healed. He couldn't help but publicize the miracle and lead others to Jesus.

The Roman Missal

The Mass texts for today are found in the "Ordinary Time" section of the Proper of Time. The Gloria is sung or said today.

The Collect asks that our lives "may be so fashioned by your grace / as to become a dwelling pleasing to you." The prayer can serve as a reminder of the connection between liturgy and life—the point of participating in worship is not to engage in ritual actions for their own sake, but rather so that our participation in ritual worship will change us to live life as God asks us to live it, so that he will truly "abide / in hearts that are just and true." The Prayer over the Offerings reiterates that such transformation should be the heart of the oblation we make; as we make our offering in union at Mass with Christ's, "may it become for those who do your will / the source of eternal reward." The prayer reminds us, however, that nothing is automatic; transformation can only occur when we are open to doing God's will. In the Prayer after Communion we pray that, "having fed upon these heavenly delights" of the Eucharist, "we may always / long for that food by which we truly live."

Other Ideas

Remind the congregation of the Ash Wednesday liturgy schedule for the distribution of the ashes. Post these clearly on the parish website and on any parish social media sites, as well as on church and rectory doors, and send it in text messages. If you do not have a marquee that can post current events, it may be wise to purchase a vinyl sign noting standard liturgy times. Make sure that many pastoral care workers are lined up to help take the ashes and Communion to the sick and homebound.

M
O
N **16** (#335) green
Weekday

The Lectionary for Mass

◆ FIRST READING: Often we see Cain's murder of Abel as central to today's story, yet the heart of the story is God's divine mercy given to Cain in the face of his sin. After Cain pleads with God that his punishment of no longer being able to till the soil and forever wandering on earth is intolerable, God promises protection for those who would attempt to kill Cain. God's abundant mercy shows forth to Adam and Eve as well, as they give life to another son, Seth.

◆ RESPONSORIAL PSALM 50: The connection to the First Reading is in the psalm's mention of slandering the child of one's own mother. The psalm reminds us that we are to keep the Lord's covenant, lest we face the Lord's judgment. God will call us to task for our infidelity, but God's mercy will prevail. For this, we offer thanks.

◆ GOSPEL: After the miracle of the feeding of the 4,000 and having seven baskets of food left over, Jesus and his disciples travelled to the region of Dalmanutha on the west shore of the Sea of Galilee. Once there, the Pharisees approach Jesus directly and demand a sign from heaven that would prove he is the Messiah. Frustrated to the core of his very being, Jesus tells them he will give no sign. Has he not taught enough, performed enough miracles, and exorcised enough demons for them to believe? How often when we cannot sense the presence of Jesus, do we ourselves wish for a sign instead of resting in the One who is the Messiah and has done so much for us already!

T U E **17** (#336) green
Weekday

Optional Memorial of the Seven Holy Founders of the Servite Order / white

The Lectionary for Mass

◆ FIRST READING: A result of human evil, the Lord began to regret that which he created and issues a warning about the destruction of all living creatures. Yet Noah finds favor with the Lord, another sign of God's mercy. Noah and his household, along with representatives of all living creatures board the ark. The Lord saves them from the devastating flood. As we celebrate Ash Wednesday tomorrow and begin our Lenten journey, we remember God's saving grace in Christ Jesus through the waters of Baptism.

◆ RESPONSORIAL PSALM 29: This psalm is a testimony to God's prevailing power over all the earth. God is present in the earth's storm and enthroned over the mighty waters of the flood. The only fitting response is for us to give glory to God. Through God's reign, blessing and protection are ours.

◆ GOSPEL: We can understand the Pharisees not being willing to accept Jesus as the Messiah without a sign from heaven, but the disciples? Jesus cautions the disciples not to become like the Pharisees who refuse his authority and rebel against him. Questioning the disciples and us, Jesus asks whether they and we still do not understand who he is. We now have all of Lent to ponder anew who Jesus is for us.

Today's Saints

The Founders of the Order of Servites were seven young men with one vision — to "be of one mind and one heart" (*Rule of St. Augustine*, the adopted Rule of the Servites, available from www.domcentral.org/trad/rule.htm) through common prayer, works of charity, and a special devotion to Mary, the Mother of God. Living in thirteenth-century Florence, the Founders of the Order of Servites (Friar Servants of Mary) were inspired to abandon their homes and businesses to seek a life of prayerful seclusion, eventually establishing themselves on Monte Scenario, called the "sounding mountain." These Friar Servants of Mary paid homage to Mary by living a humble and simple life. Their lifestyle drew young men from all over, which ultimately led to their establishment as a religious order. In the eighteenth century, a holy woman by the name of St. Juliana Falconieri was attracted to the lives of the seven holy founders and decided to consecrate her life to God, laying the foundation for the Servite Sisters.

A Lenten Reminder

Tomorrow is Ash Wednesday. Have you burned the blessed palms for the distribution of ashes?

LENT AND HOLY WEEK

The Liturgical Time

The Calendar

The Meaning / The Lectionary for Mass

LENT is the season of endings becoming beginnings. It mirrors and prepares us to celebrate the mystery of the Cross, where the end of mortal life becomes the beginning of eternal life. The readings inspire us to take up again and more firmly the practice of making ends meet by saying "no" in order to be free to make new beginnings by saying "yes." That is the essential dynamic of balanced Lenten asceticism.

The Lectionary is built in counterpoint. On the one hand, the Sunday readings unfold facets of the Paschal Mystery we prepare to celebrate and embrace. We hear that a world sodden with sin required a cleansing flood, as our sin requires Baptism received or renewed. Between sin and redemption lies a long history of temptation, epitomized here in the confrontation between Jesus and the Tempter (First Sunday of Lent). Our redemption costs the sacrifice of the beloved Son in whom burns the Fire of God. Among the conflicting voices of good and evil, we are charged to listen to this chosen Messiah (Second Sunday of Lent) and follow him through law and Cross into the glory of God (Third Sunday of Lent). Exile to the land of sin and death calls out for deliverance given through the Cross (Fourth Sunday of Lent). Liberation through the new covenant made in Christ's blood forges a new people of God, fed and strengthened by the Eucharist (the risen Christ), and thus made responsible to turn and feed the world. The resurrection that awaits, reaching back from Easter future, seizes us and transforms us into disciples and servants in service of all those God loves (Fifth Sunday of Lent). Palm Sunday returns to what lies between now and then: the journey of Jesus from acclaim to desolation through suffering and death. There Christ's ultimate "no" to the voices of evil, clamoring at him through human weakness (the unfaithful disciples) and cruelty (the judges, torturers, and executioners) becomes the ultimate "yes" to love too deep and far-reaching for us to understand. What appears to be the final end becomes in fact the greatest of beginnings.

The first dramatic chapters of this story unfold further in the Holy Week weekdays, culminating in the Chrism Mass where the Lent-weary Church gathers at the sacramental gateways of Baptism, Confirmation, Ordination, and Anointing of the Sick, all celebrations of the great Paschal Mystery toward which Lent builds.

In counterpoint to the Sunday readings, the weekday selections entwine our own everyday story with the sweeping story of Christ. Where the Sunday readings provide the model and the "why," the weekday readings supply the basic "how" and "what." The traditional Lenten practices of prayer, fasting, and almsgiving are given flesh, and a very enriched flesh at that, through Old and New Testament stories and exhortations. Fasting, we learn, is a far more comprehensive way of saying "no" than merely giving up large helpings or favorite foods. Fasting extends from food to material goods. Physical fasting strengthens us to abstain from more difficult "noes": ceasing to treat others in ways that fail to reflect the holiness of God, in whose image we were made to live in love. Further, it requires us to refuse bias and prejudice, narrow expectations and judgments, all that confines us in a world too small for God's ways. This recurring theme is punctuated with reminders of our covenant identity, of God's startling mercies, and of the hope that lies before us. Jesus's renunciation of life on the Cross is the greatest icon of human fasting.

However, "no" without "yes" is barren. Through abstaining from ways of eating, accumulating, thinking, and doing, we are drawn forward into ways of feeding others, giving to others, making judgments and acting on the love we see in God's covenant law, old and new, and in the life and death of Jesus. Here we are urged to take up the works of justice and mercy which are the larger definition of almsgiving. Perhaps the most challenging of mercy's works is the forgiveness of others at a depth matching God's forgiveness of us. Our underlying "yes" is "yes" to living in God's image in all our relationships, with family, friends and strangers alike.

The illusion that self is source and center is the root of all sin. We are reminded on the contrary that neither "yes" nor "no" is possible without prayer, lest our motives and goals dwindle into petty pride and selfishness. Besides specific instructions regarding prayer, the readings offer models, including the Our Father and numerous prayers for forgiveness.

Through all these themes are woven repeated references to the imagery of the great Easter sacraments of life for which we prepare: fire and light, water, bread, and oil, as well as the essentials of word and community. The symbolism of the oil is developed specifically in the readings for the Chrism Mass.

Into this rich tapestry of Lenten weekday readings, the two solemnities of St. Joseph and the Annunciation might seem an intrusion, focusing as they do on the beginning rather than the end of Jesus's human life. However, they remind us that the Cross begins with the Incarnation when the Word "emptied himself" into a life of obedient love that led him to death, as the reading from Philippians 2 on Palm Sunday points out. Mary and Joseph are presented as living icons of the corresponding human obedience to God's plan, a key Lenten attitude of self-giving that underlies all our "noes" and "yeses." They are a summary of all that the Lenten readings teach us about discipleship to the crucified and risen One.

The Roman Missal

THE texts for Lent in *The Roman Missal* are found immediately following the Mass for the Sunday after the Epiphany of the Lord, the

Feast of the Baptism of the Lord. Like Advent and Christmas Time, every day for Lent and Holy Week has its own Mass. Each day has a proper Entrance Antiphon, Collect, Prayer over the Offerings, Communion Antiphon, and Prayer after Communion. Formularies begin with Ash Wednesday and continue up to and including the texts for the Chrism Mass on Thursday of Holy Week (Holy Thursday), after which the section for the Sacred Paschal Triduum begins.

Universal Norms on the Liturgical Year and the General Roman Calendar (UNLY) explains that "Lent is ordered to preparing for the celebration of Easter, since the Lenten liturgy prepares for celebration of the Paschal Mystery both catechumens, by the various stages of Christian Initiation, and the faithful, who recall their own Baptism and do penance" (27). Thus, it is not surprising to find both penance and initiation as themes that emerge in the Missal texts throughout the time of Lent.

Careful selection of texts by parish liturgy committees can greatly enhance a community's entrance into the proper Lenten spirituality. Given the penitential nature of Lent, it would make sense to highlight the Penitential Act. You might consider using the Confiteor more frequently, or perhaps even exclusively, if your community uses it rarely at other times of the year. Lent would also be a good time for singing the Penitential Act as a way of highlighting it. Musical notation is provided in the Missal for singing all three components, that is, the priest's introduction, the invocations by the priest, deacon, or another minister, and the priest's conclusion (the absolution). Notice how a minister other than the priest or deacon may announce the invocations before the assembly's response of "Lord, have mercy" or "Christ, have mercy;" taking advantage of this option could greatly enhance the singing if a cantor, for example, were more musically adept than the priest or deacon. Of the sample invocations given in Appendix VI, Forms III, IV, and perhaps V seem to especially correspond to the Lenten themes. Additionally, using the Greek *Kyrie, eleison* and *Christe, eleison* rather than the English words could be another way to highlight the Penitential Act during this liturgical time.

Of course, the Alleluia is omitted at every occasion, including solemnities and feasts, throughout the entirety of Lent. The *Gloria* is also omitted, although it is used on the Solemnities of St. Joseph and the Annunciation, and at the Chrism Mass.

Priest celebrants, liturgists, and preparers need to know their way around *The Roman Missal* during Lent in order to take full advantage of different options and to be sure they are using the correct texts. There are four Prefaces of Lent, designated I–IV. Prefaces I and II can be used on weekdays (except for Ash Wednesday) and should be used on Sundays that do not have their own Preface prescribed. Prefaces III and IV are used on the weekdays of Lent, including Ash Wednesday. Specific Prefaces are prescribed for the First and Second Sundays of Lent, placed with the orations (not with the Prefaces), as well as for the Third, Fourth, and Fifth Sundays of Lent (also located right there with the orations) when the Year A readings are used (that is for the scrutinies). When the Year A readings are not used, Prefaces I or II of Lent are used on those three Sundays, not the Preface that is given immediately following the Prayer over the Offerings (read the rubrics carefully). Also, there are two Prefaces of the Passion of the Lord: the first is used during the Fifth Week of Lent, and the second is used on Monday, Tuesday, and Wednesday of Holy Week.

It must also be noted that when the scrutinies are celebrated, proper texts (including Collect, Prayer over the Offerings, and Prayer after Communion) for the First, Second, and Third Scrutinies respectively are to be used; these can be found in the section Ritual Masses: I. For the Conferral of the Sacraments of Christian Initiation, 2. For the Celebration of the Scrutinies.

Given the importance of this liturgical time, Lent might be a good time to regularly chant the introductory dialogue and Preface to the Eucharistic Prayer, if this is not already being done. Also, Lent is a good time to use one of the Eucharistic Prayers for Reconciliation, especially the first one, with its explicit references to God's constant offer of pardon to sinners, to the present time being a time of grace and reconciliation to turn back to the Lord, and to Jesus's willingness "to be nailed for our sake to the wood of the Cross" as he outstretched his arms on the Cross "to become the lasting sign of your covenant." Even though those prayers have their own Prefaces, it is permissible to use the Preface of Lent that might be prescribed for that day and yet still use the remainder of one of the Eucharistic Prayers for Reconciliation. Consider using Eucharistic Prayer for Reconciliation I more frequently.

Any of the three acclamations for "The Mystery of Faith" are fitting for Lent: the first and third call specific attention to the Paschal Mystery as they mention the Lord's Death and Resurrection, while the second connects participation in the Eucharistic banquet with the proclamation of the Lord's Death. One might argue that the third option, with its particular mention of the Cross, has a certain obvious link to the season and might be especially or perhaps even exclusively used throughout all of Lent and perhaps even throughout all of Easter Time, to connect the forty days of Lent with the fifty days of Easter Time. Whichever acclamation is chosen, communities should consider using a different one than is used at other times, or at least changing the musical setting.

Finally, every day of Lent has a proper Prayer over the People. The custom of a daily prayer over the people in Lent seems to have originated in the *Gelasian Sacramentary* of the seventh century and, after not being included in the Missal of Paul VI, has reappeared with the third edition of *The Roman Missal*. A rubric indicates that the prayer is optional on weekdays; the prayer is required on Sundays, however, including Palm Sunday of the Passion of the Lord. Note the proper structure when a Prayer over the People or a Solemn Blessing is used at the end of Mass: after the priest says, "The Lord be with you," and the people respond, "And with your spirit," the deacon, or, in his absence, the priest himself, says the invitation, "Bow down for the blessing." Then the priest outstretches his hand over the people and says the prayer, with all responding "Amen."

Children's Liturgy of the Word

DURING Lent we are asked to engage in three practices, prayer, fasting, and almsgiving (or acts of charity). For young children, Lent might be viewed in negative terms in that they may be giving up their favorite foods or television shows. It is important to help the children to understand why they give up these things. While they may not understand the word "conversion" they do understand that sometimes in order to grow closer to someone we love, we may need to do things we might not want to do or to deny ourselves things we do want; in other words, to make sacrifices for

the good of another person. They also learn to say they are sorry when doing something wrong and to seek forgiveness. Even the youngest of children, by encouraging to pray more, can understand this. Encouraging them to pray more or to share some of what they have with others and to abstain from some of the things they enjoy are the beginnings of conversion and growing closer to God. Looking at Lent this way teaches children to be positive about this great season of preparation for Easter.

◆ READINGS: It is important to note that the readings in the *Lectionary for Masses with Children* during Lent can only be used when celebrating a children's Liturgy of the Word apart from the main worship space. This is because the readings for this season are so rich and so important that they need to be read from the regular Lectionary translation. This year, the readings on the Third, Fourth and Fifth Sundays are taken from the Gospel according to John. It is important to note, however that when catechumens are present at Mass the readings for Year A, also from the Gospel according to John, are used because of their connection to the scrutinies that are celebrated at these liturgies as part of the Rite of Christian Initiation of Adults. It would be wise, if the children's Liturgy of the Word is celebrated at a Mass where the scrutinies occur, to use these Cycle A readings with the children at their Liturgy of the Word in order that they will be hearing the same readings as the adults in the larger worship space. Following Mass, families should be encouraged to discuss the readings. Encourage this as a Lenten practice that hopefully develops into a regular occurrence year round. LTP has a number of resources that can assist parents in reflecting on and discussing the readings.

◆ ENVIRONMENT: Every liturgical season has a character all its own that is reflected in the environment of the worship space. Lent presents a stark contrast from the other seasons of the year. The children should immediately notice that something is different when they enter the space on the First Sunday of Lent. Keep it simple and do not overload the space with too many symbols of the season as the absence of decoration speaks for itself. Flowers are not be used during Lent. If possible obtaining a large cross for the space will help the children focus on the sacrificial character of the season. The liturgical color is violet and this can be used in cloths or a simple banner that can also be used in procession. Violet is the color of repentance and reminds us that we, as sinners, are always in need of repentance.

A Lenten activity calendar, such as *Forty Days and Forty Nights: A Lenten Ark Moving Toward Easter* by LTP, would be helpful for the children to take home to help them live out the season. Some parishes also have a Lenten project for the children such as a mite box or rice bowl that children can use to put change in for the poor that engages them in the Lenten practice of almsgiving.

◆ MUSIC during Lent does not need to be solely focused on our need for repentance or on sorrow for Jesus's Passion and Death. It does not need to be somber or sad. The parish music director should have some suggestions appropriate for children, including a seasonal psalm. If you usually have instrumentalists it might be beneficial to make a change for Lent and sing acapella or introduce simple chants. It is always a good idea to familiarize children with the musical traditions of the Church and most children will respond well to this.

We do not sing the Alleluia for the Gospel Acclamation during Lent indicating that we are on a journey of repentance awaiting the joy that will come at Easter. Since the Alleluia is a proclamation of great joy, translated as "Praise God," we refrain from this great acclamation until the Easter Vigil when we sing it with great excitement and jubilation. On the First Sunday of Lent, briefly explaining this reason before singing the Lenten acclamation would be helpful to the children and helps acclimate them to the change in response.

Singing a simple response to the petitions, such as "Lord, have mercy" or "Lord, hear our Prayer" is a change that would engage the children in a new way, again showing them that this season is different.

The Saints

LENT has such primacy in the life of the Church; have you ever noticed that? And not just for your daily Mass goers and large/active families; plenty of Catholics who won't bother to go to church for months at a time will be absolutely certain to come not only on Christmas and Easter but also on Ash Wednesday. In my hometown, plain (cheese) pizza is a common Friday dinner even for lapsed Catholics who have no qualms about

using their Good Friday work holiday merely to start the weekend's partying early. "What are you giving up for Lent?" receives much more attention than "What are you doing for Easter?"

The liturgical calendar is a bit leaner during Lent, too. With the exception of the enormously important solemnities of St. Joseph and the Annunciation, Lent contains a conspicuous absence of saint's days. Days that are usually obligatory memorials become optional in the face of the important prayers of the Lenten liturgies. In the post-Conciliar liturgical revision, the celebration of important saints including Benedict, Gregory the Great, Thomas Aquinas, and Matthias were moved from the day on which each died (his birthday into eternal life) to another day of eternal significance, explicitly so that their feasts could be celebrated properly without concern for the more subdued character of Lent.

It's the same principle that inspires families to delay the celebration of a birthday when it falls on Good Friday. "There is an appointed time for everything, and a time for every affair under the heavens. . . . A time to weep, and a time to laugh; a time to mourn, and a time to dance" (Ecclesiastes 3:1, 4). As we fast and abstain from meat, dessert, television, or what have you, we also hold back somewhat from the joy of celebrating our brothers and sisters who are already sharing in Christ's Easter victory. But when that day comes — how full will our joy be!

The Liturgy of the Hours

MUCH like everything else in the life of the Church, the Liturgy of the Hours is a bit more subdued during Lent. It's more than just the absence of Alleluias; the whole Office is just a little more reserved, although the intensity does increase at Holy Week.

Especially notable are the Offices of Holy Saturday, which truly reflect the spirit of the day. No sacraments until the Vigil, save only the sacraments of healing. Little to do but prepare for the day to come. The Office of the day roots us in this reality! "Though sinless, the Lord has been put to death. The world is in mourning as for an only son" (*Liturgy of the Hours*, Holy Saturday, Morning Prayer, Antiphon 1). I know many laypeople who almost never pray the Office of

Readings, yet look forward to it every Holy Saturday. The harrowing of hell is a mystery upon which we so rarely meditate, and yet it is marvelous: Jesus has been quite literally everywhere we could possibly ever go, including hell itself!

Then there is the matter of Holy Saturday's Vespers. Easter is *the* ultimate feast of Christianity, yet Evening Prayer just before the feast still speaks of our waiting! Our Christ remains in the tomb, as far as we know. Unlike any ordinary solemnity, the Paschal feast keeps us waiting: we have to pray through Vespers and up to eight Scripture readings before we even get the Alleluia back!

Holy Saturday holds just one example of the genius inherent in the Divine Office. The riches of the Church are there, just waiting to be mined, by whoever is willing to do so.

The Rite of Christian Initiation of Adults

L ENT is the final preparation for those who will be fully initiated at the great Easter Vigil. The major rites of the RCIA are meant to be celebrated publically and normally during the Sunday Eucharist, not in the rectory basement or a meeting room. Since these rites are celebrated with the elect it is a very public time for them. For those who are apprehensive about standing in front of the community assure them of the community's love and support.

If catechumens and members of the elect are dismissed from the Sunday Eucharist find one acclamation for the dismissal and use it year after year. This is especially true if these folks are dismissed from various liturgies in a parish from week to week. Even if the musical leadership of multiple Masses in the parish is done in various styles, (contemporary, traditional, bilingual), find one acclamation that will work for all Masses and stick to it. This will be a challenge for some pastoral musicians, but remember musicians are to help facilitate the prayer of the gathered Church, which includes the catechumens and elect. If these folks and the community hear a different acclamation from week to week the dismissal may seen disjointed and unfamiliar. Both the assembly and those journeying toward the Easter sacraments

need to be able to identify with a common acclamation for this ritual moment.

Catechumens who will be attending the Rite of Election are sent to the bishop from the Sunday assembly (see RCIA, 106–117). If candidates (the already baptized) are being sent for recognition, then the alternate rite (RCIA, 536–546) is used for both groups. After the Homily the catechumens are presented to the pastor who seeks testimony as to their readiness to enter into the time of purification and enlightenment. They are asked to respond robustly to their convictions and their sponsors also offer testimony on their behalf. The catechumens now sign the *Book of the Elect* during the Rite of Sending to Election but candidates do not sign the book. The *Book of the Elect* is then taken to the cathedral to be presented to the bishop. After the catechumens sign the book, prayers are offered asking God's guidance and strength for the ongoing faith journey. Now the catechumens are dismissed from the Sunday assembly to continue to reflect on the Word of God.

The conclusion of the period of the catechumenate leads into the Rite of Election, or enrollment of names for those who are unbaptized, and the Rite of Calling the Candidates to Continuing Conversion for those who are baptized. This is a very significant and important step in the RCIA process. It is usually celebrated on the First Sunday of Lent at the cathedral, led by the bishop. All of the catechumens and candidates, their godparents (for catechumens) and sponsors (for catechumens and candidates) gather together on this day. It often involves hundreds of people coming together for this occasion. The Church formally ratifies the catechumens' readiness for the Sacraments of Initiation, and the candidates' willingness to be received into full communion with the Catholic Church. In turn the catechumens—from now on known as the elect—publicly acknowledge their desire to receive the Sacraments of Initiation, and the candidates request to be received into full communion with the Catholic Church. It is God who elects—chooses—them. We don't do the picking out of these people, rather it is God's action. Our responsibility as Church is to offer support and prayer.

Where there are both catechumens (unbaptized) and candidates (baptized) in a diocese there is the option of a combined rite at this stage. This rite is formally known as the (combined) Celebration of the Rite of Election of Catechumens and the Call to Continuing Conversion of

Candidates Who are Preparing for Confirmation and/or Eucharist or Reception into the Full Communion of the Catholic Church (See RCIA, 547–561).

The Period of Purification and Enlightenment usually corresponds with Lent and is intended to be a period of increased introspection and coming nearer to God. The aim of this period is to do away with what is weak and sinful, and establish what is holy. During this period the elect undertake a number of rites, including the scrutinies and presentations. The outlines of these rites are as follows: First Scrutiny (Third Sunday of Lent) [RCIA, 150–156]; the Presentation of the Creed (Third Week of Lent) [RCIA, 157–163]; Second Scrutiny (Fourth Sunday of Lent) [RCIA, 164–170]; Third Scrutiny (Fifth Sunday of Lent) [RCIA, 171–177]; the Presentation of the Lord's Prayer (ideally the Fifth Week of Lent) [RCIA, 178–184]. For the scrutinies, it is appropriate to chant a litany during the exorcism rite and the rite may be followed by a song or psalm. The scrutinies use the Gospel accounts from Year A of the Sunday Lectionary: the woman at the well; the man born blind, and the raising of Lazarus. These Gospel accounts help the elect and the community to address the reality of sin and evil which keep us from Christ. The scrutinies help the elect to achieve an intimate knowledge of Christ in the Church—a genuine self-knowledge. In this knowing, and asking for healing, we move to a more intimate knowledge of Christ and his Church. It is a time of serious examination and true repentance (see RCIA, 142).

After the Homily the elect come forward with their godparents and the rite follows with an invitation to silent prayer. During this time the priest, godparents, and RCIA team members lay hands on the elect in silence. The elect kneel if they are able. Resist the temptation to fill this time with instrumental music; rather, allow the elect and the entire community to embrace the power of silence. What follows are intercessions or a litany for the elect that conclude with the prayer of exorcism. Now the elect are dismissed from the Sunday assembly to reflect on God's word.

The period of purification and enlightenment is a time of renewal for the entire community to be aware, not simply about the "sins" of the elect, but the sins of the whole community. The Sunday assembly needs to recognize our ongoing sins along with those of the elect (see RCIA, 145).

The candidates meanwhile prepare for the Sacrament of Reconciliation with an optional Penitential Rite (see RCIA, 464–472). This takes place on the Second Sunday of Lent.

The Presentation of the Creed (see RCIA 157–161) is given to the elect during the Third Week of Lent and the Presentation of the Our Father (see RCIA, 178–84) during the Fifth Week of Lent. Consider scheduling these rites during a celebration of Morning or Evening Prayer when a greater number of community members can be present.

The Sacraments of Initiation

MANY parishes do not celebrate the Sacraments of Initiation—Baptism, Confirmation, first Holy Communion—during the Lenten season. However, other than the prohibitions listed in *The Roman Missal* for when these sacraments may be celebrated, these celebrations may take place during Lent. Think about all the groups of people preparing for the new life of the sacraments in the parish: parents preparing for the Baptism of a child; children preparing for first Holy Communion; young people preparing for Confirmation. Encourage them to participate in the parish's Lenten formation sessions. Find special ways for young people to understand what Lent is about and to experience it in a way that will help get them ready for the sacraments they are to receive during the Easter season.

In case of emergency, one should not, of course, hesitate to administer the sacraments, whether to an infant or to an adult. The RCIA provides two forms for the initiation of adults outside of the Easter Vigil. The first, Christian Initiation of Adults in Exceptional Circumstances (see RCIA, 331), is intended for situations where "sickness, old age, change of residence, [and] long absence for travel" (RCIA, 332) prevent the catechumen from participating in the Rite of Acceptance and the Easter Vigil. The second is an order for the Christian Initiation of a Person in Danger of Death (see RCIA, 370–399), which includes the giving of Holy Communion as Viaticum.

The Rite of Penance

As we begin our annual Lenten retreat we are signed with the ashes on Ash Wednesday and hear the words "Repent, and believe in the Gospel." This is the time when the entire Church enters into the period of purification and enlightenment as we journey along with our elect and catechumens who are preparing for the Easter sacraments. Lent is also the great baptismal season where the faithful members of God's holy Church prepare to renew baptismal promises at Easter. Again, ongoing catechesis is essential. Unfortunately many still do not understand that Lent is filled with both "baptismal and penitential aspects" (CSL, 109). Through frequent and careful celebrations of the sacrament of penance we strive to "perfect the grace of baptism . . . as we bear in our body the death of Jesus Christ" (RP, 7b).

Lenten catechesis on the sacrament can be expanded to include formation on the many ways we live out continual repentance through works of mercy and acts of justice. Catechesis on confessing our sin should move us from a laundry list of sins to being able to understand that confession of sins "comes from true knowledge of self before God" (RP, 6b). Ongoing catechesis should provide people with opportunities to deepen their knowledge of self in light of relationship with the triune God. Again the *Catechism of the Catholic Church* (CCC) is an excellent place to consult for ongoing catechesis. People still ask, "Why confess sins to a priest?" Help people to understand the role of the priest as "Good Shepherd who seeks the lost sheep" and the "Good Samaritan who binds up wounds" or the "Father who awaits the prodigal son and welcomes him on his return home"; the priest then is the "sign and the instrument of God's merciful love toward the sinner" (CCC, 1465).

The penitential celebrations found in Appendix II of the *Rite of Penance* may be celebrated as a way to increase the community's ongoing conversion while living out one's baptismal call. In the appendix you will find a celebration for Lent. Consider scheduling communal penance services, using Form II from the ritual, with neighboring parishes. Ask someone in your deanery or vicariate to create a schedule of these celebrations for your local area and publishing them in parish bulletins and websites. Don't forget to provide opportunities for the celebration of the sacrament in nursing homes, retirement centers, and with the sick and homebound. In addition, work with neighboring parishes to schedule a celebration of the sacrament for people with special needs.

The Rite of Marriage

The father of my goddaughter once said to me, a few months after his wedding, "My wife is my Cross, to whom I am nailed in my daily Crucifixion." This did not strike me at the time as the height of both theology and romance, as the rapture in his voice indicated that it should, but over the years I've developed some appreciation for the idea.

In former days, the Nuptial Mass was strongly discouraged — or even forbidden — during Lent, because the solemnity with which a wedding is celebrated is at variance with the more subdued character of the Lenten season. (Weddings were permitted, of course, but only outside of Mass.) But, as my friend observed above, solemnity is not the only hallmark of a Marriage celebration. The sacrifice is every bit as real, as important, even if rejoicing in it is a supernatural grace rather than a natural one.

Fortunately, God is generous with granting such graces. What time is more appropriate than Lent for meditation upon the beauty of sacrificial love, which is foundational to every marriage? "Husbands, love your wives, even as Christ loved the church and handed himself over for her" (Ephesians 5:25). This model of Christ-like love is before our eyes in a more focused way during Lent, providing a unique opportunity for all attending the wedding — especially if it is a wedding Mass — to meditate upon and promise of self-sacrifice for the good of the beloved, just as Christ sacrificed himself for us.

The Pastoral Care of the Sick

While Lent is a focused time of prayer, almsgiving, and fasting for all Catholics, it is a particularly focused time of formation for the candidates and catechumens involved with RCIA. Most parishioners have some contact with the newly initiated, whether through the scrutinies throughout Lent, the Triduum liturgies, or even just praying for them in the Universal Prayer each week.

But because the sick are not able to be present at these celebrations, they usually lose all knowledge of these inspiring soon-to-be Christians and fully intiated Catholics, and, whether they realize it or not, their Lent is somewhat impoverished as a consequence.

Additionally, many of these infirm parishioners have spent most of their lives serving others, and may even need a bit of prodding to be comfortable letting others take care of them. Here is an opportunity, then, for a great service at a perfect time: prayer partners!

Depending on the parish demographic, it might be possible to set up each catechumen or candidate with one sick or elderly parishioner, and even possible for them to develop a relationship over these weeks of prayer. It might instead be more reasonable to ask each sick person to pray for all the newly initiated, and each convert to pray for all the infirm. Perhaps the sick could receive photos and brief conversion stories, even if the almost-Catholics are never able to meet them. The permutations are endless, but the spiritual benefit seems apparent: match up a group of people who are going through a very formative time with a group of people who have ample time to pray and intercede. A fruitful Lent indeed, awaits all involved.

The Order of Christian Funerals

A FUNERAL liturgy may not be celebrated on the Sundays of Lent and texts including Alleluia are omitted during this season. Six of the Gospel texts for the funeral Mass are drawn from the Passion narratives along with three selections from John 11, the account of the raising of Lazarus, and these would be most appropriate for use during this season. Masses for the Dead are found in *The Roman Missal* under four categories: 1) For the Funeral; 2) On the Anniversary; 3) Various Commemorations; and 4) Various Prayers

for the Dead. Make sure to acquaint yourself with these different options and choose the texts that are most suitable for your situation.

The Book of Blessings

T HE *Book of Blessings* figures prominently on the first day of the great season of Lent. The Order for the Blessing and Distribution of Ashes for use on Ash Wednesday is found in chapter 52. This is the order that is used when ashes are blessed and distributed outside the celebration of Mass (the texts for use during Mass are found in *The Roman Missal*).

Although the blessing and distribution of ashes is most often done within the celebration of Mass, most parishes also schedule one or more celebrations of a Liturgy of the Word, which is the context for the order found in the *Book of Blessings*. The order is lead by a priest, deacon, or trained lay minister. The *Book of Blessings* is very helpful in providing texts and rubrics to follow when a lay person is presiding. In this case, the order presumes that the ashes are already blessed, as there is no prayer of blessing given for when a lay minister leads the celebration.

This order is equally useful for those who may visit the homebound on Ash Wednesday. Distributing blessed ashes to those who are separated from the community because of sickness or physical condition is a wonderful way to unify the whole parish for the start of the great season of Lent.

This year, the Solemnity of St. Joseph, Spouse of the Blessed Virgin Mary is celebrated during the fourth week of Lent, on March 19. The *Book of Blessings* provides an Order for the Blessing of a Saint Joseph's Table. It notes the custom of blessing bread, pastries, and other food, adding the point that an important part of the custom is to "give a large portion of [the food that is blessed] to the poor" (BB, 1679). The order is given in a Liturgy of the Word format as well as a shorter, simpler rite for use.

Other orders of blessing that might be used during this season are:

◆ Blessing of Pilgrims (chapter 8): while the connection may not seem obvious today, making a pilgrimage is actually an ancient penitential act. Today many people do so as a spiritual practice during Lent.

◆ Blessing of a Child Not Yet Baptized (chapter I.IV.B): many parents are preparing to baptize their child in the Easter season. In this case this celebration would be very appropriate during Lent.

◆ Blessings of Catechumens (Chapter IV.III): many parishes that have a year-round catechumenate have both catechumens and elect during Lent.

The Liturgical Environment

THE title of the forty-day period of preparation for Easter in English is, at its root, a name for spring. Once again, this draws our attention to the amount of light we experience in the winter season, especially as it derives from the old English word for "to lengthen;" what lengthens in spring is, of course, the hours of daylight. As the primary liturgical environment is the natural environment, we should allow the return of the light and of spring to frame whatever liturgical environments we produce. It also blends seamlessly with the call of Lenten repentance, to grow in quiet, interior ways through prayer, fasting, and almsgiving, preparing to celebrate the return of life at the Easter feast.

What this means for environment is that visually quiet simplicity should be the rule, possibly with slowly growing reminders of the spring's coming. The seasonal color is violet. If a parish has different sets of vestments, the redder violet should be used for Lent. Like Advent, there is a mid-season change to rose, in this case for the fourth Sunday, called *Laetare* Sunday, which provides a kind of transition towards the more solemn end of the season culminating in Holy Week. If you choose to veil statues and crucifixes, they should not be veiled until after *Laetare* Sunday, beginning with the Fifth Sunday of Lent. If this is done, it requires some forethought, especially in more ornate churches, as it can lead to a somewhat haphazard effect if some pieces are covered while others remain unveiled.

In most places in the Northern Hemisphere, Lent will see a major transition from winter to spring. Consider using plants and environment that highlight that change. In the north, birch trees provide a beautiful but stark reminder of the winter with their bare white bark. Bulbs might be planted in pots so that they will begin to appear during the season of Lent. With some foresight and planning, these might be timed to be at their height for the Easter Vigil. While Lent does mirror the forty-day fast of Jesus in the wilderness, desert themes are often overused, and should be carefully considered, particularly in non-desert climates. One parish with which I am familiar regularly places potted cacti around the baptismal font which both makes no botanical sense and erects a barrier to the baptismal waters which are the source of our Lenten growth.

In some places, a practice of emptying the baptismal font and holy water stoups has arisen. In some parishes, they are even filled with sand. In 2000, the Congregation for Divine Worship and the Discipline of the Sacraments, responding to an official request for clarification, replied that this practice is not allowed. The font may be emptied after the Evening Mass of the Lord's Supper (Holy Thursday), as new water will be blessed at the Vigil; it is not to be empty for the entirety of Lent. Lent is a season in which we strive to live more fully into our Baptism—denying people access to the font and the holy water stoups actively works against this emphasis.

Near the beginning of Lent, or even before, those responsible for the liturgical environment should gather with the liturgical preparation team and discuss the liturgies of Holy Week. There are many things which need to be prepared, and developing a checklist and talking through each of the liturgies can help make sure that nothing is forgotten. *Guide for Sacristans*, written by Paul Turner and Corinna Laughlin (LTP), can help think through these liturgies from the standpoint of what preparation will be required and what items need to be procured. Also be attentive to the liturgical colors of each day of Holy Week (red for Palm Sunday, violet for Monday–Wednesday; for Triduum, see below).

Palm Sunday of the Lord's Passion combines the festive character of the procession with the solemn reading of the Passion of the Lord from the Gospel according to Mark. The environment, therefore, has to strike a balance between these two extremes. Limiting it to branches, palms, and other greenery but using a sufficient number of these may strike an appropriate balance. The liturgy on this day requires, among other items, palms. These need to be ordered well ahead of time. Most American parishes order palm fronds which are imported from abroad and not always sustainably harvested. Eco-palms are available from a variety of suppliers, although they may require a little more pre-ordering time. For a hyper-local solution, consider using branches from trees local to your area. The use of palms for this liturgy is a modern addition, made possible by refrigeration and long-distance transport; the rubrics merely call for "branches." Whether you choose to use palms or not, a variety of greenery (different kinds of palms/branches from different kinds of trees), can be used in enlivening the liturgical environment for this Sunday. Broad-spanning palms can be quite striking, particularly when displayed in front of the scarlet paraments of the day.

The Palm Sunday liturgy begins with the reading of an extra Gospel and the blessing of palms in a different place, followed by a procession into the church. Consider where this procession might begin. It can be difficult to hear outside, and hearing the Gospel is certainly important. Consider using a portable sound system, or beginning the liturgy in a secondary space you might have access to. This has the added benefit of mitigating the effects of bad weather. The Palm Sunday procession can also be an opportunity for ecumenical cooperation if there are several churches in your area. The procession could begin in a common space for the reading of the Gospel and the blessing of palms, before processing to the various churches for the rest of their liturgies. If your priest vests in a cope for the procession, you will have to make arrangements for him to change into the chasuble upon reaching the church, especially if the presidential chair is not near the sacristy. This should be done simply and without fanfare.

The Liturgical Music

Lᴇɴᴛ is the annual time where the principle of "noble simplicity" (CSL, 34) can shine forth. *The General Instruction of the Roman Missal* suggests that instrumentation is used "only to support the singing" (GIRM, 313) and *Sing to the Lord: Music in Divine Worship* supports this principle (STL, 114). Yet, some communities carry this to extremes leading to a great deal of angst between ministers. A broader interpretation of this principle may be called for. This might include simpler accompaniments and arrangements of hymns and songs, and less energetic expression and more subdued presentation of the music. More a cappella singing and less amplification of singers and instruments would be a worthy exercise to embrace during this holy season. Instrumentalist might find this season to be challenging when they regularly employ preludes, postludes, and interludes as part of the liturgy. Yet, with the rich treasury of sacred instrumental music composed for this season I don't believe this principle should be taken to extremes. A balance must be discovered to ensure that the treasury of sacred instrumental music can be performed during the season of Lent.

Consider one of the following musical settings of the Kyrie: "Russian Orthodox Kyrie" arranged by John Bell, or any of the "Kyries" from the Music of Taizé by Jacques Berthier, available from (GIA). Choose a processional chant for the Communion Rite that can be sung over the five weeks so the assembly can truly experience their "union in spirit by means of the diversity of their voices, to show joy of heart, and to highlight more clearly the 'communitarian' nature of the procession to receive Communion" (GIRM, 86).

Two settings of Gospel Acclamations for Lent with Lectionary verses include "Lenten Gospel Acclamation" by Michael R. Prendergast and Joseph Sullivan (OCP) and "Praise to You, Word of God: Gospel Acclamation and Verses for Lent and Holy Week," by Charles Gardner, (WLP).

Many communities see an increase in the number of people attending daily mass during Lent. If you haven't already been doing so, consider singing the Responsorial Psalm at daily Mass. Musical settings are available in *Responsorial Psalms for Weekday Mass* by Anthony Ruff, ᴏsʙ, published by The Liturgical Press.

Choose appropriate acclamations to accompany the rituals of Sending to Election, the Penitential Scrutiny for Candidates, Scrutinies for the Elect and music for the dismissal.

Celebrations of communal penance (Form II of the *Rite of Penance*) are popular during Lent. Every hymnal and music resource contains a topical and liturgical index with a list of music appropriate for these celebrations. If you are looking for a litany for the examination of conscious consider the "Penitential Litany: Lead Us to Act Justly," by Michael R. Prendergast and Joseph B. Sullivan (OCP). The text based on Micah 6:8 contains dozens of verses directly from the *Rite of Penance*.

At the beginning of Holy Week the Church continues to scale the holy mountain of Easter. Holy Week has as its purpose the remembrance of Christ's Passion, beginning with the messianic entry into Jerusalem. Along the way we are accompanied by the ancient chant, Mode VII, "Hosanna to the Son of David," (see Paul Ford's arrangement in *By Flowing Waters*) an antiphon from Matthew 21:5 and "All Glory Laud and Honor" (*Gloria, laus et honor*) by Theodulph of Orleans (760–821). This tune, paired with a text of great scriptural imagery (Psalm 24:7–10, Psalm 118:26–27, Matthew 21:1–17, and Luke 19:37–38) escorts the Church along the path to the heart of the liturgical year, the Sacred Paschal Triduum.

Consider chanting the Passion on this day, you will find a musical setting by Bob Batastini from GIA publications. Additional settings of the sung passion are found in *Sung Gospels for Major Solemnities in Multiple Voices* by Anthony Ruff, OSB (The Liturgical Press). I suggest ending the Passion (Palm) Sunday liturgy in silence. The cantor can simply say something like the following: "Today's liturgy ends in silence in anticipation of the events of this most holy week; please leave quietly." I have found this to be a powerful way to call the assembly's attention to their preparation for the Sacred Paschal Triduum.

During Holy Week the Chrism Mass is celebrated with bishops, priests, and people of the diocese where the oil of the catechumens and the oil of sick are blessed and the sacred chrism is consecrated. Consider "Ritual Music for the Chrism Mass: The Blessing of the Oils" by Jay Hunstiger and Delores Dufner (OCP).

Liturgical Ministers

ONE Easter as an adult, I spent Holy Week at my parents' parish rather than my own. From the choir area, I watched the action in the sanctuary with my customary keen eye, excited about the glorious little ways in which the Sacred Paschal Triduum makes Christ present. However, looking as someone who has studied the rubrics keenly, I got the distinct impression that no one in the sanctuary felt my confidence in the liturgies. Sure enough, immediately after the Holy Thursday Evening Mass of the Lord's Supper, my sister—who had been one of the principal servers—rejoined the family and announced, "We didn't practice any of that before Mass; we just went with it."

In that particular case, I can excuse the overwhelmed new pastor whose permanent deacon (and head altar server trainer) had just retired and moved away. But even apart from the great loss of the beautiful liturgical minutiae of the Triduum, what a squandered opportunity for community and catechesis! The Triduum liturgies are indeed complex and require rehearsal of the practical elements. Such rehearsals can easily be interlaced with catechesis on the Paschal Mystery, and can be structured so as to naturally build community among the liturgical ministers.

In some places, the hours of adoration in the evening on Holy Thursday are filled by different parish ministries, including the liturgical ministries. This is a beautiful starting point, if insufficient on its own.

Despite the extra burdens laid on the shoulders of liturgical ministers during these most sacred days, the Triduum liturgies ought to be a time of great joy and deep prayer for them as much as for the parishioners and visitors who fill the pews on these nights. It is very easy to fall into the trap of doing a merely passable job, but with the proper preparation—a few practical rehearsals laced with spiritual catechesis—the Sacred Paschal Triduum truly becomes the seedbed of prayer and communion with God.

Devotions and Sacramentals

ONE of the most popular Lenten devotions is the public celebration on Fridays of the Stations of the Cross. Many meditations exist, classic and modern, and can easily be purchased or printed for a congregation to pray together. A performance of the Living Stations of the Cross can also be quite moving, and can affect its actors for weeks. When I was in high school, preparing the parish's Living Stations was the youth group's task: two narrators read (one the meditations, one the prayers), and actors dressed in draped-over bedsheets froze in place, then moved into the next position between stations. To get this right, however, we had to rehearse the stations at least once a week through all of Lent: a profound opportunity to keep our young minds focused on the reason for the season (while here we thought we were just hanging out with our friends)!

There are too many worthy Holy Week devotions to consider them all here, so let us touch upon only one more: on Holy Thursday night, adoring Our Lord at the altar of repose at seven churches. Originally, this was a repetition of the ordinary Roman custom of visiting the seven pilgrim churches on particular holy days, under which circumstances indulgences could be obtained. The indulgences are no more, and the selection of churches no longer matters, but the practice of adoring the Lord in this way — often praying two Stations of the Cross at each church — has remained alive in urban areas where such visits are geographically possible, ushering in the Sacred Paschal Triduum with admirable devotion.

The Parish and the Home

THE forty days of Lent are also marked by promises of the soul to be a better person, to sacrifice, pray, fast, and offer almsgiving and other acts of service. For these forty days it is acceptable to dive deep and sit with the messiness of our lives and prepare the muck to be offered and transformed. Those on the periphery of the journey will choose to "give up" something. Engage in the depth of the journey. Encourage those who give Homilies to teach about the wisdom of the inner journey. If you work in a parish create a list of reflective questions to have in the pews at each service you offer — for this day is the best day to evangelize and feed the multitudes. What is the ash they will choose to receive and wear? Is it more than a sign of faith? Is it a call?

Brainstorm with your parish staff (or your spouse) as to the meaning of giving something up and what to do instead of the perceived pleasure. For adults, we comprehend more and need to choose to give something up that takes time away from us knowing Christ in our lives. Should one choose to give up chocolate, each time they desire to have chocolate, what can be done instead to bring kindness to another person? If one gives up watching a sitcom, replace that time by giving it to God reading Scripture or another devotion or even journaling and spending time in quiet. For children it might simply be to teach a lesson about sacrifice so that at some point they can understand the sacrifice of love on a Cross and to teach that others needs are just as, if not sometimes more important than, our own.

There are six weeks of Lent and each Sunday we are to call ourselves, and those who walk with us, deeper into the dusty path that leads into the desert and eventually to the Garden of Gethsemane with Jesus. We require training and support to be able to give up what we think brings us ultimate joy. Offer or create small faith communities just for Lent (or once again incorporate weekly family prayer services at home to talk about the week and the promises you each made). The time commitment then is not overwhelming for adults, but the fire may be lit to want more after the six weeks end.

Each person on your staff (or in your family) is vital and this allows them to walk the path of their life in knowing God. Unite together and share the gift of your lives to help others understand the call to serve and witness. Collaborate with your parish staff to make the trip to Calgary holistic and so transformative that each year people will crave the time to not just give something up but to "get away" into the richness of prayer and community that our faith provides for us. From your collaboration, bring in different speakers on topics that will tough the everyday journey. Maybe you can be one of those speakers. For, while we walk individually and need to clear out the cobwebs of our spiritual lives during this journey, this is also a time to make sure that we reach out to others and ebb away any silos that might exist in our lives. Jesus could not walk or work to achieve his objectives alone, neither can we.

Mass Texts

◆ DISMISSAL FOR CHILDREN'S LITURGY OF THE WORD

Blessed children,
as you enter into this Lenten journey
you are asked to put aside all that will sidetrack you.
Put down your iPads, iPhones, iPods, and "I wants,"
and free yourself from all distraction,
so that you may hear what God truly wants
as you explore the Sacred Scriptures.
The Word of God teaches us all

and calls us ever closer to God throughout this holy season of Lent.
May you always find wonder and joy
in the gift God is offering you now.
Go in peace.

◆ Dismissal for Catechumens and Elect

For those of you participating in the Rites of Christian Initiation,
you have already experienced a long journey this year.
You have nearly reached the fullness of your journey toward full communion
in the Catholic, Christian tradition.
Do not weary now or let the devil tempt you.
Continue on your way.
You are bound to have trials
and wonderful "aha" moments
of transformation and transfiguration.
May you always find blessings now and in every day
as you continue to turn toward God in your life.
Trust in Jesus and the Cross to lead you home safely.
Go in peace.

◆ Introduction to the Mass

Too often we think of Lent as a time of penance when we should be recalling that the Gospel acounts of Lent teach us that it is a time of growth. Together with Jesus we face temptations, transfigurations, tearing down old temples and facades, and the struggle to find the faith that, through God's great mercy and love, he will build us and restore us. Let us then keep this hope alive through all our Lenten journey.

◆ Universal Prayer or Prayer of the Faithful

Introduction

Through desert wildernesses, high mountaintops, or bustling cities, Jesus always walks with us. Trusting in this, let us bring our prayers before God who loves us.

Intercessions

1. For Pope Francis, that he may teach us to "Blow the trumpet in Zion" and teach us all to return to the Lord through his joyful example of prayer, fasting, and almsgiving, we pray to the Lord: Lord, hear our prayer.

2. For all nations and peoples stricken with poverty, that God may hear their cries and all people may share generously with them, we pray to the Lord: Lord, hear our prayer.

3. For those who feel alienated from God because of sin, that they may find the strength, courage, and trust to ask God for forgiveness and mercy, we pray to the Lord: Lord, hear our prayer.

4. For our catechumens, elect, and candidates, that they may be ever strengthened on their journey of faith, and for all of us, that we may draw example from their zeal for the Lord, we pray to the Lord: Lord, hear our prayer.

5. For each of us gathered here today, that we may find our strength and hope in Jesus and follow his example to move beyond fear and bear our crosses and burdens joyfully, we pray to the Lord: Lord, hear our prayer.

Concluding Prayer

O loving God,
like Jesus, we are all on a journey toward Jerusalem, our heavenly city.
From the moment of our conception and birth, we follow your path as best we can.
Sometimes we stray, but you gently call us back or show us the way again and again.
We ask that you might hear these humble prayers, that they may draw us ever closer to you,
in this time of Lent and always.
Through Christ our Lord.
Amen.

February
Month of the Passion of Our Lord

WED 18 (#219) violet
Ash Wednesday

About Ash Wednesday

In the early Church, when Lent was a time for the reconciliation of public penitents, the penitents would come to the church at the beginning of Lent, that is, on Ash Wednesday. They would wear a penitential garment, suggesting sackcloth, and be sprinkled with ashes. Then they would be ritually expelled from the assembly to do their penance for forty days, returning to the church on Holy Thursday, when they would be readmitted to the sacraments.

With time, the expulsion of penitents disappeared, but the ashes remained and became a call to penance of all the faithful. In the Scriptures, sackcloth and ashes are the signs of penance.

The practice of using ashes from the palms of the previous year's Palm Sunday is a relatively new element of the liturgy, first appearing in the twelfth century. It adds another layer of meaning to this rich rite, reminding us of where we are headed—to the glory of Easter.

The Lectionary for Mass

The Letionary commentaries for the Lenten readings were provided by Genevieve Glen, OSB. The commentaries on the Responsorial Psalm were provided by Anne Elizabeth Sweet, OCSO.

◆ FIRST READING: The first step on the Lenten road is to change directions. We must turn back from the fascinating byways where we've wandered, the dead ends we've chosen, the roads to dark places. We must turn instead toward God from wherever we are right this minute. And not half-heartedly either. God wants our whole heart's attention because the heart houses the pilot who decides which way to take.

◆ RESPONSORIAL PSALM 51: Fully aware of sinfulness, the psalmist prays for God's help and for the clean heart, which alone can see God.

◆ SECOND READING: We can walk the Lenten road because Jesus came to get us in the deserts of sin where we've made our home. It's a demanding road, but we do not travel alone. And no, let's not even think about waiting till tomorrow morning or next Tuesday when we will have had more sleep, caught up with our to do list, or whatever other excuse delays us. The Lenten invitation is urgent. The time is now.

◆ GOSPEL: Danger awaits the Lenten traveler at the very first step. We can stop to look in the mirror, check out those ashes, compare penances with a friend, and decide we're looking pretty good. However, God has an uncomfortable habit of looking past appearances to learn what's in the heart, where no one else can see. And God's is the opinion that matters.

The Roman Missal

All the prayers and texts are proper for the day and can be found at Ash Wednesday in the Lent section of the Proper of Time toward the beginning of the Missal.

There is no Penitential Act today, since it is replaced by the distribution of ashes.

The Collect speaks of the "campaign of Christian service" that is begun today—a campaign that is begun with fasting. The proper focus of Lent is laid out for us: it is a time to "take up battle against spiritual evils" so that "we may be armed with weapons of self-restraint." Over and over again throughout the entirety of Lent the Mass prayers will remind us that the journey of Lent is more than just "giving something up," and it is more than just simply doing outward acts of penance; rather, the prayers call us to a true metanoia, a change of life with practical consequences for the way we live.

The rite for the blessing and distribution of ashes takes place after the Homily. The priest celebrant, with any necessary ministers (for example, the bookbearer, and someone to hold the vessel with water, if needed), goes to the place where the vessel(s) with ashes is (are). Hands remain joined for the introduction (the rubric for which does *not* indicate "these or similar words"), and then he leaves a brief period for silent prayer. Then, with hands extended, he prays one of the two prayers of blessing. While both prayers contain the gesture of making the Sign of the Cross over the ashes, the gesture has a somewhat different focus in each of the two prayers: in the first, the priest is asking the grace of God's blessing on those "who are marked with these ashes," and in the second, the blessing is invoked more specifically on the ashes themselves. Consequently, the gesture should match the action according to the words of the prayer.

The prayers very clearly speak of the journey of conversion. The first prayer, during which the people are blessed, highlights the Lenten observances of acts of humility and works of penance that the faithful will undertake; and it asks for God's blessing that those who undertake these practices "may be worthy to come with minds made pure / to celebrate the Paschal Mystery of your Son." The second prayer focuses more on the ashes and their purpose and meaning: receiving the ashes on our heads is an acknowledgement that "we are but ashes / and shall return to dust." Therefore, we ask, that as a result of our observance of Lent, our gain may be twofold—not only pardon for sins, but also "newness of life / after the likeness of your Risen Son."

After the prayer, the priest sprinkles the ashes with water, but this is done in silence, without his saying anything.

Either one of two formulae is used to impose ashes: "Repent, and believe in the Gospel" or "Remember that you are dust, and to dust you shall return." Although there is no stated rule about it, there might be a certain logic in using the first formula if the first prayer of blessing is used, and the second formula if the second prayer is used, since in some way the themes of the prayers and the formulae of imposition seem to correspond to each other. Say the words of imposition exactly as they are given; don't alter them or try to "personalize" the phrase; it is the Church who calls each of her members to repentance, not you personally. The rubric states simply that ashes are placed on the head of all those present who come up, as the formula is said. Customarily, this is done by the priest (or deacon or minister) dipping his (or her) thumb in the ashes, and then tracing the ashes on the person's forehead in the Sign of the Cross, although, technically, there is nothing that requires this. (Interestingly, we know, for example, that historically ashes have also been sprinkled on the top of peoples' heads.)

Singing is to take place during the imposition of ashes, and several possibilities are spelled out in the Missal. There are three suggested antiphons that can be used in connection with the verses of Psalm 51; a responsory is also suggested, or another appropriate song may be sung.

Be sure to provide the means for priests and other ministers to wash their hands after the distribution of ashes. Pre-moistened towelettes sometimes work better than plain water, although water and towels should also be available.

After the imposition of ashes (and the ministers washing their hands), the Universal Prayer takes place; the Creed is not said. After the Universal Prayer, Mass continues as usual.

If the blessing and distribution of ashes takes place outside Mass, then all moves forward as described above, including all the readings and their chants as at Mass, but then, after the Universal Prayer, the priest simply blesses and dismisses the faithful, using the Prayer over the People given at the end of the Mass formularies. Interestingly, there is no specific mention in the rubrics that the Our Father is prayed when the blessing and distribution of ashes occurs outside Mass; they simply direct that the rite is concluded with the Universal Prayer, the Blessing, and the Dismissal of the faithful.

The Prayer over the Offerings highlights the journey of conversion we are undertaking at the beginning of Lent and are marking by the offering of this sacrifice, a journey that will come to its completion in the days of the Sacred Paschal Triduum; we ask that "we may turn away from harmful pleasure / and, cleansed from our sins, may become worthy / to celebrate devoutly the Passion of your Son."

The Preface to be used today is either Preface III or Preface IV of Lent. Preface III speaks of the fruits of self-denial: pride that is humbled and works of kindness, specifically in feeding the poor; Preface IV speaks of how bodily fasting serves to "restrain our faults, / raise up our minds, / and bestow both virtue and its rewards." Both Prefaces are short and to the point, in keeping with the starkness of this day's liturgy. Also, today might be a good day to use the Eucharistic Prayer for Reconciliation I, with or without its proper Preface, to highlight the tone of the liturgical time,

and to provide a stark contrast with Ordinary Time if this prayer has been used rarely, if at all, recently.

For the Dismissal, the priest is to use the Prayer over the People. There is no indication that this dismissal text is optional. The prayer is prayed with the priest's hands extended over the people. The prayer asks that God will pour out on us "a spirit of compunction" as a result of our doing penance, again pointing to the inward, spiritual conversion that should take place as a result of the outward actions. The actual Blessing and Dismissal take place as usual.

A visit can be scheduled to all the sick and homebound on Ash Wednesday to share already-blessed ashes. There is a simple order in the *Book of Blessings*, chapter 52. A priest, deacon, or lay minister may distribute ashes, but the lay minister excludes the prayer of blessing. The lay minister should bring already-blessed ashes.

Other Ideas

Every year the parish gets inundated with requests about Lenten fasting and rules for abstinence, times for Reconciliation services, and the requirements for Easter duty, counting the days of Lent, and so on. Create a brochure listing the answer to many of these FAQs and a calendar of events for Lent and Holy Week. This brochure could be included as a bulletin insert, a downloadable PDF on the parish website, a handout to be distributed at religious education sessions, and posted on parish blogs or social media sites. Sometimes those of us who work for the Church can assume everyone should know what feels like basic facts to us, but it isn't necessarily so. Don't be condescending, but don't assume anything. Providing your congregation with as much correct information as possible will help all stay involved.

Collaborate with other Catholic churches in the area to provide information on Reconciliation opportunities, parish missions, or moments of renewal available in the entire area.

Here is a quick summary of the abstinence rules: According to Church law, Ash Wednesday and Good Friday are observed as days of fast and abstinence (*Code of Canon Law* [CCL], 1251). In the United States, all the Fridays of Lent are days of abstinence. Abstinence is to be observed by all over the age of 14 (CCL,1252). Those between the ages of 18 (CCL, 97 §1) and 59 [inclusive] (CCL, 1252) are bound by the law of fast.

Today is also usually observed as the Collection for the Church in Central and Eastern Europe. The USCCB website describes this as "Supporting the Catholic Church in Central and Eastern Europe to follow the light of Christ out of darkness . . . ."

CRS Rice Bowl (formerly "Operation Rice Bowl") also begins today. The organization's website includes a variety resources (www. crsricebowl.org).

T H U 19 (#220) violet
Thursday after Ash Wednesday

The Lectionary for Mass

◆ FIRST READING: How many Lents does this year make it? One? Forty? Lent can lose its urgency with repetition, but the urgency is always there. Lenten choices—to do good or ill or nothing, to pray or watch TV, to carry someone else's groceries or just rush to our own car—are in fact a matter of life or death. They cause few ripples on life's surface, but they eventually determine where the journey ends, because Lent is a rehearsal for all of life, not just the span from here to Easter.

◆ RESPONSORIAL PSALM 1: Fidelity to God's law is the source of true happiness and flourishing life. The one who is faithful thrives, like a beautiful tree with deep roots and leafy branches in abundance.

◆ GOSPEL: Those Lenten sacrifices—they can look so inconsequential, so inconvenient, so artificial. Even as the day after Lent begins, we can start to rewrite our resolutions, trimming off a bit here, a bit there. "Be reasonable," whispers the voice from the Eden's fruit tree. "Be good to yourself. Treat yourself." The question, though, is the one put by today's Gospel: what is real gain, what is real loss? The choice is ours.

The Roman Missal

All the texts are proper for today. The Collect asks for God's help and inspiration so that what we do (especially during the time of Lent) may always begin in God and be brought to completion by him. The Prayer over the Offerings asks for pardon such that, having received that pardon, the "offerings we set upon this sacred altar" may truly be oblations that give honor to God. Use one of the four Prefaces of Lent. While any one of the four is appropriate, since today's account of the Gospel speaks explicitly of denying oneself, perhaps Preface III, with its explicit mention of self-denial, would be a good choice. The Prayer after Communion acknowledges the blessings we have received from God while beseeching from him "pardon" and "salvation."

There is a Prayer over the People provided every day during Lent for the end of Mass. While the prayer is optional on weekdays, it is a good practice to use these special prayers to highlight the liturgical time. The prayer acknowledges that God has "made known to your people the ways of eternal life;" within the context of Lent, we can think of those ways of eternal life being the ways of penance (prayer, fasting,

and almsgiving). The prayer goes on to ask that this same path to eternal life may lead to God who is "the unfading light."

F R I 20 (#221) violet
Friday after Ash Wednesday

The Lectionary for Mass

◆ FIRST READING: Fasting is one of the three great traditional works of Lent. However, the prophet reminds us that diet is not the determinant of holiness. Love is. Lifting the emotional yoke that chafes others' shoulders, refusing to reap a profit at others' expense, ceasing to hoard abundance from Providence's warehouses when others need it, these are the real "noes" engraved on the key that opens the narrow gate onto the road to life.

◆ RESPONSORIAL PSALM 51: The repentance God desires is conversion of heart.

◆ GOSPEL: Jesus's disciples had to fast from many cherished certainties, from the security of job and family, from all the hopes and plans they no doubt had, in order to be free to learn new ways of thinking, doing, and being from their Teacher. When ultimately they had to fast even from Jesus's daily companionship, they discovered they knew how to follow him even in dark hunger. And so will we.

The Roman Missal

The Collect of the Lenten weekday acknowledges that we have begun works of penance; this is in keeping with the nature of these weekdays before the First Sunday of Lent acting as a kind of introduction to the liturgical time. The prayer asks for perseverance, "that we may have strength to accomplish with sincerity / the bodily observances we undertake." The Prayer over the Offerings for the day prays for interior conversion to occur as a result of the sacrifice we offer this day: "that it may make our intentions acceptable to you / and add to our powers of self-restraint." The Prayer after Communion petitions for healing and forgiveness, in that it asks that as a result of our partaking in the Eucharist, "we may be cleansed of all our misdeeds, / and so be suited for the remedies of your compassion."

One of the four Prefaces of Lent is used today. While any one of the four is appropriate, you might consider using Preface IV, since it specifically mentions fasting, and would therefore echo the Gospel.

Even though the Prayer over the People is optional on weekdays, it would be good to use it to highlight the liturgical time.

S A T 21 (#222) violet Saturday after Ash Wednesday

Optional Memorial of St. Peter Damian, Bishop and Doctor of the Church / violet

The Lectionary for Mass

◆ FIRST READING: Saying no to selfishness is not enough. Love is not a negative. To take food we thought we needed and give it to someone hungrier, to abandon our own comfort to care for one afflicted with fear or loneliness or grief, to substitute a kind word for malicious gossip, or to worship when we would rather do something entertaining, all seem small enough, really. Yet the prophet's promises of reward suggest that none of them is as insignificant as we might imagine.

◆ RESPONSORIAL PSALM 86: Of ourselves, we are poor and helpless. We need God, God's help, and God's deliverance. We need to learn God's wisdom.

◆ GOSPEL: Isaiah begins to draw attention away from our behavior to God's, from our meager selfishness to God's extraordinary generosity. The Gospel points

away from us to Jesus, who fasts from respectability in order to open a place for himself in the lives of sinners, there to make present in the flesh God's healing mercy.

The Roman Missal

The Lenten Collect entreats God for protection, asking him to "look with compassion on our weakness." The Prayer over the Offerings asks for inner purification through the sacrifice "of conciliation and praise," which will be offered. The Prayer after Communion prays that the nourishment we receive in the Eucharist "may be for us a help to reach eternity."

One of the four Prefaces of Lent is used today, and any one of the four is appropriate. Preface II of Lent might be especially considered for use, since its references to the renewing and purifying of hearts and to being "freed from disordered affections" would go well with the Gospel story of the call and conversion of Levi.

Even though the Prayer over the People is optional on weekdays, it would be good to use it, to highlight the liturgical time.

Today's Saint

St. Peter Damian (1007–1072), born to a large Italian family, entered a Camaldolese Benedictine monastery comprising hermit monks who followed an austere life of fasting and prayer. Dedicating himself to the study of Scripture and the Fathers of the Church, he gained a reputation among the hermits as being both a gifted scholar and spiritual guru. Although he lived in a monastery, removed from the world, St. Peter was a powerful voice of reform in the Church. He spoke out against clerical abuses, challenged bishops to recommit themselves to their vocation, and announced the need for a reformed papacy. Recognized for his ability to lead, he was made Abbot of his

monastery and later installed as Bishop of Ostia. As bishop, he never lost sight of his calling to be a monk. He was so influential in the Church that Pope Leo XII declared him a Doctor of the Church.

☀ 22 (#23) violet First Sunday of Lent

The Lectionary for Mass

◆ FIRST READING: The First Sunday of Lent confronts us with the reason, the means, and the cost of salvation through the mystery of Christ's dying and rising. This is the story that shapes our Lenten work of conversion. Genesis recalls the dreadful return of the waters of chaos to flood and cleanse a world sodden with sin. Even when human history is at its nadir, though, hope rises in the darkness under the sign of the rainbow to reassure us that the destruction we have brought on ourselves is not the end of our story.

◆ RESPONSORIAL PSALM 25: This psalm is an acrostic poem where each verse begins with the successive letter of the Hebrew alphabet. This detail is lost on us as we read, pray, or sing the English translation of this psalm. But what should not be lost on any of us is the psalm's reference to the compassion of the Lord, a compassion made known in the aftermath of the great flood, a compassion that is the source of redemption and model for human relationship. The cry of the psalmist becomes our own prayer: "Teach me your paths." Teach us to be more loving, teach us to know and live your truth. Teach us your compassion and lead us to your justice. And with the psalmist we remember that divine compassion will not falter, will not give up on us. For that is God's promise of old to all generations. God has made his covenant and, in doing so, he shows us the way.

◆ SECOND READING: The suffering, death, and descent into hell which we proclaim in the creed take Christ into the very heart of darkness where those swamped in the disaster of death await deliverance, promised to all by the rainbow. The Cross is the new ark which will carry them and all of us to life through the waters not of the flood but of Baptism. We begin Lent with a preview of the mystery we will celebrate at Easter.

◆ GOSPEL: Armed with the hope of the covenant and the promise of Baptism, we find the courage to read the story of Jesus's own journey into the desolation of the desert, the place of death and life, where wickedness and grace contended in the story of Israel. Without the detail of Matthew and Luke, Mark gives stark warning of the confrontation between evil and grace that awaits us as we follow Jesus's lead on our Lenten journey from sinfulness to salvation through Baptism celebrated or renewed at Easter.

The Roman Missal

The Gloria is omitted today. The Creed is said.

The Collect on this First Sunday of Lent sets the program, as it were, for the liturgical time that lies ahead and has the character of a prayer that is inaugurating something to be undertaken. We pray that "through the yearly observances of holy Lent," our understanding of "the riches hidden in Christ" may grow, and that our conduct may reflect those riches of living life in Christ. The Prayer over the Offerings also has the characteristic of launching the sacred time of Lent as it acknowledges that the offerings we make this day "celebrate the beginning / of this venerable and sacred time." Consequently, the prayer asks that we be given the right dispositions to make the offering properly. The Prayer after Communion speaks of the nourishment that comes to us in the Eucharist in terms of the three traditional virtues of faith, hope, and charity, noting the good effect that is had on each; it then, in a clear allusion to today's account of the Gospel, goes on to ask "that we may learn to hunger for Christ, / the true and living Bread, / and strive to live by every word / which proceeds from your mouth."

The Preface to be used for this Mass is given on the pages right there along with the other texts for the Mass. The reason this Preface, "The Temptation of the Lord," is used today is obvious, since the Gospel reading for the First Sunday of Lent is always the account of the temptation of Jesus from one of the Gospel accounts. Consider chanting the Introductory Dialogue and the Preface today; if this is not the regular practice of your community, this can be a way of powerfully drawing attention to the solemnity of Lenten time (but be sure to prepare and rehearse your assembly as needed, especially if your people are not familiar with the responses!).

The Prayer over the People is required, not optional, on the Sundays of Lent, and the text is given right after the Prayer after Communion.

Sending of the Catechumens for Election

The *Rite of Christian Initiation of Adults* includes an optional Rite of Sending of the Catechumens for Election. If your diocese celebrates the Rite of Election on the First Sunday of Lent, as suggested by the RCIA, then consider celebrating this Rite of Sending in your parish. Celebrating the rite is yet another way to catechize the entire parish about the meaning of RCIA and the journey the catechumens (soon to be elect) undertake. Also, the rite provides yet another opportunity for the catechumens to be supported in prayer by, and to receive the good wishes of, those who will soon be their brothers and sisters in Baptism. The rite takes place after the Homily at Mass and is described in numbers 106–117 in the RCIA.

Other Ideas

Today is the special collection for National Black and Indian Missions. Hold them in the communal prayers, and consider a speaker or getting information to the congregation via bulletin and web (http://blackandindianmission.org).

M O N 23 (#224) violet
Lenten Weekday

Optional Memorial of St. Polycarp, Bishop and Martyr / violet

The Lectionary for Mass

◆ FIRST READING: Holy does as holy is. God, the all-holy, is and acts out love. The Church defines holiness as love (see *Lumen gentium*, 40) and judges the holiness of sainthood candidates by the degree of their charity. The trek toward an honest Easter affirmation of our identity as people baptized into communion with the all-holy, all-loving God in Christ requires a sharp look at whatever treatment of others smacks of love's opposites.

◆ RESPONSORIAL PSALM 19: Today's antiphon comes from the Gospel according to John. Jesus's words are indeed Spirit and life! The last stanza of today's psalm can be seen in connection with the practical commands set forth in today's First Reading regarding our behavior toward others.

◆ GOSPEL: Jesus ups Leviticus's ante. It is not enough to refrain from unloving behavior. Wherever we fail to act out God's love toward others, whether we do active harm or not, we have betrayed our baptismal identity by denying in practice the reality of Christ's Body into which Baptism immersed us. Belief in Christ requires belief in the whole Christ, where even the most unappealing and inconvenient of our neighbors has a value far beyond what shows on the surface.

The Roman Missal

Only by conversion and understanding of "heavenly teaching" can we benefit from the good works we offer to God this Lent (Collect). In the Prayer over the Offerings, we pray that the offering we make to God may change our lives, reconcile us to the Father, and bring us forgiveness. In the Prayer after Communion, we pray that the power of the sacrament we receive may bring us "help in mind and body" and "the fullness of heavenly healing." The Eucharist is food for body and soul. The Prayer over the People is a simple prayer that asks that God's people may receive the grace to see what needs to be done — and the strength to do it.

Today's Saint

St. Polycarp, an esteemed Christian leader, lived during the first half of the second century and was a friend to many who personally knew Jesus. He converted to the Christian faith under the influence of Saint John the Evangelist. Saint Polycarp later became Bishop of Smyrna, in Turkey, around the year 96 AD. He fought many of the gnostic heresies that were beginning to overtake the early Church. When there was a controversy over the celebration of Easter, the Churches in Asia Minor sent Polycarp as their representative to discuss the issue with Pope Anicetus. The Romans tried to burn him at the stake (when he was in his late 80s) but, failing that, finally stabbed him to death with a dagger.

T U E 24 (#225) violet
Lenten Weekday

The Lectionary for Mass

◆ FIRST READING: Prayer is rooted in God's Word. Unlike the broken words that litter our daily landscape, from advertising jingles to evasive courtesies, God's Word comes with today's unbreakable guarantee. If we allow it in, it will go to work on us, turning us into renewed human beings, a renewal we can celebrate at Easter as our own personal resurrection from whatever deaths that have turned bits of us back into less-than-alive lumps of clay. The hitch is this: if we close the door to the Word, God will honor our decision.

◆ RESPONSORIAL PSALM 34 is a prayer of thanksgiving and praise for God's deliverance. In light of today's First Reading, it is interesting to note the words in the stanzas of the psalm. There is the word-in-action of God's deliverance in the first stanza. There are the words of the poor, the just, and the afflicted that are not without fruitful effect when addressed to the Lord.

◆ GOSPEL: Prayer in its fullest is collaboration between God's words and ours. Babbling empty words to One whose word is never empty is rather discourteous. It's like hiding behind the bushes of words so God won't find us. If we don't really want to be left there to our own devices, Jesus says, "Match your words to God's. Make them simple, direct and honest." The Lord's Prayer is not a sacrosanct script but a pattern to guide us when we pray.

The Roman Missal

The Collect calls our attention to "the chastening effects of bodily discipline," specifically, the way such discipline brings clarity to our minds (which can be made "radiant" as a result) and strengthens our yearning for God. This prayer is yet another reminder of the inward transformation that is the goal of our outward Lenten practices. The Prayer over the Offerings acknowledges that the gifts we bring are from God's bountiful goodness; it then asks that the offerings of bread and wine, "temporal sustenance," be transformed to give us eternal life. The sacramental principle is being referred to here, as the prayer prays that tangible signs be transformed to convey spiritual realities of grace. The Prayer after Communion prays that today's celebration of the mysteries may help us to keep the proper perspective in life: namely, that "by moderating earthly desires / we may learn to love the things of heaven."

Any one of the four Prefaces of Lent can be used today.

Even though the Prayer over the People is optional on weekdays, it would be good to use it, to highlight the liturgical time.

W E D 25 (#226) violet
Lenten Weekday

The Lectionary for Mass

◆ FIRST READING: In the cautionary tale of Jonah in Nineveh, ancient imperial capital of Assyria, one of Israel's greatest enemies, the Ninevites are generally bad news to the prophet and his people. But God's word reduces them to abject repentance at a single hearing because they "believed God." Here we see in action what was said of God's word in yesterday's first reading.

◆ RESPONSORIAL PSALM 51 is one of the penitential psalms, focusing as it does on the humble sinner's plea for God's mercy. Note that the prayer is not only for forgiveness, but also for a renewed and purified heart.

◆ GOSPEL: Jesus grieves the hardness of heart that makes his own people such a stubborn audience when even the pagan Ninevites and the foreign Ethiopian queen have recognized and accepted the transforming power of God's word. If we are tempted to look privately down our noses at the Ninevites because we already believe—don't we?—we might do well to pay attention not to their drama but to their humble receptivity. Nothing blocks the power of Jesus's message like the illusion that we don't really need it.

The Roman Missal

The Collect for today asks that the good works of our bodily self-denial may bear fruit by our being "renewed in mind"—again emphasizing the need for the outward behavior to have an effect on our interior disposition, our spiritual life. The Prayer over the Offerings asks that just as God makes the gifts offered become the sacrament, so too may he "let them become for us an eternal remedy." The prayer can remind us that regardless of the objective truth of the offerings of bread and wine becoming the Body and Blood of Christ, nothing automatic happens to us as a result of the transformation of those elements; instead, they will only be the "eternal remedy" they are supposed to be in our lives if we are open to them and cooperate with God's grace—and that only happens with the proper interior conversion and disposition. The Prayer after Communion prays that the nourishment of the sacrament may "bring us unending life."

Any one of the four Prefaces of Lent can be used today. While any one is appropriate, the First Reading and the Gospel, with their emphasis on responding to the call to conversion, might make Preface II of Lent, with its focus on Lent as "a sacred time / for the renewing and purifying of their hearts," or Eucharistic Prayer for Reconciliation I with its proper Preface (". . . you constantly offer pardon / and call on sinners / to trust in your forgiveness alone . . . / Even now you set before your people / a time of grace and reconciliation . . ."), good choices for today.

Even though the Prayer over the People is optional on weekdays, it would be good to use it, to highlight the liturgical time.

THU 26 (#227) violet
Lenten Weekday

The Lectionary for Mass

◆ FIRST READING: Esther, fictional Jewish queen of Persia during Israel's exile, continues Lent's urgent appeal for humble prayer. She and her people were in danger of annihilation at the hands of an unscrupulous government official. She had already shown that she had power over the king, but she was wise enough to put her trust not in her own schemes but in the fidelity and power of God. Later in the story, God does indeed grant her prayer.

◆ RESPONSORIAL PSALM 138 is a prayer of thanksgiving for the Lord's favorable answer to a cry for help. The thankful awareness of God's saving deeds in the life of the one who prays is echoed in each stanza. How can we make the awareness, the thanksgiving of this prayer our own?

◆ GOSPEL: Queen Esther asked for God's help with no guarantee of success except her trust in God's love. Jesus exhorts us to do the same. Our tendency to get caught up in the question of prayers that seem to go unanswered may deafen us to the small, poignant question hidden in this familiar passage. God will always grant the good we ask for, open the door when we knock, help us to find what we seek. The question is: will we do the same in return? Love is not a one-way street.

The Roman Missal

The Collect acknowledges our complete and utter dependence on God and asks that he may bestow on us "a spirit of always pondering what is right and of hastening to carry it out." More than just good intentions are needed during Lent; we must be sure to follow through with concrete actions so that, as the prayer goes on to ask, we may "be enabled to live according to your will." The Prayer over the Offerings expresses the proper stance of humility we should bear when offering the Sacrifice, as it entreats God for mercy for those "who approach you in supplication" and that he might "turn the hearts of us all towards you." The Prayer after Communion prays that the sacred mysteries we have been given in the Eucharist may be "a healing remedy for us, / both now and in time to come."

Any one of the four Prefaces of Lent can be used today.

Even though the Prayer over the People is optional on weekdays, it would be good to use it, to highlight the liturgical time.

FRI 27 (#228) violet
Lenten Weekday

The Lectionary for Mass

◆ FIRST READING: God reiterates more openly the subtle question of yesterday's Gospel: is my way unfair or rather are yours? The concept that we who are created in God's image and incorporated into Christ through Baptism should surely mirror the ways of God's love runs like a thread through the Lenten readings. Perhaps here what we are challenged to reflect is God's extraordinary willingness to cast all our own sins, however hideous, into an unremembered past out of the overriding love that wants only life for us.

◆ RESPONSORIAL PSALM 130: Echoing a theme from the First Reading, today's psalm asks: if the Lord remembers sin, who can live? Psalm 130 is a psalm of repentance and confident trust in the Lord's mercy.

◆ GOSPEL: Jesus holds up the mirror. What does God's intense desire for forgiveness and reconciliation look like in practice? God seeks us out with an immediacy that we can imitate by dropping anger and insults, grudges and grievances, and even the best of our Lenten sacrifices on the spot and going to repair the breach we have made in our relationships. The threat that ends the gospel emphasizes the urgency: do it now!

The Roman Missal

In today's Collect, we ask that we may be "so conformed to the paschal observances" that the penance ("bodily discipline") we have begun may be fruit "in the souls of all." The use of the word "paschal" in this third edition of *The Roman Missal* highlights for us the Lent and Easter connection and reminds us that we do penance during Lent not for its own sake, but for the sake of sharing more deeply in new life with, through, and in Christ who is risen. In asking God to accept our sacrificial offerings, the Prayer over the Offerings reminds us that it is God's will that we are reconciled to him, and our salvation is restored, through the offering of the Eucharistic Sacrifice. The Prayer after Communion uses the captivating phrase "holy refreshment of your Sacrament" in asking that the Eucharist cleanse us of old ways

and "take us up into the mystery of salvation."

Any one of the four Prefaces of Lent can be used today. Consideration might also be given, in light of the Gospel's call for us to be reconciled with one another (especially before bringing our gifts to the altar), to using Eucharistic Prayer for Reconciliation II, as it describes in its Preface how it is through the power of the Spirit "that enemies may speak to each other again, / adversaries join hands, / and peoples seek to meet together" and how the Spirit "takes away everything that estranges us from one another."

Even though the Prayer over the People is optional on weekdays, it would be good to use it to highlight the liturgical time.

SAT 28 (#229) violet
Lenten Weekday

Lectionary for Mass

◆ FIRST READING: On Monday, the Word urged us to be holy as God is holy. All week the readings have set before us the "statutes and decrees" of love that define our lives as people of the covenant promised on Sunday. The covenant is entirely mutual: if we translate our sometimes vague desire to be holy into plain obedience to these commandments of love, God will in fact make us holy, "a people sacred to the LORD," the goal of our Lenten work.

◆ RESPONSORIAL PSALM: The stipulations of the covenant agreement are spelled out in the law. Psalm 119 acclaims the wisdom of God's law and the blessedness of those who faithfully observe it.

◆ GOSPEL: We have come full circle, from Monday's exhortation that we be holy as God is holy to today's

call to be perfect as our heavenly Father is perfect. "Perfect" might scare off anyone who has suffered the curse of perfectionism, but it really means "be complete, be finished, be whole" as God is. We see what that looks like in Jesus, who will summarize in the Passion story what it really means to love even our enemies.

The Roman Missal

Today's Collect prays for the turning of our hearts toward the eternal Father so that "we may be dedicated to your worship." That dedication, however, includes "carrying out works of charity," thus pointing to an understanding of worship that goes beyond liturgy to include the "liturgy of one's life," for example, living a life of love, which is the sacrifice pleasing to God. The Prayer over the Offerings, in acknowledging that we are restored by "these blessed mysteries," also asks that they "make us worthy of the gift they bestow." Thus, we are reminded that our participation in offering the sacrifice is not through our own merit, but because we have been made worthy of that participation only as a gift from God in the first place. The Prayer after Communion prays for "unceasing favor" and "salutary consolations" for those who have shared in the "divine mystery" of this celebration of the Eucharist.

Any one of the four Prefaces of Lent can be used today. While any one is appropriate, one could find in either Preface I or Preface III echoes of today's account of the Gospel's challenge to be perfect as our heavenly Father is perfect.

Even though the Prayer over the People is optional on weekdays, it would be good to use it to highlight the liturgical time.

March
Month of St. Joseph

☀ 1 (#26) violet
Second Sunday of Lent

The Lectionary for Mass

◆ FIRST READING: Lent is a journey in faith through dark places toward the promised light. Abraham's faithful obedience took him to the brink of his son's death by his own hand as he prepared to sacrifice to God the very gift God had given to fulfill the promise of countless descendants. In Abraham's story, faith and obedience are rewarded by reprieve. But a surprise reprieve at the end did not lessen the cost of that long journey made in fear and grief to the place of sacrifice, knowing that knife and altar awaited.

◆ RESPONSORIAL PSALM 116: Filled with awe in the presence of the Lord who has "loosed my bonds," the psalmist writes, "I am your servant." It is indeed a psalm of gratitude and pledged faithfulness. God, who rescues his servant from the cords of death, regards the death of his faithful ones as precious. We see a God who cares for humanity in all its frailty, imperfection, and possibility. God loves his people and asks only for obedience in return.

◆ SECOND READING: God's love chose to take no reprieve from the sacrifice of the beloved Son, for the cost of reprieve would have been the loss of all those others who would become God's children by adoption. Yet even here, in this relentless story of love's ultimate sacrifice, the promise of Easter shines through the clouds.

◆ GOSPEL: The stories of God speaking on the desert mountaintop to Moses from a cloud of fire and to Elijah in profound silence, commanding each of them to go to the people with the word of life, come together here to identify Jesus as the one in whom the fire dwells unseen and of whom the voice says, "This is my beloved Son." We are charged to listen and to follow through the twisting desert paths before us to the final fulfillment of the promise of life made again and again to God's wandering people.

The Roman Missal

The Gloria is omitted today.

The Collect for the Second Sunday of Lent clearly connects with the Gospel reading of the Transfiguration. The prayer's opening address to God refers to him as the one who has "commanded us / to listen to your beloved Son." It goes on to ask that we might be nourished "inwardly by your word," gain "spiritual sight made pure" and therefore "rejoice to behold your glory." The imagery in the prayer all but puts us in the Transfiguration scene. The Prayer over the Offerings makes a strong connection between Lent and Easter as it looks forward to "the celebration of the Paschal festivities;" we ask that we may be prepared for those festivities by being cleansed of our faults and sanctified in body and mind through the offering of this Sacrifice. The Prayer after Communion is a prayer of gratitude, expressing thanksgiving that "[as] we receive these glorious mysteries," we are allowed "while still on earth / to be partakers even now of the things of heaven." The prayer reminds us that the Church's celebration of the Eucharist is also a participation in the heavenly, eschatological banquet.

The Preface to be used for this Mass is given on the pages right there along with the other texts for this Mass. Titled "The Transfiguration of the Lord," the Preface clearly recalls and gives the meaning of the Transfiguration: "to show, even by the testimony of the law and the prophets, / that the Passion leads to the glory of the Resurrection." Thus is the centrality of the Paschal Mystery reaffirmed. Consider chanting the introductory dialogue and the Preface today; if this is not the regular practice of your community, this can be a way of powerfully drawing attention to the solemnity of Lenten time (but be sure to prepare and rehearse your assembly as needed, especially if your people are not familiar with the responses!).

The Prayer over the People is required, not optional, on the Sundays of Lent, and the text is given right after the Prayer after Communion.

Other Ideas

In regions where appropriate, you may wish to remind people that next week is Daylight Savings Time and to be sure to turn clocks ahead so they don't miss Mass next weekend.

MON 2 (#230) violet
Lenten Weekday

The Lectionary for Mass

◆ FIRST READING: In this portrait of contrasts, the prophet offers a shamed confession of the covenant people's unfaithfulness to the covenant law, their disobedience to God's messengers sent to restore them to covenant life, and now the consequence: they are scattered to the four winds. The prophet appeals to God who is faithful, compassionate, and forgiving. Our own fidelities may be less dramatic, and our appeals for mercy more subdued, but what matters is that God is no less merciful now than then.

◆ RESPONSORIAL PSALM 79: Fittingly, our antiphon pleads that the Lord will not deal with his people as they deserve. The context of the psalm is the aftermath of the destruction of Jerusalem and the Temple — viewed as punishment for sin by biblical authors, as is the subsequent exile. The first two stanzas ask for God's forgiveness.

◆ GOSPEL: Again Jesus adds a twist. Prayer for forgiveness, dramatic or subdued, must match the reality of our lives. If we hope for mercy, we must again mirror God's forgiveness in our treatment of others. The passage hints that by scouring out grudges and resentments, we make room for the gift of God's forgiveness. A heart walled and filled with enmity toward those who have hurt or harmed us is closed to God's mercy.

The Roman Missal

The Collect of the Lenten Weekday acknowledges that the reason we "chasten our bodies" is for the sake of "the healing of our souls," again reminding us that the outward practices of Lent must penetrate into our inner life. The prayer goes on to ask that we will be enabled to abstain from all sins and have our hearts strengthened so we can "carry out your loving commands." The Prayer over the Offerings, in asking God to accept our prayers, also asks that we might be "set free from worldly attractions." The Prayer after Communion asks that this sharing in Communion may both "cleanse us of wrongdoing / and make us heirs to the joys of heaven."

One of the four Prefaces of Lent is used today. While any one of the four is appropriate, Preface I might be a good one to pick up on the themes of the First Reading and the Gospel today.

Even though the Prayer over the People is optional on weekdays, it would be good to use it to highlight the liturgical time.

T U E 3 (#231) violet
Lenten Weekday

Optional Memorial of St. Katharine Drexel, Virgin / violet

The Lectionary for Mass

◆ FIRST READING: The prophet offers God's answer to our pleas for forgiveness. Words are not enough, no matter how earnest and eloquent. Far from the angry rejection we might fear, God pleads with us to take the actions that will translate our words into reality: fast from wrongdoing and do right by the helpless. In the Bible, widows and orphans, representing all those without personal recourse against ill treatment, are especially beloved by God, so again we are asked to mirror God's love.

◆ RESPONSORIAL PSALM 50: Like the First Reading, the psalm is concerned with true righteousness. The ritual offerings are in place but the dispositions of heart (the true sacrifice of praise) are not. It is this that God desires. See all of the third part of Psalm 50 for the details of what is required.

◆ GOSPEL: God is infinitely patient with sinners but has no tolerance at all for fakes. If we mouth all the right words of repentance and do all the good deeds reputed to earn divine approval, but keep a sharp eye on the approval of other people, we have mistaken self-love for the love God demands. Humility is the key to true conversion of heart.

The Roman Missal

The Collect brings to the fore our utter and complete dependence on God as it reminds us that without God "mortal humanity is sure to fall." Consequently, the prayer goes on to ask that God's constant help

might keep us from all harm and be brought to salvation. The Prayer over the Offerings acknowledges that these mysteries that we celebrate are the means by which God works his sanctification within us; therefore, we ask that we may "be cleansed of earthly faults / and led to the gifts of heaven." The Prayer after Communion for the Lenten Weekday asks that "the refreshment of this sacred table" may bring both "an increase in devoutness of life" and "the constant help of your work of conciliation."

One of the four Prefaces of Lent is used today. While any one of the four is appropriate, perhaps either Preface II, with its references to having our hearts purified and our being "freed from disordered affections," or Preface III, with its reference to humbling "our sinful pride," would work well today.

Even though the Prayer over the People is optional on weekdays, it would be good to use it to highlight the liturgical time.

Today's Saint

St. Katharine Drexel (1858–1955), a wealthy and worldly heiress from Philadelphia, did not spend her fortune on houses or jewelry, but on the establishment of institutions and missions dedicated to the marginalized. Due to her financial means, she had the privilege of traveling to various parts of the country in which she became keenly aware of the oppression of Native Americans and African Americans. She dedicated her entire life, including the founding of a religious community known as the Sisters of the Blessed Sacrament, to the empowerment of these groups through education (i.e., launching the first Catholic college for African Americans, and starting 145 Catholic missions and twelve schools for Native Americans). Regarding the purpose of the Sisters of the Blessed Sacrament, St. Katherine said, "Ours is the spirit of Eucharist—the total gift of self" (as quoted on the website of the Archdiocese of Philadelphia, www.archdiocesephl.org/rigali/cardhom/drexel04.htm).

W E D 4 (#232) violet
Lenten Weedkay
Optional Memorial of St. Casimir / violet

The Lectionary for Mass

◆ FIRST READING: In an apparent non sequitur, we are suddenly confronted with a preview of Jesus's Passion cast in terms of Jeremiah's experience. However, it ceases to be a non sequitur when we recognize that Jesus himself did all that the prophets and the Gospel readings have been demanding of us in terms of putting God's laws of love into practice, without regard for the consequences. And Jesus is the leader we follow.

◆ RESPONSORIAL PSALM 31: The antiphon echoes Jeremiah's plea for God's help. The second stanza is a perfect parallel to the first part of the text from Jeremiah. The first and third stanzas speak of the trust the psalmist—and Jeremiah—had in the Lord's deliverance.

◆ GOSPEL: "Cup" is a recurring biblical image for "destiny," one we associate with the Garden of Gethsemane (the translation in the Lectionary is "chalice"). Jesus leaves no doubt at all that the "cup" threatened by Jeremiah will spill over not only into his own future but also the future of all those who want to follow him. Ironically, the road to the glory Zebedee's wife asks for her sons is through the bitter dregs of humiliation, suffering and death. Lenten repentance will not spare us the cup but rather strengthen us to choose it with Christ.

The Roman Missal

In the Collect, we ask God to keep his "family," the Church, "schooled always in good works," to surround us with his protection, and to lead us to heaven. Lent is this school for our souls.

The Eucharist is a "holy exchange" (Prayer over the Offerings). We offer to God the sacrifice his Son offered for us, and in return, God gives us forgiveness. The Communion we have received is our "pledge of immortality." We pray that it may "work for our eternal salvation" (Prayer after Communion).

The Prayer over the People asks God for everything we need to live the Christian life: grace and protection, health, love, and devotion.

Today's Saint

St. Casimir was a prince of Poland and of the Grand Duchy of Lithuania. Born in the royal palace in Kraków, he was heir apparent to the throne. When the king went to Lithuania, Casimir was left in charge of Poland from 1481 to 1483, and it is said that he ruled with great justice and prudence. Casimir was known for his piety and devotion. Weakened by fasting, he developed a lung disease that was probably tuberculosis, and died. St. Casimir is buried in the cathedral of Vilnius, in Lithuania.

T H U 5 (#233) violet
Lenten Weekday

Lectionary for Mass

◆ FIRST READING: The dark clouds that gather over Jesus's path and ours might send us scurrying for support to the strong men and women we admire and trust and sometimes thrust before us as a shield to protect us, while we cower in the safety of their shadow. Instead, we must step out to take responsibility for our own decisions and their consequences. We will do that in no uncertain terms when we renew our baptismal promises at Easter. Now is the time to practice the decisiveness that will require.

◆ RESPONSORIAL PSALM 1: Our antiphon echoes the true blessedness and happiness of the one firmly rooted in the Lord. The stanzas continue this theme and point to God's law as the ground in which we remain firmly planted in the Lord.

◆ GOSPEL: The rich man is a vivid icon of a man who refused to take responsibility. He did no harm to the beggar at his door; he simply did him no good. To do no harm was demanded of us last week as Lent's first asceticism, but its real purpose is to free us to do the good asked of us if we would really reflect God's love. Love is the greatest sacrifice, as the cross teaches. Let us join the rich man in looking back at our lives from beyond death's door. What has really mattered?

The Roman Missal

Today's Collect brings to mind how the purification we undergo during Lent can restore us to innocence, as it asks that being caught up in the fire of the Holy Spirit, "we may be found steadfast in faith and effective in works." The Prayer over the Offerings again highlights the necessary connection between our exterior behaviors of Lenten disciplines and our interior dispositions and conversion: those disciplines are supposed to both be a sign of and bring about the inward, spiritual realities. The Prayer after Communion prays that the sacrifice we have just celebrated may truly be active and strong within us.

Any one of the four Prefaces of Lent assigned for the day could be used equally appropriately. Even though the Prayer over the People is optional on weekdays it would be good to use it today to highlight the liturgical time.

F R I 6 (#234) violet
Lenten Weekday

The Lectionary for Mass

◆ First Reading: Jealousy blinded Joseph's brothers to the point where they decided to kill him, their own flesh and blood. They would have gained nothing but the grief of their father, whom they claimed to love. Ironically, Joseph, sold into slavery for a handful of silver, later saved them and all they valued from death. Joseph is yet another Old Testament preview of what awaits Jesus.

◆ Responsorial Psalm 105: Today's psalm tells a bit more of Joseph's story: how the evil inflicted upon him by his brothers worked unto good in the hands of God. Joseph's ability to interpret dreams won his release from his Egyptian prison and led to a position in Pharaoh's royal court.

◆ Gospel: Jealousy likewise blinded the tenants to the point where they decided to kill the heir to the vineyard so they could take over. What did murder get them? Their own destruction. Their story is a preview of the story of Jesus as it should logically have turned out, had not God so oddly opted to script the Easter events according to the pattern of Joseph's story instead. Fortunately for all of us, whatever role we play in the story, the logic of mercy prevails over the logic of vengeance in every story God writes.

The Roman Missal

The Collect notes the purifying effect that the practice of penance has and so goes on to ask that, being purified, we may be led "in sincerity of heart / to attain the holy things to come." The Prayer over the Offerings again connects the offering of our worship at the sacrifice of the Mass with the way we live our everyday lives in a reciprocal relationship: it asks that God's grace may both prepare us "for the worthy celebration of these mysteries," and that we may be led to the celebration "by a devout way of life." The Prayer after Communion expresses how the Eucharist is a foretaste of the fullness of the kingdom yet to come as it asks that "Having received this pledge of eternal salvation," we may "attain the redemption you promise."

Any one of the four Prefaces of Lent would be equally appropriate today. Even though the Prayer over the People is optional on weekdays it would be good to use it today to highlight the liturgical time.

S A T 7 (#235) violet
Lenten Weekday

Optional Memorial of Sts. Perpetua and Felicity, Martyrs / violet

The Lectionary for Mass

◆ First Reading: The logic of vengeance, which we do sometimes attribute to God, would require that God tread underfoot the sinners rather than our sins. Scripture is not bashful about speaking of God's anger, but often, as here, it seems to be the anger of love thwarted by our determination to stick our fingers into the fire despite all warnings. Fingers burned, we turn fearfully to confront God's rage, only to find instead the Divine Physician busy with burn cream and bandages, delighted that we have survived in spite of ourselves.

◆ Responsorial Psalm 103 praises God's benefits: forgiveness, healing, and deliverance from that which threatens to destroy. From the depths of the sea to the heights above the earth, as far as east is from west—it is the image of a cross, his unbounded love, his immeasurable forgiveness.

◆ Gospel: Once again we see the logic of love triumph over the logic of vengeful punishment. The story is so familiar that we might fail to consider the alternative ending if the younger son, penitent—or at least hungry—were to return home to a door barred by a wounded father who refuses all pleas for forgiveness. Instead, it is the righteous, or self-righteous, older brother who is shut out of the party, but only by his own blind jealousies and resentments.

The Roman Missal

The Collect for today twice uses a this-life/next-life-to-come contrast; first, it acknowledges that in being granted "glorious healing remedies while still on earth" we are already "partakers of the things of heaven;" second, it asks that we might be guided through this present life to be brought "to that light in which you dwell." The Prayer over the Offerings points to the fruits that can be gained from our participation in this sacrifice, namely, being restrained from "unruly desires" and being led "onward to the gifts of salvation." The Prayer after Communion directs our attention to the inner workings of the sacrament, specifically our request that it "fill the inner depths of our heart" and "make us partakers of its grace."

Prefaces I–IV are the choices once again today. While any one is appropriate, perhaps Eucharistic Prayer for Reconciliation I, with its own Preface, would be a good choice for today, insofar as that Preface tells how God is rich in mercy, offering constant pardon, how he never turned away despite how humanity broke the covenant again and again, and how now is a time for turning back. These themes would complement the parable of the lost son in today's account of the Gospel.

Today's Saints

Saints Perpetua and Felicity are Christian martyrs who died on March 7, 203. Perpetua was a noblewoman of Carthage in North Africa and Felicity her slave. The account of their imprisonment is thought to have been written by Perpetua herself, one of the first writings by a woman in Church history. The sufferings of the two women were compounded by the fact that Perpetua was a new mother, separated from her unweaned baby, and Felicity was in the last month of pregnancy, anxious about her unborn child. Two deacons bribed the guard and were able to get into the jail, bringing Perpetua's baby with them, and she was able to keep him with her and nurse him. In spite of attempts by her father to persuade her to deny her Christian faith, Perpetua kept her resolve. For refusing to sacrifice to the gods, Perpetua, Felicity, and four companions were condemned to be thrown to the beasts in the games. Because of a law forbidding the execution of pregnant women, Felicity feared that she would be separated from the others, but she gave birth two days before their day of execution. Eventually, a basilica was built in Carthage over the site of their grave; an ancient inscription with their names can still be seen. Saints Felicity and Perpetua are patron saints of mothers, pregnant women, and the city of Carthage.

8 Third Sunday of Lent
(#29)   violet

The Lectionary for Mass

◆ FIRST READING: Today's readings continue the reflections begun last Sunday. Exodus spells out the covenant law which Moses received on Mount Sinai, this episode explaining some of the reasons and significance of Moses's appearance with Jesus on the Mount of Transfiguration. The covenant law sets out the road we are to follow across life's desert as we seek to grow into the holiness into which we are baptized in Christ, the new covenant.

◆ RESPONSORIAL PSALM 19 provides a glorious affirmation of the gift of the law of the Lord. It is a love song that cherishes the law of the Lord. The "law of the LORD is perfect," trustworthy, right, clear, pure, and true. It enlightens the people and is the source of wisdom. It is more precious than gold. It is the law that forms God's people and draws them near. It is the law that defines this newly established covenant.

◆ SECOND READING: We proclaim Christ crucified, a stumbling block to many, but to those who are called, the wisdom of God. In Luke's account of the Transfiguration, Moses and Elijah converse with Jesus about his "exodus," the passage through death to life we are preparing to celebrate and live through the Easter sacraments of Baptism and Eucharist. To celebrate, never mind participate in, a death, and such a cruel death, seems utterly senseless to anyone who has not known Christ and the power of his Cross. We walk in the light of a wisdom that would be folly without hope in the Resurrection, our ultimate goal.

◆ GOSPEL: On the Mount of Transfiguration, the disciples caught a glimpse of the fire that burns in the depth of the mystery of Christ. From Moses's first encounter with God in the bush that burned in Horeb, God accompanied his people through the desert in a fiery cloud that eventually filled the Holy of Holies in the Jerusalem Temple. Jesus, in whom the fire still burns, claims to be the new Temple, no longer susceptible to destruction by enemies, even on the Cross, but still and forever present with God's people.

The Lectionary for Mass: Year A Readings (RCIA)

◆ FIRST READING: Tired and unsure of their future, the Israelites demand that Moses fix their intolerable situation. Moses himself is tremendously frustrated and minces no words with God. God answers the plea of his messenger with instructions to obtain water from the rock in Horeb. The people demanded water, but they really wanted God to send them a sign of his presence. It is a very human story because it reveals the truth that it is easy to trust that God is in our midst when everything is going well in our lives.

◆ RESPONSORIAL PSALM 95 is sung jubilantly by a people who have found the one true God. Yet, the psalm's final verse refers to that failure of faithfulness. But, even when we are not faithful, God is.

◆ SECOND READING: Paul's writing is complex, but his message is simple: Christ died for all humans and, in doing so, proved God's great and unconditional love for all. That supreme and generous act is the source of our hope and the reason for our trust.

◆ GOSPEL: In this Gospel, Jesus initiates a conversation with a woman of Samaria who is sitting alone at the town well in the noonday heat. She is so dumbfounded by this that she forgets her societal status and blurts, "How can you . . . ask me . . . for a drink?" Thus begins one of the longest and most fascinating conversations of the New Testament. Jesus asks for a drink, but then reveals he is the source of water that will quench thirst for all eternity. The woman then reverses the dialogue and says, "Give me this water." At this point, the conversation shifts and the testimony of faith begins to unfold. Jesus, aware that she has been married five times, tells her to get her husband. In doing so, Jesus recites details of her life that no stranger could know. She asks Jesus if he is the Messiah. And the world is forever changed with these words: "I am he, the one speaking who is with you." She is the first to hear the news and share it with others. Some have said she is the first missionary to proclaim the news. What we remember is that this woman stands in a long line of witnesses who have journeyed in faith before us. Buoyed by their faith, we are called to continue that journey today

The Roman Missal

The Gloria is omitted today. There are two sets of Mass formularies that might be used today: one is the Mass for the Third Sunday of Lent; the other is "For the First Scrutiny."

The Collect for this Sunday mentions the three traditional Lenten practices of prayer, fasting, and almsgiving and identifies them as a remedy for sin. After doing so, the prayer asks that God, looking "graciously on this confession of

our lowliness," may lift us up by his mercy, despite the fact that we are "bowed down by our conscience." The Prayer over the Offerings reminds us that if we are going to "beseech pardon for our own sins," then we must be willing to forgive our neighbor; the two are connected.

There is a Preface that is given on the pages right there along with the other texts for this Mass — "The Samaritan Woman." It is to be used when the Gospel story of the Samaritan woman is read. Referring explicitly to the Samaritan woman, this Preface speaks of the thirst for faith, and of how faith is in the first place a gift given by God. Consider chanting the introductory dialogue and the Preface today; if this is not the regular practice of your community, this can be a way of powerfully drawing attention to the solemnity of Lenten time (but be sure to prepare and rehearse your assembly as needed, especially if your people are not familiar with the responses!).

The Prayer after Communion relates how the Eucharist we receive here and now on earth is a foretaste and sign of the heavenly reality that it sacramentalizes. The prayer uses an interesting appellation for the sacrament: "the pledge / of things yet hidden in heaven." We ask that our participation in the Paschal Mystery celebrated in the Mass comes to "true completion."

The Prayer over the People is required, not optional, on the Sundays of Lent, and the text is given right after the Prayer after Communion.

First Scrutiny

If your parish is celebrating the First Scrutiny with the elect, then, according to a rubric in the Missal, the proper prayers should be used; these Mass formularies are found in the "Ritual Masses" section of the Missal, under segment I — For the Conferral of the Sacraments of

Initiation; #2 — For the Celebration of the Scrutinies; A — For the First Scrutiny. Here is provided a Collect, a Prayer over the Offerings and a Prayer after Communion. The Preface assigned is the Preface of the Third Sunday of Lent, the same Preface found at that Mass as described above. There are also special inserts to be used in the Eucharistic Prayers, particular ones for Eucharistic Prayers I, II, and III (since those insert texts are given separately from the Eucharistic Prayer itself, some preparation will have to be done to avoid an awkward delay caused by the flipping of pages back and forth; the insert text can be copied onto a card and affixed or attached in some way to its proper place in the Eucharistic Prayer being used). There is no Prayer over the People given for the Mass for the First Scrutiny; however, this does not mean one cannot be used. Presumably, the priest would have a choice from either the Prayer over the People for the Third Sunday of Lent or even Solemn Blessing #5, "The Passion of the Lord."

The Mass orations for the First Scrutiny are beautiful prayers that focus intently on the elect's approaching initiation. The prayers refer to the elect directly, in the Collect as "these chosen ones," in the Prayer over the Offerings as "your servants," and in the Prayer after Communion as "those you are to initiate through the Sacraments of eternal life." The Collect describes how they will be "fashioned anew through your glory" as the dignity that was lost by original sin will be restored when they "come worthily and wisely to the confession of your praise." The Prayer over the Offerings is the same prayer that was used on Friday of the Second Week of Lent, but it takes on a whole new layer of meaning used in this occasion as it includes those who are preparing for the sacraments. The Prayer after

Communion asks the Lord to give help and protection to those whom he is preparing to initiate.

For the actual ritual of the scrutiny itself, consult RCIA, 150–156. The scrutiny takes place after the Homily.

Other Ideas

Friday, March 13, is the anniversary of the election of Pope Francis. Include a special intention for Pope Francis in the Universal Prayer.

MON 9 (#237) violet
Lenten Weekday

Optional Memorial of St. Frances of Rome, Religious / violet

The Lectionary for Mass

Please note that the optional readings for the Third Week of Lent may be used on any day this week (#236).

◆ FIRST READING: One of the most difficult asceticisms is to abandon expectations too narrow to make space for the unexpected work of God. The imperious army commander, perhaps expecting an obsequious welcome, mysterious incantations, and elaborate potions, nearly sacrifices healing to his disdain for the unpretentious package in which it comes.

◆ RESPONSORIAL PSALM 42: Like the deer that yearns for life-giving streams, the psalmist thirsts for God and prays for enlightenment on the way to God's dwelling place.

◆ GOSPEL: Sadly, the faithful worshippers with whom Jesus grew up do allow their rabid biases to deprive them of the healing that Jesus, a mere carpenter's son, could have brought them. Religious narrow-mindedness can strangle the divine offers of new life before they can take root just because they break out of the boxes in which we would like to confine even God. Freedom is an essential dimension of conversion of heart if we would

welcome Christ, the life-bringer, with open doors at Easter.

The Roman Missal

The Collect for today notes how the Church needs God's compassionate cleansing and protection, because without it, the Church cannot stand secure; the prayer reminds us that unlike any human society or association, the existence of the Church is rooted in God, and without that divine union, she does not exist. The Prayer over the Offerings refers implicitly to the holy exchange that takes place in the Liturgy of the Eucharist: we offer our gifts of bread and wine as tokens of our service, indeed, of our very selves, and we pray that they will be transformed into the "sacrament of salvation." The Prayer after Communion prays that our sharing in the sacrament will result in purification and unity.

Any one of the four Prefaces of Lent can be used today. While any one is appropriate, you might also consider using Eucharistic Prayer for Reconciliation II with its own Preface. The themes of universality and of salvation being extended to those thought to be outsiders as presented in the readings would be continued in phrases such as the Church's being "an instrument of your peace among all people" and bringing together "those of every race and tongue" to "the unending banquet of unity" that are found in the second part of the Prayer.

Even though the Prayer over the People is optional on weekdays, it would be good to use it to highlight the liturgical time.

Today's Saint

St. Frances (1384–1440) was born in Rome to wealthy parents. Although she wanted to enter a monastery, her parents married her off to Lorenzo Ponziano, commander of the papal troops in Rome. It was a happy marriage that lasted 40 years. Her husband was often away at war,

and Frances spent her time praying, visiting the poor, and caring for the sick. Eventually, her example inspired other wealthy women to do the same. Frances founded a lay congregation of Benedictine Oblates now known as Oblates of Saint Frances of Rome.

TUE 10 (#238) violet
Lenten Weekday

The Lectionary for Mass

◆ FIRST READING: Daniel's prayer calls on history, promise, political disaster, and loss of reputation to bolster the plea for forgiveness, but God actually needs no elaborate convincing. The Divine Mercy stands waiting to pour out healing as soon as a contrite and humble heart flings open the doors to welcome it. Real contrition promises to set aside all other concerns to grow into the life God so eagerly offers.

◆ RESPONSORIAL PSALM 25: Today's psalm is yet another plea that God will remember the covenant promises of old and act with mercy. The first and last stanzas reiterate the psalmist's prayer that God will reveal his way.

◆ GOSPEL: There are conditions attached to God's offer of mercy, though. The one Jesus keeps repeating during Lent is that we do for others what we are asking God to do for us: forgive over and over and over again until the broken relationship is healed. And if it is broken again, forgive again. God does, and we are made in God's image.

The Roman Missal

We pray in the Collect for God's continued grace, that we may dedicate ourselves to his "holy service," and receive his help in our need. We pray in the Prayer over the Offerings that the sacrifice we offer may cleanse us of sin, and be pleasing to God. In the Prayer after Communion, we ask for "pardon and protection" through our sharing in the Eucharist. In the Prayer over the People, we ask God to drive sin away from us, so that we may remain safely under his protection.

WED 11 (#239) violet
Lenten Weekday

The Lectionary for Mass

◆ FIRST READING: On Monday, we read about a leper who wanted to set the rules for his own healing. How ready we can be to forget past Lents and Easters, and to forget all that God has done for us by playing by a different set of rules than our own expectations would dictate—for example, the rule that the dead stay dead. How adamant we can be about making our own rules even for holiness rather than listening carefully and traveling by the paths God sets out for us.

◆ RESPONSORIAL PSALM 147: The heart of the close relationship God has established with Israel is the word, the law, he has spoken to them.

◆ GOSPEL: Obedience itches. Casual Gospel readers may fondly imagine that Jesus threw out all of God's directives for holiness in favor of "anything goes, as long as it feels right." Jesus argues instead that he has come neither to throw out God's word nor to write a new set of commandments. He has come rather to live out before our eyes, teaching as he goes, the depth to which keeping God's laws of love must take us. Redemption is not novelty but fidelity.

The Roman Missal

Today's Collect reminds us that we can look on our Lenten observance as a school of prayer, and it also speaks of our being nourished by God's Word. Thus, the prayer goes on to ask that in that schooling and nourishment we may be totally devoted to God, and united with him

(and with one another) in prayer. The Prayer over the Offerings entreats God to accept the prayers of his people along with the sacrificial offerings they make, and it asks God to defend those who celebrate those mysteries "from every kind of danger." The Prayer after Communion requests that as a result of our being fed at the heavenly banquet of the Eucharist, we may be cleansed and made worthy to receive God's promises.

Any one of the four Prefaces of Lent designated for today could be used to equal benefit.

Although the Prayer over the People is optional on weekdays, it would be good to use it to highlight the liturgical time.

THU 12 (#240) violet
Lenten Weekday

The Lectionary for Mass

◆ FIRST READING: Imagine finding written on your tombstone, "Died of not listening to the word of life." Deafness of heart is a tragedy chosen rather than inflicted. We can make ourselves deaf by locking ourselves into coffins walled with unbreakable prejudice, narrowness of mind, or simply wrongs unexamined and reiterated until we can imagine no alternatives. To ignore the gift of life is to refuse it. What a shame!

◆ RESPONSORIAL PSALM 95: The theme of listening is echoed in today's Psalm 95, particularly in the antiphon and the last stanza of the psalm. Only through true obedience to his word can we offer a fitting sacrifice of praise; only then, do we truly let ourselves be guided by the Lord our shepherd.

◆ GOSPEL: Jesus paints yet another dimension of selective deafness of heart. We can dismiss the speaker, be it a prophet, a teacher, or Jesus himself, by blackening the name of the one whose words we dislike.

Or we can simply sit on the fence, watch Jesus debate opponents, and take no side lest we be discomforted by a commitment. But Jesus says that fence-sitting is a commitment—against rather than for.

The Roman Missal

There is somewhat of a sense of urgency in today's Collect, which takes note of the journey we are on toward the celebration of Easter. Referring to that upcoming feast as "the worthy celebration of the Paschal Mystery," the prayer asks that as that feast draws closer, "we may press forward all the more eagerly" toward it. Thus, we are again reminded of the ultimate purpose of our Lenten journey, which is to share in the risen life of Christ celebrated at Easter. The Prayer over the Offerings asks that we be cleansed "from every taint of wickedness" in order that the gifts we offer will be pleasing to God. The Prayer after Communion points out that those who receive the sacrament are raised up; the prayer then goes on to ask that, so raised, "we may come to possess your salvation" both in what we celebrate and in the way we live life as disciples.

Any one of the four Prefaces of Lent would be equally appropriate today.

Continue to use the Prayer over the People given for the day at the end of Mass to highlight the liturgical time.

FRI 13 (#241) violet
Lenten Weekday

The Lectionary for Mass

◆ FIRST READING: To worship God is to participate in Christ's Lenten and Easter work of returning to Eden. But which God? It wasn't only in ancient Israel that people were tempted to set up the products of their own work, or even the work itself, on an altar, and sacrifice even their children to it in a mistaken act of worship. Hosea offers a criterion for discernment: does the God who claims all your loyalty return compassion, healing, and a fruitfulness that will feed the true hungers of the heart for beauty, shelter, bread, and wine?

◆ RESPONSORIAL PSALM: Returning to the Lord means listening and obeying his word. We hear the Lord reminding Israel of what he has done for them in the stanzas of today's psalm and calling them to hear and obey. Then they will find life and blessing. What foreign gods do we worship? What are we called to hear and obey?

◆ GOSPEL: One way to evade the question is to grow a plethora of gods, ranking the God Jesus preaches in some vague heaven while devoting heart, understanding, and strength to the gods of our creation. But do they transform our selfishness to love of neighbor?

The Roman Missal

The Collect for today specifies what we want God's grace to do for us: we ask that "we may be constantly drawn away from unruly desires" and more closely obey the "heavenly teaching," which has been given to us as a gift. In the Prayer over the Offerings we ask that the offerings will be pleasing to God and beneficial for us. In the Prayer after Communion we pray that as a result of sharing in the sacrament, God's strength will be at work in us completely, "pervading our minds and bodies" and bringing us "the fullness of redemption."

Any one of the four Prefaces of Lent can be used today. While any one is appropriate, perhaps Preface II has a certain resonance with the Gospel, with phrases in the Preface such as the renewing and purifying of our hearts, and our being freed from disordered affections.

Continue using the Prayer over the People given for the day as a way of underscoring Lenten time.

SAT 14 (#242) violet
Lenten Weekday

The Lectionary for Mass

◆ FIRST READING: Lent tempts us to dwell on sacrificing the pleasures of food and ownership. To concentrate on saying no to whatever we have given up without turning to say yes to whatever aspects of love God asks of us tends to go the way of Ephraim and Judah's morning cloud and dew, which evaporate in the heat of a long day. Self-satisfaction is like a meal that requires course after course to keep us from feeling hungry again. Love given away leaves the giver well filled.

◆ RESPONSORIAL PSALM: Our antiphon is the last line of the reading, only here "love" (Hosea 6:6; literally "covenant love") is rendered as "mercy" (antiphon). Psalm 51 is a penitential psalm. Again, there is the reminder: sacrifice apart from a contrite heart means nothing.

◆ GOSPEL: It may be an accident of English translation that the Pharisee recites his list of sacrifices "to himself." But it is also a discomforting truth. The Pharisee, having impressed the ego he has mistaken for God, seems untroubled by the answering silence. The tax collector, icon of a true Lent of the heart, addressed God with a humble confession of sin, asking no affirmation at all but only mercy. And God heard and granted his prayer.

The Roman Missal

The Collect connects our observance of Lent with what they are oriented toward, namely, celebrating with joy the Paschal Mystery at Easter; that is the focus our hearts should be set on. The Prayer over the Offerings prays simply that it is by God's grace that we can approach

the celebration of the mysteries, and so we ask that our minds may be made pure. The prayer includes an interesting phrase about the mysteries, as it asks that we may offer God "fitting homage in reverently handing them on." The phrase can remind us of how our celebrations of the Eucharist are not isolated actions, but instead should be seen as actualizations that perpetuate the one offering made by Christ, that offering made present in our space and time through the Spirit. The Prayer after Communion asks for heavenly assistance so that we might seek God with all our hearts and be granted what we request. Perhaps too we can hear the phrases "minds made pure" and "fitting homage" in light of the virtue of humility that is emphasized in the Gospel.

While any one of the four Prefaces of Lent can be used today, perhaps Preface III with its reference to God's will that we "humble our sinful pride" would echo the Gospel reading.

Even though the Prayer over the People is optional on weekdays, it would again be good to use it.

☼ 15 (#32) violet or rose
Fourth Sunday of Lent

The Lectionary for Mass

◆ FIRST READING: Here we read of the tug-of-war between the paradoxes of Lent. On the one hand, we hear of the infidelities of God's people and, on the other, their exile rescinded by a liberator. As sinners, we live in exile from the home God has built for us in Christ, but as pilgrims of hope, we are gradually brought home through the work of conversion.

◆ RESPONSORIAL PSALM 137: This psalm is a perfect response to the Chronicles reading that precedes it at today's liturgy. Banished to Babylon, the people remembered their homeland and "sat and wept." The psalm laments the great loss that the exile imposed and confirms that the people have learned a painful lesson. With a promise to repent and return to the Lord, the haunting refrain establishes a firm amendment of purpose: "Let my tongue be silenced, if ever I forget you!"

◆ SECOND READING: The language of exile and return is powerful, but not powerful enough to describe the true tragedy and joy of our deepest alienation and reconciliation. Cut off from the fullness of life in Christ, whether partially or completely, we are literally dead, even if we walk and breathe on life's surface. Mercy poured out from the Cross as grace cleanses and restores us to the vibrant beauty of humanity made and living in the image of God.

◆ GOSPEL: In the desert, the unfaithful people died of serpent bites — a haunting reminder of Eden — but were saved by the sight of a serpent sign ordered by God. We die of the bite of our fallen humanity but are saved by that same humanity nailed to a cross to raise us up again. Our deliverer is no Persian king or bronze image but the very Son of God, sent to bring us out of exile and death into the light of life. Let us recall that in the Bible, the only source of light was fire, the fire burning in Christ, the true light of the world.

The Lectionary for Mass: Year A (RCIA)

◆ FIRST READING: This passage introduces the great King David to posterity. We first find David in the fields tending his sheep, not in royal surroundings. It is a reminder that God's ways often challenge human presumptions. God has sent Samuel to Bethlehem to anoint one of Jesse's sons. Jesse presents seven sons, and Samuel thinks Eliab is the one. But the Lord reminds Samuel that lofty stature is not God's measure of success, for "the LORD looks into the heart," rather than at the exterior appearance. When none of the seven proves to be the chosen one, Samuel asks, "Are these all the sons you have?" Sure enough, there is one more. David, the youngest, is tending the sheep. When David appears, the Lord pronounces, "this is the one." Samuel anoints David in the presence of his family to establish that David is filled with the Lord. From now on all would know that David's power and authority came from God.

◆ RESPONSORIAL PSALM 23: It is no accident that this psalm is paired with the Samuel reading, for it continues the shepherd theme, inviting us to reflect on the image of God as our shepherd. In our times, shepherds are not a fixture of daily life as they once were. In the time of David, shepherds were guardians and caretakers for sheep, who were dependent on them. The shepherd fed them and protected them. If they were lost, they could not find their way home without the shepherd. The message to us is that the Lord is our shepherd who will walk with us through every dark valley. When we feel lost, he will lead us to safety. When we feel trapped, he will give us courage. When we feel alone, he will lead us to his table of plenty. No wonder this is a beloved psalm, for indeed, it reminds us that the Lord will always lead us home.

◆ SECOND READING: The letter to the Ephesians is written from a post-Resurrection understanding that Christ Jesus destroyed the power of darkness with his victory over death. The passage for the Fourth Sunday of Lent is part of a section of Ephesians (4:25 — 6:20) that outlines ethical guidelines for Jesus's followers. Though addressed to the people of Ephesus, this letter has significance for the entire body of Christ, the Church. This particular excerpt advises all to "live as children of light, for light produces every kind of goodness and righteousness and truth" (Ephesians 5:8–9). But what would define a life of light that is "pleasing to the Lord" (Ephesians 5:10)? The beginning of the chapter holds the key: "live in love, as Christ loved us" (Ephesians 5:2). Those who follow Christ the Light will learn that love of each other in the Lord identifies us as Christian.

◆ GOSPEL: For people blessed with eyesight, it can be very difficult to understand what it must have been like to be the blind man in this Gospel passage. Think about a man who has been blamed all of his life for his own blindness. Think about his willingness to trust Jesus. Imagine him feeling the mud on his eyes and his walk to Siloam to wash. Consider his feeling of vulnerability as his parents left him on his own to explain this miracle. And think of his courage in response to the Pharisees' questions. He called Jesus a prophet whose power clearly came from God. When asked a second time, his pointed response, "I told you already and you did not listen" (John 9:27), placed him among Jesus's disciples. In his final encounter with Jesus, the former blind man makes a tremendous assent to faith with the words, "I do believe, Lord" (John 9:38). John wanted to address a community dispute between disciples of Moses and Jesus. One group thought Jesus was a sinner;

the other, that he was from God. When asked to take a side, the blind man at first ignored the theological dispute: "One thing I do know is that I was blind and now I see" (John 9:25). Pushed further, he said, "we know that God does not listen to sinners" (John 9:31). It's a statement of courage that puts the blind man at odds with the authorities of his faith community. Now he sees. His trust in Jesus filled him with courage to speak the truth. Will we have this same courage?

The Roman Missal

Traditionally, this Fourth Sunday of Lent marks a joyful relief amidst the seriousness and somberness of the many weeks of preparation for Easter. Hence, today is called *Laetare* Sunday, a name that comes from the Entrance Antiphon for this Mass. Rose-colored vestments may be worn, and the altar may be decorated with flowers. However, the Gloria is still omitted today.

Also, as with the previous Sunday, there are two sets of Mass formularies that might be used today: one is the Mass for the Fourth Sunday of Lent; the other is "For the Second Scrutiny."

The Collect for this Sunday recalls how God has reconciled the human race to himself through his Word; salvation was accomplished through the Paschal Mystery of the Word-made-flesh, Jesus. It is because of God reconciling us to himself (something we could not have accomplished) that we can make the petition the second part of the Collect offers: that "the Christian people may hasten / toward the solemn celebrations to come." Thus does the prayer orient us toward Easter.

The Prayer over the Offerings mentions the joy that characterizes today as it notes that we place our offerings before God "with joy." We are also reminded of the inherently missionary nature of the Eucharist—how it is not something just for ourselves, but rather how it impels us to look outward to serve the world—as the prayer goes on to note that we present these offerings "for the salvation of all the world."

The Preface that is given on the pages right there along with the other texts for this Mass, "The Man Born Blind," is to be used today. Do not use Preface I or II of Lent; that is meant for other years when that Gospel is not read. Using the motif of humanity's being led out of darkness into "the radiance of the faith," the Preface relates how being "born in slavery to ancient sin" (that is, original sin) is to be in darkness, and how we are led out of that darkness "through the waters of regeneration." The theme of the Sacrament of Baptism as enlightenment could not be clearer here, a reference so appropriate as the Church approaches the Easter Vigil when the elect will be baptized and the faithful will renew their baptismal promises. Consider chanting the introductory dialogue and the Preface today; if this is not the regular practice of your community, this can be a way of powerfully drawing attention to the solemnity of Lenten time. Be sure to prepare and rehearse your assembly as needed, especially if your people are not familiar with the responses!

The Prayer after Communion continues the focus on light as it acknowledges how God enlightens everyone who comes into the world, and it asks that he will illumine our hearts so "that we may always ponder what is worthy and pleasing to your majesty and love you in all sincerity."

The Prayer over the People is required, not optional, on the Sundays of Lent, and the text is given right after the Prayer after Communion.

Second Scrutiny

If your parish is celebrating the Second Scrutiny with the elect, then, according to a rubric in the Missal, the proper prayers should be used; these Mass formularies are found in the "Ritual Masses" section of the Missal, under segment I—For the Conferral of the Sacraments of Initiation; #2—For the Celebration of the Scrutinies; B—For the Second Scrutiny. Here is provided a Collect, a Prayer over the Offerings, and a Prayer after Communion. The Preface assigned is still the Preface of the Fourth Sunday of Lent, the same Preface found at the Mass described above. A rubric notes that there are also special inserts to be used in the Eucharistic Prayers, particular ones for Eucharistic Prayers I, II, and III, and the texts for those may be found in the texts for the First Scrutiny. Since those insert texts are given separately from the Eucharistic Prayer itself, some preparation will have to be done to avoid an awkward delay caused by the flipping of pages back and forth. The insert text can be copied onto a card and affixed or attached in some way to its proper place in the Eucharistic Prayer being used.

There is no Prayer over the People given for the Mass for the Second Scrutiny; however, this does not mean one cannot be used. Presumably, the priest would have a choice from either the Prayer over the People for the Fourth Sunday of Lent or even Solemn Blessing #5, "The Passion of the Lord."

In the Collect for the Second Scrutiny, we ask God to give the Church "an increase in spiritual joy" (echoing the joyfulness of *Laetare* Sunday); it also makes reference to the elect, asking "that those once born of earth may be reborn as citizens of heaven." The Prayer over the Offerings continues the tone of the Sunday as it notes how we place the offerings, "which bring eternal remedy," with joy before the Lord and, in so doing, we pray that we may fittingly present them "for those who seek salvation." Thus, the elect preparing for initiation are at the heart of the Church's prayer at the offering of the Sacrifice this Sunday. The Prayer after Communion petitions the Lord to sustain, correct, protect, and direct us.

For the actual ritual of the scrutiny itself, consult RCIA, 164–170. The scrutiny takes place after the Homily.

Other Ideas

The Catholic Relief Services Collection occurs today (the same group that manages CRS Rice Bowl). Refer to this website for more information (www.crsricebowl.org/).Mentioning and praying for this cause today ties in with our traditional disciplines of prayer, fasting, and almsgiving.

MON 16 (#244) violet
Lenten Weekday

The Lectionary for Mass

Please note that the optional readings for the Fourth Week of Lent may be used on any of the remaining days of this week (#243).

◆ FIRST READING: With Easter not quite yet in sight, the Lectionary scatters hints across our Lenten path that something new will walk the land in place of the grief and sorrow that have blanketed the world for so long. The cause of grief and sorrow will disappear as life replaces the death that has always come too soon.

◆ RESPONSORIAL PSALM 30: Fittingly, today's response is a song of thanksgiving for the experience of deliverance from death (first stanza) and sorrow (second and third stanzas). God has answered the psalmist's prayer.

◆ GOSPEL: The readings from John's account of the Gospel that continue all week make clear that the cause of our joy will be Jesus, the force of life who already, before

the Passion, drives out sickness and death because he is no ordinary prophet or wonderworker but someone altogether new. To bring new life, though, he must drive out old expectations and judgments. The "no" of Lent includes "no" to all that keeps us from a resounding "yes" to a world and a worldview made new by Jesus's Passover from death to life.

The Roman Missal

The Collect speaks of the renewal of the world that takes place through the sacred mysteries and, acknowledging God's eternal design, asks that he will give his help to us now. Thus, does the prayer convey a confidence in the future that God provides for us, a future that is beyond our reckoning since the mysteries through which God renews the world are "beyond all telling." We may read into this text a Christian optimism that has its foundation in the Resurrection of Christ. The Prayer over the Offerings continues this sense of optimism in the future and new life because of God's saving activity as it asks that as a result of the offering, "we may be cleansed from old earthly ways / and be renewed by growth in heavenly life." The Prayer after Communion asks for renewal and perseverance as the Eucharist renews us "within and without."

Any one of the four Prefaces of Lent is equally appropriate today.

Although the Prayer over the People continues to be optional on weekdays, its consistent use would mark the daily liturgies of Lent in a significant way.

TUE 17 (#245) violet
Lenten Weekday

Optional Memorial of St. Patrick, Bishop / violet

The Lectionary for Mass

◆ FIRST READING: On Good Friday, we will hear that water flowed

from the heart of Jesus pierced on the Cross by the soldier's lance. Jesus claimed to be the new Temple. From the crucified and risen Christ flow the waters that will bring to life all whom they touch. The waters will water new trees of life that will feed and shade all who come. Here hunger and thirst are finally quenched, as Jesus promises the woman at the well.

◆ RESPONSORIAL PSALM 46 acclaims Jerusalem, the city where God dwells, the city whose strength is the Lord. It is a city watered by life-giving streams. Such was the vision of both Ezekiel in today's First Reading and John in the Book of Revelation (22:1–2).

◆ GOSPEL: The old waters of the pool have served their time. Now comes the Source of new waters of life. The man wasted from a lifetime of illness—an image of sin in texts like Psalm 38, as Jesus seems to acknowledge in telling the man later not to sin anymore—is reborn to a new life at Jesus's word. But first Jesus asks the crucial question: "do you want to be well?" He will not impose the gift of new life on one who would really prefer to remain unchanged. The freedom to say no to life is a terrifying gift.

The Roman Missal

In another reminder of how the journey of Lent leads to the celebration of new life through Christ at Easter, today's Collect speaks of being prepared "to welcome worthily the Paschal Mystery" as a result of having our hearts shaped during this liturgical time by "the venerable exercises of holy devotion." The Prayer over the Offerings acknowledges that the gifts we offer at the Eucharist are gifts that the Lord himself has first bestowed on us; thus, the prayer notes how those offerings serve to "attest to your care as Creator," and we ask that they "effect in us the healing /

that brings us immortality." The Prayer after Communion points to the purification and renewal of our minds and help for our bodies, "now and likewise in times to come," that comes to us through "this heavenly Sacrament" of the Eucharist.

Any one of the four Prefaces of Lent is equally appropriate today. In light of the First Reading, Preface I would be a most appropriate choice. The First Reading reflects on the use of water as a symbol reminding us of the healing and new life that comes to us through Baptism and the Gospel account's emphasis on Jesus who brings healing and restoration, and as a reminder of the Sacraments of Initiation celebrated at the Easter Vigil. Preface I of Lent refers to awaiting "the sacred paschal feasts," and our participation in the mysteries by which we have been reborn, and being led "to the fullness of grace / that you bestow on your sons and daughters."

Although the Prayer over the People continues to be optional on weekdays, its consistent use would mark the daily liturgies of Lent in a significant way.

Today's Saint

Many legends have developed around St. Patrick (390–460), from driving snakes out of Ireland, to using the shamrock to explain the Trinity; however, his popularity stems beyond these stories, to his missionary zeal and astonishing ability to inspire faith. He was sold into slavery at a young age and eventually freed, and so he wanted people enslaved by doubt and skepticism to know the liberation found in Jesus Christ. Although he had little education, he was appointed Bishop of Ireland. His many accomplishments include the conversion of Ireland, ordination of clergy, consecration of virgins, and organization of missions to evangelize Europe. St. Patrick's life

has a universal appeal; therefore, his feast day is celebrated by the Roman Catholic Church, the Church of England, the Episcopal Church in America, and the Evangelical Lutheran Church in America. He also makes an appearance on the Russian Orthodox calendar. Today is a solemnity and Holyday of Obligation in Ireland.

WED 18 (#246) violet
Lenten Weekday

Optional Memorial of St. Cyril of Jerusalem, Bishop and Doctor of the Church / violet

The Lectionary for Mass

◆ FIRST READING: Isaiah sustains on our now lengthy Lenten journey with another preview of the Sacred Paschal Triduum ahead: those imprisoned in sin's dark cell will find themselves blinking in the light of the candle whose flame is Christ; the hungry and thirsty will be fed at the Lord's own table; all will be brought out of exile to the mercy, joy, and comfort of our true home in God's house. So, when we imagine ourselves abandoned on this long road across the desert, let us find hope in the covenant promise: "I will never forget you."

◆ RESPONSORIAL PSALM 145: Fittingly, this song of praise highlights the mercy God shows toward his people. The first line of the first stanza, in fact, is the very way God describes himself to Moses on Mount Sinai. The last line of the last stanza, with its theme of calling on the Lord, is a nice connection with the first line of the First Reading.

◆ GOSPEL: The ultimate promise of Lent is more than freedom, more than light, more than food and drink, more than home. These are all signs and doorways, images and aspects of the one great promise: life in Christ, now our hope, one day our sole reality, because even Easter is sign and promise of the final

fulfillment to come when the tomb of time breaks open into eternity.

The Roman Missal

The Collect focuses on our need to admit our guilt and seek pardon for our sins; we can do so with confidence, however, for the prayer rightly names God as the one who "reward[s] the merits of the just / and offer[s] pardon to sinners." At this point in Lent, if we have grown weary of the need to do penance, this prayer can refresh and renew the theme of repentance. The Prayer over the Offerings uses motifs contrasting the old and the new, asking that "the power of this sacrifice" will "mercifully wipe away what is old in us, / and increase in us grace of salvation and newness of life." The prayer can remind us that each and every celebration of the Eucharist, insofar as it is our participation in the Death and Resurrection of Christ, is an opportunity to receive new life from God in being raised up with Christ through the offering of the sacrifice. The Prayer after Communion for the Lenten Weekday identifies the Eucharist as a heavenly gift that bestows "a heavenly remedy on your people," asking that it not bring judgment on those who receive that gift; thus, we are reminded of the need to receive the Eucharist worthily, not presumptuously.

One of the four Prefaces of Lent is used today. While any one of the four is appropriate, perhaps, in light of the Collect's focus on repentance, either Preface III, with its direct reference to self-denial and humbling our sinful pride, or Preface IV, with its mention of how bodily fasting restrains our faults, would be good options.

Even though the Prayer over the People is optional on weekdays, it would be good to use it to highlight the liturgical time.

Today's Saint

St. Cyril of Jerusalem (c. 315–386), bishop of Jerusalem and Doctor of the Church, is venerated as one of the great theologians of the early Church. Like his contemporaries, he was embroiled in the Arian controversy and was exiled three times for teaching that the Son is fully divine. Cyril is best known for twenty-three lectures to catechumens, encompassing introductory teachings through post-baptismal mystagogy. From them we learn much about catechetical methods and liturgical practices in the early Church, as well as the development of teaching on the Eucharist. He was much loved by the people of Jerusalem during his lifetime for his charitable works and generosity — he even sold gifts from the emperor to raise money for the poor. Cyril is one of the Greek Fathers of the Church and is venerated by Catholics, Anglicans, and the Orthodox alike. He was named a Doctor of the Church by Pope Leo XIII in 1883.

(#543) white

THU 19 — Solemnity of St. Joseph, Spouse of the Blessed Virgin Mary

About this Solemnity/Saint

St. Joseph (first century) was an honorable and just man who took the Blessed Virgin Mary, the Mother of Jesus, as his wife. While engaged to Mary, Joseph found out that she was pregnant, but he knew he was not the father. After an angel appeared to him in a dream, in which he was told that the child was from the Holy Spirit, he courageously moved forward, and still planned to marry his beloved Mary and protect the soon-to-be Messiah. St. Joseph, a carpenter by trade, appears at various points in the four Gospel accounts, including Luke's genealogy (see Luke 3:23), the infancy narratives (see Matthew 1—2; Luke 1—2), and the flight into Egypt (see Matthew 2:13–15). Although he disappears from the Gospel after Jesus's early years, he continues to be a source of inspiration and veneration for many.

The Lectionary for Mass

◆ FIRST READING (I): Nathan's words to David foreshadow the birth of Jesus, but in the context of Lent they also point to the promise of a doorway opening onto the vista of eternity, the door opened by Jesus's Death and Resurrection. In accepting responsibility for Mary and protecting the Child, Joseph will care for the future of all the children of God born to new life in Christ.

◆ RESPONSORIAL PSALM 89: The psalmist sings of God's love and fidelity, particularly manifest in his promise of an everlasting covenant and everlasting kingship to David.

◆ SECOND READING: Joseph, who "follow[ed] the faith of Abraham," is both heir and guardian of the promise Abraham received, that his progeny would be countless, not merely in the physical sense but, even more importantly, in the sense of all those who would become children of God. We will see this promise realized yet again in the Easter sacraments.

◆ GOSPEL (I): We could have no better Lenten model than Joseph, who is asked to leave behind the carefully constructed world of laws that has hitherto defined and circumscribed his righteousness so that he is free to travel forward into an unknown future governed not by written laws but by God's astonishing mercy.

◆ GOSPEL (II): In his few Gospel appearances, Joseph never speaks. He merely does what he is asked to do in faith and without protest. Even the losses that his obedience entails do not deter him. His willingness to endure whatever suffering it takes to do what God wants of him makes him a powerful model and intercessor for our Lenten work.

The Roman Missal

All the Mass texts for this solemnity, which are proper for the day, are found in the Proper of Saints at March 19. The somberness of Lent is put aside today, and the Gloria is sung or said.

That God chose St. Joseph to watch over the Holy Family and care for Jesus is echoed in the Collect, as that prayer reminds us that the beginnings of human salvation were entrusted to the "faithful care" of St. Joseph. However, the prayer asks that just as the beginnings of salvation were entrusted to the care of St. Joseph, so may the Church "constantly watch over" the continued unfolding of those mysteries. The Church, as the guardian and caretaker of the mysteries of salvation, is herself entrusted to the guardianship and care of St. Joseph, as Patron of the Universal Church.

The Creed is said or sung today in observance of the solemnity.

The Prayer over the Offerings focuses on the theme of offering worthy service. The parallel is drawn in petitioning God that "just as Saint Joseph served with loving care / your Only Begotten Son, born of the Virgin Mary, / so we may be worthy to minister / with a pure heart at your altar." The "we" in the prayer refers to all who offer the sacrifice, not just the ordained or other liturgical ministers; rather, all who bring the offering of their sacrifice to be joined with Christ's sacrifice are the ones who minister at the altar and therefore must beg for a pure heart, so that a worthy sacrifice may be offered.

The Preface assigned for today is given right there along with the other Mass texts for the Solemnity of St. Joseph in the Proper of Saints. Its title is "The Mission of St. Joseph" and it speaks of the saint as a "just man" and a "wise and faithful servant." Although we often recognize and preach about Mary's *fiat*, let's not forget that in his own way Joseph too had to make a fiat that required openness, trust, and abandonment to the will of God, and so he is rightly called "just" and a "wise and faithful servant."

The Prayer after Communion continues the theme of protection associated with St. Joseph as it asks God that "the family you have nourished / with food from this altar" may be defended "with unfailing protection" and that the gifts we have been given from God may be kept safe.

Honoring St. Joseph

We remember the foster father of Jesus, or, as his title has been reflective of in recent calendars, the spouse of Mary, on March 19 each year. On this solemnity, it is the custom to bless bread, pastries, and other foods to be given to the poor (see BB, 1679). Some Italian parishes have the custom of having meatless dishes to share during a potluck. This comes from the time when the Italian women prayed to St. Joseph for their husbands' safe return while at sea or at war. The women would refrain from eating meat until their husbands returned. While there are many traditions and customs, see the *Book of Blessings*, 1691, for the Litany of St. Joseph that may be said during this break from the Lenten fast. Ask schoolchildren and religious education students this day to attend Mass or participate in a St. Joseph's Table celebration to remind us of the importance of this holy and righteous man. If St. Joseph is the patron of the parish, a low-key celebration of coffee, juice, and pastries might be appropriate. If the parish has an image of St. Joseph, place flowers and candles around it. If the parish is not doing a traditional St. Joseph's Table, the

assembly could be encouraged to bring food for the poor to Mass. Before the final blessing, people can be invited to bring their offerings forward and place them in baskets. The Litany of St. Joseph could be sung at this time. Then the blessing prayer is said over the baskets and the final blessing and dismissal is given.

F R I 20 (#248) violet
Lenten Weekday

The Lectionary for Mass

◆ FIRST READING: The drumroll intensifies, like thunder on a darkening horizon before the storm breaks. We are offered a disturbing preview of the mental workings of Jesus's enemies couched with astonishing accuracy in this Old Testament description of the wicked planning the destruction of the good. Their motives? Not Jesus's evildoing, but Jesus's reproach of their evildoing! Their derisive look at Jesus's firm conviction that God will vindicate him only heightens the tragedy of their own lack of any understanding of God's ways.

◆ RESPONSORIAL PSALM 34: The Lord does not abandon the just into the hands of their foes, but delivers them.

◆ GOSPEL: And here the preview begins to become reality as Jesus's enemies actively work toward his death. Even the chorus of Jerusalem bystanders admits and then denies that Jesus is the Christ. They may all know many things, even what the grapevine says about the Messiah, but they have failed to know the one thing necessary: who God is, and who Jesus is. Lent requires that we give up even mistaken certainties to surrender our entire inner being to God in Christ.

The Roman Missal

The Collect for the Lenten Weekday reminds us that the penances we

undertake during Lent are gifts that have been given to us from God as "helps for us in our weakness." As a result, those helps have healing effects on us, effects that we should receive with joy and reflect in the way we live daily "a holy way of life." The Prayer over the Offerings asks for cleansing so that we might approach the source of this sacrifice with purity; thus, does the prayer remind us that our worship can never be mere outward ritual, but must always draw us more deeply into the mystery being celebrated. The Prayer after Communion for the weekday uses the contrast between old and new to ask that we leave former ways behind and "be renewed in holiness of mind." The prayer reminds us that reception of the sacrament is never a passive reception but must represent the offering of self and the openness to transformation of a life that is continually being renewed in Christ.

Any one of the four Lenten Prefaces that are designated as options for today would be as good a choice as another.

Even though the Prayer over the People is optional on weekdays, it would be good to use it to highlight the liturgical time.

S A T 21 (#249) violet
Lenten Weekday

The Lectionary for Mass

◆ FIRST READING: The irony grows: the lamb led to slaughter will become the new Paschal Lamb whose blood poured on the wood of the Cross will save the world from death; the tree cut off will become the new Tree of Life; the name to be spoken no more will become the Name above all other names (see Philippians 2). But the greatest irony is that God's vengeance upon the destroyers will be forgiveness given from the cross.

◆ RESPONSORIAL PSALM 7: The psalmist, too, knows the rage of his foes and cries out for God's help and protection. God is sure refuge.

◆ GOSPEL: Division arises as opinions vacillate about Jesus's identity, as he had predicted it would when he claimed to bring not peace but the sword that would slice even bonds which once united families. The final sentence catches the tragedy in a nutshell: "Then each went to his own house." Isolation is complete. Yet it is this very isolation that Jesus, from Galilee, would heal on the Cross.

The Roman Missal

The Lenten Collect once again reminds us that without God we can do nothing: "without your grace / we cannot find favor in your sight." The Prayer over the Offerings points out that even in bringing our oblations we are not yet perfected, and we may in some way be defiant of God's will; nonetheless, in our offering to God, we pray that he will assist us in conforming our will to his own. This prayer, then, reminds us of the willingness to have our will transformed. This must be an inherent part of participating in the offering of the sacrifice. The Prayer after Communion for the Lenten Weekday again asks for purification so that we may be pleasing to God.

One of the four Prefaces of Lent is used today. While any one of the four is appropriate, perhaps Preface II, with its references to having our hearts purified and our being "freed from disordered affections," would be a good choice for today.

Even though the Prayer over the People is optional on weekdays, it would be good to use it to highlight the liturgical time.

☀ **22** (#35) violet
Fifth Sunday of Lent

The Lectionary for Mass

◆ FIRST READING: The new life we are promised is not individualized deliverance but deliverance from the isolation of our sin into the embrace of the new covenant forged in Christ and written in our hearts by the Paschal gift of the Holy Spirit breathed out by God upon a world renewed by the Death and Resurrection of Jesus. Love for one another will be its fruit and its sign, for love is the law and gift of the new covenant in Christ's blood.

◆ RESPONSORIAL PSALM 51 is considered one of the most beautiful penitential psalms of the Scriptures. As we pray it this day, it is appropriate to join our own need for divine forgiveness and compassion with the needs of our ancestors in faith. With the psalmist, the Hebrew people beg the Lord for the gift of forgiveness. They yearn for a clean slate, forgiveness of sins, and a new beginning. Remembering the promise of the New Covenant, they ask for clean hearts. They know they need a fresh start and they know they need the Spirit's daily presence to help them make that start and succeed. In return, they will teach sinners the way of the Lord.

◆ SECOND READING: The promise of a new covenant, or a covenant renewed, fills us with hope, but the Letter to the Hebrews reminds us of

its cost, both for Christ and for us. Obedience even unto death, death on a cross, is the only road from dead fruitlessness to a harvest of living wheat, ready to be baked into life-giving bread.

◆ GOSPEL: Christ himself is the grain of wheat buried in the earth to rise again and bear much fruit for all who have been willing to follow him through the deaths of Lent, small or great, to the light of the newly risen son. The wheat harvest, ripened in that sun, will yield bread for all the hungry. We who have been fed on the life-giving Bread that is Christ can then in turn feed the world in which we have been planted. Lent and Easter are never only about the self but always about the whole humanity to which we belong.

The Lectionary for Mass: Year A (RCIA)

◆ FIRST READING: Ezekiel served on God's behalf during the time of the Judean exile in Babylon in 593 BC. Like prophets before and since, Ezekiel was both a taskmaster and cheerleader, demanding that the people turn from wayward lives and encouraging them to place their hope in the Lord. This reading conveys a message of hope as it interprets Ezekiel's famous vision of dried bones scattered throughout the plains (37:2–10). The Lord has told Ezekiel to "prophesy over these bones, and say to them: Dry bones, hear the word of the LORD! . . . I will bring spirit into you, that you may come to life" (Ezekiel 37:4–5). Even though the people live in exile like dead bones on the plain, God has not forgotten them. He promises that he will raise them from their graves of hopelessness and bring them "back to the land of Israel" (Ezekiel 37:12). He will breathe his spirit into them and give them new life. It is not a story intended as a direct commentary on the resurrection from the dead.

It is instead a message of God's faithfulness to the people of Israel. Though bound in exile, they must know and remember that God will set them free.

◆ RESPONSORIAL PSALM 130: "With the Lord there is mercy, and fullness of redemption" (Psalm 130:7). The psalm's refrain holds the promise of redemption and new life for the people of Israel.

◆ SECOND READING: In this passage, Paul wants us to know that, through Christ's Death and Resurrection, we now belong to God in a very special way. God has sent his Spirit to remain with us and help us. Paul begins by saying that the goal of human life is to please God. He cautions that self-absorption (living in the flesh) presents a big trap that drags us away from God. But Paul also reminds his readers that the Spirit dwelling within all believers is the source and strength for living faithful lives. When distracted by things of the world, God's Spirit will help the faithful focus on what matters most. When tempted to place trust in the things of this world, Christ will help the faithful remain fixed on grace. When selfishness threatens love, the Spirit of God will help the faithful to live for others. Paul promises that, with the Spirit, believers can live righteously and thus participate in divine life.

◆ GOSPEL: Can you imagine receiving a phone call with the news that your best friend who lives nearby is dying and thinking to yourself, "I'll just wait four days and see what happens"? Of course not. That is our clue that John's narrative about Jesus's friend Lazarus speaks not of the bonds of human friendship, but rather of the power of Jesus. It helps to think of this Gospel passage as six acts of a dramatic tableau. The first act establishes the purpose of the drama: "This illness is . . . for the glory of God" (John 11:4). The

second recounts Jesus's decision to return to Lazarus's hometown even though it is dangerous to do so. The third act puts Jesus and the disciples in Bethany, where they learn that Lazarus has been dead for four days, enough time for the rabbinic scholars to believe Lazarus's soul had left his body. The fourth act introduces Martha, who first chastises Jesus and then professes her belief that his power comes from God. Martha sends for Mary as the scene changes once more, and Mary goes to meet Jesus, with the crowd of mourners accompanying her. These are the people who will return to Jerusalem with news of this miracle, fueling the call to condemn Jesus of Nazareth. The climax of the drama begins with Martha's final assertion of Lazarus's death. Jesus calls on the Father ("that they may believe that you sent me," John 11:42) and then calls for Lazarus. As Lazarus emerges from the tomb, Jesus gives a final instruction: "Untie him and let him go" (John 11:45).

The Roman Missal

The Fifth Sunday of Lent can be seen as a turning point in the Lenten journey as we enter the final days of the liturgical time, with less than two weeks left before we begin the Sacred Paschal Triduum. The Missal contains a rubric pointing to a practice that can serve as a visual reminder to the assembly that we have reached this point in Lent: the practice of covering crosses and images in the church may be observed beginning with this Sunday. Images and statues are covered until the beginning of the Easter Vigil; crosses, however, are uncovered sooner, remaining covered only until the end of the Celebration of the Lord's Passion on Good Friday. Consider doing this in your church so that the faithful continue to be engaged in the somberness and tone of Lent through the visible environment of the worship space.

Also, as with the previous two Sundays, there are two sets of Mass formularies from which to choose today: use either the Mass for the Fifth Sunday of Lent if you are not celebrating the Third Scrutiny, or the Mass for the Third Scrutiny if you are celebrating that ritual.

The Gloria continues to be omitted today.

With the celebration of the Lord's Passion approaching, the Collect for today specifically mentions how "your Son handed himself over to death." Recalling that act of love, the prayer asks that we may "walk eagerly in that same charity." The events of the Paschal Mystery are to be for all Christians, not just some remote example lived by Jesus, but rather the actual pattern of living that is grafted onto our lives, a pattern that we imitate daily.

The Prayer over the Offerings prays that because God has "instilled in your servants / the teachings of the Christian faith," we may be purified "by the working of this sacrifice." We can glean from this prayer several different levels of meaning. The phrase "teachings of the Christian faith" can certainly call to mind for us those who are being formed in the faith as they prepare for the Sacraments of Initiation; it can also remind us of our own formation and education in Christianity, a gift that has been instilled in us by the Lord himself, through the Holy Spirit, through those who formed and educated us. We can also remember that "the teachings of the Christian faith" are more than just doctrinal principles, but rather include a whole way of living life and looking at the world. The purification we ask for should involve the transformation to embrace Christian living in all its aspects.

The Preface that is given on the pages right there along with the other texts for this Mass, titled simply "Lazarus," is the Preface that is to be used today if the Year A readings are done for RCIA, and the Gospel account of Jesus raising Lazarus is the text assigned for the day. Consider chanting the introductory dialogue and the Preface today; if this is not the regular practice of your community, this can be a way of powerfully drawing attention to the solemnity of Lent (but be sure to prepare and rehearse your assembly as needed, especially if your people are not familiar with the responses!).

The Prayer after Communion is ecclesial in its focus, as it prays that through the sacrament "we may always be counted among the members of Christ, / in whose Body and Blood we have communion." The prayer is a reminder to us of a proper Eucharistic theology that understands Communion not only as union with Christ, but also as union with his Body, the Church; the liturgical act of receiving Holy Communion, although intensely personal, is never private—it is always a corporate action of the Body.

The Prayer over the People is required, not optional, on the Sundays of Lent, and the text is given right after the Prayer after Communion.

Third Scrutiny

If your parish is celebrating the Third Scrutiny with the elect, then, according to a rubric in the Missal, the proper prayers should be used; these Mass formularies are found in the section "Ritual Masses," under segment I—For the Conferral of the Sacraments of Initiation; #2—For the Celebration of the Scrutinies; C—For the Third Scrutiny. Here we find a Collect, a Prayer over the Offerings, and a Prayer after Communion. The Preface assigned is still the Preface of the Fifth Sunday of Lent, the same Preface described above. A rubric notes that there are also special inserts to be used in the Eucharistic Prayers, particular ones for Eucharistic Prayers I,

II, and III, and the texts for those may be found at the texts for the First Scrutiny. Since those insert texts are given separately from the Eucharistic Prayer itself, some preparation will have to be done to avoid an awkward delay caused by the flipping of pages back and forth. The insert text can be copied onto a card and affixed or attached in some way to its proper place in the Eucharistic Prayer being used. There is no Prayer over the People given for the Mass for the Third Scrutiny; however, this does not mean one cannot be used. Presumably, the priest would have a choice from either the Prayer over the People for the Fifth Sunday of Lent or even Solemn Blessing #5, "The Passion of the Lord."

The elect are specifically mentioned in all three of the orations for this Mass for the final scrutiny. The Collect makes explicit reference to their initiation as it prays that "these chosen ones" who have been "instructed in the holy mysteries" may "receive new life at the font of Baptism / and be numbered among the members of your Church." Of course, as we pray for those preparing for initiation, we cannot help but call to mind our own initiation and so be renewed in our own commitment to the faith. The Prayer over the Offerings acknowledges the faith that is already at work in the elect, noting that God has instilled in them as his servants "the first fruits of Christian faith." The Prayer after Communion prays for unity among all God's people, asking that as they submit themselves to God, they may obtain the grace of living out their joy at being saved and "remember in loving prayer those to be reborn." It is the role of all the faithful to pray for those preparing for the sacraments; the work of supporting those coming to the faith is work that belongs to every member of the Church.

For the actual ritual of the scrutiny itself, consult RCIA, 171–177. The scrutiny takes place after the Homily.

Other Ideas

This Wednesday is the Solemnity of the Annunciation of the Lord. Although it is not a Holyday of Obligation encourage parishioners to attend Mass because it is an important day on the Church's calendar. This is the last week before Holy Week. Make sure that all liturgical ministers are scheduled, that vestments are cleaned, and go through your basic sacristy checklist. You can refer to G. Thomas Ryan's, *The Sacristy Manual, Second Edition* (it was updated in 2012 by Corinna Laughlin). Perhaps it is time to consider purchasing the second edition of this classic text, also available from LTP.

MON 23 (#251) violet
Lenten Weekday

Optional Memorial of St. Turibius of Mogrovejo, Bishop / violet

The Lectionary for Mass

Please note that the optional readings for the Fifth Week of Lent may be used on any of the remaining days of this week (#250).

◆ FIRST READING: Two figures of women condemned to death introduce the two weeks traditionally known as Passiontide, the last part of Lent when all eyes are on the One who will himself undergo condemnation. Susannah, innocent of the sin with which her accusers charge her, is delivered by the wisdom of Daniel. A dark thread weaves her story into the unfolding of the Passion to come. When Jesus, innocent of the wrongdoing of which he is accused, suffers condemnation, there will be no deliverance.

◆ RESPONSORIAL PSALM 23 might be Susanna's song, trusting in God even in "the dark valley" (23:4).

◆ GOSPEL: The second woman accused of adultery and condemned to death by the scribes and Pharisees, also "elders" of their community, claims no innocence. Nevertheless, like Daniel, Jesus turns the accusation back onto the accusers. And they also claim no innocence. The Deliverer does not require a sinless past, only recognition of one's truth and a decision to "sin no more."

The Roman Missal

As we begin the last days of Lent, the Collect for the Lenten Weekday invites us to more and more deeply focus on entering into the Paschal Mystery and to dying and rising with Christ, particularly as that mystery will be celebrated during the Sacred Paschal Triduum, which is rapidly approaching. Thus, the prayer asks that Christ's passage will be ours: "grant us so to pass from former ways to newness of life, / that we may be made ready for the glory of the heavenly Kingdom."

The Prayer over the Offerings reminds us that the fruit of bodily penance must be "a joyful purity of heart." We might ask ourselves, after all these days of Lent so far, whether such joyful purity of heart has truly increased in us as a result of our Lenten practices. It is that same joyful purity of heart that is supposed to be the acceptable offering brought to the sacrifice. The Prayer after Communion for the Lenten Weekday asks God that we may be cleansed of our faults through the sacraments and, in an image of being raised up with Christ, requests that we may "hasten our steps upward toward you."

In keeping with the shift to the period of late Lenten time, starting today there is no longer a choice among Prefaces; rather, Preface I of the Passion of the Lord is the Preface assigned for today. It speaks explicitly of the Passion of Christ and of the "wondrous power of the Cross" that reveals both God's

judgment on the world and the "authority of Christ crucified." Consider using this Preface even if you are using one of the Eucharistic Prayers for Reconciliation (you are not required to use the Preface that goes with the Eucharistic Prayer for Reconciliation).

Continue to use the suggested Prayer over the People at the end of Mass, even though it is optional, especially in these final days of Lent.

Today's Saint

St. Turibius of Mogrovejo (1538–1606) was born into the Spanish nobility and dedicated his life to bringing Christianity to the native peoples of Peru as the missionary archbishop of Lima. He traveled the whole of his enormous diocese, usually on foot, evangelizing and baptizing as he went. Among those he baptized and confirmed were St. Rose of Lima and St. Martin de Porres. Saint Turibius also founded the first seminary in the Western Hemisphere and built roads, schools, chapels, hospitals, and convents. He is remembered for his defense of the native peoples against the injustices of the Spanish government.

TUE 24 (#252) violet
Lenten Weekday

The Lectionary for Mass

◆ FIRST READING: In this odd passage, the Israelites in the desert are bitten by serpents and healed by a bronze serpent on a pole. In the Gospel, the people are heirs to the sin that has afflicted all of humanity since Eden, as are we all. Like the Israelites, they will soon be healed by the very being that poisoned them, their humanity, raised on a cross, as we will see on Good Friday. This humanity, now borne not by sinners but by Jesus, the Word of God made flesh, redeems us all from death.

◆ RESPONSORIAL PSALM 102: In the midst of their distress, perhaps

after their exile in Babylon as the second stanza of the psalm suggests, Israel cries out for God's help.

◆ GOSPEL: Who is this man, Jesus? His hearers do not understand. Today Jesus tells us much about himself: he is from above, not of this world; he is sent by the Father who is always with him. What is more, Jesus is the great "I AM," the name God revealed to Moses in the burning bush. The "lift[ing] up" of the Son of Man (on the Cross) parallels the lifting up of the serpent. Both were a source of healing and life.

The Roman Missal

The Collect today contains an important petition, namely, that we may persevere in obeying God's will. Again, the prayer seems to recognize our need for encouragement and strength to maintain the long discipline of Lent. There is an interesting result of that perseverance that is mentioned: so that "the people dedicated to your service / may grow in both merit and number." Perhaps this phrase could remind us of the importance of giving good example to those preparing for initiation; our witness as we persevere through Lent can have a direct effect on their coming into the faith.

The Prayer over the Offerings recognizes the reconciliation that is brought about between God and humanity as a result of our participation in the sacrifice; through it, we can ask God, who is full of compassion, to pardon our offenses. The Prayer after Communion notes how a constitutive dimension of being human is to seek what is divine.

The Preface assigned for today is Preface I of the Passion of the Lord, as it will be every day this week. Use this Preface even if you are using one of the two Eucharistic Prayers for Reconciliation (you are not required to use the Preface that goes with the Eucharistic Prayers for Reconciliation).

Although the Prayer over the People continues to be optional on weekdays, its continued use would mark this late Lenten Weekday in a significant way.

W E D (#545) white
25
Solemnity of the Annunciation of the Lord

About this Solemnity

It is Luke who tells of the angelic annunciation to Mary of Jesus's birth (1:26–38). Through the angel Gabriel, the Spirit of God comes to Mary in the most unfeasible way, asking the impossible. As a young woman engaged to be married, being found pregnant would have meant her death in the culture of the time. She risks hurting Joseph, bringing shame on their families, and setting herself up for execution because she is sure of one thing: God calls her to be Mother to the Son of God. Mary is special because her faith is stronger than her fear. She does not see the road ahead but knows that God wills for her to journey it nonetheless. Trusting in God above all, she consents her will, becoming the first and most important vessel of bringing Christ's presence into the world.

The Lectionary for Mass

◆ FIRST READING (1): The recalcitrant Ahaz evaded the act of faith asked of him by disguising his refusal in pious-sounding words. God's Word achieved its promise nevertheless. Let Ahaz be a warning to us: our own evasions do not prevent God's work, except in our own hearts. Mary, Mother of Jesus, stands as Ahaz's polar opposite, as we hope to do.

◆ RESPONSORIAL PSALM 40: Today's antiphon is particularly appropriate given Mary's acceptance of the angel's word. God desires a listening heart, an obedient heart above all.

◆ SECOND READING: Again we hear that the one sacrifice necessary is obedience to God's will, as we see not only in the Incarnation of the Word but also in his obedience "unto death, / death on a cross" (Philippians 2). The Incarnation celebrated and the Passion and Resurrection to be celebrated in days to come are two panels that tell a single story, the story of our redemption.

◆ GOSPEL: The Lenten texts often exhort us to listen to God's Word. Mary listened in the most profound way possible. She received the divine Word with every fiber of her being, even to giving it her flesh and every moment of her history from that time on. Our obedient faith can never be more than a pale copy of hers, but she sustains us by example and intercession through our own growth in Lenten openness to God's word and work in us.

The Roman Missal

All the Mass texts for this solemnity are proper for the day and can be found in the Proper of Saints at March 25. As with the Solemnity of St. Joseph last week, the somberness of Lent is again put aside. The Gloria is sung or said.

The theology underlying the words of the Collect reflects the understanding that as a result of the Incarnation, humanity is given a share in divinity. Not unlike the prayer the priest prays at the mixing of a little water into the wine, ("By the mystery of this water and wine / may we come to share in the divinity of Christ / who humbled himself to share in our humanity"), this Collect asks, insofar as God willed that his Word should take on human flesh, that we "may merit to become partakers even in his divine nature."

The Creed is said today in observance of the solemnity. Today is one of two times (the other being at the Masses on the Nativity) when all genuflect, instead of bow, at the words "and by the Holy Spirit was

incarnate of the Virgin Mary and became man." Be sure your assembly is prepared for this; the priest can give a brief explanation of this in his introduction to the Creed.

The Prayer over the Offerings highlights that it is the Church that is making this offering (notice what this means in terms of liturgical theology — the entire assembly makes the offering, not just the priest), and, in so doing, she (the Church) is recognizing that her life began with the Incarnation of the Son. In God's acceptance of this offering, we pray that the Church "may rejoice to celebrate his mysteries on this Solemnity."

The Preface assigned for today is given right there along with the other Mass texts for the Solemnity of the Annunciation of the Lord in the Proper of Saints. Titled "The Mystery of the Incarnation," it relates Mary's hearing "with faith" about the Christ who was to be born "by the overshadowing power of the Holy Spirit." The text goes on to relate how, by bearing the child in her "immaculate womb" the promises made to the children of Israel were fulfilled and the hope of the world was realized.

The Prayer after Communion expresses our confession in Jesus as "true God and true man" as among the "mysteries of the true faith," and asks that we may attain eternal joy "through the saving power of his Resurrection."

No Solemn Blessing or Prayer over the People is designated for the end of Mass, but if you desired to use one, certainly Solemn Blessing #15, "The Blessed Virgin Mary," would be appropriate for today.

T H U (#254) violet
26
Lenten Weekday

The Lectionary for Mass

◆ FIRST READING: Lent could become intolerable if we were not so often reminded that we are pursuing the fulfillment of a promise made by One who keeps all promises, even so apparently impossible a promise as the one made to Abraham. The solemnities of St. Joseph and the Annunciation have set before us two strong figures whose obedient faith, like Abraham's, served the fulfillment of the promise in a way they could never have imagined. Let them give us courage to persevere toward the promise kept at Easter.

◆ RESPONSORIAL PSALM 105: The psalmist calls the descendants of Abraham to remember their covenant responsibilities and remind them of all God has done on behalf of their people.

◆ GOSPEL: The Lenten Lectionary readings are peppered not only with powerful stories of people throwing caution and comfort to the wind in order to make possible the mystery that unfolds before us at Easter but also with the tragedies of people who refused, overcome by the limitations of small, immovable expectations.

The Roman Missal

The Collect places before us in a powerful way our need for God: it states that we plead before him and we place our hope in his mercy. It also asks for perseverance in "holy living," reminding us again that the sacrifice we celebrate at the Eucharist must be put into the concrete practice of love and self-giving in our daily lives. Only then can we rightly ask, as we do in this prayer, to "be made full heirs of your promise." The Prayer over the Offerings reminds us of the missionary nature of the Eucharist, calling us beyond just our own needs, as it asks that the sacrificial offerings may both "profit our conversion / and the salvation of the world." That the offering of the Eucharist is the Church's work for the salvation of the whole world must never be forgotten. The

Prayer after Communion expresses both the earthly and the heavenly effects of the Eucharist, as it is the sacrament by which we are fed "in the present age" and through which we hope to be made "partakers of life eternal."

As with the other days this week, the Preface assigned for today is Preface I of the Passion of the Lord, and it should be used even if you are using one of the Eucharistic Prayers for Reconciliation (you are not required to use the Preface that goes with the Eucharistic Prayer for Reconciliation).

Also as with the other days of Lent, continue to use the Prayer over the People.

FRI 27 (#255) violet Lenten Weekday

The Lectionary for Mass

◆ FIRST READING: Jesus, foreshadowed by the suffering prophet Jeremiah, knew the whispers of listeners-turned-enemies that afflicted Jeremiah. Yet even on the eve of their worst plots successfully carried out, Jesus refused to turn back from the road God had laid out before him. And he was rescued, as the prophet hopes to be, not by being spared suffering and death but by being sustained through them with the trust that enables him to say on the Cross, "Father, into your hands I commend my spirit!"

◆ RESPONSORIAL PSALM 18 echoes the prayer of Jeremiah: trust in God in the midst of overwhelming distress, and the experience of God's deliverance.

◆ GOSPEL: Jesus gives his enemies chance after chance to exchange their stubborn refusal for faith, but their only response is to try to arrest him. He will not give up on them, but they have already given up on him. The loss will be theirs, but also God's. Jesus understands as they do not that in the tragic refusals

of those who reject the gift of salvation, the cost is always mutual.

The Roman Missal

There are two options for the Collect today. The first prayer is a prayer for pardon, asking that we will be set free from "the bonds of the sins / we have committed in our weakness." The second option notes how in this liturgical time the Church imitates the Blessed Virgin Mary "in contemplating the Passion of Christ," and therefore the prayer goes on to ask that through her intercession "we may cling more firmly each day / to your Only Begotten Son and come at last to the fullness of his grace." Thus, in a certain sense, this second prayer puts us at the foot of the Cross along with Mary, clinging to Jesus even throughout his Passion and Death, and prepares us well to enter into the celebration of Holy Week. The Prayer over the Offerings highlights the place of worship at the center of Christian life, as it asks "that we may be worthy / to serve ever fittingly at your altars, / and there to be saved by constant participation." "Constant participation" can remind us that life itself is to be liturgical, as the offering of our life as a sacrifice to God is to occur not only at the ritual celebration, but as a way of life every day. The Prayer after Communion asks that we might have the "unfailing protection" the sacrifice brings to us so that it will "always drive far from us / all that would do us harm."

The Preface assigned for today is Preface I of the Passion of the Lord; remember to use it even if you are using one of the Eucharistic Prayers for Reconciliation (you are not required to use the Preface that goes with the Eucharistic Prayer for Reconciliation). Continue to use the Prayer over the People as well.

SAT 28 (#256) violet
Lenten Weekday

The Lectionary for Mass

◆ FIRST READING: Sin has always broken bonds and scattered the people whom God so urgently wants to be one in the family of love so eloquently described in the Easter liturgies. Here is one of the compelling statements of God's plan for the future, with all transgression and false gods banished into memory and all the flock gathered under the single Good Shepherd. The resurrection we will soon celebrate is not a matter of individuals plucked from death but all humanity made one in the living Christ.

◆ CANTICLE: Today's response, actually taken from the prophet Jeremiah, and which is likewise spoken during the time of exile, reiterates the promise of restoration and return.

◆ GOSPEL: That ingathering of scattered humanity, each person isolated from the next by selfish sin, is not the product of God's wishful thinking or ours but of Jesus's own decision to take love to the Cross. With typical Johannine irony, Caiaphas forestalls the passing disintegration of the nation of God's people but at the price of the death of the One in whom the people will be bonded irrevocably together for all eternity.

The Roman Missal

Today's Collect begins with a clear reference to Baptism, as it states that God has made "all those reborn in Christ / a chosen race and a royal priesthood." It then goes on to ask that we will be given "the grace to will and to do what you command." The Prayer over the Offerings notes that the gifts we offer come from our fasting; here we can be especially reminded that since the acceptable sacrifice to God is a humble and contrite heart, our fasting and other Lenten penances should have that precise effect, producing hearts (and lives) that can be a gift offered to God. The Prayer after Communion prays that the nourishment we have received in the Body and Blood of Christ "may make us sharers of his divine nature." It thus highlights the transformative aspect of Eucharistic Communion, namely, that we become what we receive. The divine life given to us in our Baptism (referred to in the Collect) is nurtured and strengthened in the Eucharist.

Preface I of the Passion of the Lord is assigned for the last time today, and it should be the Preface used even with one of the Eucharistic Prayers for Reconciliation (you are not required to use the Preface that goes with the Eucharistic Prayer for Reconciliation).

Use the Prayer over the People, even though it is optional, to reinforce the themes of the liturgical time.

SUN 29 (#37, Gospel; #38) red
Palm Sunday of the Passion of the Lord

About Palm Sunday

Branches of palm, olive, or sometimes even budding willow, are ancient symbols of victory and hope, as well as of new life. The procession celebrating Jesus's entry into Jerusalem overflowed with praise and excitement, as onlookers waved these triumphant branches and proclaimed their blessings. Yet, in a few days, they will cry "Crucify him!" The crowd's change of heart illustrates the problem of holding God to our expectations. The crowd expected a liberating leader, the Messiah, to free them from Roman oppression. Jesus instead takes up his Cross and invites us to do the same. Through his Death and Resurrection he is indeed a liberator, but from death and sin, not from Rome. But unable to see past their need, the crowd's disappointment turns into anger and a death order. As we enter Holy Week, Palm Sunday teaches us to let God be God, and to trust in God's wisdom not only to meet but shatter and exceed our expectations.

The Lectionary for Mass

◆ GOSPEL AT THE PROCESSION WITH PALMS: Jesus entered Jerusalem in triumph and left in ignominy. He entered carried by a donkey colt, hailed by the crowds with branches and hosannas. He left walking, even stumbling under the weight of the Cross, to the place of execution outside the city walls, jeered there by the bystanders. Lent is a season of paradox, a season of contradictions, a season of successes and failures, culminating in the great paradox of the Cross, where all apparent failure yields to the ultimate triumph of life over death.

◆ FIRST READING: During his public ministry, Jesus did speak to the weary, the hopeless, the sick, and the grieving, a word that roused them to new purpose, the purpose of the gospel. Jesus continues to do so today, as we gather to hear the word proclaimed. But the prophet does not hide the cost. Jesus did indeed appear to be disgraced and shamed in the eyes of his short-sighted enemies, but opposition did not keep him from his appointed mission, as it must not keep us, his disciples.

◆ RESPONSORIAL PSALM 22: The words of the psalmist's lament are filled with complaint and self pity. He is mocked, scoffed at, and insulted by those around him, who say, "He relied on the LORD; let him deliver him." Yet he cannot give up on the Lord. So complain he does (22:17–18, 19), but then reminds the Lord to "be not far from me; / O my help, hasten to aid me" (22:19). These words speak of a familiar relationship that allows him to trust in the midst of great human misery. Fearful, angry, and in great need, the psalmist turns to the Lord, whose name he will ever praise and proclaim. So, too, we are encouraged to turn to the Lord in times of trouble, to speak our hearts, to complain, and to cry out with fear and loneliness. It is thus that the relationship between human and divine grows richer and deeper so that we can pray with the psalmist, "hasten to aid me."

◆ SECOND READING: This great early Christian hymn takes us through the overarching mystery of the Cross, which begins with the Word's self-emptying in the Incarnation and continues through a life of human suffering, even to the obedience of death on a cross. But the glory of Easter already shines through the dark chapters of Jesus's life, beckoning us forward in his footsteps.

◆ GOSPEL: In this shortest and most stark of the Passion narratives, the evangelist weaves into the simple unfolding of events, threads of older Scriptures that illumine the underlying meaning of what is happening. Some are heavy with literary irony: passages that tell the deeper truth about the Christ are quoted against him when in fact they validate his person and his mission beyond the wildest dreams of his opponents. Truth speaks with many voices but will not be silenced, not even by the stillness of death.

The Roman Missal

A careful reading of the Missal by all those involved in the preparation of today's liturgy will help ensure a smooth flow to the ritual. All the texts are found in the "Holy Week" section of the Missal that follows Saturday of the Fifth Week of Lent in the Proper of Time.

All Masses today take place with the Commemoration of the Lord's Entrance into Jerusalem, "to accomplish his Paschal Mystery," in the words of the Missal; that Commemoration takes place using one of three forms: the Procession, the Solemn Entrance, or the Simple Entrance. The Missal indicates that the Procession (the first form) or the Solemn Entrance (the second form) takes place before the principal Mass and that the Solemn Entrance, but not the Procession, may be repeated before other Masses that are usually celebrated with a large gathering of people (note, therefore, that the Missal envisions the first form, the Procession, taking place only once, whereas the Solemn Entrance may be used at as many Masses as is deemed pastorally advantageous in light of the gathering of the people).

First Form: The Procession

This form of the commemoration takes place with all gathering at a place other than inside the church to which the procession will go — either a smaller church, or perhaps a parish center room, or perhaps even outside. The faithful already hold palm branches.

The priest and the deacon wear red vestments; the priest may wear a chasuble, or he may wear a cope and then change into a chasuble when the procession is over. At the appointed time, the priest, deacon, and other ministers go to the place where everyone is gathered. The Missal does not indicate that this is any kind of a formal procession *per se*, so it can be an informal gathering of the clergy and ministers as they arrive at the place of beginning. The Missal does state, however, that "meanwhile" (while the ministers are assembling, or perhaps even while all are gathering, not just the ministers, to create a prayerful environment as all arrive) an antiphon or an appropriate song is sung; the antiphon suggested is from chapter 21 of Matthew's account of the Gospel: "Hosanna to the Son of David; blessed is he who comes in the name of the Lord, the King of Israel. Hosanna in the highest."

After this singing and when all have arrived, the priest begins with the Sign of the Cross and the usual liturgical greeting for Mass, followed by an introductory address. For this introduction, he may use the words given in the Missal (#5, at Palm Sunday of the Passion of the Lord); if he uses his own words, it is important that he convey the invitation for the faithful to participate actively and consciously in the celebration this day.

After the address, the priest says one of the two prayers of blessing. Only the first option includes the gesture of making the Sign of the Cross by the priest; the second one does not. The first prayer specifically asks God to bless the branches, and then goes on to ask that we "who follow Christ the King in exultation, may reach the eternal Jerusalem through him." The second option focuses more on the people "who today hold high these branches to hail Christ in his triumph," asking for their faith to be increased and their prayers to be held, so that they "may bear fruit for you by good works accomplished in him." Whichever prayer is used, however, the branches are next sprinkled after the prayer, in silence.

Then the deacon, or the priest if there is no deacon, proclaims the Gospel account of the Lord's entrance according to the proper cycle of Lectionary readings in the liturgical year; the Missal states this is done "in the usual way," meaning that there should be the greeting "The Lord be with you" and the announcement "A reading from the holy Gospel according to . . ." as is always done. Incense may also be used here. The third edition of *The Roman Missal* has the texts for this first Gospel reading right there in the Missal, which makes things much easier.

The Missal notes that after the Gospel, a brief Homily may be given. The key word concerning this Homily would seem to be "brief," if one were to be given at all—it's optional. Then an invitation is given by either a priest, deacon, or lay minister, using the words in the Missal or similar ones, to invite the people to begin the procession.

The procession is led by the thurifer, if incense is used, followed by a crossbearer. The Missal specifically points out that the cross that is carried should be "decorated with palm branches according to local custom." The cross is carried between two ministers with lighted candles. Behind this follow the deacon with the *Book of the Gospels*, the priest, the ministers, and then the faithful (note that the priest celebrant is not at the end of the procession, but rather walks before the people). Singing takes place during this procession, with various options suggested in the Missal; other appropriate songs may of course be chosen.

Keep in mind in your preparations that it will be important to choose music that will be able to be sung easily by the choir and the people as they move along in procession. Think through the route that will be used and how the movement will affect peoples' ability to sing. Think of ways to maintain the singing. *Sing to the Lord: Music in Divine Worship*

(STL, 93–94) points out that while recorded music should not normally be used in liturgy, the use of recorded music to accompany communal singing during a procession outside is an exception. Therefore, if necessary, look into resources for having pre-recorded music broadcast. For example, your choir could record the singing ahead of time, and then that recording could be broadcast outside via a bell tower or some other external speaker system, and that music would support and enhance the assembly's singing while they are processing to the church.

The Missal notes that a second song or a responsory is sung as the procession enters the church; thus, the music should change.

Then, as the procession enters the church, the priest goes to the altar, venerates it, and, if appropriate, incenses it. The people, meanwhile, continue to process into the church. He then goes to his chair, changes from cope to chasuble if necessary, and, when all are in the church, the singing ends. The priest goes right into the Collect of the Mass, and then Mass continues in the usual way; the other Introductory Rites are omitted.

The Second Form: The Solemn Entrance

This form of the entrance is used at Mass when the first form, the procession, is taking place or has taken place at another Mass, or when a procession outside the church cannot otherwise take place for some reason.

In this case, the priest, ministers and, if possible, a small group of the faithful gather somewhere other than the sanctuary, but preferably at a place where the people can see the rite. All are already holding branches in their hands.

An antiphon or another song is sung while the priest approaches the place where the rite is to begin, and then the Sign of the Cross, liturgical

greeting, introduction, blessing and sprinkling, and proclamation of the Gospel all occur as described above. After the Gospel, the priest, ministers, and small group of the faithful process solemnly through the church to the sanctuary while an appropriate song is sung. Then, arriving at the altar, the priest venerates it and then goes to the chair, where, omitting the Introductory Rites, he says the Collect of the Mass after the singing ends. Mass then continues in the usual way. The Missal makes no provision for the priest to wear a cope in this form of entrance; he wears the chasuble.

Third Form: The Simple Entrance

Essentially, this form of entrance is the same as any other Sunday: the priest proceeds to the altar while the Entrance Antiphon with its psalm or some other suitable song is sung; he arrives at the altar, venerates it, and then goes to his chair; and then he begins Mass with the Sign of the Cross, greets the people as usual, and Mass continues. In this form, the usual Introductory Rites would occur.

At the Mass

The Collect highlights the theme of humility, as exemplified both in Christ's taking flesh and in his submission to the Cross. It asks that "we may heed his lesson of patient suffering" in order to "merit a share in his Resurrection." This is the mystery we enter into this day and this week, culminating in the Sacred Paschal Triduum. Through the celebration of the liturgy, we seek to participate in the mystery of his dying and rising; through that participation, we seek to be transformed so that our lives may more closely be a reflection of his way of humility.

There are special instructions for the proclamation of the Lord's Passion: it is to be read without candles and without incense, and there is to be no greeting before the proclamation and no signing of the book. It is customary in many places to have several people participate in the reading of the Passion, not just the priest and deacon. However, the part of Christ should, if possible, be read by the priest. Only a deacon asks for the blessing of the priest before reading the Passion, as he does before reading the Gospel. Your community may wish to consider chanting the Gospel; this is a wonderful way of highlighting the solemnity of the day.

The Missal goes on to note that there should be a Homily after the narrative of the Passion, but interestingly the adjective "brief" is used again.

The Creed and the Universal Prayer take place as usual.

The Prayer over the Offerings underlines how our celebration of the liturgy is a participation in the once-and-for-all sacrifice of Christ, which is made present in our time and space, and it asks that through the Passion of Christ, we may have reconciliation with God and feel the effects of God's mercy, even though "we do not merit it by our own deeds."

The Preface assigned for today, "The Passion of the Lord," is given right there in the Missal along with the other texts for this Mass. The Preface is a very succinct proclamation of how Christ, though innocent, "suffered willingly for sinners" in order to save the guilty.

The Prayer after Communion prays that having been nourished with the sacred gift of the Eucharist, we may be led to the fullness of life through Christ's Resurrection. The Prayer over the People, required for today, sets the perfect tone for Holy Week and the Sacred Paschal Triduum as it asks God to look on us as the family "for whom our Lord Jesus Christ did not hesitate to be delivered into the hands of the wicked and submit to the agony of the Cross."

Other Ideas

Today presents a long, full liturgy, but don't cut corners to save time. Rather, choose simple psalm and Mass settings, and do not extend the music beyond the action. If your Mass times are close together, the parking lot may be the biggest problem. Consider adding some parking assistants or valet service today, especially for your elderly parish members.

30
MON (#257)   violet
Monday of Holy Week

The Lectionary for Mass

◆ First Reading: On Passion Sunday, we hear the full horror of Jesus's tortured suffering and death unfold. However, the Holy Week readings, culminating in the reading of the Passion according to St. John on Friday, take us deeper into the mystery. We are asked to recognize that God's plan forges meaning and hope out of the darkness. The Sufferer is no victim of circumstance but an active partner in the "victory of justice" which will emerge from the tomb on Easter Sunday.

◆ Responsorial Psalm 27: With the Lord as light and salvation, the psalmist confidently and courageously faces his adversaries. There is no cause for fear.

◆ Gospel: Mary of Bethany recognizes what Judas does not. With prophetic insight, she anoints the Messiah — whose title means "anointed one" — for the climax of his mission. Judas can see no deeper than common sense, blinded in this case by desire for personal gain. Jesus's gathered enemies can see no farther than a religious and political threat. Jesus credits Mary's insight as the true one: he is the one sent to achieve the work of redemption through his very death and burial.

The Roman Missal

The Collect today asks that we be "revived" through the Passion of Christ: the prayer acknowledges our weakness and our failure, but also implicitly recognizes that, every time we celebrate the Paschal Mystery in liturgy, we share in the new life that is brought to us through the Lord's Passion, Death, and Resurrection. The Prayer over the Offerings reminds us that the mysteries we celebrate here "cancel the judgment we incurred." We can recall that it is through the liturgy that the work of our redemption is accomplished, and therefore we can petition that these same mysteries may "bear for us fruit in eternal life." The Prayer after Communion notes how these sacred mysteries are a remedy to bring us eternal salvation.

The fact that we are now in Holy Week is marked by the assignment of a new Preface — Preface II of the Passion of the Lord is assigned for today. The Preface makes specific mention that "the days of his saving Passion and glorious Resurrection are approaching." In view of this, it might be better to use this Preface and not replace it with the proper Preface if one of the Eucharistic Prayers for Reconciliation is used (you are not required to use the Preface that goes with the Eucharistic Prayers for Reconciliation). In fact, it might be advantageous to highlight a certain starkness of these days of Holy Week through using an economy of words; along those lines, perhaps Eucharistic Prayer II would be a good choice for these last three days before the Sacred Paschal Triduum. Its direct statement of "At the time he was betrayed and entered willingly into his Passion" makes it perhaps especially appropriate for these three days.

The Lectionary for Mass

◆ FIRST READING: This second Song of the Suffering Servant continues to name the Servant as the new Israel, in and through whom light will dawn on a darkened world as the salvation accomplished through the Passion spreads "to the ends of the earth."

◆ RESPONSORIAL PSALM 71: The psalmist in distress cries out for God's deliverance. God is — and has been even before the psalmist's birth — rock, refuge, stronghold, and teacher. The experience of salvation leads to grateful proclamation of the Lord's deliverance.

◆ GOSPEL: What Isaiah foretold of the Suffering Servant, what Mary of Bethany proclaimed by her anointing, Judas Iscariot, Simon Peter, and indeed all the disciples except John, Mary the mother of Jesus, and the other faithful women will betray, deny, or flee in the days to come. The hard reality of the Gospel, which John describes as the ultimate conflict of darkness and light, is too much for them to bear, as it can be for all of us. However, after the resurrection, Jesus does not betray or deny or flee them but welcomes them back.

The Roman Missal

Today's Collect prays that we may receive pardon through our

celebration of "the mysteries of the Lord's Passion." The Prayer over the Offerings asks that we may be given a share in the fullness of the sacred gifts in which we have been made partakers. The Prayer after Communion makes a connection between the earthly liturgy and the heavenly liturgy as it asks that having been nourished by the saving gifts in this present age, we may be made "partakers of life eternal." Preface II of the Passion of the Lord, first used yesterday, is again assigned for today.

April
Month of the Holy Eucharist

The Lectionary for Mass

◆ FIRST READING: The Word made flesh lives the word of salvation he proclaims to all who will hear. His fidelity is obedience to the work God has given him. His love is made visible in his own decision to the turn the other cheek when he is beaten, tortured and humiliated for the salvation even of his enemies. Those who accuse him of wrong will fade before the dawning of the true Light.

◆ RESPONSORIAL PSALM 69 is a psalm of lament, vividly describing the sufferings endured by one of

the chosen people — all for the sake of God. The last stanza attests the psalmist's confidence that God will deliver him.

◆ GOSPEL: Judas is finally unable to bear the burden of his own betrayal. Lest Jesus's statement of "woe" satisfy too quickly our easy desire for defeat and revenge upon the villain of the story, let us recall his plea for forgiveness on the cross. His statement of woe may be read as dire warning of the ill to befall the betrayer, or it may be read as an expression of his defeated and grieving love for the disciple who turned away and then died of his own despair. Love, not vengeance, is the Gospel Jesus died for.

The Roman Missal

The Collect for this Mass continues to powerfully highlight for us the mood of Holy Week and the central mystery we are celebrating during the Sacred Paschal Triduum. First, the prayer expresses how Christ submitted "to the yoke of the Cross."

Preface II of the Passion of the Lord, used on the previous two days, is once more assigned for today, and the connection throughout these last three days of Lent can be maintained if, having used Eucharistic Prayer II on Monday and Tuesday, it is used again today.

SACRED PASCHAL TRIDUUM

The Meaning

THE Paschal Triduum (the "Three Days") is the heart of our liturgical year and celebrates the heart of our faith, the Paschal Mystery of Jesus Christ: his life, Passion, Death, and Resurrection. One long feast, it goes from sundown to sundown, beginning with the Evening Mass of the Lord's Supper, through Good Friday, reaching its high point in the Easter Vigil, and closing with Evening Prayer of Easter Sunday. The Great Easter Vigil is the preeminent liturgy of Easter—the preeminent liturgy of the entire liturgical year. Forty days of Lent prepare us for this Paschal feast. Fifty days unfold afterward in its celebration.

In spite of the fact that the Church has been urging us for forty years about the ways to keep the Triduum, many people seem not to have heard of it. Thursday is still thought to be the anniversary of the Last Supper, and Friday that of the Passion or the reenactment of the Stations of the

Cross. The liturgies become Passion plays, historical reenactments, celebrated as if Jesus must die all over again. Remember the words of the *Constitution on the Sacred Liturgy,* "the rites should radiate a noble simplicity. They should be short, clear, and free from useless repetition. They should be within the people's powers of comprehension, and normally should not require much explanation" (CSL, 34).

But how will our assemblies know how to keep Triduum if the parish leadership does not visibly do it well? Their example is as powerful as any bulletin announcement or booklet. The Homilies must be strong summons to participate in one continuous liturgical celebration that lasts three days, not a "go-to-church" request but an enthusiastic invitation into the Paschal Mystery. The differences between what is liturgy and what is devotion must be made. There is a fasting from meetings and classes. All liturgical preparation and rehearsals are done, save the heightened preparation of the elect and the intense focus on prayer.

The Lectionary for Mass

WE begin the Triduum celebration with the Holy Thursday Eucharist. The Scripture accounts we hear of the Last Supper address the heart of our faith. We believe the Eucharist is the Body and Blood of Christ and that Jesus told us this and commanded us to eat and drink in remembrance of him. We are also called to engage in service to our neighbor, following Jesus's example of washing the disciples's feet.

On Good Friday, we journey with the Lord, the innocent servant of God, who has taken our sins upon himself as he walks the path to Calvary. At the end, Jesus says, "It is finished." It doesn't mean, "It is over." It means, "It is accomplished" or "It is perfected." He has completed the task he was given. He hands over his spirit.

We end on that most sacred night when we gather at the Easter Vigil to rejoice in the Good News of Christ's Resurrection. All of Lent has led to this pivotal night of the entire liturgical year; even Advent and Christmas prepared us for this night. Everything we celebrate for the next fifty days until Pentecost results from our belief that Jesus is risen from the dead.

◆ FIRST READINGS: On Holy Thursday, the First Reading from Exodus is the remembrance of the Passover meal preceding the Exodus, and on Good Friday, the First Reading is from another one of the servant songs in Isaiah. At the Easter Vigil, there are seven Old Testament readings. Their proclamation makes the saving works of God throughout history present and real to us.

◆ RESPONSORIAL PSALMS: The psalms of Triduum are suitable to each of the three days. On Holy Thursday, the refrain used with Psalm 110, which comes from the New Testament's first letter of Paul to the Corinthians, speaks of the blessing cup as participation in the Blood of Christ. Good Friday's Responsorial Psalm each year is Psalm 22, and its refrain contains the words of the Gospel according to Luke spoken by Jesus as he hangs on the Cross: "Father, into your hands I commend my spirit" (Luke 23:46). The seven Responsorial Psalms of the Easter Vigil, which correspond to the seven Old Testament readings, abound with themes of the glorious nature of the earth and the Lord himself, the Lord's faithfulness to his people, the salvation the Lord offers, and the joyful nourishment that comes from following the Lord and his Word.

◆ SECOND READINGS: On Holy Thursday, the Second Reading from Paul's first letter to the Corinthians gives the oldest written account of the Eucharist and reminds us of what we celebrate each time we gather together to pray the Eucharistic liturgy. On Good Friday, the Second Reading is from the letter to the Hebrews. This letter speaks of the high priesthood of Jesus Christ. In particular, Good Friday's passage emphasizes the sacrifice of the High Priest's own life as an offering for sin.

◆ GOSPEL: During the three days of Triduum, the Gospel readings present Jesus's example in his washing of the feet of his disciples on Holy Thursday, John's account of the Passion which emphasizes Jesus as Isaiah's servant of the Lord who is the one High Priest on Good Friday, and Matthew's account of the women at the empty tomb and their announcement of the Resurrection to Jesus's disciples.

The Roman Missal

WHEN it comes to preparing for these days, nothing can take the place of carefully reading the prayers and rubrics in the Missal, and this should be the starting point for all those who prepare and minister at these liturgies. Although at first they may seem complicated because the liturgies contain components we only do once a year, there is really nothing that should scare us or that we need overly complicate. A thorough reading of the rubrics, rich discussion and detailed preparation about enacting the choreography in your particular worship space, and competently-run rehearsals for all those involved (including actually walking through the movements, so that a kind of "muscle memory" is facilitated, rather than just simply verbally explaining what will happen) will help ensure that when the time for celebration comes, everyone will be free enough from worry and distraction so that all may prayerfully enter into the ritual. Such preparation reveals how there really is an inner beauty and logic to the liturgies in and of themselves that allow us to encounter the mystery we are celebrating when we allow ourselves to be swept along by the ritual flow. Such careful preparation and rehearsal helps to prevent confusion that creates a kind of "theatrical performance" atmosphere that hinders not only the ministers but the entire liturgical assembly from becoming engulfed in the mysteries being celebrated. Be sure to include those who are in charge of the Rite of Christian Initiation of Adults in discussions, so that everyone involved can work together harmoniously from the very beginning of the process.

Those who prepare the liturgies for the Sacred Triduum should consider ahead of time the question of what book will be used at the actual celebration. Certainly, one could make a case for using the Missal book itself, since this is what it is for—it is appropriately noble and dignified, and it is therefore worthy of use; it bears the weight of mystery. However, it is also true that at times the book can be confusing to use, what with its page turns and the listing of various options; this can be especially true when it comes to initiation at the Easter Vigil. Sometimes it becomes necessary to annotate the Missal with post-it notes or other markings, but then doing so begins to detract from the dignity of the book, thus lessening its desirability as

an appropriate tool. Thus, it is not uncommon for parishes to make their own ritual books for the priest celebrant, with the texts the priest will need in order and laid out using only the options selected. Such a book has the advantage of being able to include specific rubrics and choreography as needed for a particular worship space. If such a book is used, however, be sure that it too is one that is noble, dignified, and capable of bearing the weight of mystery. Binders appropriate for this are provided by liturgical supply companies. Here's a hint if you use such binders: use plastic sheet protectors for the pages. Such protectors provide for easy grasping and page-turning since they are thicker than just sheets of paper; be sure to use non-glare ones, to keep it easy for the priest to see the pages.

The rubrics given right at the beginning of the section on the Sacred Paschal Triduum in the Missal are important, as they highlight the centrality of these liturgies. These celebrations are referred to as "the greatest mysteries of our redemption" as they keep the memorial of the Lord "crucified, buried, and risen" (Triduum rubric, 1). Special mention is given to the Paschal fast, which is to be "celebrated everywhere on the Friday of the Lord's Passion and, where appropriate, prolonged also through Holy Saturday as a way of coming, with spirit uplifted, to the joys of the Lord's Resurrection" (ibid.). Parishes would do well to catechize parishioners on the meaning of the Paschal fast, which is different from the Lenten fast. During Lent, we fast as a way of doing penance and of trying to cooperate with the grace of conversion; during the Triduum, we fast as a way of preparing for the great mysteries that are about to be celebrated. The fast during the Triduum is not one of penitence, but one of joy, of, in a sense, almost being too excited to eat, because our focus is totally captivated by the mysteries of redemption being made present to us in our midst. The emptiness of the stomach thus becomes a sign of our openness to die and rise with the Lord in these most holy of days.

The rubrics themselves point to the need for a sufficient number of lay ministers and the need for careful instruction in what is to be done; nothing is to be left to haphazardness. Singing is also given prominence: "The singing of the people, the ministers, and the Priest Celebrant has a special importance in the celebrations of these days, for when texts are sung, they have their proper impact" (Triduum rubric, 2). All, then, should set aside the proper time required to rehearse the singing of texts, including taking the time to prepare the assembly for their sung responses if this is something they are not already familiar with. In fact, the rubric goes on to highlight how the faithful should be given proper catechesis on the rites of the Triduum so that they can truly participate as actively and fruitfully as is intended by the Church. In addition to articles in their bulletin, many parishes hold special workshops or mini-courses on the Triduum for their parishioners, to give them a basic understanding of the liturgies of these days. Such gatherings would be wonderful opportunities to do a *lectio divina* of the Missal prayers with the people, so that they come to their liturgies with their ears, minds, and hearts prepared to receive the proclaimed texts.

Finally, the introductory rubrics end with a challenge to smaller communities. These days are so important that attention is to be given to gathering the faithful in as large an assembly as possible, where the resources for ministers and singing are plentiful. Thus, even though a community may gather regularly for Eucharist, the members of smaller communities must do an honest self-appraisal and ask if they have the necessary resources, specifically in terms of numbers of ministers and musical ability, to carry out the rites with the appropriate festivity and dignity. The Missal gives a certain emphasis to such communities joining with larger ones for these most sacred celebrations: "Consequently, it is desirable that small communities, associations, and special groups of various kinds join together in these churches to carry out the sacred celebrations in a more noble manner" (Triduum rubric, 3).

There are detailed rubrics for each day of the Sacred Triduum.

Children's Liturgy of the Word

THE children's Liturgy of the Word is usually not celebrated during these three days and rightly so. The nature and solemnity of the liturgies call for the entire assembly to be gathered in one place. In addition, the *Lectionary for Masses with Children* does not provide readings for the Triduum and does not envision a separate Liturgy of the Word for Children during this time. Families, however, should be encouraged to bring their children to one or all of these most holy celebrations. The symbols of these liturgies speak very well to children who often engage with wonder and awe at the sights and sounds of the Triduum, sometimes better than the adults.

The Saints

THE Three Days, the Paschal Triduum, are the primary days of celebration throughout the entire liturgical year. As such, there are no observances of the saints on Holy Thursday, Good Friday, Holy Saturday, or Easter Sunday.

If your parish feast day (which would be ranked as a solemnity) would normally fall on one of these dates, the observance is moved to the next available day on the calendar. Because the days of the octave of Easter are treated as a solemnity, the next available day is not until Monday of the Second Week of Easter.

The Liturgy of the Hours

EVENING Prayer is to be prayed only by those who will not participate in the Evening Mass of the Lord's Supper.

The two mornings of Good Friday and Holy Saturday could include a combined celebration of the Office of Readings and Morning Prayer. The practice is recommended by the *Ceremonial of Bishops* (296), the *General Instruction of the Liturgy of the Hours* (210), and *Paschale Solemnitatis* (40, 62).

Compline, or Night Prayer, could be a fitting conclusion to Adoration of the Blessed Sacrament on Holy Thursday. The Paschal Triduum officially concludes after Evening Prayer on Easter Sunday, not with the Easter Vigil. This liturgy resonates with abundant Alleluias and antiphons and is the perfect way to conclude the Triduum. Invite the entire community, and especially the neophytes, to join in this prayer.

The Rite of Christian Initiation of Adults

THE Paschal Triduum is at the heart of the RCIA and of the liturgical year. The period of inquiry, catechumenate, and period of purification and enlightenment have all led to this moment. The elect and catechumens should participate in all of the liturgies of the Paschal Triduum. On Holy Thursday they are dismissed from the celebration following the washing of the feet. Since they have been dismissed on a regular basis they can break open the word on their own, allowing a catechist or team member to be part of the entire Holy Thursday liturgy. On Good Friday, consider a short dismissal following the Adoration of the Cross.

Central to the elect's final grounding are the Preparation Rites on Holy Saturday (RCIA, 185–205). This is the time for the elect to gather for prayer and "refrain from their usual activities . . . and as far as they can observe a fast" (RCIA 185.1). Consider celebrating the preparation rites as part of Morning Prayer so that a greater number of the community can participate. The celebration includes the Recitation of the Creed (RCIA, 193–196). This consists of the elect "giving back" to the Church the Creed that was presented to them during Lent. The Ephphetha Rite (RCIA, 197–199) includes the ritual opening of the ears and mouth of the elect. This ritual action prepares the elect to robustly profess their faith before the whole Church, into which they will be baptized. In addition, the presentation of the Lord's Prayer, if it was not celebrated during the Fifth Week of Lent, may also be included in the celebration. It is important to note that the choosing of a baptismal name (RCIA, 200–202) is not normally celebrated in the dioceses of the United States (see RCIA, 33.4).

If infants will be baptized at the Easter Vigil consult the *Rite of Baptism of Children*. The rite indicates that the rite of reception and the anointing with chrism and exorcism should take place before the vigil (see RBC, 28). It would be appropriate then to include these preparation rites during the Saturday morning celebration.

In many communities throughout the United States and Canada, the Paschal Triduum is celebrated employing more than one language, for example, Spanish and English or French and English or other languages. For the entire Triduum, including the preparation rites, be sure to employ readers, musicians and ministers of hospitality.

The RCIA employs a great deal of preparation and the pastoral musicians of the community must enter into this preparation with candidates, elect, members of the RCIA team, and catechists in order for the rites to be celebrated fully and robustly, as we stand together in Christ.

At the Easter Vigil the celebration of the Sacraments of Initiation—Baptism, Confirmation, and Holy Eucharist—take place. For those who are candidates, the opportunity to celebrate the Sacrament of Penance will already have been made prior to the vigil. The elect celebrate all three sacraments while the candidates (having already been baptized) only celebrate Confirmation and the Eucharist.

Take time to review the pastoral introduction to the third step of the initiation process: the Celebration of the Sacraments of Initiation (RCIA, 206–217). Central to the celebration on this night is the baptismal liturgy. Priest celebrants, musicians, and RCIA teams will need to consult both the RCIA, 218–230, and *The Roman Missal*, 37–58, for texts and rubrics. If you are also celebrating the Rite of Reception into the Full Communion of the Catholic Church, you will also need to consult RCIA, 562–594. These combined rites are found in the United States ritual, but the combined rites are not celebrated in Canada. Likewise, if infants are to be baptized at the vigil consult the *Rite of Baptism for Children* (RBC, 28). Good pastoral practice would not separate families when celebrating the initiation rites. Therefore, if members of the elect or candidates have infants or children under the age of seven or eight coming for Baptism, they too should be baptized at the vigil. Likewise, children who have reached the age of reason who are related to the elect or candidates would celebrate the Sacraments of Baptism, Confirmation, and receive their first Communion.

Full, open, and robust symbols are to be employed in the celebration of the liturgies of initiation. The preferred means of adult Baptism is either by immersion or pouring water over the person being baptized (see the *National Statutes for the Catechumenate in the United States*, 17). The "General Introduction" to *Christian Initiation* maintains that immersion "is more suitable as a symbol of participation in the death and resurrection of Christ" (RCIA, 22). In addition the guidelines of the USCCB for the building and renovation of churches, *Built of Living Stones* (BLS), call for a font that is large enough for the Baptism of adults by either of these means (see BLS, 69). If your parish does not have a font that can accommodate either of these methods of Baptism, consider beginning a conversation about the possibility of having a permanent baptismal font with living water added to your liturgical environment. In the meantime, when there is not a font large enough to accommodate Baptism by immersion, a temporary font may be constructed for use.

Consider inserting the names of those who will be baptized into the Litany of the Saints if they are actual names of saints. If possible, have a procession of the elect that leads to the font and is led by the Paschal candle. Following the litany is the blessing of the baptismal water (see *The Roman Missal*, 44–45), and if at all possible the Paschal candle is lowered into the font once or three times. This ritual action is done during the words of the blessing that call down the Holy Spirit upon the water that is being blessed.

At that point, the elect are invited to renounce sin and profess their faith in the Blessed Trinity. This response should be robust so that all in the assembly may hear. The elect may be vested in a garment of a dark color for their Baptism. Infants coming for Baptism can already be dressed in a white garment. Then the elect receive the lighted candle, lit from the Paschal candle by their godparent. It is good to give the newly baptized a substantial candle that can either be decorated by godparents or others from the community, or a candle can be purchased (even one that matches the parishes Paschal candle). Many candle companies carry a more substantial candle.

Next the neophytes are confirmed if there are no candidates for full communion. The celebration includes the invitation and silent prayer with the priest extending his hands over those to be confirmed while calling for the sending of the Spirit. The Christ oil—the sacred chrism—should be lavishly poured over the newly baptized. Godparents and RCIA members can continue to rub the oil onto the head and cheeks of the neophytes. The priest who baptizes the adults or children of catechetical age has the faculty to confirm. It is not necessary to seek delegation from the bishop since the faculty comes from the law itself. It is important to note that the Confirmation of any newly baptized adult or child of catechetical age cannot be deferred to a later time, except in extreme circumstances. Children of catechetical age must be

confirmed. The pastor and even the bishop cannot defer Confirmation to a later time since this is prohibited by canon law (CCL, 885.2).

Afterward, the neophytes who were baptized in living water go to a separate place to change into their Easter cloths. Then the candles of all in the assembly are relit. Take the Paschal candle and process it through the church so that the assembly may take their light from the Christ candle.

If the Rite of Reception into the Full Communion of the Catholic Church is to be celebrated, the renewal of baptismal promises and the Rite of Reception begins immediately after the neophytes have been presented their candles. First the assembly renews their baptismal promises, which is followed by a sprinkling with baptismal water. In some communities the entire assembly is called to process to the font and bless themselves while the *Vidi aquam* ("I saw water flowing") or another chant or song that is baptismal in character is sung (see *The Roman Missal*, 56).

Next those who are to be received are called forward. Situate them in a place facing the assembly with their sponsor standing next to them or behind them. The priest invites them to make a profession of faith (see RCIA, 585). This profession may be made as a group or individually. Make sure that you provide the text on at least a 6"×8" card and ask the candidates to proclaim their profession robustly. Then the priest goes to each person to receive them with the approved formula (see RCIA, 586). If at all possible the priest should commit to memory the text so that he may give his full attention to each candidate. Now both the neophytes and the candidates receive the Sacrament of Confirmation.

The Universal Prayer follows. Since the neophytes have been dismissed on a regular basis from the Sunday assembly, they will now join with the entire community in bringing to bear the priestly character of Baptism. Formularies of the Universal Prayer for Easter are found in Appendix V, #8 in *The Roman Missal*.

As the Liturgy of the Eucharist begins consider inviting some of the neophytes to bring forward the gifts of bread and wine. If at all possible encourage the priest celebrant to chant the Eucharistic Prayer along with the dialogue and preface.

The RCIA offers a marvelous suggestion for an invitation to Holy Communion (RCIA, 243). It calls for the priest, just before the invitation, to remind the neophytes, and the gathered assembly, of the preeminence of the Holy Eucharist, which is the culmination of their initiation and the center of the whole Christian life.

These rites can also be celebrated outside of the Easter Vigil; however, this should be exceptional for the unbaptized—for example, if someone is near death or is being deployed into military service. At some college campuses that have spring breaks during Holy Week, initiation for both the baptized and the unbaptized is often done during the weeks after Easter, so more of the community can be present. The circumstances for the baptized candidates are more flexible.

When initiation rituals of water, oil, and table-sharing are done carefully and lavishly in our presence, and when we are attentive—stirring up our own baptismal consciousness, helping us embrace daily dying and burial with Christ—this prompts us to promise to live no longer for ourselves, and urges us to live, in deed, what we proclaim in ritual action.

The elect are now called neophytes, and they are considered to be full members of the Christian faithful.

The Sacraments of Initiation

Accarding of the *Rite of Baptism for Children*, the Baptism of infants can be celebrated at the Easter Vigil in order to bring out the Paschal character of the sacrament (see RBC, 9). However, give this option careful consideration. The demands of the Easter Vigil (with its late hour), various elements, and time considerations might make it difficult for the parents and family, as well as for the infant. When would it be appropriate to celebrate an infant Baptism at the Vigil? If one of the elect has an infant that is not baptized, it would be an appropriate occasion for the child's initiation as well. Then again, the next day, Easter Sunday, might be a better choice because of its much simpler liturgy. Whatever the choice, the parents need to be well prepared.

The Rite of Penance

Communal penance services are to "take place before the Easter Triduum and should not immediately preceed the Mass of the Lord's Supper" (*Paschale Solemnitatis* [PS], 371). Individual celebrations of the sacrament may be celebrated on Good Friday and Holy Saturday according to the same instruction (PS, 61 and 67). It only makes sense pastorally to offer the sacrament on these days to allow the faithful to have full access to their Easter duty.

The Rite of Marriage

The Paschal Triduum is not an appropriate time for the celebration of a wedding, and all the energy and resources of a parish community are focused on the Three Days. Be sure that couples who are preparing a spring or Easter wedding know this well in advance (see PS, 61 and 75).

The Pastoral Care of the Sick

Holy Communion should be taken to the sick directly from the Evening Mass of the Lord's Supper; "directly from the altar" say the rubrics (PS, 53). Remember that ministers may not keep consecrated hosts overnight. On Good Friday, Holy Communion may be taken at any time, but on Holy Saturday it may only be given as Viaticum. The readings and a copy of a Homily or reflection could be taken to the sick and homebound, along with the prayers of the community. The Anointing of the Sick in situations of emergency can take place at any time during the Paschal Triduum.

The Order of Christian Funerals

THE funeral Mass may not be celebrated during the Paschal Triduum, but on Good Friday, *Paschale Solemnitatis* tells us that "funerals are to be celebrated without singing, music or the tolling of bells" (PS, 61). Since this directive is rather harsh, it would be best to schedule the funeral liturgy before the Paschal Triduum or during the Octave of Easter. Assure the family of the community's prayer for the deceased during the Triduum.

The Book of Blessings

BECAUSE the primary liturgies of the Three Days are the Mass of the Lord's Supper on Holy Thursday, the Liturgy of the Lord's Passion on Good Friday, and the Paschal Vigil on Holy Saturday night, the *Book of Blessings* is a secondary resource.

One order of blessing that is appropriate is the Order of Blessing of Food for the First Meal of Easter (chapter 54). Many parishes have the custom of gathering on Holy Saturday morning or afternoon and blessing baskets of food with which the faithful will "break fast" after the Vigil or on Easter Sunday Morning. If the parish schedule allows, it can also be used on Easter morning.

The Liturgical Environment

EACH day of the Triduum has a distinct character, but the worship of the Three Days forms one liturgy. The environment should try to underline both unity and difference.

The Evening Mass of the Lord's Supper has white as its liturgical color. Like Palm Sunday, this Mass has a transitional character. It celebrates the institution of the Eucharist and is festive, but also has a somber character underlined by the foot-washing and the silencing of the bells and organ after the Gloria. Noble simplicity is a good rule for the environment at this liturgy. If there is a choice, this is an appropriate time to bring out the more festive set, along with any more festive altarware, much as one would bring out Grandma's special table cloths and china for important family celebrations. If more ornate altarware is to be used, make sure that it is big enough. The paten will have to hold hosts for both the Holy Thursday and Good Friday liturgies; many older chalices are not sized to hold wine for the entire assembly.

Give careful consideration to the *mandatum*. Its location in the liturgy usually requires that it be set up and taken down in the course of the Mass, so everything used should be easily movable. Chairs will have to be set out for those having their feet washed, bowls for water will need to be brought out and moved without spilling water on the floor. Towels are another necessity. Consider using a carpet, especially if the church's floors are wood or stone. This will provide a more comfortable experience for those with bare feet. It can also help define a space in the middle of the church, adding focus to the rite.

The offering at Holy Thursday is traditionally distributed to the poor. Some parishes underline this by collecting food stuffs and other gifts along with money on this day. If this is to be done, it will require some consideration about how it will work and where the items collected will be placed.

Following the liturgy, there is a procession with the Eucharistic host to an altar of repose. This should be outside of the church, in a location which can be appropriately set up for the occasion. Wooden screens can provide a backdrop, as can carefully arranged drapery. A tabernacle should be provided on a stand, and the space sufficiently defined so that it feels like a solemn liturgical space. This can often be accomplished with arrangements of candles and plants. Consider using some of the greenery from Palm Sunday, along with some of the Easter plants for this environment. The liturgy evokes the night of prayer at Gethsemane, and so a vibrant garden setting is appropriate, although not required. Simplicity can also be quite effective. Sufficient chairs should be provided, along with kneelers if they are available, for those who choose to stay and pray following the service. Because each parish has different spaces available to them, consider what options you have open to you and how you can make it work as a liturgical space. Early preparation will provide time to procure what is necessary for this liturgy.

After the liturgies, the altar is to be stripped, crosses are to be removed or veiled, and the font may be emptied in preparation from the Good Friday Liturgy. If the altar of repose is close to the church, be careful to work quietly, so as not to disturb those in prayer.

The Good Friday environment is very plain. The color of the day is red, although it appears only in the vesture of the ministers. The altar remains bare. Candles are removed from the sanctuary, as are crosses, if this is possible. A single, large cross is carried in during the service for veneration. It may be veiled in violet or unveiled, but must be light enough to be carried in. It may be honored with candles and incense, and a stand should be prepared to hold it throughout the day for the peoples' veneration and private prayer. The altar is briefly dressed with a corporal and candles for the Communion. These are returned to the sacristy after Communion is finished, when any remaining Blessed Sacrament is returned to the Altar of Repose.

The Vigil in the Holy Night of Easter is the most complex liturgy of the year. Attending to its structure can help prepare the environment and all its parts. These are the *Lucenarium* (service of light), the Liturgy of the Word, the Liturgy of Baptism, and the Liturgy of the Eucharist. The environment should underline these major actions and not get in the way of the assembly's participation. The liturgical color is white or gold.

Light continues to be the central theme at the Vigil. The service cannot begin before local astronomical twilight, when the sky is truly dark, and must be concluded before sunrise. Your diocesan liturgical office should publish the time of astronomical twilight, or it can be found online. The lighting of the fire begins the service, and requires a space clear of flammable objects and tripping hazards. There should be enough space for the parish to gather around the fire, and potentially sound amplification so that the celebrant can be heard during the opening rites. The fire itself should be of significant size. Wood should be obtained early and kept in a dry place so that it lights easily. Have a taper handy to light the paschal candle from the fire, and someone standing by with a fire extinguisher in case things go wrong. Someone should stay with the fire until it is extinguished after the assembly has processed into the church.

The Paschal candle should have been procured well in advance and be of a proportional size to your space. While you may be restricted as to diameter because of the stand you already have, consider buying the tallest candle that will work in your space. It should be of good quality wax and may have the year, the *Alpha/Omega*, and a cross on it. If it does not, these are inscribed with an awl by the priest celebrant onto the wax as part of the opening rites. If they are already on the candle, he traces them with his finger. If you have two stands for the candle, place one by the ambo for the *Exsultet* and the other by the font. You will also need smaller candles for all the baptized of the assembly. While many parishes use very small tapers for this, larger candles that people can take home and burn throughout the Easter season might be considered.

Following the service of light, the Liturgy of the Word consists of at least three, and preferably seven, readings from the Old Testament with their psalm responses, an Epistle reading with its psalm response, and the Gospel. There should be sufficient light for the assembly to follow the worship aid, but the ambo may be highlighted with a spot. Plants may be used to enhance the location of the Paschal candle and the ambo, along with the altar and the font.

The Liturgy of Baptism requires careful consideration. Baptism by immersion or submersion is highly recommended, and many parishes do not have fonts which will allow this. A temporary font can be installed for Easter Time, so long as it does not look flimsy or cobbled-together. If the water can be warmed, this is also to be encouraged. Those to be baptized can wear their own clothes or a darker robe which will not become transparent when wet. After they are baptized, they may be presented with an alb (the white robe of the baptized), and given time and a space to change into it. If the priest or deacon is to enter the font with those to be baptized, he will also require a dry alb to change into after the rite. Most churches have floors which will be slippery to those with wet feet. Place a towel or mat at the entrance to the font. Towels for those baptized to dry off will also be necessary, along with baptismal candles, chrism, and a basin and towel for the celebrant to wash his hand. Lemon juice can help cut the oil.

After the Baptism, tools for sprinkling the assembly with water will be necessary — a bowl with fairly straight sides (to avoid spilling) and an aspergillium. This can be easily made of several small fir branches wired together.

The Liturgy of the Eucharist is no different from a normal Sunday, except for perhaps somewhat more solemnity. If the parish has a special set of vessels, this would be an appropriate time to use them. Many older chalices do not hold much wine, so be attentive that there will be enough for those who will commune.

The Liturgical Music

THIS is the season that calls for all the musicians in the faith community to come together to form one large choir. The liturgies of the Three Days are not assigned to different groups—it is one liturgy that unfolds over three days—all parish musicians must be present for this. The music used during the Triduum should come back year after year and the repertoire should be incorporated into the liturgical year. Pastoral musicians and other liturgical ministers must step up to the plate and show forth the "Church" by celebrating the Triduum as a united community. If we truly embrace the fact that the liturgy is the "Sacrament of Unity" (CSL, 26) then the musicians from various church choirs in the parish must come together to form one ensemble of musicians for the Triduum. This may take a few years to accomplish, but this once-a-year opportunity to celebrate the Paschal Mystery as "one" community will over time allow musicians from different choirs to build more sincere conversations with one another, not just the perfunctory "hello" on the way into or out of Mass. When the parish musicians embrace this model, they will not only be concerned about the quality of the music but the quality of relationships with each other and the entire faith community's experience of the heart of our faith, the Paschal Mystery.

Thursday of the Lord's Supper: At the Evening Mass

The liturgy begins with the keynote of Galatians 6:14. Consider using the choral introit *"Nos autem gloriari"* by Christopher Tietze (WLP) or one of the several musical settings based on this text: "Glory in the Cross" by Dan Schutte (OCP); "We Should Glory in the Cross" by Ricky Manalo, Gerard Chiusano, and Stephen Dean (OCP); *"Que Nuestro Único Orgullo/*We Should Glory in the Cross" by Bob Hurd (OCP); or "Glory in the Cross" by Steve Janco (GIA). During the singing of the "Glory to God" the church bells or individual bells are rung.

The antiphon, *Mandatum novum*, "I give you a new commandment, that you love one another as I have loved you, says the Lord" (John 13:24) is chanted as feet are washed. The Communion antiphon "This is the Body that will be given up for you; this is the chalice of the new covenant in my Blood, says the Lord; do this, whenever you receive it, in memory of me" (1 Corinthians 11:24–25). Any familiar Communion chant that echo's this text is appropriate for this night. The ancient chant, *Pange lingua*, "Sing, My Tongue, the Savior's Glory" (a hymn composed by St. Thomas Aquinas) is sung as the Sacrament is carried in procession and all leave the church in profound silence (although some may stay for time with the Blessed Sacrament in the chapel of reservation).

A plethora of music and musical styles may be used for the washing of the feet. Consider some of the following: "Jesus Took a Towel" by Chrysogonus Waddell, "This Is My Example" by Francis Patrick O'Brien, "So You Must Do" by Marty Haugen, and "Song of the Lord's Command" by David Haas (all from GIA). "The Sacrament of Service" by Alan J. Hommerding (WLP) and "Jesu, Jesu" with text by Tom Colvin and melody based on the Ghana folk song CHEREPONI (Hope Publishing Company) also works well. The following pieces from OCP also serve this ritual moment well including: "As I Have Done For You" by Dan Schutte, "Faith, Hope, and Love" by Ricky Manalo, "No Greater Love/*No Hay Amor Más Grande*" by Bob Hurd and "Great Is the Love/*Hay Gran Amor*" by Jamie Cortez.

On this night *The Roman Missal* indicates there "may be procession of the faithful in which gifts for the poor may be presented with the bread and wine." *The Roman Missal* suggests that the ancient hymn "*Ubi Caritas/*Where true charity is dwelling, God is present there" accompany this procession.

At the altar of repose consider reading from John's account of the Gospel (chapters 13–17) through the evening interspersed with silence and short Taizé style chants. The collection *Hear the Prayers that Rise*, edited by Barbara Bridge and Mercy Sister Suzanne Toolan, contains several possibilities (OCP). Adoration of the Blessed Sacrament could continue through midnight concluding with Night Prayer about 11:45 PM (see WLP's "Christ Our Light" for one model).

Friday of the Passion of the Lord [Good Friday]

We celebrate an austere form of the Liturgy of the Word followed by Adoration of the Cross and then Communion with the reserved Sacrament. At liturgy on this day we contemplate the victory over the power of sin and death, which Jesus Christ won on the Cross of Calvary. The Collect may be chanted by the presiding minister and several fine settings of Psalm 31 are available including "I Place My Life" by Rory Cooney and "Father, I Put My Life in Your Hands" by Howard Hughes (both from GIA); "*Padre, en Tus Manos*/Father into Your Hands" by Bob Hurd and "Father, I Put My Life in Your Hands" by Randall DeBruyn (both from OCP); "*Padre, en Tus Manos*/Father, into Your Hands" by Eleazar Cortés and "Into Your Hands" by Chrysogonus Waddell (both from WLP). The texts proclaim the "suffering servant," the prototype of God's chosen people, Israel (see Isaiah 52:13 — 53:12). Psalm 31 gives expression to the desolation which all human beings experience, and which the "high priest" experienced in its fullness. John's account of the Passion (John 18:1—19:42) is most effectively proclaimed when it is sung. Settings include the chant arranged by Robert Batastini (GIA) or Columba Kelly (OCP) and a contemporary setting by Christopher Walker (OCP). *The Passions of Holy Week Bilingual Illuminated Edition for Multiple Voices* by Charles Rohrbacher is available from Liturgical Press.

The Solemn Intercessions are marked with gesture and silence. Consider having a deacon or another minister chant the introduction on this night. A beautiful bilingual setting "General Intercessions for Good Friday/*Oración Universal del Viernes Santo*" by Dolores Martínez is available from OCP or Kevin Keil's Good Friday Intercessions (OCP). You may also want to consider adding a short acclamation for the people to sing, such as "*O Christe Audi Nos*" by Jacques Berthier (GIA).

Adoration of the Cross follows as a minister chants, "This is the wood of the cross, on which hung the Savior of the world" and the people respond "Come, let us worship." Several chants, hymns, and acclamations can be used as the people come forward to adore the one cross. The *Ceremonial of Bishops* suggest removing shoes and coming forward barefoot, "as a sign of humility" to adore the cross. Consider using the strong acclamation "Holy is God, Psalm 116–117" by Howard Hughes (GIA). This psalm sings out the *Trisagion*, meaning "Thrice Holy," the standard hymn of the Divine Liturgy in most of the Eastern Orthodox Churches, Oriental Orthodox Churches, and Eastern Catholic Churches. By singing this psalm as we begin the Adoration of the Cross we can stand in solidarity with and pray for unity of the Churches of the East and West. Take into account the diversity of your assembly this day and find hymns, acclamations, psalms, or ostinatos that can be sung by both choir and assembly. The Adoration of the Cross is not the time for a choir concert but rather a time for a wide variety of musical responses by both assembly and choir.

The choice of the Communion chant for this liturgy requires some reflection: *The Roman Missal* suggests Psalm 22 and *Sing to the Lord: Music in Divine Worship* reminds us that the "Communion song might reflect themes of the Gospel reading of the day" (STL, 191). Rather than using a standard Communion song that reflects the liturgical action of eating and drinking the Body and Blood of Christ consider using a processional chant (psalm) that echoes the Passion.

The Easter Vigil in the Holy Night

The *Exsultet* must be sung and the traditional chant in *The Roman Missal* is the best choice; it is normally proclaimed by the deacon or cantor. Consider having the deacon or cantor proclaim the Easter Proclamation from the illuminated volume augmented with magnificent illustrations by artist Charles Rohrbacher, deacon of the Diocese of Juneau (The Liturgical Press).

The Easter Alleluia is intoned and then the cantor or choir sings the verses to the psalm. The Alleluia raises a half step after each verse.

Sacramental initiation and the renewal of Baptism at Easter help us to focus on a theology of the liturgical year and "being born anew in Christ." *Sing to the Lord: Music in Divine Worship* stresses the importance of singing acclamations during the celebration of Baptism and Confirmation (see STL, 206). First, the Litany of the Saints is sung and those who are coming for Baptism may process through the church on the way to the font. While the traditional chant setting is the best choice, other settings of the litany work well including that by John Becker or by Grayson Warren Brown (OCP). The blessing of water is best chanted and can be found in *The Roman Missal*. Consider adding a short response for the people to sing along the way such as "Blessed Are You O God," "Blessed Be God, O Blessed Be God," or an "Alleluia." During the actual Baptisms an acclamation such as "You Have Put on Christ" (the setting by Howard Hughes, GIA, and Stephen Dean, OCP, both work well). Many communities sing an "Alleluia" at the end of each Baptism. An acclamation, ostinato, or hymn could be sung during the Rite of Confirmation. A plethora of "water acclamations" and songs can be sung as the assembly is sprinkled with the new baptismal water. These include: "Springs of Water" by Thomas Savoy (you will need a very fine cantor and organist to pull this setting off and the brass parts are splendid); "Springs of Water" by Jeremy Young; "Rite of Sprinkling/Springs of Water" by Don Fellows, and "Springs of Water, Bless the Lord" by Marty Haugen (all from GIA.) Lynn Trapp's piece based on the hymn tune ASSURANCE, "Springs of Water, Bless the Lord," is available from OCP. The traditional African American Spiritual "Wade in the Water" also works well during this ritual action.

For the Universal Prayer consider the "Trilingual Intercessions" by Michael Hay (WLP). This is a great option to encourage the assembly to sing in three languages: English, Latin, and Spanish. A multilingual setting, "*Exaudi Nos/ Hear Us, O Lord*" by Rufino Zaragoza and Paulist Ricky Manalo include responses in twenty languages (OCP).

Make sure to choose service music and processional chants for Communion that are well known by the people. A festive concertato or other choral arrangement of one of the standard Easter Hymns is a fitting end to the great vigil.

The Liturgical Ministers

B ECAUSE of the particular needs of the Paschal Triduum, practice and rehearsal should be the main concern of all liturgical ministers. As once-a-year celebrations, they can be intimidating. As has been noted in this introduction already, ample time for rehearsing will help the ministers tremendously as they offer service to the liturgies of these most solemn of days.

Encourage and offer adequate opportunities for the lectors to practice their assigned readings in the church. Make sure the sound system is turned on so that they can practice and become familiar with the microphone. For those liturgies in which lighting is altered (e.g., the Easter Vigil), be sure all liturgical ministers are aware of this and that they are prepared for it. Designate someone to turn the lights on at the appropriate times.

Ushers and greeters should know the specific needs of each liturgy, what to provide to those attending each liturgy, and the processional routes that will be used.

Sacristans should have all the liturgical items prepared and readied. Be sure that all vessels, vesture, and other needed items have been cleansed. Be sure that everyone is aware of where each item needed will be placed and that they are accessible to liturgical ministers. For example, where will the blessed and consecrated oils be placed so that they can be presented during the Preparation of the Altar and the Gifts during the Evening Mass of the Lord's Supper? Who will make sure they will be placed in the proper place? Who will be involved in the presentation (e.g., ushers, those presenting each oil, the priest celebrant)?

Cantors and musicians should know the repertoire thoroughly and should have practiced it well before the Paschal Triduum begins. If there is singing during any of the processions, they should know how they will take part and how they will sustain the singing throughout (e.g., the procession to the altar of repose if it is in a building different from where the Mass is celebrated: where will cantors and other singers be placed within the procession to ensure the singing is sustained?).

Devotions and Sacramentals

I N many countries, it is a long-standing custom for the faithful to make a pilgrimage on the evening of Holy Thursday, visiting the altar of repose at seven different churches, often including the cathedral church, until the period of adoration concludes at midnight. Sometimes the Rosary is said on the journey from church to church.

Good Friday has inspired many different devotional practices, from Passion plays, like the famous one in Oberammergau, Germany, to dramatic processions with the "dead Christ," as in Spain and Portugal (*Directory on Popular Piety and the Liturgy* [DPPL], 142). The DPPL urges respect for these traditions, for through them the faithful "intuit much of the significance" (142) of the mysteries celebrated on Good Friday. At the same time, though, the Directory cautions against trying to integrate such devotional practices into "solemn liturgical action of Good Friday for such would constitute a distorted celebrative hybrid" (DPPL, 143). The "Tre Ore," or "Three Hours," is an American original, which developed in Lima, Peru, in the eighteenth century. In this service, which usually begins at noon and concludes at three o'clock, the faithful seek to keep company with Jesus during the hours he hung on the cross. The service is celebrated in a variety of ways. It can include the Stations of the Cross, the Rosary, sermons on the words Jesus spoke from the cross (the seven last words), music, Scripture, and silent prayer.

In some areas, it is the custom to observe on Holy Saturday the "Ora della Madre," the hour of Mary, a vigil of prayer with Mary. The Blessed Virgin Mary, as she is represented in Christian tradition waiting near the Lord's tomb, is an icon of the Virgin Church keeping vigil at the tomb of her Spouse while awaiting the celebration of his Resurrection (see DPPL, 147).

In some countries, notably in the Philippines, a beautiful procession takes place at dawn on Easter Sunday. Prior to the first Mass of Easter, a group of the faithful bearing an image of the sorrowful Mother sets out for the church. From another direction, a procession accompanies an image of the risen Christ. The two images meet at the church, "so as to show that Our Lady was the first and full participant in the mystery of the Lord's resurrection" (DPPL, 149). After the procession, the Mass of Easter begins.

The Parish and the Home

WHEN the greatest gift is given there are no words that can bring forth what it means to the person who receives. To those who believe in the essential goodness of our Roman Catholic faith, this is the Triduum. There are no words, nothing else that can be done. While not environmentally friendly, the most beautifully wrapped packages are the ones to which most people are first drawn. As the ritual of these three days are already provided, how we then present this gift is what matters most. People came out in unprecedented numbers to begin Lent; they received the outward sign, a present of sorts, on their forehead to be counted as part of the fold. Who is present as the finish line draws near? Being marked with ash is important, but receiving the essential instructions of how to live this life is necessary. However your parishioners/family can hear this, craft the words. Allow this message to be clearly and wonderfully heard.

We need all ages to be present together and living out what they will profess to believe. The invitation also now matters just as much as the external wrapping of the gift to come. Create your Holy Thursday service into one that is full of the immense warmth and intimacy that Jesus offered to his disciples. To do this, listen to the hearts of the faithful on your commissions and who speak for the larger community. Involve multiple generations in the preparation to add the touch that makes your community who they are and allows you, as minister in the church, to gift others. Pour this richness of all ages into the Holy Thursday liturgy, the institution of the Eucharist, and our instructions to serve. Create unique invitations to your parish to allow everyone to understand why, as the Jewish child asks, this day is so different from any other day. For on this day, we combine the history of our Jewish family members and watch as Jesus transforms the Passover into a meal of his life for us. He defies all practical tradition and the ego of his headstrong disciples and shows us that to lead is to serve.

Invite trained parents and children to be readers, music ministers, greeters, and servers— together. The act of washing feet is humbling and being in relationship with your community allows you to best know how to turn this into the great soul gift that it can be. Know the stories of pain and transformation in your parish and invite some members to have their stories briefly shared to the community before their feet are washed and they, in turn, go out to begin washing the feet of others. Watching feet being washed is one dimensional. Calling one first to have their feet washed and then to wash another's feet transcends. Create the space in your parish to offer a peaceful garden—time in adoration to sit with Christ before the wounds of passion are hammered in on Good Friday.

Many churches already include children and teens in their Living Stations of the Cross. Continue to invite, include, and immerse the entire community in the ritual. The best way to offer this prayer is to dive deep into the meaning and mystery yourself and, from this place of absolute uncertainty of how and why God did what God did, create your prayer. Your spirit is now where Christ lives and only you can uncover the words, song, and ritual to wash over your community and family in a time when hearts are stirred to tears at the reality of why our faith communities exist. Every word matters. Every song counts to touch someone's soul. While this experience happens year after year, let nothing be rote this year. Find something new to include in the offering of Good Friday prayer and then create the bridge of transformation into the Easter Vigil.

Mass Texts

◆ Universal Prayer or
Prayer of the Faithful

Please note the texts below should not be used on Good Friday. Please refer to The Roman Missal *for the Solemn Intercessions on this day.*

Introduction

Lord, you call us to eat at this heavenly banquet, and offer us the mandate to serve you. Hear the prayers that we dare to bring before you.

Intercessions

1. For our Holy Father, Pope Francis, that, through his example, we may stoop to wash the feet of those around us, we pray to the Lord; Lord: hear our prayer.

2. For our bishops and parish priests, that as they serve *in persona Christi* they may have the humility and love of Jesus, we pray to the Lord: Lord, hear our prayer.

3. For the leaders of nations, that they may work for peace throughout the world, especially in war-torn countries, we pray to the Lord: Lord, hear our prayer.

4. For the sick and the dying and those who may be experiencing the Passion of Christ in a special way,

that they may offer their sufferings joyfully to God, we pray to the Lord: Lord, hear our prayer.

5. For those who have gone before us, that, as we sing our Easter song, we remember them with joy and hope in the Resurrection, we pray to the Lord: Lord, hear our prayer.

6. For all guests and parishioners who are gathered here this Sacred Triduum, that they may experience the Body of Christ and the presence of the Lord (presence of the risen Christ) here within this congregation, we pray to the Lord: Lord, hear our prayer.

Conclusion

God of great mercy and compassion,
it is through your love
that we learn to enter
into the Paschal Mystery.
From foot washing and adoration
to Passion and Resurrection,
you are always present.
Hear our prayers,
for you know all that we need.
Bless us with your kindness as you answer them.
Through Christ our Lord.
Amen.

Dismissal for Catechumens and Elect

The Holy Triduum is a single extended feast that incorporates us into the events of Christ's Death and Resurrection. The mystery of salvation becomes less mysterious when we live it by entering the tomb of the font and then rising to put on the garment of new life in Christ. Your lives manifest this mysterious reality to our community. With gratitude for your fidelity to Christ's call and for the power of your witness we pray that you will fully embrace your new identity in Christ and live it faithfully till the end of your days.

April
Month of the Holy Eucharist

(#39) white

**Thursday of
Holy Week
(Holy Thursday)
Evening Mass of
the Lord's Supper**

T
H
U
2

About the Triduum/Evening Mass of the Lord's Supper

This evening Lent ends and the Church enters the Sacred Paschal Triduum, gathering to pray, building toward the prolonged vigiling of Saturday night. This evening's celebration, the Mass of the Lord's Supper, is the threshold liturgy of the Triduum. It commemorates the institution of Eucharist and the priesthood, as well as Jesus's command of love and service. It should be the only parish Mass today, even if varied language groups make up the parish community. Another Mass is celebrated only with permission of the bishop, and it should not dissuade people from attending the principal Mass. Aside from the possibility of the Chrism Mass, no other Masses are celebrated today. (Please note that since the Chrism Mass is not celebrated in parishes, the editors of this year's *Sourcebook* chose not to include commentary so to allow more comments on parish Triduum liturgies.)

Preparing this liturgy and the others of the Triduum can be enormously stressful if not reviewed well in advance. Avoid scheduling rehearsals during Holy Week; conduct them instead during the last few weeks of Lent. While there should be one overall coordinator for the Triduum liturgies, it helps greatly to have people responsible for each ministry and willing to rehearse each group. Rehearsals calm anxiety and ministers will be able to identify the processional routes, the stations for the washing of the feet, musical cues for movement, the location of readings and petitions, as well as the placement of needed liturgical items.

It is interesting to note that the Missal gives a series of instructions for the whole Sacred Paschal Triduum; these are listed before the rubrics for Thursday of the Lord's Supper. Liturgy committees would do well to take note of these important instructions and reflect on how they can best be implemented in their parish celebrations.

First, the centrality of these days as the preeminent days for celebrating the Paschal Mystery is noted, since on these three days the Church solemnly celebrates "the greatest mysteries of our redemption, keeping by means of special celebrations the memorial of her Lord, crucified, buried, and risen" (rubric for Triduum, 1).

The Paschal fast is also mentioned. The fast is to be kept everywhere on the Friday of the Lord's Passion, but the Missal goes on to recommend that it be prolonged through Holy Saturday. Catechesis about this Paschal fast might be useful for parishioners, because its meaning differs from that of the Lenten fast. While the Lenten fast is centered on penance, conversion, and renewal, the Paschal fast is more focused on preparation and anticipation (in a sense, almost being too excited to eat!); it is a way of preparing to come, "with spirit uplifted, to the joys of the Lord's Resurrection" (rubric for Triduum, 1). The Paschal fast helps us to enter into *kairos*, the "time outside of time" that characterizes the continual anamnesis of the Three Days, which, in some sense, are actually one.

A second rubric cautions that a sufficient number of lay ministers is required in order to fittingly celebrate the Sacred Paschal Triduum. Thus, what is true all year long must be especially in evidence during the Church's most sacred days, namely, that liturgical celebrations are diversified actions celebrated by the entire Body, and that a variety of ministers is needed, in proper number, so that the fullness of the Church's liturgical ministries may be in evidence. While "good enough is never good enough" is a maxim that should always apply to the Church's liturgical celebrations, the necessity of allowing the rites to be celebrated in all their fullness, which includes an adequate number of lay ministers, is heightened during these days.

In actuality, the point about lay ministers simply underscores the importance of the full, conscious, and active participation of the faithful during the celebrations, and this is the point that is highlighted next. The Missal points out that the "singing of the people, the ministers, and the Priest Celebrant has a special importance in the celebrations of these days, for when texts are sung, they have their proper impact" (rubric for Triduum, 2). Thus, the Missal is calling on communities to sing the rites during these days, and indeed these are the days to sing as many of the texts as possible — maybe even all of them! Furthermore, the full participation of the faithful is so important that the Missal makes a special reminder to pastors to catechize their people about the meaning and order of the celebrations. If we take this seriously, then we understand that catechesis about the Sacred Paschal Triduum through bulletin articles, preaching, workshop sessions, and adult education courses is as important a part of liturgical preparation as are the flow charts, gathering of props, and sprucing up of the environment and the vestments.

A third notation specifies that the liturgies of the Sacred Paschal Triduum "are to be carried out in cathedral and parochial churches and only in those chosen churches in which they can be performed with dignity, that is, with a good attendance of the faithful, an appropriate number of ministers, and the means to sing at least some of the parts" (rubric for Triduum, 3). For some, this might be a challenge to a radically new understanding of the rites. The liturgies of these days are not formalities or simple prayer experiences that can be performed perfunctorily just for the sake of giving people a nice experience; they are liturgies that are supposed to be powerful expressions of the very heart of what we believe and who we are. Thus, it is essential that these liturgies be celebrated with the dignity and fullness of expression that their nature demands. Small communities and other groupings of the faithful—small communities of religious, nursing homes or other institutions, schools, and even mission parishes—may need to ask some very difficult questions about their ability to celebrate these liturgies properly, and perhaps consider joining with larger communities.

The Lectionary for Mass

◆ First Reading: In this reading, God commands Moses and Aaron to institute the feast that would be known as Passover. At the time, the community of Israel was suffering in bondage in Egypt. This passage comes in the midst of the description of the ten plagues which convinced Pharaoh to free the people of Israel from their captivity. Passover came to mean the meal and the date fixed on the Jewish calendar. For the first observance, a family slaughtered a lamb or a goat, eating the meat, but sprinkling the blood on the two doorposts of each home. The blood became a sign for the angel responsible for the tenth plague to "pass over" the homes and spare the life of the firstborn. Ever since this event, the Jewish community has celebrated Passover each year.

◆ Responsorial Psalm 116: Several verses from a song of thanksgiving form the Responsorial Psalm. The overall purpose of this Psalm is to give thanks to God, but the Lectionary designates these verses because they especially fit the themes of Holy Thursday. The psalmist gives thanks by taking up "the cup of salvation" (116:13). The Psalm proclaims, "Precious in the eyes of the Lord / is the death of his faithful ones" (116:15). These verses foreshadow the Eucharistic cup that Jesus shared at the Last Supper, as well as his own Death looming on Good Friday. The refrain is lifted from the same epistle that gives us the Second Reading; it is not a verse from the Psalm. As Christians experiencing anew the last days of Jesus, rooted in the meal traditions of our ancestors, we sing, "Our blessing-cup is a communion with the Blood of Christ." Normally, the Responsorial Psalm echoes a theme from the First Reading or the Gospel. This is a rare instance when it pertains to the Second Reading, which is yet to be proclaimed.

◆ Second Reading: Saint Paul tells how Jesus instituted the Eucharist. With minor variations, this account also appears in Gospel accounts by Matthew, Mark, and Luke. Scholars tell us, however, that Paul wrote these epistles before the evangelists wrote their Gospel narratives. Therefore, this is the oldest account of what happened at the Last Supper, the version that lies closest to the years of Jesus's life. At this point in his letter, Paul is probably responding to some specific questions from the Corinthians. Apparently, they had asked about the proper way to celebrate the Eucharist. Paul hands on to them what others had told him. Paul says that the supper took place on the night before Jesus was betrayed, that Jesus took bread, gave thanks, said, "This is my body that is for you," and commanded his followers to "do this in remembrance of me" (11:24). Jesus repeated this command upon taking up the cup, which he called "the new covenant in my blood" (11:25). Paul says we proclaim the death of the Lord until he comes whenever we "eat this bread and drink the cup" (11:26). These words address the heart of Catholic faith. We believe that our Eucharist is the Body and Blood of Christ, that Jesus told us this, and that he commanded us to eat and drink in remembrance of him. This passage is the key that unlocks the meaning of Holy Thursday.

◆ Gospel: Jesus gives his followers a model of discipleship when he washes their feet. In John's account of the Gospel, at the Last Supper, when the reader expects to find the institution of the Eucharist that appears in Matthew, Mark, and Luke (the synoptic accounts of the Gospel), and even in Paul's First Letter to the Corinthians, it is not there. Instead, John gives a mystical interpretation of the Eucharist in the washing of the feet. Just as Paul's letter unlocks the meaning of Holy Thursday, John's narrative unlocks its implications. As Jesus stoops to wash feet, Simon Peter resists until Jesus warns him, "Unless I wash you, you will have no inheritance with me" (13:8). His statement probably alludes to Baptism, which became an initiation rite for all the followers of Jesus. Importantly, Jesus advises the disciples, "If I, therefore, the master and teacher, have washed your feet, you ought to wash one another's feet" (13:14). Whenever we engage in selfless, humble service to our neighbor, we follow the model that Jesus gave.

The Roman Missal

Before the Mass texts are given, the Missal lists special instructions that pertain to the celebration of the Evening Mass of the Lord's Supper, some of which are worth highlighting here. First to be noted is that the Mass is celebrated in the evening, "with the full participation of the whole local community and with all the Priests and ministers exercising their office" (Thursday of the Lord's Supper, rubric 1). Thus once again the importance of the community gathering as the one body with a variety of roles and ministries in evidence is affirmed; in fact, it is ancient tradition that all Masses without the participation of the people are forbidden on this day (see PS, 47). Another rubric mentions that flowers are permitted as decorations, but there should be moderation; we are not yet at Easter. This moderation applies to the place where the Blessed Sacrament will be reserved after Mass; *Paschale solemnitatis* specifies that that space must be conducive to prayer and meditation, and therefore demands sobriety, and abuses are to be suppressed (see PS, 49). Nor is the place of reservation to be made to resemble a tomb, because the chapel of repose is not representing the Lord's burial; rather, it is for the custody of the Eucharistic bread that will be distributed in Communion on the next day (see PS, 55).

The Entrance Antiphon, taken from chapter 6, verse 14 of Paul's letter to the Galatians, sums up the mystery we are celebrating throughout the days of the Sacred Paschal Triduum. It's a mystery that can only be understood by living in its truth: "We should glory in the Cross of our Lord Jesus Christ." How is it possible to find glory in the midst of suffering and death? It's possible because through Christ's suffering and Death "we are saved and delivered." That's the mystery that is the heart of the Christian faith, the mystery that is celebrated in every liturgy, and the mystery that is the *raison d'être* of the Christian life—it is the Paschal Mystery that through Christ, with him, and in him, death becomes life and self-emptying leads to fullness.

The Gloria returns this evening, and it should be sung with joy and

fullness; the Missal mentions that bells are rung. Outdoor bells should be rung in the carillon; bells inside the church may be rung by choir members, or altar servers and other ministers, perhaps even by members of the assembly. After this joyous ringing out of the glory of God, the bells are to remain silent until the Gloria of the Easter Vigil. To further highlight the seriousness and uniqueness of the days of the Triduum, a rubric notes that "during this same period [between the Gloria of the evening Mass on Holy Thursday and the Gloria at the Easter Vigil], the organ and other musical instruments may be used only so as to support the singing."

The Collect for this Mass draws our attention to this night's Eucharist being linked to the Last Supper, which is referred to in the Second Reading, with the meaning of the supper being clear: it is the meal Jesus "entrusted to the Church" as "the banquet of his love," "a sacrifice new for all eternity." The effects of participating in that sacrificial banquet are also made clear: we are to draw "from so great a mystery the fullness of charity and of life."

This evening is one of the rare occasions when the Missal specifies for the homilist the themes he is to touch on. The priest's Homily is to shed light on "the principal mysteries that are commemorated in this Mass, namely, the institution of the Holy Eucharist and of the priestly Order, and the commandment of the Lord concerning charity." As will be noted several times below, the connection between participation in the Eucharist and living a life of love cannot be overlooked, and that connection should be at the core of the meaning of this Mass. The institution of the ministerial priesthood is commemorated because of the close connection between priesthood and the Eucharist; it is the priest who acts in the person of Christ the Head (*in persona*

Christi capitis) within the liturgical assembly and without whom the Eucharist cannot be celebrated. Notice, however, that there is nothing in the ritual for this evening about priests renewing their promises; the place for that is at the Chrism Mass and it has no place in this liturgy. It is something that is meant to be led by the bishop; there are no texts for it at the evening Mass, and it should not be added.

Sacrificial charity and sacrificial living are ritualized in the Washing of Feet, which, as the Missal notes, follows the Homily. Although technically optional, the ritual has such power that one might rightly question why a community would not celebrate it. The unique power of this startling gesture should be allowed to stand on its own and should not be obscured by gimmicks or adaptations. Yes, it is uncomfortable, especially (and ironically), not for the one doing the footwashing, but for the one having his or her feet washed (it's not unusual for people to be shy and reticent about doing this); yes, it is countercultural; yes, it can be awkward. However, all three can also be said about Christian humility and sacrificial love. Resist the temptation to weaken the gesture by changing it to a washing of hands. Nor is there any foundation in the Missal for anyone other than the priest celebrant to wash feet; he functions as the sacramental image of Christ the Head at all other parts of the Eucharist, so why should there be the need to mute this representation during this rite, which is part of the Eucharist? True, all are called to wash one another's feet, that is, serve one another, but the same call to service (and unity) is true of every Eucharist, and the priest exercising his liturgical function alone at other times does not negate or lessen the assembly's participation in the mystery; the same is true here. Therefore, also to be avoided is diminishing the power of the gesture by having others, whether they be clergy or laity, join the priest celebrant in washing feet.

The rite is simple and straightforward. The Missal tells us: "The men who have been chosen are led by the ministers to seats prepared in a suitable place. Then the priest (removing his chasuble if necessary) goes to each one, and, with the help of the ministers, pours water over each one's feet and then dries them." Some comments are in order.

Although the Missal uses the word "men" for those who are chosen to have their feet washed, in fact in many United States parishes, women as well as men have their feet washed. The United States Conference of Catholic Bishops has a statement about the meaning of the Washing of Feet, which would, at least as of this writing, still allow for the practice of including women (see http://www.usccb.org/prayer-and-worship/liturgical-resources/triduum/holy-thursday-mandatum.cfm). Also, no specific number is mentioned, and therefore it need not be limited to twelve. While twelve is a customary number, any number can be used, and the people chosen should adequately reflect the make-up of the community. People of all ages, including young children, may be asked to have their feet washed; people of different races and language groups may be included; at least one of the elect, preparing for initiation at this year's Easter Vigil, may be included.

Next, the only location mentioned is "a suitable place." Therefore, there is no need for this rite to take place exclusively in the sanctuary; in fact, there are several reasons that would argue against that practice. Certainly, the visibility of the rite would be an important factor. Having multiple stations throughout the church would allow for a maximum number of people to be up close to the action as it is taking place. (This is also one way of reinforcing what is true for all liturgy — that the liturgical action takes place in the entire worship space, not just in the sanctuary.) Additionally, there can be something very touching — part of the meaning of humble service — to have the priest celebrant move throughout the assembly, going to those before whom he will kneel, rather than having them come to him. However, the suitability of various locations must be carefully considered: how will chairs be placed and then removed in such a way that this action does not draw undue attention to itself? Will the priest be able to kneel easily enough, and will the necessary ministers have access to assist him? What about numbers of pitchers, basins, and towels — how will they be made available, taken away, and who will see to this? None of these details are insurmountable; they need only be thought through in advance so that specific needs can be prepared for and the action can be carried out smoothly, with a minimum of distraction.

Also of interest is the statement that the priest removes his chasuble if necessary; given the action to be performed, one would think it is necessary, for ease of movement. However, there is no mention of the priest tying a towel around his waist, which is nonetheless a custom that many priest celebrants do; the Gospel for the Mass mentions that Jesus did so before he washed the disciples' feet. The rubric goes on to mention that the priest goes to each person and, assisted by ministers, pours water over each one's feet and then dries them. The plural "feet" is used, which would seem to indicate that both feet of each person are to be washed, not just one. (Many priest celebrants have the custom of kissing the feet of the people as well, after washing them.)

While the rite should not be unduly prolonged, neither should it be hurried; the fact that several examples of antiphons are given in the Missal indicate this. The meaning of the rite is revealed in the antiphons: it is all about Jesus's example of love, humble service, and sharing in Jesus's life by following him.

After the washing of feet, the priest washes and dries his hands, puts the chasuble back on, and the Mass continues with the Universal Prayer as usual. The Creed is not said. After the Universal Prayer, Mass continues with the preparation of the altar and the presentation of the gifts.

Rarely does one find in the Missal a specific rubric about the procession with the gifts, but there is one given here: it is mentioned that gifts for the poor may be presented along with the bread and wine, with those gifts being carried in procession by the faithful. This harkens back to the ancient practice of the Church, where everyone brought something for the offering, and some of the offerings would be set aside for the poor. Such a procession would be a stark reminder of the practical charity that must be a consequence of our participation in the Eucharist — we cannot truly share bread at the Eucharistic table unless we are also sharing bread with the hungry outside the Eucharist. Perhaps these offerings on Holy Thursday can be an impetus for catechizing the faithful at other times about the offering of self that is the heart of our participation in the Eucharistic sacrifice. Certainly the sight of everyone processing forward to bring their gifts to the altar, with the gifts of bread and wine that will be transformed through the power of the Spirit being carried last, would be a powerful sign of the participation of all the faithful. The Missal's suggestion of the antiphon to be chanted, *Ubi caritas*, "Where true charity is dwelling,

God is present there" highlights the unity of meaning between the footwashing, which was just completed, and the bringing forward of the offerings for the celebration of the Eucharist.

The Prayer over the Offerings offers a succinct summary of the very essence of liturgical theology: "whenever the memorial of this sacrifice is celebrated / the work of our redemption is accomplished" (one suspects that the homilist could well include this theme in his preaching). To the degree that we are aware of and appreciate what is taking place in our midst here and now (the work of our redemption), that is the degree to which we can be said to be participating worthily in the mysteries.

The Preface assigned for this Mass is Preface I of the Most Holy Eucharist, and the text, with musical notation, is given along with the other texts for this Mass; one could argue that this is revealing the Church's preference for the priest celebrant to chant the Preface (see comments above about singing during the Triduum). The text itself zeroes in on the core of Eucharistic theology. As it recalls Christ offering himself "as the saving Victim," it also notes how the Eucharist was instituted as the pattern of his sacrifice, and therefore the offering of the Eucharist is the memorial of his offering and sacrifice. Participation in the Eucharist means to join one's own offering with the self-offering of Christ that is made present through anamnesis. This is further emphasized as the Preface goes on to note, "As we eat his flesh that was sacrificed for us, we are made strong, and, as we drink his Blood that was poured out for us, we are washed clean."

The complete text for Eucharistic Prayer I, the Roman Canon, is given along with the other texts for this Mass. This allows for an easy use of the special inserts for the *Communicantes* ("In communion with those"), the *Hanc igitur* ("therefore, Lord, we pray"), and the *Qui pridie* ("On the day before he was to suffer"), which are used at this Mass. However, while it might be argued that, given these special inserts, there is a certain preference for using the Roman Canon, it is not required (as indicated by the rubric at number 17, "When the Roman Canon is used . . . "), and so Eucharistic Prayer III could also be used. (Prayer II because of its brevity would not be appropriate, and Eucharistic Prayer IV is disqualified because of its proper Preface.)

There is a special rubric concerning Holy Communion: after distribution, a ciborium with hosts for Communion tomorrow is left on the altar. The Prayer after Communion makes an eschatological reference as it asks that "just as we are renewed by the Supper of your Son in this present age, so we may enjoy his banquet for all eternity." This is the last prayer that will be proclaimed at this liturgy; the transfer of the Blessed Sacrament follows immediately.

The transfer of the Blessed Sacrament is rather simple and direct. After the Prayer after Communion, the priest, after putting incense in the thurible, goes to the Blessed Sarament and incenses it three times. He puts on a white humeral veil, rises, takes the ciborium, and uses the ends of the humeral veil to cover it.

A procession is then formed, led by a minister with a cross, flanked by ministers with lighted candles; although the people are not mentioned, if the place of repose is in another location, the assembly will join the procession, following these ministers. Other ministers with lighted candles may follow the assembly, preceding the minister carrying the smoking thurible, who is directly in front of the priest carrying the Blessed Sacrament. During the procession, a suitable Eucharistic chant is sung; the Missal suggests *Pange, lingua*, excluding the last two verses (the *Tantum ergo*), and it might be argued there is a certain fondness for using this chant.

Upon reaching the place of repose, the priest places the ciborium in the tabernacle, but leaves the door open. Placing incense in the thurible, he incenses the Blessed Sacrament while kneeling and while the *Tantum ergo* or another Eucharistic chant is sung. After this, the tabernacle door is closed.

Next comes a period of adoration in silence (note that the door is to be closed before the period of adoration). After a period of silence, the priest and ministers rise, genuflect, and then depart, but with no formal procession — this is simply a functional leaving of the ministers, not a ritual departure. Adoration by the faithful before the Blessed Sacrament continues, but the Missal notes that midnight is a demarcation point for adoration: "after midnight the adoration should take place without solemnity" (rubric 43). However, there is no requirement to continue adoration past midnight, but only "for a suitable length of time during the night." Thus, there is nothing to prevent a parish closing the period of adoration at midnight.

Notice that there is no formal or specific dismissal to this liturgy; thus, emphasizing that the liturgies of the Sacred Paschal Triduum are, in some sense, one continuous liturgy. After the liturgy, at an appropriate time, the altar is stripped and crosses are removed from the church, if they can be; if not, they should be veiled (number 57 of *Paschale solemnitatis* notes that the veil should be red or purple, unless they have already been veiled on the Saturday before the Fifth Sunday of Lent). This stripping is done without any ritual or solemnity.

The Missal makes a final note that if for some reason the Passion of the Lord is not celebrated in the same church on the next day, then Mass ends in the usual way, and the Blessed Sacrament is reserved in the tabernacle as usual, without any procession or adoration.

Other Ideas

The altar of repose should be a beautiful, well prepared space, and not an afterthought. The more inviting it is, the more likely the congregation will pray for a while after the liturgy. Make sure that all hospitality ministers, choir members, and liturgical environment team members model silence and calmness well to the assembly. Keep the lights semi-dimmed and the people will depart in silence. Or, better yet, bring the choir to the altar of repose, and have them sing "Stay Here and Keep Watch" or something else to bring the people to prayer.

(#40)   red

F
R   **3**   **Friday of the**
I   **Passion of the Lord**
           (Good Friday)

About Good Friday

On this day, the parish community gathers to prayerfully recall the Death of Jesus "in the hope of their resurrection" (Prayer over the People, Good Friday). Because his Resurrection is inseparable from his Death, the Lord's Passion is truly celebrated. We remember last night's words from St. Paul, "We should glory in the Cross of our Lord Jesus Christ, / in whom is our salvation, life and resurrection, / through whom we are saved and delivered."

A rubric in the Missal describes how the environment in the church expresses the somber mood of the day: the altar should be completely bare, without cross, candles, or cloths. The liturgy is to begin at three o'clock in the afternoon or later; a time before then is not

envisioned. It is a liturgy consisting of three parts: the Liturgy of the Word; the Adoration of the Cross; and Holy Communion.

The liturgy may be repeated later with the permission of the diocesan bishop, and this is important. For people who work and/or who would otherwise be unable to attend the afternoon liturgy but who are looking to attend a service to mark the day, it would be preferable for them to be able to experience the liturgy of the Church. Certainly devotional celebrations such as Stations of the Cross can be scheduled on this day, but as much as possible we should be encouraging people to pray the official liturgies of the Church. Finally, there is a specific rubric mentioning that this liturgy "by its very nature" may not be celebrated in the absence of a priest; therefore, a deacon may not preside.

The Lectionary for Mass

◆ FIRST READING: The Lectionary subtitles this passage the fourth oracle of the Servant of the Lord, but it is often called the fourth song of the Suffering Servant. Near the end of the book of the prophet Isaiah, we meet a figure called God's servant, who represents God but suffers greatly for the sins of others. The figure may have been a historical person at the time of Isaiah or a representation of the people of Israel. Christians read these four passages with a very specific insight: they prophesy Jesus, the servant of the Father, who suffered for our salvation. The passage opens with a startling description of this servant. He was "spurned and avoided by people, / a man of suffering, accustomed to infirmity" (Isaiah 53:3). In the most moving verses, read with a lump in our throats, we realize that the servant's suffering should have been ours: "Yet it was our infirmities that he bore, / our sufferings that he endured. . . . / We had all gone astray like sheep . . . /

but the Lord laid upon him / the guilt of us all" (Isaiah 53:4, 6). On Good Friday, these verses come to fulfillment in the crucified Jesus.

◆ RESPONSORIAL PSALM 31 appeals to God for rescue. The psalmist is desperate, "an object of reproach, / a laughingstock to my neighbors, and a dread to my friends" (Psalm 31:6). But the Psalm does not dwell in despair. It trusts that God will redeem the one in distress. This singer is so convinced of salvation that the Psalm concludes with an exhortation to the hearer: "Take courage and be stouthearted, / all you who hope in the Lord" (Psalm 31:25). The refrain for the Psalm comes from the Gospel according to Luke. It was spoken by Jesus on the cross. Jesus, who must have known its words by heart, quotes Psalm 31 when he makes his appeal for rescue: "Father, into your hands I commend my spirit" (Luke 23:46).

◆ SECOND READING: The sufferings of Jesus enabled him to empathize with our weakness, making him a powerful mediator of mercy and grace. The Letter to the Hebrews explains the role of Jesus as the greatest of all high priests. This passage describes the events of Jesus's Passion: "In the days when Christ was in the flesh, he offered prayers and supplications with loud cries and tears to the one who was able to save him from death" (Hebrews 5:7). These words resemble the Gospel accounts of Jesus suffering his agony in the garden of Gethsemane. But the passage does not linger on Jesus's suffering. "[H]e was heard" (Hebrews 5:7). The Father, who could save Jesus from death, did, through his Death and Resurrection.

◆ GOSPEL: This passage in the Gospel according to John is one of the most sublime testimonies to the glory of God. The narrative moves through several scenes, but it constantly teaches the meaning of

Jesus's life, Death, and Resurrection. We hear it each year on Good Friday.

Early on, John presents "Jesus, knowing everything that was going to happen to him" (John 18:4). Jesus is no innocent bystander. He is the omniscient God in control of the events that follow. Three times in the opening confrontation he says, "I AM," boldly claiming the name that God revealed to Moses in the burning bush. His enemies end up proclaiming the truth about Jesus in spite of themselves. Caiaphas had told the Jews that, "it was better that one man should die rather than the people" (John 18:14), fulfilling Isaiah's fourth oracle. Pilate, unable to get a straight answer from Jesus about his identity, asks, "What is truth?" (John 18:38). But it is Pilate who has an inscription made for the cross that calls Jesus, in three languages, the King of the Jews. The soldiers plait a crown from thorns and wrap Jesus's aching body in purple cloth, intending to mock, but instead acknowledging his kingship.

While the enemies of Jesus unintentionally speak the truth, his friend Peter intentionally denies Jesus three times. From the cross, Jesus takes matters into his own hands, entrusting his mother and the disciple whom he loved to each other. From these faithful disciples the Church will be born. Before he dies, Jesus says, "It is finished" (John 19:30). That doesn't mean, "It's over." It means, "It is accomplished," or "It is perfected." He has completed the task he was given. He hands himself over to God. John has Jesus dying on the cross on preparation day, the day before Passover, so that we will see in the slaughtering of the Passover lambs a contemporaneous symbol of the One who gave his life that others might live.

The Roman Missal

Just as last night's liturgy had no formal ending, so today's has no formal beginning — one liturgy flows into the next in the unity of these days. Wearing red Mass vestments, the priest and deacon simply go to the altar in silence and, after reverencing it, prostrate themselves; all others in the assembly kneel. Then, after a period of silence, the priest rises and goes to the chair. He should take care to make sure that the period of silence is noticeable. It has been said that true silence begins only when the shuffling, rustling, and other noises end, and so the priest should allow for a prolonged period of true silence on this particular day.

At the chair, the priest prays the prayer. This prayer is not a Collect, and the invitation "Let us pray" is omitted, further showing both the stark nature of this liturgy and the way this liturgy flows from the previous one. The priest has a choice from among two prayers. The first option asks God to remember his mercies and to protect his servants, because they are the ones for whom Christ shed his blood and established the Paschal Mystery. The overt use of the phrase "Paschal Mystery" is striking, and it reminds us of the total mystery we are celebrating through the Sacred Paschal Triduum. The second option asks that just as we have borne "the image of the man of earth," that is, Adam, so too, "by the sanctification of grace," may we "bear the image of the Man of heaven." Bearing the image of Christ is possible because by his Passion he "abolished the death inherited from ancient sin."

The Liturgy of the Word takes place, with the Lord's Passion read in the same way as it was read on Palm Sunday of the Lord's Passion. After the reading of the Passion, a brief Homily is preached; the rubric goes on to mention that at the end of the Homily "the faithful may be invited to spend a short time in prayer" (rubric 10). Certainly this day above all others calls for noticeable periods of silence.

The Solemn Intercessions follow. A deacon or lay minister sings or says the invitation while standing at the ambo. Then all pray in silence for a while, followed by the priest saying or singing the prayer with his hands extended. A rubric mentions that it is traditional for all to kneel for silent prayer after each invitation to prayer, as the deacon may add, "Let us kneel" and "Let us stand." While technically optional, one could argue a certain preference for following this tradition on this day: it highlights the solemnity of the intercessions, and the unusual gesture serves to further mark off the rites of the Sacred Paschal Triduum as rites that occur only once a year to mark our central and holiest days. A key element, however, would be to make sure the people are left to kneel silently for a long enough period of time, lest the kneeling and standing become simply a distracting (and perhaps unintentionally comical) series of down-and-up, down-and-up movements.

There are ten intercessions provided by the Missal: for the Holy Church; for the pope; for all orders and degrees of the faithful; for catechumens; for the unity of Christians; for the Jewish people; for those who do not believe in Christ; for those who do not believe in God; for those in public office; and for those in tribulation. The titles reveal the universality of these prayers as the Church expresses her concern and intercedes for the whole world. It is significant that on one of her most solemn days, the Church spends so much time pleading for the well-being of the entire world.

Following the Solemn Intercessions, which conclude the Liturgy of the Word, comes the second part of the liturgy, the Adoration of the

Holy Cross. The Holy Cross is first shown, and then it is adored; there are two forms for the showing, and there are two ways that the adoration may take place.

In the first form of the showing, the deacon, accompanied by one or more ministers, goes to the sacristy and then returns in procession, accompanied by two ministers carrying lighted candles, carrying the Cross, which is covered with a violet veil, through the church to the middle of the sanctuary. There the priest receives the cross and, after uncovering a little of its upper part, elevates it while singing the "Behold the wood of the Cross. . . ." After responding, "Come, let us adore," the people kneel and adore the cross in silence for a brief period while the priest stands and holds the cross up. Then the priest uncovers the right arm of the cross, again raising it, and then singing "Behold the wood of the Cross. . . " and the rest taking place as the first time. Lastly, he uncovers the cross completely and the same sequence of events occurs. In the second form of showing, the priest or the deacon, accompanied by one or more ministers, goes to the door of the church and takes up the unveiled cross as the ministers take up lighted candles. Then, in procession, they move through the church to the sanctuary, stopping in three locations — just inside the entrance to the church, in the middle of the church, and in front of the entrance to the sanctuary — at which times the priest or deacon elevates the cross, sings "Behold the wood of the Cross" with all responding "Come, let us adore." A rubric states that also in this second form the people are to kneel and adore the cross in silence for a brief moment, as in the first form.

For the Adoration of the Cross, one option is to have the priest or deacon, after carrying in the cross, hand over the cross to ministers to hold at the entrance to the

sanctuary, or at some other suitable place, with candles placed to the right and left of the cross. At that location, the priest celebrant, possibly with chasuble and shoes removed, approaches the cross, followed by the clergy, lay ministers, and the faithful, all coming in procession. The sign of reverence to the cross can be varied: a simple genuflection, a kiss, or some other meaningful gesture. Consider inviting everyone to remove their shoes before approaching the cross; there is nothing that forbids this, and the strangeness of this gesture not only reinforces the uniqueness of the days of the Triduum, but also makes a statement about the holiness of the ground we walk in adoring the instrument of our salvation.

It is clearly stated that only one cross should be used for adoration, so parishes should avoid using multiple crosses. When the assembly is so large that approaching individually is not feasible, a second option is given for the adoration. (It should be noted, however, that several people can approach the cross and venerate it at the same time, to accommodate a larger number of participants. There is no need to rush this part of the liturgy, and the music that is suggested [see below] would seem to indicate that more than just a brief time should be accorded to the adoration.) In this second option, the priest, "after some of the clergy and faithful have adored" (the Missal does not specify who these "some" are) takes the cross and invites the people in a few words (of his own choosing — no text is given) to adore the Holy Cross, after which he holds the cross high for a brief time while the faithful adore it in silence. The Missal suggests and gives the texts for an antiphon, the Reproaches, and/or the hymn *Crux fidelis* to be sung during the adoration; other suitable songs may be used as well, and a rubric mentions the *Stabat Mater* as another possibility,

in addition to some other "suitable chant in memory of the compassion of the Blessed Virgin Mary."

When the adoration is finished, the cross is carried to its place at the altar, where it stands with lighted candles, which are placed either around the altar, on it, or near the cross. The third part of the liturgy, Holy Communion, now begins with the altar being prepared with a cloth, a corporal, and the Missal being placed on it. While this is being done, the deacon, or, in his absence, the priest, wearing a humeral veil, brings the Blessed Sacrament from the place of repose to the altar while the assembly stands in silence. The Missal specifically notes that the deacon or priest uses "a shorter route," indicating that this is not in any way to be an elaborate procession; it is simply more of a functional bringing of the Blessed Sacrament to the altar for Holy Communion, although appropriate marks of honor for the Real Presence are nonetheless used — the humeral veil, and two ministers with lighted candles accompanying the Blessed Sacrament. As the Blessed Sacrament is placed on the altar, candlesticks are placed on or around the altar.

If the deacon brought the Blessed Sacrament to the altar, the priest goes to the altar once the ciborium is uncovered, and he genuflects upon arriving there. He then introduces the Lord's Prayer, which is prayed with its embolism and doxology, followed by a private prayer of the priest, his genuflection, and then the "Behold the Lamb of God . . ." with the response, "Lord, I am not worthy. . . ." Communion is then distributed, during which Psalm 22 or another appropriate song may be sung.

When the distribution of Holy Communion is completed, the Blessed Sacrament is taken by the deacon or another minister to a place prepared outside the church. Of note here is that there seems to be a preference for the priest not to do this; if a deacon is not present, then perhaps another minister would be a more appropriate choice. No mention is made of candles accompanying the Blessed Sacrament, so this too is a simple action of returning the sacrament to its place of repose, and is in no way a procession or movement with a great deal of solemnity; this is in keeping with the tone of the day. If required, the Blessed Sacrament may be placed in the tabernacle, although it would appear the preference is to use a place outside the church.

The liturgy ends as starkly as it began. After the Blessed Sacrament has been removed, the priest prays the Prayer after Communion. Then follows a simple dismissal: the deacon or priest invites the people to bow down for the blessing, the priest extends his hands over the people and prays the prayer; and then they simply depart after genuflecting to the cross. There is no procession by the ministers or the faithful; it is a simple dispersing.

After the liturgy, the altar is stripped, but the cross remains with two or four candlesticks; people should be encouraged to pray before the cross.

Other Ideas

So much of the liturgical year is focused on the Gospel message about Jesus's journey towards Jerusalem. Well, we are finally here, as we embrace the Passion of Christ this day. One of the "extras" of the day is a Collection for the Holy Land. But this service has no traditional offertory, and ushers passing around baskets in the middle of prayer would be extremely anti-climatic. Some parishes simply leave an envelope in the end of pews and allow parishioners to place the envelopes to be placed in baskets at the entrances of the church. Realistically this will mean chaos at the doors instead of solemn

silence — and potentially less offering. Perhaps a better solution is to wait until just a few minutes before the service begins, and then have someone come out and speak on behalf of the Holy Land funds.

Has your priest toured Jerusalem? Then he could give a more passionate presentation then someone simply reading a prepared script. If you have followed this rhythm for a few years, as soon as he starts speaking, the ushers could begin handing out the baskets. A solo cello piece or brief choral number could cover this action and set the appropriate solemn mood for the service, and help people settle in to pray.

violet

SAT 4 Holy Saturday Morning and Afternoon

About Holy Saturday

Christ was in the tomb; he lay in darkness in the womb of the whole world. Holy Saturday commemorates that day and has a character all its own. It is a quiet day of meditation, reflection, and anticipation, especially for the elect preparing for Baptism. Although there is much to do, don't let it just be a day for decorating the church. During the day, invite people to pray Morning Prayer and vigil in front of the crucifix in the barren church.

There is no Mass during the day, and Holy Communion may be given before the Vigil only as Viaticum. Reconciliation and Anointing of the Sick may be celebrated today. Ministers to the sick should make every effort to visit the sick during Good Friday and Holy Saturday, sharing with them some of the readings and bringing the prayers of the community. During the day today we continue the Paschal fast. The elect should be fasting in preparation for their Baptism, and the faithful may join them in solidarity of spirit. This recommendation

dates back to about the year 100 AD, where it appeared in the *Didache*. Linked to the past, we continue this discipline in a prayerful spirit. The climax of the Sacred Paschal Triduum, the Easter Vigil, begins after darkness has fallen, officially forty-five minutes after dark. You can find the exact time for the setting of the sun in your area by consulting the Navy website (http://aa.usno.navy.mil/data/docs /RS_OneYear.php). The Easter Vigil launches us into Easter Time, and it should not be confused with Holy Saturday itself.

(#41)   white

SAT 4 Holy Saturday Easter Sunday of the Resurrection of the Lord: The Easter Vigil in the Holy Night

About the Easter Vigil

Shattering the darkness, the great Paschal candle is lit with the Easter fire, five wax nails of incense are imbedded, and it becomes the symbol of the crucified Christ. The Paschal Mystery, already celebrated in various ways since the Evening Mass of the Lord's Supper, is clearly and joyfully announced from the very beginning of the Vigil liturgy. It is in the light of the Paschal candle that the liturgy continues to unfold. The Easter Vigil is the most beautiful of all liturgies. Ranking highest among the celebrations of the liturgical year, it should rank highest in the spiritual life of the parish community, not a small task in places where Christmas is considered the high point. Encourage all parishioners to take part by offering good, solid catechesis and invitations in advance. If the community has been involved in the journey of the catechumens, they will want to be present and surround them for this celebration.

The four parts of the Easter Vigil move us through a gradual unfolding of the Paschal Mystery of Christ. The great fire immediately dispels the gathering gloom. The Liturgy of the Word reveals the path of God's plan throughout salvation history. The Liturgy of Baptism draws the elect through the baptismal waters into the promise of eternal life and renews the baptismal belief of the faithful. The Liturgy of the Eucharist brings the celebration to the climax of the banquet of the Lamb, as we experience the presence of the risen Christ in our midst.

The Lectionary for Mass

◆ FIRST READING: The entire Bible opens with an account of how and why all things came to be. The heavens and the earth exist by the will of God. At the time these verses were written, science had not advanced beyond a rudimentary understanding of biology and zoology. The Catholic Church does not expect members to believe literally in the words of this story. Genesis, however, defends a vital belief that we recite at the beginning of our weekly Profession of Faith: God is the Creator of heaven and earth. The Easter Vigil is the pivotal night of the entire liturgical year. Lent has led up to this night; even Advent and Christmas Time have been preparing for this night. Everything we celebrate for the next fifty days results from our belief that Jesus is risen from the dead. Christ's Resurrection from the dead makes our own resurrection possible. As faithful followers, we believe that God created us, and that God will re-create us at the end of time. Our destiny is prefigured in the Baptisms we celebrate in Catholic churches throughout the world on this night. To reaffirm the foundation of our belief in a new creation, the Easter Vigil offers us the story of the first creation. Since God created everything out of nothing, it is not so hard to believe

that God can re-create everything out of something.

◆ RESPONSORIAL PSALM, OPTION 1: Psalm 104 is a song of praise to God for the wonders of creation. It imagines the earth fixed upon a foundation, covered with the waters of the oceans, surmounted by waters enclosed in the sky, high above the tops of the mountains. Water, birds, cattle, and grain all supply the needs of humanity, the crown of God's creation. It would be enough if this Psalm praised God for the wonders of nature, but it does something more. It praises God for the way nature is renewed each year and from one generation to the next. The verse we use for the refrain calls upon God to send the Spirit to renew the face of the earth. This quality of creation, its inherent ability to renew, makes this Psalm a perfect choice for the Easter Vigil. On this night, we praise God for the Resurrection of Christ, for the new life bestowed upon the newly baptized, and for the promise of eternal life revealed throughout God's Word.

◆ RESPONSORIAL PSALM, OPTION 2: As an alternative to Psalm 104, a different song of creation may follow the First Reading: Psalm 33. It, too, praises God for the wonders of nature. This Psalm envisions that the waters of the ocean are contained as in a flask, confined as though in cellars in the deep. Notably, Psalm 33 includes morality among God's creations. God's word is "upright," all God's works are "trustworthy," God loves "justice and right," and the earth is full of God's "kindness." Here is echoed the belief from the First Reading that what God made is "good." We praise God not just for the things that are, but for the goodness of things that are. Christians interpret one of the verses of this Psalm as a prophecy for our belief in the Holy Trinity: "By the

word of the Lord the heavens were made; / by the breath of his mouth all their host." In one verse we find references to the Lord, the Word, and the breath, images of the Triune God, preexisting all that is.

◆ SECOND READING: This is one of the most difficult passages in the entire Bible, and it is hard to hear it without feeling squeamish about the God who would make this request, Abraham who would fulfill it, and Isaac who would be the innocent victim. There is a happy ending, but not before the story turns our stomachs. Adding to the grim nature of God's request is that Abraham had no son until he was over one hundred years old. God had promised that Abraham's progeny would be as numberless as the sands on the shore of the sea, but the patriarch was not yet a father of one. Now, at incredibly advanced ages, Abraham and Sarah had become first-time parents, and this was the son God wanted him to sacrifice. The story is retold at the Easter Vigil because it foreshadows the life of Jesus. He was an only child, as was Isaac. He was innocent, yet walked up a hill carrying on his shoulders the wood of his sacrifice. But there, the similarities end. Isaac was saved from death; Jesus was saved through death.

◆ RESPONSORIAL PSALM: Those in the most difficult circumstances yearn for the confident trust of Psalm 16. When things go wrong, we turn to God for assistance. Sometimes we demand help; often we hope against hope for it. But Psalm 16 exudes confidence: "with [the Lord] at my right hand I shall not be disturbed." This Psalm flows naturally from the story of Abraham and Isaac. Abraham, too, possessed the charism of confidence. He believed that, even in the most difficult circumstances, God would be faithful to the covenant. Psalm 16 fits the Easter Vigil because of its references to death and life. This Psalm appears each week in Thursday's night prayer from the Liturgy of the Hours. Before going to bed, Christians pray these words, confident that wakefulness will follow sleep, and life will follow death.

◆ THIRD READING: This paradigmatic reading from the Old Testament must be proclaimed in every celebration of the Easter Vigil. The liturgy encourages the use of all the Old Testament readings at the Vigil, but permits a smaller number for exceptional circumstances. This reading is never omitted because it roots our understanding of Baptism and resurrection. In the story, Egypt has enslaved the Israelites, and God has appointed Moses to lead them from the clutches of Pharaoh into freedom. Their only route traverses the Red Sea, which parts for their passage, but returns to swallow up the pursuing forces of Pharaoh, his chariots, and his charioteers. On the other side of the waters, Israel is poised to enter the Promised Land. The Exsultet and the blessing of baptismal water, which are both heard in the Vigil, point out the significance of this passage, and hence of this night. God freed Israel from its foes through water, and God will free the catechumens from the clutches of Satan and sin through the waters of Baptism. Set free from Pharaoh, Israel entered the Promised Land. Set free from sin, the neophytes enter the life of grace as members of the Body of Christ. At the center of all this imagery is Jesus Christ, who was set free from death to life through the mercy of the Father.

◆ CANTICLE: The Responsory that follows this reading from Exodus also comes from Exodus. It is the very song that Israel sings upon reaching the dry shores on the other side of the Red Sea. It retells the events of this Passover night: the loss of Pharaoh's chariots in the Red Sea and the redemption of God's Chosen People when God "planted them on the mountain" (Exodus 15:17). Throughout the song, the people give praise to God. It is the Lord who has covered himself in glory. Yes, they have experienced freedom from slavery, but they do not rejoice in their own accomplishment. They praise God.

◆ FOURTH READING: This passage from the prophecy of Isaiah meets Israel at a very different moment in history. Many years have passed since the dramatic rescue of the Chosen People from the hand of Pharaoh. The people have dwelled in the Promised Land and have enjoyed too much prosperity. They have been lured away by other beliefs. But God did not relinquish the covenant. Isaiah uses a startling image: "The LORD calls you back, / like a wife forsaken and grieved in spirit" (Isaiah 54:6). God says through Isaiah, "For a brief moment I abandoned you, / but with great tenderness I will take you back" (Isaiah 54:7). God compares this event to the days of Noah, when God swore never again to cover the earth with the waters of wrath. God is not angry with the Chosen People. God takes them home. God still takes pity on us in our sin. Even those who have not yet been baptized are God's children. God is yearning to receive them with great tenderness as they enter the waters of Baptism. Catholics who have spent this Lenten season in repentance can hear these consoling words and take heart that God has noticed their penance, heard their prayers, and is anxious to renew with them the everlasting covenant of mercy.

◆ RESPONSORIAL PSALM: We thank God for release from a serious threat, not for just any unexpected gift. The writer of Psalm 30 experienced death threats from enemies. Death seemed near, but somehow God rescued the singer "from among those going down into the pit" (Psalm 30:4). At the time, it seemed as though there was no way out, but in retrospect, it seems as though God's anger lasted "but a moment" and his good will lasts "a lifetime" (Psalm 30:6). This Psalm takes up the main theme of the Easter Vigil: the triumphant Passion of our Lord Jesus Christ. He could have sung this Psalm himself: "O Lord, you brought me up from the netherworld. . . . / At nightfall, weeping enters in, / but with the dawn, rejoicing" (Psalm 30:4, 6). All the participants in the Easter Vigil can sing this along with Christ. Those to be baptized are to be lifted from their former way of life to membership in the body of Christ. Those who have already been baptized have expressed sorrow for their sins and experienced the joy of God's mercy. With Christ, we are all brought up from the netherworld on this night that shines more brightly than the dawn.

◆ FIFTH READING: Isaiah offers a second prophecy for our reflection. It extends again to a people who had drifted from the covenant, but who discover that God's mercies are without end. The prophecy opens with an invitation to drink water, a symbol that will occupy center stage at the Easter Vigil in the next part of the ceremony. We cannot live without water, and our relationship with God slakes our spiritual thirst. The Lord is near, and Isaiah urges us to call upon him, forsaking the ways of sin. The risen Christ is very near to all who seek him. Catechumens have left the desert of life-without-Christ, and the faithful have abandoned their sins through the penance of Lent. The waters of the covenant will renew us. Strengthening the image of water, God speaks through Isaiah about the effectiveness of rain and snow. They come down from the heavens and do not return there "till they have watered the earth, / making it fertile and fruitful." God's word does that in our lives. It comes to us like living water, and it produces the effect for which it was sent.

◆ CANTICLE: Isaiah supplies not just the two previous readings, but also the Responsory for the second one. Like the passage from Exodus that follows the Third Reading, this canticle resembles the structure and content of a Psalm, but it exists in another book of the Bible. The Lectionary offers us this passage to follow the previous reading because of the similarity in the way it applies the image of water, and because it comes from the same biblical book. The Canticle rings forth with praise of God. The singer proclaims, "I am confident and unafraid" (Isaiah 12:2). God is the source of salvation, just as a fountain is the source of life-giving water. On this Easter night, preparing for the celebration of Baptism, we are reminded of all that God promises, and how confidently we stand in faith.

◆ SIXTH READING: Changing the tone of the evening, the prophet Baruch chides Israel for forsaking the fountain of wisdom. He ascribes the troubles of Israel to the people's infidelity to the covenant. The solution? "Learn where prudence is, / where strength, where understanding" (Baruch 3:14). To know wisdom is to know God. Just as creation unveils the wisdom of God, so to know the wisdom of God is to draw near to our Maker. On this wondrous night, we grasp the wisdom of God's plan. The plan existed from the beginning of creation, but it was revealed to human beings slowly, through history. At the time of Baruch's prophecy, people still did not fully comprehend that Jesus would reveal the resurrection. Yet even without complete knowledge, people were able to perceive the wisdom of God in imperfect ways. Hearing this

reading, and standing on the other historical shore from the Passion of Christ, we praise God for the gift of revelation made plain to us. Those who are approaching the waters of Baptism have come to the same insight. They put their faith in the Resurrection of Christ, and they participate in his life because of the interior wisdom they have received.

◆ RESPONSORIAL PSALM: Psalm 19 has two parts, and these verses come from the section that revels in the beauty of God's word. It resembles Psalm 119, the longest in the Bible, which meditates line by line on the word of God through a variety of synonyms and attributes. These verses of Psalm 19 praise the "law," "decree," "precepts," "command," and "ordinances" of the Lord; they gladden the heart and enlighten the eye. This Psalm builds upon the theme of wisdom from the previous reading. We come to know God through meditation on his decrees. God revealed these to us in the covenant, so they detail the wisdom that exudes from the very being of God. For Christians, Jesus Christ is the perfect expression of God's wisdom. He is God's wisdom. He is the Word made flesh. For this reason, the Lectionary gives us a refrain taken from the Gospel according to John, not from the Psalm itself. The verse is spoken by Peter after Jesus has given the discourse on the Bread of Life. The teaching revealed the very reason Jesus came: to offer us eternal life through the eating of his body and drinking of his Blood. Many of those who heard him speak these words, however, turned away. Jesus looked fearfully at his closest followers and asked if they, too, were going to leave him now. Peter said no: "You have the words of everlasting life" (John 6:68c). That statement of faith becomes the refrain we sing to a Psalm that praises the wisdom of God. It also foreshadows the initiation of those

who will share Holy Communion for the first time at this Mass.

◆ SEVENTH READING: The prophet Ezekiel addresses a people who had experienced exile from their homeland because of their infidelity, but learned now that God had not abandoned them. As a sign of renewing the eternal covenant, God offered the people cleansing and renewal through the gift of a new spirit. Israel's sin was not covered up, but it was forgiven, and the people grew stronger in faith. On a night when the waters of Baptism contain the symbolism of new life, this passage prophesies all that Christianity has to offer. Those who have failed to love God as they should are cleansed from all sin. Some are baptized and others will renew their baptismal covenant through promises and holy water. All will experience the gift of the new spirit that God places in the heart of believers. God never goes back on the covenant; it is eternal. Even though we sometimes fail to keep the covenant, God always gives us the opportunity to renew it.

◆ RESPONSORIAL PSALM, OPTION 1: The Lectionary offers three possible Responsories to the Seventh Reading. The first, from Psalm 42, is sung whenever Baptism will be celebrated at the Vigil. The Psalm asks God for the gift of God's light and fidelity, so that those who receive it may approach the dwelling place of God, and specifically the altar of God. These verses eloquently prophesy the journey of the catechumens, who thirst for the waters of Baptism, and attain it through the light and fidelity that God extends to new believers through the covenant. Having been refreshed by the waters of Baptism, the neophytes come to the altar of God, where they participate in Holy Communion, the intimate union that makes them fully the body of Christ, a dwelling place for God most high.

◆ CANTICLE, OPTION 2: In this song of praise, we thank God for all that he has accomplished. This is exactly the Responsory that follows the Fifth Reading of the Easter Vigil. It is offered again as one of the alternatives following the Seventh Reading. In practice, it could logically be sung here whenever the seven readings are abbreviated and the Fifth Reading has been eliminated. But the Responsory may be used twice on the same night. Here, the English Lectionary recommends it as one of the options if Baptism is not celebrated during the Vigil. This may seem puzzling because the image of water is so strong at the beginning of these verses. In fact, the liturgical books are not consistent on this point. The Ordo Lectionum Missae actually recommends this Psalm, not the previous one, when Baptism is to be celebrated.

◆ RESPONSORIAL PSALM, OPTION 3: Tradition calls seven of the 150 psalms penitential. This one is perhaps the greatest of them. It expresses the remorse we feel after sinning and our cries for forgiveness. These particular verses, coming at the end of the psalm, focus on renewal. Although we have sung this text often during Lent, we may complete its sentiments at the Vigil, when we put our sinful ways behind us and seek a clean heart. These verses work well after the passage from Ezekiel, which employs a similar image—a new heart. In reestablishing the covenant with us, God remakes us. We reenter the covenant not as the same people, but as those who have known sin, repented of it, received forgiveness, and resolved not to sin again. This Psalm is recommended for an Easter Vigil that does not include Baptism. It more nearly suits the faithful

Christians coming for renewal after observing a rigorous Lent.

◆ EPISTLE: Through Baptism, we enter the mystery of his Death and Resurrection. After hearing and singing up to fourteen passages from the Old Testament (seven readings and seven responsories), the New Testament makes its bright appearance. We hear Paul say, "We know that Christ, raised from the dead, dies no more; death no longer has power over him" (Romans 6:9). This is the first scriptural proclamation from tonight that Jesus is risen. Paul compares the Resurrection of Christ and Baptism. This passage underscores our liturgical practice of celebrating Baptism at the Easter Vigil. It also affirms our preference for baptizing infants on any Sunday, our weekly observance of the Resurrection.

◆ RESPONSORIAL PSALM/GOSPEL ACCLAMATION: This psalm gives many reasons for thanksgiving. It opens with the simple assertion that the Lord is good, and that "his mercy endures forever" (Psalm 118:1). It then announces the power and deeds of God's right hand. Two of the verses prophesy the meaning of this Easter night. You can imagine Jesus singing this Psalm: "I shall not die, but live, / and declare the works of the Lord" (Psalm 118:17). Christians can affirm, "The stone which the builders rejected / has become the cornerstone" (Psalm 118:22). His enemies thought they had put Jesus to death, but he has become the cornerstone of life. The refrain for this Psalm is a triple Alleluia. It doubles as the Gospel Acclamation. No words can fully express the joy of this night, so we resort to a Hebrew acclamation that needs no translation: Alleluia! Throughout Lent, we have abstained from singing that word. We have introduced the Gospel with a different acclamation of praise. But now, the word returns.

Our "fasting" from the Alleluia is over. We rejoice that Christ is risen.

◆ GOSPEL: The women see a large stone and wonder who will roll it back for them. Then the women are amazed to see a young man clothed in white. They hear the most important news that has ever been spoken: "[Jesus] has been raised; he is not here." They see the empty tomb. They receive the commission to report this good news. The young man instructs them to tell the disciples—and Peter. Apparently, Peter was going to need a special message because of his misbehavior and his doubts, but also because of his leadership among those who would hear the word.

The Roman Missal

The Missal gives several introductory and explanatory rubrics for the celebration of the Easter Vigil. Some comments about them are noted here.

This night's Vigil is explicitly described as "the greatest and most noble of all solemnities." The importance and grandeur of this evening celebration cannot be emphasized too strongly, and parishes must resist any temptation to abbreviate the rites or to enact them in a perfunctory way. Feeble excuses such as "it's too long for the people" are in fact insulting to the people of God—their spiritual wherewithal when the rites are done in all their fullness is quite hearty; let's not shortchange the people of God on "this most sacred night."

It is to take place "during the night, so that it begins after nightfall and ends before daybreak on the Sunday. This is an absolutely crucial and non-negotiable point, as strongly stated by PS, 78: "This rule is to be taken according to its strictest sense. Reprehensible are those abuses and practices that have crept into many places in violation of this ruling whereby the Easter Vigil is celebrated at the time of day that it is customary to celebrate anticipated Sunday Masses." The starting time, then, is to be after nightfall: thus, depending on the date of Easter and in what part of the country you live, the time will vary.

The Easter Vigil is made up of four parts: the Solemn Beginning of the Vigil or Lucernarium; the Liturgy of the Word; the Baptismal Liturgy; and the Liturgy of the Eucharist.

First Part: The Solemn Beginning of the Vigil or Lucernarium

The Vigil begins with the church in darkness. The Missal states that "a blazing fire is prepared in a suitable place outside the church," and that the people gather around the fire. The intent is clear that this is to be a bonfire, more than just a few small flames flickering from a table-top hibachi. As a later rubric describes, the blessing of fire may be adapted if difficulties arise constructing a bonfire. In such cases, the people may gather in the church as usual, and at the door of the church the rites of blessing the fire and preparing the candle take place.

The liturgy begins with the Sign of the Cross and the priest offering a greeting to the people "in the usual way"—presumably, using one of the liturgical greetings for Mass; unlike the Good Friday liturgy, the Easter Vigil is a Mass. The priest then instructs the people about the meaning of this night, "in which our Lord Jesus Christ / passed over from death to life," and that we keep this memorial in "the sure hope / of sharing his triumph over death / and living with him in God." The instruction may be given using the exact words in the Missal or similar words of the priest's own choosing.

The priest then blesses the fire, after which the candle is prepared. The rubric simply states that one of the ministers brings the Paschal candle to the priest; while therefore

any minister may do this, perhaps it is fitting, if a deacon is carrying the candle into the church, for him to be the one to do this, in a sense taking custody of the candle. The lines of the cross, the alpha and omega, and the numerals of the current year are cut into the candle; this preparation of the candle is not optional. Thus the rite presumes that a real candle that is actually prepared in this way is used; *Paschale solemnitatis* clearly states that it "must be made of wax, never be artificial, be renewed each year, be only one in number, and be of sufficiently large size so that it may evoke the truth that Christ is the light of the world" (PS, 82). Plastic tubes that hold oil canisters and have permanent symbols, where only the last numeral changes from year to year, should be avoided at all costs!

After the cutting of the cross and other signs have been made on the candle, five grains of incense may be inserted in the form of a cross, with the accompanying words. This part is optional.

Next the priest lights the Paschal candle from the new fire with the accompanying words sung or said. A little careful preparation and rehearsal will ensure that all goes smoothly at the beginning of the Vigil; it can become rather awkward managing the various items needed and matching the gestures to the words, and making sure all the necessary things are handy, so think this through ahead of time.

Once the candle has been lit, the procession forms. Ministers take burning coals from the fire and place them in the thurible, and the priest puts incense into the thurible in the usual way. A deacon, if present (otherwise, any other suitable minister), carries the candle. The order of procession is: first the thurifer with the smoking thurible, then the deacon or other minister with the candle, followed by the priest with other ministers,

and finally the people, all carrying unlit candles. Note that the priest precedes the people, and that candles are not yet lit.

The same three stations as used for carrying in the cross on Good Friday are used again: the door of the church, the middle of the church, and in front of the altar. At each station the candle is lifted high and "The Light of Christ" is sung, with the peoples' response. Only the priest's candle is lit after the first "Light of Christ" and its response; then, after the second, the people's candles are lit; after the third, the Paschal candle is placed in its stand that is located next to the ambo or in the middle of the sanctuary.

The Missal is clear that it is at this time that the lights are turned on in the church, although the altar candles are not yet lit. Although there has arisen the custom of not turning the church lights on until later, usually during the Gloria, it is clear that the rubrics do not call for this. The powerful symbol of the light of the Paschal candle is being emphasized in that once it is brought into church, its brightness completely illumines everything.

With the Paschal candle in its stand, the priest goes to his chair, and after handing his candle to a minister so his hands are free, he puts incense in the thurible and blesses the incense as at Mass. The deacon asks for and receives the blessing from the priest in preparation for singing the Easter Proclamation (*Exsultet*). The blessing is the same one given before the Gospel at Mass, except that the words "paschal praise" are used instead of the word "Gospel." After receiving the blessing, the deacon incenses the book and the candle, and then proclaims the Easter Proclamation at the ambo or at some other lectern; the assembly remains standing and holds lighted candles. The choice as to whether to use the ambo or some other lectern can be made based on the arrangement of your church; presumably, if the ambo were some significant distance from the Paschal candle, it might be advantageous to use a lectern that is right next to the candle.

It is possible for someone other than the deacon to sing the *Exsultet*, with the Missal specifically mentioning the priest celebrant or a concelebrating priest, although a lay cantor is another possibility. One presumes the decision will be made according to which person will be able to proclaim such an important piece best. Note the omission of certain lines in the case of a layperson singing the Proclamation. Immediately after the Proclamation, all extinguish their candles.

Second Part: The Liturgy of the Word

This Vigil is referred to as "the mother of all Vigils," and so nine readings are provided, seven from the Old Testament and two from the New, an Epistle and a Gospel reading. Considering the importance of this liturgy, all nine readings should be considered, "so that the character of the Vigil, which demands an extended period of time, may be preserved." Liturgy committees and preparers, and indeed all parishioners, should understand that the Solemn Easter Vigil is not just another Mass, nor is it even just "a long Mass;" it is a Vigil, and a Vigil takes time. It is part of the experience of "time outside of time," the sacred time of the Triduum that was begun on Holy Thursday night and is reaching its climax this night. Any attempts to truncate or abbreviate the experience should be avoided. The Missal is clear that using all nine readings is the norm and is preferred. Nonetheless, the Missal does admit of the possibility of reducing the number of readings "where more serious pastoral circumstances demand it." One might take special note of the deliberate

use of the word "serious," which is weightier than just preference, impatience or, as noted above, a misguided sense that the people cannot handle it. In the case of a shortened Liturgy of the Word, at least three readings should be read from the Old Testament, both from the Law and the Prophets, and the accompanying Responsorial Psalms should be used; additionally, the reading of chapter 14 of Exodus and its canticle is always to be used—it cannot be omitted.

The priest gives an instruction, using the words of the Missal or his own words, to invite the people to listen to the Word of God "with quiet hearts" and reminding them to meditate on how God has saved his people throughout history and especially by sending his Son as Redeemer.

The Missal gives prayers to follow each of the Scripture readings; in some cases, the priest has a choice between two prayers.

After the last Old Testament reading followed by its Responsorial Psalm and prayer, the altar candles are lit and the priest intones the Gloria. Since the Missal gives the notation for the priest to sing, there would seem to be indicated a preference that the priest do this. After he intones the Gloria, the assembly then takes up the hymn. Bells are rung during the hymn, but no further specification of this is given; it simply says "according to local custom," so this can be left open to the creativity of the parish—perhaps the choir rings bells, or servers, or even members of the assembly who have brought their own, or any combination or all of these! When the Gloria is concluded, the priest prays the Collect.

After the Collect, the Epistle is proclaimed. After the Epistle, all rise and the priest solemnly intones the triple Alleluia, with the Missal specifically noting that he raises the tone by a step each time, and

all repeat after him. However, if the priest is not capable of singing this properly, it is possible for a cantor to do so. Incense is placed in the thurible as usual, and the deacon receives the blessing as usual. Only incense is carried in procession with the *Book of Gospels*; the Missal explicitly states that candles are not used. Finally, there is a rubric stating that the Homily is not to be omitted. The importance of preaching on this holiest of nights is underscored by this rubric.

Third Part: Baptismal Liturgy

The Baptismal Liturgy begins after the Homily. The rites take place at the baptismal font, so the priest goes there with the ministers, unless there is to be a procession to the font (see below). If, however, the font is in a location where it cannot be easily seen by the faithful, then a vessel with water is placed in the sanctuary. Notice the importance given to the participation of the entire assembly—it is crucial that they be able to see what is going on. This is in keeping with the main thrust of the renewal of the liturgy.

Next, the elect are called forward and presented by their godparents or, in the case of small children, are carried by their parents and godparents. It is admittedly odd that the Missal refers to them as catechumens when, in fact, the terminology used in the *Rite of Christian Initiation of Adults* refers to them as the elect. The Missal does not give any specific texts for this calling forward and presentation.

If there is to be a procession to the baptistery or to the font, it begins now, and the order of procession is clearly noted: a minister with the Paschal candle leads the procession, followed by those to be baptized and their godparents, then other ministers, the deacon, and lastly the priest. (Thus, if there is to be a procession to the font, the priest and the ministers do not immediately go there.) The Litany of the Saints, given in the Missal, is sung during the procession. Names of some saints may be added, especially the saint for whom the parish is named, and other patron saints, for example, of those to be baptized. Also, if there are candidates to be baptized, the priest adds a prayer at the end of the litany.

If there is no procession to the font, the priest addresses the assembly using the words given in the Missal, or words similar to them. The Missal provides a text not only for the case when Baptisms are to take place, but also for the case if no one is to be baptized, yet the font is still to be blessed.

There is a third possibility: that no one is to be baptized, and that no font is to be blessed. In that instance, there is no Litany of the Saints, and the Blessing of Water takes place at once (see below).

After all have arrived at the font and the Litany ends, the priest blesses the baptismal water, with has hands extended during the prayer. The Missal gives the text of the prayer first with musical notation and then without, indicating a certain preference for singing the prayer. The prayer includes the gesture of lowering the Paschal candle into the water either once or three times and then holding the candle in the water for the remainder of the prayer, with an acclamation sung (or said) by the assembly as the candle is lifted out of the water. If no one is to be baptized and if the font is not to be blessed, there is a completely different introduction and blessing prayer for the priest to use.

When Baptisms are to take place, they take place immediately after the blessing of the baptismal water and the acclamation of the people. The Missal first directs the priest to the appropriate ritual (that is, either the *Rite of Christian Initiation of Adults* or *Rite of Baptism*

for Children) for the prescribed questions and answers concerning the renunciation of sin. There is also a mention that if the anointing of adults with the oil of catechumens has not already taken place at some point before this (that is, as part of any earlier preparatory rites), then it is to occur now. This, however, conflicts with the *Rite of Christian Initiation of Adults*, 33.7, which states that in the United States, "the anointing with the oil of catechumens is reserved for use in the period of the catechumenate and in the period of purification and enlightenment and is not to be included in the preparation rites on Holy Saturday or in the celebration of initiation at the Easter Vigil or at another time." As of this writing, this point would seem to be in need of clarification.

Next the priest questions the adults, and the parents and godparents of children, about the faith, again as indicated in the respective rites. Interestingly, the Missal admits of an option that, should the number of those to be baptized be very large, the priest may, immediately after the response of those to be baptized and the parents and godparents of children, also ask for and receive the renewal of baptismal promises of the entire assembly. Presumably, this option is offered as a way of not unduly prolonging the ritual when the numbers are large.

After the professions of faith, the priest baptizes the elect and the children (here the Missal does refer to the adults as the elect!). While no mention is made of the manner of Baptism, it would be good to reflect on what the *Rite of Christian Initiation of Adults* and *Rite of Baptism for Children* ritual books say about the suitability of and preference for immersion.

After the Baptisms, the infants (children under the age of discretion) are anointed with chrism (this is the anointing on the crown of

the head, as described in the *Rite of Baptism for Children*). Next, white garments are given to all the newly baptized, adults and children, followed by the lighting of the baptismal candles from the Paschal candle. The Missal states that the Rite of Ephphetha is omitted for the infants.

The explanatory rites completed, there is a procession back to the sanctuary (unless, of course, these rites have occurred in the sanctuary), in the same order as before, and with the newly baptized carrying their lighted candles. The Missal suggests singing the baptismal canticle *Vidi aquam* during this procession, or some other appropriate song.

Finally, the Missal notes that once the procession has returned to the sanctuary, the adults are to immediately receive the Sacrament of Confirmation according to the proper ritual book. (Priests who baptize an adult or a child over the age of discretion have by law the faculty to confirm, and should do so.)

After the Rites of Baptism and of Confirmation are complete, or after the blessing of water if there have been no Baptisms, the renewal of baptismal promises for the assembly takes place (unless this has already been done when those to be baptized did so, as mentioned above). All in the assembly hold lighted candles (although it does not make sense for the newly baptized to participate in this, since they have just done so; it can be powerful for them to watch the "veteran" Catholics renew what they themselves just did for the first time). The introduction to the questions, which may be said by the priest using the exact words in the Missal or other similar words, makes reference both to the Paschal Mystery (the very meaning of what we are doing) and the fact that this celebration comes as the fruition of the Lenten observance; the reference to Lent serves to reinforce a sense of the "Ninety Days," so to speak, of Lent-Easter. Two forms of questions for the renunciation of sin are given, and then there are the traditional questions for the profession of faith, followed by a conclusion by the priest. The priest then sprinkles the assembly with the blessed water while an appropriate baptismal song is sung, perhaps the *Vidi aquam*.

A rubric indicates that during the sprinkling the newly baptized are led to their place among the faithful. In practice, the adults may need some time to put themselves together, especially if Baptism was done by immersion. Drying off, changing clothes, and getting ready to rejoin the assembly can take place in another location while the assembly renews their baptismal promises and are sprinkled, with the neophytes rejoining the assembly during or immediately after.

After the sprinkling, the priest returns to the chair and the Universal Prayer is prayed in the usual way; the Creed is omitted. The Missal makes specific mention that the newly baptized participate in the Universal Prayer for the first time; it's a significant moment for them as they exercise this important function of the priestly people of God — that of interceding for the needs of others and of the whole world — and its importance should not be lost on them or on the entire assembly.

Fourth Part: The Liturgy of the Eucharist

After the Universal Prayer, the Mass continues as usual with the beginning of the Liturgy of the Eucharist. The Missal makes specific mention of the desirability of having the bread and wine brought forward by the newly-baptized adults and/or by the parents or godparents of newly-baptized children. Thus is their participation in the offering of the sacrifice for the very first time duly highlighted. Needless

to say, high priority should also be given to bringing forward and consecrating all the bread that will be needed for Holy Communion; it is fitting, given the newness of life that is central to this celebration, that any consecrated bread remaining from Good Friday has perhaps been consumed, or at least, is not used for this Paschal celebration.

The Prayer over the Offerings makes yet another explicit reference to the "paschal mysteries," asking that the Lord accept our prayers along with these sacrificial offerings, so that we might be brought "to the healing of eternity" through those mysteries.

Preface I of Easter is the Preface prescribed for this Mass, and the phrase "on this night" is used. The Preface succinctly announces the Paschal Mystery: "by dying he has destroyed our death, and by rising, restored our life."

There are special inserts that are to be used in the Eucharistic Prayer; be careful, as these can be tricky because the inserts are found in the Ritual Masses section toward the back of the Missal, under "I. For the Conferral of the Sacraments of Initiation; 3. For the Conferral of Baptism." Eucharistic Prayer IV would be excluded from use this night, because of its proper Preface, but Prayers I or III would be good choices (II would perhaps not be appropriate to the solemnity of the occasion, due to its brevity, although there is nothing to absolutely forbid it). Eucharistic Prayer I, the Roman Canon, has these three special inserts and proper forms: at the *Memento Domine* ("Remember, Lord, your servants"), found in the Ritual Masses section; a proper form of the Communicantes, used from the Mass of the Easter Vigil until the Second Sunday of Easter, and found right within the text of the Prayer; and a proper form of the *Hanc igitur* ("Therefore, Lord, we pray") with two variations: one

variation is found right within the text of the prayer itself, used from the Mass of the Easter Vigil until the Second Sunday of Easter, and a second variation is found in the Ritual Masses section, with this second variation perhaps being a better choice for use this night if Baptisms have occurred. The inserts for Eucharistic Prayers II and III are found in the Ritual Masses section and are inserted in the places as indicated in the rubrics (there is only one insert for each prayer).

The Missal reminds the priest that before the "Behold the Lamb of God . . . " he may briefly address the newly baptized "about receiving their first Communion and about the excellence of this great mystery, which is the climax of initiation and the center of the whole Christian life." Those words in and of themselves can be the basis for the priest's remarks, and one would think it most beneficial to take advantage of this opportunity to offer extemporaneous remarks to highlight this important moment in the lives of the newly initiated and of the entire community.

The appropriateness of the newly baptized along with their godparents, their Catholic parents, spouses, and the catechists, indeed, the entire assembly, all receiving Communion under both kinds is highlighted, and it is hoped that this is a common practice of the parish.

The Communion Antiphon, taken from chapter 5 of 1 Corinthians, refers to Christ as "our Passover" and enjoins us, since he has been sacrificed, to "keep the feast with the unleavened bread of purity and truth." The Prayer after Communion asks God to pour out on us "the Spirit of your love" so that the nourishment of the Eucharist might make us "one in mind and heart." Once again, unity is emphasized as the goal of receiving Holy Communion.

The text for a Solemn Blessing is given and should be used. A rubric indicates that this Solemn Blessing may be replaced by the final blessing formula from the *Rite of Baptism of Adults or of Children*; interestingly, while such a formula is given in the rite for children, there is no such formula in the rite for adults. Use of the formula from the rite for children would make sense if only children were baptized this night; otherwise, stick with the text given in the Missal. Lastly, the dismissal is chanted, by the deacon or by the priest, with the double Alleluia. This solemn dismissal is used throughout the Octave of Easter—that is, also on Easter Sunday, on the weekdays of Easter Week (within the Octave of Easter), and on the Second Sunday of Easter. It is not used, however, on the other weekdays or Sundays of Easter Time, being used again only at Pentecost.

Other Ideas

A liturgy professor used to tell his students "it doesn't matter how much you have rehearsed for a liturgy, how well trained the servers are, or how long the reader has prepared. When everything seems just 'perfect,' that is the moment that a dog will walk in front of the altar during the consecration." This story was not shared to be irreverent, but to be a simple reminder that anything can happen during the liturgy. When you add darkness, fire, water, lights, sprinkling, and a two-and-a-half-hour-plus liturgy, it is all up for grabs. If you are preparing an outdoor fire, have a backup fire of alcohol and salt in case of inclement weather. Test your microphones to make sure they will function outdoors. Make sure there are fire extinguishers handy, fresh batteries in the wireless mics, and extra ones nearby, and try to have some medical personnel from the congregation present. Hospitality

ministers should be nearby. Prepare extra seating and orders of worship.

(#42, or Gospel #41, or at an afternoon or evening Mass, Gospel #46) white

Easter Sunday: Solemnity of the Resurrection of the Lord
5 SOLEMNITY

About Easter Sunday

The celebration of the Resurrection of Jesus Christ continues into Easter Sunday morning. Easter Sunday marks the end of the Triduum and is the first day of the Easter Octave. The celebration of the Triduum concludes after Vespers and the great fifty days begin. Forty days of fast yield to fifty days of feast. On Easter Sunday, many of those who were present the night before return, especially the neophytes. In addition, there may be many people attending who have not been to church in a while. Have plenty of hospitality ministers to greet and seat them. Have enough seats and enough worship aids so all can participate. Insert words of welcome and a description of the parish into the worship aid or bulletin. Perhaps you will make them feel so welcome that they will return to church because of you.

It is not surprising that in many parishes some of those baptized at the Easter Vigil, those still "wet behind the ears," wake up on Easter Sunday morning and go to Mass.

Their excitement cannot be contained. If this is the case, invite the neophytes to wear the white garment donned at the Easter Vigil to Easter Sunday Mass. Some parishes celebrate the receptions into full communion and/or the completion of sacramental initiation at a Mass or Masses on Easter Sunday morning. Others schedule these events on Sundays during Easter Time. This laudable practice helps distinguish the baptized from the unbaptized at the Easter Vigil. Without the additional ceremonies, the Vigil is celebrated much more smoothly, and Easter Time, the great fifty days, then takes on the characteristic of being an extended time of initiation. Be sure to include the names of the neophytes in the Universal Prayer (Prayer of the Faithful) at the Sunday Masses on Easter Sunday and throughout Easter Time. If the parish celebrates Easter Evening Prayer, consider inviting the neophytes to that celebration.

The Lectionary for Mass

◆ FIRST READING: Peter and Cornelius received a divinely inspired vision that led them to one another. They must have recognized the gift of that grace because it was extremely unlikely that a Jew (Peter) would be a guest in a Gentile home. What they heard remains ours today as we hear the First Reading: Jesus of Nazareth, anointed by God with the Holy Spirit, healed many people. He was put to death but was raised by God. We have seen him and have eaten with him. He has sent us to preach this Good News. And this is the truth we speak to you today: "Everyone who believes in him will receive forgiveness of sins through his name." Peter took a very bold step that day to broaden the mission of the followers of Jesus. Because of the vision he received, Peter had come to believe that all people were to be included in the great work of preaching the story of Jesus Christ. The Good News could not and should not be contained, for it is meant for all people for all time.

◆ RESPONSORIAL PSALM 118: The psalmist gives voice to the great joy of the people, expressing their overwhelming gratitude for the faithfulness of the Lord.

◆ SECOND READING (OPTION 1): The Colossians reading urges us to die to self in order to focus on the Lord, for having been baptized in Christ, the concerns of the world should diminish in meaning. For those who are caught up in the things of this world, however, this reading is an invitation to reorder our lives. On the day of glory, the worldly things that can consume human hearts will have no significance.

◆ SECOND READING (OPTION 2): Some have called this Corinthians reading the first Easter sermon. Leading up to this passage, Paul has chastised the people for their wicked behavior. Now he makes it clear that to honor the Paschal sacrifice and live as the new life demands, Christians have a responsibility to one another to live with sincerity and truth.

◆ SEQUENCE: This Sunday, the Church sings a sequence—an ancient, poetic song that precedes the singing of the Gospel acclamation. The Easter Sequence, *Victimae paschali laudes*, is a song of praise to the Paschal Victim that also reflects the Gospel account of Mary's encounter with the risen Lord.

◆ GOSPEL: Mary Magdalene is the first person at the tomb in all four Gospel accounts. In John's account of the Gospel, the anointing of the body has already taken place, but Mary is still the first person on record to go to the tomb. She is the messenger who then brings Peter and the Beloved Disciple to see that the stone has been moved. Cloths lay on the ground, the head cloth arranged in a separate place, all to indicate that this is not the scene of a robbery. Time and future appearances of the Lord will add believers to the community.

The Roman Missal

The Gloria is used today, and of course, today is a day for great flourish and solemnity in the selection of musical settings.

The Collect uses the important phrase "on this day." Our participation in the liturgy on this day is our participation in the salvation won for us and made present for us; therefore, it is on this day that God, through his only begotten Son, has "conquered death / and unlocked for us the path to eternity." Therefore, we pray that "we who keep the solemnity of the Lord's Resurrection" may rise to new life through the renewal brought by the Holy Spirit.

The Creed is said today, although it may be replaced by the rite of the renewal of baptismal promises. The text for it is not given again at the Mass during the Day; the priest will need to refer to the text used at the Easter Vigil. In the Prayer over the Offerings, we express that we are offering the sacrifice by which

the Church "is wondrously reborn and nourished" filled with "paschal gladness." Preface I of Easter is again, as at the Vigil, the Preface assigned for today. Because of this, use of Eucharistic Prayer IV is again precluded, and perhaps Eucharistic Prayers I or III would be better choices than Eucharistic Prayer II, given the festivity of the day. The only inserts or special forms to worry about are the "In communion with those" and the "Therefore, Lord, we pray" as indicated within the text of Eucharistic Prayer I; there are no other special inserts.

The three-part Solemn Blessing from the Easter Vigil may be used again at this Mass, and the dismissal with the double Alleluia is used, preferably sung.

Other Ideas

Recall everything that we have said recently about issues with overflow seating, parking, orders of worship, and things that can go wrong will go wrong. This is also true today. There will be many guests present so make sure there are extra ministers of hospitality. Be sure that maintenance staff or extra ministers of hospitality are scheduled, as the bathrooms will receive a lot of extra wear and tear today and throughout the Triduum. There are many liturgical jokes about "Chreasters," that is, those who only attend Christmas and Easter Mass, but recall that the hospitality that is shown to these people and the welcome they receive may determine when you see them again.

EASTER TIME

The Meaning / The Lectionary for Mass

THE Easter Triduum culminates with the Easter Vigil during which, in symbol, song, and story, we proclaim Jesus risen from the dead. This Easter joy and celebration continues for fifty days as we delve into the richness of the Easter mysteries, Jesus's Passion, Death, Resurrection, Ascension, and glorification, culminating in the sending of the Spirit at Pentecost. For John's account of the Gospel, the premier narrative of the whole season, as well as for the whole Gospel narrative, these are parts of one interrelated event. *Universal Norms on the Liturgical Year and the General Roman Calendar* describe Easter Time in this fashion: "The fifty days from Easter Sunday to Pentecost are celebrated in joyful exaltation as one feast day, or better, as one 'great Sunday'" (UNLY, 22).

However, these Easter mysteries pack such power and meaning that, as humans, we need time to digest, dissect, and reflect on their meaning for our lives. That is why Church tradition and wisdom celebrates Easter Time for fifty days. All fifty days are days *of* Easter, not days *after* Easter. The Lectionary readings for the season are meant to help us unpack these rich Easter mysteries.

John's account of the Gospel, along with Luke's Acts of the Apostles, dominates the entire Easter season. Except for the Octave of Easter, on weekdays, and on the Sundays of Easter, Acts and John are consistently proclaimed, with no readings from the Old Testament, save for the Responsorial Psalms. This follows ancient Lectionary traditions and provides a way of unpacking the effects of the Easter mysteries on the early Jesus communities after the Spirit's descent at Pentecost, as well as on his disciples while Jesus is still with them.

The Octave of Easter, the first eight days of the Easter celebration, proclaims readings from Acts and different Gospel passages that highlight the beginning and growth of the Jesus communities after Pentecost, as well as affirm the reality of the true and living presence of the risen Christ. Peter in Acts preaches and cures in the name of the risen Christ, while the Gospel accounts tell of the discovery of the empty tomb and various appearances of Jesus to his disciples, constantly connected with meal scenes and obvious Eucharistic themes. During the Easter season the readings from Acts narrate how the early Jesus communities grew and sustained themselves, highlighting many of the individuals who played significant roles in preaching the word and bringing others to Christ. Among these many ministers of God's love manifested in Jesus, Acts centers on the ministries of Peter and Paul, giants in the faith and trend setters in proclaiming the word to Gentiles. We also learn of the many conflicts among the Jews, between believers and non-believers in Jesus, as well as among Jewish believers who struggled over how to reach out and welcome Gentiles into the Jesus communities.

From the second to the seventh week of Easter, Acts and John are consistently proclaimed. The Responsorial Psalms focus on God's great deeds done on behalf of the people, both in the past and the present moment, evoking joy, praise and thanksgiving from all who have seen and experienced the Lord's mighty deeds. Many of the readings from John come from Jesus's public ministry before his Death and Resurrection. Yet, read in light of the Easter mysteries, they are heavily laden with Resurrection meaning and significance.

Jesus's "I AM" statements—I AM the Way, the Truth, and the Life (John 14), I AM the Good Shepherd (John 10), I AM the Vine (John 15), I AM the Bread of Life (John 6), I AM the Light of the World (John 12)—take on new depths of meaning in light of the Resurrection. God so loved the world that nothing would be spared to restore that love relationship, not even the sending of an only son (John 3). Jesus promises his disciples that he will always be with them. He commissions them to go into the world to carry on his mission, empowered by his Spirit, whom he promised to send once he returned to the Father. As we approach Pentecost, Jesus's high priestly prayer for his disciples and for the world (John 17) is proclaimed on the Fifth, Sixth, and Seventh weeks of Easter. As Pentecost nears, the Lectionary prepares us by focusing on Jesus's promise of the Advocate, the Spirit who will teach us, guide us and maintain us in the truth that Jesus spoke from the Father.

The Sundays of Easter in Year B focus on proclamations primarily from Acts, 1 John, and the Gospel according to John. Acts allows us to experience the joy, enthusiasm, and excitement of the early communities who accepted Jesus as Messiah and lived out the implications of his coming for themselves and for all people, as they were guided and empowered by the Spirit.

John's first letter picks up many of the Johannine Gospel themes, consistently asserting that God is love and the one who loves abides in God in a mutual indwelling. Such indwelling calls us to love one another the way God has loved us. Only in this way can we truly manifest that we love God.

John's account picks up rich theological themes and images that have endured the ages and captured the imagination of all disciples. All the "I AM" passages mentioned above, along with the deep intimacy that God offers us in Christ, provide rich food for thought and reflection on how we can cultivate our deep relationship with God, in and through the person of Christ.

The exaltation of the risen Christ at the Ascension is celebrated according to Luke's time sequence in Acts, that is, forty days after Easter. The First Reading proclaims Luke's account of the Ascension, while the Gospel proclaims the brief account of Jesus commissioning his disciples before his Ascension, narrated in the longer ending to Mark's account.

Finally the Great Fifty Days or the "Great Sunday" closes with the Feast of Pentecost. Like the Ascension, the First Reading proclaims the Pentecost narrative, unique to Luke in Acts, as God gifts Jesus's disciples, 120 in all including Mary, Jesus's mother, with the Spirit, showering all with the power to enact unity of mind and heart in the midst of diversity. John's account of the risen

Christ breathing his Spirit upon the disciples on Easter Sunday is proclaimed as the disciples are instructed to be instruments of forgiveness and reconciliation to the world. Paul's First Letter to the Corinthians speaks of the Spirit's many gifts given for the benefit of all, and of the Spirit's work among us enabling us to be one body even though we have many parts.

During Easter Time, the Lectionary functions as a school of faith, providing the curriculum needed for us to grow in deeper relationship with God in and through the risen Christ. Multiple passages call us to reflect on the meaning and significance that the Easter mysteries have in our lives here and now. Like the disciples, we too have been called to intimacy with Christ. We too have been empowered by the Spirit to be instruments of forgiveness, reconciliation, and unity to the world. We too have been offered the assurance that death, evil, and calamities will never have the last word. Do we have the courage and conviction to believe such "good news" and live our lives accordingly?

The Roman Missal

THE Easter Time section in the Missal begins following the page for Holy Saturday, thus, beginning with Easter Sunday of the Resurrection of the Lord—first, the Easter Vigil in the Holy Night, followed by the Mass during the Day, and then each day of Easter Time starting with the days within the Octave of Easter. Some rubrics are mentioned that are applicable for the entire season. One of these concerns the use of the solemn dismissal with "Alleluia, Alleluia": it is used at the Vigil, at the Mass during the Day, and at Masses throughout the Octave of Easter (see *The Roman Missal*, Sunday of the Resurrection, 69 and 78); it is not, however, to be used at every Mass throughout Easter Time, which is a common mistake made by priests and deacons. After the Second Sunday of Easter, use of the solemn "Alleluia, Alleluia" dismissal ceases, and it is not used again until Pentecost (both the Vigil and the Mass during the Day). A second rubric to be noted concerns the Paschal candle: "The paschal candle is lit in all the more solemn liturgical celebrations of this period." Given its prominence during Easter Time and its centrality as a symbol of the Resurrection, a legitimate argument could

be made that the Paschal candle should be lit at all liturgical celebrations during Easter Time.

Once again, careful selection of texts by parish preparation committees can greatly enhance a community's celebration of the entire fifty days of Easter Time, providing continuity even toward the end of the season when a sort of fatigue about its being "one great Sunday" begins to set in. In the later weeks of Easter Time it is especially important to maintain the particular aspects of the liturgical season that have been used throughout. One of the most obvious examples of this is the Rite for the Blessing and Sprinkling of Water, in place of the Penitential Act, which can be found in Appendix II of the Missal. Although the rite has been moved to an Appendix, it is no less a viable option than it was in the former Sacramentary, where it was placed as an option along with the Penitential Act. It is meant to be used on Sundays, especially in Easter Time, and so it would not be used on weekdays. If the Rite for the Blessing and Sprinkling of Water is not used, then the Penitential Act occurs as normal.

There are five Prefaces designated for Easter Time, and these follow Preface II of the Passion of the Lord. Preface I is the Preface assigned to the Easter Vigil, to the Mass on Easter Sunday, and to each of the Masses during the Octave; the priest is to use the proper phrase from among the choices of "on this night" (at the Vigil) "on this day" (on Sunday and during the Octave), and "in this time" (throughout the remainder of Easter Time). Highlighting the Paschal Mystery in a very simple and direct way, this Preface announces that "by dying he has destroyed our death, / and by rising, restored our life." Preface II speaks of aspects of our new life in Christ, in that "the halls of the heavenly Kingdom / are thrown open to the faithful" because of Christ's dying and rising. Preface III speaks of Christ as our eternal intercessor, using Paschal imagery such as "the sacrificial Victim who dies no more" and "the Lamb, once slain, who lives for ever." The fourth Preface uses the motif of restoration as it announces that "the old order [is] destroyed, / a universe cast down is renewed, / and integrity of life is restored to us in Christ." Lastly, Preface V is similar to III in that it highlights Christ as Priest and Victim, describing how he shows himself to be "the Priest, the Altar, and the Lamb of sacrifice" for our salvation.

Easter Time might be a good time to regularly chant the introductory dialogue and Preface to the Eucharistic Prayer. If this was done throughout

Lent, it becomes a good opportunity to link the two seasons, highlighting the "ninety days." If it was not done during Lent, then this would be a good time to institute the practice as a way of highlighting the festivity of the season.

Children's Liturgy of the Word

EASTER Time focuses on the Resurrection of Christ from the dead, and as such it is a time to put all our efforts into preparing beautiful liturgies. It is also the time in which we recommit ourselves to Christ through our renewal of our baptismal promises. The Asperges Rite, the sprinkling of holy water upon the assembly symbolizing this renewal, is enjoyed by children and also connects with them as a reminder of their own Baptism. Easter Time lasts for fifty days ending on the Solemnity of Pentecost. During this time we continue to celebrate with great joy the feast of the Resurrection and anticipate the coming of the Holy Spirit on Pentecost.

◆ READINGS: Unlike the rest of the year when the First Readings are taken from the Old Testament, during Easter we read from the Acts of the Apostles attributed to Luke. These readings tell us what happened following the Resurrection and Ascension of Jesus and how the early Church was formed. The Second Readings during this season are taken from the First Letter of John. This beautiful letter speaks of the love of God and love of each other. It would be best to choose this letter if only utilizing one reading in addition to the Gospel. Choose a reader who would read them with the tenderness in which they were written.

◆ ENVIRONMENT: White is the color of this joyous season. White is the color of joy and what greater joy is there than the Resurrection of our Lord. Gold and silver are other colors that can be used. White banners with bright, spring-colored accents can be used to lead the dismissal procession adding another festive element to this holy season or they can be displayed in the children's worship space.

No doubt the main worship space in the parish will be filled with flowers symbolizing our great joy at the Resurrection; however, the main symbols of Easter are not the flowers. The Paschal candle that was lit at the beginning of the Easter Vigil symbolizes the Light of Christ that pierces the darkness and lights our way, leading us back when we stray away from God through sin. It is the main symbol of this season and it is kept lit during the entire season. If lighting a candle in the children's worship space, connect it to the Paschal candle in the larger worship space which is lit during this entire season, and remind them that we carry that light in our hearts by virtue of our Baptism. The other prominent symbol reminding us of Baptism is the font through which new Christians entered into the life of Christ and his Church at the Easter Vigil and through which we all became part of the family of God. Having a bowl of holy water near the entrance of the children's space and asking them to bless themselves when coming in, especially if there wasn't a sprinkling rite as part of the Penitential Act at the beginning of Mass, again reminds them of their own Baptism.

Flowers decorating the space are quite appropriate, but do not overdo it in a small space. Instead of ordering additional flowers for the children's space, ask the children to bring flowers from their garden if possible, remembering to have an adequate number of vases to put them in. If there was a large cross displayed during Lent, draping it with a while cloth symbolizes the Resurrection.

Music for Easter Time should fill us with great joy. The Alleluia has returned and should be sung with gusto. If you retired a banner with Alleluia written on it during Lent, this is the time to return it by asking a few children to unfold it or to process it in during the Gospel Acclamation. This is also a good time to introduce a new setting of the Alleluia, perhaps one that utilizes bells or other simple hand-held instruments. Ask your music director for suggestions. Many parishes use seasonal psalms and responses with the children, but the Lectionary also allows for an Alleluia to replace the psalm response during Easter Time. This response can be a repeat of the Alleluia used at the Gospel or it could be a different setting.

The Saints

THE process of venerating the saints began with the martyrs. Their martyrdom was clearly seen as a share in Christ's Cross, and the early Christians began to celebrate them on the day of their death, that is, their "birthday" into eternal life. Gradually this practice expanded to include those holy Christians who had died more peacefully. But at its root, our veneration of the saints is a celebration of Christ's victory over death. Especially after the long, quiet weeks of Lent, what better time to commemorate the saints than during Easter, the primordial feast of the Church?

The analogy is made in apologetics that praying through the saints is little different from asking Grandma to request that favor you want from your uncle, rather than asking him first yourself. Well, to take it a step further, praying through the saints is kind of like asking your mentor or supervisor to request a favor from his good friend, the owner of the company. During Easter, however, it's like he's asking the boss to give you a raise at the party celebrating the best fiscal year the company has ever had! Jesus's victory over sin and death is sacramentally more present to us during Easter Time, and the saints, who are this very minute sharing in the fruits of that victory, are glad to request for us graces that would give us a greater sharing in the same victory.

Celebrating the saints during Easter in no way detracts from the Resurrection of Jesus Christ. It only heaps glory on top of glory, as praise offered to them redounds directly to God himself.

The Liturgy of the Hours

ALLELUIA! Alleluia! After forty days of abstaining from this word, it is suddenly absolutely everywhere! And nowhere is this more evident than in the Divine Office. Every single antiphon ends with at least one Alleluia, sometimes two, and it continues this way straight through to Evening Prayer II of Pentecost, the very last liturgy of Easter Time.

The Octave of Easter is a bit unusual. We are supposed to be celebrating the very day of the Resurrection for eight days straight, because this feast is so important that even its very beginnings can't be exhausted in one day. However, most of us have to return to the daily grind by Easter Monday or Tuesday. While the day's Masses retain a Gloria and lots of Alleluias, there's no Creed, often even no music. How to keep the spirit of the

Resurrection alive in our hearts? One option: The Liturgy of the Hours.

Each day during the Octave of Easter, the antiphons, psalms, and canticles are taken entirely from Easter Sunday, with only the reading and what follows coming from the day. In the mornings, this just feels like a string of feasts. After all, anyone who prays Morning Prayer with any regularity becomes quite familiar with those psalms of Sunday Week I before too long. Where the real genius lies, I think, is in Evening Prayer. The Octave of Easter is the only time we pray the evening psalms from Sunday Week I on any weekdays. Returning to Psalm 110 day after day really roots you in the reality of Christ's priesthood, his victorious kingship, and our participation in them. The Liturgy of the Hours truly sanctifies our time, bringing home by repetition the festivity of the Sunday, of Easter Day itself.

The Rite of Christian Initiation of Adults

EASTER Time is the period of post-baptismal catechesis or mystagogy (RCIA, 244–251). Mystagogy, "to reveal" or "to uncover the secrets, or the mysteries" is a fifty day period lasting from Easter Sunday until Pentecost, which marks the end of the Easter season each year. The mysteries to be unpacked during the fifty days are rooted in the Paschal Mystery of Christ's Death and Resurrection and the invitation to a new life in Christ through the sacrament of Baptism. Mystagogy is described as "a time for the Community and the Neophytes together to grow in deepening their grasp of the paschal mystery and in making it part of their lives through meditation on the Gospel, sharing in the Eucharist, and doing the works of Charity" (RCIA, 244).

The primary setting for the Period of Mystagogy is at the Sunday assembly during the fifty days of Easter (see RCIA 247). If the neophytes wear white robes during Easter Time, a tradition in many communities, make sure members of the assembly sit with them and help them navigate their way through the celebration of the Eucharist.

This period often comes to a close with the celebration of Mass for new Catholics held at the local diocesan cathedral. The conclusion of the mystagogy period marks the end of the initiation process. Now the neophytes enter into a lifelong process of Christian Formation along with the rest of the faithful.

The Sacraments of Initiation

THE Fifty Days are an especially appropriate time for the rites of initiation, with the special sacramental identity and liturgical character of this season. The Sundays of this season are a fine time to baptize infants within the celebration of Mass. While the Easter texts must be used rather than the ones from the rite, they are beautifully appropriate.

Depending on episcopal availability, Easter may be the season in which Confirmation is celebrated for those baptized as infants. Celebrations should stress the gift of the Holy Spirit, not the achievements of the candidates. Avoid the use of stoles on those being confirmed, as these symbols are part of clerical clothing.

While there is no specific time of the year for the celebration of first Eucharist, it most often takes place during Easter Time. If at all possible, celebrate this sacrament within the Sunday assembly as we do the other initiation rites. This allows the entire community to rejoice with the children. Some parishes celebrate special first Communion Masses, while others incorporate children into the regular Sunday celebration when children are ready.

Because Lent has such a strong penitential character, the Sacrament of Reconciliation is less often celebrated during Easter Time. Nevertheless, your parish community should know when the sacrament is available.

Children preparing for first Eucharist may not yet have celebrated the Sacrament of Reconciliation. Prepare, then, a special liturgy that encourages parents to come to Penance services as well. The newly baptized need not rush toward the celebration of this sacrament because Baptism has wiped away all sin.

The Rite of Penance

THE *Catechism of the Catholic Church* encourages frequent celebration of the Sacrament of Penance and frequent celebration of the Eucharist that "strengthens our charity, which tends to be weakened in daily life; and this living charity *wipes away the venial sins*" (CCC, 1394). The *Catechism* goes on to speak of both personal sin and social sin. As the *Catechism* reminds us, "[We] have a responsibility for the sins committed by others when *we cooperate in them*: by participating directly and voluntarily in them; by ordering, advising, or approving them; by not disclosing or not hindering them when we have an obligation to do so; by protecting evil-doers" (CCC, 1868).

Prepare to celebrate the sacrament with neophytes sometime during Easter Time. These folks having just celebrated the scrutinies and will understand the need for ongoing conversion. Make the sacrament available for those who are preparing to celebrate the Sacrament of Confirmation, their sponsors and family members.

Additional catechesis is needed to raise awareness of the role of conversion and reconciliation. Some questions we might ask would include: What do we need to do to emphasize the ecclesial dimensions of the sacrament? In what ways can we lead people into the powerful mystery of reconciliation? How might we foster an interior disposition of conversion? In what ways can we continually call people to repentance through works of mercy and acts of charity?

The devotion of the Pentecost Novena (celebrated between Ascension and Pentecost) has been gaining popularity in many circles. Consider scheduling a communal penance service on one of the days of the novena. For more information consult the USCCB (www.usccb.org/prayer-and-worship/prayers/). Consider preaching on the text of the *Veni Sancte Spiritus* on Pentecost which includes such images as "heal our wounds our strength renew" and "wash the stains of guilt away."

The Rite of Marriage

WHAT better time to celebrate a joyous occasion than Easter? Yet, St. Paul might argue that a wedding is somewhat less appropriate during Easter than at another time, because of the eschatological consciousness that Easter Time brings, particularly toward the end, as we celebrate the Ascension and Pentecost (see 1 Corinthians 7:25–40).

However, our eminent forefather's admittedly personal interpretation notwithstanding, it is extremely appropriate to witness the covenant between husband and wife during this time when we celebrate the fulfillment of God's covenant promises to his chosen people! Marriage "is a great mystery, but I speak in reference to Christ and the Church" (Ephesians 5:32). This too-often-overlooked aspect of the marriage liturgy is in high relief during Easter, as Christ's love for his Church—and the gifts that brings—are on center stage.

The Pastoral Care of the Sick

THE Paschal Mystery is a source of joy indeed, even to those whom health impedes from participating in its glorious liturgies. However, after the octave has passed, that joy naturally begins to fade, and we must rest on supernatural means in order to sustain it.

The sick and suffering, by virtue of their great share in Christ's Passion but also simply because of fewer time constraints, are privileged intercessors. As they rejoice in his Resurrection and look with expectant hope to the day when he calls them to join him in heaven, they are yet firmly rooted in this earthly life and their loved ones here with them.

Yet they likely remain disconnected from the life of the parish at large. However, if the parish were to bring its intentions to those parishioners who are confined to their home or institution: what a wealth of grace just waiting to be tapped into!

During the latter part of Easter and the early part of Ordinary Time, parish life becomes busy with joyous events. Even before wedding season begins, classes of children usually come to receive first Penance, Confirmation, and first Holy Communion! While intercession carries its own eternal rewards, it also brings with it the consolation of easing meditation upon these sacraments, two of which can—and should—be received over and over again. *Confirmandi* can be encouraged to earn some of their service hours by doing housework for homebound parishioners, returning a corporal work of mercy for a spiritual one, and

giving the adults a chance to meet some of the recipients of their intercession.

Especially during the latter part of Easter, when the whole Church is focused on the prayer "Come, Holy Spirit," the opportunities for bringing the resurrected Christ to others are offered no less to the sick than to the healthy.

The Order of Christian Funerals

EASTER Time is one of the most appropriate times in the liturgical year for the celebration of a funeral. "In the face of death, the Church confidently proclaims that God has created each person for eternal life and that Jesus, the Son of God, by his death and resurrection, has broken the chains of sin and death that bound humanity" (OCF, 1). With the light of the Paschal candle, the sprinkling with the baptismal water of Easter, and the placing of the pal (the baptismal garment), the glory of Easter shines through the funeral liturgy.

The *Order of Christian Funerals* includes prayers for when the body is transferred to the church or the place of committal (see OCF, 119–127). These prayers include welcoming the body to the church for the vigil with the funeral elsewhere, the body to the church for early visitation by the family or friends, and the body to the cemetery from the funeral home. These times of prayer are short and are marked by deep scriptural faith and confidence in God. These rites may be lead by a deacon or a lay leader of prayer.

Consider choosing readings from Easter Time which are most appropriate for the funeral liturgy. The *Order of Christian Funerals* encourages choosing readings from the Acts of the Apostles or those from the Book of Revelation for the First Reading (see OCF, 345). Homilists and those who offer a reflection on the readings can make connections to the Resurrection event.

The Paschal candle holds a prominent role in the funeral liturgy and in some places leads the procession into the church at the vigil or the funeral liturgy.

The Book of Blessings

As has been noted, at the heart of every order of blessing is the praise and thanks that the Church offers to God for the good things that God has done for us. What better time than during the great fifty-day feast of Easter to gather and to bless the Lord! As the *General Introduction* notes, "the ancient curse upon us was thus changed into a blessing: when 'the glorious Sun of Justice, Christ our God, appeared, he freed us from the age-old curse and filled us with holiness'" (BB, 2).

Beginning on Easter Day, when the Order for the Blessing of Food for the First Meal of Easter (chapter 54) might take place, the *Book of Blessings* helps us to raise our praise and thanks, echoing the Alleluia of Holy Saturday night! Similarly, the Order for Blessing of Homes during the Easter Season (chapter 50) would be specific to the season.

Other blessings, however, while not necessarily pertinent to Easter Time, may be appropriate because of what's going on in the lives of parishioners or because of the civic calendar.

- The Orders for the Blessing of Religious Articles (chapter 44): the Blessing of Rosaries (chapter 45), and the Blessing and Conferral of a Scapular (chapter 45) may all be used should these items be given as gifts for first Holy Communion, Confirmation, or graduation.

- This year, Mother's Day falls on the Fourth Sunday of Easter. The Order of Blessing of Mothers on Mother's Day can be found in chapter 55.

- Memorial Day falls during the sixth week of Easter. Parishes might use the Order for Visiting a Cemetery (chapter 57) to mark this day.

Because Easter coincides with the beginning of spring, many blessings from Part II: Blessings Related to . . . Various Forms of Human Activity may be appropriate:

- The Orders for the Blessing of Various Buildings or Structures (chapters 10–20)

- The Order for the Blessing of Fields and Flocks (chapter 26)

- The Order for the Blessing of Seeds at Planting Time (chapter 27)

- The Order for the Blessing of Boats and Fishing Gear (chapter 22)

- The Order for the Blessing of an Athletic Event (chapter 29)

The Liturgical Environment

While Easter Sunday Mass still properly belongs to the Triduum, it can also be considered as part of the fifty-day celebration of Easter TIme. This season has several sections, which can be attended to in designing the environment. First, there is the day itself, which is part of the Sacred Paschal Triduum. Second, there is the Octave of Easter, the eight days from Easter Sunday to the Second Sunday of Easter. Each of these days is a solemnity and an extension of Easter Day. There is also the season of Easter, reaching until Pentecost. There is a tendency to functionally allow the season to run its course before Pentecost, especially as everyone gets busy with the end of the school year and the beginning of summer. This tendency is to be resisted, and the environment can help in this effort.

The Second Sunday of Easter has also had the title Sunday of Divine Mercy on the Roman calendar since 2001. The devotion to the Divine Mercy should lead back to the Mystery of the Resurrection, especially on this Sunday within the Octave of Easter. If images of the Divine Mercy are incorporated in the environment, it should be in a way that harmonizes with the Easter environment and underlines that this is a part of the celebration of Easter, not a different celebration distracting from the Easter solemnity.

The entire season has white or gold as its color. Red reappears at Pentecost. There is no need for the environment to be especially elaborate, as it is intended to draw attention to the actions of the liturgy. Adorning the liturgical *loci* (font, altar, ambo, Paschal candle) is certainly appropriate. This can draw the eye to these places and reinforce the joyful fecundity of God's grace which the season celebrates. In preparing for Easter Time, consider setting aside some funds for refreshing the plants throughout the season. Easter lilies, in particular, will not last throughout the season, although removing the anther from the flowers (the yellow, fuzzy part) can extend the life of the flowers somewhat and cut down on allergic reactions. If you use lilies or other flowering plants, they need not be replaced with other flowers. Consider adding more greenery, as this mirrors the natural progression from flowers in spring to green in summer without denuding the sanctuary during the festive season.

The Paschal candle should remain in the sanctuary throughout Easter Time. It should be lit for each liturgy. This is another reason to get the largest candle that fits your space, as a larger candle will better survive the many hours of burning which it will receive during the season. It should be fitted with a follower (usually made of brass or glass). This will help the candle burn more evenly and longer, as well as prevent messy spills of wax. Particularly in a large-diameter candle, large amounts of liquid wax can be held in the follower, so extinguish the candle carefully, preferably by snuffing it rather than blowing it out.

There are often extra liturgies during Easter, first Communions and Confirmations, weddings, Baptisms, and so on. These are entirely appropriate during the season, but the liturgical environment and the liturgies should not allow Easter Time to go uncelebrated or be de-emphasized. Consider adding to the Easter environment in ways that enhance what is already there rather than eclipse it. These additions can add to Easter joy and help extend the season through to its finish at Pentecost.

The end of Easter Time with Pentecost means the change from white and gold to red. Red vestments and paraments can be striking, especially when well executed. The tongues of fire which lit upon the Apostles can also provide inspiration for Pentecost environment, although flame as a motif can be overdone. There are also plenty of red-blooming flowers which are usually in season around Pentecost.

worshipers' minds may be turned to the "punchline" of the Gospel of the day.

On Pentecost we sing the squence, "Come, O Holy Spirit, Come / *Veni Sancte Spiritus.*" Chant Mode I, sometimes called the "golden sequence," is attributed to Stephen Langton, archbishop of Canterbury (1228). Other musical settings for Pentecost based on the text of today's sequence include "Come, O Holy Spirit" (HYMN TO JOY); "Come, Holy Spirit, on Us Shine" (O FILII ET FILIAE); "By the Waking of Our Heart" (Manalo); "ENVÍA TU ESPÍRITU" (Hurd); and "*Veni Sancte Spiritus*" (Walker).

Many communities will celebrate the Order of Crowing an Image of the Blessed Virgin Mary during the month of May. Don't forget to consider the hymn "Be Joyful Mary" (*regina caeli*) with its 17th century text for use during the Sundays of Easter Time.

Infant Baptism could fittingly be celebrated on any Sunday of Easter Time — including Pentecost — during the Sunday Eucharist. Look at all the options for including music when celebrating the rite. The rite suggests the text "You have put on Christ; in him you have been baptized. Alleluia, alleluia." A plethora of settings are available from the various music publishers. An excellent option is by Howard Hughes (GIA). When all the Baptisms are complete this acclamation can be sung in a cannon and the octavo contains festive hand bell parts as well.

Liturgical Ministers

THE Easter season is such a busy time! It's packed with liturgical events — Confirmations, weddings, ordinations and first Masses, and first Communions, on top of those special Masses for other major events. Life outside of the Church is a whirlwind at this time of year, too, with graduations, end-of-year concerts and plays, Mother's Day, weddings, sports, and the beginning of summer vacations.

With all these things going on, it's rather a miracle if one's liturgical ministers show up at all for their scheduled Masses! The big, special ones usually work out okay, but the ordinary Masses? It is very tempting to declare them prohibitively inconvenient, and not important enough to overcome the difficulty.

The Liturgical Music

THE two common psalms of Easter Time are Psalm 118 and Psalm 66. Many musical settings of these psalms are available from the Catholic music publishers. The Lectionary also includes the option for Alleluia to be used as the refrain for the psalm on both Sundays and weekdays. Paul Ford's *By Flowing Waters* (The Liturgical Press) includes six melodies that can easily be memorized by the assembly (160–61 and 169–70).

Bob Hurd's collection *One with the Risen Lord* (OCP) contains 18 chanted psalms mostly meant to be sung during Communion so that the

My father received a voicemail recently to the effect of: "Hey, I'm out of town this weekend, can you cover for me tomorrow? If not . . . oh, well. They'll figure something out." This is epidemic of a greater problem that seems to be omnipresent: meeting one's obligations if it's reasonably convenient, but if not, it's not worth worrying over, something will work out.

All of which is so sad, especially during Easter Time! Liturgical ministries are ministries of evangelization, ministries that bring Christ's Resurrection to his people. But when parishioners are more involved in their weekend trips than their weekend parish—or even just busy keeping up with their children's social lives—unless they are intentional about balance, other things will overwhelm and push out Church time, and even if it does not all disappear, it will shrink. And, of course, it is during this busy season that everyone could use a little more Paschal joy in their lives.

How to counteract this? The ideas are as varied as congregations can be. E-mails? Phone calls? Personal invitations? Strict attendance policies? Loose attendance policies? Scheduling a backup minister for most Masses? The possibilities are endless. But so long as we keep in sight that the reason this matters is because Jesus Christ destroyed death and wants to take us to heaven with him, to be with him forever, we should be just fine.

Devotions and Sacramentals

ONE of the most powerful devotions of Easter Time is the Pentecost Novena, sometimes called "the original novena," as it is modeled after the nine days the Apostles and disciples spent secluded in prayer between the Ascension of Jesus into heaven and the descent of the Holy Spirit at Pentecost (see Acts of the Apostles 1:14; 2:1).

This novena has received strong support (and, previously, indulgences) from popes in recent centuries, and has been highly recommended to all the faithful as an annual opportunity to open our hearts—indeed, our whole lives—more and more deeply to the Holy Spirit.

This novena can be a pastoral difficulty in those dioceses where Ascension is celebrated on Sunday rather than Thursday, but even if the novena must be begun in anticipation of the liturgical feast, it still provides a worthwhile opportunity not only to receive divine grace but also to meditate upon the gifts of the Holy Spirit and one's openness to his works.

After all, at Easter we receive the greatest gift we could possibly receive: redemption, eternal life, participation in the glory of the Trinity. What better way to carry forward this gift than to request the Holy Spirit to direct the rest of our lives to it?

The Parish and the Home

WITHIN the great celebration of Easter, our daily lives are also hoping to come to life amidst the longer days of sunlight and the warmer weather calling us out of our homes. Connect with neighbors and greet them with Resurrection joy. Surprising others with a "Happy Easter" long after Easter day allows for small teachable moments beyond the church walls. Revel in the miracle of creation and allow for purposeful treasure walks to see what aspect of the world has come to life that day. See the world through the eyes of a child, looking for bird's nests awaiting new life, shapes in the clouds, and robins searching for food. Like Christmas Time, Easter Time is meant to be lived in vibrant joy for others to see and join the multitudes wanting to live for Jesus Christ.

When Ascension comes, don't let the sun go down on your hope. This is a day when the reality of our human emotions can be recognized and honored. Truly place yourself in the shoes of the disciples. But then, gifted with the creative love showering down upon the whole Church, allow the strength to reinvigorate your baptismal call, preparing for the Holy Spirit about to come.

At Jesus's first miracle, the Wedding of Cana, the best wine came at the end of the party. Is it possible to have something better than Jesus conquering death? The reality of knowing that answer is in every moment of life we trust Jesus fully living in us. His promise is that the Spirit will come and this unseen reality will provide each person with all the gifts necessary to speak the message of Christ to the world. Pentecost is the birthday of the entire Church, a day when Christ could not be contained to one people, one language, but had to be shared to all. Recommit yourself to the promise of your Confirmation. The Church as a whole can be sealed with the gifts of the Holy Spirit by your "yes!" to living as a firm believer and constant witness.

Mass Texts

◆ DISMISSAL FOR CHILDREN'S LITURGY OF THE WORD

Boys and girls,
throughout this season of Easter,
you will hear the word "alleluia"
many times in our songs and in our prayers.
It means "Praise God."
As you explore the Sacred Scripture this season,
you will experience Jesus as he first appeared after
    his death,
and as he prepares the people
for the coming of the Holy Spirit.
If you listen closely, you too will say "Praise God,
    Alleluia!"
Go in peace.

◆ DISMISSAL FOR CATECHUMENS

Dear catechumens,
as we move through Easter Time,
you will indeed encounter the risen Christ
in the Scriptures and in those around you.
Marvel at this mystery,
and find your hope within it
as you go forth with an "alleluia"
on your tongue and in your heart.
Go in peace.

◆ INTRODUCTION TO THE MASS

Throughout these fifty days of Easter, we will learn how Jesus Christ our Savior appeared to the faithful after his Death and Resurrection. Many of these stories seem familiar to us, as they are recurring themes we hear in some format each year. The texts may be the same, but each time the readings are proclaimed, they become alive and new. They are not something that happened 2,000 years ago, but the Word of God, as it relates to your life, your family, and the events from the daily news. So find your joy in Scripture and breaking bread this day, knowing that God has indeed done great things for us.

◆ UNIVERSAL PRAYER OR PRAYER OF THE FAITHFUL

Introduction

"Alleluia, Alleluia, give thanks to the Living God," as we bring our prayers, petitions, and praise before him.

Intercessions

1. For Pope Francis, who serves as shepherd of the Church, that he may follow the example of Jesus, the Good Shepherd, in all his actions and words, we pray to the Lord: Lord, hear our prayer.

2. For our government leaders, that they may learn to work together for the common good of all people, we pray to the Lord: Lord, hear our prayer.

3. For all who are like Thomas or who find their faith wavering, that they may put their trust and hope in the risen Lord, always recalling his faithfulness and Divine Mercy, we pray to the Lord: Lord, hear our prayer.

4. For all those who are grieving the loss of loved ones, that they may remember the promises of this Easter season, and sing the resurrection song, we pray to the Lord: Lord, hear our prayer.

5. For all those who will be receiving Sacraments of Initiation, that they may be forever zealous and joyful as God is working in their lives, we pray to the Lord: Lord, hear our prayer.

6. For all of us gathered here this day, that we may keep the resurrected Christ alive in our hearts, as we joyfully await the coming of the Holy Spirit, we pray to the Lord: Lord, hear our prayer.

Conclusion

O God, our Father in heaven,
you sent us Jesus Christ,
your only begotten Son,
who suffered, died, and rose for us
that we might have eternal life.
We ask that you might hear our humble prayers
and in your mercy and love answer them as you will.
Through Christ our Lord.
Amen.

April
Month of the Holy Eucharist

(#261) white
Monday within the Octave of Easter
SOLEMNITY

The Lectionary for Mass

◆ FIRST READING: Peter addresses the crowd of Jews who were in Jerusalem for the pilgrimage feast of Pentecost. Jesus, whom they killed by means of "lawless men," was raised up by God and "exalted at the right hand," the place of honor. From there, Jesus "poured forth" the promised Spirit that he had received from the Father. Quoting Psalm 16, Peter asserts that Jesus is the fulfillment of the promises made to David, and that he would rule on David's throne forever. They, as Jesus's disciples, are living witness to the Resurrection.

◆ RESPONSORIAL PSALM 16: Quoted in today's First Reading, Psalm 16 manifests complete trust and confidence in God, no matter how difficult life becomes. In the midst of suffering and pain akin to death, the psalmist turns to God knowing that God hears, responds, and rescues even from the throes of death. The psalm is perfectly fulfilled in the person of the resurrected Jesus.

◆ GOSPEL: Two contrasting responses to Jesus's Resurrection are evident. The women, the first Resurrection witnesses in all the Gospel accounts, are "overjoyed" at the empty tomb and the announcement that Jesus is alive. Their joy must have burst at their encounter with Jesus and in being able to touch him once again. The women are commissioned as the first apostles, sent to tell the others of the "good news" that Jesus is alive. Meanwhile, the chief priests are conspiring and doing damage control by trying to cover up the reality of the empty tomb by bribes and media spinning.

◆ SEQUENCE: See the commentary by Paul Turner on page 170. The sequence may be used each day during the Octave of Easter.

The Roman Missal

The Gloria is sung or said today, as it is every day within the Octave of Easter.

The Collect makes explicit reference to the newly baptized who were initiated at the Easter Vigil as it refers to the "new offspring" given to the Church by God. The prayer goes on to ask that all of us may hold fast to the sacrament (that is, sacramental initiation and consequent life of grace) we have received.

The Prayer over the Offerings asks that the Lord accept our offerings such that, "renewed by confession of your name and by Baptism," we may "attain unending happiness." The prayers of this Mass continue to echo the sacramental initiation that is integral to the understanding of the Easter mystery.

Preface I of Easter is assigned for today, and, as specified at the text for the Preface, the phrase "on this day" is used. If Eucharistic Prayer I, the Roman Canon, is used, the special inserts are used.

The solemn dismissal with the double Alleluia is sung or said today, as it is throughout the Octave of Easter.

TUE **7** (#262) white
Tuesday within the Octave of Easter
SOLEMNITY

The Lectionary for Mass

◆ FIRST READING: Peter continues his Pentecost witnessing to Jesus's Resurrection by reminding the people of what they did to Jesus. The people are "cut to the heart" by his words as they ask him and the other apostles for guidance. "Repent and be baptized" is their response, for in Jesus there is forgiveness, reconciliation, and peace in the gift of Jesus's Spirit. This is the "good news" for all who respond in faith to Jesus's call. Peter's witnessing leads many to seek Baptism and about "three thousand persons were added that day."

◆ RESPONSORIAL PSALM 33: Because the Lord is just and upright, loving and caring for all, God can be trusted and relied upon, no matter how difficult life becomes. Hope and trust in the Lord leads to deliverance even from famine and death. God's steadfast covenant love, translated here as kindness, suffuses the earth and becomes a living reality for all those who put their hope and trust in the Lord. Never despair. Turn to the Lord for forgiveness, reconciliation, and new life.

◆ GOSPEL: As Mary Magdalene discovers the empty tomb she weeps fearing that Jesus's body has been taken away. Jesus appears to her but in her grief she fails to recognize him till he speaks her name. Overwhelmed with joy, she reaches out to embrace him, attempting to hold him close once more. However, Jesus commissions her to go and tell the others what she has experienced, and how Jesus has returned to the Father. Mary becomes the first apostle to witness to the Good News of Jesus's Resurrection.

The Roman Missal

The Gloria is once again sung or said today.

The Collect mentions that God has bestowed on us "paschal remedies," a reference to the Easter sacraments. These sacraments bring us the opportunity to possess "perfect freedom" such that the joy we experience now is destined to reach fulfillment in heaven.

The Prayer over the Offerings brings an eschatological focus as it asks that not only may we not lose the gifts we have received (and in this season we can be reminded of the gift of new life through the sacraments, which keep us under God's protective care), but also that we might "attain the gifts that are eternal."

Preface I of Easter is again assigned for today, and, as specified at the text for the Preface, the phrase "on this day" is used. If Eucharistic Prayer I is prayed, remember to use the special inserts.

The Prayer after Communion asks that as we have received "the perfect grace of Baptism," so we may be prepared "for the reward of eternal happiness."

W E D 8 (#263) white
Wednesday within the Octave of Easter
SOLEMNITY

The Lectionary for Mass

◆ FIRST READING: Peter and John, typical religious Jews, are on their way to pray at the temple when they encounter a cripple man begging for alms. Instead of averting their eyes, they encounter the man as a child of God by looking at him and he at them. In that encounter they share with the man the most valuable thing that they now possess as followers of Christ. Invoking Jesus's name, they bring Christ's love, care, and healing to the crippled man, whose immediate response is one of joy in praising God with his whole being. Others marvel at his healing, but do not yet know it's true source is Jesus.

◆ RESPONSORIAL PSALM 105: The psalm's refrain exhorts all those who seek the Lord to rejoice. In seeking the Lord, we come to know all the good things that the Lord has done and continues to do for us and for all creation. God's love and wisdom, God's forgiving and healing ways prevail, since God always remembers the loving, faithful covenant established with all creation through Abraham and Isaac. The healed crippled man's

fitting response is praise of God, rejoicing in the concrete manifestation of God's faithful love and touch.

◆ GOSPEL: The encounter between Jesus and two disciples on the road to Emmaus is instructive of where and how all disciples encounter and come to know Jesus. Preoccupied with their own disappointment in Jesus, the two fail to recognize him, even though he walks with them. Jesus unpacks for them the Scriptures about his needing to suffer so as to enter into his glory. While at table with them, they come to recognize him in the breaking of the bread, but Jesus immediately vanishes from their sight. Luke, writing several generations after Jesus's Resurrection, asserts that we encounter Jesus whenever we reflect on Scripture and break bread together.

The Roman Missal

The Gloria is once again sung or said today.

The Collect gives voice to the joy we receive as we celebrate "year by year" the solemnity of the Lord's Resurrection, and asks that we may "reach eternal joys" through our celebration of "these present festivities." The phrase "these present festivities" can be appropriated in a broad sense to include the whole of Easter Time, in addition to specifically pointing to the days of the Octave.

The Prayer over the Offerings asks God to receive "the sacrifice which has redeemed the human race," and to "accomplish in us / salvation of mind and body." The phrasing can remind us of the totality of redemption—mind and body—that has been won for us in the Paschal Mystery, and can also be seen as an echo of the healing power that comes through Jesus's Resurrection, as proclaimed in the First Reading.

Preface I of Easter is again used today, as is the phrase "on this day."

If Eucharistic Prayer I is used, the special inserts are also again used.

The Prayer after Communion gives voice to the old/new motif as it asks that through the sacrament we may be cleansed from our old ways and transformed into a new creation.

T H U 9 (#264) white
Thursday within the Octave of Easter
SOLEMNITY

The Lectionary for Mass

◆ FIRST READING: Peter uses the people's reaction of marvel at the healing of the crippled man to testify that this miracle was done in Jesus's name. Jesus was the one predicted long ago by Moses and later prophets. Peter reminds them again that, through their ignorance, they rejected the one sent by God in favor of a murderer. God raised Jesus up, sent here to bless all. Anyone who believes in him and calls upon his name will be forgiven and reconciled to God. The people are advised once again to repent and be converted.

◆ RESPONSORIAL PSALM 8: The psalm refrain glories in the name of God whose wonders are evident throughout the earth. All that we have and enjoy, all that nourishes and gives life, is given to us as a blessing by God. The psalm marvels at this concrete manifestation of the unimaginable love and care that God has for all human beings. Jesus is the ultimate manifestation of God's love. Peter asserts that in Jesus, God has blessed us beyond measure.

◆ GOSPEL: As the two from Emmaus report to the other disciples their meal encounter with Jesus, he appears in their midst with a greeting of peace. Startled, the disciples think they are seeing a ghost. To assure them, Jesus shows them his wound marks and asks for something to eat. Overcome with joy, the disciples are instructed by Jesus as he "opened their minds to understand the Scriptures" that were fulfilled in him. They are now to carry on his mission of forgiveness and reconciliation to the world by being "witnesses of these things."

The Roman Missal

The Gloria is sung or said today, as it is every day within the Octave of Easter.

The Collect makes explicit reference to "those reborn in the font of Baptism," continuing the central place of initiation in the Mass prayers this week. The prayer notes that God has brought many nations to confess his name, and so asks that the baptized "may be one in the faith of their hearts / and the homage of their deeds." This reminds us that one is baptized into a community of faith and into a life that must be lived in union with all the other baptized.

The Prayer over the Offerings states that the sacrificial offerings of this Eucharist are offered for those who have been baptized, and also "in hope of your increased help from heaven." The request for increased help can be understood as not only for the newly baptized, but for all the baptized.

Once again Preface I of Easter is the Preface to be used for today, and the phrase "on this day" is used. If the Roman Canon is used, be sure to use the special inserts.

In the Prayer after Communion, we once again have the celebration of the Eucharist referred to as "this most holy exchange," such that the transformation that has occurred in this offering might give us God's "help in this present life / and ensure for us eternal gladness."

FRI 10 Friday within the Octave of Easter
SOLEMNITY

The Lectionary for Mass

◆ FIRST READING: Peter and John are arrested by the temple guards for disturbing the people by preaching and witnessing to Jesus's Resurrection. Despite this, many were moved by their witnessing and came to believe, greatly augmenting Jesus's disciples. Peter and John testify before their prosecutors to Jesus's name and the path of salvation that Jesus offers to all who believe. The cripple man, the sinner, even those who rejected Jesus can all be healed and achieve salvation by believing in Jesus and the power of his name.

◆ RESPONSORIAL PSALM 118: This thanksgiving psalm celebrates God's gracious care and concern for all, especially the downtrodden and oppressed. God's care is manifest in the frequently prayed Easter refrain, "The stone rejected by the builders has become the cornerstone." Peter quotes this verse in the First Reading, accusing the Jewish leaders (the builders) of rejecting Jesus (the stone), whom God raised up and made the cornerstone (the savior), through whom all who believe will be saved. Every Eucharist is a thanksgiving song to God for making Jesus our cornerstone.

◆ GOSPEL: The risen Jesus appears to his disciples on the shores of the Sea of Galilee, as they are in their boats fishing unsuccessfully. They recognize him only after he instructs them to cast the net once again and they haul a huge catch. Coming to shore, they are fed by Jesus who nourishes them physically and spiritually. In breaking bread and sharing fish, the evangelist is connecting this experience of the risen Lord with the celebration of Eucharist. The risen Jesus becomes

our food, our source of nourishment and eternal salvation.

The Roman Missal

The Gloria is sung or said today.

The Collect reminds us that the Paschal Mystery is the covenant established by God that reconciles us to him, and it goes on to ask that what we celebrate in faith may be expressed in our deeds, thus giving voice to the very purpose of worship—namely, that it might transform us to live out the self-offering of the Paschal Mystery that we commemorate at liturgy.

The Prayer over the Offerings makes another reference about "the solemn exchange brought about by these paschal offerings," an exchange that brings us "from earthly desires / to a longing for the things of heaven."

As with all the days this week, Preface I of Easter is assigned for today, and, as specified at the text for the Preface, the phrase "on this day" is used. If Eucharistic Prayer I, the Roman Canon, is used, the special inserts are used.

The Prayer after Communion prays that God may keep safe those he has saved and redeemed, so that "they may rejoice in his Resurrection." The prayer makes an explicit mention of the Passion of the Lord, a remembrance that is traditional on Fridays, even during Easter Time.

SAT 11 Saturday within the Octave of Easter
SOLEMNITY

The Lectionary for Mass

◆ FIRST READING: The cure of the crippled man by Peter and John in the name of Jesus still bothers the Jewish leaders but they are not certain how to deal with the disciples because of the people's support of them. They warn the disciples not to speak in Jesus's name any longer. The disciples respond that it is impossible to keep silent about what they have seen and heard. Sternly warned once again not to speak in Jesus's name, they are released for fear of the people who were continually praising God for the good that the disciples had worked among them.

◆ RESPONSORIAL PSALM 118: Again, we pray different verses of Psalm 118, a thanksgiving psalm of praise, structured around a communal liturgical context. The verses clearly express what must have been in the minds of the disciples as they are arrested and severely censured. In times of trial, the Lord does answer and gives strength to endure the struggle, ready to rescue us even from death. In the presence of the assembled community, the psalmist articulates the very thoughts of the disciples as they are released: "I give thanks to you (Lord), for you have answered me / and have been my savior."

◆ GOSPEL: Mark's longer ending, probably added later, summarized several appearance scenes that are detailed further in other Gospel accounts. The passage focuses on the reality that Jesus is now risen and present among us. The various encounters of the risen Lord with believers are to emphasize this very fact. The others refuse to believe their words till they see for themselves. Jesus reprimands the eleven for not believing the testimony of others. The passage ends with Jesus commissioning them to go into the world and proclaim the Good News to "every creature."

The Roman Missal

The Gloria is sung or said today.

The Collect again refers to the initiations that took place at the Easter Vigil as it acknowledges God as the one who gave "increase to the peoples who believe in you." Further explicit mention of initiation is found in the reference to the chosen ones clothed "with blessed immortality," the ones who were "reborn through the Sacrament of Baptism." Thus, Baptism continues to play center stage in the meaning of the Easter Octave, even on this late day.

The Prayer over the Offerings continues the motif of initiation as it refers to "the renewal constantly at work within us," asking for that renewal to "be the cause of our unending joy." That renewal is constantly at work within us, however, through our participation in the liturgy, which is the primary way we share in Christ's Death and Resurrection; thus the prayer includes the petition "that we may always find delight in these paschal mysteries."

Preface I of Easter is to be used today, although today is the last weekday for which it will be exclusively assigned. The phrase "on this day" is again used, as are the special inserts for Eucharistic Prayer I if that prayer is selected.

The Prayer after Communion, asks that those renewed by eternal mysteries "may attain in their flesh / the incorruptible glory of the resurrection." Thus we are also reminded that "putting on Christ" has eternal, eschatological effects.

(#44) white

12 Second Sunday of Easter (or Sunday of Divine Mercy) Octave Day of Easter

About this Sunday

The Sunday of Divine Mercy is a day established by Pope John Paul II as "a perennial invitation to the Christian world to face with confidence in divine benevolence the difficulties and trials that humankind will experience in the years to come" (May 23, 2000, the Congregation for Divine Worship and the Discipline of the Sacraments). In a way similar to Passion Sunday (Palm Sunday) or the Fourth Sunday of Easter (Good Shepherd Sunday), the Second Sunday of Easter bears the additional title of Sunday of Divine Mercy.

This is not a new solemnity or feast, nor does it celebrate a new or separate mystery of redemption, but rather, it leads into the continuing celebration of God's mercy during Easter Time. As the Octave Day of Easter, the Lectionary readings and prayer texts highlight the mystery of divine compassion that underlies the Church's Easter faith.

The Lectionary for Mass

◆ FIRST READING: Luke's description of the early Jesus communities pictures the believers being of one heart and mind, with no needy person among them. How realistic this was we do not know. However, it is the ideal that all believers strive for in making real God's reign which Jesus proclaimed. The Apostles, bearing witness to the risen Christ, were highly esteemed, and were entrusted with the distribution of goods to those in need. They modeled for the community Jesus's demand that all leaders be faithful in their responsibilities and ever vigilant about proclaiming Christ and not themselves.

◆ RESPONSORIAL PSALM 118: With the psalmist, we give thanks for the Lord's goodness, whose covenant love is everlasting. This psalm of trust and confidence praises the Lord for being "my strength and my courage," always present in our struggles, and whose loving mercy endures forever. God is at work restoring the fortunes of anyone rejected for being just, holding them up as the model, the cornerstone of God's building. The risen Christ is that cornerstone, and we are called to rejoice in what God has done for Jesus, and for us who believe.

◆ SECOND READING: Those who claim to love God show this most clearly by loving the children of God. Believing in Jesus and following through on God's loving command, which Jesus modeled through his words and actions, makes us begotten of God and responsible for one another. Such faith, articulated in our actions, conquers the world, understood as the place that finds it difficult to believe and accept Jesus. The risen Christ has already conquered the world, and through the Spirit's power, we too are called to model our lives on his. Easter Time invites us to deepen our baptismal call.

◆ GOSPEL: The risen Christ greets his fearful disciples with peace, commissions them to carry on his mission, and breathes his forgiving and reconciling Spirit upon them. They are overwhelmed with joy. Thomas who was not present refuses to believe until he is able to

see and touch Jesus for himself. A week later, Jesus appears and invites Thomas to see and touch. Thomas, overwhelmed by the risen Christ, makes one of the most profound belief statements ever by addressing Jesus as "my Lord and my God." Jesus proceeds to praise all those like ourselves who have not seen and yet have believed. Easter Time allows us the time to deepen our faith and intimate relationship with the risen Christ.

The Roman Missal

As the eighth day of the Octave of Easter, this Sunday completes the Easter Octave, and the Missal texts continue to strongly emphasize the meaning and effects of sacramental initiation. Historically, this day was given the name *dominica in albis* — the last day for the neophytes to wear their white baptismal garments.

Keep in mind, given the baptismal character of all of Easter Time, that the Rite for the Blessing and Sprinkling of Water is a good option to take advantage of. The rite may be used as a memorial of Baptism in place of the Penitential Act at the beginning of Mass on Sundays, and parishes and liturgy preparation groups would do well to do this on all the Sundays (and any other major celebrations) during Easter Time. The rite is found in Appendix II at the back of the Missal. The priest and ministers enter as usual, and the priest greets the people as usual. Then, standing at the chair (or perhaps going to the baptismal font), with a vessel containing water to be blessed nearby, he calls the people to prayer and then blesses the water; be sure to use the third option, the prayer during Easter Time. Salt may be blessed and added to the water if that is the custom of the people.

After this, the priest sprinkles himself, the ministers, and the people, ideally moving throughout the church. One of the chants suggested

in the Missal or some other appropriate song is sung during the sprinkling. After the sprinkling, the singing ends, and the priest returns to his chair and prays the closing to the rite. After this prayer, the Gloria is sung.

The Collect is replete with the language of initiation: acknowledging that our faith is kindled "in the very recurrence of the paschal feast" (the celebration of the Eucharist), it asks that "all may grasp and rightly understand" the meaning of their initiation, which is spoken in terms of being washed, being reborn, and being redeemed. The reference to grasping and rightly understanding could be understood as the journey of mystagogia, that is, of unpacking the mysteries that were celebrated at the Easter Vigil.

The Prayer over the Offerings asks God to accept our oblations and, in an optional phrase, the oblations "of those you have brought to new birth," referring of course to the neophytes. The prayer goes on to ask that those "renewed by confession of your name and by Baptism" may "attain unending happiness," reminding us again of the promised eschatological fulfillment that is the consequence of being initiated into the mysteries.

Preface I of Easter is assigned for today, although today will be the last Sunday for which it will be the only one to be used; the phrase "on this day" is again the proper phrase to be used among the possible choices. Consider chanting the introductory dialogue and the Preface today, and every Sunday during Easter Time; if this is not the regular practice of your community, this can be a way of powerfully drawing attention to the festivity of the liturgical time, and in particular if this was the practice during Lent, this can be a way of highlighting the continuity of the liturgical times (but be sure to prepare and rehearse your assembly as needed, especially if your people are not familiar with the responses!). If Eucharistic Prayer I is selected, the proper forms of the "In communion with those" and the "Therefore, Lord, we pray" are still used, as it is the Octave of Easter.

The Prayer after Communion prays that "our reception of this paschal Sacrament" may have an ongoing effect in our life, both in mind and in heart. The phrase "paschal Sacrament" should be understood in a broad sense; while it can refer to the Eucharist itself, it should be seen as encompassing in a wider sense our participation in the totality of the Easter mystery: the Paschal Mystery and the sacraments of initiation, of which the Eucharist is the climax.

If a Solemn Blessing is to be used, it is the Solemn Blessing for Easter Time, found at number 6 in the "Blessings at the End of Mass and Prayers Over the People" section of the Missal immediately following the Order of Mass. Notice how the third section of the blessing continues the baptismal theme of Easter by its specific reference to that sacrament.

Finally, for the last time until Pentecost, the solemn double Alleluia dismissal is used.

Other Ideas

Many people do not understand the difference between devotional and liturgical prayer. Sometimes, the lines are incredibly blurry. Divine Mercy is one of those days. Divine Mercy Sunday is the official title of the day, and although the Lectionary readings for the Second Sunday of Easter are about mercy, the Second Sunday of Easter is to remain the focus—not the Divine Mercy. Any devotional Masses should be later in the day, separate from normally scheduled Sunday services. Similarly, Divine Mercy chaplets and novenas should not be incorporated into the liturgy and

should be scheduled later in the day. It may be important to explain this to the congregation in the bulletin or the Homily, and invite parishioners to come back later for the Chaplet of the Divine Mercy.

MON 13 (#267) white
Easter Weekday

Optional Memorial of St. Martin I, Pope and Martyr / red

The Lectionary for Mass

◆ FIRST READING: Peter and John tell of their arrest and warnings by the chief priest and the elders to the gathered disciples. The disciples respond in prayer concerning the reality that persecution and suffering are part and parcel of God's plan. Quoting the Old Testament, they speak of others rejecting the Lord and God's anointed. Jesus was also rejected by the people, and the disciples are to expect nothing less. Despite rejection and persecution, the disciples pray for God's help in speaking "your word with all boldness." Their prayer is answered with the gift of the Spirit, filling them with boldness to continue speaking the word of God.

◆ RESPONSORIAL PSALM 2: The disciples in the First Reading quote Psalm 2 as they affirm that rejection of the Lord and God's anointed was known by God. However, the Lord is king of the universe, enthroned in heaven, and no one can thwart God's plans. We are God's anointed, specially chosen to ultimately overcome with boldness all those who think that they can undo God's eternal plans.

◆ GOSPEL: Jesus's conversation with Nicodemus, unique to John's account of the Gospel, emphasizes the role of the Spirit in giving all believers new birth and entrance into God's kingdom. John typically has Jesus's conversation partners delve deeper into what Jesus is saying, enabling the Johannine Jesus to

explain and explore the issue further. While Nicodemus thinks of natural birth, Jesus explains that being born again in the Spirit involves a rebirth into the reality and wisdom of what God is about, and what God intends for all humanity. In this fashion, the Spirit enables us to enter and make real the reign of God among us.

The Roman Missal

Remember, since we are now outside the Octave, the Gloria is no longer used on weekdays, and the double Alleluia dismissal is discontinued, as are the special inserts for Eucharistic Prayer I.

The Collect for the Easter Weekday links this week to last week's strong emphasis on initiation by referring to participants in this Mass as "we, who have been renewed by paschal remedies." Those who are thus renewed are made new creations — they transcend "the likeness of our earthly parentage." Having thus been made new, the prayer asks that we may reach our final fulfillment in eternity, "transformed in the image of our heavenly maker."

The Prayer over the Offerings gives voice to the joy both of the liturgical time and of the eternal joy that God wants for us, as it recognizes God as the one who has given us cause for gladness and as it asks that "the gifts we bring / may bear fruit in perpetual happiness." The Prayer after Communion for the Easter Weekday recalls the eschatological element in every celebration of the Eucharist, begun here on earth and pointing to fulfillment in the heavenly banquet, as it asks that "those you were pleased to renew by eternal mysteries / may attain in their flesh / the incorruptible glory of the resurrection."

Any one of the five Prefaces of Easter may be used today. While any one of the five is appropriate, perhaps, in light of the Collect's reference to renewal and initiation, and the Gospel's references to being "born from above," either Preface II—with its references to children of the light rising to eternal life—or Preface IV—as it speaks about the old order being destroyed, the renewal of the universe, and life being restored in Christ—would be good choices.

Today's Saints

Saint Martin I was a Roman of noble birth and had a reputation for intelligence, learning, and charity. He fought against the Monothelite heresy, which claimed that Jesus had two natures—human and divine—but only one will. At that time, the government was deeply involved in theological controversies. If the Church was torn by doctrinal conflicts, the emperors felt it threatened public order. They sought peace at all costs, even sacrificing orthodoxy. Martin was tried by Emperor Constans II in Constantinople, and was imprisoned and exiled. He died from mistreatment at the hands of fellow Christians in 655.

T U E 14 (#268) white Easter Weekday

The Lectionary for Mass

◆ First Reading: This description of the early communities of Jesus's followers highlights the perennial Christian attitude that must be developed toward wealth and possessions. Going contrary to our typical human attitude to own, possess, hoard and keep, Jesus's community was and is still encouraged to share possessions with those in need so that there exists "no needy person" among us. Community leaders are to ensure that the shared wealth is distributed "to each according to need." Barnabas, a future companion of Paul, is introduced as a model of what true Christian community living entails.

◆ Responsorial Psalm 93: The psalmist affirms that the Lord is king, robed in majesty and girt about with strength. Our God, the creator of all things, is enthroned above and everlasting. Because of this, whatever the Lord has decreed can be trusted, for holiness befits God's house. A community that shares, along the lines of our First Reading, is truly one that befits God's house. We are to share with all in need because all things belong to our creator God and not us. We are to share with all in need because it is the decree of the Lord and it typifies the holiness required of all who claim to reside in God's house.

◆ Gospel: Jesus continues to challenge Nicodemus by insisting that "you must be born from above." Nicodemus desires to know how this can occur. Jesus reprimands him insisting that anyone who claims to be a "teacher of Israel" should understand what he is saying. Belief in heavenly realities is what Nicodemus seems to lack. Jesus claims to speak with authority and knowledge because he is the Son of Man, the one who has come down from heaven, and will return there. Using the image of the serpent lifted up by Moses in Numbers to save people who were dying because of snake bites, Jesus asserts that those who look up at the crucified Son of Man will have eternal life, and thus be born from above.

The Roman Missal

On the weekdays of Easter Time, the Prayer over the Gifts and the Prayer after Communion are repeated week by week. Commentaries are included for these prayers on the Easter Sundays when they occur. Each day has its own unique Collect, however, which is briefly commented on below. "With great power the Apostles bore witness to the resurrection of the Lord Jesus," we hear in today's First Reading

(Acts of the Apostles 4:33). The Collect for today reminds us that we, too, are called to that apostolic task, "to proclaim the power of the risen Lord."

W E D 15 (#269) white Easter Weekday

The Lectionary for Mass

◆ First Reading: As the Apostles continue to preach about Jesus and to work many signs in his name, the high priest and the Sadducees were jealous of their popularity, arrest them and put them in jail. An angel of the Lord frees them from bondage and commissions them once again to proclaim and teach the Good News of Jesus to all. The Jewish leaders are not certain what to make of their escape and puzzle over the significance of this new movement and teaching. Hearing that the Apostles are teaching in the temple, guards are sent to arrest them again, but without force because they feared the reaction of the people who followed the apostles.

◆ Responsorial Psalm 34: The psalm declares that our God hears the cry of the poor. As a result, the psalmist invites all to bless and glorify the Lord who hears and delivers those who call upon the Lord. In our distress the Lord hears and delivers. Blessed are all those who fear and take refuge in the Lord for they will "taste and see how good the Lord is." The psalm connects the Apostles in the First Reading with those who fear and call upon the Lord. In their cry, the Lord hears and delivers them from all their enemies.

◆ Gospel: Jesus's conversation with Nicodemus continues with the Gospel narrator stressing that God loves the world immensely, and will not hold anything back in manifesting that love to all who believe, not even the only-begotten Son. The Son came into the world not to condemn but to save. Those who believe in him will be saved. The difficulty lies with those who choose not to open themselves to the immensity of God's love manifested in Jesus. These tend to prefer their way of doing things and not God's, thus cutting themselves off from the truth and light which Jesus offers. These condemn themselves to darkness because they prefer themselves and their own pettiness over God. Whoever is open to God's ways manifested in Jesus will live in the light forever.

The Roman Missal

The weekday Collect continues to situate us with the privileged Easter Time by announcing that "we recall year by year the mysteries / by which, through the restoration of its original dignity, / human nature has received the hope of rising again." We can hear echoes of Christ as the new Adam in this prayer. The Prayer over the Offerings, which will be used again on the Fifth Sunday of Easter, again uses the phrase "wonderful exchange," highlighting the important aspect of liturgical theology that it is the very gifts we offer that become the vehicle for our participation in the life of God. That sharing in God's life was begun at Baptism and becomes more and more pervasive through our participation in the Eucharist—the prayer entreats: "as we have come to know your truth, / we may make it ours by a worthy way of life." The Prayer after Communion will also appear again on the Fifth Sunday of Easter; the motif of the old being made new is employed to announce the transformation that is offered to us in the Eucharist: "lead those you have imbued with heavenly mysteries / to pass from former ways to newness of life."

Among the choices of the Easter Prefaces, perhaps Preface II, with its theme of new life in Christ and its explicit mention about "children of light" rising to eternal life, would be a good choice to echo the Gospel. Preface IV, with its mention of "integrity of life" being restored in Christ, could work as well.

THU 16 (#270) white
Easter Weekday

The Lectionary for Mass

◆ FIRST READING: The Apostles are brought before the Sanhedrin and questioned by the high priest as to why they continue preaching in Jesus's name, after they were specifically warned not to do so. The Jewish leaders are offended and worried by the fact that the Apostles are blaming them for the spilling of Jesus's blood. Peter's response sums up the Apostles's attitude, "We must obey God rather than men." Peter continues to assert that this Jesus whom they had killed has been exalted by God as savior, granting repentance and forgiveness of sin to all who are open to listen. Since they are witnesses to these things, they are motivated by the Spirit to proclaim this message to all. Infuriated, the Jewish leaders desire to do away with them.

◆ RESPONSORIAL PSALM 34: The psalm refrain again asserts that the Lord hears the cry of the poor. The just, the brokenhearted, those crushed in spirit, and all those who take refuge in the Lord are heard and rescued from all distress. To "taste and see how good the LORD is" is to know and experience the Lord as savior, ready to forgive all who seek repentance. Peter in the First Reading emphasizes this key characteristic of who Jesus is and what being an apostle entails. Turning to the Lord and obeying "God rather than men" is the heart of discipleship. All who do so are near to the Lord who hears the cry of the poor and rescues all from distress.

◆ GOSPEL: John's account of the Gospel shifts to an encounter between Jesus and John the Baptist. As that encounter ends, either the Gospel narrator or John the Baptist himself highlights what gaining eternal light entails. Similar to the ending of the Nicodemus encounter, we hear the distinction made between the one who knows and speaks of heavenly things, versus the one who only speaks of earthly things. Jesus is the one to whom God has revealed all things and he can be trusted to reveal to us all that is heavenly. Those who listen, obey, and believe in God's Son will have eternal life while others will only experience God's wrath. The apostles "obey God rather than men."

The Roman Missal

The Collect for today stresses that it is the "paschal sacrifice" which reconciles humanity to God.

FRI 17 (#271) white
Easter Weekday

The Lectionary for Mass

◆ FIRST READING: The trial of the Apostles for preaching in Jesus's name continues with the advice of the Pharisee Gamaliel, a member of the Sanhedrin. Using various examples, Gamaliel advises that the Jesus movement be allowed to run its course to see if it has its source in God or in humans. If of human origin, it will eventually come to naught. However, if from God, then they would be putting themselves in opposition to God. Do they really want to go there? Gamaliel persuades the council. The council still has the disciples flogged and again warns them not to preach in Jesus's name. The Apostles are filled with joy that they were able to suffer "for the sake of the name," and continue to publically preach and proclaim Christ.

◆ RESPONSORIAL PSALM 27: The psalmist seeks to dwell in the house of the Lord, for the Lord is "my light and my salvation . . . my life's refuge." Those placing their trust and confidence in the Lord, always seeking to dwell in God's house, will definitely experience "the bounty of the LORD" here and now, no matter life's difficulties. The Apostles in our First Reading continue preaching Christ's message despite the suffering they endured. Seeking to be with the Lord enables them to experience the Lord's bounty. Being able to suffer because of seeking to dwell in the Lord's house brings not pain but great joy.

◆ GOSPEL: John's account of the multiplication of the loaves and fishes emphasizes Jesus's ultimate desire to be true food and nourishment for all. In questioning his disciples regarding the care of those following him, he already knows what he desires and how he will accomplish it. While the disciples get the 5,000 organized, it is Jesus who gives thanks and distributes the loaves and fish to each person. All are satisfied and there are plenty of leftovers gathered. This sign of abundance is understood by all as an indication of the presence of the last great prophet who would bring about God's final reign. However, Jesus is not yet ready for the fulfillment of his "hour" and seeks solitude over the people's praise and adulation. Throughout John's account of the Gospel, Jesus will continue to be the source of food and nourishment to all who seek such a rich banquet.

The Roman Missal

In the Collect, we come before God in earnest prayer, asking him to make our hearts "worthy" to give him praises.

S
A
T
18
(#272)   white
Easter Weekday

The Lectionary for Mass

◆ FIRST READING: As the early Jesus communities grew, greater organizational structure was needed to address the needs of all. In caring for the needs of widows, the Hellenists (Greeks) felt that they were being slighted in favor of the Hebrew widows. Since the apostles needed to devote themselves to prayer and preaching the word, they decide to appoint others who would pay greater attention to meeting the needs of the growing communities. Stephen and six other men are selected and officially designated for this work of service by the laying on of hands. The number of disciples greatly increased and even Jewish priests were attracted to the Jesus communities in large numbers.

◆ RESPONSORIAL PSALM 33: This psalm of trust enjoins all to turn to the Lord who showers mercy and love upon all creation. Praise and thanksgiving are fitting responses to God's care for us. The Lord is trustworthy in all things enfolding all creation in covenant love. God's eyes shine upon all who trust and who act with justice and right. God will preserve all from harm and nourish us even in times of famine. The Apostles, following through on God's loving-kindness, ensure that all needs are met by appointing others who will manifest God's love to all they encounter.

◆ GOSPEL: Following the multiplication of the loaves and fish, Jesus departs alone, while his disciples get into a boat. During the stormy crossing, they see Jesus walking on the sea near the boat, and they began to be afraid. Jesus calms their fears by assuring them that, "It is I. Do not be afraid." With that, they soon miraculously arrive at their destination. The incident clearly highlights the theme in John's

account of the Gospel of Jesus being the divine one come down to dwell among us. In the Old Testament only God could walk on water, thus taming the chaotic forces of nature which were attributed to the sea waters. When John has Jesus state "It is I," he is attributing to Jesus the same "I AM" title that God does in the conversation with Moses on Mt. Sinai. Clearly the incident confirms Jesus as divinity dwelling among us.

The Roman Missal

There are two options for today's Collect. In the first, we beg God to "set aside . . . / the bond of sentence" written by our sins and cancel it through the Resurrection of Christ. In the second, we see "the gates of mercy" flung wide through the Paschal Mystery, and we pray that we may "never stray from the paths of life."

19
(#47)   white
**Third Sunday
of Easter**

The Lectionary for Mass

◆ FIRST READING: Peter's speech to his fellow Jews in Jerusalem for the feast of Pentecost accuses them and the Jewish leaders of maneuvering to do away with God's servant, Jesus. Peter accused them of putting to death the "author of life," but God raised him from the dead, and they are living witnesses to the risen Christ. This was all part of God's plan, announced by the prophets, that God's Christ or

Messiah would suffer. None of that matters, for God now calls all to repent and be converted, so that sins are wiped away and forgotten. God invites all to the same repentance and conversion.

◆ RESPONSORIAL PSALM 4: The psalmist prays in confidence asking God to "let your face shine on us." No matter what we have done, if we turn back to the Lord in fidelity and trust, God will answer, restore us and put gladness into our hearts once more. The Lord is the only one who can relieve our distress and bring security and peace to our hearts and minds. This is the essence of what Peter is preaching to his fellow Jews and to us today.

◆ SECOND READING: As believers, we are called to a life of love. When we falter in that love, we should not be overwhelmed for we have Jesus, our advocate with the Father. Through his word and deeds, Jesus has reconciled the whole world to the Father. All we have to do is turn to God for forgiveness and reconciliation. This is best manifested when we love others the way God has loved us. No one can truly claim to love God and not follow through on love of others. They fool only themselves. We are to keep God's word and grow daily in our love of others.

◆ GOSPEL: Another appearance of the risen Christ to his fearful disciples stresses that Jesus is not a ghost but is really and truly risen. Showering them with peace, he affirms his living presence by asking for something to eat. The disciples, overwhelmed with joy, are instructed by Jesus as he opens "their minds to understand the Scriptures" that were written about him. Having previously instructed them, he now reiterates how the Scriptures predicted that the Messiah would have to suffer and die, but rise on the third day. In this manner repentance and forgiveness of sin would

be preached to all. They and we are witnesses to these things. This Easter Time, examine how you are a faithful witness to the risen Christ.

The Roman Missal

It would be a good idea to again use the Rite for the Blessing and Sprinkling of Water, as discussed for the Second Sunday of Easter. The rite is found in Appendix II at the back of the Missal and replaces the Penitential Act. The Gloria is sung today.

The Collect describes how God's people have been "renewed in youthfulness of spirit" and rejoice "in the restored glory of our adoption." Such references to youthfulness, restoration, and adoption maintain the imagery of the new life given to us at Baptism that would be recalled in the Rite of Blessing and Sprinkling of Water. The prayer ends by reminding us that such Easter joy goes beyond the present moment — there is a fitting eschatological reference as we ask that "we may look forward in confident hope / to the rejoicing of the day of resurrection." Our present participation in the mystery of Christ's Death and Resurrection cannot be separated from the way that participation points toward its future fulfillment.

The Prayer over the Offerings continues the joyful tone of the texts by describing the Church as "exultant" as we offer these gifts, again asking that the offerings will "bear fruit in perpetual happiness."

Any one of the five Easter Prefaces may be selected for today; if Preface I is chosen, remember that the correct wording is "in this time." Consider chanting the introductory dialogue and the Preface today, and every Sunday during Easter Time, in order to highlight the ongoing festivity of the season.

The Prayer after Communion also has an eschatological focus, as it reminds us that our participation

in the Paschal Mystery at the Eucharist always looks forward to its fulfillment in "the incorruptible glory of the resurrection."

You might consider using the solemn blessing for Easter Time, found at number 6 in the "Blessings at the End of Mass and Prayers over the People" section of the Missal immediately following the Order of Mass. Remember that a regular formula for dismissal is used, not the solemn double Alleluia.

Other Ideas

Often we speak of mystagogical cathechesis, that is, mystagogy as an initiation into all that is not fully realized. During Easter Time, the neophytes are to reflect more deeply on the mysteries they just experienced. But, why limit the experience to the neophytes? Provide sessions for the congregation. Coffee and mystagogy could be wonderful as people get a chance to share how they found Christ in the liturgies of the Triduum, or this Sunday's liturgy, or in a general way. Just because something is designed for a new person, doesn't mean it isn't something that could be really good for all those involved.

Are there any announcements about first Communions or Confirmation that need to be mentioned during the annoucements? Or training sessions for new liturgical ministers? Sometimes the spoken word does more than the written one when it comes to recruiting volunteers!

M O N 20 (#273) white Easter Weekday

The Lectionary for Mass

◆ FIRST READING: Stephen, one of those appointed by the Apostles to be of service to the community is described as being "filled with grace and power . . . working great signs and wonders among the people." Some Hellenistic Jews debate with Stephen, jealous of his wisdom. They stir up the people against Stephen with accusations of blasphemy against Moses and God. Bringing him before the Sanhedrin they falsely accuse him. The charges center on Stephen preaching that Jesus would destroy the temple and change the customs of Moses. Stephen is described by the onlookers as having the face of an angel. In the Old Testament, Joseph and Moses, who were intimate with God, have faces that are like those of an angel. Luke places Stephen among that august company.

◆ RESPONSORIAL PSALM 119: The way of the Lord, God's decrees and statutes, are a delight to the psalmist, leading to a deeper understanding of the Lord and the true path of life. The psalm verses readily connect with Stephen in today's First Reading, who despite slander and false witnesses both from the people and their leaders, stays the course of God's path, making God's ways his delight, and always choosing the way of truth. The psalm refrain affirms that all those who attune themselves to God's ways, God's laws, will be blessed, regardless of what happens to them. Like Stephen, such blessed people will have faces like those of an angel.

◆ GOSPEL: After the multiplication of the loaves and fishes and Jesus walking on water, the crowd seeks Jesus out in Capernaum. Jesus reprimands the crowd for they seem to be following him not because they believe in the deeper reality of his signs but because they ate the loaves and were filled. The crowd is urged not to work for food that perishes but for food that endures to eternal life. Only the Son of Man can give eternal life. The crowd inquires of Jesus as to what they can do to accomplish the works of God, and gain eternal life. Jesus clearly asserts that to do the work of God is to believe in him, the one whom

God sent to guide us in doing the work of God.

The Roman Missal

The Collect for today gives voice to the motif of putting off the old self, noting how we have been conformed to the nature of Christ "through the healing paschal remedies." Thus, being remade in this way should result in our living as Christ did. The Paschal Mystery of dying and rising with Christ, and its effects for the way we are supposed to live life, continues to be present in this Collect, appropriate for Easter Time. The Prayer over the Offerings, heard on the Thursday after the Second Week of Easter, continues the theme of being conformed to the Paschal Mystery, a conformation expressed here as being effected by the rising up of our prayers "together with the sacrificial offerings" which leads to a purification through the graciousness of God. The Prayer after Communion notes how the Resurrection of Christ has restored us to eternal life and asks for an increase of "the fruits of this paschal Sacrament"—particularly, the strengthening of our hearts.

Any one of the five Easter Prefaces may be used today; the readings don't seem to necessarily suggest any one more appropriate than another, although perhaps Preface I, focusing in general on the Paschal Mystery, with its mention that "dying he has destroyed our death, / and by rising, restored our life," would resonate well with the orations.

TUE **21** (#274) white
Easter Weekday

Optional Memorial of St. Anselm, Bishop and Doctor of the Church / white

The Lectionary for Mass

◆ FIRST READING: Stephen, falsely accused, defends himself against the people and the council by blaming

them for opposing the Holy Spirit and for killing the prophets God sent to foretell the coming of the righteous one, Jesus. He further accuses them of receiving the law but not observing it. The people are infuriated by his accusation, cover their ears to avoiding listening to his charges, and attack him. Stephen does not seem to even notice them as he has a vision of God's glory and Jesus standing at the right hand of God. Mob-like, they stone Stephen to death and he, like Jesus, asks God to forgive them. Saul is briefly introduced as looking on and consenting to the execution.

◆ RESPONSORIAL PSALM 31: This trust psalm links clearly to the events that Stephen is experiencing. As Stephen is being stoned, he commends his spirit to Jesus, picking up the refrain of "Into your hands, O Lord, I commend my spirit." The Lord is Stephen's "rock of refuge . . . and fortress." Stephen actually sees the glory of God as the "plottings of men" overtake him. Stephen trusts in God's loving kindness and faithful love that, no matter what happens, the Lord "will redeem me" and "save me." The psalm articulates that trust in God that enables all disciples to carry on despite life's challenges and difficulties.

◆ GOSPEL: The Johannine Bread of Life discourse continues with the people asking Jesus for a sign so that they can believe in him. Is he greater than Moses who gave them manna in the desert? Jesus clarifies that Moses did not give them manna but God did, stating once again that they are to focus not just on material things but on the bread of God, or the spiritual nourishment that comes down from heaven and gives life to the world. Again the crowd misunderstands by requesting that Jesus give them this bread always. Jesus responds with the first of seven "I AM" declarations in John's account of the Gospel asserting that "I am the bread of life." True and lasting nourishment is coming to know Jesus as the bread come down from heaven and believing in him.

The Roman Missal

Today's Collect continues Easter Time's overall emphasis on sacramental initiation with reference to "those reborn of water and the Holy Spirit," as it asks for "an increase of the grace you have bestowed;" this increase is available through the Eucharist, which is the culmination of and renews the life of grace begun at Baptism. The Prayer over the Offerings, recently used this past Sunday, expresses the joy of the Church, a joy that originates in the new life given at Easter and finds fulfillment in the happiness of the Kingdom of God. The Prayer after Communion, also repeated from Sunday, asks that those who have been renewed by eternal mysteries—pointing to how every celebration of the Eucharist is our present participation in the Paschal Mystery—may "attain in their flesh / the incorruptible glory of the resurrection," thus, like the Prayer over the Offerings, reminding us of the eschatological fulfillment that awaits us.

Any one of the five Easter Prefaces may be used today. Perhaps, in light of the First Reading from Acts, which portrays Stephen's death as paralleling Jesus's, we could find in Preface V of Easter, with its mention of Christ our Passover being sacrificed, its reference to the oblation of Christ's Body, and its mention of Christ "commending himself to you for our salvation," an echo of both Jesus and Stephen handing themselves over in death.

Today's Saint

Saint Anselm was born around the year 1033 in Aosta, then part of the Kingdom of Burgundy, today part of Piedmont in the Italian Alps. Hearing of the reputation of his countryman, Lanfranc, who was prior of the Benedictine abbey of Bec in Normandy, Anselm entered the monastery there at the age of twenty-seven. When Lanfranc was named abbot of Caen, Anselm succeeded him as prior of Bec, and fifteen years later in 1079, he became abbot. In 1070, Anselm's mentor Lanfranc was made archbishop of Canterbury in England, and when he died in 1109, William II of England seized the lands and revenues of the archdiocese and left the office of archbishop empty (at this time, bishops were appointed by kings). Finally in 1093, public pressure forced William to appoint Anselm archbishop of Canterbury. Anselm's term as archbishop was not easy. He was forced into exile twice because of his support of the Gregorian Reform, which tried to do away with lay investiture, the power of secular authority to appoint bishops. Anselm is a Doctor of the Church and is called the Father of Scholasticism for his works of theology, especially the *Proslogion*, an argument for the existence of God based on reason, and his treatise, *Why God Became Man*, on the saving action of the Incarnation. He is also celebrated in the Anglican and Lutheran Church.

W E D 22 (#275) white Easter Weekday

The Lectionary for Mass

◆ FIRST READING: Following upon the martyrdom of Stephen, Acts recounts a severe persecution of Jesus's disciples in Jerusalem, scattering all to the countryside and Samaria. As Stephen is lamented and buried, Saul takes up the battle cry against the Jesus communities by seeking them out and imprisoning them. The scattered disciples begin preaching the word wherever they land, with Philip, one of the seven men selected to serve the Jerusalem community, preaching the word in Samaria. Many paid attention to the words and healing signs he was performing, and great joy was experienced there. Jesus's commission to spread the word to all is beginning to be actualized outside of Jerusalem.

◆ RESPONSORIAL PSALM 66: The joy of Samaria in hearing and seeing Philip's words and healing actions is the theme that runs through the psalm. God has done marvelous things for the people, exemplified by the Exodus experience, and God continues to do marvelous things again, even in Samaria. Therefore, all on earth are called to "shout joyfully to God" marveling at "how tremendous are your deeds." All are invited to "come and see the works of God." Philip could have easily used this psalm in preaching the word and manifesting God's love for all.

◆ GOSPEL: Jesus reiterates that he is the bread of life and anyone who believes in him will never hunger or thirst. Some choose not to believe. Facing that reality, Jesus clarifies his identity and mission for them. The Father welcomes all, and has sent Jesus to gather all and not reject anyone. Jesus's primary mission is to "not lose anything of what the Father gave me." Those who do come to Jesus and believe will be assured of eternal life on the last day. Jesus repeats it again to make sure that his identity and mission from the Father are clear to all. How they respond to his person and mission is now clearly in their court. Jesus will continue to invite all to belief, even with his very dying breath.

The Roman Missal

Today's Collect emphasizes God's initiative in saving us, as it points to "those you have endowed with the grace of faith," and it again reminds us to look beyond our present participation in the Paschal Mystery toward our full participation as it asks that God give us "an eternal share in the Resurrection of your Only Begotten Son." The Prayer over the Offerings speaks of the ongoing power of the Paschal Mystery in our life, asking that "the renewal constantly at work within us / may be the cause of our unending joy." We should always remember that the effects of the Lord's Resurrection are ongoing in our lives, especially through the liturgy (in the words of the prayer, "these paschal mysteries"). In the Prayer after Communion we once again hear the felicitous phrase "holy exchange" as we pray that this exchange—this liturgical celebration—"may bring your help in this present life / and ensure for us eternal gladness."

Any one of the five Easter Prefaces may be selected for today; perhaps Preface II, with its theme of new life in Christ, would resonate well with what was said above concerning the orations.

T H U 23 (#276) white
Easter Weekday

Optional Memorials of St. George, Martyr / red; St. Adalbert, Bishop and Martyr / red

The Lectionary for Mass

◆ FIRST READING: Philip continues his ministry by responding to an angel who directs him to an Ethiopian eunuch desiring clarification concerning certain Scripture passages that he is reflecting on. Seeing that the eunuch was open to a deeper understanding of God's word, Philip proceeds to instruct him concerning Jesus, by applying the passage from Isaiah to Jesus. As they approach water, the eunuch requests Baptism and Philip baptizes him. The Spirit obviously desires Philip to continue his ministry since he is snatched up and delivered to another locale to proclaim the word. Meanwhile, the eunuch, filled with joy, continues his journey home. The passage emphasizes

what openness to God's word can do for all who are willing to listen and believe.

◆ RESPONSORIAL PSALM 66: The psalm once again picks up the theme of joy that enveloped the eunuch as he came to know Jesus and was baptized by Philip. The psalm refrain was most likely on the lips of the eunuch as he exclaimed, "let all the earth cry out to God with joy." Joy is the result of realizing that God "has given life to our souls and has not let our feet slip." The eunuch sought deeper understanding and desired to draw closer to the Lord. With the psalmist, he must have shouted out "Blessed be God who refused me not / my prayer or his kindness!" Today, we too are invited to "cry out to God with joy" in thanksgiving for all that the Lord has done for us.

◆ GOSPEL: As Jesus continues his Bread of Life discourse, he stresses the Father's initiative in drawing all people to God through Jesus. God desires that we draw close to Jesus, the one whom the Father sent, thus allowing God to teach us and to enter into deeper knowledge and awareness of the Father. Believing in Jesus, the one God sent, results in eternal life. Jesus claims once again to be the bread of life that, unlike their ancestors who ate the manna and later died, those who eat of Jesus, the Bread of life, will never die. The passage concludes with Jesus affirming that, unlike the manna, the bread that he will give is his very self, "my Flesh for the life of the world."

The Roman Missal

The Collect points to our ongoing celebration of the fifty days of Easter Time, and the mystery we focus on, as it asks that we experience God's "compassion more readily / during these days when, by your gift, / we have known it more fully." The mention of having been "freed

from the darkness of error" can, of course, call to mind the illumination that occurred at Baptism, another theme that runs throughout Easter Time. The Prayer over the Offerings expresses how this "wonderful exchange" makes us partakers of the very life of God (that is, in the liturgy the very work of our redemption is accomplished). Being made sharers in the life of God, however, the prayer reminds us that we must "make it ours by a worthy way of life." The Prayer after Communion returns to the old way of life/new way of life motif, asking that we be led to the new way.

Among the Easter Prefaces to be used today, perhaps either II, with its reference to "children of light" or IV, with its statement that "the old order [is] destroyed, / a universe cast down is renewed, / and integrity of life is restored to us in Christ" would continue the themes found in the orations.

Today's Saints

Saint George (c. † 303) was a soldier from Syria who was in the guard of emperor Diocletian. Although historians feel that he did, in fact, exist, the details of his life have been obscured by the many legends that grew up around him. *The Golden Legend*, a thirteenth century collection of saints' stories, relates the account of George slaying a dragon. He is honored by Catholics, Anglicans, Lutherans, the Orthodox, and even adherents of Islam. Saint George is shown in art as a soldier on a white horse slaying a dragon, while carrying a white shield with a red cross. This red cross on a white background is known as Saint George's Cross and is on the flags of several countries, including England and Greece.

Saint Adalbert (c. 959–997) came from a wealthy Czech family. He became bishop of Prague before the age of thirty, but resigned because paganism persisted among the Christians there. Adalbert went to Rome and became a Benedictine monk, but in 993, after only four years, the pope sent him back to Prague to resume his role as bishop. He founded the first monastery in the Czech region, but during an uprising, all of his brothers were murdered, and Adalbert had to flee Prague. Adalbert then went to evangelize in Hungary and Poland, where he was welcomed by the rulers. He then went to Prussia where, following the custom of Christian missionaries, he chopped down the sacred oak trees to show the people that the trees were not supernatural. For this he was executed in April, 997. He is honored by both the Catholic and Orthodox Churches and is a patron saint of Bohemia, Poland, and Prussia.

F R I 24 (#277) white
Easter Weekday

Optional Memorial of St. Fidelis of Sigmaringen, Priest and Martyr / red

The Lectionary for Mass

◆ FIRST READING: This is one of several versions of Saul's conversion, his acceptance of Jesus as the long awaited Messiah and Son of God. This does not mean that Saul, a lifelong Jew and a Pharisee, left Judaism behind and became a Christian. Rather, Saul always remained a Jew, who accepted Jesus as the Messiah, and who began preaching that message to all who would listen. Saul was transformed from a persecutor of Jesus's disciples to an active advocate of Jesus and the new age that was initiated with his coming. The narrative highlights the Spirit's role in Saul's new way of seeing and understanding which will bring him great pain and sorrow as well as great joy and gain. Such is the fate of any disciple who chooses to follow the way of the Lord.

◆ RESPONSORIAL PSALM 117: The shortest of all the psalms is used to highlight what Jesus predicts will be Saul's mission and ministry, "to carry my name before Gentiles, kings, and children of Israel." The refrain, taken from Mark's account of the Gospel, emphasizes the universality of the Lord's commission to "go out to all the world and tell the Good news." Saul will see himself as the Apostle to the Gentiles, carrying out the Lord's universal commission to the end of the earth. Saul's key message is summarized in the second verse of the psalm when it proclaims that we praise the Lord "for steadfast is his kindness towards us, and the fidelity of the LORD endures forever."

◆ GOSPEL: The Bread of Life discourse continues with the crowd questioning how Jesus can give them his flesh to eat. Jesus reiterates that unless they eat of his flesh and drink of his blood, they will not have life within them. This obvious Eucharistic reference does not mean that we are literally eating Jesus's flesh and drinking his blood. Rather flesh and blood refer to Jesus's entire living person. When we share Eucharist, we become one with the entire living person of Jesus, the risen Christ, and we commit to giving of ourselves for others, the way Christ gave of himself for us. This intimate communion is what nourishes us and insures eternal life. Without intimate union and belief in Jesus, we will die. With Jesus and the intimate nourishment that he provides, we will live forever, even when we die.

The Roman Missal

The Collect for today emphasizes new life: since we have "come to know / the grace of the Lord's Resurrection," we pray that we "ourselves rise to newness of life." The prayer reminds us of the agency of the Holy Spirit as it acknowledges that this rising to newness of life will occur "through the love of the Spirit." The Prayer over the Offerings entreats that what we do at this liturgy will become the pattern of our entire lives — that "the oblation of this spiritual sacrifice" may "make of us an eternal offering to you." The Prayer after Communion asks that since "We have partaken of the gifts of this sacred mystery," that it effects in our life a "growth in charity." The directness of this prayer reminds us that the fruits of the Eucharist must always be made manifest in our love toward one another.

The various references to living in newness of life, and the Gospel's reference to having life because of our feeding on the Bread of Life might make Easter Prefaces I or II likely candidates for use today.

Today's Saint

Saint Fidelis of Sigmaringen (1578–1622) was a German Capuchin. He studied at the University of Freiburg, and after finishing he taught philosophy, but in spite of his learning, he was known for his penitential practices, prayerfulness, and humility. In 1612, at the age of thirty-five, he joined the Capuchins and took the name Fidelis, which means "faithful." Fidelis was known for his charity and prayer, and when he became superior of a Capuchin friary, many in the local area returned to Catholicism as result of his influence. At the behest of the Habsburgs, who ruled parts of Europe at the time, Fidelis went to the north of France to preach to the people who had left the Church. Although he was protected by Austrian soldiers, he was captured by Calvinists, who murdered him when he refused to renounce his faith.

SAT 25 (#555) red
Feast of St. Mark, Evangelist

The Lectionary for Mass

◆ FIRST READING: We hear of Mark in the closing greeting of Peter's letter. In the preceding verses, Peter exhorts believers to humility, to trust in the Lord, to discipline and vigilance, and to being on guard against the devil. Heavenly glory awaits us after our suffering.

◆ RESPONSORIAL PSALM 89: Through their written accounts of the Gospel of the Lord, the evangelists did indeed sing the goodness of the Lord. Their words are light through which we may walk in the light of the Lord's countenance, rejoicing in his name all the day.

◆ GOSPEL: The risen Christ commissions his Apostles to proclaim the Gospel to the whole world, promising them the assurance of signs and wonders as confirmation of their message. Having sent the Apostles as his messengers, the risen Christ ascends to heavenly glory.

The Roman Missal

The prayers for the feast are found in the Proper of Saints. The Gloria is said or sung today. Preface II of Apostles is used.

In the Collect we pray that we may learn from the Gospel according to Mark to "follow faithfully in the footsteps of Christ." The Prayer over the Offerings is a prayer for the Church, that she may "always persevere / in the preaching of the Gospel." We pray that the Communion we have received may make us strong in the faith which Saint Mark proclaimed (Prayer after Communion).

Today's Saint

Saint Mark (first century) is the traditional author of the Gospel account that bears his name. Although he has been identified with John Mark and Mark, the cousin of

Barnabas, the earliest tradition sees him as a distinct individual, one of the seventy disciples sent by Jesus to preach before the Crucifixion. According to Hippolytus, a writer of the second to third century, he had such difficulty with Jesus's teaching on the Eucharist that he left but was later brought back by Saint Peter. Subsequently, he traveled with Peter and worked as his interpreter, wrote the Gospel based on Peter's preaching, and became bishop of Alexandria in Egypt. The Coptic Church claims him as their first bishop and parts of their liturgy are attributed to him. Their tradition says that he was martyred at Alexandria in 68 AD.

☀ 26 (#50) white
Fourth Sunday of Easter
Good Shepherd Sunday

About this Sunday

The Fourth Sunday of Easter is traditionally referred to as *Good Shepherd Sunday*. Hearing the Shepherd's voice, followers recognize and know it is their God. Safe in the knowledge that they cannot be taken from the hand of the Shepherd, those who hear his voice follow as faithful believers willing to go where God calls and sends them. When all the clamor of false voices and seductive distractions threaten to overwhelm, we have only to listen carefully to be led to do the work of the Father.

The Lectionary for Mass

◆ FIRST READING: Peter clearly explains to Jewish leaders and elders that the healing of a cripple was done in the name of Jesus, the Nazorean. Accusing them of having crucified Jesus, Peter asserts that God foiled their plan by raising Jesus from the dead. Quoting Psalm 118 Peter claims that God made Jesus, the stone they rejected, the cornerstone of God's building, the stone that holds the whole building together. As a result, "there is no other name under heaven . . . by which we are to be saved." Salvation is assured to anyone who lives and acts in the manner of Jesus, the cornerstone of God's building.

◆ RESPONSORIAL PSALM 118: Peter quotes the psalm refrain to show how Jesus, the stone rejected by others, has been raised by God and made the cornerstone. This psalm of trust and confidence images God as good and full of mercy, whose loving kindness and covenant love endures forever. God is our savior, who answers us in time of need, and restores all those who have been rejected and abandoned. Such wonders that God does on our behalf can only elicit praise, thanksgiving, and blessing of God now and always. Easter Time calls us to praise and bless God always.

◆ SECOND READING: By God's gracious gift in Christ Jesus, we are now children of God. This gift is ours, despite the refusal of the world, the place of unbelief, to acknowledge us as such. What we shall be when the end time comes, we do not yet know. However, as children of God, we do know that when that time comes, we shall know, see, and be like the Lord always. This is our Easter hope and prayer.

◆ GOSPEL: On this Good Shepherd Sunday, we hear one of Jesus's clear "I AM" statements, "I am e good shepherd." Shepherds e scripturally understood to be e leaders who are to model for thers the care and concern that od has for all people. As the Good hepherd, Jesus contrasts himself ith the hired hand, other leaders ho work for pay and are not conerned for the sheep. He is the good hepherd because he cares for the heep even to the point of laying own his life for them. Jesus's love f the sheep extends to all of God's reature, even those who are not of his particular fold. Jesus desires ll to be one, loving and caring for ne another the way he freely and illingly loves and cares for us. All his is exactly the will of the Father, nd Jesus models that life perfectly.

he Roman Missal

Continue to use the Rite for the Blessing and Sprinkling of Water, as discussed for the Second Sunday of Easter, or, if you haven't been using t, consider beginning to do so. This ite, found in Appendix II of the Missal, replaces the Penitential Act. The Gloria is sung today.

The Collect refers to God's peole as "the humble flock" who ask o "reach / where the brave shepherd has gone before." This, of course, echoes the Gospel reading today, which gives this Fourth Sunday of Easter its popular title of *Good Shepherd Sunday.*

The Prayer over the Offerings, previously used on Saturday within the Octave of Easter, Tuesday after the Second Sunday of Easter, and Wednesday after the Third Sunday of Easter, continues to express our Easter joy by asking that "we may always find delight in these paschal mysteries" and reminds us that the renewal brought about by our participation in Jesus's Death and Resurrection is "constantly at work within us."

While any one of the five Easter Prefaces may be selected for today, certainly Preface III with

its reference to Christ as "the Lamb, once slain, who lives for ever," would be appropriate. Continue or begin chanting the introductory dialogue and the Preface today, in order to highlight the ongoing festivity of Easter Time.

The Prayer after Communion also employs the shepherd imagery, even mentioning the "eternal pastures," which we hope to settle in. Interestingly, the prayer mentions how we are redeemed "by the Precious Blood of your Son," thus giving a nod to the importance of the shedding of Christ's Blood as the offering of himself and therefore of the importance of regularly offering Holy Communion under both kinds as a sign of our participation in the Paschal Mystery.

You might consider using the solemn blessing for Easter Time, found at number 6 in the "Blessings at the End of Mass and Prayers over the People" section of the Missal. Remember that a regular formula for dismissal is used, not the solemn double Alleluia.

Other Ideas

Many people have never seen a real sheep. Sheep are pictured as cute, clean little lambs — an adorable pet. In reality, sheep are not very bright and they need a lot of care including someone to guide them, sheer them, care for hoofs, and dock their tails. For many children involved in programs like 4-H, the sheep is a "starter animal." Instinctually, sheep will follow each other and try and stay together. If they are separated, they will work desperately to return to the flock. When we hear the parable of the lost sheep, it may not dawn on us that that the lone sheep may have been trying to find his way back to Jesus, the Good Shepherd. There is a picture that floats around the internet of "Shrek the Sheep" who was lost in the rocks and craigs for over six years. He was almost unrecognizable, and

could barely see, because he was so overgrown. When sheered, his wool weighed sixty pounds compared to the average ten. It is a powerful metaphor for what happens when we become estranged from God for a long time, and burdened with our sins. Reconciliation serves us as a good sheering.

MON 27 (#279) white
Easter Weekday

The Lectionary for Mass

◆ FIRST READING: As Gentiles, non-Jewish converts, accept the word of God, Peter is reprimanded by fellow Jewish disciples not for preaching to or baptizing Gentiles (see Acts of the Apostles 10), but for entering their houses and eating with them. Peter recounts the vision of clean and unclean foods that he had before encountering Cornelius in Acts of the Apostles 10: "What God has made clean, you are not to call profane." Peter justifies his actions by recalling the Lord's words that you are to be baptized with the Holy Spirit. If the Lord sent the Spirit upon the Gentiles as well, who was he to stop God from acting? The others began glorifying God for having brought "life-giving repentance to the Gentiles too." This would not be the end of the matter, but for now the Jewish disciples are pleased.

◆ RESPONSORIAL PSALM 42: Thirst for the living God sums up the psalm as well as the desire of the Gentiles in our First Reading. Our desire for meaning and purpose in life often drives us to thirst and search for God, the only one who ultimately satisfies. Such longing is compared to the demanding thirst for water, a thirst that only water can quench. Another comparison is the search for a place where one feels at home when all else seems out of place. Once these are satisfied, then joy and gladness enters, with thanks and praise of God as the only appropriate response. The Gentiles in our First Reading must surely have experienced such yearning and desire, as we do also.

◆ GOSPEL: John 10 focuses on Jesus as the Good Shepherd, in contrast to strangers, thieves, and robbers. The whole chapter is a response to the attack on Jesus by some Pharisees during the cure of the blind man episode in John 9. Jesus contrasts his leadership style, one of care and concern for the sheep, with that of some of the Pharisees, who seem to care only for themselves. Jesus insists that the sheep know better and will follow him because he provides safety, care, nourishment, and life. They will not follow leaders who are thieves come to steal, slaughter, and destroy. "I came so that they might have life and have it more abundantly."

The Roman Missal

The image of light, so central to the meaning of Baptism and of Resurrection, is used in the Collect for the Easter Weekday as the prayer addresses God as "perfect light of the blessed." The prayer prays for a fulfillment of the life of light and grace begun at Baptism as it asks that we may "rejoice in the full measure of your grace / for ages unending." The Prayer over the Offerings, previously prayed on Monday after the Second Sunday of Easter, on the Third Sunday of Easter, and on Tuesday after the Third Sunday of Easter, continues to speak about the joy of Easter, a joy that will reach fulfillment in "perpetual happiness." The Prayer after Communion, previously heard on the same days as the Prayer over the Offerings, also points us to look forward, in this prayer, to attaining in our flesh "the incorruptible glory of the resurrection."

Any one of the five Prefaces of Easter may be used today, although Preface V, with its mention of Christ's bringing "the sacrifices of old to fulfillment" might resonate with the First Reading from the Acts of the Apostles.

TUE 28 (#280) white Easter Weekday

Optional Memorials of St. Peter Chanel, Priest and Martyr / red; St. Louis Grignion de Monfort, Priest / white

The Lectionary for Mass

◆ FIRST READING: We read today of the Spirit's work in spreading God's word from Jerusalem to other corners of the world, now focused on the Gentiles in Antioch. In going out to the Gentiles, "the hand of the Lord was with them" signifies that this was God's doing, guided by the Spirit. No longer would the word of God be limited to just Jews, but would reach out to all. This controversial stance will create tension and division among Jews and Gentiles. But for now, Barnabas is commissioned by Jerusalem to preach in Antioch, and he searches out Saul to help him in spreading the word. And, "it was in Antioch that the disciples were first called Christians."

◆ RESPONSORIAL PSALM 87: "All you nations, praise the Lord" is a fitting summary of the spread of God's word to the Gentiles of Antioch. The psalm praises God for having established Zion, Jerusalem and its temple, as the holy city from which all goodness and grace flows into the whole world. All who are open to God's word and carry it out in their lives are wondrously connected to God's holy city, Jerusalem. Just as the Jerusalem Church sent Barnabas to Antioch, so all who listen to God's word are connected with Jerusalem. The psalm sums it up with the phrase, "all shall sing . . . 'My home is within you.'"

◆ GOSPEL: In winter, during the feast of the Dedication better known as Hanukkah, Jesus is confronted by some Jews who demand that he speak plainly concerning his identity; namely, is he the Christ, the Messiah, or not? Jesus tells them that he has spoken plainly about his identity many times and his signs testify to that but they fail to believe, because they are not among his sheep. If they were, they would hear, know, and believe. Jesus asserts that he is the true Shepherd, commissioned so by the Father, who handed over all the sheep to him. Those who listen and believe are among his sheep. He will give them eternal life and no one will ever snatch them away from him. Jesus has so enfleshed God that the Father and he are one, and everything he does is done with the will and desire of the Father.

The Roman Missal

The Collect for the weekday is very simple and direct: it asks that by "celebrating the mysteries of the Lord's Resurrection, / we may merit to receive the joy of our redemption." The prayer reminds us that if we have died with Christ, then we shall also live with him, and that every Eucharist is a participation in the Paschal Mystery of the Lord's Death and Resurrection. The Prayer over the Offerings, used before, points to the joy of sharing in these Paschal Mysteries and of the renewal of life that is "constantly at work within us" as a result of our participation in them; the Prayer after Communion, also previously heard, prays that "this most holy exchange" may bring us not only divine assistance now, but also "eternal gladness" in the future. Any one of the five Prefaces of Easter may be used today.

Today's Saints

Saint Peter Chanel (1803–1841) was born in France and ordained in

1827, when he was twenty-four years old. After reading letters of missionaries, the desire to evangelize grew, and in 1831 he entered the newly founded Society of Mary (Marists). After the new order was approved by Pope Gregory XVI, they were asked to send missionaries to the South Pacific region. Chanel left France in 1836, the superior of a group of Marists. They traveled to the Canary Islands and Tahiti, and Peter ended up at Futuna. The local king was threatened by the missionaries, and when his son requested Baptism, he arranged for Peter's murder. Peter Chanel is the patron saint of Oceania, the area in the South West Pacific that encompasses Australia, New Zealand, and the islands of Polynesia, Melanesia, and Micronesia.

Saint Louis Grignion de Montfort (1673–1716) was born in Britanny. He developed his devotion to the Blessed Virgin Mary when young, and a benefactor paid his way through the famous seminary of Saint-Sulpice in Paris. After his ordination in 1700, he discerned the need for an order of priests dedicated to Mary. Eventually, this group became the Company of Mary and an order of women, the Daughters of Wisdom. Saint Louis Marie is thought of as a founder of the area of theology known as Mariology, and is famous for his books, *True Devotion of Mary*, the *Secret of Mary*, and the *Secret of the Rosary*. His preaching on the mercy of God served as a powerful antidote to Jansenism, a Calvinist-influenced movement that was prevalent at the time. Louis de Montfort wore himself out with preaching and died in 1716, only sixteen years after his ordination.

WED 29 (#281) white
Memorial of St. Catherine of Siena, Virgin and Doctor of the Church

The Lectionary for Mass

◆ FIRST READING: Antioch is now the focal center of the missionary activity of both Barnabas and Saul. Peter and Jerusalem become a backdrop to Antioch and the spread of God's word from there. The passage evidences other traveling prophets and teachers who spread the message to other parts of the empire. As the community gathered for worship, the Holy Spirit speaks demanding that Barnabas and Saul be set apart for yet unspecified work. Attuned to the Spirit, the community lays hands on them and sends them off. They sail to Cyrus and begin preaching in the synagogue and market place. The Spirit is continually at work guiding the mission of all disciples.

◆ RESPONSORIAL PSALM 67: The universality of God's justice and reign moves the psalmist to invite all the nations to praise the Lord. God rules the people with equity and guides the nations so that God's ways may be made known throughout the earth. The psalm picks up on the saving guidance of the Spirit that leads Barnabas and Paul to set out to spread the word to all nations, so that God's ways may be known by all. It is fitting therefore that all the nations be called upon to praise the Lord.

◆ GOSPEL: This summary statement of Jesus reiterates many of the key themes of John's account of the Gospel. Believing in Jesus involves access to the Father, because whoever fully sees Jesus sees the Father who sent him. Jesus came as light into the world not to condemn the world but to save it. Those who do not believe and observe Jesus's words ultimately condemn themselves since they refuse to be open to God's ways and thoughts as expressed fully by Jesus. Whatever Jesus says and does is exactly the way the Father has instructed him. Those who listen and follow through on Jesus's words and actions will have eternal life.

The Roman Missal

The prayers for this Mass, all proper for the day, are found in the Proper of Saints section of the Missal, at April 29.

The Collect reminds us that St. Catherine was "on fire with divine love / in her contemplation of the Lord's Passion / and her service of your Church." Therefore, we invoke her intercession that, by our participation in the mystery of Christ, we may "ever exult in the revelation of his glory." The Prayer over the Offerings asks that, insofar as we have been instructed by the teaching of St. Catherine, "we may give ever more fervent thanks / to you, the one true God" as we offer this sacrifice commemorating her. The Prayer after Communion calls to mind how the Eucharist unites all members of the Church throughout time, as it acknowledges that the Eucharist has nourished us and conferred eternal life upon us just as it did St. Catherine in her time. The Preface chosen could appropriately be one of the five Prefaces of Easter, highlighting that we are still in Easter Time. The priest celebrant could also choose one of the two Prefaces of Saints, or the Preface of Holy Virgins and Religious.

Today's Saint

Saint Catherine of Siena (1347–1380) was a Dominican tertiary (lay member) and mystic, the twenty-fourth of twenty-five children. In spite of family opposition, she dedicated herself to Christ at a very young age, and at the age of sixteen, she withdrew from her family to lead a life of intense prayer. When she emerged, she began to dedicate herself to care of the sick and poor. Her joyful spirit attracted a number of followers. After a series of mystical experiences, Catherine felt compelled to write letters to those in secular and Church authority, which she dictated to her friend, the Dominican Raymond of Capua. Her influence became so great that papal legates consulted her. At this time, the popes had moved their residence from Rome to Avignon, France. Catherine begged Gregory XI to return to Rome, which he did in 1377. Saint Catherine died in 1380 at the age of thirty-three, leaving behind her writings, the *Dialogue on Divine Providence*, letters, and prayers. She is represented in art holding a lily and wearing the habit of a Dominican tertiary, and she is the patron saint of Europe and Italy. In 1970, Pope Paul VI made her a Doctor of the Church, one of the first women, along with Teresa of Avila, to be so honored.

THU 30 (#282) white Easter Weekday

Optional Memorial of St. Pius V, Pope / white

The Lectionary for Mass

◆ First Reading: Saul, now using his Roman family name of Paul which he does as he ministers to the Gentile world, is in Antioch in Pisidia (Asia Minor), distinct from Antioch in Syria where he began his travels. He has taken the leadership among his fellow missionaries and at the synagogue service he gets up to exhort the people. After reviewing some key elements of God's interaction with the Jewish people, Paul speaks of Jesus as the long promised savior descended from the house of David. John the Baptist witnessed to Jesus, and Paul is now witnessing to him as well.

◆ Responsorial Psalm 89: The psalm offers praise to God for having blessed the people through David, his servant. Paul's exhortation in the synagogue picks up on God's faithfulness at work through all generations, always exercised in covenant love and kindness toward the people. God anointed David and was faithful to him. God's faithfulness and mercy have continued to be with the house of David, gifting us with Jesus, the long promised descendant from David's house. In Jesus, God has exalted David's house and line, while at the same time bringing salvation and covenant love to all.

◆ Gospel: Upon washing the feet of his disciples, Jesus challenges them with his action parable of service. If he as master and lord has done this for them, they are to do this for one another. Understanding and following through on what Jesus has modeled for them is the heart of discipleship. Not all will follow through as Jesus predicts Judas's betrayal according to God's preordained plan. Jesus uses his foreknowledge of this plan as a manifestation of his divine nature (I AM) to his disciples. The passage ends with Jesus identifying with his disciples in the same way that he identifies with his Father. Whoever receives his disciples receives Jesus and whoever receives Jesus received the Father who sent him. Intimacy and union with God through Jesus is the key component of discipleship.

The Roman Missal

The Collect for the Easter Weekday continues to remind us of the effects of Baptism as it acknowledges God as the one who, "through the wonder of rebirth," restores human nature "to yet greater dignity than at its beginnings;" we can recall the early Church's references to Baptism as regeneration. The Prayer over the Offerings reminds us of the transformation that we must be open to in every celebration of the Eucharist as it asks that, as our prayers and sacrificial offerings rise

up to God, so may we "be conformed to the mysteries of your mighty love." The Prayer after Communion connects the restoration that has come to us in Christ's Resurrection with the ongoing strength we receive from the Eucharist as "the fruits of this paschal Sacrament." Any one of the five Easter Prefaces would seem to be as good a choice as any other today.

Today's Saint

Saint Pius V (1504–1572) was pope immediately following the Council of Trent (1545–1563). He was a reformer who saw the laxness that had overtaken the Church, and he fought to overcome it by paring down the papal court and enforcing the decrees of Trent. He is best remembered for promulgating the 1570 edition of *The Roman Missal*, which was used until the liturgical reforms of the Second Vatican Council, and for reforming the Liturgy of the Hours. He was a Dominican friar, and after he was elected to the papacy, he continued to wear his white habit. Since then, it has been customary for the pope to wear a white cassock.

May
Month of Our Lady

FRI 1 (#283) white Easter Weekday

Optional Memorial of St. Joseph the Worker / white

The Lectionary for Mass

◆ First Reading: Paul continues his exhortation to both Jews and God-fearers, mostly Gentiles interested in Judaism, in the synagogue in Antioch by telling them that the good news of Jesus, the long-promised messiah, is the word of salvation for all. The Jewish leaders in Jerusalem "failed to recognize him" and condemned him, thus fulfilling the Scriptures. But

God raised Jesus up who appeared to many who had traveled with him, now witnesses to the Good News. Jesus's Resurrection and saving acts on our behalf are the fulfillment of the promises made long ago to our fathers. We are the beneficiaries of God's faithful promises, and Jesus is that gift.

◆ RESPONSORIAL PSALM 2: The psalm refrain, "you are my Son; / this day I have begotten you," is quoted by Paul in his exhortation to the people in Antioch as proof of God's promise fulfilled in raising up "my Son," Jesus, from the dead. This coronation psalm was used at the installation of a new king in Israel. Kings were believed to be appointed and established by God and were usually referred to as God's son. God would protect the king and make him strong and powerful, thus showing the mighty power and goodness of God toward the people, and other nations as well. Today, we apply the psalm to Jesus, not merely a symbolic son of God but the actual Son of God, come to save and redeem all nations.

◆ GOSPEL: Part of Jesus's farewell discourse to his disciples at the Last Supper, this passage manifests Jesus's concern for his disciples once he departs from them. He counsels them to not let their hearts be troubled. The intimacy he has with them moves him to understand his departure as similar to that of a bridegroom leaving for his father's house to prepare a special place for his bride. After the place is prepared, he will return to take them with him so that "where I am you also may be." Responding to Thomas's concern about not knowing the way, Jesus clearly states that "I am the way and the truth and the life." Once Jesus dies and is resurrected, they will clearly know the way back to him and to the Father. For now, they are to believe in him, trust, and remain steadfast till he returns.

The Roman Missal

Referring to God as the "author of our freedom and of our salvation," the Collect goes on to note how we have been redeemed "by the shedding of your Son's Blood," thus incorporating verbal imagery that resonates with the fullness of the Eucharistic sign—both Body and Blood. The Prayer over the Offerings reminds us that the gifts we offer in this celebration point to heavenly gifts as the prayer asks that we might "attain the gifts that are eternal." The Prayer after Communion gives voice to the dynamism of the Paschal Mystery as it asks that those who have been "redeemed by the Passion of your Son" may "rejoice in his Resurrection." Any one of the five Easter Prefaces may be used today, although perhaps using Preface I, II, or IV, with their explicit mention of the life we share in Christ, would provide an echo of the Gospel reading.

Today's Optional Memorial

The optional Memorial of Saint Joseph the Worker is a relatively new addition to the calendar. It was introduced by Pope Pius XII in 1955, as an alternative to secular May Day celebrations of the worker, which originated in Communist countries and which did more to promote Communist propaganda than to promote the worker. Pope Pius XII urged workers to look to Saint Joseph the carpenter and to see the dignity inherent in human labor, which could become a source of holiness. The prayers for today from *The Roman Missal* call Joseph our "wise and faithful servant" who is our patron as we "complete the works [God] set us to do."

(#284) white

S A T
2
Memorial of St. Athanasius, Bishop and Doctor of the Church

The Lectionary for Mass

◆ FIRST READING: Paul's exhortation at the synagogue in Antioch has ignited the interest of the city. The following sabbath almost the whole city gathers to hear him. The synagogue Jews are jealous of Paul and Barnabas and they contradict, slander, and even incite others to expel them from there. For their part, Paul and Barnabas explain that they felt obliged to preach the word first to Jews. But since they rejected the word, they would now turn to the Gentiles, so that they might know and accept the light that is Jesus. This will become a consistent pattern for Paul in Acts no matter where he travels. Those who heard the word and believed "were filled with joy and the Holy Spirit."

◆ RESPONSORIAL PSALM 98: The psalm links well with Paul and Barnabas proclaiming the word to Jew, Gentile, and all the nations. The refrain declares that "All the ends of the earth have seen the saving power of God." We are to sing a new song because the Lord has made salvation open to all. In sending forth Jesus, God has manifested justice, kindness, and faithfulness toward all nations. As Paul and Barnabas speak of the graciousness of God in Jesus, the nations, represented by both Jew and Gentile, are filled with joy and the Holy Spirit. While some will reject the word, those that accept and believe joyfully sing to the Lord a new song.

◆ GOSPEL: Continuing his farewell discourse, Jesus asserts that in knowing him, they also know the Father. Philip's request that Jesus show them the Father seems to exasperate Jesus. "Haven't you got it yet?" seems to be the gist of Jesus's response. Whoever sees Jesus sees the Father. What Jesus says and does have their origin in the Father. Whoever believes in Jesus will do the same works and even greater, because in his return to the Father, Jesus will continue to be with them. "Whatever you ask in my name, I will do," is the assurance that Jesus will continue to be with them even beyond death and will continue to aid them in their ministry. Jesus continues to be with them and us whenever we gather to continue doing the works that he has done.

The Roman Missal

The prayers for this Mass, all proper for the day, are found in the Proper of Saints section of the Missal, at May 2.

The Collect acknowledges St. Athanasius "as an outstanding champion of your Son's divinity" and asks that we may grow in knowledge and love of God because of the saint's teaching and protection. The Prayer over the Offerings notes how St. Athanasius professed "an unblemished faith" and asks that as we commemorate him, so may we witness to the same truth as he did, and thus be brought to salvation. The Prayer after Communion professes the true divinity of Christ, the doctrine St. Athanasius upheld, and petitions that we may be given life and protection through that same divinity of Christ, which we also profess.

The Preface chosen could appropriately be one of the five Prefaces of Easter, highlighting that we are still in Easter Time. The priest celebrant could also choose one of the two Prefaces of Saints, or the Preface of Holy Pastors could also be used.

Today's Saint

Saint Athanasius (295–373), bishop of Alexandria and Doctor of the Church, contributed immensely to the development of doctrine and spirituality. He defended the teaching of the First Council of Nicaea

(325 AD) that Jesus was both fully human and fully divine. The Arians, who taught that Jesus was not divine, unleashed a series of attacks upon Athanasius, resulting in exile not just once, but five times in his life, amounting to seventeen years out of the forty-five he was bishop. During one of these exiles, he wrote the influential biography of the renowned hermit and monk Saint Anthony of Egypt. This spiritual classic, entitled *Life of Antony*, has been and continues to be read by people longing to remove worldly distractions that keep them from mystical union with God. He is also noted for two other works: *On the Incarnation* and *Discourses against the Arians*. Many titles have been bestowed upon him, including defender of faith, champion of orthodoxy, mystical theologian, and spiritual master. Athanasius is venerated by the Eastern Orthodox as well as Western Christians and is especially revered by the Coptic (Egyptian) Orthodox.

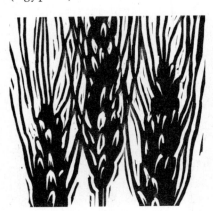

(#53)   white
3 Fifth Sunday of Easter

The Lectionary for Mass

◆ FIRST READING: After Saul accepts Jesus as the long awaited Jewish Messiah, he goes to Jerusalem to connect with the disciples. Because of his history, they are afraid of him until Barnabas speaks well of Saul, his acceptance of Jesus, and his preaching in Jesus's name. Once

accepted, Saul speaks out boldly and debates with Hellenists who are so upset at him that they try to kill him. With help Saul escapes to Caesarea and returns to his hometown of Tarsus. Despite all this, Luke claims that the Church is at peace, growing, being built up and accompanied by the Spirit's wisdom and guidance. Even amidst apparent dissension, the Spirit's peace and wisdom continues to embrace Jesus's followers both then and now.

◆ RESPONSORIAL PSALM 22: This lament psalm speaks of the psalmist feeling abandoned by God, alone in life's suffering. Despite such feelings of abandonment, the psalmist turns to God, realizing that God is the only hope. In today's verses, the psalmist already anticipates God's help and promises to fulfill the vows made to God, especially in caring for the poor and needy. Confident that God will answer and relieve the suffering, the psalmist praises God and promises to let all generations, past, present, and to come, know of God's justice, care, and love. Saul in our First Reading could have easily prayed this prayer and so can we.

◆ SECOND READING: This passage, rich in Trinitarian theology, invites all to "love not in word or speech but in deed and truth." God does not condemn us but desires us to trust that, if we keep the Commandments, we will receive all that we ask for. Keeping God's Commandments demands believing in Jesus and loving one another in the same manner that Jesus loved us. In so doing, we are assured, through the Spirit gifted to us, that we will remain in Jesus and he in us. Such divine intimacy with Father, Son, and Spirit is a treasured gift that must be continually cultivated if is to impact our daily lives.

◆ GOSPEL: Jesus's "I AM" statement, "I am the vine, you are the branches," speaks of intimacy and fruitfulness in discipleship. If we are to produce rich fruit, we have to be not only connected to Jesus, the life-giving vine, but we also have to be open to being pruned by the Father, the vine-grower. Being pruned involves living according to Jesus's words and actions. Those who choose otherwise will wither and die. In believing and living the Jesus lifestyle, we will have intimacy with Jesus, be fruitful and life-giving, and give honor to God, who will be receptive to all that we ask for. This was a good program for disciples then and continues to be a rich program now for all who desire to be disciples.

The Roman Missal

Continue to use the Rite for the Blessing and Sprinkling of Water, as discussed for the Second Sunday of Easter, or, if you haven't been doing it, there's no reason why it cannot be used this week. This rite, found in Appendix II of the Missal, replaces the Penitential Act. The Gloria is sung today.

Even though we are at the Fifth Sunday of Easter, the season is still reverberating with the joy and enthusiasm of the sacramental initiation that occurred at the Easter Vigil: the Collect makes explicit reference to "those you [God] were pleased to make new in Holy Baptism." The prayer goes on to ask that those newly baptized will "bear much fruit / and come to the joys of life eternal." The meaning of Baptism continues to be center-stage in the liturgical theology of Easter Time.

The Prayer over the Offerings, using the important notion of "the wonderful exchange effected in this sacrifice," prays that we might truly come to live the divine life we encounter in the exchange: "that, as we have come to know your truth, / we may make it ours by a worthy way of life."

Any of the five Easter Prefaces may be selected for today. Continue to chant the introductory dialogue and Preface in order to highlight the ongoing festivity of Easter Time, especially if it is not your practice to do so during Ordinary Time.

The Prayer after Communion speaks of the ongoing dynamic quality of a life lived dying and rising in Christ, a dynamism animated by the Eucharistic food, as it asks that God be with us to "lead those you have imbued with heavenly mysteries to pass from former ways to newness of life."

Consider using the Solemn Blessing for Easter Time, found at number 6 in the "Blessings at the End of Mass and Prayers over the People" section of the Missal. Remember that a regular formula for dismissal is used, not the solemn double Alleluia.

Other Ideas

The fifty days of Easter get to be a long haul as the rest of the world has moved on and the only Easter items you may find are a few things in the clearance basket at the grocery or hobby store. So we have to continue to make our liturgies fresh and inviting.

Spring in a parish can get really crazy and busy. If you didn't do infant Baptisms during Lent, there will be a plethora of them during Easter Time. There are also first Communions, Confirmations, May Crownings, and *Quinceañeras*. It is easy for a parish calendar and a congregation to get overwhelmed. Communicate any upcoming events well. One of the problems associated with these happy days is that often people get into an "event" mentality rather than a prayerful mode. It might be wise to have someone give an extended welcome, pointing out restrooms, worship aids, and any specifics, for example "no flash photography" or "please do not block the aisles." Sometimes things that are obvious to us are not obvious to guests!

Similarly, you may wish to incorporate an extended prelude, to help keep folks calm. Explain to the assembly before the liturgy that it is a "pray-lude" and invite them to enter in to the moment.

MON 4 (#285) white
Easter Weekday

The Lectionary for Mass

◆ FIRST READING: Paul and Barnabas, after being attacked for their work, move to Lystra where they heal a lame man. The inhabitants, observing the miracle, consider them to be Greek gods and begin offering sacrifices to them. Paul and Barnabas, scandalized by this, proclaim that they are human beings just like themselves. They came to preach worship not of idols but of the living God who created and sustains all life. While God allowed people to choose their own path, God always manifested signs of care and concern in providing rain and nourishment for all. The passage calls us to pay attention to signs all around us of God's care, love and sustenance for all creation.

◆ RESPONSORIAL PSALM 115: The psalm refrain and verses link clearly with the points that Paul and Barnabas were making to the Greeks who took them for gods. Humans are not responsible for the glory, wonder, and joy of creation but God is. Idols are handworks of humans. God is justice, mercy, and truth, and all glory belongs to God. God has gifted humanity with the earth and our only appropriate response is to give God glory and thanks. This perspective is essential to remember whenever we veer off into thinking that what we have is ours and no one can tell us different. What we have is God's. We have been entrusted with it. Give God the glory.

◆ GOSPEL: Jesus's farewell address continues with Jesus's assurance that anyone who keeps his Commandments manifests love of him and of the Father. Jesus and the Father will love those people in return and actually make their dwelling with them. Such indwelling is to take place now and not in some future end time. Those who do not keep Jesus's words do not love and are not open to having Jesus and the Father dwell with them. Jesus continues to comfort his disciples and us with the promise of the Holy Spirit, the Advocate who will teach and remind us of everything that Jesus said and did. Such assurance is comforting whenever we feel uncertain about following through on Jesus's words and deeds.

The Roman Missal

The Collect brings to mind the pilgrim nature of our spiritual journey as people given new life in Christ — in other words, even though we have been made new, we are nonetheless always "on the way" — as it asks that we may have the Lord's "perpetual help" in being "defended from all wickedness" and thus "make our way by means of your heavenly gifts." Perhaps we might hear in this prayer a certain "pep talk" to keep alive the elation we felt at the Easter Vigil and early in Easter Time. The Prayer over the Offerings speaks to how the offering of ourselves in the Eucharist should lead us to be open to be transformed into the likeness of Christ — "conformed to the mysteries of your mighty love." The Prayer after Communion also reminds us of our status as new creations as it affirms God as the one who restores us "to eternal life / in the Resurrection of Christ;" having thus been made new, we must be more receptive to "the fruits of this paschal Sacrament."

Any one of the five Easter Prefaces would work well today; in view of the orations, Preface I or IV might perhaps be considered in particular.

TUE 5 (#286) white
Easter Weekday

The Lectionary for Mass

◆ FIRST READING: Some Jews incite the people and have Paul stoned and left for dead outside Lystra. Paul, with the help of disciples, survives and returns to the city, deciding with Barnabas to return to Antioch in Syria where they began their missionary journey. Along the way Paul and Barnabas stop at places where they had preached and do two things. They encourage the people to be faithful despite difficulties, suffering, or persecutions. They also appointed "elders" (presbyters) to maintain and sustain the leadership in those communities. Arriving at Antioch, they praised God for all the great work that had been accomplished through them among the Gentiles. All are greatly impacted by the Gentiles that are now Christ's disciples.

◆ RESPONSORIAL PSALM 145: The psalm refrain easily links with Paul and Barnabas as the Lord's friends who have traveled about making "known . . . the glorious splendor" of the Lord's kingdom. This thanksgiving psalm speaks of the "faithful ones" making known to all the Lord's might and glorious splendor evident everywhere and forever. The only fitting response is praise and blessing of God forever. Jesus's message, which we as disciples commit ourselves to, is to make known God's glorious kingdom to all creation.

◆ GOSPEL: Jesus continues to console his disciples upon his impending death by wishing them a peace that is lasting and not ephemeral, and by not allowing their hearts to be troubled. They should be glad that he is returning to the Father for he will be in a better place. However, he wants them to be prepared so that as the "ruler of the world" (Satan, death) approaches, they should not worry or be afraid. Ultimately the ruler has no control over him, but is merely the path to ultimate victory and return to the Father. For John, this is part of God's plan to bring about lasting victory over sin and death and to reconcile the world. This is the basis on which we too are invited to face death and to trust in the Father, the one who guarantees eternal life.

The Roman Missal

In the Collect for the Easter weekday we pray for "constancy in faith and hope" that we may never doubt the promises we have learned from God. The petition is especially apropos in light of the weekday Gospel reading where Jesus exhorts his hearers to not let their hearts be troubled or afraid. Indeed, we can be reassured at this offering of the sacrifice as the Prayer over the Offerings reminds us that we have cause for "great gladness." One of the reasons for that great gladness can be found in our hope, given voice in the Prayer after Communion, that we may attain in our flesh "the incorruptible glory of the resurrection."

Any one of the five Easter Prefaces may be used today, with perhaps Preface III, describing how Jesus "never ceases to offer himself for us" and how he "defends us and ever pleads our cause before you," providing a nice resonance with the reassurance we hear, and trust we are asked to have, in the words of the Gospel reading for the day.

WED 6 (#287) white
Easter Weekday

The Lectionary for Mass

◆ FIRST READING: The passage brings to a head a conflict that splintered the early followers of Jesus. Some Jewish disciples were insisting that if Gentiles wanted to follow Jesus, they had to become Jews first by being circumcised and following the Mosaic law. Paul, Barnabas, and others debate the issue strenuously and decide that the matter has to be resolved in Jerusalem with the Apostles. On traveling to Jerusalem, they tell of the great wonders that the Lord has worked among the Gentiles and all are pleased. In Jerusalem, certain Jews insist on Jewish observance by the Gentiles. A meeting is set to address the matter.

◆ RESPONSORIAL PSALM 122: This pilgrimage psalm speaks of the great joy in traveling to Jerusalem, the Holy City, to encounter the presence of the Lord, in the house of the Lord. Jerusalem, city of David, is where the decrees and judgments of the Lord are discussed and made active. The obvious reference is to Paul, Barnabas, and the others traveling to Jerusalem to discuss with the Apostles the fate of the Gentiles, and to decide how they are to be welcomed as followers of the Lord. Much is at stake here and Jerusalem is the fitting place for that decision.

◆ GOSPEL: Jesus uses the well-known image of the vine, the branches, and the vine dresser to exhort his followers to remain in him, even when he is gone. Jesus is the true vine who gives life and sustenance to his followers, the branches. The Father is the vine grower who needs to prune the vines if true and abundant fruit is to result. Pruning is done on the basis of whether one desires to remain in Jesus, the vine, or refuses to do so. Those who refuse are pruned away so that good fruit will result. Rich fruit results from being connected to Jesus's words and doing the works that he did. In all this, the Father is glorified.

The Roman Missal

The close connection between Easter and Baptism continues to be highlighted in the weekday Collect as God is addressed as the "restorer

and lover of innocence" and as we hear about those who have been "set free from the darkness of unbelief," asking that they "may never stray from the light of your truth." The baptismal imagery of innocence and moving from darkness to light is clear. Baptismal themes can continue to be heard in the Prayer over the Offerings with its reference to "the renewal constantly at work within us." The Prayer after Communion first asks that "this most holy exchange"—this liturgical celebration—may bring us God's help in this life, and then it looks forward to asking for "eternal gladness."

Any one of the five Prefaces of Easter are equally appropriate for today, although if the priest celebrant wished to emphasize the Johannine Gospel theme of the intimate union between Jesus and his followers (the vine and the branches), perhaps either Preface I or Preface III would provide this emphasis most fittingly.

THU 7 (#288) white
Easter Weekday

The Lectionary for Mass

◆ FIRST READING: Peter addresses the council in Jerusalem concerning his experience with the Gentile convert Cornelius, as the council discusses the subject of how to welcome the Gentiles as followers of Jesus. From that experience, Peter concludes that Jews and Gentiles are both saved "through the grace of the Lord Jesus." Paul and Barnabas speak of the signs and wonders that the Lord worked among the Gentiles through them. Finally James, the leader of the Jerusalem community concurs with Peter, and the others, and suggests a compromise. Nothing is to be imposed on the Gentiles other than refraining from idolatry, unlawful marriage, blood, and meat of strangled animals. Jesus's saving grace

is the key component in welcoming anyone who desires to know and follow Jesus.

◆ RESPONSORIAL PSALM 96: This praise psalm picks up on the key insights of the council in Jerusalem which approved the disciples' mission to "proclaim God's marvelous deeds to all the nations." All nations and people are invited to sing and bless the Lord as the faithful ones announce the Lord's salvation, glory, and wondrous deeds to all. The Lord is king of the universe who creates, loves, and sustains the world, governing the nations with justice and equity. The universal and inclusive nature of our God is something that all disciples need to understand and emulate, if God's kingdom is to be fully realized.

◆ GOSPEL: Jesus clarifies for his disciples what it means to remain in him and he in them. The intimacy that he has with the Father, he now shares with them. He continues to invite them to remain in his love. They can be assured of remaining in his love if they keep his commandments, just as he remains in his Father's love by keeping his commandments and doing everything that the Father desires. If they remain in him by following through on his words and deeds, then complete and fulfilled joy will be theirs. The intimacy that God desires with us through Jesus is beyond anything that we could ever hope for or imagine. Let us strive to remain in Jesus always.

The Roman Missal

The weekday Collect contains a richness in describing what God does for us through Baptism: we are sinners, yet are made just; we are pitiable, yet are made blessed. Therefore, we can ask God to "stand by" his works and gifts and, in so doing, give "the courage of perseverance" to "those justified by faith." It is that redeemed people who are made "partakers of the one supreme Godhead," as the Prayer over the Offerings describes, through "the wonderful exchange effected in this sacrifice." Indeed, it is only Baptism that makes true participation in the holy exchange possible (Baptism is the entrance into the Church and the doorway to the Eucharist). Thus, the Prayer after Communion notes that those who have been imbued with these heavenly mysteries are rightly "to pass from former ways to newness of life." Any one of the five Prefaces of Easter might be used equally well today.

FRI 8 (#289) white
Easter Weekday

The Lectionary for Mass

◆ FIRST READING: After the compromise decision arrived at in Jerusalem, the Apostles and the elders send Paul, Barnabas, and others to Antioch to announce the news to the Gentiles, not only in Antioch but also in Syria and Cilicia. Gathering the communities together, the letter from Jerusalem is read, declaring that despite what others have said, they do not need to be circumcised or follow the law of Moses. Rather they are to refrain from fornication, idolatry, blood, and strangled animals. The people were delighted with the news that they were not restricted in following Jesus. Reflect on how often we place unnecessary restrictions on others when God doesn't.

◆ RESPONSORIAL PSALM 57: This thanksgiving and praise psalm exudes the relief and grateful feelings that the Gentiles must have experienced when they heard the liberating news from Jerusalem. The psalmist praises God who is merciful and faithful. As a result, we can rest steadfast in God who assures us that no matter what happens, God will be there to forgive

and rescue. The Gentiles who heard the letter must have responded joyfully with the psalm's response, "I will give you thanks among the peoples, O Lord."

◆ GOSPEL: Jesus continues to clarify for his disciples the elements that constitute true love and friendship. Love is not merely a feeling but manifests itself most clearly in actions. Being willing to lay down one's life in love for the other is the greatest act of love. Love is concern for the other, wishing nothing but the best for another. Friendship consists of being open and sharing all that one knows with the other. Jesus had done this consistently with his disciples and therefore they are no longer servants but friends. Jesus initiated the bond of friendship with them and they are to continue that bond with him and with all they come across. Concern for others will guarantee God answering whatever they ask for. Love manifests itself in selfless action on behalf of others. Jesus is the best model.

The Roman Missal

The Collect for today first notes how we have been "rightly conformed to the paschal mysteries;" this can remind us of how we have been remade through our participation in the Death and Resurrection of Christ, first through Baptism. Then the prayer goes on to ask that "what we celebrate in joy / may protect and save us with perpetual power," thus pointing to the ongoing effects we hope our participation in liturgy will have. The Prayer over the Offerings points to another aspect of the transformation that must occur in us: as we ask God to accept "the oblation of this spiritual sacrifice," we beg that we will be made into an eternal offering to him. The Prayer after Communion reminds us that the liturgy we just celebrated was something that Christ commanded

us to do in memory of him, and so we pray that it "may bring us growth in charity."

Although any one of the five Easter Prefaces would be appropriate for today, perhaps one could find a resonance with today's Gospel reading, where we hear about the love of laying down one's life for one's friends, in Preface III of Easter.

SAT 9 (#290) white
Easter Weekday

The Lectionary for Mass

◆ FIRST READING: Paul continues his missionary journey announcing to all along the way the Apostles' decision. As a result the communities began to grow "stronger in faith and increased in number." Paul encounters Timothy whom he considers a good candidate for missionary work, but because he has a Jewish mother and a Greek father, he was not circumcised. Paul decides to circumcise him so as not to engage in a useless battle with other Jewish disciples. Often we too restrict others from following Jesus because of our own prejudices and biases. Paul receives a vision in which a Macedonian seeks to hear the Good News, requesting his help. Paul decides to travel with others to spread the good news of the Lord to Macedonia.

◆ RESPONSORIAL PSALM 100: This psalm of praise invites "all the earth to cry out to God with joy." Our God made us and cares for us the way a shepherd cares for the flock. We belong to the Lord who is good, and whose covenant love endures forever. The Lord is always faithful and can always be relied upon. With this good news, Paul, Timothy, and others travel to unknown lands and territories to tell others of God's faithful love and care, fully expressed in Jesus. Every day we too are to cry out to the Lord with joy for the very same reasons that the psalmist offers us.

◆ GOSPEL: Jesus continues to counsel his disciples by warning them about the world's hatred of them as much as they hated him. Here the world is understood as those who refuse to believe in Jesus's words and deeds. Jesus chose them, and because they responded and believed, they are no longer of the world, resulting in being hated by the world just like Jesus. Their words and actions will be scrutinized just as they scrutinized Jesus and eventually killed him. Because they do not know the Father, they care nothing for the Son, or the ones the Son chose as his own. The disciples are forewarned about the difficulties and dangers of discipleship. Our response, like theirs, should be that no matter the challenges we choose to remain in him just like he has chosen to remain in us.

The Roman Missal

Today's Collect, even at this late stage in Easter Time, continues to place Baptism center-stage as it reminds us that God confers on us heavenly life "through the regenerating power of Baptism" (recall that "regeneration" was another way of referring to Baptism in the ancient Church). Eschatological fulfillment is also a major theme in this prayer. It asks that those rendered "capable of immortality" (through Baptism) may indeed "attain the fullness of glory," that is, in heaven. The Prayer over the Offerings also refers to attaining the eternal, as does the Prayer after Communion with its petition that, having been "redeemed by the Passion of your Son," we may "rejoice in his Resurrection."

Of the five Easter Prefaces that can be used today, it is Preface IV of Easter, with its mention of "the old order destroyed," that perhaps provides an echo of the Gospel reading of the day, in which Jesus

talks to his disciples about being hated by the world.

☀ **10** (#56)   white
Sixth Sunday of Easter

The Lectionary for Mass

◆ FIRST READING: In entering the home of the Gentile Cornelius, Peter takes a radical step for a Jew. In a vision, Peter has come to an awareness of God's inclusive nature and boldly states that "God shows no partiality. Rather in every nation, whoever fears him and acts uprightly is acceptable to him." Peter is interrupted by the Spirit who proceeds to descend upon all. As Jewish believers are astounded that the Spirit is gifting both Gentiles and Jews, Peter responds by saying that if Gentiles are acceptable to the Lord, then who are we to stand in God's path. He orders Cornelius and his entire household to be baptized. Often we too need to scrutinize our beliefs and actions to make certain that we are not standing in God's path.

◆ RESPONSORIAL PSALM 98: Jumping off Peter and the Baptism of Cornelius's household, the psalm revels in the fact that "the Lord has revealed to the nations his saving power." All are invited to sing a new song to the Lord who has done wondrous deeds by making salvation and justice known and available to all people. God's covenant love and faithfulness are made

known to Israel and to all the ends of the earth. Such inclusiveness calls for new joyful songs that all can sing. We would do well to examine our own inclusiveness and that of our communities.

◆ SECOND READING: We are exhorted to love one another because love is of God, and whoever loves knows God and is begotten by God. God is love. That love is clearly manifested by the Father taking the initiative in sending Jesus to show love's depth, even to the point of being willing to die for another. Whoever does not love, does not know God. Easter Time invites us to reflect on how we practically and realistically demonstrate our love of God.

◆ GOSPEL: In his farewell address to his disciples, Jesus exhorts them to love one another as he has loved them. The depth of love is the willingness to die for the other. Jesus has chosen them, revealed all that the Father commanded him, and promises to love them and remain in them. All he asks in return is to remain in him by loving one another. Intimacy with God rests on our willingness to believe in and imitate Jesus in loving one another even unto death. Our communities would certainly be different if we all took this message to heart in all our dealings and encounters.

The Roman Missal

Continue to use the Rite for the Blessing and Sprinkling of Water, as discussed for the Second Sunday of Easter. If you haven't been doing it, there's no reason not to use it this week. This rite, found in Appendix II of the Missal, replaces the Penitential Act. The Gloria is sung today.

The Collect situates this celebration within the ongoing festivity of the fifty days of Easter Time as it refers to our celebration "with heartfelt devotion of these days of joy, / which we keep in honor of the risen Lord." Also, the key connection between liturgy and life is affirmed as we ask "that what we relive in remembrance we may always hold to in what we do."

The Prayer over the Offerings also prays for the liturgical celebration to have an ongoing effect in our lives as it petitions that "we may be conformed to the mysteries of your mighty love." Such transformation, however, is a result of God's grace, not our own efforts alone, as the prayer recognizes our need to be purified by God's graciousness.

Any one of the five Easter Prefaces may be used equally appropriately today. Continue to chant the introductory dialogue and Preface in order to highlight the ongoing festivity of the season, especially if it is not your practice to do so during Ordinary Time.

The Prayer after Communion affirms both that we have been restored to eternal life "in the Resurrection of Christ," and that we are asking for the "strength of this saving food" to bear fruit in our life. The prayer reminds us that our reception of Holy Communion should always have the effect of increasing our love for one another.

Consider using Solemn Blessing for Easter Time, found at number 6 in the "Blessings at the End of Mass and Prayers Over the People" section of the Missal. Remember that a regular formula for dismissal is used, and not the solemn double Alleluia.

Other Ideas

The *Book of Blessings* inlcudes a blessing for mothers (BB, 172). This may be used at the Concluding Rite. Be sure to include a petition in the Universal Prayer. Be sensitive. There are many people in our pews today with various stories and situations and some of them are difficult. While nothing can compare with the bond of motherhood, remember all those mothers who raise foster

children, step children, or serve as spiritual mothers (*Ammas*) or mentors to others.

May 13 is the optional Memorial of Our Lady of Fatima and is a good opportunity for the May Crowning. If you can, try and avoid making it a "parish school" event and include both day school and religious education families.

If you live in a rural region, chances are the people still celebrate "rogation days" and bless the land. To the old farmer, these days are as important as the *Farmer's Almanac*. Respect these traditions and pray well for those who raise our crops and food.

People still get very confused about when Ascension is—is it on Thursday or Sunday? Announce this well, explain why it may be moved to Sunday—advertise in bulletins, on the web, parish blog, and on parish social media sites.

MON 11 (#291) white
Easter Weekday

The Lectionary for Mass

◆ **First Reading:** Paul and companions (we) arrive in Philippi. On the Sabbath they seek a synagogue, a gathering for prayer, and instead they encounter a group of women. One of those women, Lydia, a dealer in purple cloth, pays attention to Paul's words and over a period of time she and her whole household are converted to Christ. Her occupation probably provided well for her and her family, and she invites Paul and his companions to stay in her home. Usually Paul would refuse because he did not want to be a burden on anyone. She prevails upon them and eventually a strong friendship is born between Lydia and Paul, and her household becomes a gathering place for the community of Philippi. One of Paul's most endearing letters is to his beloved community at Philippi.

◆ **Responsorial Psalm 149:** This praise psalm emphasizes the reality that the Lord takes delight in people and all creation. This alone should be enough reason for praise but the psalmist clearly asserts that the Lord "adorns the lowly with victory." In our First Reading, Paul encounters women, not men, in Philippi and they become the first ones to be attentive to his words and are converted to Christ. Through Paul's words, they became aware of the psalmist's reason for praising God. Paul spoke of God's great love for all manifested in Christ. What better reason to praise God is there?

◆ **Gospel:** Jesus's farewell discourse continues by focusing on two components of discipleship: witnessing and persecution. Upon Jesus's return to the Father, he will send the Advocate, the Spirit of Truth who will testify to Jesus. The disciples too are called to testify because they have seen, heard, and been with Jesus from the beginning. From here, Jesus shifts to warning his disciples to hang in there when things get really bad. Others will persecute them because of their connection to Jesus and because of their refusal to believe or come to know Jesus or the Father. In warning them, Jesus wants to prepare them for the worst so that they will not be surprised or give up. Such is Jesus's care and love for all.

The Roman Missal

In the Collect, we ask for "the fruit produced by the paschal observances," that Easter may have an effect in our lives. Continue to use any of the Prefaces for Easter.

TUE 12 (#292) white
Easter Weekday

Optional Memorials of Sts. Nereus and Achilleus, Martyrs / red; St. Pancras, Martyr / red

The Lectionary for Mass

◆ FIRST READING: This well-known passage from Acts tells of the beating and imprisonment of Paul and Silas in Philippi. A miraculous earthquake opens their cell and loosens their chains, yet none escape. The jailer, thinking himself disgraced contemplates suicide, until Paul intervenes. The jailer, recognizing the power of Paul's God asks "What must I do to be saved" Paul, with Christian believers through the ages, responds, "Believe in the Lord Jesus and you and your household will be saved." Having cultivated and instructed them in the word of the Lord, the jailer and his family are all baptized and care for Paul and Silas as members of his family. Such is the power of God's word to move mind and hearts.

◆ RESPONSORIAL PSALM 138: This thanksgiving psalm recounts the response of one who, in time of trouble, has been heard by the Lord and saved. The refrain sums up the psalm's theme "Your right hand saves me, O Lord." The psalm emphasizes the fact that when one calls on the Lord, one is heard and the Lord responds. "When I called you answered me; / you built up strength within me." Both Paul and Silas, along with the jailer and his family, can definitely attest to this characteristic of the Lord. Their fitting response is praise and thanksgiving for God's love and saving power.

◆ GOSPEL: Jesus's impending departure from his disciples, namely his death, along with his prediction of similar fates for his disciples, fills them with grief. But Jesus insists that it is for their benefit that he leaves so as to send the Advocate. The Advocate "will convict the world" on three fronts: sin, righteousness, and condemnation. The Advocate will refute the arguments of those who refused to

believe and accept Jesus's identity and words. Sin is linked to proving the sinfulness of their refusal to believe. Righteousness is linked to proving that Jesus's return to the Father is God's righteousness with regards to Jesus. Condemnation is linking to the fact that, in Jesus's death, the ruler of this world along with death have been defeated. The Advocate continues to be with us in our struggle to know and believe in Jesus.

The Roman Missal

The Easter Time weekday Collect prays that "we may in truth receive a share / in the Resurrection of Christ your Son." The Prayer over the Offerings, prays that "we may always find delight in these paschal mysteries." The Prayer after Communion, also a familiar one by now, reminds us of "the holy exchange, / by which [God has] redeemed us." Any one of the five Prefaces of Easter can be used today. Since in today's Gospel we hear how Jesus will be going to the Father and the disciples will no longer see him, perhaps Preface III of Easter with its reminder that "He never ceases to offer himself for us but defends us and ever pleads our cause before you" would be an apt choice.

Today's Saints

Not much is known about Saints Nereus and Achilleus (second century). They must have been important figures because the Roman Christians built a church over their grave in the late fourth century. An inscription composed by Pope Damasus describes them as soldiers who converted to Christianity and were martyred.

Saint Pancras (c. † 304) was brought before Emperor Diocletian, who asked him to sacrifice to the Roman gods. Pancras refused, even when promised wealth and power, and the emperor ordered him to be decapitated. He was only fourteen

when he was martyred, in about the year 304.

WED 13 (#293) white
Easter Weekday

Optional Memorial of Our Lady of Fatima / white

The Lectionary for Mass

◆ FIRST READING: Paul's speech to the Athenians starts from the reality they know and tries to move them to a deeper awareness of the divine, and to an understanding of Jesus's mission and ministry. Jumping off a statue named for "an Unknown God," Paul attempts to link this unknown god to the Lord, creator of all, by quoting from well-known Greek philosophers and by affirming that we are all God's offspring. Our God demands that all repent, and in Jesus, whom he raised from the dead, there is reconciliation and forgiveness of sin. Philosophically, the Greeks see the resurrection as an absurdity and therefore refuse to allow Paul to continue. Some came to believe but not many and so Paul leaves Athens for Corinth.

◆ RESPONSORIAL PSALM 148: This powerful praise psalm speaks of God's name and majesty presiding over heaven and earth. "Heaven and earth are full of your glory" is the aspect of God that Paul was trying to elucidate for the Athenians. By coming to this recognition, all would acknowledge that God is our creator and sustainer. We belong to God and turning to God in love and repentance is the fitting response for any believer. Such a relationship with God evokes praise and thanksgiving for all that God has done and continues to do for us throughout creation and in history.

◆ GOSPEL: Jesus continues to console his disciples upon his departure by stressing that, even though they can't bear to hear what he is saying, when the Spirit of truth comes, they will be guided in the path of discipleship without stumbling. The Spirit of truth, either the Advocate or Jesus himself, will return and will continue to guide and reaffirm everything Jesus has said and done. Jesus stresses the consoling reality that his death will not separate him from them. Rather, he will continue to be present and real to them, guiding and sustaining them in truth and discipleship. They have to trust him and be attuned to his presence with them in a new manner. He will not abandon them but will continue to be present with them always.

The Roman Missal

The Collect today reminds us how every celebration of the Eucharist unites us with the Communion of Saints: we participate in the fruits of Jesus's Resurrection now, through our liturgical celebration of the mysteries, while the saints already share in the fullness of the Resurrection in the kingdom. In the Prayer over the Offerings we again hear of "the wonderful exchange effected in this sacrifice," which should become the pattern for every aspect of our life; growing in that conformity to the life of Christ is the goal of liturgical celebration. The Prayer after Communion presents the effects of our participating in the "heavenly mysteries" as passing "from former ways to newness of life."

Today's Optional Memorial

Today the Church honors Mary as Our Lady of Fatima. In 1917, in a tiny, rural town of Portugal, the Blessed Virgin Mary appeared to three shepherd children on the thirteenth day of six consecutive months, beginning on May 13. During these apparitions, the lady urged the children to pray for sinners and above all to pray the Rosary. On October 13, the last of the apparitions, the children were joined by a crowd of around 70,000 people, who witnessed what became to be called "The Miracle of the Sun." Today pilgrimage to the site of the apparitions continues all year round. The largest crowds gather on May 13 and October 13, when up to a million of the faithful come to pray and participate in processions, both during the day and at night, by the light of tens of thousands of candles.

THU **14** (#58) white

Solemnity of the Ascension of the Lord
HOLYDAY OF OBLIGATION

About this Solemnity

The distinct celebration of the Ascension of the Lord was unknown in the first three and a half centuries. The chronology of dating the Ascension to forty days after Lent exists only in the Acts of the Apostles. In the Gospel according to Luke, the Ascension appears to have taken place much earlier, even on Easter Day. The original ending to Mark's account of the Gospel did not include the Ascension at all, and it can only be inferred from Matthew's conclusion. When fourth-century Egeria mentions a celebration forty days after Easter in Bethlehem, it may have been for the Holy Innocents. But by the fifth century the observance seems to be universally accepted.

In the dioceses where today is celebrated as the Ascension, it is a Holyday of Obligation.

The Lectionary for Mass

◆ FIRST READING: Luke's account of the Ascension in Acts of the Apostles differs from his account of the Ascension in his Gospel account. Here, the Ascension signals the beginning of the Apostles' ministry. Unlike the Gospel which has Jesus ascend late on Easter Sunday, Acts has Jesus stay for forty more days, instructing the apostles concerning their mission to preach the Kingdom of God. Before ascending, Jesus commissions them to be his witnesses to the ends of the earth, and instructs them to wait for the Father's promise of the Spirit who will empower them for ministry. As he ascends, the apostles' heavenly gaze is shattered by two men in white who predict that Jesus will return in the same way that they saw him departing. In the meantime, their work and ours is to carry on Jesus's mission till he returns.

◆ RESPONSORIAL PSALM 47: The psalm invites all people to clap their hands and shout for joy as it images God mounting a heavenly throne amidst shouts of joy and trumpet blasts. God is the king of all the earth, reigning over all nations and peoples. The psalm clearly articulates the joy in heaven upon the return of the victorious Jesus, enthroned at the right hand of his heavenly Father. We too take joy in and celebrate the reality that Jesus now rules over all, making God's reign real, active, and effective.

◆ SECOND READING: Ephesians speaks of Christ being raised and seated at the right hand of God. God put all things under Christ's authority (feet), making him head over all the believers, unifying and filling all things in every way. Because of this, we who believe are gifted with much power, enabling us to have hope and to offer that hope to all we encounter. As we prepare to celebrate Pentecost, we pray that God gift us with the Spirit of wisdom and revelation resulting in deep knowledge, awareness and intimacy with God and with all creation.

◆ GOSPEL: Mark's longer ending to his Gospel account mentions the Ascension, with Jesus taken up to heaven and seated at the right hand of God. The focus of the passage is on Jesus's commissioning his disciples, along with instructions concerning their mission. They are to proclaim the Gospel to every creature, leaving the choice up to them as to whether they believe and are baptized or not. Signs will accompany those who believe: heal the sick, drive out demons, speak new languages and encounter deadly things that will not harm them. With Jesus enthroned in heaven, they went forth and the Lord was with them, confirming their word through signs. Such is still the mission of every disciple, always assured that Jesus is with us in all our witnessing.

The Roman Missal

Two sets of Mass formularies are given for the solemnity, one for the Vigil Mass and one for the Mass during the Day. A rubric before the texts for the Vigil Mass explains that where the Solemnity of the Ascension is not observed as a Holyday of Obligation, it is observed on the Seventh Sunday of Easter.

◆ AT THE VIGIL MASS: The Collect for the Vigil proclaims that Jesus ascended to the heavens "today," thus affirming once again the convergence of past, present, and future in liturgical celebration. The prayer goes on to assert a key point about the meaning of the Ascension, as is indicated in both of the Prefaces—namely, that the Ascension is not about Jesus leaving us as much as it is a continuation of sharing in his glorified, risen existence. Thus, the Collect goes on to remind us of his promise and asks that "we may be worthy for him to live with us always on earth, and we with him in heaven."

Remember that the Creed is said today as is the Gloria.

The Prayer over the Offerings reiterates that Christ is our High Priest seated at the right hand of God, appropriate imagery for the Solemnity. Because he intercedes for us, we can dare to ask to "approach with confidence the throne of grace and there obtain your mercy."

The Preface assigned for this Mass is either Preface I or Preface II of the Ascension. Preface I makes explicit that the purpose of Christ's Ascension was "not to distance himself from our lowly state," but rather so that we "might be confident of following where he, our Head and Founder, has gone before." Preface II states the same thing in a slightly different way, noting that the purpose of the Ascension was so that "he might make us sharers in his divinity." As with the Sundays of Easter Time, it would be a good idea to chant the introductory dialogue and Preface today.

If the Roman Canon is used as the Eucharistic Prayer for this celebration, remember that there is a proper form of the *Communicantes* ("In communion with those . . . "); it is found within the prayer itself, on the page that lists the several different forms of the *Communicantes*.

There is a special Solemn Blessing specifically for the Ascension of the Lord that can be used for the final blessing at the end of Mass, and it would be good to make use of it. We're not at Pentecost yet, however, so the solemn double Alleluia dismissal is not yet used. Stick with one of the usual dismissal formulae.

◆ AT THE MASS DURING THE DAY: There is no reason not to use the Rite for the Blessing and Sprinkling of Water, especially if it has been used on the Sundays throughout Easter Time. Baptism into the Paschal Mystery means immersion in the fullness of the mystery, which includes Christ's ascended glory. The rite is found in Appendix II of the Missal and replaces the Penitential Act. The Gloria is sung today.

The priest celebrant has a choice from among two Collects for today. The first option sets a tone of gladness and joy as it notes that "the Ascension of Christ your Son / is our exaltation" because we, his Body, are "called to follow in hope"

where he, our Head, has gone. The reality that liturgy is at its core a celebration of our participation in the mysteries of Christ cannot be stated emphatically enough, and this prayer is yet another example of how this truth is basic to the meaning of liturgical celebration. The second prayer asks that, since we "believe that your Only Begotten Son, our Redeemer, / ascended this day to the heavens," we may be granted to even now dwell in spirit "in heavenly realms." Notice too, the important assertion of "this day," an important reference to the salvific reality being made present in our own time and space.

The Creed is said today.

The Prayer over the Offerings makes use of the important concept of "this most holy exchange," this time asking, in light of the particular solemnity we are celebrating, that through it "we, too, may rise up to the heavenly realms."

See the comments about the Vigil Mass for some thoughts about the two options for the Preface, which are the same for the Mass during the Day, and for the proper insert if Eucharistic Prayer I is used.

The Prayer after Communion reminds us that through the liturgy, we can share in heavenly realities even while still here on earth; because of that, we have the hope of being united with the Lord fully one day.

As with the Vigil Mass, it would be good to use the special Solemn Blessing specifically for the Ascension of the Lord as the final blessing at the end of Mass. Since we're not at Pentecost yet, one of the usual dismissal formulae, not the solemn double Alleluia dismissal, is used.

THU **14** (#564) red
Feast of St. Matthias, Apostle

In some dioceses, today is celebrated as the Feast of St. Matthias. The commentaries that follow are regarding this day.

The Lectionary for Mass

◆ FIRST READING: After Jesus's Ascension, the men and women who followed him gathered together in prayer. Peter recognized the need to find a replacement for Judas among the Apostles and cited scriptural evidence in support. The qualifications: the person should have accompanied Jesus during his time on earth, from his baptism until his Ascension. Notice the petition of their prayer: "You, Lord . . . show which one . . . you have chosen." It is the Lord who chooses; the praying assembly must be open and receptive.

◆ RESPONSORIAL PSALM 113: Matthias, counted among the twelve leaders of God's people, gives new meaning to the words of this song of praise. Notice the reference to the enthroned Lord in the third stanza, now understood with reference to Jesus.

◆ GOSPEL: The one sent in Jesus's name must be centered (remain, dwell) in Jesus's love. Here is the source of joy, the sustenance needed for bearing fruit. It is Jesus who has chosen that person to be friend, to be messenger, to love as he or she is loved by Jesus.

The Roman Missal

If the Solemnity of the Ascension of the Lord is celebrated on Sunday instead of today, please use the prayers proper to the Feast of St. Matthias found in the Proper of Saints. The Gloria is said or sung today. One of the Prefaces of the Apostles is used. The Collect alludes to the fact that Saint Matthias was chosen by lot to take the place of Judas among the Twelve. We pray that, through his intercession, we may "be numbered among the elect."

Today's Saint

Matthew (first century), referred to as the tax collector, is one of the twelve Apostles and and traditionally honored as the author of the first of the four accounts of the Gospel. His Gospel has a twofold purpose: one, to announce that Jesus is the eternal king of all creation; and two, to encourage faith in the face of doubt, especially regarding persecution. We have very little information about him, other than he invited Jesus to his home to dine with societal outcasts (see Matthew 9:9 –13), and that he preached the Good News after the Resurrection. Tradition says he began preaching in Judea, then moved on to Ethiopia, Persia, Syria, Macedonia, and possibly Ireland. He is venerated as a martyr, even though there is no historical evidence to validate this claim.

F R I 15 (#295) white
Easter Weekday

Optional Memorial of St. Isidore / white

The Lectionary for Mass

◆ FIRST READING: Paul, receiving a vision of support and encouragement from the Lord, stays on in Corinth for over a year and a half. The Jews of the city, disgusted with Paul, seize him and drag him to Gallio, the Roman proconsul of Achaia, for judgment and condemnation. Gallio, typical of Roman officials, despises the Jews and wants nothing to do with them over a matter of no concern to Rome. While the Jews beat Sosthenes, a synagogue official most likely sympathetic to Paul, Gallio washes his hands of this internal squabble, allowing Paul to continue ministering to the Corinthians until he moves on to Syria, accompanied by Priscilla and Aquila. The Spirit must have been working through Gallio as well allowing Paul's ministry to continue unhindered.

◆ RESPONSORIAL PSALM 47: All people are invited to clap their hands and shout praises to God who is king over all the earth. God's throne is in the heavens from which God rules with justice and might, announcing salvation to all. Paul, along with both Jews and Greeks who have come to believe and be baptized, are all included in this call to praise God. As Paul continues to persist in his ministry and continues to bring more people to the Lord, he must have turned to this psalm many times, and so should we.

◆ GOSPEL: Jesus continues his consolation of the disciples by focusing on the pain that they will experience when he is no longer with them, and the joy that will be theirs when they see him again. As a woman in labor feels pain, they too will be in pain. It will be real and hard to bear. But just as a woman no longer remembers the pain but rejoices at the birth of her child, so too will their anguish and pain be forgotten once they see and experience him again. The joy will be so overwhelming that nothing will get in the way, not even questions. Jesus encourages them to ask the Father for anything in his name, and it will be granted. That joy in the resurrected Jesus is ours now and will be even more glorious when we see him again.

The Roman Missal

The Missal acknowledges that in some regions the Solemnity of the Ascension, observed on the Seventh Sunday of Easter, has not yet been celebrated, and so it provides a choice for the Collect.

The first Collect is the one to be used if the Ascension was celebrated the day before. It acknowledges that God restores us to eternal life through Christ's Resurrection, and so it asks that we be raised up "to the author of our salvation, / who is seated at your right hand." The prayer then goes on to confess how our Savior will come again in majesty, therefore asking that "those you have given new birth in Baptism / may be clothed with blessed immortality." Notice how the prayer skillfully weaves together various themes we have been hearing throughout Easter Time, incorporating them with the most recent aspect of a focus on Christ's Ascension into glory.

The second Collect is the correct choice for those places where the Solemnity of the Ascension is celebrated on the upcoming Sunday. This prayer more generally asks that what God has promised may be accomplished so that "all your adopted children" (we can hear the language of Baptism here) may attain what has been foretold—eternal life and happiness.

The Prayer over the Offerings, in a somewhat similar theme as the second Collect, begs both that the blessings that have been given by God may not be lost, and that we may "attain the gifts that are eternal." The Prayer after Communion echoes this petition. The choices for the Preface today include any one of the five Prefaces of Easter or the two Prefaces of the Ascension. For communities that celebrated the Ascension yesterday, it would be most beneficial to highlight the unique nature of these days as time in between the Ascension and Pentecost by using one of the Ascension Prefaces. For other communities, one of the Easter Prefaces should be used.

Today's Saint

Today we honor Isidore the Farmer, rather than the Doctor of the Church, Isidore of Seville. Isidore the Farmer was born in Madrid to poor parents who sent him to work for a landowner. He was very devout and married a like-minded woman, Maria, who also became a saint. Isidore attended daily Mass and was often late arriving at the fields, but he managed to get his work done nonetheless. He shared

the little he had with the poor. He is the patron of farmers; it is fitting to remember him in the Northern Hemisphere's agricultural season.

(#296) white
Easter Weekday
S A T **16**

The Lectionary for Mass

◆ FIRST READING: Paul begins another missionary journey to communities he had visited previously and brings strength to all the disciples along the way. In Ephesus, we are introduced to Apollos, an Alexandrian Jew who was filled with a fiery passion for Jesus and used Scripture authoritatively to establish to others that Jesus is the Christ. Priscilla and Aquila find his teaching somewhat deficient (we are not told how) and proceed to instruct him "more accurately." He, like Paul, and with the support of others, travels to Achaia, and proves very helpful to the communities established there. We see in Apollos, and others like him, God's Spirit at work in many people, making certain that the Word of the Lord would become known throughout the world.

◆ RESPONSORIAL PSALM 47: Similar to yesterday's psalm, the invitation to clap hands and praise God is once again extended to all. God is the king of all the earth, rules all, and invites the princes of the nations to sit with God's special people, the Jews. Together, we all belong to God who is supreme over all. The Spirit's work in Acts manifests this significant quality of God who, through people like Paul, Apollos, Priscilla, and Aquila, invites all to come to know the Lord and work together to make God's kingdom and reign known throughout the earth.

◆ GOSPEL: Jesus, in consoling his disciples, stresses his intermediary role with the Father by encouraging

them to "ask the Father in my name," and it will be given to you. Jesus assures them that a time is coming when he will no longer speak in "figures of speech" but speak plainly about the Father. On that day they will know the Father and when they ask God, God will answer them directly, without Jesus as intermediary. The relationship with God will be direct because they have loved Jesus and he has come from the Father. He came from the Father and now he is leaving to return to the Father. This rich intimacy with God through Jesus is something we are all called to strive for in our life as disciples.

The Roman Missal

Notice that there are two options for the Collect today, to be used depending on when the Solemnity of the Ascension of the Lord is observed.

(#60) white
17 Seventh Sunday of Easter

Editorial Note: In some dioceses, the Solemnity of the Ascension of the Lord is transferred to the Seventh Sunday of Easter. If this is the case in your diocese, please use the readings and prayer texts from the Ascension. Please see page 210 in this Sourcebook for commentary.

The Lectionary for Mass

◆ FIRST READING: Luke recounts the reason and process that went into the selection of Matthias as a replacement for Judas. The setting is the upper room, traditionally associated with the Last Supper, with about 120 persons present. This will be the setting for the Spirit's descent on Pentecost. It was God's plan that Judas betray Jesus, and so it is fitting to replace him so that the twelve Jesus chose can be witnesses to his Resurrection. Zeroing in on two candidates who accompanied them from the baptism of John to the Lord being taken up, they prayed, cast lots and Matthias is chosen. Both divine and human elements are integral to any good Christian decision making.

◆ RESPONSORIAL PSALM 103: God's majesty and power, set up in the heavens and ruling over all, is celebrated with praise and blessing showered upon God. God's covenant love for us surpasses all boundaries, and God's mercy continually forgives and forgets our transgressions. These are at the heart of God's many benefits which the psalmist invites all to remember and never forget. This is exactly what Jesus came to tell us and show us about God through his actions and care for us, even to the point of death.

◆ SECOND READING: God is love. God shared that love completely with us by sending Jesus. God initiates love of us and invites us to love one another in the same manner. In this way, God establishes intimacy with us and we with God. The concrete sign of this intimacy is the gift of the Spirit that has been given to all. In testifying to Jesus as the Savior of the world, we testify to God's love of us and we are challenged to love one another in return. Discipleship challenges all to love as God loves and Jesus modeled.

◆ GOSPEL: Jesus prays for unity among his disciples, comparable to the unity he has with his Father. He protected them while with them, except for Judas who chose his own path. But now that he will leave them, Jesus asks the Father to protect them from the world and the evil one. These forces choose not to believe and come to know the Father, not Jesus, the one whom the Father sent. Armed with the Father's protection, Jesus sends them into the world, already consecrated and armed with the truth, to love one another as Jesus has loved them and consecrated himself for them. The Pentecost Spirit will facilitate much of what Jesus prays for and the Spirit is still at work in our communities as well.

The Roman Missal

If you are in a region that observes the Solemnity of the Ascension today, refer to the comments on page 210 for the celebration of Mass today. What follows is for the Seventh Sunday of Easter.

Continue to use the Rite for the Blessing and Sprinkling of Water, as has been done, it is hoped, on all the Sundays of Easter Time. If this has not been the case, it can nonetheless still be used today if desired. Remember that this rite, found in Appendix II of the Missal, replaces the Penitential Act. The Gloria is sung today.

The Collect acknowledges the paradoxical nature of what we celebrate with the Ascension: that Christ is both with the Father in glory and, at the same time, present among us; the prayer therefore asks that we may indeed "experience, as he promised, until the end of the world, his abiding presence among us." Though the "ascension" and "abiding presence" seem to contradict each other, theologically they are actually different aspects of the same reality.

The Prayer over the Offerings conveys the dynamism of what takes place in liturgical action, as it asks that through the sacrificial offerings we make, "we may pass over to the glory of heaven." Thus are we once again reminded that in every liturgical celebration the work of our redemption is being accomplished.

Although the choice of the Preface may be taken from among the five Easter Prefaces or the two Ascension Prefaces, it would seem to be pastorally advantageous to use one of the two Prefaces of the Ascension. This would highlight the unique segment of Easter Time in which we find ourselves, and also continue to echo themes that have been announced in the Collect and the Prayer over the Offerings. In any event, continue to chant the introductory dialogue and Preface.

The Prayer after Communion continues the idea that the celebration of the liturgy accomplishes the work of our salvation. Here, the prayer asks that "what has already come to pass" in Christ as Head of the Church may also "be accomplished in the body of the whole Church."

Use the solemn blessing for Easter Time, found at number 6 in the "Blessings at the End of Mass and Prayers over the People" section of the Missal, and one of the regular formulae for dismissal is used.

Other Ideas

Historically, the Ascension used to be the end of the Easter season. Even though the emphasis is moving closer to the coming of the Holy Spirit, the Advocate, it is still Easter. The liturgical environment and music should reflect this. You should still be using the same Mass settings you have been, and other musical pieces, for example, seasonal psalms, and so on. The Paschal candle should still be lit and kept in its place near the ambo.

MON **18** (#297) white
Easter Weekday

Optional Memorial of St. John I, Pope and Martyr / red

The Lectionary for Mass

◆ FIRST READING: Paul is in Ephesus where he comes across some disciples who were unaware of the Holy Spirit and had been baptized only with the baptism of John. Paul clarifies that John's baptism of repentance pointed to Jesus, the one who came after him and that the Holy Spirit is connected to Jesus. Once they are baptized in Jesus, they receive the gifts of the Spirit, enabling them to speak in tongues and to prophesy. Paul continues debating in the synagogue concerning the meaning and understanding of God's kingdom, made real in Jesus. We too are challenged to see Jesus as the Christ who is intimately connected to the Spirit's presence among us.

◆ RESPONSORIAL PSALM 68: Throughout this Easter Time, the psalms have called us to praise, joy, and thanksgiving for the many marvelous deeds that God has done for all humanity. This praise psalm again invites us to "sing to God, O kingdoms of the earth." God's gracious love and care are for everyone, and in Jesus and the Spirit, all people are made beneficiaries. The Lord scatters enemies but protects and cares for the orphan and the widow. Prisoners and those forsaken find a home in the Lord. This is the message Paul clarifies for the uninformed disciples and for those he debated with in the synagogue. This should clearly be our message also.

◆ GOSPEL: The disciples interject that Jesus is now speaking clearly and they understand perfectly and believe that he came from God. By this interjection, Jesus realizes that they still have little understanding of what will happen to him. In an attempt to console them, he tells them that when "the hour," his Death, arrives, they will all scatter and leave him alone with the Father. He does not want them to be overwhelmed with remorse but to "have peace in me." The world that does not believe in him will cause him and them pain, but again Jesus consoles them by insisting that he has conquered the world. As the disciples and we struggle with our own weakness, Jesus continues to be our source of hope and consolation.

The Roman Missal

The Easter Time weekday Collect today prays specifically for the power of the Holy Spirit to come to us, that we may keep God's will in mind and "express it in a devout way of life." The Spirit transforms us to live the Christian life. The Prayer over the Offerings, while not explicitly mentioning the Holy Spirit, does pray that "this unblemished sacrifice" might purify us, thus calling to mind the purifying fire of the Spirit, as we ask for "the force of grace from on high" to be imparted to our minds (can we hear reference to the Spirit's gift of Wisdom?).

The Prayer after Communion reiterates a petition that we have made frequently during Easter Time, that, being "imbued with heavenly mysteries," we might "pass from former ways to newness of life." Certainly, it is the Spirit who breathes new life into us.

Although the choice of the Preface may be taken from among the five Easter Prefaces or the two Ascension Prefaces, strongly consider using one of the two Prefaces of the Ascension as a way of highlighting the unique liturgical time in which we find ourselves, in between Ascension and Pentecost in days that pray for the coming of the Spirit.

Today's Saint

Saint John I († 526) was a native of Tuscany and was elected pope when quite elderly. Despite his protests, he was sent by the Arian King Theodoric to Constantinople, where he was to convince Emperor Justin to moderate his decree against the Arians. Theodoric threatened reprisals against Orthodox Christians in the West if he failed. When John returned, Theodoric had him arrested on suspicion of conspiring with the emperor. He died in prison of ill treatment.

19

T U E (#298)   white
Easter Weekday

Lectionary for Mass

◆ FIRST READING: Paul's final speech to the elders of the community in Ephesus highlights his mission and the responsibility he felt to ensure that his communities grow and thrive. Summoning the community leaders, he tells them of being Spirit-directed to Jerusalem to face imprisonment and hardships. Paul considers this inconsequential, as long as he can continue his ministry "to bear witness to the Gospel of God's grace," experienced fully in Jesus. Sensing that he will not see his beloved communities again, he counsels them to carry on because he "did not shrink from proclaiming to you the entire plan of God." Paul had done his work faithfully and well, and now leaves them in God's hands. Such an approach is essential and demanded of all disciples.

◆ RESPONSORIAL PSALM 68: A repeat of yesterday, this praise psalm again calls all kingdoms to sing to God. The verses speak to Paul's situation concerning his impending hardships in Jerusalem. The psalm asserts that God provides for the poor and needy. Our God "is a saving God" who bears our burdens and even "controls the passageways of death." As Paul traveled to Jerusalem, this psalm must have been a constant companion and source of solace.

◆ GOSPEL: Often referred to as Jesus's high priestly prayer, Jesus

MAY

concludes his farewell speech to his disciples by praying to God on their behalf. With his hour here, Jesus asks that he complete the task given to him by the Father, with honor and glory. Eternal life consists in knowing the Father and the one whom the Father sent, Jesus. His life has been devoted to letting his disciples know all about the Father. Therefore Jesus prays for them that, in the midst of the world that does not believe, they continue to believe and give glory to God. In this manner, Jesus is glorified in them and will continue to be so because he is returning to the Father while they remain in the world. With no concerns about the difficulties, a disciple's testimony of Jesus continues to give glory to both the Father and to Jesus.

The Roman Missal

Continue to use either the Easter or Ascension Preface.

WED 20 (#299) white
Easter Weekday

Optional Memorial of St. Bernardine of Siena, Priest / white

The Lectionary for Mass

◆ FIRST READING: Paul continues his farewell speech to the elders of Ephesus charging them "to keep watch over yourselves and over the whole flock." He warns them of "savage wolves" who pervert the truth and draw the flock away from the fold. Using himself as an example, he encourages them to be steadfast in their ministry and not to strive for material benefit but rather use all that they have to take care of the needy, as he did while he was with them. After prayers and a tearful farewell, Paul is escorted to the ship heading for Jerusalem. Luke models Paul's farewell to the elders on Jesus's own challenging and consoling farewell to his disciples in John's Gospel.

◆ RESPONSORIAL PSALM 68: All kingdoms are again invited to sing to God. Each time a different aspect of God is highlighted, evoking songs of praise. Today, we praise God's power and majesty used to aid and exalt all who believe and turn to God. God's goodness and power is shared with all who acknowledge God's majesty, wonder and power. This is an integral component of Jesus's prayer to his Father in the Gospel. In the disciples' witnessing, he and the Father are both honored and glorified. Paul in the First Reading also counsels the elders to do everything so as to give God the glory and not themselves.

◆ GOSPEL: Jesus continues his prayer by asking the Father to keep the disciples united as one, just as Jesus and the Father are one. Jesus prepared them by revealing to them all that the Father desired. But like Paul in the First Reading, Jesus is aware that they will need help and protection since they will remain in the world, which refused to know and believe in him. They are in the world but are not of the world. They are now of God and Jesus asks the Father to consecrate them in truth so whatever they do or say will give glory to the Father. Commissioned to spread what they know to the world, Jesus prays that as he has consecrated and given of himself for them, they too might give of themselves for the world.

The Roman Missal

The Collect for today, in continuing to include reference to the Holy Spirit, prays for one of the chief gifts of the Spirit, that of unity—specifically, in this prayer, that the Church might be "united in purity of intent." The Prayer over the Offerings relates how the sacrifice we offer was instituted by God's command, and asks that the sacred mysteries we celebrate (namely, the Eucharist) as "our dutiful service" in the present "graciously complete the sanctifying work / by which you are pleased to redeem us." Thus, are we again reminded how all liturgical celebration goes beyond the present moment to bring us along the path of a future fulfillment. The Prayer after Communion asks for an increase of grace, particularly the grace to always be ready to receive so great a gift as "this divine Sacrament." The prayer can remind us that even our hunger for the gift of the Eucharist is itself first a gift from God. The choices for the Preface today include any one of the five Prefaces of Easter or the two Prefaces of the Ascension. It would seem most beneficial to highlight the unique nature of these days as time in between the Ascension and Pentecost by using one of the Ascension Prefaces.

Today's Saint

Saint Bernardine of Siena (1380–1444) was an Italian Franciscan, a priest, and a preacher. He was orphaned young and raised by a pious aunt. While still a student, he helped care for the sick during an outbreak of the bubonic plague, contracted the disease and almost died. Bernardine joined a strict branch of the Franciscans, called the Observants, around 1402. Known as the "apostle of Italy," he preached devotion to the Holy Name of Jesus, popularizing the use of the monogram I.H.S. and encouraging his hearers to burn unnecessary luxuries in "bonfires of vanities."

THU 21 (#300) white
Easter Weekday

Optional Memorial of St. Christopher Magallanes, Priest, and Companions, Martyrs / red

The Lectionary for Mass

◆ FIRST READING: Paul, now in Jerusalem, is in the hands of the Roman tribune who calls together members of the Sanhedrin to discuss the accusations against Paul.

216 EASTER TIME: MAY

Knowing that his audience comprised both Pharisees who believed in the resurrection of the dead and Sadducees who didn't, Paul states that the reason he is being tried is his belief in the resurrection of the dead. The group immediately divides over the issue and dissension arises among them. The tribune, fearing that Paul, a Roman citizen, might be killed, sends troops to rescue Paul. Later Paul is consoled by a vision that he will bear witness to the Lord in Rome, just as he has done in Jerusalem. Paul's hardships are not over, by any means.

◆ RESPONSORIAL PSALM 16: The psalm expresses a strong sense of trust and confidence in God who sustains and protects us even in death. The refrain captures it well as the psalmist prays, "Keep me safe, O God; you are my hope." The Lord keeps us safe, holds fast our lot, counsels us, does not abandon us even in death, and shows us the path to life. As Paul struggled both in Jerusalem and in Rome, this psalm was definitely a source of solace and strength, allowing him to place all hope in the Lord, even in the face of death.

◆ GOSPEL: Jesus concludes his prayer by praying for all those in the world who will believe through the disciples's witness, so that all may be one. Jesus thanks the Father for gifting him with the disciples, for through them, he and the Father will continue to be made known to the world. Even though he wishes them to be with him, as he is with the Father, Jesus consoles them, knowing the hardships they will face the world in his name. Yet, in being commissioned to witness to the world, Jesus will continue to dwell with them, sharing with them the same love and care that he has for the Father and the Father for him. Such rich intimacy with his disciples is the same rich intimacy that Jesus shares with us today.

The Roman Missal

The choices for the Preface today include any one of the five Prefaces of Easter or the two Prefaces of the Ascension. It would seem most beneficial to highlight the unique nature of these days as time in between the Ascension and Pentecost by using one of the Ascension Prefaces.

Today's Saints

Saint Christopher Magallanes was a Mexican priest whose years of ministry coincided with an extreme anticlerical era in Mexico. He was falsely accused of promoting rebellion and arrested while on his way to celebrate Mass. Christopher was killed without trial after absolving his executioners, saying, "I die innocent, and ask God that my blood may serve to unite my Mexican brethren." He and his companions died between 1915 and 1928. He was canonized by Pope John Paul II on May 21, 2000, along with twenty-one priests and three laymen, also martyred for resisting the anti-Catholic Mexican government of the 1920s.

FRI 22 (#301) white
Easter Weekday

Optional Memorial of St. Rita of Cascia, Religious / white

The Lectionary for Mass

◆ FIRST READING: The passage relates the conversation concerning Paul that Festus, a Roman official in charge of Paul, has with Herod and his sister Bernice in Caesarea. Paul, as a Roman citizen, has appealed his case to the Roman emperor and awaits arrangements to travel to Rome for trial. Meanwhile, Festus is not quite certain what to charge Paul with because he is not aware of why the Jewish leadership despises Paul over "a certain Jesus who had died but who Paul claimed was alive." So Festus and Paul are in a holding pattern until arrangements can be made to escort him to Rome.

Paul must have struggled greatly with the uncertainty of the situation, not to mention his inability to carry on his ministry.

◆ RESPONSORIAL PSALM 103: This praise psalm asks that all remember the Lord's many benefits, the Lord whose throne is set in the heavens. God's kindness or covenant love toward those who fear him surpasses all expectations. God's forgiveness of transgressions is beyond anything we could ever imagine. This is the kind of kingdom that God had established in the heavens. Such love and care, such forgiveness and reconciliation can only elicit blessing and praise from all those who fear the Lord. No matter the hardship, Paul can still praise and sing joyfully to the Lord.

◆ GOSPEL: This post-Resurrection encounter between the risen Jesus and Peter seeks to reconcile Peter and Jesus, after Peter's three-fold denial of Jesus. In rehabilitating Peter and restoring him to his leadership position, Jesus three times questions him concerning his love, countering Peter's threefold denial. In each case, the love Peter expresses for Jesus is actualized by Jesus as love that should drive Peter to care and pasture of others. Reconciled and restored, Peter is invited to follow Jesus. As is clear from the text, such following will lead to Peter's death, modeled on Jesus, the one whom he loves and desires to be with. Discipleship is summed up in love of Jesus that drives one to love others as Jesus loved us, even to death on a cross. Like Peter and Paul, disciples always face this challenge.

The Roman Missal

The weekday Collect acknowledges God as the one who has "unlocked for us the gates of eternity" through the "glorification of your Christ / and the light of the Holy Spirit." The phrase "light of the

Holy Spirit" can call to mind the enlightenment that takes place in Baptism; thus, Easter Time themes of Resurrection, Ascension, and our sharing in those realities through Baptism all come together. The fruits that we ask for in this prayer are deeper devotion and stronger faith. The Prayer over the Offerings also provides an explicit reference to the Holy Spirit; in this prayer, it is to the coming of the Spirit that we await at Pentecost, a coming that will "cleanse our consciences." The Prayer after Communion refers to our Eucharistic celebration as a banquet that, we pray, will bring everlasting life.

Today's Saint

Saint Rita of Cascia lived in Italy from 1377 to 1457. Against her wishes, her parents arranged for her to marry a man who ended up abusing her. She had two sons with him; both followed their father's bad example. Rita's husband converted toward the end of his life, but he was murdered by an old enemy. Her sons died soon after. Rita was refused entrance to an Augustinian monastery several times because she was a widow, but eventually she was admitted and lived there until her death. She is depicted with a wound in her forehead because she asked to suffer in union with Jesus and was given a wound from a thorn in his crown.

SAT **23** (#302) white
Easter Weekday

At the Morning Mass

The Lectionary for Mass

◆ FIRST READING: This is the last that we hear of Paul in Acts. He is under house arrest in Rome, yet still able to meet others, interact, and even continue preaching. Calling the Jewish leaders together, Paul desires to clarify that he has done nothing to deserve the death penalty. Paul's intent has always been for "the hope of Israel" and for this, he is imprisoned. Luke concludes Acts with Paul remaining under house arrest for two full years, receiving all, and "with complete assurance and without hindrance" proclaiming the kingdom of God and teaching about the Lord Jesus Christ. Paul ends his ministry the way he began it. He is faithful to the very end.

◆ RESPONSORIAL PSALM 11: The psalm images the Lord seated in the heavens, beholding all creation while searching both the just and the wicked. The wicked are despised. Since the Lord is just by nature, the Lord loves just deeds and the just, the upright ones, will see and "gaze upon your face, O Lord." Paul, having been righteous up to his last breath, would be assured that he would soon gaze on the Lord's face and dwell with the Lord always.

◆ GOSPEL: As John's account of the Gospel comes to a close, Peter desires to know the fate of the Beloved Disciple. Jesus basically says that it is not really a concern of Peter, for he is to focus on following him, even to the Cross. The Beloved Disciple is following in a different mode and that should not be a concern for Peter. Was this rivalry between two different modes of discipleship? All we know is that there are many ways to follow Jesus. We are told that the Beloved Disciple has written these stories down to testify to Jesus. Not all are included for they would be impossible to contain in books. The implication is that the story of Jesus continues to be told by all those that have seen, heard, and experienced Jesus in their own time and space. These are the stories that we continue to recount to this day.

The Roman Missal

Notice how the Missal's designation of "At the Morning Mass" clearly distinguishes this Mass from the Vigil of Pentecost, which will be celebrated later the same day, in the evening.

The Collect, perhaps somewhat curiously, does not specifically mention the Holy Spirit (except in the Doxology, of course), but it does convey a sense of completion or coming to a close with its phrase about "we who have celebrated the Paschal festivities" — throughout these fifty days. The prayer goes on to ask that we may "hold fast to them in the way that we live our lives," thus affirming the goal of all liturgical celebration — that what we celebrate in ritual (dying and rising; offering ourselves in union with Christ) may be lived out in daily life. The Prayer over the Offerings does explicitly mention, in a way that connotes a sense of anticipation and excitement, that the Holy Spirit is indeed "coming near," as it asks that the event "prepare our minds for the divine Sacrament, since the Spirit himself is the remission of all sins."

The notion of our being prepared fits well with this point in the liturgy at the Prayer over the Offerings as part of the Preparation of the Gifts; the mention of the remission of sins reminds us of one of the fruits of participation in the Eucharist, namely, forgiveness. The Prayer after Communion uses the old/new motif that we have heard so often throughout Easter Time, as it begs that "as we have been brought from things of the past to new mysteries [both in this Eucharistic celebration and throughout the whole fifty days of Easter Time, which are coming to a close today], so, with former ways left behind, we may be made new in holiness of mind [the concrete transformation to be brought about through our participation in the mysteries]."

The choices for the Preface today include any one of the five Prefaces of Easter or the two Prefaces of the

Ascension, but certainly one of the Prefaces of the Ascension of the Lord could be used to good pastoral advantage at this Mass, the last one for Easter Time this year.

(#63)   red

23/24 Solemnity of Pentecost

About this Solemnity

The Greek word for Pentecost (*Pentekostē*) means "fiftieth," and in early Christianity it referred to the entire fifty days of Easter. The roots of Pentecost can be found in the Jewish festival of Weeks (Shavu'ot), the fifty-day celebration following Passover (Exodus 23:16). It was a harvest festival in which the first fruits of the harvest were offered to God in gratitude. It eventually became associated with the giving of the Torah on Mount Sinai. Early Christians reinterpreted the Jewish festival as a commemoration of the coming of the Holy Spirit, since Acts records that the Holy Spirit came to the disciples when the festival of Pentecost was fulfilled (see Acts 2:1–11). The celebration of Pentecost may begin on Saturday afternoon or evening with the Vigil. By the end of the fourth century in the West, Pentecost became a time for the initiation of those not baptized at Easter. Thus, a night vigil was added like the Easter Vigil for this purpose. With this early history in mind, this is a most appropriate time to initiate those

who were not ready at the Easter Vigil, or (not and) to celebrate the Reception of Baptized Christians into the Full Communion of the Catholic Church (see RCIA, 473).

The Lectionary for Mass

Extended/Shortened Vigil Mass

◆ First Reading (option 1): This story recounts the origin of the many and varied languages spoken by humankind. Such diversity was viewed as both a punishment and a check by the Lord to stop humans from the kind of self-assertion evidenced in their attempt to "make a name" (Genesis 11:4) for themselves through their own efforts. Such misguided and uncontrolled drives could be disastrous. Unable to understand one another because of their diverse languages, the people were dispersed throughout the world. At Pentecost, the disciples' gift of tongues would overcome these barriers and serve the proclamation of the Gospel and the faith of those from far off lands who heard them.

◆ First Reading (option 2): The Jewish festival of Pentecost, fifty days after Passover, commemorated the giving of the Law on Mount Sinai. Note the reference to Passover ("how I treated the Egyptians" [Exodus 19:4]) at the beginning of the reading. The Israelites, as God's people, have a special relationship with God and accordingly stand out above all other nations on earth. The people acknowledge this and agree to be faithful to God's covenant with them.

◆ First Reading (option 3): The prophet's words at the time of the Babylonian Exile bear witness to the powerful impact the Spirit of the Lord had in his life. Not only are his visions the result of the Spirit's work in his life, the prophet is led to understand that it is the Spirit of the Lord who is the source of all life. It is this same Spirit who will

enliven the dry bones of the Israelites. God's people will be raised from the graves of their exile and be restored to life and to homeland.

◆ First Reading (option 4): The prophet looks toward a time when God's Spirit would be poured out upon *all* people. Later in the reading, the phrase "the day of the Lord" (Joel 3:3) is used with reference to the day of judgment, a terrible day marked by signs in the cosmos. This text from Joel is cited by Peter in his speech after the coming of the Spirit upon Pentecost (see Acts 2). A day of judgment has come with the Death, Resurrection, and Ascension of Jesus. Cosmic signs of darkness (see Luke 23:44–45) and fire (see Acts 2:3) are evident. Judgment is at hand. All who believe in Jesus will be saved.

◆ Responsorial Psalm 104: This hymn of praise acclaims all the works of God's creation. The verses chosen for today's response focus in particular on the greatness and majesty of the Creator. The responsorial antiphon acknowledges that it is through the life-giving breath of God that all things live (see also the last stanza with its allusion to Genesis 2:7).

◆ Second Reading: Through Baptism, believers have received the Spirit of God, the first-fruit of the new creation. Yet, the life of God is still coming to be realized within us. Until the day of our death, we—and all creation—are in labor pains as this new life comes to birth. The Spirit we have been given works within us and prays within us until all is accomplished.

◆ Gospel: Set within the context of the Jewish Feast of Booths, or Tabernacles (commemorating the time of Israel's desert wanderings after the exodus from Egypt), Jesus speaks of the water he will provide for all who are thirsty in his day—and our own. This living water will arise from within us, from deep within our hearts. It is the water of life of his Spirit. It is the gift to be given after Jesus's glorification through his death and exaltation on the cross.

Mass during the Day

◆ FIRST READING: Pentecost was one of the three pilgrimage feasts of the Jews, when all who were able came to the Temple in Jerusalem, thus the presence of so many foreigners in Jerusalem that day. All the disciples were gathered in one place. Acts of the Apostles 1:13–14 identifies these disciples as the Eleven; Mary, the mother of Jesus; the women who journeyed with Jesus from Galilee to Jerusalem (see Luke 8:1–3; 23:49); and his relatives. The cosmic sign of the strong driving wind attracted the crowd. (In Greek, the language in which Acts was originally written, the same word is used for both "wind" and "spirit.") Note also the sign of "fire." The fruit of the Spirit's presence and work is the disciples' ability to proclaim the Gospel in various tongues and be understood by those who heard them.

◆ RESPONSORIAL PSALM 104: As at the Vigil Mass, Psalm 104 is used, with the same antiphon. There is some variation in the stanzas. Today's addition in the last stanza voices the desire that both God's glory and God's joy in his creation endure. The psalmist is intent on being pleasing to the Lord and finding joy in him. A beautiful theme for each of our lives!

◆ SECOND READING: The contrast between the Spirit and the flesh — and their respective fruits — is emphasized in today's reading. The flesh represents anything that is opposed to God; the Spirit, that which is enlivened by God's power and presence. Paul's command to live by the Spirit points to the choice we have in

the matter. Which fruits are more evident in our lives?

◆ GOSPEL: The setting of today's text is Jesus's last discourse to his disciples, at table with them the night before he died. Jesus promises to send, an Advocate on their behalf, the Spirit of truth. Note the intimate workings between the Father, the Son, and the Spirit and how the disciples are drawn into this by the power of the Spirit at work in their lives. On their part, the disciples must receive what the Spirit declares to them and testify on Jesus's behalf.

The Roman Missal

◆ EXTENDED VIGIL: The Missal gives rubrics and texts to be used for the extended celebration of a Pentecost Vigil, and it is hoped that every parish will take advantage of such a celebration for its parishioners. Instructions are even given if a parish wishes to celebrate First Vespers (Evening Prayer I) in common. This might be something for communities to consider as a way of highlighting the Liturgy of the Hours as something that is meant to be prayed by every baptized Christian, not just the clergy.

If Evening Prayer I is not to be celebrated communally and Mass is to begin in the usual way, then all is done as usual for the beginning of Mass, including the Kyrie (Lord have mercy), after which the priest prays the Collect of the Mass. This would be an ideal occasion to use the Rite for the Blessing and Sprinkling of Water, found in Appendix II at the back of the Missal, especially if your parish has been doing this on all of the Sundays of Easter Time. Even if you have not been making use of this rite, today is a perfect occasion to do so as it brings together the themes of Paschal Mystery, Easter Time, Baptism, and the Holy Spirit, and its use allows the enactment of the ritual to convey the sense of fullness

and completion so appropriate for this solemnity. Remember that this rite takes the place of the Penitential Act. It's important to note, however, that in this extended Vigil, the Collect would be prayed by the priest immediately after the concluding prayer "May almighty God cleanse us of our sins . . . ," not the Gloria, which comes later (see below).

The Collect for this extended Vigil is specified as the "Grant, we pray, almighty God, that the splendor . . ." text, which is the second option for the Collect under the Simple Form of the Vigil Mass (the texts for which follow this first section for the Extended Form). The prayer is replete with imagery appropriate to the Holy Spirit: it speaks of the splendor of God's glory shining forth upon us; it mentions "the bright rays of the Holy Spirit;" it asks that "the light of your light may confirm the hearts of those born again by your grace," thus giving voice to baptismal themes.

After the Collect, an address is given to the people, using the exact words in the Missal or words similar to them. The address asks the people to follow the example of Mary, the Apostles, and the disciples who persevered in prayer and who awaited the Spirit as promised by the Lord. We follow that example by listening "with quiet hearts" to the Word of God, meditating "on how many great deeds God in times past did for his people" and praying "that the Holy Spirit, whom the Father sent as the first fruits for those who believe, may bring to perfection his work in the world."

After this follows an extended Liturgy of the Word modeled on the Liturgy of the Word at the Easter Vigil. The Missal refers us to the readings proposed as options in the Lectionary, with a Responsorial Psalm and a prayer corresponding to the reading following each one. (It is possible to have a period of sacred silence in place of any of the Responsorial Psalms.) The Missal then goes on to give the texts for prayers that correspond to each of the readings and their subsequent psalms. It is then after the fourth reading that the Gloria is sung.

When the Gloria is completed, the priest then prays the Collect in the usual way; this time, the Collect used is the text found as the first one given as the Collect for the Simple Form of the Vigil Mass, the "Almighty, ever-living God, who willed the Paschal Mystery. . . ." After this, the reading proclaims the Epistle, Romans 8:22–27, and everything continues in the usual way. The texts for the remainder of the Extended Form of the Vigil Mass are taken from the Simple Form of the Vigil Mass, which follows in the Missal. Commentary on those texts is provided below.

◆ Simple Vigil: If the Extended Form of the Vigil is not being celebrated, then all occurs as usual at Mass; however, there are still proper texts that must be used for the Vigil Mass, distinct from the Mass during the Day.

As with the extended form of the Vigil Mass, the simple form would be an ideal occasion to use the Rite for the Blessing and Sprinkling of Water, found in Appendix II at the back of the Missal, especially if your parish has been doing this on all of the Sundays of Easter Time. Even if you have not been making use of this rite, consider doing so now. Remember that this rite takes the place of the Penitential Act. The Gloria immediately follows the prayer the priest prays as the conclusion to the Rite for Blessing and Sprinkling of Water.

In the simple form of the Vigil, either one of the two Collects given in the Missal may be used. The second prayer was discussed above, under the extended form. The first option highlights the liturgical time of the fifty days of celebrating the Paschal Mystery ("Pentecost" referring to the fifty-day time period of "a week of weeks"), after which it emphasizes a central theme associated with the Holy Spirit, that of unity. Evoking the story of the Tower of Babel from Genesis, the Collect makes explicit reference to "the confusion of many tongues" and therefore presents "heavenly grace" (the Spirit) as the agent for bringing together "into one great confession of your name" that which had been scattered through human pride and sin.

The Prayer over the Offerings begins with a line that sounds like the epiclesis in a Eucharistic Prayer: "Pour out upon these gifts the blessing of your Spirit, we pray, O Lord . . ." How appropriate on a day when we celebrate the coming of the Holy Spirit! The second part of the prayer makes the important point that the purpose of invoking the Spirit upon the gifts is so that the Spirit will come upon those who receive those gifts: "so that through them your church may be imbued with such love. . . ."

The Preface assigned for today is the Preface of Pentecost, the text for which (both with and without musical notation) is given along with the texts for the Mass during the Day, two pages further along (this might be a little confusing; the priest celebrant should be sure to check this ahead of time). Given the festivity of the day, it would be a good idea to sing the introductory dialogue and the Preface, especially if this has been the custom on Sundays throughout Easter Time. Note that if Eucharistic Prayer I, the Roman Canon, is used, there is a proper form of the *Communicantes* ("In communion with those . . ."), which mentions the traditional image of the Holy Spirit as tongues of fire.

The Prayer after Communion notes how the Eucharistic gifts of the Body and Blood of Christ ("the gifts we have consumed") are indeed gifts in the Spirit (since the bread and wine were transformed by the power of the Spirit). Having feasted on those gifts touched by the Spirit, we can rightly petition the Lord to make us "always be aflame with the same Spirit" that was poured out on the gifts, the same Spirit also "wondrously poured out" on the Apostles.

A formula for Solemn Blessing is suggested, the formula titled "The Holy Spirit" (number 8 under "Blessings at the End of Mass and Prayers over the People"), and it would be good to use this formula. Since it is Pentecost, the solemn dismissal with the double Alleluia returns for use one last time before Easter Time next year.

◆ Mass during the Day: As with either the extended form or the simple form of the Vigil Mass, the Mass during the Day provides an ideal occasion to use the Rite for the Blessing and Sprinkling of Water, found in Appendix II at the back of the Missal, especially if your parish has been doing this on all of the Sundays of Easter Time, and strong consideration should be given to this. Remember that this rite takes the place of the Penitential Act. The Gloria immediately follows the prayer said by the priest at the end of the Rite.

In the Collect for this Mass, the universality of the gifts of the Spirit is emphasized as we ask God to "sanctify your whole Church in every people and nation." Additionally, we ask that the Spirit who was at work "when the Gospel was first proclaimed" still fill the hearts of believers.

In the Prayer over the Offerings we pray for the Spirit to do something very specific for us in this liturgy: that he "may reveal to us more abundantly the hidden mystery of this sacrifice." In other words, we are asking the Spirit to help us to enter more deeply into the mystery we are celebrating and to help us to understand better the meaning of what we do at this Eucharist. With such insight and understanding, we can be led into all truth — not only in terms of what we do at liturgy, but also in terms of the meaning of all of life.

The text for the Preface, both with and without musical notation, is proper for today and is given right there at the place in the Missal along with the other texts for the Mass during the Day. See above for commentary on the Preface, as well as for notes concerning the proper insert if Eucharistic Prayer I is used.

The Prayer after Communion communicates to us a dynamic quality of the ongoing power of God conveyed through the Eucharist, a heavenly gift bestowed upon the Church; the prayer asks "that the gift of the Holy Spirit poured out upon her may retain all its force." If we are open to such heavenly gifts, then the spiritual food we receive will gain us the "abundance of eternal redemption." The way our Eucharistic celebrations on earth nourish us in our pilgrimage toward the heavenly banquet can never be forgotten.

The formula titled "The Holy Spirit" (number 8 under "Blessings at the End of Mass and Prayers over the People") is suggested for use as the final blessing, and it would be good to do so. Remember that since it is Pentecost, the solemn dismissal with the double Alleluia is used today, one last time before Easter Time next year.

Other Ideas

Chances are, this will be the last week for your parish choir before summer vacation. If so, be sure to recognize and thank them for their diligent service in enhancing the liturgy of the Church. Announce any times for special Memorial Day services and include a "prayer for graveside" in the bulletin or on the order of worship.

ORDINARY TIME (DURING SUMMER AND FALL)

The Meaning

AFTER our full participation in the forty days of Lent, the three days of the Sacred Paschal Triduum, and the fifty days of Easter Time, we now return to counting or numbering the weeks, not the days, of the liturgical year. Ordinary Time, which will take us through the summer and fall, comprises the thirty or so weeks that are not marked by major feasts. According to the *Universal Norms on the Liturgical Year and the General Roman Calendar,* "besides the times of year that have their own distinctive character, there remain in the yearly cycle thirty-three or thirty-four weeks in which no particular aspect of the mystery of Christ is celebrated, but rather the mystery of Christ itself is honored in its fullness, especially on Sundays. This period is known as Ordinary Time " (UNLY, 43).

As we are often reminded, the naming of this liturgical time is from the Latin *ordo*, which refers both to a counting or numbering and an order. While ordinary may suggest something usual or customary, this liturgical time is significant for our continued growth in faith, both as individuals who continue to be transformed by our observance of the liturgical year and as a community that seeks to conform to the light, life, and love revealed to us by Jesus. Ordinary Time allows us to integrate our experiences of Lent through Pentecost. Through the Scriptures, we learn more about the life of Jesus and the early Church; through our observance of various feasts and solemnities, we learn more about the saints, our Catholic tradition, and the Church community over time.

Understanding the long span of Ordinary Time in this way helps us to see its rich potential for the faith community. In addition to major solemnities (Most Holy Trinity; Most Holy Body and Blood of Christ (*Corpus Christi*); Our Lord Jesus Christ, King of the Universe) and feasts of the Lord (Transfiguration; Exaltation of the Holy Cross), we will celebrate and honor Mary on the Solemnity of the Assumption and throughout the months of May and October. These observances, along with the feast days of the saints, nurture our own desire to live as faithful Christians and as active participants in the Church. They help us to focus on our liturgical prayer life throughout the year, until we come to November 29, 2015, when we will once again count our days as we begin a new year of grace.

The Lectionary for Mass

PREPARE yourself to spend time with two very gifted storytellers! The vivid and often pointed descriptions of the ministry of Jesus offered in the Gospel accounts of Mark and Luke make the twenty-six weeks of Ordinary Time in the summer and fall anything but "ordinary," as we will see.

The First Readings in these weeks between Pentecost and the start of a new liturgical year in Advent offer twenty stories from the Old Testament and sixteen from the New. Many of the Old Testament offerings reveal the roots of the laws about which Jewish authorities are challenging Jesus. Some offer stories of ancestors in faith who are held up as examples to the Apostles and other disciples, such as Jonah.

The Epistles draw from Paul's letters to the communities at Corinth, Collosae, Thessalonica, and Rome. We hear Paul's passion for his ministry and his commitment to the successful development of these small but growing groups of Christians. (There were, for example, probably about 200 people to whom he wrote the letter to the Corinthians; during his lifetime, there were never more than the equivalent of today's largest Catholic parishes in the entire world!) Aware of their struggles but convicted by his hope in Christ and his faith in them, the letters temper firm direction with compassion for the challenges they are facing.

Each day's psalm offers refrains that amplify the meaning of both the First Reading and the Gospel. Sometimes, we hear just two or three verses of an extremely long psalm, such as Psalm 119. We hear a number of the psalms that served in the Temple liturgy and many that speak to the precious centrality of the Temple in the life of Israel. These illuminate the conflicts between Jesus, the Pharisees, and others regarding Jewish pious practice, including the practices of the Temple.

Our intimate daily walk through the Gospel accounts of Mark and Luke offers vivid descriptions of the day-to-day preaching and teaching of Jesus, including many of his most compelling parables. We also see him grappling with challengers, hearing each Evangelist's account of key altercations. We see him affirming but also expanding the teachings of Judaism, and also hear of the episodes in which his understanding of God's law is either applauded or critiqued.

We also hear Jesus speak about what it means to follow him—the practical realities, such as care for each other and those in need, and the challenging elements, like the unavoidable fact that we must carry his Cross. In the resistance and slow understanding of the disciples, we find ourselves: people in need of his love, his instruction, and his promise; often confused or resistant, but still listening. Jesus's critique of those who preach religion at the expense of God's mercy and those who choose comfort over following him are relevant to all who would bring his message to those in need in our own age.

The Roman Missal

ORDINARY Time resumes after Easter Time with the Tenth Week in Ordinary Time, starting on the Monday after Pentecost. *The Roman Missal* notes that each Sunday in Ordinary Time has its own proper Collect, Prayer over the Offerings, and Prayer after Communion, as well as Entrance and Communion Antiphons. There are no formularies for ferial weekdays. (Note: since there are no formularies for the Thirty-Fourth Sunday in Ordinary Time, orations for weekday Masses may come from the page with the title "Thirty-Fourth Week in Ordinary Time.")

Continue to explore the rich options in the Missal for weekdays by using the orations not only from the previous Sunday, but from any Sunday in Ordinary Time whose prayers seem to be relevant to the readings or to the life of the worshiping community. Also continue to use the Masses for Various Needs and Occasions and Votive Masses from time to time, again with an eye toward the spiritual good of the community. There are some rich themes that can serve to powerfully connect the celebration of the Eucharist with the everyday faith life of believers: there are Masses "For the Nation or State" (#21), "For the Preservation of Peace and Justice" (#30), "For Charity" (#40), and "For Giving Thanks to God" (#49). Don't forget to also include "For Ministers of the Church" (#8; particularly if your parish is going through some form of ministry renewal or recruitment, as many do in the fall) and "For Vocations to Holy Orders" (#9).

The Eucharistic Prayers for Masses of Reconciliation should also be used from time to time, and would be appropriate with Masses "For Reconciliation" (#16) and "For the Forgiveness of Sins" (#38), for example.

We are contemporary disciples of Jesus; we are also his Church, his presence in our world today. The feast of the Dedication of the Lateran Basilica on November 9 speaks not only of this splendid cathedral in Rome, but also of our own reality as Church (see especially the Second Reading for this day). We are the dwelling place of God—such has God made us, so we must become. It is an awesome responsibility and challenge for us to become what we are called to be. The Scriptures, particularly those found in the Lectionary for Mass, are a primary instrument in our formation. May this Ordinary Time of the liturgical year be for us an extraordinary time of becoming who we are as individuals and as Church.

Children's Liturgy of the Word

◆ SUMMER: While parishes might put the children's Liturgy of the Word on hiatus during the summer months due to vacations, continuing the dismissal of the children assures continuity throughout the year. Even if the children's Liturgy of the Word is not celebrated during the summer months, summer provides a good opportunity to spend time evaluating how well the children's Liturgy of the Word is proceeding and to engage in ongoing education and formation of those involved in the children's Liturgy of the Word. Informal meetings with prayer leaders over the summer months to discuss the readings and work on presentation skills are a good way to prepare for the fall. Practicing giving reflections to each other and getting positive feedback can only help prayer leaders hone their skills. This is the time to order the resource *Children's Liturgy of the Word 2015–2016: A Weekly Resource* from LTP for each member of the children's Liturgy of the Word team including the priests and deacons. Other recourses such as LTP's *Celebrating the Lectionary* or *Celebrating Sunday for Catholic Families*, aid prayer leaders in formulating reflections and understanding the Scriptures as related to children.

◆ SUMMER READINGS: The first two Sundays in the period of Ordinary Time immediately following Pentecost celebrate two important solemnities, the Solemnity of the Most Holy Trinity and the Solemnity of the Most Holy Body and Blood of Christ (*Corpus Christi*). These two solemnities celebrate what are probably the most important dogmas of the Catholic faith, that of Three Persons in One God—Father, Son, and Spirit—and the reality of the Eucharist as the Real Presence of Christ. The Sundays of Ordinary Time pick up with the Eleventh Sunday on the Sunday following *Corpus Christi*. The Gospel stories from Mark focus on the ministry and miracles of Jesus. Children love miracle stories and these stories tell of Jesus's great compassion for people. Since the Gospel according to Mark is the shortest of the four Gospel accounts, during Year B, beginning with the Seventeenth Sunday and ending with the Twenty-First Sunday, we hear from the Gospel according to John. The readings are taken from the sixth chapter, the "Bread of Life Discourse." These beautiful and important readings may be challenging to explain to children but they are significant because they point to the identity of Christ and especially speak of his presence in the Eucharist.

◆ SUMMER ENVIRONMENT: Entering into Ordinary Time will again present a marked contrast in the worship environment both in the church or larger worship space and in the children's space where their Liturgy of the Word is celebrated. The liturgical color for Ordinary Time is green as it was during the winter period. Recall that green represents growth and hope. Unlike winter however, the image of growth is more prominent during this time of year, especially if children bring flowers from their home gardens to decorate the space. Reduced numbers of children in attendance during the summer months due to vacation season may necessitate creating a smaller area within the children's worship space, always making sure the space is welcoming for visitors over the summer.

◆ SUMMER MUSIC: Summer is a time when many music ministers go on vacation and it may be more difficult to consult with someone regarding the choice of music. *Children's Liturgy of the Word: A Weekly Resource* from LTP gives suggestions, or consult with the music director before summer begins for ideas. Young visitors who may not be familiar with the acclamations or seasonal psalm may necessitate a brief rehearsal after the children enter the worship space.

◆ FALL: As the fall approaches and children get ready to go back to school, the parish should be ready to welcome the children back. For the children, it is a time of new beginnings. In the parish it is a time for new beginnings as well, as there may be changes in the pastoral staff, parish music programs are starting up again, and new people may be involved in the children's Liturgy of the Word. In addition, some of our regular children may now be of an age where they no longer are dismissed, but new children will be coming to participate in the Liturgy of the Word for the first time. The few weeks prior to the start is a good time to re-introduce the children's Liturgy of the Word to the

parish via the bulletin or parish website, a brief announcement, or flyers sent home through the parish school or the religious education office. If there are parent meetings ask for a few moments to present it to the parents and ask for volunteers to help as chaperones, to help with the environment or to learn how to become prayer leaders. It will be good to consult *Children's Liturgy of the Word for 2015–2016: A Weekly Resource* (LTP) for more information on preparation for the children's Liturgy of the Word. It's a good idea to have a copy of both publications for all on your parish liturgy preparation team in addition to those who work on the children's Liturgy of the Word.

◆ FALL READINGS: Beginning with the Twenty-Second Sunday we return to the Gospel according to Mark and begin to enter into the fall months of Ordinary Time. In the Gospel accounts of the next few months we learn what is needed to live as followers of Christ, concluding with signs of the end times preparing to lead us into Advent. Christ the King ends Ordinary Time focusing on Jesus as the King of the Universe.

From the Twenty-Second to the Twenty-Sixth Sunday we hear an almost continuous reading from the Letter of James. In his letters, James also teaches his readers what is needed to live as Christ's followers in a straightforward manner. If only one reading in addition to the Gospel is chosen for the children's Liturgy of the Word, selecting the readings from this letter might be the better choice; it is simple enough that children can understand, especially if using the Lectionary for Masses with Children in your sessions.

◆ FALL ENVIRONMENT: When the fall approaches, especially if the Liturgy of the Word with Children was not celebrated during the summer, it is time to evaluate the children's space to make sure it is welcoming, safe, and arranged in such a way that the children will be actively engaged. If area rugs or mats are used for sitting, do some need to be replaced or cleaned? How accessible is the room for children with disabilities? If someone other than a team member sets up the space, such as a sacristan or member of the parish staff, make sure that a diagram or written instructions are available to ensure the space is ready before Mass begins. Remember this is being used as a worship space even if the space is normally used as a classroom or meeting room.

During the fall, utilizing symbols of harvest helps remind the children of the great gifts that

God has bestowed upon his people and our need to offer him praise and thanksgiving. Cloths and banners are still green but switching to a different shade of green changes the environment a bit but still keeps with the liturgical season.

◆ FALL MUSIC: As fall approaches check with the music director to find out if new acclamations or hymns will be introduced to the assembly during the fall. If the parish has a school it is a good idea to work with the music teacher when selecting music. If there is a particular acclamation or song that is sung as the children are dismissed, this is a good time to make a change making sure it is something that the entire assembly can easily sing without resorting to picking up a hymnal. An acclamation or hymn refrain is a good choice. Make sure the music is only long enough to accompany the dismissal of the children.

The Saints

SOME find this stretch of Ordinary Time long and boring, which is somewhat understandable, since it lasts longer than the seasons of Advent, Christmas, Lent, Triduum, and Easter combined! Still, "boring" is hardly appropriate, particularly considering the feasts of the saints and of the Lord that fall during these summer and autumn months. The two midsummer solemnities are so often overlooked in pastoral practice: the Nativity of Saint John the Baptist (June 24) and Sts. Peter and Paul (July 29).

John the Baptist is undoubtedly one of the most important saints in the calendar. "Among those born of women, no one is greater than John" (Luke 7:28), Jesus himself tells us. We celebrate him liturgically three times: in the womb (Visitation), at his birth (Nativity), and at his death (Passion) — not to mention his obvious presence in the Lectionary. Of these three, it is John's birth that receives the highest honor by the Church's calendar; how very unusual! There is something about his birth that is greater even than his death.

Peter and Paul — where to begin? We can all trace our faith to these Apostles: the Jews to Peter, the Gentiles to Paul. Again, each has his own individual feast (the Chair of Peter, February 22, and the Conversion of Paul, January 25), but again these are ranked lower than their corporate

celebration here. Not to undervalue the work of the other Apostles, but it was fundamentally through the leadership of these two men that God brought Christianity to the world. How could we fail to honor their memory, to call upon their intercession!

Both are solemnities, observances in the highest degree. When these solemnities fall on a Sunday, they are to be celebrated in place of the Sunday's liturgy! Yet when they fall on a weekday, how often do they receive no more fanfare than an optional memorial? Sure, the congregation is surprised by the Gloria and Creed, but that is all. How sad!

These saints are everyone's patrons in a special, particular way, and making this present to unsuspecting parishioners is a great grace. What a celebration it would be if, for instance, a parish hosted a bonfire on St. John's Eve (see the *Directory on Popular Piety and the Liturgy*, 225) — building community by celebrating the advent of him who was first to announce the Light of the World!

The Liturgy of the Hours

IF during Easter your parish scheduled the communal praying of the Liturgy of the Hours, seriously consider maintaining this practice during Ordinary Time. When celebrating the Hours, the faithful exercise the common priesthood of their Baptism, offering praise to God and interceding on behalf of the Church and of the world. With concerted effort, the parish could strive to establish the Liturgy of the Hours as a regular practice. For example, if there is a day during the week when daily Mass is not celebrated, this is a perfect opportunity to pray Morning Prayer. Likewsie, a parish could commit itself to celebrate Evening Prayer one day a week. It could be scheduled so that people are able to participate as they come home from work. This liturgy gives the Church the opportunity to praise God for the blessings of the day and to ask for his blessing during the coming night.

The Rite of Christian Initiation of Adults

DISMISSALS of catechumens continue on each Sunday. Consider inviting readers from the parish to lead the dismissal catechesis and the breaking open of the word. In communities where readers are those of every race, language, and way of life, the catechumens will be enriched by the readers' lived experience with the proclamation of the word and their own cultural insights and lived experiences.

Now is a good time to provide training and formation for sponsors and godparents. Consider providing copies of LTP's *Guide for Sponsors, Fourth Edition* by Ronald Lewinski. Help sponsors and godparents explore the difference, in discerning their role, when sponsoring catechumens or candidates.

Be sure someone in the parish is free to meet with those inquiring into the life of the Catholic Church. Anytime a person comes to our door we need to welcome, embrace, and include them in a process. To say "come back in September when our program starts up again" must no longer be the norm. Take your lead from Pope Francis who posed the following question to the faithful, in an address on May 29, 2013, "What do I do to make the church a community where everyone feels welcomed and understood, everyone feels the mercy and love of God who renews life?" Be ready to welcome people at all times during the year when they knock on the door.

Remember that the RCIA explains that the Rite of Acceptance into the Order of Catechumens may be celebrated at any time throughout the liturgical year. Perhaps scheduling two or three dates throughout the year to celebrate this rite would be a good thing.

Provide ongoing formation and catechesis for the liturgical assembly with bulletin inserts or e-mail blasts. Consider joining Team RCIA (www.teamrcia.com/) where you will find articles, video clips, and courses on the RCIA.

The Sacraments of Initiation

THE ritual Masses for the sacraments can be celebrated on any weekday that is not a solemnity. Baptisms may be celebrated on any Sunday in Ordinary Time, preferably during a parish Mass so that the community may be present and the relationship between Baptism and Eucharist is clearly evident. The Sacrament of Confirmation and first Holy Communion may also be celebrated during a Sunday parish liturgy, since all sacraments are ecclesial and communal celebrations.

The Rite of Penance

CONSIDER scheduling a catechetical fair on the Sacrament of Penance. Invite catechists and those who work preparing children for first reconciliation and provide them with stimulating catechesis about the rite. Expect to hear questions such as, "I have never heard a proclamation of the Scripture before celebrating the sacrament individually with a priest. When was that introduced?" "When did they change the Act of Contrition?" Use the *Rite of Penance* and the *Catechism of the Catholic Church* as your starting point for preparing the catechists. Develop materials and handouts that can be shared with parents, the first teachers of their children.

With our catechesis we need to think harder about the interrelation of spiritual direction, pastoral counseling, other therapeutic practices, and sacramental reconciliation. People should be instructed that when they entered the chapel for reconciliation they should be conscientious of others who are waiting to celebrate the sacrament and not extend their time with the confessor that may in turn pose an undue burden on others. Priests or other spiritual counselors need to be available to meet the needs of people who are facing a more serious situation. Throughout the year in the bulletin, the parish website, and even during a Homily at Mass let people know that they can have access to the priest or another minister in the parish to talk to about important issues. Keep extending an invitation to those who have been away, hurt, or alienated by the Church. Consider posting the times of when the sacrament is celebrated in neighboring parishes on the church door each Saturday.

The Rite of Marriage

THE Holy Trinity is a difficult mystery to explain. Three distinct Persons, yet one substance; one God, with no beginning or end. The Father is, was, always has been, and though the Son and the Spirit were before time, they are yet from the Father (since one cannot speak of "before" and "after" without time).

Why such a lofty theological discussion in the section for Marriage? Because married love is an image of the love and communion of the Holy Trinity. The Father willed the Son into being so as to love him. The love between them was so strong that it could not be contained in what we would consider an ordinary manner, but burst forth into a third Person, the Holy Spirit.

The love between a husband and wife is so strong, so blessed, that it likewise produces a third person — and sometimes a fourth, and a fifth, and a sixth. . . . The Father blesses their love, which resembles his, with a participation in his creating power.

How lovely would be a wedding celebrated on Trinity Sunday! Just a perfect confluence of theological concepts that explain each other more perfectly.

The Pastoral Care of the Sick

DESPITE parishioners and staff members disappearing for vacations, this stretch of Ordinary Time may well provide a perfect opportunity for a parish-wide service of the Anointing of the Sick — since not all who are sick are unable to come into the church for a special occasion! This, of course, requires extra catechesis about the appropriate recipient of the sacrament, but there is no rush, no upcoming major events to distract from whatever is needed. It can be accomplished leisurely, with great flexibility to the needs of the parish.

The Order of Christian Funerals

IF the parish priest or staff members are away during the summer months be sure someone is available to minister to families at the time of death. Arrange for priests in neighboring parishes or institutions to be on call for celebrating the funeral Mass. Be pastorally present to people before talking about details such as financial obligations or the time for scheduling the funeral.

November is the time when the Church rehearses for death. It is the time for us to tell the stories that feed our symbolic life, the time to learn about death in a less demanding drama than when we are faced with the death of a sister or a brother in our midst. The Sunday Gospel accounts of November offer us a chilling testimony to the serious side of the future. November is the time to encourage people to examine their own funeral preparations. This is a good opportunity to create parish funeral packets for parishioners and prepare teams to help households, especially the elderly and infirmed, fill out these forms. LTP's *Now and at the Hour of our Death: Instructions Concerning My Death and Funeral* includes information about living wills, durable powers of attorney, funerals, burial, and cremation. It is a must-have resource to put in the hands of every family in the parish. Encourage families to give the book as a gift to family members and friends during the upcoming Christmas season.

The Commemoration of All the Faithful Departed (All Souls' Day) is celebrated on November 2, following the Solemnity of All Saints, November 1. The choice of November 2 is traditionally attributed to St. Odilo, the fifth abbot of Cluny. It was established as a time to offer special prayers and to sing the Office of the Dead. The modern view of death derives in part from pre-Hispanic times. The Aztecs played a very important role in the development of this tradition. Through their history this festival emerged as one of intricacy and varied interpretation. The Spanish Conquest of 1521 brought about the combination of Catholic approaches and indigenous beliefs. The Day of the Dead was revealed as a result of a mixture of pre-Spanish/Indian ritual beliefs and was joined with ritual and dogma of the Catholic Church. In some cases, people celebrating this holiday will attend Mass and pray for the faithful departed; while still others will go to the cemetery to visit, bless, and decorate graves. Many customs are associated with the Day of the Dead celebration. In the home an altar is made with an offering of food upon it. It is believed that the dead partake of the food in spirit and the living eat it later. The "ofrendas" or offerings are beautifully arranged with flowers, marigolds (*cempazúchitl*) which are the traditional flower of the dead. There is a candle placed for each dead soul, and they are adorned in some manner. Incense is also used. Mementos, photos, and other remembrances of the dead are also adorning the ofrenda. Papier-mâché and sugar skulls are popular, as are cardboard coffins from which a skeleton can be made to jump out. In some of the rural villages of Mexico images of angels, birds, chalices, and crosses are also used. Consider building an "altar of the dead" in your own community and invite parishioners to bring photos of deceased loved ones and place them on the altar. Ask them to tape their name and phone number to the back of the photos so they can be returned at the end of November.

At the conclusion of the funeral liturgy is the Final Commendation and Farewell. This rite is a final farewell by the members of the community, an act of respect for one of their members, whom they entrust to the tender and merciful embrace of God (see OCF, 146). The rite contains silence and prayer and reverencing with incense while the Song of Farewell is sung. Since the Song of Farewell is the most important song to be sung during the funeral liturgy it is important for the whole community to know the song by heart and join in singing it at the funeral. Consider using the song as the closing song during the Sundays of November at the Sunday Eucharist, so that the whole community becomes familiar with the text and tune. The incensing of the body signifies respect for the body as the temple of the Holy Spirit and the body may also be sprinkled with holy water as a reminder that through Baptism the person was marked for eternal life (see OCF, 147). Before the procession to the place of committal (see OCF, 176) the priest or deacon says: "in peace let us take our brother/sister to his/her place of rest."

Consider putting together a funeral choir, perhaps of retired parishioners, who can serve as a core group to assist in the assembly's full participation in the funeral liturgy. Likewise provide good hospitality by providing a funeral lunch or reception following the funeral. Consider scheduling funerals at the same time as the daily morning Mass, or cancelling daily morning Mass when there is a funeral, and encourage these faithful ones to attend the funeral liturgy.

The Book of Blessings

RECALL that many of the orders of blessings found in the *Book of Blessings* are not limited to any one liturgical season. Most, in fact, can be celebrated throughout the year, whenever the need arises within the life of a parish or the lives of individual parishioners. Because of this, parishes can be quite creative in terms of how they integrate these blessings into the liturgical and ritual life of the parish.

As the "General Introduction" to the *Book of Blessings* reminds us, orders of blessing "should truly contribute to God's praise and glory and should serve to better God's people" (BB, 11). Thus, their use in the liturgical life of the parish should be a strong consideration throughout the liturgical year. "At all times and in every situation," the "General Introduction" reminds us, "the faithful have an occasion for praising God through Christ in the Holy Spirit, for calling on divine help, and for giving thanks in all things" (BB, 13).

The Liturgical Environment

REVISING the environment is the natural environment, the summer is a time of (slow) growth, warmth, and plenty of light. The themes of "light in the darkness" and "anticipation" fade as we continue to count the Sundays of Ordinary Time. After the half-year marathon from Advent through the Paschal seasons, somewhat of a slowing down is appropriate. It can also provide time to reflect on how the liturgical environment worked in the previous year along with enough time to prepare to do things differently if there are areas requiring improvement. Scheduling a meeting of your group to discuss the seasons one at a time, with pictures, if you have them, can give you time both to thank people for their work during the year and to consider what improvements you might want to make in the next year. Moreover, many organizations finalize the budget in the spring or summer, so if you are planning on making an unusual expense (such as a new set of vestments), this may be the time you need to get it into a budget and find the money to pay for it.

New items for the liturgical environment can be quite pricey, especially those of better quality. If you have talented tailors or seamstresses in your community, they are not difficult to make, although they are somewhat different from other sewing projects with which most contemporary sewers are familiar. It can also be difficult to find high-quality fabrics in a sufficient width, although the internet has made this somewhat easier. Fabric woven for upholstery is usually woven wider, although it is often stiff or of materials which do not suit vestments. Many vestment manufacturers will sell you fabric by the yard if you inquire, although it can be quite pricey. If you decide to design vestments or paraments on your own, allow the color to be the primary symbol. Appliqué and embroidery can be quite distracting, and can overshadow the color of the season. Contrasting colors can be used for emphasis, but the primary color of the item should be the liturgical color of the season for which it is intended.

New non-fabric items can also be quite expensive, both because it is a small market and most of them are hand-made. Some church suppliers provide a consignment service for parishes or religious houses who are selling items they no longer need, and these can provide a more affordable source of such items, and reducing the waste of producing something new. If you are replacing your own liturgical items, consider donating the old ones to parishes that cannot afford new ones. Several charities facilitate such exchanges online, or you might ask those responsible for partnership relationships with parishes or dioceses if such items could be put to good use.

The summer can also be a good time to consider the liturgical spaces outside of the sanctuary. Are there improvements that can be made to the grounds to help the church be more welcoming to those who come to the liturgy? Are there places where you start processions that can be improved to better host those liturgies? What about the location of the altar of repose on Holy Thursday? Are there other liturgies which take place in other parts of your parish? How can they better host the liturgical actions?

Fall is not a different liturgical season than Ordinary Time in Summer, but it does have a different feeling and different emphases. Green continues to be the color of the season, but the space might begin to incorporate more other colors of the harvest season, especially with plants which are found in your region. The readings of Ordinary Time begin to be colored by more attention to the "last things" in the fall, especially as we enter the month of November with the Solemnities of All Saints (November 1), All Souls' (November 2), and move toward the Solemnity of Our Lord Jesus Christ, King of the Universe, which falls on the last Sunday before Advent (November 22 in 2015). Advent's double focus on the coming of Christ at Christmas and his coming finally to complete the redemption of all things is anticipated, at least in the second part, at the end of Ordinary Time. The end of the liturgical year draws our attention to the end of time, underlined by the harvest imagery of the readings and of the season.

Before we get there, however, fall brings a return to normalcy in parish life. School starts up, people are at church more regularly, and parish activities resume their normal rhythm. Energies are often high, but it is time to consider how the environment can help turn focus to the more triumphant and solemn emphases which are coming. Several feasts and traditional celebrations can be used to begin the turn toward the later emphases of the fall. The environment for these feasts need not be ornate. A simple cross, perhaps the one used for veneration on Good Friday, works for the Exaltation of the Cross, while simple white vestments and flowers would be appropriate for the angel feasts.

October is historically celebrated as the Month of the Holy Rosary and this is to be encouraged. However, as an extraliturgical devotion, the Rosary should not be overly emphasized in the liturgical environment, especially in ways that would distract from the central actions of hearing the word and receiving the sacrament. On October 7 (Memorial of Our Lady of the Rosary), it might receive somewhat more central emphasis, perhaps with the temporary addition of a statue of Our Lady of the Rosary to the church, perhaps with roses, especially if such additions are customary ways of celebrating feasts in your parish. The celebration is, however, a memorial, and should celebrated as such.

November's emphasis on memory of the departed faithful begins with its first days, and continues through the month. Many parishes set up a book where people can inscribe the names of those who have died for prayer. If this is done, it should be a book worthy of the task. A plastic three-ring binder with college-ruled notebook paper is not sufficient. A nicely-bound blank book could be used, or, perhaps, the three-ring could be covered in a fabric which coordinates with the vestments for All Souls' Day, and good-quality paper could be added. LTP published the *Book of the Names of the Dead* which provides an elegant way to record the names of those who have died. It should be displayed somewhere where it will be seen, but not interfere with the liturgy. Often, they are displayed at the back of the church or in the narthex, with a seven-day candle and some greenery. A careful, inviting setup can also encourage parishioners to inscribe the names of their loved ones and to browse the book and pray for those whose names are inscribed.

The Solemnity of Our Lord Jesus Christ, King of the Universe, was added to the liturgical calendar by Pius XI in 1925. It is a fitting celebration to the end of Ordinary Time and transitions nicely into the Advent call to prepare for the coming King. Christ's kingship is eschatological, already present in the Church but to be fulfilled for all things at the end, and so cannot be divorced entirely from the idea of the last things, for which harvest is an appropriate image. This solemnity gives a pre-vision of the coming fulfillment of the reign of Christ, which we will then spend Advent being asked to prepare for. It serves as both the fulfillment of the story as told throughout the liturgical year and as a transition back into Advent. In the United States, it often falls on the Sunday before or after Thanksgiving (in 2015, it is the Sunday prior), and can easily incorporate harvest themes, although they are not the central motif. In preparing the environment, consider how the liturgy acts as a foretaste of Christ's complete reign. How can that be made more clear? What other kingdoms are we called to renounce? What would that look like? How is your Eucharistic liturgy already the Kingdom of God? What does your parish need to repent of and renounce to follow Christ without hesitation? Can the environment support such choices?

The Liturgical Music

CONSIDER building a seasonal repertoire of the common psalms, 19, 27, 34, 63, 95, 100, 103, and 122, as found in the Lectionary at #175. These are the texts that appear in the Lectionary most frequently during Ordinary Time. They can be used as processional chants for entrance or Communion as well as the Responsorial Psalm. If you have Spanish speaking members in your assembly consider building a repertoire of bilingual psalms as well. You will find these collections of bilingual psalms especially helpful: "¡*Aclama, Tierra Entera*! / Sing, All You Lands!" (WLP) and "*Cantaré Eternamente* / For Ever I Will Sing": Volume I & II (OCP). GIA also publishes a number of bilingual psalms by Tony Alonso.

Ordinary Time is a fine period to review acclamations and service music for use with the assembly. Before introducing new service music or acclamations be sure that the current repertoire used in the parish is so well known that it falls on the lips of the assembly as a shout of joy because "ideally, the people should know the acclamations by heart and should be able to sing them readily, even without accompaniment" (STL, 115a).

Consider building a repertoire of bilingual, multilingual, and ethnic songs, hymns, acclamations, ostinatos, and litanies for use with your assembly. The music from Taizé (GIA) is a good place to start. OCP's music resource for contemplative prayer "Hear the Prayers That Rise" contains Taizé style music that can be easily learned by the assembly and help to build up this repertoire.

November is the time to strengthen the funeral repertoire of the community. The *Order of Christian Funerals* suggests that "efforts should be made to develop and expand the parish's repertoire for use at funerals" (OCF, 32). Begin by using a setting of Psalm 23 as the Communion chant for the four Sundays of November along with the "Song of Farewell" as the concluding song on the same Sundays. Since the "Song of Farewell" is the most important song to sing at the funeral, it will never be sung robustly until the entire assembly knows it well. Many beautiful settings of this ritual song exist including the eleventh century chant (Mode VII and Mode VIII), *In paradisum*, and, *Chorus, angelorum*. "Song of Farewell" by Ernie Sands (OCP), "Saints of God" by Richard Proulx

(GIA), and "Saints of God" by Steven Janco (GIA) are other versions of this sacred text. If you are in search for a musical setting of the intercessions for the funeral vigil that employs the text found in the ritual book consider the setting based on the *Dies Irae,* Chant Mode I, by Michael R. Prendergast (OCP).

During the summer months take time to study the liturgy documents. If you have not read *Sing to the Lord Music in Divine Worship* published by the United States Conference of Catholic Bishops, now would be a good time to do so. It is available as a single volume from the USCCB but it is also included in a compendium of liturgical documents from LTP (*The Liturgy Documents, Volume I*).

Remember that the most beautiful sound is that of the singing assembly. For all in parish musical leadership, it is essential to move away from any sound reinforcement once the people begin singing and let this unifying voice of the assembly join with the angelic hosts in proclaiming a new song to the Lord.

Liturgical Ministers

A PRIEST classmate once told me a story, with great excitement, about the altar server appreciation days he'd held at his previous parish. An essential part of his altar server program was consistently assuring these kids that they were important! They weren't just filling space; they were performing difficult tasks, the complexity of which increased as they climbed the "ranks." Twice a year, he'd host a big party for them all, to emphasize in a particular way the special nature of their ministry.

Before the festivities began, he would set up a table in the church basement, where the party was invariably held. And on that table he would place every single candle he could find — except, of course, for the few needed on the altar in the meantime. He would put two tapers next to the table, with a matchbook and a stopwatch. The pair of altar servers who lit, then snuffed all the candles in the shortest amount of time won the prize! Needless to say, the kids got a kick out of an adult encouraging them to play with fire, no matter the circumstance, and really seemed to get

the message that they were spending their Sunday mornings doing something really important.

Over the summer is the most difficult time to keep track of altar servers, between the lack of school structure and vacation season, but it can be a perfect time to take the server program "to the next level," whether that means giving some servers advanced training or just throwing a party with silly contests. Their ministry is tied to vocation, and supporting their ministry in a way that encourages discernment is an uncommon but good use of this part of Ordinary Time.

Devotions and Sacramentals

D EVOTIONS and popular piety comprise "all the rest" of the Church's prayers, everything the People of God pray that is not strictly liturgical. This does not mean, however, that it is good for the two types of prayer to be completely discrete, for through the liturgical year, the Church consecrates time itself.

Some of this connection is quite natural: for instance, most consecrations to the Blessed Virgin Mary aim to end on one of her feasts. Others are less obvious at first, and less commonly known, like the consecration to the Sacred Heart on the Solemnity of Our Lord Jesus Christ, King of the Universe. These prayers, though completely separate from the liturgy itself, help to bridge the gap between liturgy and ordinary life.

In a similar way, sacramentals extend the liturgical life of the Church into the workaday life of the Christian. One can pray with a blessed Rosary or prayer book; keep holy water in a little font in the house, as a reminder of its inhabitants' Baptism; slide a blessed crucifix in a drawer or secure it on the wall of an office; even use a dash of holy salt in one's cooking! These items are not to be used with superstition, as if all that's needed for the conversion of an irreligious child is to hide enough green scapulars under his bed; sacramentals are tangible reminders of the Lord's promise to take care of us, and of our pledge to continue to pray and intercede. Just as our words can enhance and deepen the prayers of our hearts, so can sacramentals intensify the prayers of our words.

The Parish and the Home

SUMMER: Warmer days coupled with vacation plans and school ending means that our bodies are ready to be nourished in playtime along with relationships being renewed. But, it also seems to mean that our spiritual lives can too easily take the backseat to our lives. In families, parents and children look forward to the lack of scheduled time without religious education and required meetings. Yet everyone needs to remember that now is also the time to nourish the mundane, the counted time between the big feasts in preparing our lives to rest in the presence of God. Being called indoors on a perfect day (or coming to Mass on a gracious morning which too easily pulls one to the golf course) is never desired. Our lives are to be tempered with grace, markers of faith that remind us who we are, even when we want to take a break from all the routine. While Easter has ended and the big feasts are over, the first three weeks of Ordinary time are bold reminders of our Catholic faith.

Consider Trinity Sunday—no other Christian faith starts and ends every single prayer with the Sign of the Cross. Sit with this simple act which is incredibly unique to us as Catholics. Look up the teaching of St. Patrick and even his full prayer, the *Lorica of St. Patrick*. We pray calling upon three Persons of one God, this is powerful.

The following week we are called to note another difference from our fellow Christian brothers and sisters. As Catholics we focus on the actual Body of Christ; we have crucifixes in our homes and wear them around our neck. Why? The Solemnity of the Most Holy Body and Blood of Christ allows us to settle into meaningful differences. Catholic children are taught to recognize Jesus's body on a cross, a very hard concept to teach to an innocent mind. We know that through his physical life on earth (playtime and friend time included) his body becomes our blessing and sustenance. In the transubstantiation of the bread and wine, our belief in the Eucharist not only sets us apart from other faith traditions, but also transforms us. On this day celebrate this depth of prayer and go back to the day of your first Eucharist. Does the white dress or suit with folded hands and simple faith still inspire you today?

Finally, though not celebrated on Sunday, remember the Feast of the Sacred Heart of Jesus. Jesus's heart burns in loving passion for us. As we go about our days in a slower pace at work (hopefully), relaxing by splashing waves of the ocean or at the pool on the weekends, find time to sit in the summer sun with recognition that you are deeply loved and held in a heart that desires to encompass all you are and desire to be. When we slow down we can fill our lives with distractions or choose moments to retire into the quietness of our soul to remind us of all we are called to do in this world, through him, with him, and in him. Mass does not leave us; the instructions of life still remain edged into our living steps.

As the routine of the year has now turned into possible leisure of the moment, time to honor each aspect becomes the recognized gift of prayer. St. Francis of Assisi once spoke that we are to be living prayer—not just people who do the rituals with reverence but that what we do in church becomes who we are at all times. We are fed in a home to give back to others. More than the barbecues and adult beverages that accompany recreational time, summertime can both feed us spiritually and allow us to be that blessing and gift to another. Find and name God so clearly in nature, in all living things. Encourage all those around you to stop, become keenly aware of the gift of time and love of Christ, to surrender to stillness, and then go on living and being God's gift back to the world.

◆ FALL: While fall does not "officially" begin until mid-September, living in any family unit means that by mid-August summer is ending and a new time begins. To transition from the rest of the summer into the usual busyness and inevitable chaos of the fall months, we need strength from above. Allow the cycle and feasts of the Church to continue to help you to pause with fuel to forge ahead with the schedule now filling in the calendar.

Amid busier days at work and weather slowly shifting and teasing us alternately with exceptionally warm days mingled with the cool days to come, find time to breathe and not forget the summer lessons. With the pace of life picking up, requirements come back from parish ministries to show up to classes, become a teacher, or commit to a new group or ministry. Parish staff members are called to remember that, like teachers assigning homework, there are strings of attachment pulling each person in many directions and the focus needs to remain on the essential, not the extravagant.

There aren't many notable feast days in this segment of ordinary time, for by the time we arrive at All Saint's Day and All Souls' day, most of consumer society has already pulled us into Christmas mode. It is still time to allow the soul to soak in the message of Jesus.

All Saint's Day reminds us that we are one of many who are called to worship God. The saints before us are our teachers and role models. Children in Catholic schools or religious education classes are usually called upon to research a saint. No matter our age, we are called to constantly grow to serve God through our words, in our choices, and in all our actions. This is what the saints show to us. Many of us have our favorite saint and this is a time to call upon their example in their prayer life to help us, but also to reach into the lives of other saints to inspire us to move forward in our spiritual walk.

Time will move quickly during this fall Ordinary Time and all too soon the intensity of Advent preparation will begin. Constantly pause in intentional prayer. Make sure your parish staff relishes the moments to nourish each other and to build the relationships that you will need to survive in the coming months of beautiful craziness in the liturgical year. Don't allow the natural busyness of contemporary life to consume you, for after all, as living saints, you are the models of faith-filled living to each member of the parish family.

Mass Texts

Summer

◆ DISMISSAL FOR CHILDREN'S LITURGY OF THE WORD

My dear children, it is summer,
and for many of you,
that means a vacation from school.
However, we never cease from praising God,
or growing closer to him.
So we continue to listen and share the Word of God.
During these weeks,
God continues to call his disciples,
and send them forth.
As you go listen to the Word of God,
be sure to look for God speaking around you
in nature and in all of life.

Go now, that the seed of God
may be planted deep within you.

◆ DISMISSAL FOR CATECHUMENS AND ELECT

My dear friends,
these weeks we exeperience many changes in environments
and hear and speak of wheat fields and mustard seeds.
Jesus calls us to follow him,
to take times of silence,
and to live lives worthy of the Gospel.
May you be strengthened in your attempts to bear fruit
and grow stronger in your faith.
May you never be discouraged,
and find the strength to turn to God in your need.
Take heart,
knowing that God can do great things
when we cannot.
Find your hope in him now.
Go in peace.

◆ INTRODUCTION TO THE MASS

May the peace of Christ be with you all. During these summer weeks, we hear much about nature in our readings. Vines and wheat, caring for the things God created, and human nature, as Jesus invites others to follow him. Because of the shortness of the Gospel according Mark, we will explore a portion of John's account for six weeks as we hear his "bread of life" discourse. Let us then enter into this liturgy with open ears and hearts, as we experience God in all whom we meet.

◆ UNIVERSAL PRAYER OR PRAYER OF THE FAITHFUL

Introduction

Vine and branches, loaves and fishes are just a few of the ways God leads and calls us nearer. And so we trust him as we offer these prayers.

Intercessions

1. For our Holy Father, Pope Francis, that through his example of simplicity and poverty he may teach us all to share our loaves and fishes, we pray to the Lord: Lord, hear our prayer.

2. For government leaders, that they may strive to make sure that all people have their fill to eat, warm shelters, and enough to care for their basic needs, we pray to the Lord: Lord, hear our prayer.

3. For farmers and ranchers and those who produce our foods, and all who work in the food service and grocery industries and in food shelters, that they know the sacred task to which they are called, we pray to the Lord: Lord, hear our prayer.

4. For all travelers, that they may reach their destinations safely, and for the safety of all road construction workers, we pray to the Lord: Lord, hear our prayer.

5. For those who keep us safe, they in turn may be protected and return home safely, we pray to the Lord: Lord hear our prayer.

Conclusion

God of all creation,
you have made us to serve and love you.
Draw us closer to you,
that we may praise you in all our actions and our
    words.
Hear our fervent prayers and answer them as you
    will.
Through Christ our Lord.
Amen.

Fall

◆ DISMISSAL FOR CHILDREN'S LITURGY OF THE WORD

Dear children,
just as your lives and rhythms may be in transition
as you return to school or begin new activities,
we begin to see changes in our Scriptures,
and in Jesus's life.
Jesus is telling us about the end times
and the direction his ministry will take.
We invite you now to journey with him
as he travels toward Jerusalem.
Go in peace.

◆ DISMISSAL FOR CATECHUMENS

As we break open the life of Christ
and the life of being a Christian,
we know that it is not easy.
Some weeks we will hear how difficult it was
for Jesus and his disciples on the journey.
As those preparing to enter into a deeper
    relationship with the Church,
you will run into naysayers,
or those who will challenge you for your faith.
Be strong and courageous,
taking up your cross and following Christ your
    Lord.
Go in peace.

◆ INTRODUCTION TO THE MASS

In these dark days, we begin to experience the eschatological nature of the Scriptures as they point us toward the "already but not yet." Jesus does not show fear as he approaches Jerusalem and his death. Rather, he continues to turn to God in prayer for strength and support. Passing on his message to others becomes more and more imperative. Let us then enter into this liturgy with that same sense of urgency, as we strive to follow Jesus ever more closely, in this world and the next.

◆ UNIVERSAL PRAYER OR PRAYER OF THE FAITHFUL

Introduction

As we follow Jesus toward Jerusalem, we offer our prayers now that we may find the strength for the journey.

Intercessions

1. For Pope Francis, and all Church leaders, that they may have the wisdom to lead us all toward our destiny, we pray to the Lord: Lord, hear our prayer.

2. For government officials, that they may respect life in all its forms and govern and legislate accordingly, we pray to the Lord: Lord, hear our prayer.

3. For students, educators, and catechists, that they may always teach the laws of love and instill in all the desire to follow Jesus, we pray to the Lord: Lord, hear our prayer.

4. For those who are called to the priesthood or religious life, for those who are called to Marriage, and those who are called to live the single life, that each may take up daily the cross that has been been prepared for them, and embrace Jesus's direction in their lives, we pray to the Lord: Lord, hear our prayer.

5. For all those who serve as volunteers at ministries within the parish, and for all those whose parish life flows out into their ministries and volunteering in the larger community, that they may always remember to return to Jesus as their source of strength and inspiration, we pray to the Lord: Lord, hear our prayer.

6. For our parish that we may always find examples and inspiration in the Word of God, the Eucharist, and Christ working in each of us, we pray to the Lord: Lord, hear our prayer.

Conclusion

O God of wonder,
you call us to serve you and be your people of faith.
At times it is difficult to respond.
The way seems dark and filled with trials.
Instill in us the courage, strength, and hope to
respond with joy.
Hear the prayers we offer now
and know those which we hold deep in the silence
of our hearts.
Through Christ our Lord.
Amen.

May
Month of Our Lady

Except for the days of the First and Thirty-Fourth Weeks in Ordinary Time, The Roman Missal does not provide prayer texts for the weekdays in Ordinary Time. Instead, priest celebrants and those who prepare the liturgy may select from among the prayers provided for the Sundays in Ordinary Time. Your diocesan Ordo will provide suggestions. On days celebrated as optional memorials, prayers may be from the Sundays of Ordinary Time (for the ferial weekday), the Proper of Saints, or the Commons. Always refer first to the Proper of Saints—it is there you will find guidance for selecting from the Commons. On all Saturdays during Ordinary Time that do not have an obligatory memorial, a memorial of the Blessed Virgin Mary may be celebrated. The prayers may be selected from the Common of the Blessed Virgin Mary. Commentary below is only provided for Sundays, solemnities, feasts, and obligatory memorials.

MON 25 (#347) green
Weekday

Optional Memorials of St. Bede the Venerable, Priest and Doctor of the Church / white; St. Gregory VII, Pope / white; St. Mary Magdalene de' Pazzi, Virgin / white

The Lectionary for Mass

◆ FIRST READING: The Wisdom literature gives us poetry and wise teaching, but not much in the way of plot. Notice how the beginning and ending of this passage express almost exactly the same idea: that God is merciful to those who repent. The lines in between tell us why we should return to God—because to praise God is a privilege of the living.

◆ RESPONSORIAL PSALM 32 is a call to just that kind of conversion and praise spoken of in the First Reading.

◆ GOSPEL: For the people of Jesus's time, wealth was seen as a sign of God's favor. No wonder, then, that this good young man is dismayed when Jesus tells him to leave all of that behind and follow him; no wonder the disciples are "amazed" (Mark 10:24). Why does Jesus say it is so difficult for the rich to enter the kingdom? In the context of the Gospel, this passage immediately follows the injunction to accept the kingdom as a child (see Mark 10:15). We are to depend on God as a child depends on its parents—absolutely and unquestioningly. The "rich" are those whose good things—whether money, or talent, or even good works—have become a way for them to measure God's favor—a burden that prevents them from wholehearted acceptance of God's way.

The Roman Missal

Sourcebook only provides Missal commentary for obligatory observances. If celebrating any of the optional memorials throughout Ordinary Time, first refer to the Proper of Saints on the date of celebration.

Today's Saints

The life of the Venerable Bede (672/73–735), a doctor of the Church, illustrates that one can transform the Church from the quiet of a monastery. As a Benedictine monk at the Abbey of Jarrow in England, he devoted his life to scholarly pursuits, including the study of Scripture, the composition of commentaries based on the ideas of Church Fathers, and extensive research and writing regarding the history of the Church in England. He is credited with educating over 600 monks and popularizing the use of AD (*Anno Domini*—in the year of our Lord) to refer to the Christian era. Although known as "Venerable," this title is not in reference to the ranking of canonization. Saint Bede was canonized in 1935.

Saint Gregory VII (c. 1028–1085) joined the Benedictine monks, but was eventually called beyond the cloister to serve the larger Church as pope. Recognized as one of the greatest reformer popes, Saint Gregory instituted what is known as the Gregorian reform. Through this reform he wanted to end rampant and widespread abuses in the Church; in particular, nepotism, clerical marriage, and lay interference in the appointment of bishops and abbots. He was removed from the papal office twice by bishops under the control of Emperor Henry IV due to his arduous efforts to eliminate the power of temporal rulers in Church matters.

Mary Magdalene de' Pazzi (1566–1607), daughter of a noble Florentine family, was a Carmelite mystic who prayed tirelessly for the Church.

TUE 26 (#348) white
Memorial of St. Philip Neri, Priest

The Lectionary for Mass

◆ FIRST READING: The Old Testament is full of sacrifice, which was the center of temple worship. But it is also full of passages like this one, which reminds us that the sacrifice God loves best is faithful love and obedience. It is not the amount we give back to God that matters—what matters is that we give in proportion to what God has given us.

◆ RESPONSORIAL PSALM 50 expresses the same sentiment. We hear God speaking in this psalm. The people are observant of the letter of the law, with their burnt offerings—but God wants instead a sacrifice of praise.

Today's Gospel comes on the heels of yesterday's account of the rich young man, who "went away sad, for he had many possessions"

(Mark 10:22). Peter and the others have indeed given up everything to follow Jesus — and the unspoken question is easy enough to hear — what then? What will their reward be? Jesus responds to their unspoken question: the rewards are unimaginable, but the road is a hard one. And God does not measure success the way we do.

The Roman Missal

The prayers for this Mass are all proper for the day and can be found in the Proper of Saints section of the Missal at May 26.

The Collect asks that through the Holy Spirit we may be filled with the same fire as filled the heart of St. Philip Neri. The Prayer over the Offerings prays that we may imitate the example of St. Philip by always giving ourselves "cheerfully / for the glory of your name." Thus is a connection made between the giving of ourselves at this offering of the sacrifice and the need to give of ourselves entirely in our whole lives. The Prayer after Communion requests that as we have fed upon the food of the Eucharist ("these heavenly delights") so too may we "always long for that food by which we truly live."

Today's Saint

Saint Philip Neri (1515–1595) spent much of his life hearing confessions and providing spiritual direction. He was considered somewhat of a clairvoyant due to his ability to "read" the hearts of people. Fundamental to the counsel he provided was the belief that unreasonable fears prevent people from living in right relationship with God and others. As a priest ministering in Rome, he offered discourses on Scripture, gradually evolving into afternoons of Scripture study, music, reading the lives of the saints, and personal reflection on the part of both clerics and laymen. These meetings became known as

the "oratory," thus leading to the foundation of the Oratorians, a congregation of diocesan priests bound by the bond of love rather than religious vows and dedicated to the spiritual well-being of souls. One of its most esteemed members was Cardinal John Henry Newmann.

WED 27 (#349) green Weekday

Optional Memorial of St. Augstine of Canterbury, Bishop / white

The Lectionary for Mass

◆ FIRST READING: The author of the book of Sirach interrupts the flow of good advice with this impassioned prayer to God not to forget his people. It is the fruit of long reflection on the words of Scripture, which is the story of God's covenant with Israel. The writer prays that God will continue to write that story — "give new signs and work new wonders" (Sirach 36:5).

◆ RESPONSORIAL PSALM 79, a prayer for deliverance, has the same intensity of pleading that we hear in the First Reading.

◆ GOSPEL: As Jesus leads the way to Jerusalem, where he is to be handed over to death, the disciples are debating. They are "amazed" and "afraid" (Mark 10:32) at his destiny of suffering, but at the same time James and John long to be with Jesus in his glory. All Jesus promises them, however, is that they will share the cup of his suffering. Then Jesus gathers the Twelve and tells them what leadership is really about in his kingdom. It is not about having places of glory. It is a leadership of humility and service.

Today's Saint

When Saint Augustine of Canterbury († 604) joined a group of monks in Rome, little did he know that someday he would become the first Archbishop of Canterbury

and hold the title "apostle of the English." At the request of Pope Gregory the Great, Saint Augustine led a mission of monks to evangelize Anglo-Saxons in Britain. Although King Ethelbert of Kent had reservations about their arrival, he gave them housing in Canterbury and allowed them to preach. They used relics, heroic stories about the saints, and ancient vessels to inspire faith in the people. Their missionary endeavors proved to be successful, eventually leading to the Baptism of King Ethelbert and his people. Saint Augustine built the first cathedral and school at Canterbury, and later founded the first monastery in close proximity to the cathedral. Within the ecumenical movement he is an icon of unity — a time when Rome and England were of one mind.

THU 28 (#350) green Weekday

◆ FIRST READING: The author of Sirach bursts into praise of God, who is beyond human understanding, whose wisdom is as infinite as his works are marvelous. The passage ends with a question: "can one ever see enough" (Sirach 42:25) of the splendor of God's works? And the unspoken answer is clear — a resounding no!

◆ RESPONSORIAL PSALM 33 is a call to praise of God the creator, full of the same wonder and delight we heard in the First Reading.

◆ GOSPEL: Jesus is on his way to Jerusalem; the disciples are weighed down with concern about the sufferings he will undergo — and with questions about their own place in the kingdom. Perhaps this is why people try to keep Bartimaeus from calling out to Jesus. But Jesus pours himself out for his people; he is never too preoccupied to tend to their needs. He calls Bartimaeus and in compassion restores his sight, and his insight; for even though Jesus is headed toward Jerusalem, Bartimaeus follows him.

FRI 29 (#351) green
Weekday

◆ FIRST READING: The sacred writer praises the "godly men" (Sirach 44:1) who came before him—the ancestors of the chosen people. Before he speaks of those whose names are remembered—Enoch, Isaac, Moses, Aaron—he pauses to praise those whose names are forgotten. But even these live on, the author says, in their descendants, the children of the covenant.

◆ RESPONSORIAL PSALM 149 is a song of that chosen people, praising God who is their maker and their king.

◆ GOSPEL: The Passion of Jesus draws near as he moves ever closer to Jerusalem. The mysterious incident of the fig tree is perhaps best understood figuratively. The prophets often used a fig tree as a symbol of Israel. The withered fig tree is, then, a fitting emblem for the religious authorities of Jesus's day, who have turned the worship of God into a matter of buying and selling, and who are plotting the death of the one who only spoke the truth.

SAT 30 (#352) green
Weekday

Optional Memorial of the Blessed Virgin Mary / white

◆ FIRST READING: This is the last of our readings from the book of Sirach. As the book draws to an end, the writer returns to the theme with which he began—praise of God's wisdom. He tells his own story, the story of a faithful and dutiful young man, who sought wisdom constantly, and at last attained what he sought.

◆ RESPONSORIAL PSALM 19 praises the law of God, which is all the heart can desire: perfect, trustworthy, right, clear, pure, true, just, precious, and sweet.

◆ GOSPEL: Yesterday we read about Jesus clearing the temple area. Today, the religious authorities confront him and seek to entrap him with a question about his authority. Jesus's heavenly wisdom confuses them.

The Roman Missal

Remember that on Saturdays during Ordinary Time which do not have an obligatory memorial, you may celebrate a Mass in honor of the Blessed Virgin Mary. Use prayer texts from the Common of the Blessed Virgin Mary.

☀ 31 (#165) white
Solemnity of the Most Holy Trinity

About this Solemnity

"In the name of the Father, and of the Son, and of the Holy Spirit." Christians who use this phrase repeatedly could easily lose sight of the powerful mystery it expresses. Today, Trinity Sunday, the Scriptures call for reflection on this central belief of Christianity: the Trinity. One of the greatest gifts of the Christian faith is the dogma of the triune God: God is three (tri) in one (une). Christians name God as a Trinity of Father, Son, and Spirit, but only in light of Jesus Christ does such language and insight fully emerge.

The Lectionary for Mass

◆ FIRST READING: Moses speaks to his people, reminding them of the wondrous uniqueness of their relationship with God. He takes them back to the dawn of creation and says that never has another people been favored by God as they have. Moses invites us to consider our own experience of God's care.

◆ RESPONSORIAL PSALM 33: On this Sunday, contemplating the mystery of the Trinity, we remember that God never forgets us. As a parent takes delight in watching a child, so God watches over us, always ready to come near when we call.

◆ SECOND READING: We end our Eucharistic Prayer remembering that that all honor to God comes through, with, and in Christ. Our reading from Romans reminds us that Christ's Spirit inhabits us, so that we are not only able to be led by the Spirit, but that the Spirit within us will draw us into deeper communion with God.

◆ GOSPEL: Matthew tells us that Jesus's last interchange with the disciples included a promise and a mission. The two go together. The promise is that he is Emmanuel, God who will always be with us. The mission is to share that experience of God with the entire world. All of the baptized have a share of that mission. How are you called to fulfill it?

The Roman Missal

The texts for this solemnity are found after the texts for the Thirty-Fourth Week in Ordinary Time, toward the end of the "Ordinary Time" section of the Missal, and several pages before the "Order of Mass" section begins.

The Gloria is sung or said today.

The Collect expresses for us the meaning of this solemnity not in terms of some dry theological doctrine but rather in terms of the active, dynamic power of the triune God: the Father sends into the world the Word of truth and the Spirit of sanctification and, in so doing, reveals to the human race his own "wondrous mystery." The prayer affirms that through the Trinity we know the very life of God himself.

The Prayer over the Offerings makes the important liturgical point that as we make the offering of our lives at this liturgy — "this oblation of our service" — its ultimate purpose is that by it we might be made "an eternal offering to you." The prayer expresses how in the liturgy we are swept up into the life of the Trinity so that our entire life might be lived with the same self-emptying, self-giving love as exists between the divine Persons.

The Preface, "The Mystery of the Most Holy Trinity," is proper for today and its text is given along with the other texts for the Mass; there is both a text with and without musical notation. The text reiterates the theological meaning of God being "one God, one Lord: / not in the unity of a single person, / but in a Trinity of one substance, equal in majesty."

The Prayer after Communion also gives voice to the basic statement about the Trinity nonetheless being "undivided Unity."

Since there should be a certain emphasis given to how the life of the Christian should be a reflection of and a participation in the life of the Trinity, perhaps the formula "Go in peace, glorifying the Lord by your life" would be an appropriate choice for the dismissal today.

Other Ideas

An image of the Trinity could be placed at the main door of the worship space with candles and flowers, or it could be carried in the entrance procession and placed in another suitable place. Whenever we carry something with words or an image on it from the door to the sanctuary of the worship space, we may want to reverse it so the assembly can see the image or words as it comes past them. The color for the day is white. However, since we are in Ordinary Time, some green fabric might be introduced.

June
Month of the Sacred Heart

M O N 1 (#353) red
Memorial of St. Justin, Martyr
Ninth Week in Ordinary Time

The Lectionary for Mass

◆ FIRST READING: Before this, Tobit had fled for his life for the crime of burying the victims of a despot. Now, in the very act of seeking to share his blessings, he is again called on to bury the dead. His neighbors inadvertently give witness to the real measure of the man as they mock him for being fearless in doing what is right.

◆ RESPONSORIAL PSALM 112 strikes a familiar theme proclaiming the blessedness of anyone like Tobit who demonstrates what it means to fear the Lord. Unlike dread or anxiety, fear of the Lord entails profound respect: a desire to act in a godly manner, lending generously and showing the strength of character that gives witness to those who come after. That is blessedness.

◆ GOSPEL: As Jesus is reaching the finale of his ministry in Jerusalem, he tells the parable of tenants whose life revolves around coveting a vineyard. Addressing religious leaders, Jesus exposes the destructiveness of those whose zealous, jealous "goodness" ultimately seeks nothing more than their own benefit. The self-seeking motivation of all they did became obvious when only fear for their own safety delayed their plots against Jesus.

The Roman Missal

Full texts for today's memorial are found in the Proper of Saints at June 1. Use Preface I or II of Holy Martyrs.

Today's Saint

Saint Justin († 165) was a philosopher who became one of the Church's first apologists, exploring the rational basis of faith and arguing that true philosophy would lead to Christ. We are also indebted to Justin for one of the earliest descriptions of the Mass (it can be found in the Office of Readings for the Third Sunday of Easter). His memorial is a good day to pray for theologians, philosophers, and for ourselves — that we will seek God not only with our hearts, but with our minds.

T U E 2 (#354) green
Weekday
Optional Memorials of Sts. Marcellinus and Peter, Martyrs / red

◆ FIRST READING: Even the just man grows weary. For Tobit it came when he was struck blind and had to rely on his wife's labor to support the family. When he suspects her of stealing a goat she had been given, her retort reveals the unworthiness of his accusation. Only a humble man would repeat such a story about himself.

◆ RESPONSORIAL PSALM 112: The psalm again praises the just. We remind ourselves that there is nothing to fear if we trust in God. Such deep trust will manifest itself in mature self-assurance and generosity.

◆ GOSPEL: The plot against Jesus continues with the Roman loyalists' attempt to expose Jesus as an enemy of Caesar. He deftly dodges their trap, pointing out that those who look to Caesar for benefit should also pay their share. Nevertheless, he puts priority on giving God that which is due to God: his reference to the image on the coin turns this into a command that calls us to become the image of God we were created to be.

Today's Saints

Almost nothing is known about Saints Marcellinus and Peter, except that they gave their lives for Christ during the persecution of the Church under the emperor Diocletian. Their names are included in the list of martyrs in Eucharistic Prayer I (the Roman Canon).

(#355) red

WED 3 Memorial of St. Charles Lwanga and Companions, Martyrs

The Lectionary for Mass

◆ FIRST READING: Both Tobit and Sarah have given up hope for any good in their lives. The grief they suffered was intensified by the judgmental comments of those around them; their great sorrow led them to hope for death. Then their despairing prayer brought them the blessings they needed to go on, teaching us that while God may not directly smite others or heal us, openness to grace will lead us beyond the dead ends that fill our imagination.

◆ RESPONSORIAL PSALM 25: Following the prayers of Tobit and Sarah, we lift up our very soul, our naked, most honest self to God. As we do so, we remember God's compassion, kindness, and undying promise of guidance.

◆ GOSPEL: Now, the Sadducees pose a sophomoric question to Jesus. One can imagine Jesus with tongue in cheek taking them on as he points out that eternity offers far more than earthly love. The take-home line for the day may well be that God is the God of the living—so let us live fully and bring life to others!

The Roman Missal

The prayers, which emphasize the wise teaching and doctrine of Saint Justin, are found in the Proper of Saints. The Preface of Holy Martyrs is used.

Today's Saints

Along with his twenty-two companions, Saint Charles Lwanga (1860/1865–1886) is considered a proto-martyr, one of the first martyrs of Black Africa. Saint Charles, a native of Uganda, served the kabaka, or king, as a master of pages whose primary task was to train young people in royal service. Unfortunately, he was thrust into this position during the reign of the anti-Christian king, Mwanga. As a recent convert, he felt impelled to catechize the young pages in the ways of Christianity, which led to several Baptisms. When the king found out about his actions, he demanded that Saint Charles and the newly baptized renounce their faith, but they remained steadfast in their beliefs, resulting in arrest and sentence to death. Saint Charles and six others were wrapped in a mat of reeds and burned to death. His final words were *Kotonda wange*, "My God."

(#356) green

THU 4 Weekday

The Lectionary for Mass

◆ FIRST READING: Today we see Tobiah, the image of his faithful father, wedding Sarah in spite of the story that demons killed everyone who attempted to make her their wife. Taking his life in his hands, Tobiah began the marriage with a prayer expressing his faith and hope that their marriage would fulfill God's purpose in creating man and woman. With that faith, the two began a happy life together.

◆ RESPONSORIAL PSALM 128: Today's psalm proclaims Tobiah and

Sarah's joy, even while their history reminds us that the just themselves often suffer great trials. In what seems a theme for the week, the psalm calls us back to that fear of the Lord that recognizes and trusts in God's mercy and goodness.

◆ GOSPEL: In typical fashion, Jesus responds to a person without being trapped by his question. In Jesus's eyes, there is no one greatest Commandment. Rather, the two complement each other to summarize the entire law. When we try to blend those two, we will never be far from the Kingdom of God.

(#357) red

FRI 5 Memorial of St. Boniface, Bishop and Martyr

The Lectionary for Mass

◆ FIRST READING: Now, not only is Tobiah safely married, but he has been given the means to cure his father's blindness. In addition to telling of a physical healing, this incident symbolizes the insight that can gradually come to God's suffering people. The new way of seeing is a grace that goes beyond the merely human perspective.

◆ RESPONSORIAL PSALM 146: Again, we sing a psalm of joy at what God has done. We may sing this in gratitude for what we have been given. Remembering Tobiah, we might also ask that our eyes be opened to those to whom God might be sending us today.

◆ GOSPEL: Jesus is involved in the sort of debate that delighted the rabbis as well as the crowds. The early Christians saw this interchange as an affirmation of Jesus's humanity and divinity. He was a descendant of David, and also the Lord.

The Roman Missal

The Collect is drawn from the Proper of Saints, with the remaining prayers taken from the Common of Martyrs or of Pastors. The Preface of Holy Martyrs or of Holy Pastors may be used.

Today's Saint

Saint Boniface started life as Winfrid, a member of a Benedictine monastery in England. He was elected Abbot, but resigned in order to become a missionary. The Pope gave him the name Boniface and sent him to Germany, where he served as bishop for thirty years. It is said that he won the confidence of the people when he took an ax to the sacred oak of Thor, and it immediately crashed to the ground. He was martyred on June 5, 754, as he was preparing to administer the sacrament of Confirmation.

S
A 6 (#358) green
T **Weekday**

Optional Memorials of St. Norbert, Bishop / white; Blessed Virgin Mary / white

The Lectionary for Mass

◆ FIRST READING: As the Tobit story closes, Raphael reveals his true identity to Tobiah and Tobit, first in a sermon and then in plain words. Perhaps the essence of his message and the whole book is Raphael's line: "The works of God are to be declared and made known."

◆ CANTICLE: This canticle, taken from the Book of Tobit, recaps the whole story and underlines its message. Tobit began praising God in the land of his exile. He knew the depths of anguish, and though impatient in his trials, he lost not his hope in God. He invites us to join him as he says "[N]ow, consider what God has done for you."

◆ GOSPEL: "Many rich people . . . but she, from her poverty, has contributed all she had." Here Jesus uses one example to underline two of his favorite themes: the radical nature of discipleship and the example of the poor: whether you have much or little to give, discipleship is an all-or-nothing proposition, and the poor seem to have a unique advantage when it comes to trusting completely in God.

(#168)   white
Solemnity of the Most Holy Body and Blood of Christ (*Corpus Christi*)

About this Solemnity

Today we celebrate *Corpus Christi*, the Solemnity of the Most Holy Body and Blood of Christ. In the Eucharistic feast, the gifts of bread and wine really and truly become the Body, Blood, Soul, and Divinity of Christ. Through this covenant of love, God draws us into his divine life and offers us food for our earthly pilgrimage to continue with faith and hope, confident in God's ability to transform our weaknesses and sufferings into life and joy.

The Lectionary for Mass

◆ FIRST READING: The people Moses led out of Egypt had gone through a death to their old way of life and were now on a journey toward the land and life God planned for them. By sprinkling ox blood on them, Moses ritualized their death to the old and their pledge of fidelity to the new covenant of the Law. Their sprinkling, like ours in Baptism, was an outward sign of the indelible inward change that had begun in them.

◆ RESPONSORIAL PSALM 116: As we say that we will take up the cup of salvation, we join ourselves to the Israelites with Moses and the disciples at the Last Supper. We are invited to consider what the cup of salvation has meant and means for us today. Drinking from this cup brings us into communion with Christ, making us participants in his Passion, Death, and Resurrection.

◆ SECOND READING: The Letter to the Hebrews talks about God's dwelling places in the world. Once, the Hebrews carried a tabernacle on pilgrimage with them to the Promised Land, and finally installed it in the Temple. The Letter to the Hebrews proclaims that Christ has opened a new tabernacle in the dwelling place of God. In other writings Paul speaks of Christians as new dwelling places for God, as temples of the Holy Spirit. Where do we look for God's dwelling among us?

◆ GOSPEL: In Mark's narrative of the Last Supper, we realize that God has everything prepared, but that it is up to the disciples to lay it all out, to prepare for the actual sharing around the table. Today, we might put ourselves in their sandals and ask how we are to play our part in preparing for and sharing the meal of the Eucharist. How do we prepare ourselves and what must we do so that others can fully participate?

The Roman Missal

The texts for today are found immediately following the texts for the Solemnity of the Most Holy Trinity, toward the end of the "Ordinary Time" section of the Missal. You might consider using the Rite for the Blessing and Sprinkling of Water found in Appendix II at the back of the Missal; this might help to reinforce the connection between Baptism and Eucharist, and the Eucharist as the culmination of initiation. The Gloria is sung or said today as is the Creed.

The Collect notes that in the Sacrament of the Eucharist, God has "left us a memorial of your Passion." The prayer goes on to ask that because of our revering of "the sacred mysteries of your Body and Blood," we may "always experience in ourselves / the fruits of your redemption." As this prayer speaks of the fruits of being redeemed, we must always remember that those fruits are expressed in a life of self-emptying love. Therefore, the focus is not so much on a passive contemplation of the Real Presence in the Eucharist, but, as with all liturgical celebration, how our participation in the mystery is a means of being transformed by God to live out the mystery that is being celebrated.

The Prayer over the Offerings reinforces the idea that worship of the Eucharist must be expressed in the practical living out of our lives. This prayer reinforces that one of the chief results of Eucharistic celebration must be unity: as the "one bread" and "one cup" are prayed over at the one altar around which is gathered the one Body of Christ, we see in those signs the mystery of what we are to become—"one body, one spirit in Christ," in the words of Eucharistic Prayer III.

The Preface that is given along with the other formularies for this Mass is Preface II of the Most Holy Eucharist; only the text with music is given, indicating a certain preference for chanting the introductory dialogue and the Preface itself. However, a rubric indicates that Preface I of the Most Holy Eucharist, which can be found along with the texts of other Prefaces further along in the Missal, may also be used.

The Prayer after Communion points to the important but often-overlooked eschatological dimension of the Eucharist, as it reminds us that the reception of the Body and Blood of the Lord in the present age is a foreshadowing of sharing in God's divine life for all eternity.

Noting that it is desirable for a Eucharistic procession to take place after Mass, the Missal gives instructions on how this is to be carried out. The host that will be carried in the procession should be a Host that has been consecrated at this Mass; thus it is made clear how worship of the Eucharist outside Mass is an extension of the grace of the offering of the sacrifice. If such a procession is to take place after Mass, the host to be carried in procession is placed in the monstrance when the Communion of the faithful is over, and that monstrance is set on the altar. The Prayer after Communion is then prayed, but the Concluding Rite is omitted. Instead, the procession forms immediately after the Prayer after Communion. The Missal gives no further rubrics concerning the procession; liturgy preparers should consult the ritual, *Holy Communion and Worship of the Eucharist outside Mass* for specific instructions. The Missal does note, however, that the procession need not take place immediately after Mass, but may instead follow after a public and lengthy period of adoration coming at the end of Mass.

Other Ideas

One of the most commonly heard complaints from people in the pews and clergy alike is "the lack of reverence" that is frequently shown toward the Eucharist. Many do not genuflect or bow before the Blessed Sacrament, some do not know the proper way to hold their hands to receive Holy Communion, many receive "unworthily" without finding the right disposition by attending the Sacrament of Reconciliation first, and generally congregations get pretty casual in their wardrobe choices, especially as summer is unfolding. Perhaps you can use this wonderful celebration as a time to catechize about reverence.

Include a bulletin announcement reminding liturgical ministers and the congregation about appropriate dress. For example, "We ask that ministers avoid wearing flip flops, bare midriffs, shorts, and spaghetti or strapless tops" or "ushers are to wear suitcoats in winter months and tie and button down shirt in the summer." You will be surprised at the number of positive responses you will receive from those who feel the same way.

While it is not a Holyday of Obligation, you may wish to remind the congregation that Friday is the Solemnity of the Sacred Heart of Jesus.

M O N 8 (#359) green Weekday

Tenth Week in Ordinary Time

The Lectionary for Mass

◆ FIRST READING: Any writing teacher would admonish Paul for using the word "encourage" nine times in this passage. The word, which could also have the sense of "consolation" has special meaning for Paul. Not an ordinary "You go girl!" phrase, this encouragement is rooted in what would seem its opposite: suffering or misfortune. For Paul, all of this is a share in the mystery of Christ's Passion and Resurrection. The reason for suffering is that evil still battles good. The reason for encouragement is that we know the outcome and are therefore charged to share it with others.

◆ RESPONSORIAL PSALM 34: "Taste and see the goodness of the Lord." What an invitation to follow Paul's words! To deepen our appreciation of it, we might spend time meditating on the line "Look to God that you may be radiant with joy." Whether in a time of exaltation, sorrow, or in between, the promise is that time spent savoring God's presence will teach us joy upon joy.

◆ GOSPEL: "Blessed are you." The first two readings lead up to this. Counterintuitive as the Beatitudes are, Jesus promises an inexplicable and unexpected happiness that can only come from God. Jesus believed it and invites us to do the same.

TUE 9 (#360) green
Weekday

Optional Memorial of St. Ephrem, Deacon and Doctor of the Church / white

The Lectionary for Mass

◆ FIRST READING: Paul says that Christ offered a thorough "yes" to the Father, and therefore, only through him could the fullness of divine fidelity be seen. The more complete our "Yes," the more deeply can God's Spirit work in us.

◆ RESPONSORIAL PSALM 119: This hymn of praise promises what we have heard from the saints: the more we enter into living the word of God, the more wondrous it will appear. To the extent that we seek God, our steps will be steadfast.

◆ GOSPEL: What a responsibility Christ gives us in this teaching! The more we think we can accomplish it, the further we will be from actually doing so. The only light we have to offer is the reflected light of God's grace in our lives — and that is an offering that can only be made in deep humility.

Today's Saint

After serving as head of a cathedral school in Syria, St. Ephrem (306–373), a Doctor of the Church, fled to a cave near Edessa to take up the life of a monk. While devoting himself to an austere life marked by solitude and fasting, he earnestly wrote hundreds of hymns and commentaries on Sacred Scripture.

His hymns and discourses on Scripture provided deep insight into the Paschal Mystery of Christ and opposed gnostic tendencies among various sects. At times, he would leave his cave to preach in Edessa. Crowds were attracted to his eloquent preaching; therefore, he became known as "the harp of the holy spirit." Later in life he was ordained a deacon and helped the people of Edessa weather a terrible famine.

WED 10 (#361) green
Weekday

The Lectionary for Mass

◆ FIRST READING: Paul here elaborates a favorite theme, the superiority of the new covenant over the old. It is not that he demeans the Law, but rather realizes that seeking perfection through it leads only to rigid perfectionism. On the other hand, being humble and grateful to the Spirit gives life and a joy that can never be earned but is free to those who will gratefully receive it.

◆ RESPONSORIAL PSALM 99: We acclaim God's holiness, that is, God's "otherness." Yet, even as we extol our awesome God, we recall God's closeness, guidance, and forgiveness. This is the Holy One who is both transcendent and more near than we are to ourselves.

◆ GOSPEL: Jesus's admonition to fulfill the Law is entirely in line with Paul's teaching. What Jesus criticized was making the law an idol — something to be obeyed for its own sake. Jesus's "fulfillment" of the Law, as we will see, increased its authority, teaching that every part of the Law is to lead to right relationships with God and neighbor.

THU 11 (#580; Gospel #362) red
Memorial of St. Barnabas, Apostle

The Lectionary for Mass

◆ FIRST READING: This short reading gives us a lot of information about Barnabas's role as an Apostle. Some sources say that his name was really Joseph, but he got the nickname "Barnabas" or "son of encouragement." We might let that remind us that the real meaning of evangelization is to share good news. In honor of this Apostle, may we all be sources of encouragement.

◆ RESPONSORIAL PSALM 98: As we sing that the Lord's saving power has been revealed to the whole world, we remember that that revelation comes about only through the dedication of "Apostles." We are called daily to reveal God's justice and kindness.

◆ GOSPEL: Jesus addresses his followers insisting that they must outshine the religious leaders of the day. It is one thing to observe the law, it is another to understand its purpose and fulfill it. The Reign of God happens when the law is fulfilled.

The Roman Missal

All the orations are proper for today, and can be found in the Proper of Saints at June 11. The Collect recognizes the saint for his preaching of the Gospel to the nations, calling him "a man filled with faith and the Holy Spirit." The prayer goes on to ask that the Gospel may continue to "be faithfully proclaimed by word and by deed" even down to our own day. The Prayer over the Offerings asks that the offerings we make will transform us to do that work of spreading the Gospel in the same way St. Barnabas did, "set us on fire" with the same "flame of your love, / by which Saint Barnabas brought the light of the Gospel to the nations." Either Preface I or Preface II of the Apostles is the Preface to be used today. The Prayer after Communion points to the kingdom that is revealed and anticipated in the celebration of the Eucharist, a kingdom we hope to arrive at fully one day, as it asks that "what we celebrate in sacramental signs . . . we may one day behold unveiled."

Today's Saint

Even though St. Barnabas (first century) was not one of the original Twelve Apostles, he was given the title of "apostle" by St. Luke and the early Church fathers due to his apostolic endeavors on behalf of Christianity. His original name was Joseph, but the Apostles gave him the surname Barnabas, meaning "son of encouragement." Together with St. Paul, he extended the missionary efforts of the Church beyond Jerusalem to Antioch, and after much success moved on to other places throughout Asia Minor. After parting ways with St. Paul over issues regarding circumcision and the Mosaic law, St. Barnabas embarked on further missionary journeys with John and Mark (see Acts of the Apostles 15:36–40). Tradition indicates that St. Barnabas was stoned to death, and his remains were taken to Constantinople where a church stands in his honor.

(#171) white

FRI 12 Solemnity of the Most Sacred Heart of Jesus

About this Solemnity

Devotion to the Sacred Heart of Jesus became popular in the seventeenth century through St. Mary Margaret Alacoque (1647–1690) [St. Margaret's memorial is October 16], who said that in her visions Christ told her, "Behold the heart that has loved people so, yet is loved so little in return." *Catholic Household Blessings & Prayers* includes a Litany of the Sacred Heart. Pray

this. It may also be helpful to have an extended period of prayer in the presence of the Blessed Sacrament or with the parish's image of the Sacred Heart. See Pope John Paul II's prayer, the Litany of the Sacred Heart of Jesus (*Our Sunday Visitor*, 1992), for a deeper understanding of this devotion. Encourage a night vigil until the celebration of the memorial of the Immaculate Heart of Mary the next day, Saturday, June 28.

The Lectionary for Mass

◆ FIRST READING: On this feast of love, the Book of Hosea paints a picture of God as the doting parent who thrives on being tender to his child. Then, when the child rejects that love, God will not react in anger. God will not stoop to human pettiness, but shows that love endures, no matter what response it may be given.

◆ CANTICLE: The motif of water from the springs of salvation link today's Canticle from Isaiah not only to the reference to the Exodus in today's First Reading, but perhaps even more to the blood and water that flow from the wound in Jesus's side in today's Gospel. Praise and thanksgiving are the only fitting response. Note also the reference to proclaiming the Good News throughout the earth, as Paul the apostle did (today's Second Reading).

◆ SECOND READING: Paul tells us that God's eternal purpose has been carried out in Christ. And what is that? That human beings may speak freely to God. That we may draw near to God with confidence.

◆ GOSPEL: What do we know of the heart of God? What we truly know about God, we know through Jesus, the Christ. Here, the Gospel according John teaches us that God has a heart that bleeds. That great God, a doting parent, desires to be near to human creatures. What more could we want to know?

The Roman Missal

The Solemnity of the Sacred Heart of Jesus is all about the incredible love of Christ for humanity. There are two options for the Collect. The first speaks of the Heart of Jesus as a fount of grace. We pray that we who "glory" in the Sacred Heart of Jesus may remember his goodness, and be worthy to receive "an overflowing measure of grace / from that fount of heavenly gifts." The second emphasizes the suffering of Christ, whose heart is "wounded by our sins" and yet who gives us "the boundless treasures of . . . love." We pray that we may make reparation to him as we offer our devotion. In the Prayer over the Offerings, we ask God to look at his Son's love for us in his Heart—and to let our offering be "an expiation of our offenses." The proper Preface is subtitled "The Boundless Charity of Christ." In Christ, raised high on the cross, pierced by the soldier's lance, we behold "the wellspring of the Church's Sacraments," a fountain of salvation open to all. Christ's Sacred Heart is an "open heart," offering love and life to every person. The familiar image shows the Sacred Heart of Jesus on fire, a sign of his suffering and his love. In the Prayer after Communion, we pray that we may also be "fervent with the fire of holy love," and be so drawn to Christ that "we may learn to see him in our neighbor" (Prayer after Communion).

SAT 13 (#364) white
Memorial of the Immaculate Heart of the Blessed Virgin Mary

About this Memorial

It was Pope John Paul II who raised this celebration to an obligatory memorial, a kind of liturgical sister to yesterday's solemnity of the Most Sacred Heart of Jesus. The prayers and readings for the memorial are not placed with those of the Sacred Heart; you'll find them between May and June in both the *Lectionary for Mass* and *The Roman Missal*. It always takes place on the Saturday following the Second Sunday after Pentecost (Most Holy Body and Blood of Christ/*Corpus Christi*). The prayers are in the Proper of Saints, following the prayers for the Visitation of the Blessed Virgin Mary on May 31.

The Lectionary for Mass

◆ FIRST READING: "The love of Christ impels us." To what? To recognize that we enjoy a union with God that changes absolutely everything. Paul wants us to look at every person we meet and ask ourselves "If I am in God, and God in me, what can my relationship with this person become?" Christ has already reconciled us, we have only to make it real in our lives.

◆ RESPONSORIAL PSALM 103: "Bless the LORD, O my soul; / and all my being bless his holy name . . . ." As people whom God has drawn near, we want to give praise and thanks with every fiber of our being. Praying Psalm 103 offers us the opportunity to reflect over and again on God's great love.

◆ GOSPEL: Why would Jesus forbid oath taking? An oath sets certain statements apart as assuredly, almost sacredly, truthful, thereby implying that other speech allows room for prevarication. In redeeming the loss of Eden, Jesus

demands that every word we speak be a bearer of the truth that makes us free to relate to one another in love.

The Roman Missal

The prayers for this memorial are found in the Proper of Saints, immediately following the prayers for the Visitation of the Blessed Virgin Mary on May 31. God made Mary's Immaculate Heart "a fit dwelling place for the Holy Spirit." We, too, are formed to be a "temple of [God's] glory" (Collect). In the Prayer over the Offerings, we pray that the prayers and offerings we make on this memorial may be pleasing to God, and bring us "help and forgiveness." Through the sacrament we share, we are "partakers of eternal redemption" (Prayer after Communion). We pray that God's grace may be increased in us.

☀ 14 (#92) green
Eleventh Sunday in Ordinary Time

The Lectionary for Mass

◆ FIRST READING: This reading, chosen to complement today's Gospel, is a promise to God's people. Although they are in exile, God will bring them back and plant them in their own territory. Ezekiel underlines the fact that it is God who will do this, the people can do no more than cooperate with God's grace.

◆ RESPONSORIAL PSALM 92: Praying our psalm, we thank God who

is kind and faithful. We remember the promise that God's faithful will grow like the tallest, best trees known to the people of Israel.

◆ SECOND READING: Ezekiel taught that all growth comes from God. Now Paul says we walk by faith, not by sight. That is one of the hardest things we are called to do. As a people proud of our independence, we would much prefer to make the roadmap for our lives. Nevertheless, our Christian vocation is to discern God's will, forsaking our own preferences when they impede our Christian journey.

◆ GOSPEL: Jesus's seed parables, like the reading from Ezekiel, remind us that the Reign of God is a work of human and divine collaboration. Like the farmer, we must do all we can to provide the circumstances in which God's reign can grow. When we do, all is ready for God's Spirit to breathe life into our world, be it in the garden or the soul of a people.

The Roman Missal

Without God, we "can do nothing." We ask for God's grace, that we may follow God's commands and be pleasing to him "by our resolve and our deeds" (Collect). The Eucharist is food for body and soul. We pray that this "sustenance . . . may not fail us in body or in spirit" (Prayer over the Offerings). Holy Communion is a foretaste of the promise of our union with God. We pray that this sacrament may "bring about unity in your Church" (Prayer after Communion).

Other Ideas

The readings today speak of trees, seeds, and growth. The texts fit perfectly with the summer season. Did you know that these summer months are the hardest of times for food pantries? Children are no longer receiving hot lunches at school and families have a difficult time making ends meet. Encourage your congregation to plant an extra row in their garden to share with the local food pantry. Remember those less fortunate and those who produce food in the Universal Prayer. And don't forget your local animal shelters too.

MON 15 (#365) green Weekday

The Lectionary for Mass

◆ FIRST READING: "We appeal to you not to receive the grace of God in vain." Paul lists the graces that characterize disciples as "ministers of God" (purity, knowledge, patience . . .). Today, let us meditate on Paul's list of virtues and ask for the grace to receive them and put them into practice.

◆ RESPONSORIAL PSALM 98: Our psalm invites us to recall the ways in which we have experienced God's saving activity. From God's great deeds in history to the secret graces we may have received, the purpose of it all is to allow all the ends of the earth to know his salvation. We each have our part to play.

◆ GOSPEL: As we continue to hear the Sermon on the Mount, Jesus turns expectations on his follower's heads. This time he insists that we not let evil-doers or persecutors write the script for us. When someone takes advantage of us, Jesus's prophetic way is to do the unexpected and demonstrate how a real human being acts in freedom. The trick is to turn the other cheek in a way that demonstrates our dignity and calls forth the same in the other.

TUE 16 (#366) green Weekday

The Lectionary for Mass

◆ FIRST READING: Paul is making an eloquent plea that the Corinthians share generously with other needy Christians. His point is that by giving, the Corinthians are doing far more than donating material goods. They are participating in Christ's own self-emptying for the salvation of the world. How might we do the same today?

◆ RESPONSORIAL PSALM 146: Following Paul's plea to share wealth with others, our psalm reminds us "Blessed [is the one] . . . whose hope is in the LORD." We may find it frightening to part with anything that gives us security. But, the more we place our hope in God, the less we will have to fear.

◆ GOSPEL: As Jesus outlines what it means to "fulfill" the law, he comes to this most demanding, all-encompassing command. In reality, the command to love our enemies fulfills the command against idolatry as well. If I love only those of my nation or persuasion, I am reducing God to my own concepts. Loving my enemy moves me beyond my comfortable, tribal god toward openness to the God who shares life with those I have not yet learned to love.

WED 17 (#367) green Weekday

The Lectionary for Mass

◆ FIRST READING: In today's reading, Paul continues his appeal that the Corinthians be generous. In this, he is teaching that their charity makes them channels of God's generosity. This teaching further develops 1 Corinthians 12. Paul's teaching insisted that every gift, personal or material, is given for the good of the whole community.

◆ RESPONSORIAL PSALM 112: How often do we return to the theme of the blessings of those who "fear the Lord?" One way to understand that phrase could be "blessed are they who know they are not God." Reading it that way, we are led to ponder the Sermon on the Mount as a guide to right relationship with God and all whom God has put on our path.

◆ GOSPEL: It is notable that Jesus's Sermon on the Mount deals first with human relationships and only later focuses on "religious" activities. With these instructions about how to perform works of piety, Jesus reminds us that true religious activity is directed to praise of God alone. We are invited to free ourselves from concern about anyone else's opinion. When God's grace leads us to that, we will know what it means to be poor in spirit.

THU 18 (#368) green Weekday

The Lectionary for Mass

◆ FIRST READING: Today's reading gives us a glimpse of the greatest conflict that plagued early Christianity: the question of whether the faith was a nuance of Judaism or a new, universal revelation. Those who preached "another Jesus" were demanding strict adherence to Jewish law. Paul's vision was broader, and he would not accept a diminishment of the universal Christ he had come to know.

◆ RESPONSORIAL PSALM 111: As we praise God for working in "justice and truth," we remember that God's working is greater than we can comprehend. Thus, in the middle of praising what little we can conceive, we repeat that "majesty and glory" characterize God's work, and give thanks, aware that God offers more than we can receive or appreciate.

◆ GOSPEL: The Lord's Prayer is the centerpiece of Jesus's teaching about "pious" works. It gives us an insight into Jesus's own prayer and the relationship God will share with us through faith. Meditation on each phrase will bring us closer

JUNE

to living in the love of the God who wishes to be our Father.

FRI 19 (#369) green
Weekday

Optional Memorial of St. Romuald, Abbot / white

The Lectionary for Mass

◆ FIRST READING: In this passage, Paul explains to his readers how God's strength worked through his own weakness. He names the graces of faith he received and the sufferings he has endured for the Gospel. But above all, he wants Christ to shine through as the one whose help will lead them on in faithfulness to the Gospel.

◆ RESPONSORIAL PSALM 34: As we pray this psalm of gratitude, it is good to take a few moments to remember the ways in which we have felt God's saving presence in our life. When we take time to appreciate what God has done, we will be radiant with joy.

◆ GOSPEL: Taking Jesus quite literally, we could envision the moth-eaten heart that results from nourishing on that which has no real life. This reading might remind us of St. Lawrence of Rome who, when officials detained him and demanded that he present the treasures of the Church, assembled the poor, blind, and lame and presented them to his arresting officers. Unimpressed, they sent him to torture and death on a grill. What could you present as your treasure today?

Today's Saint

Aristocratic-born Romuald led a wild life as a young person in tenth-century Italy. This changed at age twenty when he saw his father murder another man. Filled with horror, Romuald fled to a Benedictine monastery to do penance for his father's actions. Even monks found him uncomfortably holy, so he left and wandered throughout Italy, establishing his own monasteries and hermitages along the way. He eventually formed the Order of Camaldoli, a religious group of men who combined the cenobitic tradition of communal living with the eremitical (hermit) life of the Eastern monks. He lived a long life, dying of natural causes in 1027.

SAT 20 (#370) green
Weekday

Optional Memorial of the Blessed Virgin Mary / white

The Lectionary for Mass

◆ FIRST READING: Paul continues his "boast" that he has received gracious gifts from God. But still, he boasts not of his superiority, but of what God can do with weakness. Yes, he had some sort of vision, but he also suffers a "thorn in the flesh" which has taught him that God's grace alone is sufficient—for him and for us.

◆ RESPONSORIAL PSALM 34: Our praise in this psalm proclaims that God's goodness to us is so great that we can literally taste it. Like Paul, the psalmist calls us to proclaim that naught is lacking to those who take refuge in God.

◆ GOSPEL: These words of Jesus invite us to consider what attitude Christians might have in regard to worries and poverty. In the liturgy we pray to be "safe from all distress." This cannot mean that the poor must accept hunger as God's will. Rather, Jesus may be asking Christians to gaze upon the poor and ask the rest of the world "What are they to eat? What are they to wear?" Then, our focus will not be on ourselves, but on the abundance of creation and the possibilities it offers for the good of all.

21 (#95) green
Twelfth Sunday in Ordinary Time

The Lectionary for Mass

◆ FIRST READING: Job challenged God about that most disturbing question: Why do the just suffer? God did not respond directly, but rather pointed out the vast difference between humanity and divinity. If we cannot control the sea, how can we question or comprehend the designs of God?

◆ RESPONSORIAL PSALM 107: This psalm of thanksgiving for rescue does not answer the question about the why of a near-fatal storm. Rather, it gives thanks for God's presence in the time of danger as well as in times of contentment.

◆ SECOND READING: Paul says "The love of Christ impels us . . . " This reading invites us to ask how our experience and love of God compel us to live, no longer for ourselves, but for Christ.

◆ GOSPEL: Job wondered where God was in his suffering. The disciples were shocked that Jesus slept during the storm. In both cases, the ones in danger were disappointed that God didn't act as they wished. Put in very blunt terms the readings ask us to consider whether we look to God to be our servant and rescuer or our teacher and Lord.

The Roman Missal

We pray that we may honor God's name and, "set firm on the foundation of [God's] love," know his guidance (Collect). We offer "the sacrifice of conciliation and praise" and pray that it may so work in our lives that we may offer to God "a heart pleasing" to him (Prayer over the Offerings). The Eucharist renews and nourishes us. We pray that this sacrifice "may be our sure pledge of redemption," the promise of eternal life (Prayer after Communion).

Other Ideas

Today is Father's Day so be sure to offer a blessing for all dads and father figures at the end of Mass. The text in the *Book of Blessings* (#1729) may replace the Solemn Blessing. Thursday is the Solemnity of the Nativity of John the Baptist. Continue to point out some of the highlights of the weekly sanctoral calendar and encourage people to attend daily Mass.

Sometimes, liturgical ministers forget things or miss scheduled times because of vacations or family events. Encourage other ministers to check in with the sacristan or liturgical coordintators before Mass and see if help is needed. Consider investing in a ministry scheduling program that sends out automatic reminders and makes finding subs a snap. It is well worth the investment. You also may want to encourage potential ministers to "shadow" sacristans and cantors this summer. This will help "newbies" get a sense of the ministry.

M O N 22 (#371) green Weekday

Optional Memorials of St. Paulinus of Nola, Bishop / white; Sts. John Fisher, Bishop, and Thomas More, Martyrs / red

The Lectionary for Mass

◆ FIRST READING: Historians of the Bible say that Abraham migrated at a time when his civilization was threatened by internal conflict. People from the United States might resonate with Abraham because so many of our ancestors discerned that it was God's will that they move to a land that would be better for their families. Like Abraham, they sought a promised land that they would have to help create.

◆ RESPONSORIAL PSALM 33: With this psalm we sing in faith and hope. We believe that God is concerned for us and will somehow deliver us if only we wait faithfully.

◆ GOSPEL: This warning from Jesus comes at an important moment in his Sermon on the Mount and also follows up on the First Reading. People who believe God has chosen them, who have accepted Jesus's rigorous standards may become prone to judge others. Before that attitude can get very far, Jesus calls us to a reassessment of ourselves. If we don't see a problem, we might be courageous and humble enough to ask our neighbors to show us our blind spots.

Today's Saints

St. Paulinus of Nola (c. 354–431) was raised in a family of wealthy politicians in Bordeaux. His interests were varied: everything from practicing law to writing poetry, from traveling to governing. After the death of a newly born son, he and his wife, Therasia, gave away the family fortune to the poor and to the Church. Saint Paulinus and Therasia moved to Italy where they began to live, along with some other friends, a life of prayer and service. They lived in a two-story building in which the first floor provided a place of rest for the wayward and the lost, and the second floor was their place of residence based on the rhythms of monasticism. Gaining a

reputation for holiness, Saint Paulinus was ordained a priest and was eventually made a bishop of Nola.

St. John Fisher (1469–1535) and St. Thomas More (1478–1535) lived during a time of great upheaval and reformation. Both were friends and consultants to King Henry VIII, and both were executed because they would not declare the king's supremacy over the Church. Saint John Fisher, born in Yorkshire, was an astute scholar recognized for his profound insight into the complex questions of life. He held many positions of esteem, including a tutor to the young Henry VIII, Chancellor of Cambridge University, and bishop of Rochester.

St. Thomas More, born in London, was a family man characterized by a deep affection for his wife and three daughters. He, too, held many powerful positions in the Church and in society; in particular, a Parliament lawyer, Speaker of the House of Commons, and Chancellor of England.

T U E 23 (#372) green Weekday

The Lectionary for Mass

◆ FIRST READING: This incident fills in our picture of Abraham. Planning to avoid conflict, he offers Lot the opportunity to choose his own portion of the land. Here there is no hint of competition, only Abraham's wisdom and generosity. While he could have claimed the better part, he asked Lot to choose. Perhaps Abraham's faith left him no doubt that God would provide, no matter which portion of land he received.

◆ RESPONSORIAL PSALM 15: Recalling Abraham, we sing about those who do justice. The psalm does not promise prosperity, but rather knowledge of the presence of God and freedom from anxiety. Like

Abraham, the just are radically free because of their faith in Providence.

◆ GOSPEL: This is sage advice for evangelization. Abraham respected Lot's preferences. In our desire to share faith, we must honor other ways of being. Lacking sympathy for others' religious worldview, we may offer them what we see as pearls, but they perceive as pig feed. What others need us to do for them is based in their perception of the world, not our own. Jesus calls us to respect the other's culture as much as we respect our own.

(#586) white
TUE 23
Vigil of the Solemnity of the Nativity of St. John the Baptist

About this Solemnity

John the Baptist was the great prophet and herald of Jesus the Messiah. He prepared the way of the Lord and revealed Jesus to others as both the Messiah and the Lamb of God. St. John exemplifies the Christian life as one who proclaims the Gospel message of healing and repentance while he points out Christ to others and shows them the way to become united with God.

This is an ancient solemnity, reaching back to the fourth century, though the date of the celebration varied in East and West. In the East, the birth of the forerunner was celebrated on the day after Epiphany, January 7, because of the association of that feast with the Baptism of the Lord. In the West, it was celebrated on June 24, in keeping with Luke 1:36, which notes that Elizabeth was six months pregnant at the time of the Annunciation of the Lord.

The Lectionary for Mass

Commentary was provided by Anne Elizabeth Sweet, OSCO.

◆ FIRST READING: The prophet Jeremiah was but a youth when he received his prophetic call. In fact, as he himself saw it, he was too young to be about what the Lord asked. Nevertheless, the Lord reassures him: it is the Lord's Word he speaks, not his own. What is more, he will not be alone: the Lord is with him.

◆ RESPONSORIAL PSALM 71: The reference to the mother's womb in our antiphon and in the third stanza are fitting for this solemnity celebrating the birth of John the Baptist, who, as Luke attests, even in his mother's womb bore witness to his Lord. The pleas for deliverance are likewise applicable to John the Baptist who was put to death because of the word he spoke.

◆ SECOND READING: The themes of joy and the working of the Spirit in God's prophets link today's Second Reading with the Gospel announcement of the birth of John the Baptist. Believers in every generation are among those who rejoice because of the salvation that is theirs in Christ.

◆ GOSPEL: The birth of John the Baptist was announced to his elderly father, Zechariah, in a vision as he offered incense in the Temple. As with so many before him, the vision evokes fear, but God's messenger immediately reassures him and speaks of the joy that he and so many others will have because of his son. The messenger speaks of the child's future role: he will be dedicated to God as the Nazirites of old (no wine or strong drink; see Numbers 6) and will be instrumental in the conversion of many in Israel. The Spirit of the Lord will be upon him, even from his mother's womb.

The Roman Missal

Two sets of Mass formularies are given for this Solemnity, "At the Vigil Mass" and "At the Mass during the Day."

◆ AT THE VIGIL MASS: The Collect uses the interesting appellation "the Precursor" to refer to St. John, a title somewhat unfamiliar to us but one which certainly defines his role in salvation history. The prayer asks that we may come safely to the One foretold by John.

Remember that the Creed is said at this Mass.

The Prayer over the Offerings once again makes a connection between liturgy and life, petitioning God "that what we celebrate in mystery / we may follow with deeds of devoted service."

The Preface is proper for today, "The Mission of the Precursor," and the text, with and without musical notation, is located among the texts for the Mass during the Day, two pages over from the Vigil Mass texts. The Preface recalls the events associated with St. John the Baptist's life and echo the Scripture passages associated with him: how he was consecrated "for a singular honor / among those born of women"; how "His birth brought great rejoicing"; how he leapt for joy in the womb; how "He alone of all the prophets / pointed out the Lamb of redemption"; how "he baptized the very author of Baptism"; and how he gave witness to Christ by the shedding of his blood.

The Prayer after Communion emphasizes the Communion of Saints as it asks that "the prayer of St. John the Baptist / accompany us who have eaten our fill / at this sacrificial feast." There is also a plea for forgiveness through the intercession of the saint: since he was the one to proclaim Jesus as the Lamb who would take away our sins, we ask that "he implore now for us your favor."

An argument could be made that the dismissal formula "Go and announce the Gospel of the Lord" fits in well with today's focus on the life and mission of the Precursor.

W E D 24 (#587) white
Solemnity of the Nativity of St. John the Baptist

The Lectionary for Mass

Commentary was provided by Mary McGlone, CSJ.

◆ FIRST READING: Isaiah's servant song describes John the Baptist. Called before he was born, formed by God and kept hidden until the proper moment, he too wondered if his mission was in vain. But, God worked through him to fulfill a plan John couldn't fully understand. So, too, we are uniquely to be God's messengers, trusting that God can work through us, whether or not we understand how.

◆ RESPONSORIAL PSALM 139: No psalm compares to this as a meditation on God's care for each of us and desire for us to know and live our vocation. It is especially apt for moments when we, like John, may be unsure of what we are called to do.

◆ SECOND READING: Paul's short description of John summarizes the essence of the man: a charismatic preacher who was able to tell his fans and followers, "I am not [the One]." John calls us to be similar witnesses, not seeking the spotlight, but using it to point out the way to the One we trust and proclaim.

◆ GOSPEL: John's nativity account places him in the heart of Israel, born of parents who mirror Abraham and Sarah in their age, their desire for a child, and their wonder at his birth. His father's first words after recovering his speech affirmed that John's name had come from beyond, assuring that God had chosen him from before his birth. The real wonder is that the same is true for us.

The Roman Missal

◆ AT THE MASS DURING THE DAY: The Gloria is sung or said today.

The Collect speaks about the preparatory role of the Baptist as one who was raised up "to make ready a nation fit for Christ the Lord." This prayer prays that we may be directed "into the way of salvation and peace."

Remember that, because it is a solemnity, the Creed is said today.

The Prayer over the Offerings expresses why it is fitting to celebrate the nativity of St. John: it is because he "both foretold the coming of the world's Savior / and pointed him out when he came."

The text for the proper Preface used today is located immediately following the Prayer over the Offerings. See the commentary above under the Vigil Mass.

The Prayer after Communion uses the imagery of the Lamb so closely associated with John the Baptist's announcement of Jesus, and in so doing the prayer gives voice to a rich Eucharistic theology with its phrase "Having feasted at the banquet of the heavenly Lamb . . ."

As remarked concerning the Vigil Mass, an argument could be made that the dismissal formula "Go and announce the Gospel of the Lord" fits in well with today's focus on the life and mission of St. John the Baptist.

T H U 25 (#374) green
Weekday

The Lectionary for Mass

◆ FIRST READING: The writers of the Old Testament were neither scandalmongers nor saint-makers. The stories of our ancestors in the faith recount their weaknesses as well as their faith. In today's reading, we hear about Abraham's first son, Ishmael, whom God would protect and prosper, even if he wasn't to be the child of the promise.

◆ RESPONSORIAL PSALM 106: Praying this psalm with Hagar in mind,

we can recall how God transforms unfortunate or even tragic events into occasions of grace. Remembering this pattern of God's activity among us offers new perspective on whatever may be troubling us at the moment.

◆ GOSPEL: Jesus could not be more direct than he is in today's Gospel account. What we profess with our lips can be either true or self-righteous. We make our real proclamation of faith by our everyday actions. Even "driv[ing] out demons" can be a self-promoting show rather than a real offering of ourselves to free another. With these words, Jesus asks his followers to evaluate the real motivation of their behavior. The essential question is "Whom do we serve?"

F R I 26 (#375) green
Weekday

The Lectionary for Mass

◆ FIRST READING: We might ask ourselves which is more laughable, that an old couple should have a child or that a person would walk blamelessly in the presence of God. Obviously, our ancestors in the faith were less than perfect, but they did strive to be conscious of God every day of their lives. If we do the same we will share in their blessings.

◆ RESPONSORIAL PSALM 128: Our psalm invites us to really stop and notice God's blessings in our own and others' lives. Then if we develop an attitude of thanksgiving, we will keep deepening our awareness that everything we are and experience is gift.

◆ GOSPEL: This account of Jesus's healing a leper is striking in its brevity. What is hidden in the leper's phrase, "If you wish"? For us, it may serve as a reminder that God does not take away all our ills, but rather promises to be with us in sickness and in health.

SAT 27 (#376) green
Weekday

Optional Memorials of St. Cyril of Alexandria, Bishop and Doctor of the Church / white; Blessed Virgin Mary / white

The Lectionary for Mass

◆ FIRST READING: Abraham welcomes the strangers with overwhelming hospitality. In turn, he received the unlikely fulfillment of the promise that Sarah would have a child. While we believe that God will not be outdone in generosity, until we learn that there is no stranger in this world unworthy of our attention, we may miss the opportunity to welcome the God who comes to meet us.

◆ CANTICLE: God's mercy extends "in every generation." We sing Mary's hymn of praise and thanks, remembering times when we, like Sarah and Mary, have been greatly blessed by God.

◆ GOSPEL: The three people Jesus heals in this Gospel were among those prohibited from taking part in the liturgical assembly. The conditions of leprosy or being a stranger or woman were sufficient for exclusion. The migrant patriarch Abraham welcomed strangers only to discover they represented God. Jesus reached out to the marginated, declaring that human laws could not set the boundaries of the Reign of God.

28 (#98) green
Thirteenth Sunday in Ordinary Time

The Lectionary for Mass

◆ FIRST READING: This beautiful selection from the Book of Wisdom reminds us that God is the God of Life. Even more wondrous, we are created in God's own image. These are simple ideas well worth contemplating.

◆ RESPONSORIAL PSALM 30: We may not have experienced overwhelming miracles, but each of us has surely experienced God's providence in a time of need. Perhaps it happened when we were at a loss for words and they "came" to us, or we could see no way out, and an alternative appeared unexpectedly. It could well have been a healing at the hands of one of God's servants in the medical field. Whatever the circumstances, it is good for us to remember and give thanks.

◆ SECOND READING: Paul is asking the Corinthians to help a community they do not know. Why should they do it? God has been good to them, and the only fitting response is to be good to others.

◆ GOSPEL: The account of these two miracles provides an action-packed follow-up to the parable of the seed that grows overnight (Mark 4). Both the woman and the girl's father set out to put their faith into action, and thus they opened up the

space for God to work wonders for them.

The Roman Missal

The Collect contrasts light and darkness. God has chosen us as "children of light." We pray that we may not be "wrapped in the darkness of error," but remain in the "bright light of truth." We pray that our "deeds" may be worthy of the "sacred gifts" we receive in this sacrifice (Prayer over the Offerings). We pray that the "divine sacrifice" we have received may so "fill us with life" that we may "bear fruit that lasts forever" (Prayer after Communion).

Other Ideas

Today's readings speak of death and illness. We don't like to think of these aspects of life but today presents a good opportunity to invite parishioners to a preparation session for funerals or an adult faith formation session on a Catholic theology of death, suffering, afterlife, and Resurrection. Consider offering a funeral preparation workshop with information on cremation, the three parts of the Catholic funeral liturgy, and how to pick Lectionary readings and music. Invite middle-aged parishioners to attend with their parents. One may find that this helps families broach these difficult topics.

Remember those who work in health care professions or pastoral care ministers who take Communion to the sick. Include them in the Universal Prayer or consider offering a special blessing for these ministers today at the end of Mass. If the parish needs more volunteer ministers to the sick and homebound, today would be a good day to have extraordinary ministers of Holy Communion who minister to the sick and homebound speak at all the Masses (following the Prayer after Communion). A personal touch is extremely important in all minsterial roles.

Announce any special times for morning Masses or other Independence Day celebrations.

Today is also the collection for Peter's Pence, which allows the Vatican to engage in many ministries and outreach programs (www.usccb.org/catholic-giving/opportunities-for-giving/peters-pence/).

(#591)   red

MON 29 Solemnity of Sts. Peter and Paul, Apostles

About this Solemnity

Today we commemorate Sts. Peter and Paul, martyred around the year 64 AD during Nero's persecution following the Great Fire of Rome. Tradition says that Peter fled Rome to avoid arrest and saw Jesus on the road. "Where are you going, Lord," Peter asked. Jesus replied, "I am going to Rome to be crucified again." Peter turned back and was crucified upside down because he felt unworthy to meet his death the same way as Christ. Paul was arrested in Jerusalem and was sent to Rome, where he was placed under house arrest. He was slain by beheading, because as a Roman citizen he could not be subjected to the indignity of crucifixion.

The Lectionary for Mass (Vigil)

Commentary was provided by Anne Elizabeth Sweet, OSCO.

◆ FIRST READING: The story of the crippled beggar lying at the gate of the Temple who receives the gift of healing in the name of the Lord Jesus from the hands of Peter and not the alms he expected is the subject of today's First Reading. What better way to give God praise than fully using that which is restored to full health! The man walks and jumps with joy, giving God praise.

◆ RESPONSORIAL PSALM 19 declares the "glory of God" (verse 2) as spoken by creation. In the light of today's First Reading, "their" (see verse 5) refers not to creation, but to the voice of the Apostles.

◆ SECOND READING: Paul speaks to the Galatians of his encounter with the risen Jesus, a "revelation" that changed his life. Paul turned from persecutor to missionary of the Gospel, sent by the risen Lord to the Gentiles.

◆ GOSPEL: The risen Jesus commissions Peter, entrusting him with the care of the sheep of his flock. Jesus also speaks of how Peter will one day follow him, led by another to death, and ultimately to glory.

The Roman Missal (Vigil)

Two sets of Mass formularies are given for this Solemnity, "At the Vigil Mass" and "At the Mass during the Day."

The Collect continues to honor Peter and Paul together as it affirms that "through them you gave your Church / the foundations of her heavenly office"; the prayer goes on to ask that through them the Church may be assisted on her way to eternal salvation.

Remember that the Creed is said at this Vigil Mass.

The Prayer over the Offerings speaks of hopefulness and encouragement: it tells us that "the more we doubt our own merits, / the more we may rejoice that we are to be saved / by your loving kindness." We offer this Eucharist in union with the Apostles Peter and Paul who themselves, as the Scriptures so clearly tell us, were men who sinned and had their faults and weaknesses.

The Preface is proper for today, and it is found among the prayers for the Mass during the Day, a page turn away from the Vigil prayers. A text is given both with music and without; since it is a solemnity, strongly consider singing the

introductory dialogue and the Preface. The Preface mentions in tandem the attributes that are the reasons we commemorate these two Apostles: Peter is "foremost in confessing the faith" and is the one "who established the early Church from the remnant of Israel"; Paul is the faith's "outstanding preacher . . . master and teacher of the Gentiles." Thus is the mission of the Church both within Israel and beyond her to the whole world avowed.

The Prayer after Communion entreats that as we have been "enlightened with the teaching of the Apostles," so may we be strengthened by "this heavenly Sacrament."

The Solemn Blessing for Saints Peter and Paul, Apostles (#16 under "Blessings at the End of Mass and Prayers over the People") is suggested, and should be used today. It refers to Peter's "saving confession" and uses the image of the solid rock, and to "the tireless preaching of Saint Paul." It then brings the two together by highlighting "the keys of St. Peter and the words of St. Paul."

The Lectionary for Mass (Day)

Commentary was provided by Mary McGlone, CSJ.

◆ FIRST READING: This reading tells of one of Peter's prison escapes. There were some in the early Church who longed for martyrdom as a sign of their love for God. Peter and many of the other early martyrs longed not for martyrdom, but for the spread of the Gospel, and for that, they were willing to pay any price.

◆ RESPONSORIAL PSALM 34: This psalm of rejoicing in God's providence invites us to gratefully recall how God has sent "angels" to help us in times of trouble. When we remember our own time of deliverance from need, we are prepared to speak a word of encouragement to the "lowly."

◆ SECOND READING: Paul, too, recounts ways in which God has accompanied and preserved him throughout his ministry. Now he sees the end approaching and he can humbly say "I have finished the race." He invites us to ask what it is that we must do now so that when our day comes we can say the same.

◆ GOSPEL: This Gospel incident shows Peter in the best light possible as he proclaims faith in Jesus as the Son of God. But, in order to understand the whole picture, we need to read the next four verses which recall how incompletely the disciples understood Jesus and his mission. This Gospel and this feast remind us of champions of our faith and invite us to imitate their courage, knowing that even they had to grow in faith as they faced trials.

The Roman Missal (Day)

The Collect for this Mass during the Day reminds us that the Church's faith came through the Apostles Peter and Paul; it was through them that the Church "received / the beginnings of right religion."

Remember that, because it is a solemnity, the Creed is said today.

The Prayer over the Offerings asks for the powerful intercession of these two Apostles, praying that their prayer may "accompany the sacrificial gift / that we present to your name for consecration." Again we are reminded that every Eucharist is celebrated in communion with all the saints who have gone before us.

The Preface is proper for today; see the commentary for it above, under the Vigil Mass.

Although the Prayer after Communion does not mention Peter and Paul by name, it does pray that we might persevere "in the breaking of the Bread / and in the teaching of the Apostles"—notice the reference

to the Eucharist and to Tradition, without which the Church does not exist—and so live as Church as "one heart and one soul." The unity of the Church founded on the Apostles Peter and Paul is strengthened and nourished through sacrament and through authentic teaching.

As at the Vigil Mass, the Solemn Blessing for Sts. Peter and Paul, Apostles (number 16 under "Blessings at the End of Mass and Prayers over the People") is suggested for today, and should be used. The blessing mentions Peter's "saving confession" and the image of the solid rock, and Paul's "tireless preaching," also noting "the keys of St. Peter and the words of St. Paul."

(#378) green

T U E 30 Weekday (Thirteenth Week in Ordinary Time)

Optional Memorial of the First Martyrs of the Holy Roman Church / red

The Lectionary for Mass

◆ FIRST READING: Two details of Lot's story offer us food for contemplation. First, the seemingly strange prohibition of looking back reminds us that conversion demands looking forward, we are no longer to dwell on the enjoyments or the guilt of what is left behind. Second, the reading ends with Abraham understanding that God fulfilled the bargain to save the worthy in Sodom.

◆ RESPONSORIAL PSALM 26: We could well be praying this with Abraham in gratitude for God's mercy. Lest we be too convinced of our righteousness, we claim integrity but, in the next breath, ask for redemption. All of us are needy when we stand before God.

◆ GOSPEL: This miracle reveals Jesus as one with the Creator who has power over nature. At the same time, it offers us a path of hope and prayer whenever the storms of our

lives seem to be overwhelmingly dangerous. The question we must ask is whether we are ready for God to act powerfully in our lives or if we are so afraid of God's power that we would rather weather the storm alone.

Today's Saints

Today we commemorate the martyrs who died between the years 64–68 AD, around the same time as Saints Peter and Paul. The emperor Nero was accused of starting the Great Fire of Rome, and to divert attention from himself and satisfy his appetite for cruelty, he turned the blame on the Christians in Rome. They were rounded up and killed by various means: by crucifixion, by being fed to wild animals, and by being burned as torches to provide light for parties. The Roman historian Tacitus provides an independent record of their torture and death.

July
Month of the Most Precious Blood

(#379) green

W E D 1 Weekday

Optional Memorial of Blessed Junípero Serra, Priest / white

The Lectionary for Mass

◆ FIRST READING: As we watch Hagar driven out and wandering hopelessly, God's promise of care for the poor comes to the fore. This incident may remind us that the promise to one does not mean the other is forgotten. God's love is not a zero-sum contest. We may not understand God's self-revelation to and care for people of other traditions, but neither should we doubt it.

◆ PSALM 34: "The Lord hears the cry of the poor." What does that mean for us? When God heard the cry of Israel in Egypt, it was bad news for Pharaoh. We might well ask whose cry God is hearing today and what God expects of us in relation to those who are calling for help.

◆ GOSPEL: On this occasion, Jesus is in Gentile territory, and he chooses to heal a Gentile. Interestingly, this endeared him to almost no one. His own people didn't approve of interaction with the pagans, and the Garadenes were less than happy with the loss of their pigs. Jesus seemed to be left with only the approval of someone known as a demoniac. Serving the poor is not often a path to popularity.

Today's Saint

Blessed Junípero Serra (1713–1784) was a Spanish Franciscan friar, best known for founding the string of twenty-one missions that stretch from San Diego to Sonoma, California. Junípero was born in Majorca. At age 16 he entered the Franciscans. After completing his theological studies, he served as professor of philosophy at Majorca before volunteering for the missions in the "New World." Upon arrival, he went to Mexico City to dedicate his mission at the shrine of Our Lady of Guadalupe. Serra founded his first mission at San Diego in 1769, and worked his way up the coast along El Camino Real, making converts as he went. In spite of a leg injury he suffered at the beginning of his ministry, he traveled on foot whenever possible, eventually covering 24,000 miles.

THU 2 (#380) green
Weekday

The Lectionary for Mass

◆ FIRST READING: The story of Abraham's willingness to sacrifice Isaac is unintelligible to contemporary ears. If we could hear it as did our ancestors in the faith, we would find two unexpected lessons. First, child sacrifice was common among the ancients. The story of Abraham ultimately repudiates the practice as something God rejects. Secondly, Abraham becomes renowned for his obedience, making obedience more important than any sacrifice a people would offer. The people's relationship with God was thus based on love, not propitiation.

◆ RESPONSORIAL PSALM 115: Today's antiphon can easily be applied to both Abraham and Isaac: Abraham for his total obedience; Isaac, in his deliverance from death. The stanzas of today's psalm contrast the powerlessness of idols with the glory of the God of Israel.

◆ GOSPEL: In the Gospel readings over the past few days, we have seen Jesus exercise power over nature and over demons. Today, his power over sin, his power to forgive sin, is demonstrated. In Jesus's day, people considered illness to be a punishment for sin. Thus, forgiveness and healing go hand in hand.

FRI 3 (#593) red
Feast of St. Thomas, Apostle

The Lectionary for Mass

◆ FIRST READING: Paul's words invite us to rejoice in the company of the saints. How good it is to remember that we have such marvelous companions in the household of God!

◆ RESPONSORIAL PSALM 117: Our song is short and simple. Let us discover how to praise God together with all the peoples.

◆ GOSPEL: Though Thomas retains the fame on one doubting statement, we know he was also a faithful disciple whom legend credits with sharing the Gospel as far away as India. He reminds us that when we face our doubts, our faith can grow to new, unexpected proportions.

The Roman Missal

The texts for this Mass, all proper for the feast today, are located in the Proper of Saints section of the Missal at July 3. The Gloria is sung or said today, since it is a feast.

The Collect points to the Apostle Thomas's acknowledgement of the Lord as read in the Scriptures. The Prayer over the Offerings again refers to St. Thomas's confession, asking that the gifts God has given us — the gifts of faith — be kept safe. The Prayer after Communion again echoes the Gospel as the prayer asks that, in receiving the Sacrament of the Eucharist, "we may recognize him / with the Apostle Thomas by faith / as our Lord and our God." This recognition of the Lord, however, cannot be a passive gazing; rather, as a result of sacramental Communion, we must go on to "proclaim him by our deeds and by our life."

The Preface, proper for today, is one of the two Prefaces of the Apostles. Also, the Solemn Blessing formula titled "The Apostles" (#17 of the "Blessings at the End of Mass and Prayers over the People") is fittingly used as the final blessing at the end of Mass today.

Today's Saint

Thomas, also called "Didymus" or "the Twin" (John 11:16) was one of the Twelve Apostles. He is remembered for doubting the Resurrection of Christ: "Unless I see the mark of the nails in his hands and put my finger into the nail marks and put my hand into his side, I will not believe." The following week, Thomas was with the Twelve when Jesus appeared and chided him for his lack of faith: "Have you come to believe because you have seen me? Blessed are those who have not seen and have believed" (John 20:25–29). After seeing the risen Christ alive, Thomas exclaims "My Lord and my God!" According to tradition, Thomas is the only Apostle who went outside the borders of the Roman Empire to evangelize. Although there is a Gospel account attributed to him, it is not accepted in the canon of Scripture, and is, in fact of gnostic origin. The people of Kerala in South India fervently believe that it was Thomas who evangelized them. He is represented in art with a spear, the instrument of his martyrdom. He is the patron of architects and builders, and of India, where today is a solemnity.

SAT 4 (#382) green
Weekday

Optional Mass for Independence Day / white; Optional Memorial of the Blessed Virgin Mary / white

The Lectionary for Mass

The commentary was written by Anne Elizabeth Sweet, osco.

◆ FIRST READING: Today's First Reading is a beautiful message from the Lord of all comforts and consolation. Despite the punishment meted out on the wicked, God will one day restore the kingly line of the house of David and the house of Israel. The Lord is ever faithful to his promises.

◆ RESPONSORIAL PSALM 85: Today's antiphon aptly expresses the message of today's First Reading. We are all called to hear his word, to welcome his salvation.

◆ GOSPEL: The image of Jesus as Bridegroom echoes an Old Testament image for God (see Isaiah 54:6). Similarly, the glory of the end time is depicted as a wedding feast (see Revelation 21). When Jesus lived on earth, the divine Bridegroom was one of us and dwelt among us. It was indeed the beginning of a new creation.

☀ 5 (#101) green
Fourteenth Sunday in Ordinary Time

The Lectionary for Mass

◆ FIRST READING: God's communications may sometimes be more realistic than we would hope. Here, Ezekiel is called to be a prophet and warned that he will likely not find success. We might question the value of taking on such a mission. God's answer is simply, "They shall know that a prophet has been among them." No one who has heard a prophet can claim innocence through ignorance.

◆ RESPONSORIAL PSALM 123: This is a prayer designed to sustain one like Ezekiel. His heart cannot be set on accomplishment, or else he would soon find another occupation. Fixing our eyes on Christ, especially in a communal context, will show us the way through anything we need to face.

◆ SECOND READING: Paul is offering us an example of selfless discipleship. He challenges us to accept our weakness as the religious and emotional space where we can best encounter God working in and through us.

◆ GOSPEL: Perhaps the best lesson this Gospel teaches us comes from the "audience." Rather than reassess their way of thinking, they convinced themselves that Jesus, coming from a simple family known to all of them, couldn't

possibly have a new message worthy of their attention. Are we ready to hear a divine message from a simple source?

The Roman Missal

The Mass texts for today are found in the "Ordinary Time" section of the Proper of Time. The Gloria is sung or said today.

The Collect points to God's raising up of our fallen world through "the abasement" of his Son. (It is hoped that the hearers at Mass do not mishear the phrase and think that a basement, as in a cellar, is being referred to!) The image is meant to reflect the Paschal Mystery of lowliness leading to glory, which brings "holy joy," as the prayer goes on to ask for "eternal gladness" to be bestowed upon those who have been rescued from slavery to sin (that is, through the Son's act of humble love). The Prayer over the Offerings prays for purification of our lives to occur through the oblation being offered; it reminds us of the concrete changes we must make in our lives if we are going to truly live what we believe, as we pray that participating in this celebration might "day by day bring / our conduct closer to the life of heaven." The Prayer after Communion notes how the food of the Eucharist replenishes us so that "we may gain the prize of salvation / and never cease to praise you." That the Eucharist is nourishment for the journey to heaven must never be forgotten.

Any one of the eight Prefaces of the Sundays in Ordinary Time can be used. In making a choice, note how Preface I, with its mention of Jesus accomplishing "the marvelous deed," or Preface II, with its mention of his humbling himself to be born of the Virgin, could echo the theme of "abasement" (humility) mentioned in the Collect, and the meekness and humility of Christ. Preface IV's reference to experiencing daily the effects of God's care could connect with the notion of "day by day conduct" referred to in the Prayer over the Offerings and also correlate with the notion of the burdened finding rest in the Lord as described in the Gospel. Another possibility would be to use Eucharistic Prayer IV today, with its own proper Preface, because of its recap of how Jesus proclaimed the Good News of salvation to the poor, freedom to prisoners, and joy to the sorrowful of heart, which would also echo one theme from the Gospel.

Other Ideas

The congregation is going to be mindful of the holiday weekend and will be expecting to hear patriotic musical selections, especially on Saturday. Perhaps a good compromise is be to play a patriotic prelude or postlude or to use "This is My Song" FINLANDIA, "God of Our Fathers" or "Faith of our Fathers" as a closing hymn. Because there may be guests at liturgy, make sure you have enough hospitality ministers scheduled. Include petitions for the nation, the world, for peace, and for travelers in the Universal Prayer.

MON 6 (#383) green
Weekday

Optional memorial of St. Maria Goretti, Virgin and Martyr / red

The Lectionary for Mass

◆ FIRST READING: Jacob's dream included a crucial revelation. As he rested at a shrine, his inclination was to convert it, to make it a holy place for his faith tradition. Nevertheless, God's message urged him far beyond that. The God who revealed himself to Jacob was not a god of places, but the God of all, the God who is found, not in shrines, but through personal relationship. The God of Abraham and Isaac wishes to be our God too.

◆ RESPONSORIAL PSALM 19: We sing of our trust in the God who promises to be personally near us when we call.

◆ GOSPEL: The woman with the hemorrhage reminds us that sometimes we may lack the courage or words to beg God for what we need. Even when we can do no more than reach out, if we do so in hopeful faith, God can hear and respond and heal us.

Today's Saint

Although St. Maria Goretti (1890–1902) walked this earth for a short time, her life speaks to all generations. As a simple young girl born to poor farmers in Italy, she demonstrated a piety and zeal uncharacteristic of someone her age. Her life ended prematurely when she was murdered by a young man named Alessandro, because she would not succumb to his sexual advances. Right before she died, Saint Maria extended forgiveness to her attacker with the simple phrase, "for the love of Jesus." At Saint Maria's canonization ceremony, in which her family members were present, she was declared a martyr for chastity. The Passionists, a religious congregation founded by Saint Paul of the Cross, claim her as one of their own because she was raised in a parish staffed by Passionist priests.

TUE 7 (#384) green
Weekday

The Lectionary for Mass

◆ FIRST READING: Jacob is renamed because of his long struggle with an unknown being. His new name, which becomes the name of his descendants, reminds us that every people of God becomes who they are through a process of struggle. God may test us to teach us our own strength, but, God respects our freedom and will never overpower us.

◆ RESPONSORIAL PSALM 17: This could well have been Jacob's prayer after his all night struggle. When we pray with total sincerity and full of trust, we will discover how God shows mercy and hovers over to lead us safely through our distress.

◆ GOSPEL: "Ask the master of the harvest to send out laborers." God called the patriarchs to give life to a nation, then Moses to lead them to freedom. Jesus handed his mission over to his followers. Today, we need laborers to continue the work of building up the Kingdom of God. Jesus tells us we must pray that God send them, which means that we must be willing to give our part for what we pray for.

WED 8 (#385) green
Weekday

The Lectionary for Mass

◆ GOSPEL: We take a huge leap through Genesis to arrive at this summary of Joseph's history. For the next three days we will hear how Joseph allowed God to achieve the greatest good for his family through the tragedy of their selling him into slavery.

◆ RESPONSORIAL PSALM 33: The refrain of our psalm summarizes it all. We pray for the fulfillment of God's designs, which are mercy-filled plans for us. We have faith that God's plan will eventually be fulfilled, and pray that it may happen in our day.

◆ GOSPEL: Yesterday Jesus called for prayer for laborers. Today, we hear him name and commission the first Twelve to carry out his mission. Those good Israelites knew their history, and surely knew that being God's messengers was risky business. May we, like them, be ready to go where the Lord would send us.

THU 9 (#386) green
Weekday

Optional Memorial of Blessed Augustine Zhao Rong, Priest, and Companions, Martyrs / red

The Lectionary for Mass

◆ FIRST READING: Today, Joseph gives us an example by refusing to take vengeance on the brothers who betrayed him. He does not condone their action, but teaches them that God had brought a greater good out of the evil they had done. His history proved that there is no situation or problem that God cannot redeem — even if not the way we would plan it.

◆ RESPONSORIAL PSALM 105: Remembering the example of Joseph, we pray to remember the wonders God has worked in history. The prayer invites us to put our problems into God's today.

◆ GOSPEL: Were you ever moved to conversion by a preacher who was full of himself? Jesus sends out the disciples to serve others, clothed and fortified only with humility and gratitude for all that God has done for them. That, according to Jesus, is all that they will need to carry forth his mission.

Today's Saints

Between 1648 and 1930, eighty-seven Chinese Catholics and thirty-three Western missionaries, some of whom were Dominicans, Franciscans, Salesians, Jesuits, or Vincentians, were martyred for their ministry or for refusing to renounce their Christian faith. Many of the Chinese converts were killed during the Boxer Rebellion, a xenophobic uprising during which many foreigners were slaughtered by angry peasants. Augustine Zhao Rong was a Chinese diocesan priest who was tortured and killed in 1815 after the Emperor Kia-Kin issued decrees banning Catholicism. Augustine Zhao Rong and the other Chinese martyrs were canonized in 2000 by Pope John Paul II.

FRI 10 (#387) green
Weekday

The Lectionary for Mass

◆ FIRST READING: We return to the narrative about Israel/Jacob who, like his grandfather Abraham, was called to leave his homeland. God promises to go to Egypt with Jacob, assuring him that God is not a territorial god limited to a particular geography, but the God of history whose grace working in people will affect the course of events.

◆ RESPONSORIAL PSALM 37: Today we sing a song of gratitude and obedience. We celebrate our God, our refuge in distress, the One who offers us our heart's request and an eternal inheritance.

◆ GOSPEL: In our psalm we prayed that God delivers the just. In the Gospel, Jesus warns that discipleship will entail great trials, but he promises salvation to those who endure. This is where we might echo Peter who, recognizing that following Jesus would be hard, but that leaving him would be worse, simply said "Lord, to whom could we go? You alone have the words of eternal life."

SAT 11 (#388) white
Memorial of St. Benedict, Abbot

The Lectionary for Mass

◆ FIRST READING: This touching family scene portrays a major shift in Israel's self-awareness. The great nation began with three patriarchs. After Jacob's death, Joseph could have assumed leadership, even dictatorship, on the merits of saving his family. Nevertheless, he was inspired to establish a new way of being among them. No longer would there be one ruler or patriarch like the Egyptian Pharaoh, but the leaders of each tribe would collaborate together for the good of the whole.

◆ RESPONSORIAL PSALM 105: The lowly are glad when God reigns in their midst. As we pray this psalm we are invited to question ourselves about our deepest desires. If our hopes bring joy to the poor, we have aligned our hearts with God and we will give thanks together.

◆ GOSPEL: Of the many teachings we have here, the one that summarizes them all is that the vocation of a disciple is to become like the master. As such servants, we will replicate Jesus's care for those in need, all the while facing fear with the confidence that God cares for us more and better than we could imagine.

The Roman Missal

The orations, all proper today, are found in the Proper of Saints at July 11. The Collect recognizes St. Benedict as being "an outstanding master in the school of divine service," a nod, of course, to his famous *Rule*. The Prayer over the Offerings asks that we follow Benedict's example in seeking God; the Prayer after Communion prays that, by being attentive to the teaching of St. Benedict, we may serve God's designs and "love one another with fervent charity" as a result of our receiving this sacrament as a "pledge of eternal life." The Preface may be either Preface I or II of Saints or the Preface of Holy Virgins and Religious.

Today's Saint

Saddened by the immoral state of society, St. Benedict of Nursia (480–553/7) left the city to live as a hermit at Subiaco. In time, more and more men were attracted to his charismatic personality as well as to his way of life. He eventually moved a group of monks to Monte Cassino, near Naples, where he completed the final version of his

Rule, now known as *The Rule of Saint Benedict*, on the fundamentals of monastic life, including the day-to-day operation of a monastery. The *Rule* asserts that the primary occupation of the monk is to pray the Divine Office in tandem with a vowed life of stability, obedience, and conversion. The whole of the monastic vocation can be summarized in the opening line of his *Rule*, "Listen carefully." St. Benedict is considered the father of Western monasticism.

12 (#104) green
Fifteenth Sunday in Ordinary Time

The Lectionary for Mass

◆ FIRST READING: When the priest told Amos to stop his prophesying, Amos had a simple response. He told the priest that because it was not he, but God, who had called him to his vocation, no human had the authority to tell him where or how to prophesy.

◆ RESPONSORIAL PSALM 85: As we pray this psalm, we are challenged to put our heart and soul into the words we say. Are we ready to ask for the kindness and salvation God offers or do we want to fill out an order for God so that our requests will be answered according to our will.

◆ SECOND READING: Paul is calling us to rejoice in the mystery of our very being. He invites us to contemplate what it means to have been chosen "before the foundation of the world, to be holy."

◆ GOSPEL: Jesus "summoned the Twelve." They did not choose him, but he them, and he sent them. Likewise, we who are baptized have been summoned to continue Jesus's mission in the world. This is a moment to ask what gifts God has given us for the good of others.

The Roman Missal

The Mass texts for today are found in the "Ordinary Time" section of the Proper of Time. The Gloria is sung or said today.

The Collect addresses the living of the Christian life, as it reminds us that God shows the light of truth "to those who go astray," praying that "they may return to the right path." However, we must always remember that we are all among those who could at any time go astray; hence, the prayer goes on to ask that all who "are accounted Christian" may be given "the grace to reject whatever is contrary to the name of Christ." Being converted to the Gospel is an ongoing journey for us all, one that is never complete. The Prayer over the Offerings speaks to the effects of participating in the sacred meal of the Eucharist, noting that the ultimate end of the offerings (of bread and wine) is that of being consumed "by those who believe." Thus, the prayer asks that those offerings "may bring ever greater holiness" to those who consume them. The Prayer after Communion directly picks up on this by its opening reference to the action that has just taken place: "Having consumed these gifts, we pray, O Lord. . . ." Notice how participation in Eucharistic liturgy is highlighted here by the sacred actions of offering and of eating and drinking. It is only participating in the sacred actions that we can in any way hope that the "saving effects upon us may grow."

Any one of the eight Prefaces of the Sundays in Ordinary Time could rightly be used to equal pastoral advantage today.

Other Ideas

In Mark's account of the Gospel, Jesus sends the missionaries without a cloak or sandals. Perhaps this is a good week to have a presentation from a missionary or to recognize youth outreach programs in the parish.

Speaking of tunics, during the summer months be sure your altar server robes are cleaned. Enlist the help of volunteers to clean them or take them to the dry cleaners along with the priest's albs and vestments.

During these summer months, take time for relaxation and vacation. Go on a retreat, listen to music, or attend a liturgical workshop. Rejuvenate your soul and ministry!

13 (#389) green
Weekday

Optional Memorial of St. Henry / white

The Lectionary for Mass

◆ FIRST READING: It is the most natural thing in the world for oppressors to fear their victims. As we see in Exodus, fear, and its mirror image of lack of belief in one's own worth, can lead even to genocide. Thus, the Chosen People were enslaved and in danger of extermination.

◆ RESPONSORIAL PSALM 124: To pray "our help is in the name of the LORD" is to be convinced that using evil's tactics to overcome it cannot succeed in the long run. In order to make that faith a reality, we must have patience and immense, hopeful trust that God will reveal a solution that we had not imagined.

◆ GOSPEL: Jesus makes the radical demands of discipleship clear in this passage. Simply put, there is no relationship in family or community that outweighs discipleship. Jesus himself showed the way by making everyone his family, even though his blood relatives did not understand it.

Today's Saint

St. Henry II (972–1024) was a German king and Holy Roman Emperor, the only German king to be canonized. Henry had considered becoming a priest, but when his father died, he inherited his father's title of Duke of Bavaria. He became King of Germany in 1002 and married Cunegunda, who is also a saint. He had a reputation for being learned and pious, and was a positive influence in Church-state relations. At that time, secular authorities appointed bishops and often selected their political allies. Henry appointed bishops who would be good pastors, and supported them in their work. Although he waged many wars, he was not the aggressor but fought only to protect his borders and preserve peace. Henry is a patron saint of Benedictine oblates and is invoked against infertility, for he and his wife were childless.

(#390)   white

T U E
14
Memorial of St. Kateri Tekakwitha, Virgin

The Lectionary for Mass

◆ FIRST READING: What is the effect of having been rescued from death? While we may not have thought about it, even the odds that we would have been born are astonishingly small, especially if we consider the many generations before us and life's precarious conditions before our own time. Recognizing that reality, we may, like Moses, come to realize that we have something unique to accomplish during our short lifetime.

◆ RESPONSORIAL PSALM 69: The psalm refrain reminds us to turn to God in need. Later in the psalm we promise to sing praise and glorify God in thanksgiving. The most appropriate way to give that thanks is to live as though our lives were precious enough to have been saved.

◆ GOSPEL: Jesus condemns nearby cities for rejecting his offer of life. In her day, many refused to believe that the Native American St. Kateri, could be a model Christian. Today we are invited to open our eyes and hearts to see and respond to God's mighty deeds among us.

The Roman Missal

The Collect, the only prayer proper for today, can be found in the Proper of Saints at July 14. It specifically mentions both St. Kateri's Native American heritage and her innocence, praying for the unity of all believers gathered together "from every nation, tribe and tongue." The Prayer over the Offerings and the Prayer after Communion are taken from the Common of Virgins: For One Virgin. Either Preface I or Preface II of Saints would be the appropriate choice for today.

Today's Saint

St. Kateri Tekakwitha (1656–1680), called the "Lily of the Mohawks," is the first Native American to have been beatified and was recently canonized a saint. The daughter of a Mohawk chief and a Christian Algonquin, she vowed to live as a virgin. She eventually decided to convert to Christianity after a few encounters with Jesuit missionaries. Her decision to convert was not received well within her community because Christianity was seen as the religion of the oppressors. St. Kateri was a pious woman who attended daily Mass, fasted twice a week, taught children, and cared for the sick. After she died, a number of miracles and visions were attributed to her intercession. Tekakwitha was canonized in 2012.

(#391)   white

W E D
15
Memorial of St. Bonaventure, Bishop and Doctor of the Church

The Lectionary for Mass

◆ FIRST READING: Moses begins a risky conversation with God in today's reading. He recognizes God's holiness, but when he asked for a sign about his mission he was told only that God would be with him and after succeeding against the Pharaoh, he and his people would worship God in the place he was then. It is no wonder that he insisted on asking more!

◆ RESPONSORIAL PSALM 103: God promised to be with Moses. Psalm 103 invites us to celebrate God's goodness to us every day in every way.

◆ GOSPEL: Let the PHDs go to the back of the room! Education and achievement are not the measure of discipleship. Jesus praises God for the wisdom of the simple. He assures us that knowing God and being God's instrument for others does not depend on cleverness, but on grace freely received and shared.

The Roman Missal

The Collect proper for today is found in the Proper of Saints at July 15. That Collect recognizes St. Bonaventure's "great learning" and also asks that we may "constantly imitate the ardor of his charity." Both the Prayer over the Offerings and the Prayer after Communion will have to be taken from either the Common of Pastors: For a Bishop, or from the Common of Doctors of the Church. While either Preface I or II or Saints could be used, it would also be fitting to use the Preface of Holy Pastors.

Today's Saint

St. Bonaventure (1221–1274), scholastic theologian and philosopher, was born in Italy and joined the Franciscans in 1243. He studied theology at Paris with his great contemporary, Thomas Aquinas. After teaching for a time, he was chosen Minister General of the Franciscans in 1257, at a time when the order suffered from divisions, which he was able to do much to heal. Later, he was named Cardinal Bishop of Albano. Bonaventure was declared a Doctor of the Church in 1588 by Pope Sixtus V, and is called the "Seraphic Doctor" because his love of God is so evident, even in his philosophical writings. When the Council of Lyons was called to bring the Greek and Latin churches back together, Bonaventure went at the request of Pope Gregory X, but he died before the Council's work was finished, receiving the Sacrament of the Sick from the pope himself. St. Bonaventure is shown in art dressed in a Franciscan habit and wearing a cardinal's hat.

THU 16 (#392) green
Weekday

Optional Memorial of Our Lady of Mount Carmel / white

The Lectionary for Mass

◆ FIRST READING: This is the pinnacle of Moses's experience: not only does he speak to God, but he hears God's name. The only trouble is that God's name is not really a name at all and is not translatable. The closest translation is probably "I shall be who I shall be." The other hint Moses gets is that God is the God of Abraham, Isaac, and Jacob. Putting those two titles together, we can conclude that humanity can only know God through God's action in our history. We, of course, would add that God is the God revealed in Jesus Christ.

◆ RESPONSORIAL PSALM 105: Singing this, we praise God's faithfulness and recall God's great deeds in history.

◆ GOSPEL: In Jesus's day a yoke symbolized the Law. With this statement, Jesus offers an alternative to a religious life centered on fulfilling every detail of the Law. His easy yoke is nothing more or less than love of God and neighbor.

Today's Saint

Mount Carmel is part of a mountain range in northern Israel, significant to Christians for its biblical association with the prophet Elijah (see 1 Kings 18). In the twelfth century, the Carmelites were founded at a site reputed to have been Elijah's cave. They soon built a monastery here. The Carmelites honor the Blessed Virgin Mary under the title Our Lady of Mount Carmel. The English Carmelite, St. Simon Stock, is believed to have been given the brown scapular by Our Lady, and those who wear it believe they can be sure of her help at the hour of their death.

FRI 17 (#393) green
Weekday

The Lectionary for Mass

◆ FIRST READING: The establishment of the month of the Pasch, the time of Passover, as the first month of the year, gave a unique character to the Jewish calendar. Passover, like the Christian feast of Easter, symbolized a new creation, the time when God saves the people. We might ask ourselves how to maintain our awareness that we are indeed in a new creation where death, oppression, and sin have been rendered powerless.

◆ RESPONSORIAL PSALM 116: How might we offer a sacrifice of thanksgiving for God's goodness to us? The psalm suggests that the truest "return" we can make is to gratefully and wholly accept what God offers. How might we take up the cup of salvation today?

◆ GOSPEL: One would think that the Pharisees would learn: challenging Jesus leads to losing the debate. Jesus, as he did in the Sermon on the Mount, explained the heart of the Jewish law: the welfare of human beings was the purpose for which God gave the Law in the first place.

SAT 18 (#394) green
Weekday

Optional Memorials of St. Camillus de Lellis, Priest / white; Blessed Virgin Mary / white

The Lectionary for Mass

◆ FIRST READING: What a lovely, subtle detail we hear in "This was a night of vigil for the LORD, as he led them out." Here we have an image of God watching as a mother watches over a sick child. How better to remember that than to set aside one night a year to keep vigil for the Lord, remembering God's great solicitude for us.

◆ RESPONSORIAL PSALM 136: This call and response psalm sings praise and recalls God's mighty deeds. We might add our own verses from Christian history or our own salvation story.

◆ GOSPEL: In this reading we see how the earliest Christians began to interpret Jesus and his mission. Jesus's preference for secrecy might well have been an attempt to avoid being followed for his wonders rather than his message. In that, he mirrored the Servant of Isaiah's prophecy who preached without imposition or triumphalism and whose message brought more hope than amazement.

Today's Saint

Laying aside a life of violence and gambling, St. Camillus de Lellis (1550–1614) was ordained a priest and later founded the Order of Clerks Regular Ministers to the Sick (the Camillians), a religious order dedicated to the sick, especially those afflicted with the plague. Whether they were ministering in a hospital or tending to the wounded on the battlefield, the Camillians were easily identified by their black habit with a large red cross on the breast. St. Camillus implemented many innovative approaches to hospital care, including proper ventilation, suitable diets, and isolation of people with infectious diseases. He is also credited with inventing field ambulances and military hospitals. Along with St. John of God, he is patron of hospitals, nurses, and the sick.

☀ 19 (#107) green
Sixteenth Sunday in Ordinary Time

The Lectionary for Mass

◆ First Reading: The religious leaders of Jeremiah's day left much to be desired. The assurance we find in this reading is that God will find a way to care for us, even when those appointed do not live up to their calling. If we hope for leadership that cares for those in greatest need, we must also be prepared to do our part.

◆ Responsorial Psalm 23: This most well-known psalm reminds us that God is ever watching over us. It does not promise a life of ease, but rather that God will be there with us through the dark valleys.

◆ Second Reading: Paul tells us that Christ is our peace. The work of Christ was to bring together all of us who were far off and far apart. Therefore, when we offer or seek the peace of Christ, we are committing ourselves to do our part to bring about the unity that all of humanity was created to enjoy.

◆ Gospel: Here we see Jesus's solicitude for his disciples and the crowds. Like the disciples, we need to know that there is a time for rest as well as a time to respond to the needs of others. Pastors understand that there are times when the needs of the sheep prevail.

The Roman Missal

The Mass texts for today are located in the "Ordinary Time" section of the Proper of Time. The Gloria is sung or said today.

The Collect, in asking God to "mercifully increase the gifts of your grace," can be seen as setting a tone for hearing the parables in today's Gospel. The Prayer over the Offerings reminds us that Christ's "one perfect sacrifice" completed all prior offerings of the law and asks that our sacrifice, like Abel's, will be made holy; the communal aspect of our worship is highlighted as the prayer gives the reason we ask the sacrifice to be made holy: "so that what each has offered to the honor of your majesty / may benefit the salvation of all." The Prayer after Communion is a prayer used frequently in Easter Time; it asks that we "pass from former ways to newness of life" as a result of our having been "imbued with heavenly mysteries." The passage of the Paschal Mystery focused on so intently during Easter Time is, of course, at the heart of every celebration of the Eucharist.

Any one of the eight Prefaces of the Sundays in Ordinary Time may be selected for today. Using Eucharistic Prayer I, the Roman Canon, with its mention of "Abel the just" could provide a connection with today's Prayer over the Offerings.

Other Ideas

Jesus says, "Come away and be at rest for a while." This can be a difficult task if you work in ministry. A trip to the grocery store for milk turns into an hour as someone catches you to tell you what they like or don't like about your parish, Homily, music, youth program, and so on. Between cell phones, texts, tweets, e-mails, and social media, we are always "on call." People expect immediate responses. Do you establish boundaries? Do you take time for yourself? Do you find time that is sacred to you? Take time that is sacred for your prayer, reflection, music rehearsal, Homily preparation, and so on? Or times that are just to be with your family or close friends? If you don't set boundaries, you will become overwhelmed. If you are overworked and overwhelemd you will not be good to yourself nor to anyone in your parish.

M O N 20 (#395) green
Weekday

Optional Memorial of St. Apollinaris, Bishop and Martyr / red

The Lectionary for Mass

◆ First Reading: The Israelites had come to their most critical juncture: Egyptians behind them, sea before them. The consequences of following Moses became frighteningly clear: they could either return to punishment and slavery or risk everything on the God who created the sea. Betting on God was an irrevocable choice that changed them forever. Under no circumstance in the future would they be able to say that serving God was impossible; God had proven faithful in ways they could never have imagined.

◆ Responsorial Psalm 15: When we find ourselves in a situation similar to the Israelites, we would do well to remember this psalm. Perhaps we have the certainty of the Lord's glory. When we don't, we can fall back on the faith that our strength and courage will always come from the Lord.

◆ GOSPEL: Jesus juxtaposes compelling outward signs with a response of the heart. The people of Nineveh responded to Jonah's preaching without demanding miraculous demonstrations. While Jesus performs wondrous signs, they are in service of people in need. Astounding miracles produce acquiescence rather than faith in Providence.

Today's Saint

Not much is known about Saint Apollinaris (dates unknown) except that he was from Antioch, a Syrian, and the first bishop of Ravenna. Tradition says he was appointed bishop by Saint Peter himself. Apollinaris was exiled with his people during the persecution of Emperor Vespasian. As he left the city, he was pointed out as the leader of the Christians. He was tortured and executed with a sword. Saint Apollinaris is a patron saint of those suffering from epilepsy or gout and is shown in art with a sword, the instrument of his martyrdom.

TUE 21 (#396) green
Weekday

Optional Memorial of St. Lawrence of Brindisi, Priest and Doctor of the Church / white

The Lectionary for Mass

◆ FIRST READING: Multiple explanations have been put forth for this escape. Some declare it a miracle of nature, with God manipulating the flow of the sea. Others suggest natural explanations having to do with arid winds that temporarily dry out shallow water. Another interpretation points out that people on foot can pass where chariot wheels would be clogged. In the end, no matter why it worked,

the Israelites' escape assured them that God was with them and was stronger than their enemies, their doubts and fears.

◆ RESPONSORIAL PSALM 15: We might well imitate the tone of this song of triumph. Every verse points out that salvation reveals God's glory, not the might or right of the saved.

◆ GOSPEL: Jesus radically redefined family and tribal loyalty. In his culture, one's obligations were measured by the degree of blood relationship one had with another. Jesus overturned that system, proclaiming that everyone who strove to be a child of God belonged to him — and one another — as next of kin.

Today's Saint

St. Lawrence of Brindisi (1559–1619), a Capuchin Franciscan in Italy, was an astute Scripture scholar with a comprehensive understanding of ancient and modern languages. His widespread knowledge of Scripture enabled him to be an effective and powerful preacher. He served the Capuchins in several leadership capacities, ranging from provincial of Tuscany and Venice to Minister General (superior) of the entire order. He was declared a Doctor of the Church due to his extensive writings, which are primarily sermons and commentaries.

His writings bear a resemblance to the humanistic approach and optimistic view of humanity, espoused by St. Francis de Sales.

WED 22 (#397; Gospel 603) white
Memorial of St. Mary Magdalene

The Lectionary for Mass

Please note that only the Gospel is proper; however, you could choose to use all of the readings from the Proper of Saints, #603. The commentary below is about Lectionary #603.

◆ FIRST READING: Moses had the unenviable task of leading a frightened, wavering people on the road to their freedom. When they began to complain about their diet, the God who had listened to their cry for freedom also heeded their grumbling. God, who cared more about their freedom than they did, saw to it that they were amply fed as they trudged onward.

◆ RESPONSORIAL PSALM 78: As we sing of God's providence, we might realize that God's gift of food to the Israelites was natural to the desert. As we pray this psalm, we might ask that God open our eyes to see what heavenly sustenance lies unseen before us.

◆ GOSPEL: We celebrate Mary Magdalene, recalling that she was the first to whom the risen Christ appeared. Like the Israelites in the desert, she had to open her eyes to perceive who it was standing before her. When she saw, she was not only comforted beyond imagination, but missioned as the Apostle to the Apostles.

The Roman Missal

All the orations are proper for today, and can be found in the Proper of Saints at July 22. The Collect hails Mary Magdalene as the one "entrusted . . . before all others / with announcing the great joy of the Resurrection." Therefore, we pray that we may be the same kind of witness; namely, "that through her intercession and example / we may proclaim the living Christ." The Prayer over the Offerings introduces the idea of charity; it points out how the "homage of charity" offered by St. Mary Magdalene "was graciously accepted" by Jesus. We can be reminded how our participation in the Eucharist is supposed to bring about an increase of charity in us. Either Preface I or Preface II of Saints would be the appropriate choice for today.

The Prayer after Communion appropriately reminds us of the "persevering love / with which Saint Mary Magdalene / clung resolutely to Christ her Master"; sacramental Communion, itself a clinging to Christ, should also increase in us the love for Christ by which we will cling resolutely to him.

In view of the Collect's recognition of St. Mary Magdalene's role in announcing the Resurrection, it would seem that using the dismissal "Go and announce the Gospel of the Lord" would be appropriate today.

Today's Saint

Mary Magdalene is one of the most misunderstood women of the Bible. She was conflated with several other figures by medieval commentators, including Mary of Bethany (sister of Martha and Lazarus) and the sinful woman who washes Jesus's feet with her hair in Luke's account. The confusion about who she is still exists in the Church's calendar: exactly one week from today we will celebrate St. Martha, sister of a different Mary. What we do know about Mary Magdalene is that Jesus healed her, and that she was the first witness of his Resurrection.

THU 23 (#398) green
Weekday

Optional Memorial of St. Bridget, Religious / white

The Lectionary for Mass

◆ FIRST READING: There are no words to convey the enormity of an encounter with God. What we see in this passage is that God is the one who initiates the encounter and tells the people to prepare themselves. We are reminded that God can never be coerced, but only encountered with the help of grace.

◆ CANTICLE: This call and response prayer from the Book of Daniel reflects the prayer of a people almost babbling as they experience an encounter with God. In its original setting, it was the triumphal song of the three brothers who accepted martyrdom and were saved from the flames of the fiery furnace. We affirm a prayer like this in the Preface to the Eucharistic Prayer with the priest's words "It is truly right and just, our duty and our salvation, always and everywhere to give you thanks."

◆ GOSPEL: Just as God initiates interaction with humanity, so too, understanding Jesus is given, not achieved. Our best response is to pray that God continually open our hearts and minds to the Word spoken to us each day.

Today's Saint

St. Bridget of Sweden (1303–1373), a wife and mother of eight children, joined a Cistercian monastery after the death of her husband. After a series of visions, she founded the Bridgittine Order—a double monastery for men and women living in separate enclosures dedicated to learning. In another vision, she was instructed to heal the schism of the Avignon papacy by warning Pope Clement VI to return to Rome from Avignon. She was not canonized for her many and varied revelations, but for her heroic virtue. It is interesting that she shares a feast day with St. John Cassian who founded two monasteries (one for monks and the other for nuns) and who was also canonized for a virtuous life beyond reproach.

FRI 24 (#399) green
Weekday

Optional Memorial of St. Sharbel Makhlūf, Priest / white

The Lectionary for Mass

◆ FIRST READING: The Commandments we hear come directly from God. They are the divine demands made on those who wish to serve only this God. Every one of them teaches us how to be in right relationship with God, and reveals that such righteousness necessarily involves our relationships with others. Today we might ask ourselves how obedience has brought us into a deeper relationship with God.

◆ RESPONSORIAL PSALM 19: We often think of law as the minimum requirement to be fulfilled—like homework. The psalm invites us to see God's commands instead as a joyous pathway into everlasting life.

◆ GOSPEL: The explanation of the parable of the seed provides excellent commentary on what we have just heard and proclaimed. The question posed to us is how deep we want our relationship with God to be. We can observe the letter of the law and be like seed on shallow ground, or we can continually seek God's will and yield more than we could ever imagine.

Today's Saint

St. Sharbel Makhlūf Joseph Zaroun was a Maronite Catholic, born and raised in a small Lebanese mountain village. As a child he led a pious life of prayer and solitude. His favorite book was *The Imitation of Christ* by Thomas à Kempis. When he entered the Monastery of St. Maron at twenty-three, he took the name Sharbel after the second-century martyr of the Antioch Church. He lived an austere life as a hermit, eating only one meal of vegetables each day, sleeping on a pillow of wood, and a duvet filled with dead leaves. His time was devoted to prayer, contemplation, and manual labor. Many came to him for counsel and blessing. He died in 1898 on Christmas Eve.

S A T

25 (#605) red
Feast of St. James, Apostle

The Lectionary for Mass

◆ FIRST READING: This selection from St. Paul reminds us that the greatest saints are, like us, vessels of clay. But, according to Paul, it is our very weakness that allows God's grace to shine through. We often hear that message from people who have faced addiction or suffered from serious illness or a disability. They thank God for the difficulties that opened them to recognize God's power and love in their lives as never before.

◆ RESPONSORIAL PSALM 126: The refrain for our psalm speaks of the hope known only to those who have suffered greatly. Although no one seeks such trials, when they come, our faith offers hope that would be unimaginable to those who do not believe.

◆ GOSPEL: James and John were seen as the number two and three disciples and were as imperfect as any of the others. When they attempt to usurp Peter's primacy and ask Jesus to place them above the others, Jesus simply offers them his cup of suffering and reliance on the Father. Like them, we need to learn that service is the path toward sharing the Master's power.

The Roman Missal

The texts for this Mass, all proper for the feast, are located in the Proper of Saints section of the Missal at July 25. The Gloria is sung or said today, since it is a Feast.

The Collect acknowledges the martyrdom of St. James as it notes that God "consecrated the first fruits of your Apostles / by the blood of Saint James." The Prayer over the Offerings continues this recognition by referring to the saint as "the first among the Apostles / to drink of Christ's chalice of suffering." As the prayer goes on to ask that "we may offer a sacrifice pleasing to you," we cannot help but be challenged to know that such sacrifice involves our willingness to participate in that same chalice of suffering. The Prayer after Communion proclaims that we receive the holy gift of the Eucharist with joy on this feast day.

The Preface, proper for today, is one of the two Prefaces of the Apostles. Also, the Solemn Blessing formula titled "The Apostles," number 17 of the "Blessings at the End of Mass and Prayers over the People," may be used as the final blessing at the end of Mass today.

Today's Saint

The St. James we honor today is the brother of the Apostle John, one of the "sons of thunder" (Mark 3:17) who were privileged witnesses of some of Jesus's greatest signs: the raising of the daughter of Jairus from the dead, the Transfiguration, and the agony in the garden. James was the first Apostle to suffer martyrdom, slain by Herod's orders as described in Acts of the Apostles. According to legend, his remains were carried away by his friends in a rudderless boat, which drifted all the way to Spain. Many centuries later his remains were discovered, and a great cathedral was built over the spot where they were found (*Santiago de Compostela*, which became one of the most popular pilgrimage destinations of the Middle Ages). To this day, hundreds of thousands of pilgrims make their way to that remote corner of Spain to venerate the relics of St. James.

26 (#110) green
Seventeenth Sunday in Ordinary Time

The Lectionary for Mass

◆ FIRST READING: This incident takes place during a time of famine. When Elisha receives a gift of bread, he immediately gives it to a large crowd. Given the option of hoarding or solidarity, he shows us how to choose that which promises greater life.

◆ RESPONSORIAL PSALM 145: As we pray "The hand of the Lord feeds us," we need to be aware of how our own hands are often the ones God would use to help others.

◆ SECOND READING: "Live in a manner worthy of the call you have received." That might be the one command necessary for a Christian life. It reminds us that we are called by God and that, day by day, we must choose whether or not to accept the grace we are offered for the good of the whole.

◆ GOSPEL: The "sign" of the bread includes great generosity and trust. The self-sacrificing generosity of the child who offered all his food prepared the way for everyone to share, not keeping or taking more than needed, and offering the rest to the others. Today's readings remind us that God's generosity is often expressed through human hands.

The Roman Missal

The Gloria is sung or said today.

The Collect speaks eloquently of God as the firm foundation of our lives; with that foundation, we can "use the good things that pass / in such a way as to hold fast even now / to those that ever endure." The sense of the imminent-yet-not-fully-realized Kingdom of God that underlies this Collect connects well with the Gospel parables today. The Prayer over the Offerings continues to acknowledge the need to progress in the life of the kingdom, which is both here and yet-to-come: we bring our offerings from the abundance of God's gifts (the "already" of the kingdom), and we pray that "these most sacred mysteries may sanctify our present way of life / and lead us to eternal gladness" (growing in grace toward a future fulfillment). The Prayer after Communion highlights the nature of every Eucharistic celebration as an amnesis—the "perpetual memorial of the Passion of your Son."

Any one of the eight Prefaces of the Sundays in Ordinary Time may be selected for today, although perhaps Preface V, with its description of God's sovereignty over creation, or Preface VI, with its reference to how we both "experience the daily effects" of God's care (the kingdom present in our midst) and also "possess the pledge of life eternal" (a recognition of something yet to come), would be apt choices in particular.

The dismissal formula "Go in peace, glorifying the Lord by your life" would reinforce the need for us to live life in a way whereby we grow in the ways of the kingdom.

Other Ideas

There is an old expression, "If you want to get something done, ask a busy person." Busy people and generous people often go hand in hand. The miracle of the loaves and fishes is about people sharing what they have and there being plenty left over.

What are the needs of your parish? Do you need a special collection for something or more ministers in specific areas? Ask clearly and honestly for what you need and a few brave souls will come forward and pave the way. God will provide. Many times people are extremely generous if they know what the needs are. Communication is key.

Today would also be a day to take up a collection for the local food pantry, or to ask people to bring canned and boxed goods for those in need. Check with the pantry to see if they have specific needs, and advertise for them.

MON 27 (#401) green Weekday

The Lectionary for Mass

◆ FIRST READING: Was there ever a harder day for Moses than when he found his people worshipping a golden calf and the work of their own hands? Aaron has failed Moses and the people, leaving Moses to attempt to bridge the breach the people have created between themselves and God. On one hand, he will not let them off easy. On the other, he pleads with God for them, to the point of asking to lose his own life if God will not forgive them. In that, he fulfills the priestly role of a prophet.

◆ RESPONSORIAL PSALM 106: Remembering our own failures, we praise God's goodness. Thanking God for one like Moses, we are also called to be willing to follow in his footsteps.

◆ GOSPEL: These two parables speak of the extravagance of the Reign of God. In Jesus's day, as often in our own, it seems that little is being accomplished toward bringing about God's reign. But, the tiny seed begins an astounding process of growth, seen only by those who wait long enough to see it. We are not told how much yeast the woman had, but she used enough to leaven ten pounds of flour—enough to make bread for 150 people. She was a woman of generous vision!

TUE 28 (#402) green Weekday

The Lectionary for Mass

◆ FIRST READING: Moses went to the Tent of Meeting to commune with God. We see here a progression in religious imagination. On one hand, there was a sacred place in which he expected to meet God in a holy space. On the other hand, he pleas that God accompany the people along their way, thus indicating that God is tied to no place, but can be found by anyone seeking to go where God would lead.

◆ RESPONSORIAL PSALM 103: As we seek deeper communion with God, we also sing praise because we know God's love for the oppressed, God's generosity and compassion. If God can put our transgressions so far from us, might we not also forgive ourselves and others?

◆ GOSPEL: Jesus's explanation of the parable of weeds and wheat reminds us that the harvest and the sifting belong to God alone. Only God knows the heart, and only God can decide whether or not someone can be classified as an evildoer.

WED 29 (#403; Gospel 607) white Memorial of St. Martha

The Lectionary for Mass

◆ FIRST READING: We know that couples in love can have a unique glow about them. That is what the people saw in Moses. That is but one expression of how our relationship with God might show forth in our life, leading others to see it and to want what we have.

◆ RESPONSORIAL PSALM 99: As at the beginning of the Eucharistic prayer, we acclaim God's holiness. The only appropriate response to God's holiness is worship: admiration, praise, and awe.

◆ GOSPEL: In the midst of her grief, Martha first chastised Jesus for not having arrived on time to heal Lazarus. Then, in dialogue with him, she made one of the clearest proclamations of faith found in the New Testament: "I believe that you are the Messiah." She said that before Jesus raised Lazarus. Martha's witness encourages us to believe and hope, even when we have no reasonable expectation of changing a situation of tragedy.

The Roman Missal

The proper prayers for this memorial are at July 29 in the Proper of Saints. The Collect gives voice to Martha's hospitality to the Lord and asks that we too may serve Christ faithfully by serving our brothers and sisters. The Prayer over the Offerings reminds us that the offering we make at the Eucharist, and consequently the offering of our lives, must always be an offering of love; it is only that kind of offering that finds favor with God. Either Preface I or Preface II of Saints would be the most appropriate choice for the Preface today. The Prayer after Communion asks that as a result of our reception of Holy Communion we may, like St. Martha, be completely focused on serving the Lord and on growing in sincere love.

Today's Saint

Martha was the sister of Lazarus and Mary, friends of Jesus. She appears to have been a practical-minded woman, for she seems to have organized the dinner in Luke 10:38–42, and she protests when Jesus commands that the stone be rolled from the entrance to her brother's tomb after he'd been dead for three days. At the same time,

however, she is one of the few in the Gospel to profess her faith in Jesus as the Messiah: "Yes, Lord. I have come to believe that you are the Messiah, the Son of God, the one who is coming into the world" (John 11:27). *The Golden Legend* records the tradition that Martha, with her sister, Mary, and brother, Lazarus, fled Judea after the death of Jesus and landed at Marseilles. Martha is supposed to have traveled to Avignon, where she converted many to Christianity. St. Martha is shown in art bearing the tools of a housekeeper — keys or a broom — and is a patron saint of domestic servants, homemakers, cooks, and single laywomen.

THU 30 (#404) green Weekday

Optional Memorial of St. Peter Chrysologus, Bishop and Doctor of the Church / white

The Lectionary for Mass

◆ FIRST READING: The "meeting tent" was where Moses would go to encounter God, God's unique dwelling place among the people. In declaring that in himself, there was something greater than the Temple, Jesus replaced the theology that expected to find God in a place constructed by human hands, revealing that God is never contained in one locus.

◆ RESPONSORIAL PSALM 84: Our psalm bridges today's readings. We sing of the beauty of God's dwelling place and the joy we find in places of prayer, and at the same time, we pray in gratitude for God's presence in all times and places, in nature and in exemplary human beings.

◆ GOSPEL: Here Matthew returns to the teaching that the sifting of good and evil is God's task, rather than a matter handed over to our judgment. As we consider our Church practice, we too are called to make use of both the old and the

new, treasuring what has stood the test of time, remembering that God is still active among us and drawing us toward something new.

Today's Saint

St. Peter Chrysologus (380–450), born in Imola in northeastern Italy, was appointed Archbishop of Ravenna by Emperor Valentinian III. His orthodox approach to the Incarnation and other Church doctrines earned him the support of Pope St. Leo the Great. He was given the title "Chrysologus," meaning "Golden-worded," due to his flair for preaching. This title may have been given to him so that the Western Church would have a preacher equal to St. John "Chrysostom" ("Golden-tongued") of the East. Most of his writings did not survive, but the Church is graced with a number of his sermons. The remaining sermons are written with pastoral sensitivity and optimism, while challenging people to conversion and repentance.

FRI 31 (#405) white Memorial of St. Ignatius of Loyola, Priest

The Lectionary for Mass

◆ FIRST READING: The feast days of the Jewish calendar, and of our own, keep people mindful that all time is God's time. The Jewish feasts mark the normal rhythm of agricultural life, another reminder that all life and growth comes from God.

◆ RESPONSORIAL PSALM 18: With this psalm we remember and celebrate the joy we know when we allow God to be our help.

◆ GOSPEL: St. Ignatius taught his brothers to be indifferent to poverty and riches, and even to prefer poverty when given a choice. This is in imitation of Christ who left behind all Godly grandeur to live among us as a poor person of humble background. The skeptics of his day, as in our own, could not accept profound wisdom from someone who lacked an appropriate human or religious lineage. What criteria do we use in deciding who has something to teach us?

The Roman Missal

All the orations, located at July 31 in the Proper of Saints, are proper for this obligatory memorial. The Collect reflects aspects often associated with Ignatian spirituality with its references to the greater glory of God's name and fighting the good fight on earth. The Prayer over the Offerings describes the sacred mysteries we are celebrating as "the fount of all holiness." In view of this, perhaps it would be good to be sure to use Eucharistic Prayer II today, with its mention of the Lord as "the fount of all holiness." Preface I or Preface II of Saints or the Preface of Holy Pastors are all appropriate choices for today's Preface. The Prayer after Communion asks that the "sacrifice of praise" we have offered here on earth may bring us to the joys of eternity where we will "exalt your majesty without end."

Today's Saint

St. Ignatius was the founder and first Father General of the Society of Jesus, or Jesuits, and author of the *Spiritual Exercises*. Born in the Basque region of Spain, he joined the army and was severely wounded in battle. While recovering, he read about the life of Christ and the lives of the saints, and decided to emulate them. He laid his military equipment before a statue of Mary at the Benedictine abbey of Montserrat, and spent several months in a cave near Manresa. After making a pilgrimage to the Holy Land, he

enrolled at the University of Paris, and he gathered six companions who would become the first Jesuits.

August
Month of the Immaculate Heart of Mary

(#406)   white

S
A **1**
T

Memorial of St. Alphonsus Liguori, Bishop and Doctor of the Church

The Lectionary for Mass

◆ FIRST READING: The week of seven days, like the cycles of seven and fifty years, were among the Semites' unique contributions to civilization. The Sabbath is a reminder that human beings are created for more than work. The fiftieth year Jubilee, when debts are forgiven, land returns to the original owners, and sins are forgiven reminds everyone that creation itself belongs to God and is given for the good of all. No one has a permanent right to this world's goods.

◆ RESPONSORIAL PSALM 67: Today we pray that all our actions and organizations will reveal God's justice. Then, we pray with confidence that God will bless us and all the earth will recognize God's glory.

◆ GOSPEL: In contrast to a Jubilee way of life, Herod reveals himself as a weakling and a servant. John has suffered the fate of those who proclaim God's ways in a twisted society. Jesus and many of his faithful followers will share that fate, and also eternal life.

The Roman Missal

The proper orations for this obligatory memorial are taken from

August 1. The Collect points to St. Alphonsus as an example of virtue and it notes his "zeal for souls." The Prayer over the Offerings makes reference to the Holy Spirit, asking God "to enkindle our hearts / with the celestial fire your Spirit," so that we might make a holy offering of ourselves just as St. Alphonsus offered himself. Preface I or Preface II of Saints, or the Common of Holy Pastors, are the choices from which to select the Preface for today. Pointing to the stewardship and preaching of St. Alphonsus, the Prayer after Communion asks that we too, in receiving "this great mystery," may praise God without end.

Today's Saint

Following a successful career as a lawyer, St. Alphonsus Ligouri (1696–1787) lost a legal case that he believed to be a sign from God that he should change his ways and study for the priesthood. At the suggestion of a bishop friend, he founded the Congregation of the Most Holy Redeemer, also known as the Redemptorists, a community of priests dedicated to preaching, hearing confessions, and administering the sacraments. One of his most important contributions to the Church is his prolific writing in the area of moral theology. Also included among his writings are many devotional works on Mary and the saints. He influenced the Church not only through his writings, but also through his leadership as a bishop. Due to his many accomplishments, he was declared a Doctor of the Church and is recognized as one of the greatest moral theologians in Church history.

2 (#113) green
Eighteenth Sunday in Ordinary Time

The Lectionary for Mass

◆ FIRST READING: God provided bread for the complaining people, but they didn't know what it was. Happily, Moses could tell them. How often does God answer our prayers or meet our needs and we fail to recognize the gift being offered? Who has helped us see a gift in what at first appeared to us to be strange?

◆ RESPONSORIAL PSALM 78: The psalm sings of what the elders experienced and retold to their descendants over and again. While we may personally thank God for many things, do we tell our stories of blessings? Many times we tell of the hard things in our lives, but how often do we give witness to God's providence? Celebrating God's blessings is a form of evangelization and a path to better recognizing God's action in our lives.

◆ SECOND READING: Note that Paul says: "You learned Christ," not "You learned about Christ." The knowledge Paul is talking about here is comparable to the difference between knowing what a bicycle is and knowing how to ride one. To learn Christ means to let Christ so influence our heart and mind that others will know Christ by watching us. That demands a lot of practice!

◆ GOSPEL: The message from John's account of the Gospel complements what Paul said. Jesus, who said "My food is to do the will of the One who sent me," (John 4:34) says that he himself can be our sustenance. Christ, in his message and in his living Body, is the heavenly bread God continues to send to us.

The Roman Missal

The Collect points to how God constantly gives life to his creation: he creates, and he also restores what he creates and keeps safe what he restores. This is the reason we glory in God as our "Creator and guide." The Prayer over the Offerings highlights the theme of offering, which is central to every celebration of the Eucharist, as it petitions that we may be made an eternal offering to God. The Prayer after Communion returns to the theme of protection heard in the Collect, asking that those renewed with the heavenly gifts of the Eucharist might be worthy of eternal redemption.

Of the eight Prefaces of the Sundays in Ordinary Time that could be used today, Preface III echoes the idea of God's protection and restoration as it speaks of God coming to our aid with his divinity. Preface VI speaks about the daily effects of God's care.

Other Ideas

In his *Rule*, Benedict warns the monks five times against the sin of "murmering." He suggests monks should be grateful to have what they need and not to compare wants with what others have. Sadly, it seems to be our human nature to murmer. Make a change in the parish and the first thing you will here is "We've always done it that way." Parishoners may be complaining about the pastor or some of the team members, but make sure the pastor and the staff are not complaining about parishioners either. It is easy to start gossiping while venting or if someone has come into the office with unreal expectations.

One department or organization may complain because another has a larger staff, or a bigger budget, more space in the newsletter, or gets mentioned more in the homilies and intercessions. Stop yourself when you are inclined to do this and be grateful for what you have.

As our Gospel reminds us, "What can we do to accomplish the works of God?" Jesus answered and said to them, "This is the work of God, that you believe in the one he sent."

Encourage the community to come to Mass for the Feast of the Transfiguration on August 6.

3 (#407) green
MON **Weekday**

The Lectionary for Mass

◆ FIRST READING: Moses never feared a strong discussion with God. Hearing the people's lament, he turns to God and says, in essence, "You are the mother who gave them birth, then had me carry them like a foster-father. I can't carry on alone! If you don't do something, please just let me die!" That is the honest prayer of a man who loved God and his people. Are we willing to be so torn out of love for others?

◆ RESPONSORIAL PSALM 81: In reply to Moses, we hear what might be God's own grieving. God's hands are tied; God can only do for the people what they accept. God's will is to give them the best of wheat and honey.

◆ GOSPEL: Just as Jesus looks for privacy to mourn and ponder his fate, the crowds seek and find him. In response, he gives away all he and the disciples have, confident that their example will inspire generosity. The people accepted it and all "ate their fill."

TUE 4 (#408) white
Memorial of St. John Vianney, Priest

The Lectionary for Mass

◆ FIRST READING: The Book of Numbers, which has just recounted Moses's protest to God, now calls him the meekest man on earth. While he may not seem to be docile, there is no doubt that he was big-hearted and humble. Thus, when Miriam's jealousy becomes manifest in leprosy, Moses pleas on her behalf. As one who interceded and forgave, he was a forerunner of Christ. What does his example invite you to do today?

◆ RESPONSORIAL PSALM 51: This is the classic psalm of repentance. Praying it, we stand with Aaron and Miriam, challenged to let go of our pride and accept the clean heart God can create for us.

◆ GOSPEL: As Jesus walks on the water, the disciples remember God's power over nature and the Creation when God's Spirit brought order from the chaos of the waters. Jesus shares his power with the wavering Peter, showing that disciples share the power to overcome the powers of death. We need only believe.

The Roman Missal

The Collect is proper and is found in the Proper of Saints for August 4. The remaining prayers may be from those for Ordinary Time or from the Common of Pastors: For One Pastor.

Today's Saint

St. John Vianney (1786–1859) is the patron of parish priests. Although he was not academically astute and had to receive his training privately, he was ordained a priest due to his virtue. He was stationed in a small village, *Ars-en-Dombes*, in France, where he became a noted catechist, confessor, and spiritual director. Soon, he gained a reputation for working miracles, such as multiplying loaves and physical healings. Consequently, the small village became a place of pilgrimage, attracting over 300 visitors a day, from 1830 to1845, to see the "Curé d'Ars." Special train schedules as well as a special booking office had to be established in the nearby city of Lyons to accommodate the steady stream of visitors.

WED 5 (#409) green
Weekday

Optional Memorial of the Dedication of the Basilica of St. Mary Major / white

The Lectionary for Mass

◆ FIRST READING: Israel's sojourn in the desert was a long learning process. Every time they sensed danger, they wailed and railed against Moses and God. Here, Moses's envoys focus on the bad news, inducing the people to abandon their trust in God. As the reading indicates, it would take a long time for them to learn their lesson.

◆ RESPONSORIAL PSALM 106: How many times the psalm says "they forgot" while still asking the Lord to remember to love them. How many times must we repent of our forgetfulness of God's love?

◆ GOSPEL: The Canaanite woman is more like Moses than are Jesus's own disciples. She is begging Jesus to represent the God of all, not simply one nation. Her faith persuades him. May we follow her example persisting in prayer and believing that God's love is for everyone, not just one nation or denomination.

Today's Optional Memorial

Today we celebrate one of Rome's most prestigious churches, the Basilica of St. Mary Major, formerly called Our Lady of the Snows. Among its most prized possessions are relics of the manger in Bethlehem. St. Mary Major sits on the horizon of the seven hills that form Rome, along with three other papal basilicas: St. John Lateran, St. Peter, and St. Paul Outside the Walls.

THU 6 (#614) white
Feast of the Transfiguration of the Lord

About this Feast

The Feast of the Transfiguration of the Lord reminds us about the depth of mystery that surrounded Jesus Christ—mystery in the sense that we can never exhaust who he really is or categorize him in any way. Fully human, he may indeed have needed a tent or a place to camp on the mountain, like Peter asked. But just when the Apostles may have been getting really comfortable with their understanding of Jesus as friend and teacher, they catch a glimpse of his heavenly glory, challenging them to remain open to Christ communicating to them who he is as Son of God. We have moments like the Apostles each time we encounter and grapple with a new and challenging image of God in the Scriptures. Remaining humble and open to the revelatory action of God's Word and Spirit is a way to enter ever more deeply into the mystery of who God is for us in Jesus Christ.

The Lectionary for Mass

◆ FIRST READING: Daniel gives us the vision of the "Son of man" who came from God and received all power from God in an everlasting Kingdom. Jesus referred to himself as the "Son of Man" and this description would have fed his disciples' imagination.

◆ RESPONSORIAL PSALM 97: This psalm sings that the dominion of the Lord will be, not only glorious beyond imagination, but good news for all people. We proclaim it as true today, knowing that the seeds of God's justice are growing and will one day come to fruition and that Christ will be all in all.

◆ SECOND READING: What's the difference between a myth and a vision? Peter talks of the vision he had in the Transfiguration. A vision reveals the truth of what is and is to come. It is unexpected. It contains insight that lures us forward.

◆ GOSPEL: Peter and his companions knew their brother Jesus pretty well. They had been dazzled at his power and wondered what it might portend. In this incident, filled with the symbolism of their religious tradition, they received a revelation, an insight into Jesus as the Son of God. They would grapple with that insight until it became clarified through Jesus's passion and resurrection. May we continue to grapple with revelation, allowing it to expand our consciousness of God in, but not of, our world.

The Roman Missal

The orations for this feast are all proper for the feast today, and are located in the Proper of Saints section of the Missal at August 6. The Gloria is sung or said today, since it is a feast. (Since the feast is not on a Sunday this year, however, the Creed is not said.)

The Collect places the meaning of the Transfiguration not as some event that took place in the past, but rather as something that serves as an invitation to explore ever more deeply the reality of who God reveals himself to be. Thus, in the Collect we are enjoined to listen to the voice of God's beloved Son, that is, now, in the present, so that "we may merit to become co-heirs with him." We must recall that all liturgical celebration is about our entrance at the present into the mystery that is being made manifest and present through the ritual actions and the anamnesis of the Church. The Prayer over the Offerings employs imagery of the Transfiguration by referring to the "radiant splendor" of the Son. The Prayer after Communion, which also uses the imagery of

radiance and splendor, picks up the theme of transformation: we pray that the "heavenly nourishment" we have received will "transform us into the likeness of your Son." We are reminded that our reception of Holy Communion is never simply a passive reception, but it is always to be an active participation in being transformed into what we receive.

The Preface, "The Mystery of the Transfiguration," is proper for today, and is given in the pages along with the other Mass texts. Music is provided, so perhaps today would be a good day to sing the introductory dialogue and the Preface. This Preface reminds us, as with so many of the mysteries of our faith, that the reality we celebrate about Christ is a reality we are called to also experience—we are all called to be transfigured with Christ, as his Transfiguration shows us "how in the Body of the whole Church is to be fulfilled / what so wonderfully shone forth first in its Head."

FRI 7 (#411) green
Weekday

Optional Memorials of St. Sixtus II, Pope, and Companions, Martyrs / red; St. Cajetan, Priest / white

The Lectionary for Mass

◆ FIRST READING: Today we hear Moses teaching cosmic history: never, ever, has God been so close to a people and done so much for them! Therefore, the only sensible, much less holy, response is to worship and obey God.

◆ RESPONSORIAL PSALM 77: Today, let us remember the deeds of the Lord. We celebrate salvation history and God's action in our own life and times.

◆ GOSPEL: Remembering what the Lord has done is the way to find the courage to follow in Jesus's footsteps. And Jesus makes the option crystal clear: either we follow, or we lose our very self. Underneath that

simple statement, we realize that the only way to be fulfilled is to fulfill God's will. Discipleship transforms everything, beginning with our definitions of winning and losing.

Today's Saints

This third-century pope, St. Sixtus II, was best known for solving the controversy surrounding Baptism performed by heretics. He stated that the validity of Baptism should be based on the recipient's desire to be Christian and not on the errors of the baptizer. This decision restored relations with the African and Eastern Churches. Sixtus was pope for only a year before he and six of his deacons were beheaded by Emperor Valerian.

Today's other saint, Cajetan, is known for establishing the Theatines, a pioneer religious order of the Counter-Reformation, whose mission was to bring clergy back to a life of prayer, Scripture study, preaching, and pastoral care.

SAT 8 (#412) white
Memorial of St. Dominic, Priest

The Lectionary for Mass

◆ FIRST READING: Moses's message sounds so simple: "The LORD is our God, the LORD alone!" Yet, how often do we chase after lesser values, or teach our young how to "make it" instead of how to evaluate everything in the light of God's plan? The only thing to fear is failing to live up to our commitment to God. What one thing might you do today to move further toward fulfilling Moses's command?

◆ RESPONSORIAL PSALM 18: How easy it is to sing "I love you, Lord, my strength." The question before us is whether our faith is really in God or our credit cards, our popularity, or our position.

◆ GOSPEL: The disciples were confounded by their inability to heal. Yet, they were probably trying

---

to do it on their own, not relying on God's will and power. Faith the size of a mustard seed is faith that knows it must die to self to produce life.

The Roman Missal

The orations are all to be found at August 8. The Collect not surprisingly underscores Dominic's reputation as an outstanding preacher. The Prayer over the Offerings prays for protection, "through the great power of this sacrifice," for "those who champion the faith"—thus reminding us that we are called to be preachers of the truth, like St. Dominic. The Prayer after Communion again highlights St. Dominic's preaching: since the Church flourished by means of his preaching, we also ask that we might be "helped through his intercession." In view of St. Dominic's life and preaching, the Preface of Holy Pastors would appear to be the most apt choice for today, although Preface I or II of Saints could also be used.

Today's Saint

St. Dominic (1170–1221), a contemporary of St. Francis of Assisi, founded a mendicant order (those who rely on the charity of others) of men, called the Order of Preachers, or Dominicans, to preach against theological error. One of the pressing issues facing the newly established order was the Albigensian heresy, claiming that matter, specifically the body, is evil. Contrary to this heretical thinking, the Black Friars, as they were commonly known, went from town to town preaching the goodness of the body. In order to preach sound doctrine with clarity, St. Dominic exhorted his sons to engage in rigorous academic study. He eventually started a contemplative female branch of the Dominicans to support the apostolate of the men through prayer.

(#116) green

9 Nineteenth Sunday in Ordinary Time

The Lectionary for Mass

◆ First Reading: Mother Theresa is said to have remarked that God would never give her more than she could handle. But she added, "I only wish he didn't trust me so much!" When Elijah felt like that, ready to lie down and die, God sent an angel to wake him up and give him food to strengthen him. This might remind us of the warning "My child, when you come to serve the Lord, / prepare yourself for trials" (Sirach 2:1). The only consolation, known by all who serve until the end, is that God will be with us.

◆ Responsorial Psalm 34: What a change of mood, from the ordeal of serving God to "Let my soul glory in the Lord." Saints and holy people across the ages seem to agree: to the extent that we recognize and accept our own incapacity, we recognize and experience God working through us. That is not to deny our abilities, but rather to offer all that we are and are not so that God can work in and through us.

◆ Second Reading: How often have we considered the effects of our Baptism? Paul wants us to understand that Baptism has a profound effect on us. As baptized, we have become Christ's own so profoundly that Christ's Spirit lives in us, luring us toward all that we can become through sharing life with Christ. We cannot control the Spirit, but we are free to choose how much we wish to be open to God's constant offer of grace.

◆ Gospel: Throughout John's Gospel we encounter superficial understandings of Jesus's teaching. The people hearing Jesus in today's story held such a high opinion of their knowledge of Jesus's background that they blinded themselves to him and his message. They who refused to accept the living bread stand as a warning to us about the devastating effects of low expectations.

The Roman Missal

The Mass texts for today are found in the "Ordinary Time" section of the Proper of Time. The Gloria is sung or said today.

The Collect gives voice to the relationship we enjoy with God: in bold words, it reminds us that "we dare to call [God] our Father." We can dare to do so precisely because we have been given "the spirit of adoption as your sons and daughters," and so the Collect prays that the spirit of adoption may be brought "to perfection in our hearts." Our relationship with the Father is never complete; it is always capable of being deepened insofar as ongoing conversion—a conversion brought about by repeated immersions in the Paschal Mystery through the liturgy—is a constant task in the life of a Christian. We are constantly being beckoned to come closer to the Lord in faith, doing so with trust. The Prayer over the Offerings recaps that the offerings made at this celebration are to be transformed "into the mystery of our salvation" (and, therefore, we must remember, are the agents to transform us). The Prayer after Communion prays that our communion in the sacrament may "confirm us in the light" of God's truth.

Any one of the eight Prefaces of the Sundays in Ordinary Time are possible choices for today.

Other Ideas

Are there announcements about parish religious education classes or day school enrollments? Now is the time we are turning our attention to the return of reality. Do you need to recruit volunteers? Remind people to take a child safety program, for example, Virtus or Protecting God's Children.

The Solemnity of the Assumption of the Blessed Virgin Mary is on Saturday, August 15. Remind people of the Mass times today and clarify that next Saturday evening is a Mass in anticipation of Sunday; therefore, it is not a Holyday of Obligation this year. The Mass for Mary will be in the morning.

MON 10 (#618) red Feast of St. Lawrence, Deacon and Martyr

The Lectionary for Mass

◆ FIRST READING: Some Spanish speakers say thank you with a phrase meaning, "May God repay you." Paul is telling the Corinthians that God will not forget their generosity on behalf of the community in Jerusalem. Paying careful attention to his logic, we see that he is not promising a magic return on an investment, but rather pointing out that their charity itself is a seed. The more that seed is sown, the more the world will reap the fruits of generosity.

◆ RESPONSORIAL PSALM 112: This psalm proclaims that the one who is just and generous will be unshakeable, without fear. Perhaps it is trying to point out that people who share freely will never fear that others will take what they hold onto as their own.

◆ GOSPEL: The example of the martyrs offers the ultimate expression of generosity and therefore fearlessness. Jesus talks

of "hating" one's life in this world. That can be understood as a desire to reject anything that would tie us down, blinding or preventing us from achieving our ultimate goal in Christ.

The Roman Missal

The prayers for the feast are found in the Proper of Saints. The Gloria is said or sung. The simple petition in the Collect might be spoken of any saint: "grant that we may love what he loved / and put into practice what he taught." Use the Preface I or II for Holy Martyrs.

Today's Saint

Saint Lawrence († 258), one of the seven deacons of the Roman Church, fell victim to the anti-Christian persecutions launched by the emperor Valerian. Although little is known about the events leading up to his death, legend claims that he was martyred by being roasted on a gridiron. However, most historians believe he was beheaded several days after Pope Sixtus II was.

According to tradition, his death brought an end to idolatry and led to the conversion of Rome. His life has been the subject of many artistic masterpieces, including the paintings of *Fra Angelico*.

TUE 11 (#414) white Memorial of St. Clare, Virgin

The Lectionary for Mass

◆ FIRST READING: Here we witness Moses's last act on earth. The audacious, strong, outspoken leader is now ready to allow another to take over the task he started. Moses may have thought he was fading away, but his memory has remained inspiring for thousands of years.

◆ CANTICLE: This "Song of Moses" recapitulates God's faithfulness. Like so many psalms, it invites us to recall God's love expressed throughout history and to

realize that we are the ones whom God prizes.

◆ GOSPEL: Who is the greatest? Jesus first makes an example of a child. Remembering that the Aramaic word for child can also mean servant, Jesus's point refers to being "lowly." The gospel then switches from the theme of being little to being a scorned sinner. Jesus does not see the sinner as an enemy, but as the one who needs and accepts the most attention and care. Who is the greatest in Jesus's eyes?

The Roman Missal

It is the Collect, found in the Proper of Saints at August 11, that is proper for today, and it speaks of Clare's life of poverty. Consequently, the prayer goes on to ask that we too will follow Christ "in poverty of spirit" and so merit to contemplate God in the heavenly kingdom. The texts for the Prayer over the Offerings and the Prayer after Communion are taken either from the Common of Virgins: For One Virgin, or from the Common of Holy Men and Women: For a Nun. Possible Prefaces are Preface I or II of Saints, or the Preface of Holy Virgins and Religious.

Today's Saint

Inspired by the Lenten sermons of her close friend St. Francis of Assisi, St. Clare of Assisi (1193/4–1253) renounced her wealth to found the Poor Clares, or Minoresses, a community of nuns devoted to a simple, austere life of prayer. She is the patron saint of television, due to a vision she had while lying sick in bed on Christmas Eve, in which she saw the crib and heard the singing just as if she were present in the church. In art, she is often depicted holding a monstrance because she protected Assisi from attackers with the Blessed Sacrament. Her sister St. Agnes eventually joined the Poor Clares.

W E D **12** (#415) green
Weekday

Optional Memorial of St. Jane Frances de Chantal, Religious / white

The Lectionary for Mass

◆ FIRST READING: Scripture portrays Moses's death as the peaceful culmination of a well spent life. He was allowed to see the Promised Land, but not to enter it. As in yesterday's reading, Moses ultimately played the humble role of allowing someone else to enjoy the glory of leadership. Nevertheless, Scripture says: "no prophet has arisen . . . like Moses."

◆ RESPONSORIAL PSALM 66: How appropriate a psalm to remember Moses! Praying with him, we acknowledge that it is God who sets us on fire. It is God who works tremendous deeds in our history.

◆ GOSPEL: Although we may not notice it at first, Jesus's teaching here indicates that the community overcomes sin through active forgiveness. Here it is not a question of talking God into absolving someone, but of the community winning them back. Whether it happens between two, or in a larger gathering, Christ promises to be with us as we build up the community of the redeemed.

Today's Saint

Under the influence of her spiritual director St. Francis de Sales, St. Jane (1572–1641), a wealthy widow and mother from France, founded the Congregation of the Visitation of the Virgin Mary. Unusual in its time, this new community of enclosed nuns welcomed individuals with frailties due to health and age, and who were often refused admittance by other cloistered orders. She was no stranger to pain, from the death of her husband and some of her children to the death of her dear friend St. Francis, but she transformed her experiences of sorrow into moments of transformation and service to the sick. The proper Collect emphasizes her vocation to the sick, noting that she was "radiant with outstanding merits in different walks of life." The Collect asks that we may model her vocation and also "be examples of shining light." The remaining prayers may be from the Common of Holy Men and Women: For Religious.

T H U **13** (#416) green
Weekday

Optional Memorial of Sts. Pontian, Pope, and Hippolytus, Priest, Martyrs / red

The Lectionary for Mass

◆ FIRST READING: The entry of the people and the ark into the Promised Land is full of reminders of the crossing of the Red Sea. The account not only depicts God's formal entry into the land, but reminds the people that God will remain with them when they live in obedience.

◆ RESPONSORIAL PSALM 114: The only possible refrain to sing now is "Alleluia!" We remember God's faithful presence in the people's struggles for freedom.

◆ GOSPEL: No sooner had Jesus instructed the disciples to forgive than Peter asked about the limits. In some religious schools of the day there was actually a calculation of how many times one needed to forgive different people—more for a brother than a neighbor, etc. When we pray the Lord's Prayer at the Eucharist, we say "We dare to say Our Father." Far more audacious than that, if not downright foolhardy, is the petition, "forgive us . . . as we forgive." Are we ready to aspire to God's measure of mercy, or would we prefer that God use our scales of justice in relation to ourselves?

Today's Saints

Pontian and Hippolytus (✝ 235) became the target of Emperor Maximinus Thrax who despised Christians, especially their leaders. Pope Pontian and the priest Hippolytus differed in terms of orthodoxy, so much so that they rivaled each other as leaders. Hippolytus did not acknowledge Pontian as the true pope, resulting in a schism in the Roman Church and leading to Hippolytus's reign as the antipope. They eventually reconciled during their exile to Sardinia, known as the island of death, where they died as martyrs due to harsh treatment.

F R I **14** (#417) red
Memorial of St. Maximilian Kolbe, Priest and Martyr

The Lectionary for Mass

◆ FIRST READING: Joshua speaks for God reminding the people of their history, a history marked by God's favor at every turn. As citizens of the United Sates who, like those Israelites, come from immigrant roots, we might do well to recount our own history of migration out of poverty or suffering and God's deliverance as we strove to establish ourselves in a new homeland.

◆ RESPONSORIAL PSALM 136: This psalm converts history into a song praising God's everlasting mercy. Perhaps we should write our own psalm, remembering the blessings of our ecclesial and personal salvation history.

◆ GOSPEL: In speaking of divorce, Jesus stands up for the woman who, according to at least one school of thought, could be put aside for almost any motive. At the same time, he indicates that marriage is not simply a human agreement, but that God plays a role in the union of the couple. As in the Sermon on the Mount, Jesus looks for the underlying intent of the Law, a dimension too often missed when we concentrate on the literal details.

The Roman Missal

The Collect, the Prayer over the Offerings, and the Prayer after Communion are all proper for today and are taken from August 14. The Collect recognizes the saint for his "zeal for souls and love of neighbor" as well as his Marian devotion. The Prayer over the Offerings asks that through the oblations we present at this celebration, "we may learn / from the example of Saint Maximilian to offer our very lives to you." Indeed, the offering of our lives is the heart of our participation in the Eucharistic celebration. One of the two Prefaces of Holy Martyrs would probably be most appropriate today, although the Preface of Holy Pastors or even one of the two Prefaces of Saints could also be considered. The Prayer after Communion reminds us of our communion with the saints in the Eucharist, as it asks that through the Eucharist "we may be inflamed with the same fire of charity / that Saint Maximilian received from this holy banquet."

Today's Saint

Polish-born Maximilian was a Franciscan friar whose devotion to Mary continues to affect the Church today. He established the Militia of the Immaculata, a Marian apostolate that uses prayer as its main weapon in spiritual battles. His extensive writing on Mary's role as mediatrix and advocate influenced the Second Vatican Council. He was eventually arrested and sent to Auschwitz. He volunteered to die in place of another prisoner and was put in the starvation bunker. Still alive two weeks later, Maximilian was injected with a lethal dose of carbolic acid, dying with a radiant, calm look upon his face.

FRI
14
(#621)   white

Vigil of the Solemnity of the Assumption of the Blessed Virgin Mary
NOT A HOLYDAY OF OBLIGATION

About this Solemnity

This day we celebrate the promise of God expressed fully in the life of Mary, the Holy Mother of God. God invites us to eternal life, to enjoy the glorious new creation of his Son in body, soul, and spirit. Our final hope is the resurrection of our own bodies at the end of time to exist forever in this new order of creation. The Solemnity of the Assumption is our great celebration of this final hope. Mary is a pioneer for us in faith. She was the first among us to accept Jesus Christ into her life. In her bodily Assumption, she is also the first to fully enjoy eternal life at the side of her risen Son in the glory of heaven. Where she has gone, we hope to follow. We rejoice in the fulfillment of God's promise in her, as we turn to her to guide us to the side of her risen Son who reigns in heaven.

The Lectionary for Mass

◆ FIRST READING: Today's First Reading recounts David's enthronement of the Ark of the Covenant (the chest containing the tablets of the law) in the tent he had prepared for it. Mary, the Mother of Jesus, has traditionally been invoked as the Ark of the New Covenant; thus, the reading from 1 Chronicles is particularly appropriate as we celebrate the heavenly enthronement of the Blessed Virgin Mary who was the Ark of the Living Lord.

◆ RESPONSORIAL PSALM 132 was sung by Jewish pilgrims as they made their way to the temple. It recounts David's concern to establish a home for the Ark of the Covenant. Today we celebrate Mary being taken up into the heavenly temple,

enjoying her heavenly rest there with her risen and glorified Son.

◆ SECOND READING: All of 1 Corinthians 15 deals with the subject of the resurrection of the body. These concluding verses celebrate the victory Jesus has won over death. Assumed into heaven, Mary is clothed with immortality.

◆ GOSPEL: Today's Gospel seems to put Mary in the background. The opposite is true, though. It brings all believers into the foreground with her. The heavenly glory she enjoys will likewise be ours if we hear God's Word and keep it.

The Roman Missal

Two sets of Mass formularies are given for this Solemnity, "At the Vigil Mass" and "At the Mass during the Day."

The Collect puts forth for us not only the belief concerning the Assumption — that the Blessed Virgin Mary "was crowned this day with surpassing glory" — but also the central point that we hope to share that same destiny, that of being exalted on high.

Remember that the Creed is said at this Mass.

The Prayer over the Offerings refers to the sacrifice we are celebrating as a "sacrifice of conciliation and praise."

The Preface is proper for today, "The Glory of Mary Assumed into Heaven," and the text, with and without musical notation, is located among the texts for the Mass during the Day, one page-turn over from the Vigil Mass texts. Consider chanting the Preface and its introductory dialogue today. The Preface reiterates that our liturgy celebrates our (hoped-for) participation in the mystery being commemorated: it describes that the Virgin Mother of God "was assumed into heaven / as the beginning and image / of your Church's coming to perfection." Thus are we given "a sign of sure hope and comfort." It also gives an easily understandable definition of the dogma as it explains how God "would not allow her / to see the corruption of the tomb / since from her own body she marvelously brought forth . . . the Author of all life."

The Prayer after Communion prays for freedom "from every threat of harm" as a result of our partaking of the food of the Eucharist.

The Solemn Blessing formula for the Blessed Virgin Mary, number 15 under "Blessings at the End of Mass and Prayers over the People," is suggested for this Mass, and it would be fitting to use it.

<table>
<tr><td></td><td>(#622) white</td></tr>
</table>

S A T 15 Solemnity of the Assumption of the Blessed Virgin Mary NOT A DAY OF HOLYDAY OF OBLIGATION

The Lectionary for Mass

◆ FIRST READING: John wrote this fantastic, symbolic description of the woman giving birth in the face of overwhelming danger to comfort his persecuted people. God had raised Christ up; their future in God was secure, no matter what the appearances.

◆ RESPONSORIAL PSALM 45: Today's psalm reminds us of Mary's unique position in the history of humanity. Though she never dressed as a queen, she is the one to whom the Angel declared "You have found favor with God."

◆ SECOND READING: Paul reminds us that Christ was the "firstfruits" of the Resurrection. Depictions of the death or "dormition" of Mary show Christ at her bedside, receiving and carrying her into eternal life. The doctrine of the Assumption assures us of the ultimate goodness of the flesh and the

promise of our own resurrection in body and soul.

◆ GOSPEL: Mary's *Magnificat* glorifies God for all the blessings she has received. She sees God's grace as the origin and destiny of all of history, even though she had to have an inkling of the hard times that would come in between. The Church has chosen her prayer as our prayer each evening. Let us give thanks with her always.

The Roman Missal

The Collect reminds us that our final goal is to be sharers in the same glory the Virgin Mary enjoys, and therefore we should always be "attentive to the things that are above."

Remember that, because it is a solemnity, the Creed is said today.

The Prayer over the Offerings asks the Blessed Virgin Mary's intercession that our hearts may constantly long for God. Used at this place in the liturgy, we can make the connection between "longing" and "hungering" for God, a hungering that is ultimately fulfilled only by our participation in the heavenly banquet in the kingdom.

The text for the proper Preface used today is located immediately following the Prayer over the Offerings; see the Vigil Mass above for commentary.

The Prayer after Communion, as do other texts we have seen, prays that, through the intercession of the Blessed Virgin Mary, we will share in the mystery that is being commemorated and be brought "to the glory of the resurrection."

As remarked concerning the Vigil Mass, the Solemn Blessing formula for the Blessed Virgin Mary, number 15 under "Blessings at the End of Mass and Prayers over the People," is suggested for this Mass, and it would be fitting to use it.

<table>
<tr><td></td><td>(#119) green</td></tr>
</table>

16 Twentieth Sunday in Ordinary Time

The Lectionary for Mass

◆ FIRST READING: The early Christian tradition saw Wisdom as a figure of the Holy Spirit. Here, Wisdom invites the simple to come and enjoy all she has to offer. We might ask ourselves whether we can be counted as the simple who savor the banquet or if we are more like the self-proclaimed wise who are invited to forsake foolishness.

◆ RESPONSORIAL PSALM 34: This is the favorite psalm to accompany Jesus's Bread of Life discourse. Its repetition invites us to deepen our appreciation of what it proclaims. This week it underlines Wisdom's invitation to the feast. The third stanza is an offer well worth serious meditation. Let us ask ourselves how willing we are to seek deeper encounters with the God of life.

◆ SECOND READING: The message keeps being repeated. Paul calls us to act, not like fools, but to discern the will of the Lord. For him, being a fool means to follow our own will, disregarding the search for what God has in mind for us. He advises us to replace overindulgence in food and drink with being filled with the Spirit. Of course, we cannot control the gifts of the Spirit, but we can either seek them or allow the pursuit of other things to detour us from the road of Wisdom.

◆ GOSPEL: This is one of the most direct statements Jesus makes about himself in the Gospel. He says that the path to life—real life, a holy life, a fulfilled life—passes through him. Being with and in him is so essential that he refers to it as the basic nourishment we need for life. There may be many paths toward God, but none of them compare to what he says he offers. We who hear Jesus's words are faced with a choice to pursue or reject a life of communion with and in Christ.

The Roman Missal

The Mass texts for today are found in the "Ordinary Time" section of the Proper of Time. The Gloria is sung or said today.

The Collect speaks to the need to keep God as the highest priority in our lives as it asks that we might love him "in all things and above all things." Ultimately, it is God alone who can fulfill us since what he promises surpasses every human desire. The Prayer over the Offerings reminds us once again that the celebration of the Eucharist is a "glorious exchange"—we offer what God has first given to us, and, in receiving those offerings back, we receive God's very self. The Prayer after Communion expresses how partaking of the Eucharist transforms us now as it conforms us to Christ's image on earth, and then goes on to ask that "we may merit also to be his coheirs in heaven." The transformation begun through sacramental communion reaches its fulfillment in union with Christ in heaven.

Consider using Eucharistic Prayer IV today; use of this prayer means you also must use its proper Preface, not one of the Prefaces of Sundays in Ordinary Time.

Other Ideas

The images from the Proverbs reading show us a God whose name is Wisdom, who is unbelievably generous. Suggest to the assembly that

an interesting conversation around the Sunday dinner table might be about Wisdom's invitation to those who are simple to come to her house. Being simple has a fairly negative connotation in our culture. What is the Scripture trying to tell us?

MON 17 (#419) green Weekday

The Lectionary for Mass

◆ FIRST READING: We hear how Israel, surrounded by people worshipping other gods, frequently fell into their camp, bringing ruin upon themselves. While our ancestors understood their downfall as divine punishment, today we know only too well that degeneracy spawns its own disaster on the personal and societal level. Now and then, God raises up prophets who can attract us to the transformation we need. We can rightly recognize God's grace in action through such a person.

◆ RESPONSORIAL PSALM 106: When we pray like this, asking for God's mercy, we do not expect to change God, but to allow God's grace to turn us around.

◆ GOSPEL: The man who approached Jesus seemed to sincerely want to live a good life and follow Jesus's teachings. He had pretty well counted the cost and made his budget. When Jesus asked something far more radical, he wasn't ready to pay the price.

TUE 18 (#420) green Weekday

The Lectionary for Mass

◆ FIRST READING: The call of Gideon is a typical vocation story. The person called has questions, sometimes about God, and almost always about how they can carry out the task being given them. God's answer is always a promise of presence and some sort of protection. May we have the wisdom

to know that it is only with God's grace that we can become who God made us to be and do what we are created to do.

◆ RESPONSORIAL PSALM 85: Even in the midst of disaster, we can discern a call from God by the peace we find in accepting it. If God's call brings us peace, then an integral part of our vocation, whatever its details, is to share that peace.

◆ GOSPEL: More than once, Jesus admits that discipleship is hard, and in this case, nearly impossible. What he wants us to remember is that God can do for and in us what we cannot do for ourselves. True discipleship is always the result of grace working with whatever willingness we offer God.

WED 19 (#421) green Weekday

Optional Memorial of St. John Eudes, Priest / white

The Lectionary for Mass

◆ FIRST READING: This, one of the very few fables in the Old Testament, indicts Abimelech's brutal kinship. The question for the people, and for us who come after them, is what to do when wise leadership is not willing or available to serve.

◆ RESPONSORIAL PSALM 21: The psalm describes the sort of ruler God would choose for the people. What goes for the king should apply to everyone in any role of leadership: when our strength comes from God, both we and those with whom we deal know true joy.

◆ GOSPEL: Jesus explains the thoroughly counter-cultural model of life in the Reign of God. On human terms, it was right for the first workers to complain—their recompense did not meet a test of strict human justice. On the other hand, a daily wage was what was needed to survive, and the owner wanted life for all the workers.

Might we be content with a God who fosters life, not measuring one of us against the other?

Today's Saint

St. John Eudes (1601–1680), a successful preacher in France, cared for plague victims on both a physical and spiritual level. In light of the Protestant Reformation, he felt that the academic and spiritual training of priests needed to be strengthened; therefore, he established a society of diocesan priests, the Congregation of Jesus and Mary, commonly called the Eudists. Their sole purpose was directed toward the foundation of new seminaries where future priests would be equipped with the necessary tools to respond pastorally to the turbulent times. He eventually established a religious community of women, the Congregation of Our Lady of Charity of the Refuge, dedicated to the rehabilitation of prostitutes.

(#422) white

THU 20 Memorial of St. Bernard, Abbot and Doctor of the Church

The Lectionary for Mass

◆ First Reading: With Jephthah we encounter a very primitive theology: a concept of God that believed that victory had to be repaid with human sacrifice. In an ancient culture, this story explained the absolute duty to fulfill a vow. In truth, the conviction that God would demand such a sacrifice reduces God to the level of blood-thirsty pagan deities.

◆ Responsorial Psalm 40: This psalm is a corrective to sacrificial theology. Our duty is to listen to God, not to invent the sacrifices we think will make us holy.

◆ Gospel: In contrast to the death theme in Judges, Jesus likens the Reign of God to a banquet. No one is compelled to come; worthiness is not a requirement for participation. When one banqueter refuses to join the spirit of the party, we understand that he has excluded himself and cannot be allowed to spoil the celebration for the rest.

The Roman Missal

All three of the orations are proper for today, found in the Proper of Saints at August 20. The Collect describes St. Bernard with bright and energetic terms such as "zeal for your house," "a light shining and burning in your Church" and asks that "we may be on fire with the same spirit / and walk always as children of the light." Such phrases point to the remarkable influence St. Bernard had on the people of his time. The Prayer over the Offerings continues to extol St. Bernard as a role model as it refers to him as "a man outstanding in word and deed, who strove to bring order and concord to your Church." Such concord is appropriate in this prayer as it names the sacrament we offer at this celebration as "the Sacrament of unity and peace." We can never forget that unity, concord, and peace must be the fruits that result from Eucharistic celebration. The Prayer after Communion prays that the Eucharist we receive will truly have an effect on our life. Preface I or II of Saints or the Preface of Holy Virgins and Religious would be appropriate choices today.

Today's Saint

St. Bernard (1090–1153) joined the Cistercian abbey at Cîteaux, known for its strict and austere way of life. Within a short time he was noticed for his leadership; hence, he was appointed abbot of a new monastery at Clairvaux. His monastic vision at Clairvaux led to the foundation of several monasteries throughout France, Britain, and Ireland. In solitude he wrote numerous theological and spiritual classics, including his treatise *On Loving God*, eighty-six sermons on the Song of Songs, and a major work *On Consideration*, a reflection on papal spirituality. St. Bernard had a special devotion to Mary, earning him the titles "Our Lady's faithful chaplain" and "Mary's harper." Bernard was a prolific writer and had a great influence on the Church.

(#423) white

FRI 21 Memorial of St. Pius X, Pope

The Lectionary for Mass

◆ First Reading: The Book of Ruth introduces us to the plight of famine-wracked families, the precarious life of widows, and faithfulness within a family. The exemplary Ruth chose solidarity with her mother-in-law over the security of her own homeland. She even accepted Naomi's faith tradition in spite of the fact that she would be seen as a foreigner among the Jews.

◆ Responsorial Psalm 146: This could well have been Ruth and Naomi's prayer as they journeyed together. Ruth had chosen to seek her future with the God of Jacob, the God of her mother-in-law. Together they hoped in God's promise to sustain widows.

◆ Gospel: There is an ironic contradiction in the fact that the religious leaders conspiring against Jesus tried to snare him with a question about God's Commandments. The scene, in addition to the teaching about love of God and neighbor, invites us to consider why we ask certain religious questions. Do we try to trap people or justify ourselves, or do we sincerely seek information that might influence us to change?

The Roman Missal

Texts for today can be found at August 21. The Collect acknowledges the saint's desire to "restore all things in Christ" as it recognizes his intelligence and great accomplishments. The Prayer over the Offerings reminds us of the reverence with which we must always celebrate the divine mysteries, and the Prayer after Communion asks that "the power of this heavenly table" may make us "constant in the faith." The Preface of Holy Pastors would be a good choice for today since St. Pius X was a pope.

Today's Saint

Known as the pope of the Eucharist, Pius X is remembered for promoting frequent reception of the Eucharist. He did this when Jansenism, a heresy that believed Holy Communion should be reserved for only a select few, was prevalent. Stating that "Holy Communion is the shortest and safest way to heaven," Pius X issued a decree to combat Jansenism, allowing children to receive Holy Communion when they reached the age of reason (age seven), rather than waiting until they were older. Pius X's other accomplishments include reforming the liturgy, encouraging priests to give simple Homilies, reintroducing Gregorian chant into services, revising the Roman Breviary, and developing a new catechism.

(#424) white
SAT 22 Memorial of the Queenship of the Blessed Virgin Mary

Today's Memorial

Mary is truly the "Favored One of God." Her relationship with Jesus Christ was like no other, and God filled her life with grace from beginning to end because of her Son. Today we celebrate her at her Son's side in heaven. As Christ reigns in heaven, tradition teaches that God continues to favor the Mother of God, crowning her queen alongside her Son. Even in heaven, her relationship with Jesus Christ fills Mary's life with grace. On this memorial we rejoice in the fullness of hope and promise God shows us in

Mary's life. She is Queen of Heaven, as God holds nothing back from her in the glory of heaven. Mary's joy is our hope as she lovingly guides us to join her at the side of her Son in eternity.

The Lectionary for Mass

Commentary written by Anne Elizabeth Sweet, OSCO.

◆ FIRST READING: In this fraction of Ruth's history we see how God inspires others to care for the poor and thus change the course of history. Ruth, a young, foreign widow stayed with her bereaved mother-in-law and they try to survive by gleaning others' fields. Boaz eventually marries her, and through her, the Davidic line includes nationalities other than the Israelites.

◆ RESPONSORIAL PSALM 128: Praying this psalm invites us to contemplate the blessings enjoyed by truly good-hearted people. The psalm might refer to Boaz, Ruth, the saints, or some of the people who surround us.

◆ GOSPEL: Pope Francis famously remarked that pastors should smell like their sheep. That is the opposite of what Jesus saw in the religious leaders of his day who dedicated themselves to their own self-aggrandizement. Rather than exhibiting fear of the Lord, some seemed to be in the business of trying to impress even God.

The Roman Missal

All the orations for this obligatory memorial are proper for today and are located in the Proper of Saints at August 22. The Collect acknowledges the Blessed Virgin Mary as our Mother and our Queen. The Prayer over the Offerings makes explicit the connection between the offering we make and Christ's offering on the Cross, while the Prayer after Communion points to eschatological fulfillment as it

asks that through this Eucharist we "may merit to be partakers at your eternal banquet." The Preface is one of the two Prefaces of the Blessed Virgin Mary; if Preface I is used, the correct phrase to use is "on the feast day."

(#122) green
23 Twenty-First Sunday in Ordinary Time

The Lectionary for Mass

◆ FIRST READING: As Joshua asks the people to choose whom to serve, he offers the choice between the God who has done so much for them or the false gods worshipped by their ancestors and neighbors. We can understand the lure of other gods if we think of idols as work, prestige, winning, flashy possessions, clothes, and so on. When everyone around you believes those things to be necessary, it can be hard to choose the values of the Cross. This reading challenges us to ask ourselves what gets us up in the morning and motivates what we do with our days.

◆ RESPONSORIAL PSALM 34: This week, we might meditate on the line "Let my soul glory in the LORD!" How would your day be changed if everything you did was consciously done for the greater honor and glory of God?

◆ SECOND READING: This entire passage, some of which is quite bound to the culture and time in which it was written, can be summed up with the first line: Defer to one another out of reverence for Christ. Whether in the intimacy of marriage or in the life of the entire community, Paul is calling us to serve one another, in such a way that we become occasions of grace one for the other.

◆ GOSPEL: The way Jesus offers is the path of most resistance. Peter and the disciples slowly realized how difficult Jesus's road would turn out to be, but when Jesus questioned whether or not they would choose him, Peter responded that the hard road was the only one going anywhere worthwhile. Are we with him?

The Roman Missal

The Mass texts for today are found in the "Ordinary Time" section of the Proper of Time. The Gloria is sung or said today.

The Collect asks that we might love what God commands and desire what God promises. The Prayer over the Offerings reminds us that we have been gathered by God to become one people "through the one sacrifice offered once for all," and therefore we pray for "the gifts of unity and peace in your Church." The Prayer after Communion asks for completion of the works of God's mercy, thereby implying that those works have begun in our sacramental communion.

Preface I of the Sundays in Ordinary Time describes how we have been summoned "to the glory of being now called / a chosen race, a royal priesthood, a holy nation, a people for your own possession, to proclaim everywhere your mighty works"; this would certainly pick up on a theme heard in the Prayer over the Offerings. Similarly, so would Preface VIII, which speaks about the people gathered and formed as one, made the Body of Christ, and now manifest as the

Church. One of those two Prefaces might be a good choice for today.

Other Ideas

Bartholemew, Monica, Augustine, and John the Baptist — this week certainly has an allstar cast. Invite your congregation to get to know them better. They also embody the spirit of today's readings. They are saints, but incredible things were asked of them. We can think that following Christ and living a Catholic life should be good, happy, and easy. But it "ain't necessarily so." Reflect on the Tom Booth song ,"I Will Choose Christ." In reality, we need to choose Christ — to choose which house we serve over and over in life. While there may be a moment of conversion or a life changing event, for most of us the call is to choose Christ rather than serving money, alcohol, prestige, pornography, lust, or any number of things. It may be the way we respond in a moment of crisis. Sometimes, it is even a matter of choosing between "two goods" — and that is even more difficult.

The Second Reading is about Marriage. Couples need to choose to love each other each day, and Marriage is nothing if not compromise — giving up one's own will for the greater good of the couple, the family, or the spouse. May God bless you in all the paths you choose.

(#629)   red

MON 24 Feast of St. Bartholomew, Apostle

The Lectionary for Mass

◆ FIRST READING: In this vision of the New Jerusalem, John sees twelve gates to the city, each with the name of an Israelite on it. The foundation stones bore the names of the Apostles. The New Testament naming of the Twelve Apostles symbolically represented the new Israel inaugurated by Christ, open to people of all nations.

◆ RESPONSORIAL PSALM 145: The refrain of our psalm offers a summary of the life of Apostleship. We too are called to spend our lives manifesting the glory of God's reign.

◆ GOSPEL: It might be confusing that the Gospel for this feast day refers to Philip and Nathanael. The fact is that the various New Testament lists of Apostles do not match perfectly, and Nathanael may well have been another name for Bartholomew. Jesus recognized Nathanael as "true child of Israel" who would see much greater things by remaining with Jesus. We might conclude that the role of apostleship is much greater than their biographies and remember that Jesus's followers were primarily faithful Israelites who saw in him the fulfillment of their faith tradition.

The Roman Missal

The Prayers for the feast are found in the Proper of Saints. The Gloria is said or sung today. The Preface of the Apostles is used. We pray that God may strengthen us in the faith to which the Apostle Bartholomew "clung wholeheartedly" (Collect) and that through his prayers we may know God's help (Prayer over the Offerings).

Today's Saint

There is little reference in the Gospel to Saint Bartholomew (first century), other than the fact that he was one of the original Twelve Apostles. He is also mentioned in the Acts of the Apostles as one of the disciples waiting for the descent of the Holy Spirit. According to the second-century Alexandrian teacher Pantaenus, an early Christian community in India claims Saint Bartholomew as its founder. Tradition states that he preached throughout Persia, Mesopotamia, Lycaonia, and Phrygia. It is believed that he was skinned alive and beheaded at Albanopolis, on the west coast of the Caspian Sea.

TUE 25 (#426) green
Weekday

Optional Memorials of St. Louis / white; St. Joseph Calasanz, Priest / white

The Lectionary for Mass

◆ FIRST READING: Paul wants to assure his community of the sincerity of his message and the humility with which he and his companions present it. He invites us to envision what evangelization would look like if it were carried out in the manner of nursing mothers attentive to every need of their children.

◆ RESPONSORIAL PSALM 139: This psalm invites us into the depth of a thoroughly honest and loving relationship with God. It calls us to believe in God's great love more than in anything else.

◆ GOSPEL: In this section of Matthew, Jesus speaks his mind about those who claim religious authority. His colorful language makes his point all the more memorable. While he does not dispute their teaching, he names it for what it is. Proud of their mastery of minute detail, they have missed the purpose, and therefore the graced potential of God's law.

Today's Saints

Becoming king of France at the age of 12, St. Louis (1214–1270) imbued French culture with a deep sense of divine justice. Although he enjoyed the finer things in life, including good wine and food, he never lost sight of the poor. It was not uncommon for him to feed the less fortunate from his own table, but he felt this was not enough so he provided homes for them. Even with the many constraints upon his time, he managed to spend several hours a day in prayer. The priest St. Joseph Calazanz (1556–1648) formed a religious order, the Clerks Regular of the Pious School, to set up free schools for the education of poor children. He believed that education would free the young from the dismal life of the slums, basically ending the cycle of poverty, by giving them the necessary skills to build a brighter future. During the plague of 1595 he ministered to the sick with St. Camillus de Lellis.

WED 26 (#427) green
Weekday

The Lectionary for Mass

◆ FIRST READING: In this section of his letter Paul repeats a favorite theme: make your lives worthy of the God who calls you. We could spend many an hour beginning to plumb the implications of that statement. Until we have that leisure, we ought to realize that the way we live our everyday lives is the truest possible witness to what we really believe.

◆ RESPONSORIAL PSALM 139: Little children cover their eyes and believe that reality has gone away. Praying Psalm 139 reminds us that whether we seek God or try to hide, God is with us, knowing us more deeply than we know ourselves — and loving us in every moment.

◆ GOSPEL: Jesus continues his diatribe against the religious leaders around him. In their pride and hypocrisy they are the opposite of a person who would pray Psalm 139 with sincerity.

THU 27 (#428) white
Memorial of St. Monica

The Lectionary for Mass

◆ FIRST READING: As Paul writes, he reveals the profound importance that the Christian community has for him. In Christian community, we sustain and strengthen one another by our faith, and our most fervent prayer is that our love for others may increase.

◆ RESPONSORIAL PSALM 90: A community like that to which Paul gives witness knows that God's love expressed in worship and solidarity is the source of true joy. In a community that shares its faith we learn to "number our days aright, / that we may gain wisdom of heart."

◆ GOSPEL: As Matthew nears the climax of his Gospel, the message becomes more and more urgent. Whether we think the end is near or not, we are called to remain alert to the signs of God's action among us. Each of us is called to be that servant dedicated to the well-being of the family of the master.

The Roman Missal

The proper Collect for today, found in the Proper of Saints at August 27, describes St. Monica as one who wept "motherly tears . . . for the conversion of her son Augustine." The Prayer over the Offerings and the Prayer after Communion are taken from the Common of Holy Men and Women: For Holy Women, and either Preface I or Preface II of Saints is the Preface to be used for today.

Today's Saint

St. Monica (332/3–387) knew the pain of disappointment, an unfaithful husband named Patricius who drank too much, and a promiscuous son, St. Augustine of Hippo, who lived an immoral youth. Through patience and love, her husband had a change of heart, choosing to become a Christian. St. Augustine's conversion was a much more difficult task. St. Monica prayed constantly and fasted daily, but nothing seemed to work, so she consulted St. Ambrose, Bishop of Milan, for guidance. Through the intervention of God, the two of them managed to lead St. Augustine to the waters of Baptism. St. Monica exemplifies that unconditional love and persistence are portals for God's saving grace.

FRI **28**
(#429)   white
Memorial of St. Augustine, Bishop and Doctor of the Church

The Lectionary for Mass

◆ FIRST READING: It might be tempting to interpret this section of Paul's letter as saying that morality is equal to Christian spirituality. That is the road to the superficiality Jesus condemned in religious leaders. Paul's instructions here are motivated by what he said earlier, that Christians strive to live worthily in response to God's great love, not to gain it nor to prove themselves.

◆ RESPONSORIAL PSALM 97: In response to Paul, we rejoice in the God who is the source of all that is good. The more we live in God's love, the more God's light will dawn on us, sharpening our perception and bringing us gladness, no matter what our circumstances.

◆ GOSPEL: One of the less noted dimensions of this parable is the fact that women are its subject. Although it may seem subtle, Jesus's demand that they do everything necessary to be prepared for the reign of God is a reminder that among Christ's followers, gender matters no more than nationality or hair color. No one is excused from the demands of discipleship.

The Roman Missal

The Collect, the Prayer over the Offerings and the Prayer after Communion are all proper for today, located at August 28. In the Collect we pray for the same spirit as that which inspired St. Augustine to thirst for "the sole fount of true wisdom." The Prayer over the Offerings prays that this Eucharist may be for us "the sign of unity / and the bond of charity"; we can recall how that was a major theme of St. Augustine's preaching about the Eucharist. The Prayer after Communion echoes Augustinian

preaching on the Eucharist once again as it asks that "being made members of his Body, / we may become what we have received." The Preface of Holy Pastors would be a most apt choice for today, although either Preface I or II of Saints would be acceptable.

Today's Saint

St. Augustine was born to a pagan father and a devout Christian mother. This wild, unruly young man later became one of Western Christianity's most influential figures. He tried it all—living with a woman, fathering a child out of wedlock, and dabbling in Manichaeism, a heretical belief similar to Gnosticism. Through his mother's prayers and a friendship with Ambrose, he eventually converted to Christianity, was ordained a priest, and then became bishop of Hippo in 396. His prolific writing formulated theories and doctrines on original sin, just war, human will, divine predestination, the Trinity, and Christology.

SAT **29**
(#430; Gospel #634)   red
Memorial of the Passion of St. John the Baptist

Today's Memorial

For speaking the truth, John the Baptist is imprisoned, and eventually beheaded. The story of his death cries injustice to this day. Yet the courage of John the Baptist to speak the truth to Herod is also inspiring and awesome. How did he find the courage? Did he have a sense of what would be at risk? What might have sustained his spirit in prison? To answer these questions, we could look to the many people, such as political prisoners or victims of religious intolerance or ethnic persecution, who are imprisoned unjustly today for daring to speak the truth. People like Oscar Romero, Edith Stein, and Dietrich Bonhoeffer are modern-day John

the Baptists who continue to remind us of the power of the Holy Spirit that accompanies us even in the most difficult circumstances. Trusting in God's Spirit, we, too, may find the courage to speak and act for God's goodness and truth.

The Lectionary for Mass

◆ FIRST READING: Some of Paul's letters are quite harsh, but in writing to the Thessalonians he finds much to praise. Their love for each other is so great that it is known throughout Macedonia. But Paul exhorts them to continue in the way they have begun. This reading includes a short and simple guide to a happy life. Mind your own business. Work with your own hands. Live in tranquility.

◆ RESPONSORIAL PSALM 98 is a song of the Lord's coming; he will bring justice to the earth.

◆ GOSPEL: Here, we have the contrast between one who speaks the truth, no matter the cost, and one enslaved by others' perception. As we hear stories of martyrdom, the tragic characters are not the martyrs: they knew what they were doing and were willing to pay the price for their faithfulness. The pitiable ones in the stories are the ones who had to use force, who could not bear criticism, who betrayed their better selves to prove their strength or power.

The Roman Missal

The texts for the memorial are to be found in the Proper of Saints at August 29. The Collect reminds us that St. John the Baptist was a forerunner (precursor) of the Lord not only in his birth, but also in his death. We pray in this prayer that "we, too, may fight hard / for the confession" of what God teaches. The Prayer over the Offerings employs imagery and phrases closely associated with the Baptist ("make straight your paths;" "that voice crying in the desert") in the way it asks that the offerings have an effect in our lives. The text for the Preface, "The mission of the Precursor," is given along with the other texts for this Mass, and it is the same Preface as used on the Nativity of St. John the Baptist in June (the text with music can be found there if the Preface is to be sung). The Prayer after Communion prays that we will recognize both what the sacrament signifies and what it effects in us.

(#125)   green

☀ 30 Twenty-Second Sunday in Ordinary time

The Lectionary for Mass

◆ FIRST READING: As Moses presents God's law, he insists that obedience will make the people famous and assure a good life. Most of all, he underlines the fact that they are uniquely privileged in the way God is present to them and has taught them. This reading, coming at the end of the summer season, invites us to look at our religious experience and tradition and appreciate our faith heritage in the same way that Moses encouraged his people to do.

◆ RESPONSORIAL PSALM 15: When we pray "those who do justice will live in the presence of God," we are not saying that God is absent from the unjust. Rather, doing justice is our way of choosing to be conscious of and responsive to his presence. That includes an attitude

of heartfelt truth expressed that comes to light in service of others.

◆ SECOND READING: In today's language we might say that the Epistle of James is the epistle of transparency. James insists that our faith must be expressed in action for the good of others. If we are saved, then we will act like people who have nothing to worry about and who therefore can share with abandon. He goes so far as to equate work for justice with worship. In the light of that, he would ask us how we live and worship outside of the church building.

◆ GOSPEL: If we want to summarize today's Gospel with a key question, it would be "Where is your heart?" The "law" that the religious leaders were quoting to Jesus was actually scholarly commentary on God's law developed over centuries. Certainly, it was a good and healthful practice to eat with clean hands, but scrupulous attention to detail was not part of Jesus's vision of God's reign. According to Jesus, those whose religiosity focuses more on legal detail than on the needs of others block the way to God for themselves as well as for others.

The Roman Missal

The Mass texts for today are found in the "Ordinary Time" section of the Proper of Time. The Gloria is sung or said today.

The Collect reminds us of our absolute dependence on God as we turn to him beseeching that he "nurture in us what is good" and keep safe what he has nurtured; thus are we reminded of the constant care God offers us. The Prayer over the Offerings in effect points to the sacramental principle and the efficacy of symbols in liturgical celebration as it asks that this offering may "accomplish in power . . . what it celebrates in mystery." The Prayer after Communion calls the Eucharist "the food of charity," thus

reminding us that the Eucharist should bear fruit in us by stirring us up to serve God in our neighbor.

Other Ideas

St. James tells us, "humbly welcome the word that has been planted in you and is able to save your souls." This is an important message to convey to the entire congregation, but especially to those students who may be heading off to college this week. St. Mark gives us a whole list of things that can happen when one's heart is not in the right place, and many of them are the things that young people become enslaved to under the guise of "freedom" as they enter college or the work world. Freedom is not simultaneous with irresponsibility. It goes back to last week. Again we must choose Christ.

Offer a special blessing for those beginning school and for the educators who help guide and shape their minds.

Church programs will begin soon. Make sure supplies have been ordered, websites updated, and that you are as prepared as you can be. Good. Now step away from it all and take a few days off for vacation and/or retreat before everything breaks loose in the parish. You must be rested to start. You can't "welcome the Word" unless you take the time to "plant it in you."

(#431)   green

ᴹᴼᴺ 31 Weekday

The Lectionary for Mass

◆ FIRST READING: Today's text addresses the sorrow and grief the Thessalonians experience at the death of their loved ones. They are assured that they and their loved ones will be together again with the Lord when he comes in glory.

◆ RESPONSORIAL PSALM 96: Once again, the theme of the Lord's judgment is heard in the Responsorial Psalm. The Lord will come as judge. All creation rejoices in his presence.

◆ GOSPEL: This text from Luke's account of the Gospel is a sort of programmatic statement for the whole of Jesus's ministry and teaching. Empowered by God's spirit, he is sent in particular to those who are poor or imprisoned, physically disabled, or in need of consolation from the Lord. Note that Jesus is in the synagogue in his hometown of Nazareth, and he gets mixed reviews. Jesus, well-versed in the Scriptures, knows that it is often the lot of prophets to be rejected by their own. On this day, those who could not receive his word were so enraged that they tried to kill him. This is a hint of what will happen later in the Gospel.

September
Month of Our Lady of Sorrows

T U E 1 (#432) green
Weekday

The Lectionary for Mass

◆ FIRST READING: In this, the oldest existing text of the New Testament, we experience Paul's vivid theological metaphor of "light." Through Baptism all of Christ's followers are illumined; they need not worry about the darkness even as they wait upon the day of the Lord. While he may come "like a thief at night" (see Matthew 24:42–44) they can stay "alert and sober" as they wait—and be a positive example for those surrounding them.

◆ RESPONSORIAL PSALM 27: Here, the psalmist affirms the value of trusting in the Lord. Again, we experience the image of light, which can be experienced in God's holy temple. Reminiscent of Psalm 23, it reminds us that trust in God is a source of courage and promise.

◆ GOSPEL: Again we hear of Jesus's time spent teaching in the local synagogue and his impact upon those who hear him. His authority is palpable. Silencing the "demon" that possesses the man, he demonstrates that he can act as God's agent against evil. Scholars tell us that the Greek word in verse 33, *daimon*, had to do with urges that could not be controlled. We are powerless over unhealthy urges—what might we do in response?

W E D 2 (#433) green
Weekday

The Lectionary for Mass

◆ FIRST READING: Paul is effusive in the love he expresses toward the community at Collosae. He extols the fact that not only have they heard the Gospel, but they are living it—in acts of faith, hope, and love. These are the core characteristics of Christians, both then and now.

◆ RESPONSORIAL PSALM 52: The psalmist voices his deep trust in God's mercy, evoking the image of the olive tree. Olive trees grew in the vicinity of the temple in Jerusalem, their fertile blooming a testament to the presence of God.

◆ GOSPEL: The Messianic Secret, usually associated with the Gospel according to Mark, appears in the stories at Capernaum. Jesus heals with authority, first Simon's mother-in-law and next many others who were sick. He silences the demons, not allowing them to reveal his true identity. Unlike his reception in Nazareth, here the local people long to hold on to him and bring their ailing family members to him as soon as the Sabbath is complete at sunset.

T H U 3 (#434) white
Memorial of St. Gregory the Great, Pope and Doctor of the Church

The Lectionary for Mass

◆ FIRST READING: Paul writes in loving acknowledgement of this community, which he did not found but which he nevertheless supports wholeheartedly. He prays for spiritual wisdom and understanding to be theirs, and for their bonds to be strengthened. He wants them to not only know God, but to be able to live the inheritance that has been given to them.

◆ RESPONSORIAL PSALM 98: In this hymn, the Lord's victory is a source of ebullient celebration. The salvation of God is announced to all the ends of the earth, and no reaction less than the sounding of instruments in jubilation is appropriate. Truly God's salvation is good news for all. This psalm of entrance is offered almost in its entirety.

◆ GOSPEL: For the first time in the Gospel according Luke we hear Jesus described as preaching "the word of God." This first call of the disciples focuses on Simon, who is then named Simon Peter, the rock upon which the Church will be built. Despite his skepticism, he listens to Jesus and acts in faith. The catch of fish is nothing less than miraculous, and Simon and his companions are moved to leave all behind and follow Jesus. Notice that Simon first calls Jesus, Master, and then refers to him as Lord. How are each of us invited to experience God's wondrous abundance and embrace him for who he really is, in faith?

The Roman Missal

All the orations, proper for the day, are found in the Proper of Saints at September 3. The Collect points to the way St. Gregory was exemplary in his shepherding role in the Church as pope. The Prayer over the Offerings recalls the forgiveness that comes to us through the Eucharist, since it notes how "through its offering" God has "loosed the offenses of all the world." The Prayer after Communion uses the image of Christ the teacher to ask that those who have been fed with

the living bread may learn God's truth, "and express it in works of charity." The appropriate Preface to use for today would be either the Preface of Holy Pastors or Preface I or II of the Saints.

Today's Saint

St. Gregory the Great (540–604) was a mayor, a monk, a pope, and a writer. Unhappy with his life as mayor of Rome, St. Gregory allocated half of his fortune to the poor and the other half to the foundation of seven monasteries. After joining a monastery in pursuit of a simple life, he was elected to the papacy. As pope, he cared for the poor, implemented the Gregorian reforms to improve Church governance and clerical behavior, promoted the monastic vocation, and renewed the liturgy. His name is associated with Gregorian chant (plainsong) and Eucharistic Prayer II (along with St. Hippolytus). A prolific writer and Doctor of the Church, St. Gregory composed numerous theological texts and is cited 374 times in St. Thomas Aquinas's *Summa Theologiae*.

FRI 4 (#435) green
Weekday

The Lectionary for Mass

◆ FIRST READING: This Christhymn, like the one in the letter to the Phillipians, is a profound theological statement about the nature of Jesus Christ. As the "firstborn," all that is created comes through him, and all is, in turn, reconciled through the Blood of his Cross.

◆ RESPONSORIAL PSALM 100: Again we hear the kingship of the Lord extolled. Knowing who he is and all that he has done, the only response is praise and thanksgiving. All are invited to come through the gates of his temple to give thanks and blessing.

◆ GOSPEL: The Pharisees and scribes note the ways in which the

habits of the disciples of Jesus differ from their own habits and those of the followers of John the Baptist. They are drawing attention to the ways in which the old ways and his new ways contrast. Jesus answers them in logical terms, referencing the mending of clothes and the storing of wine. His disciples are called to new practices and new ways. How are all of us called to revisit our old ways of doing things as we become new in Christ Jesus?

SAT 5 (#436) green
Weekday

Optional Memorial of the Blessed Virgin Mary / white

The Lectionary for Mass

◆ FIRST READING: Paul's listeners are reminded here that they were once pagans and alienated from God. Now, part of Christ's Body — the Church — they are pleasing to God. Persevering in faith and retaining their hope in the Gospel is the key to remaining in that relationship.

◆ RESPONSORIAL PSALM 54: The psalmist cries out in great despair asking for God's protection and care. Refusing to despair, he trusts that God will save him. Consistent with the form of the "psalms of lament," God's actions lead to thanksgiving and praise.

◆ GOSPEL: In the absence of Temple piety during the Babylonian captivity, Sabbath practices became extremely important, and the prohibition of work on the Sabbath became deeply tied to the preservation of identity. Jesus sees things far more fluidly, and as an observant Jew, counters the criticism with a reference to the greatest king of Israel, David. He demonstrates that the ultimate fulfillment of God's purpose for the Sabbath is not just not doing evil, but in fact doing good.

6 (#128) green
Twenty-Third Sunday in Ordinary Time

The Lectionary for Mass

◆ FIRST READING: Isaiah's salvation proclamation begins with a call to "be strong, fear not!" No matter what struggles surround or overwhelm us with fear, trust that God comes to save. God's salvation is for all.

◆ RESPONSORIAL PSALM: This "Hallelujah" psalm calls the entire community to praise the Lord with all their being (soul). Such total praise is due because God "keeps faith forever," secures justice, feeds the hungry, and liberates the captives.

◆ SECOND READING: James counsels all followers of Christ to live lives that manifest love for all, most especially the poor and those that society easily marginalizes because of their looks, appearance, or social status.

◆ GOSPEL: Made whole by becoming able to speak and hear, the healed deaf mute becomes a sign of God's reign and saving power, realized and activated through Jesus.

The Roman Missal

The Mass texts for today are found in the "Ordinary Time" section of the Proper of Time. The *Gloria* is sung or said today.

The Collect gives a description of those gathered to enact worship:

they are redeemed, adopted by God, and are therefore "beloved sons and daughters." We pray that in belonging and in believing in Christ, we "may receive true freedom / and an everlasting inheritance." The Prayer over the Offerings designates two fruits we are hoping for as a result of making the offering this day: that it might allow us to "do fitting homage" to God's "divine majesty," and that it may unite us with one another in mind and heart. The Prayer after Communion acknowledges that the celebration of the Eucharist nourishes us with both "Word and heavenly Sacrament"; we should never forget the inherent unity of the Liturgy of the Word and the Liturgy of the Eucharist, the two parts of the Mass that are so intimately connected that they form one act of worship.

Other Ideas

Include an intercession for those who are blind or hearing impaired as well as the health care professionals who work with them. Does your parish offer a hearing-loop or other worship aids for those with difficulties? Many times people are not aware of the resources that are available to them at church—be sure to communicate these resources with members of the congregation.

Contact your diocesan deaf-ministry and invite a sign interpreter for the liturgy so that members of the deaf community can participate fully, consciously, and actively!

Because of today's readings, today presents a good opportunity to offer the Anointing of the Sick during one of the Sunday liturgies (or, at the very least, between Masses).

Monday is Labor Day—make sure the times for Masses and other liturgies are posted. Include a petition for the needs of human labor. Welcome any guests that may be visiting the parish.

MON 7 (#437) green
Weekday

Optional Mass for Labor Day (U.S.A./Canada) / white

The Lectionary for Mass

◆ FIRST READING: To follow Christ is not without struggles, as witnessed to in this letter. The mystery of God is revealed through the listening and the actions of holy ones like those in Colossae. This revelation is not reserved for Israel, but reaches out to the Gentile world through ministers like Paul.

◆ RESPONSORIAL PSALM 62: Listeners are reminded that trust in God is essential. The refrain (or antiphon) is the omitted verse 8. God alone is the refuge in which true rest can be achieved in the midst of the hardships of life.

◆ GOSPEL: Having just proclaimed himself Lord of the Sabbath, Jesus continues his ministry of healing. To lose one's right hand was to lose the instrument of all social connection (for example, eating and touching) because the left hand was reserved for personal hygiene. The affliction in this story is therefore far more grave than first meets the eye. In this healing, Jesus is bringing the man back into the community and empowers him to celebrate the Sabbath. By doing this, Jesus again fulfills the true meaning of the Sabbath.

TUE 8 (#636) white
Feast of the Nativity of the Blessed Virgin Mary

About this Feast

Exactly nine months after the Solemnity of the Immaculate Conception of the Blessed Virgin Mary (December 8), we come to a feast in honor of Mary's birth. This is one of only three "birthdays" on the liturgical calendar, the other two being the birthdays of Jesus and of John the Baptist (other days

recognize a saint's "day of death"). Today we recall the greatness of Mary and her importance in all of salvation history, as we remember her humble and obedient "yes" to give birth to Jesus Christ, the Savior of the World. So on this day we honor the life of this young woman, Mary Immaculate, called to be the Mother of God and our mother, queen of heaven and earth.

The Lectionary for Mass

◆ FIRST READING: Micah, speaking more than 700 years before the birth of Jesus, heralds the birth of the new Davidic king, who will come through his line. Notice that the mother of this king is mentioned but not the father. Christian tradition has embraced this text as foreshadowing the birth of Jesus, the Good Shepherd and Prince of Peace.

◆ RESPONSORIAL PSALM 13: This brief excerpt of the psalm offers language of trust, rejoicing and song. Each is reminiscent of the powerful descriptive language of the *Magnificat*, making this an evocative choice for today's feast.

◆ GOSPEL: Today's long form of the Gospel offers us the detailed description of the genealogy of Jesus. Matthew moves through forty-two generations — from Abraham, the father of Israel, to Christ. This directly places Jesus in the line of David, situating him as the fulfillment of God's promise. While contemporary listeners may not know all the figures, it is noteworthy that among them are prostitutes, adulterers, heathens, and murderers. This Divine King comes from the human situation to the human situation. Even the story of Joseph's frailty and courage speak to the humble beginnings of Jesus's life.

The Roman Missal

The texts for this Mass are all proper for the feast today, and are located in the Proper of Saints section of the Missal at September 8. The Gloria is sung or said today, since it is a feast.

While the Collect acknowledges that today is the Feast of the Nativity of the Blessed Virgin, the prayer also points to the birth of Christ, which is referred to as "the dawning of salvation." There are two options for the Prayer over the Offerings. The first one, in somewhat curious phrasing, asks that the humanity of God's Only Begotten Son come to our aid; it also exalts the Blessed Mother's place in salvation history with its statement that Jesus, at his birth from the Blessed Virgin, "did not diminish but consecrated her integrity." Lastly, the prayer asks that Christ may take away our wicked deeds so that the oblation we offer is acceptable to God. The second option also mentions the humanity of Christ, as it asks that we be "given strength / by the humanity of your Son, / who from her [the Blessed Virgin Mary] was pleased to take flesh." The Prayer after Communion, after noting how the Church has been renewed with these sacred mysteries, now refers to the Nativity of the Blessed Virgin Mary as "the hope and the daybreak of salvation for all the world."

The Preface, proper for today, is one of the two Prefaces of the Blessed Virgin Mary. If Preface I is used, the correct phrase to use is "on the Nativity." Also, the Solemn Blessing formula titled "The Blessed Virgin Mary," number 15 under "Blessings at the End of Mass and Prayers over the People," is suggested and should be used today. Finally, since Mary is the model disciple who shows us how to follow Christ, perhaps the dismissal formula, "Go in peace, glorifying the Lord by your life" would be appropriate for today.

WED 9 (#439) white
Memorial of St. Peter Claver, Priest

The Lectionary for Mass

◆ First Reading: The freedoms of a new life in Christ bring with them responsibilities. In particular, Christians are called to set aside the activities that might have been a part of their pagan past, including idolatry. Echoing the texts of Corinthians and Ephesians, there is no "Greek and Jew"; a new era of equality has been born.

◆ Responsorial Psalm 145: God is both praised and extolled in Psalm 145, which in its entirety presents an acrostic, with each line starting with a successive Hebrew letter. Again, God's Kingship is celebrated and proclaimed

◆ Gospel: Luke's Sermon on the Plain, a part of which is offered today, shares some but not all its material with the Sermon on the Mount in Matthew. In the manner of Moses, Jesus has come down the mountain to tell the people what God has promised them. This is offered in an active voice, today, not of a future being foretold. His listeners are being addressed directly. How do we react to both the blessings and "woes" of this poetic set of promises and warnings as injunctions for our lives today?

The Roman Missal

The Collect affirms St. Peter Claver's ministry to African slaves and echoes his personal vow as "slave of slaves." The prayer asks that we may love our neighbor as St. Peter Claver did, "in deeds and in truth." The Prayer over the Offerings and the Prayer after Communion come from either the Common of Pastors: For One Pastor, or from the Common of Holy Men and Women: For Those Who Practiced Works of Mercy. The Preface of Holy Pastors or Preface

I or II of Saints are the options for the Preface today.

Today's Saint

St. Peter Claver (1580/1–1654), a Spanish Jesuit priest, spent his life tending to the needs of African slaves in Colombia, South America. While serving as a missionary, he ministered to the slaves by providing them with food and medicine, washing their wounds, preparing them for Baptism, and witnessing their Marriages. He actively pursued lawyers to plead the cases of imprisoned slaves and prepared criminals for death. Not only did he care for the slaves, but he also preached missions to plantation owners and sailors. The "saint of the slaves," as St. Peter is often called, died after contracting a plague.

THU 10 (#440) green
Weekday

The Lectionary for Mass

◆ First Reading: We continue to hear the message sent to Collosae. Here, the writer calls listeners to embody all the positive aspects of discipleship. The list of qualities is compelling. All are supported by a heart governed by the peace of Christ, a mind that dwells on his word, and an "attitude of gratitude" for all he has given.

◆ Responsorial Psalm 150: The final hymn of the psalter, Psalm 150 boldly calls out for praise of God. All he has done is praiseworthy, and creation, musically animated and dancing, makes a joyful noise in recognition of this fact. This is not a bad day to encourage the assembly to sing fully!

◆ Gospel: The sermon now takes a turn to one of the most challenging realities of the Christian life: Love. It is insufficient simply to love those who are loveable; Christians are called to love even the most unlovable characters around them.

This is the nature of the radical love of God; it includes all. The pattern is straightforward: "Love," "do good," and "give," trusting that God will do the same and in even greater measure.

FRI 11 (#441) green
Weekday

The Lectionary for Mass

◆ FIRST READING: In the tradition of ancient discourse, the letter begins with the name of the sender, the author acknowledging the recipient, and a greeting. Here, Paul adds "mercy" to the traditional greeting of grace and peace. The next paragraph expands that theme and how God's mercy has affected Paul's life. Unlike many of Paul's other letters, Timothy addresses a single person rather than a community.

◆ RESPONSORIAL PSALM 16: The psalmist affirms his fidelity to the true God and not the false gods of other peoples. The God of Israel is God from age to age, the inheritance and comfort of believers. To him alone belongs worship.

◆ GOSPEL: Unlike in Matthew, where the warning is against the false teaching of Pharisees, here Jesus exhorts members of the community to be scrupulous in their own behavior. To teach truly in the manner of the "teacher" requires the humility to be scrupulous about blind spots and biases, and to overcome all that is inconsistent to the life to which Jesus calls his followers. Fraternal correction, in this case, begins with personal awareness and self-improvement.

SAT 12 (#442) green
Weekday

Optional Memorials of the Most Holy Name of Mary / white; Blessed Virgin Mary / white

The Lectionary for Mass

◆ FIRST READING: Paul yet again demonstrates the magnitude of his commitment to Christ Jesus by informing Timothy, his reader, of his great personal failings. Paul, the greatest sinner, has been mercifully treated. All sinners can therefore hope for the same, and for this God should be glorified.

◆ RESPONSORIAL PSALM 113: The name of God was never spoken at the time of the psalmist; to this day, the unpronounceable tetragrammaton YHWH is used. It appears almost 7,000 times in the Old Testament. Here, the psalmist praises "the name of the LORD" without saying it, but enumerates God's marvelous qualities and deeds. [In 2008, the Vatican declared that it is also inappropriate to utter the same name of God in Catholic liturgy. The third edition of the Missal accomodated the Vatican's request and familiar hymns and songs have been updated. See the Vatican news article here: http://www.ewtn.com/vnews/getstory.asp?number=90429.

◆ GOSPEL: In contemporary terms, this Gospel message might be reduced to the phrase "you've got to walk the walk." It is not enough to call Jesus "Lord." Rather, one must hear what he says and act accordingly. To do this is to create a firm foundation for one's faith, and to be in position to bear the sort of good fruit He wants. Today is a good day to inquire, "For what fruit am I known?"

Today's Optional Memorial

The Most Holy Name of Mary is the counterpart to the optional Memorial of the Most Holy Name of Jesus celebrated on January 3. Both of these optional memorials had been removed from the general calendar after the reform of the liturgical calendar in 1969. The memorials were restored with the promulgation of the third edition of *The Roman Missal*.

13 (#131) green
Twenty-Fourth Sunday in Ordinary Time

The Lectionary for Mass

◆ FIRST READING: In today's reading, Isaiah describes the servant of God as one who is willing to undergo torment. The servant expresses nothing but gratitude and recognizes God as the one who opens his ears, who keeps him from disgrace and from being proven wrong.

◆ RESPONSORIAL PSALM 116 follows the song of the servant in beautiful harmony. Whereas the servant proclaimed that God had opened his ear, we are invited to join the psalmist in singing the praise of the God who gives ear to our cries.

◆ SECOND READING: James insists that genuine faith in Christ is more than intellectual. Real faith is demonstrated through Christ-like actions, such as caring for the needy.

◆ GOSPEL: Jesus's retort to Peter's rebuke underlined the problem the disciples had to deal with. Peter had pulled Jesus aside to plead against the fate he predicted. When Jesus called Peter "Satan," the effect was not to say he was a devil, but rather a tempter. The phrase "get behind me," pointed out that Jesus, not Peter, was the teacher. The place for a disciple was following the Master's lead, not vice versa.

The Roman Missal

We pray that we may "serve [God] with all our heart" and so "feel the working" of his mercy in our lives (Collect).

We pray that the offering of each of us "may serve the salvation of all." We are one Body in Christ: the love and faith, the needs and hopes we each bring to our prayer touches others in ways we cannot imagine (Prayer over the Offerings). We pray that the "heavenly gift" we have received may so work in us that God's will may prevail over our own desires (Prayer after Communion).

Other Ideas

Initiate efforts to organize and schedule a coat drive. Invite a representative from a local homeless shelter or food pantry to make a presentation to the congregation. This could be done at Mass following the Prayer after Communion or at another scheduled event. Then help this organziation prepare for winter before the snow falls.

Are there any new ministry training sessions scheduled? Fall is a great time to recruit new members as people are adjusting to school schedules and other rhythms. Work with your religious education team to schedule a training session or a presentation for adults while youth activities are taking place. It will be a win-win situation.

Ask for help with the liturgical enrionment. Now is the time to switch to a fall theme.

(#638)   red

M O N 14 Feast of the Exaltation of the Holy Cross

About this Feast

God sent his Son into the world so that we might receive life and salvation. Today on the Feast of the Exaltation of the Holy Cross we proclaim the Good News that God transforms suffering and death into new life. Our God is a God of victory who reigns victorious, even over the evil of death. As Christians, today we rejoice in the mystery of the Cross, which brings about our freedom, salvation, and life.

The Lectionary for Mass

◆ FIRST READING: The Israelites do not overtly rebel against Moses; their behavior is far more insidious: a constant murmuring and complaining. God punishes them; serpents are sent among them. The serpent, the instrument of death, is mounted on a pole and then serves as a source of life — evocative of the Cross of Christ when read typologically, as it has been over the centuries.

◆ RESPONSORIAL PSALM 78 recounts, in its many verses, the story of the Exodus. Although the ancestors were quick to forget the gracious deeds of God, current generations can remember what God has done. Even in the face of their infidelity, God shows mercy to Israel.

◆ GOSPEL: Here, Jesus himself draws the parallel between the episode of the serpent and the Exodus as he compares the lifting up of the pole to the cross that will come. This Gospel contains the text of the Scripture citation most found in popular culture: John 3:16, seen at ballgames and elsewhere. This pericope is expressive of the magnitude of God's profligate and unreasonable love. Nicodemus, a Pharisee, opens his heart to Jesus who shares this vision of life eternal.

The Roman Missal

All the texts are taken from September 14 in the Proper of Saints.

The Gloria is sung or said today.

The Collect speaks of how the human race has been saved by Christ's sacrifice on the Cross, asking that since we know the mystery of the Cross on earth, we "may merit the grace of his redemption in heaven."

The Creed is not said at this Mass, since it falls on a Monday. The Prayer over the Offerings makes a direct connection between the offering made once by Christ in history and the offering we make today; since the Eucharist makes present for us the salvation won for us in Christ's Death and Resurrection, we can also find in this liturgical celebration forgiveness for our sins.

The Preface is proper for today, "The victory of the glorious Cross," and the text, with and without musical notation, is located right there amid the other texts for the day. This Preface puts forth a very positive theology of the Cross, not focused on Christ's sufferings, but rather on the new life that flows from his sacrifice: "where death arose, / life might again spring forth;" "the evil one, who conquered on a tree, / might likewise on a tree be conquered." There is also the possibility of using Preface I of the Passion of the Lord, the text for which is found immediately following Preface IV of Lent. This text speaks of the power of the Cross, and how that power reveals "the authority of Christ crucified."

The Prayer after Communion speaks of the passage of the Paschal Mystery as it asks that those who have been nourished at the holy banquet may, by the wood of the life-giving Cross, be brought to the glory of the Resurrection. An echo of the Good Friday liturgy can be heard in the phrase "wood of your life-giving Cross." Again, a positive theology of the Cross is espoused, as the wood of the Cross is seen as the instrument of salvation, a salvation we participate in through our sharing in the Eucharistic banquet.

TUE 15 (#444; Gospel #639) white
Memorial of Our Lady of Sorrows

Today's Memorial

This is a relatively modern celebration, included on the universal calendar only in 1814. The sorrows of the Blessed Virgin Mary begin with the prophecy of Simeon at the Presentation at the Temple, when he tells her, "Behold, this child is destined for the fall and rise of many in Israel, and to be a sign that will be contradicted (and you yourself a sword will pierce) so that the thoughts of many hearts may be revealed" (Luke 2:34–35). In art, Our Lady of Sorrows has her heart pierced by seven swords, representing the seven sorrows of tradition and the prophecy of Simeon.

The Lectionary for Mass

◆ FIRST READING: Paul recites to Timothy the qualities that should be found in good bishops and deacons. The list sounds something like a job description; in fact, these qualities would be looked for in any leader of the age — note that it is not an exclusively Christian list. Keep in mind that the bishop of the time would have presided over a community far smaller than most Catholic parishes today!

◆ RESPONSORIAL PSALM 101: This "royal" psalm offers us a vision of God having chosen the king, and through him the people of Israel. The qualities of the king are those of a faithful man of integrity and service. The refrain has the quality of a vow that is being spoken.

◆ GOSPEL: No greater tragedy might have befallen a widowed woman of Jesus's day than to lose her only son — her protection and care. Jesus, filled with compassion, raises him from the dead. This evokes memories of similar episodes with the great prophets Elijah and Elisha. The fear the people express was tied more to the ritual uncleanness that would have come from touching the coffin, although they quickly recognize that this is no ordinary person before them.

The Roman Missal

All the orations are proper for today, and can be found in the Proper of Saints at September 15. The Collect draws a direct connection between yesterday's feast and today's memorial as it reminds us that when Christ was "lifted high on the Cross," his Mother was standing close by and sharing his suffering. Thus, we ask that we, with Mary, may also participate in the Passion of Christ so as to share in his Resurrection. Of course, our participation in that Paschal Mystery is effected most completely in the liturgy. The Prayer over the Offerings describes the Blessed Virgin Mary as "a most devoted Mother" who stood by the Cross of Jesus; we can do the same by our fidelity to participation in the Eucharist. Either Preface I or Preface II of the Blessed Virgin Mary is the Preface to be used today, but if Preface I is used, then the phrase "on the feast day" is the correct phrase to use. The Prayer after Communion relates how our participation in "the Sacrament of eternal redemption" is a participation in the Paschal Mystery, including the suffering of Christ.

Although the Missal does not mention it, there is nothing to prevent the use of Solemn Blessing number 15, "The Blessed Virgin Mary," at the end of Mass today, particularly if your weekday Mass will see an increased attendance because of a particular devotion to the Blessed Mother under this title.

WED 16 (#445) red
Memorial of Sts. Cornelius, Pope, and Cyprian, Bishop, Martyrs

The Lectionary for Mass

◆ FIRST READING: Timothy offers us a compelling image of the Church: it is the household of God. This is an image that the Fathers of the Second Vatican Council highlighted (see *Lumen gentium,* 6). What qualities make up a healthy household? How do we fulfill them as God's people?

◆ RESPONSORIAL PSALM 111: Here the psalmist invites us to remember the works of God, and through that, come to even greater faith in God. Recognition of God's deeds leads to praise.

◆ GOSPEL: This Gospel passage has a close parallel to one in Matthew. Here we experience the inconsistency and double standards Jesus faced. John is condemned because he is too ascetic; Jesus because he is not. The listeners are like cranky unsatisfied children. Where are we holding double standards in our lives and our faith?

The Roman Missal

The Collect, the Prayer over the Offerings, and the Prayer after Communion are all found at September 16, proper for this obligatory memorial. The Collect hails these two friends as "diligent shepherds" and "valiant Martyrs," and as the prayer asks that we may "spend ourselves without reserve / for the unity of the Church," we can remember that it was for their efforts to preserve that unity that these two saints were martyred. The Prayer over the Offerings connects the Eucharist we offer with the Eucharist offered by Sts. Cornelius and Cyprian, as it notes how the Eucharist "gave them courage under persecution" and asks that it will "make us, too, steadfast in all trials."

The Preface of Holy Pastors would be a fitting choice today, although one of the Prefaces of Saints could also be used. Since their names are mentioned in Eucharistic Prayer I, perhaps today would be a good day to use the Roman Canon. The Prayer after Communion asks that "through these mysteries which we have received," and by the example of these holy martyrs we might be "strengthened with the fortitude of your Spirit / to bear witness to the truth of the Gospel."

Today's Saints

St. Cornelius († 253) and St. Cyprian († 258) lived during the persecution by the Emperor Decius. St. Cornelius, the pope, faced the issue of whether or not Christians who renounced their faith during the persecutions should be welcomed back into the Church. With great compassion he publicly declared that these individuals may return to the Church after a period of penance. St. Cyprian, Bishop of Carthage, spent much of his life in hiding due to the persecutions, but this did not stop him from offering pastoral guidance and dispensing wisdom to the people of his diocese. Through letters he urged the people to remain faithful to their Christian call. Both Sts. Cornelius and Cyprian shared the same fate — a martyr's death.

T H U 17 (#446) green Weekday

Optional Memorial of St. Robert Bellarmine, Bishop and Doctor of the Church / white

The Lectionary for Mass

◆ FIRST READING: Paul addresses his young colleague Timothy and exhorts him to confidence. He has all the gifts he needs to succeed in Ephesus. Today is a good time to reflect on how well we receive and respect the giftedness of the young.

◆ RESPONSORIAL PSALM 111: We hear Proverbs 9:10 as a verse quoted in Psalm 111. This is a selection from the text that offers the Wisdom Woman's instruction on how to become wise. Proverbs addresses itself to several audiences, including the young — similar to Paul's instruction to Timothy.

◆ GOSPEL: The contrast between the absence of basic hospitality by the host and the overflowing generosity of the woman with the alabaster flask is stark. Notice that it is through forgiveness ("hence") that the woman is empowered to show great love. This calls to question our own practices of hospitality, and what comes first to mind when we are wronged. Is it forgiveness?

Today's Saint

St. Robert Bellarmine (1542–1621), bishop and Doctor of the Church, was an astute scholar with a knack for diplomatically responding to the controversies of his day. As a Jesuit priest embroiled in the Protestant Reformation, he sensitively communicated through word and writing the Catholic perspective, especially regarding the relationship between Church and state. One of his most important contributions to the Church is a three-volume work, *Disputations on the Controversies of the Christian Faith*, which explained Catholic fundamentals in a non-defensive, systematic way. St. Robert, a devotee of St. Francis of Assisi, demonstrated heroic virtue by praying for his opponents, living simply, and embracing spiritual discipline.

F R I 18 (#447) green Weekday

The Lectionary for Mass

◆ FIRST READING: Paul tells Timothy to teach, and to do so without the fractiousness found in other, "false" teachers. In effect, we see a clear illustration of the Gospel

heard earlier in this cycle, in which it is by the "fruits" that one knows the tree. Notice the fruits Paul points to in the second paragraph.

◆ RESPONSORIAL PSALM 49: Like Psalm 27, Psalm 49 offers images of trust in God. Here, the wealthy are impugned for trusting in their riches rather than in the Lord. This invites a moment of reflection on where we place our trust and how we use our financial blessings.

◆ GOSPEL: The story of the woman who washes Jesus's feet (now universally recognized as someone other than Mary of Magdala) tells us something about his companions. The Twelve are with him, as well as women who had been cured. The fact that Mary, Joanna, and Susanna are named indicates their stature in the community. These are the people who funded the ministry of Jesus. Reclaiming the stories of the women disciples is critical for contemporary followers of Jesus, male and female alike.

S A T 19 (#448) green Weekday

Optional Memorials of St. Januarius, Bishop and Martyr / red; Blessed Virgin Mary / white

The Lectionary for Mass

◆ FIRST READING: Paul begins closing his letter to Timothy with a strong personal challenge; he anticipates Jesus's arrival soon. The phrase "unapproachable light" is a beautiful image of the dwelling place of the Divine. Tertullian will echo it in referring to God as "light from light," a phrase that will be incorporated into the Creed at the Council of Nicaea.

◆ RESPONSORIAL PSALM 100: Like the other psalms of kingship, Psalm 100 invites celebrating God in his temple. Explore these images. Are they reflected in the demeanor of the assembly at Mass?

◆ GOSPEL: This vivid and instructive parable also appears in the Gospel accounts of Mark and Matthew. Luke offers not only story but an interpretation. Luke points to the fact that those who hear are called to act upon what they hear. God is doing his work, but it is incumbent upon humankind to receive God's word and have it "bear fruit through perseverance."

Today's Saint

St. Januarius († 305) was Bishop of Benevento in Italy during the Diocletian persecutions. After suffering the fate of a martyr, being thrown to wild beasts and then beheaded, his relics were transported to Naples, where it is said that a vial of his blood liquefies on three feast days related to his life: today; the day he supposedly prevented an eruption of Mount Vesuvius in 1631 (December 16); and the Saturday before the first Sunday in May, commemorating the transfer of his relics. He is the patron saint of blood banks and Naples, where he is referred to as San Gennaro.

(#134)   green

☀ 20 Twenty-Fifth Sunday in Ordinary Time

The Lectionary for Mass

◆ FIRST READING: The wicked are characterized as believing that life is short, that we were born by chance and we will soon be no more. Therefore, life is always ripe for revelry as we use our strength against the weak. But the response of Wisdom goes on to say that "they erred, / . . . / For God formed man to be imperishable; / . . . / the souls of the just are in the hand of God" (2:21 — 3:1).

◆ RESPONSORIAL PSALM 54: An appeal to the name of God implied an appeal to God's strength and faithfulness: the essence of the divine character. It was a way of asking God to become visibly active in the petitioner's life. The whole of the psalm, like the Responsorial itself, proclaims faith that God will care for the unjustly oppressed one.

◆ SECOND READING: In today's passage, James returns to the topic of division, this time both within the individual and in the community. The cause is jealousy and selfish ambition. The jealousy James condemned had generated conflicts that he compared to war and murder.

◆ GOSPEL: The death that Jesus was going toward was politically and physically appalling. Religiously, it was considered proof of the person's God-forsakenness. Jesus, seeing the disciples' opinions about rank, declares that God is to be found where they least expect or want to go. The just one will suffer, but God will not abandon him.

The Roman Missal

The Mass texts for today are found in the "Ordinary Time" section of the Proper of Time. The Gloria is sung or said today.

The Collect notes how all the commands of God's sacred law are grounded in one foundation: the unity of love of God and love of neighbor. The Prayer over the Offerings prays that we may truly possess what we "profess with devotion and faith"; since the context for this possession is asking God to receive our offerings, then it is the offering of ourselves in union with Christ that we are professing, and it is the offering of ourselves in union with Christ that we pray will become more and more a reality through our participation in the offering of the Eucharist. The Prayer after Communion also makes an important connection between liturgical celebration and everyday life: it asks that redemption might be ours "both in mystery [liturgical celebration] and in the manner of our life."

Any one of the eight Prefaces of the Sundays in Ordinary Time are appropriate for today.

Other Ideas

Today is Catechetical Sunday. Following the Prayer after Communion, bless parish catechists as well as parishioners who teach in public and Catholic schools. You might even consider including parents, since parents really are the primary teachers of the faith. The blessing is found in chapter 4 of the *Book of Blessings*.

(#643)   red

MON 21 Feast of St. Matthew, Apostle and Evangelist

The Lectionary for Mass

◆ FIRST READING: This exquisite reading from Ephesians not only affirms the magnificent hope of the Christian calling, but the gifts that God bestows so that it might be fulfilled. Everyone receives grace in Baptism; our challenge is to recognize giftedness and bring it to the fullest possible expression.

◆ RESPONSORIAL PSALM 19 reminds us that all that God created, so magnificently recounted in Genesis, proclaims his glory. We easily imagine the Angels created for unending praise. What would life look like if we saw ourselves and all the earth created for the same purpose?

◆ GOSPEL: On the Feast of St. Matthew, we hear the calling of this disliked tax collector. He will become a powerful disciple. When the religious authorities challenge Jesus's choices, he cites Hosea's beautiful exhortation: "I desire mercy, not sacrifice." Pope Francis has been reminding us that Christ came for sinners and that we, his contemporary followers, must be agents of God's infinite mercy.

The Roman Missal

The prayers for the feast are found in the Proper of Saints. The Gloria is said or sung today. Preface II of Apostles is used. In the Collect we pray that we may learn from the Gospel according to Mark to "follow faithfully in the footsteps of Christ." The Prayer over the Offerings is a prayer for the Church, that she may "always persevere / in the preaching of the Gospel." We pray that the Communion we have received may make us strong in the faith which Saint Mark proclaimed (Prayer after Communion).

Today's Saint

According to tradition, Matthew and John were Apostles. Mark was not, although he could have been an eyewitness to the events he describes in his Gospel. He is thought to have been a friend and disciple of Peter, and we know from New Testament references that he ran into some difficulties with Paul. We know that his account of the Gospel of Jesus Christ was written in Rome between 60 and 70 AD, following the martyrdom of Peter and Paul. Mark's symbol is a winged lion, an allusion to the desert wilderness with which his Gospel begins. Mark is the patron saint of Venice, and his relics are venerated in the great cathedral of San Marco.

TUE 22 (#450) green
Weekday

The Lectionary for Mass

◆ FIRST READING: In the Book of Ezra, we hear of the rebuilding of the temple and the role Persian King Darius played in that achievement. The restoration of God's house is a pivotal moment in the history of Israel. Scholars argue about the historicity of the timing of the Passover; even when read theologically, it speaks powerfully to what has been returned to the Jews, who have suffered in their exile in Babylon.

◆ RESPONSORIAL PSALM 122 invites us to share in the uncontained joy of the people of Israel when they have the privilege of coming to Jerusalem and the temple where God dwells. We hold the belief that God is among us in the Eucharist, and can bring the same joyful expression into our "pilgrimage" to our place of worship each day.

◆ GOSPEL: For Jesus, being part of God's family is not only about earthly bonds of familial ties and tradition. Those who act on God's word are the brothers and sisters of Jesus. It is important not to read hostility into this text; there is perhaps no better example of someone who heard and acted upon God's word than Mary, the mother of Jesus.

WED 23 (#451) white
Memorial of St. Pius of Pietrelcina, Priest

The Lectionary for Mass

◆ FIRST READING: The people of Israel have been rewarded by their experience of a plural culture (the restoration of the Temple) but they have also been affected negatively through a loss of identity that has come with intermarriage. Now that Judah and Jerusalem are restored, it is time to return to observances of the law.

◆ CANTICLE: The song of praise that Tobit offers in response to the exhortations of the angel Raphael is included in the text for today. Interestingly, the verses focused on Jerusalem and the restoration of the Temple are not offered, but the sections about praise of God are presented.

◆ GOSPEL: The mission of the Twelve is specific: Heal the sick and proclaim God's kingdom. Jesus offers practical advice. Take nothing: this journey requires dependency and vulnerability. Do not be discouraged: when you are thwarted move on without malice or being upset. They must have been listened too, because they report success. How do we make our faith complicated? Simple?

The Roman Missal

The Collect, found at September 23, is the prayer that is proper for today. The Collect acknowledges the stigmata that Padre Pio received as it notes that God, "by a singular grace, / gave the Priest Saint Pius a share in the Cross of your Son." Thus do we ask in this prayer to "be united constantly to the sufferings of Christ." The Prayer over the Offerings and the Prayer after Communion come from either the Common of Pastors: For One Pastor, or from the Common of Holy Men and Women: For Religious. Consider using the Preface of Holy Pastors as the Preface for today, although Preface I or II of Saints or the Preface of Holy Virgins and Religious could also be considered.

Today's Saint

Early in life St. "Padre" Pio of Pietrelcina (1887–1968), a Capuchin priest from Italy, demonstrated an unquenchable thirst for God. While praying one day before a crucifix, he received the stigmata. After an examination by a doctor, it was determined that there was no natural explanation for the wounds.

He also experienced other mystical phenomena, including bilocation, and "reading the hearts" of those who sought counsel and forgiveness in the Sacrament of Reconciliation. These two miraculous gifts enabled him to lead both the sinner and devout closer to God. Upon his death the stigmata were no longer visible.

THU 24 (#452) green Weekday

The Lectionary for Mass

◆ FIRST READING: The prophet Haggai speaks to the second group of exiles returning to Jerusalem from Babylon. His name means "festival" and scholars speculate that among his goals was the restoration of the festival celebrations of Israel in the restored second Temple.

◆ RESPONSORIAL PSALM 149: The psalmist reminds us what gives God delight. Among them are the actions to which Haggai will later exhort the people. Notice that God who loves his people is particularly generous to the "lowly" (see verse 4).

◆ GOSPEL: People are buzzing with interest in Jesus. Herod is among them. This person about whom he has heard is not John—he has executed John after Salome's wily actions. The word translated as "perplexed" can also mean confusion and indecision. Notice that his piqued interest causes Herod to seek more information.

FRI 25 (#453) green Weekday

The Lectionary for Mass

◆ FIRST READING: Haggai speaks to a community of people that includes members who knew the Temple in all its glory in its first form. Clearly the second iteration is more modest. Through Haggai God reassures listeners that his spirit is still with them despite their travails.

◆ RESPONSORIAL PSALM 43: This lament comes from someone who lives north of his people and who cannot join the faithful worshippers in the Temple of Jerusalem. Still, this person, who is in distress and is distant, knows that God will bridge all places of separation.

◆ GOSPEL: Yesterday we read of Herod's wonderment over Jesus. Here, we see him inquiring of the disciples about the questions people are asking. The answer that he is the anointed one of God—the Christos—is in many ways a very Jewish answer. But this anointed one will need to suffer; he will not look like the Davidic King of Israel's expectations.

SAT 26 (#454) green Weekday

Optional Memorials of Sts. Cosmas and Damian, Martyrs / red; Blessed Virgin Mary / white

The Lectionary for Mass

◆ FIRST READING: Like his contemporary Haggai, Zechariah offers visions of God's zeal for his people and the rebuilding of his Temple. In this second vision, he sees a man with a measuring line and hears words of reassurance from an angel. The theme of reconstruction is underlined here, emphasizing God at its center.

◆ CANTICLE: The poem of the third chapter of Jeremiah is offered in place of a psalm today. The themes of God as the good shepherd who gathers the flock, redeems them, and transforms sorrow is offered, an ideal complement to the reading from Haggai.

◆ GOSPEL: As in the Gospel according to Mark, we experience the "messianic secret" in various passage of the Gospel according to Luke. Jesus asks the disciples to attend to what he is saying—he will be handed over. But they are not clear what this means and remain reluctant to ask. He continues preparing them for a future that will look quite different from their religious and cultural expectations.

Today's Saints

Sts. Cosmas and Damian († 287) were brothers, possibly twins, who practiced medicine without accepting money for their services. They are known in the East as the *anargyroi*, meaning "moneyless ones" or "moneyless healers." As vibrant witnesses to the Christian faith, they were arrested during the Diocletian persecutions. When they refused to renounce their faith and engage in idolatrous worship, they were beheaded and cast into the sea.

27 (#137) green Twenty-Sixth Sunday in Ordinary Time

The Lectionary for Mass

◆ FIRST READING: God bestowed the spirit on the elders, and they prophesied as a result. Only God could choose to give or to withhold the spirit. Moses, more aware than others that the spirit was a free gift, did not cling to status. He not only affirmed the liberty and unpredictability of God's activity, but wished that everyone would be so gifted.

◆ RESPONSORIAL PSALM 19 has three focal points: creation's

testimony to God's goodness, the beauty of God's law, and the human desire to serve God well. The psalmist admits that no one, no matter how faithful or vigilant, can be perfect. Our only recourse is to turn to God, who will cleanse and guide us.

◆ SECOND READING: James writes in the context of the impending end of the world. He warns the rich that they have stored up treasures for the last days, but the end times that are coming will reverse all their hopes. That which they could have spent on others will not only be rusted, but the money and moth-eaten garments will actually testify against them.

◆ GOSPEL: Jesus wastes no time in refocusing the disciples' priorities. If someone performed a mighty deed in Jesus's name, that was a sign of the person's solidarity with Jesus and his ministry. The disciples believe that Jesus is acting with the power of the Spirit of God; therefore, they should recognize that anyone who does the kind of works he does is also graced with power from that same Spirit.

The Roman Missal

The Mass texts for today are found in the "Ordinary Time" section of the Proper of Time. The Gloria is sung or said today.

We hear the Collect how God shows his power principally by pardoning and showing mercy. Thus are we prepared to hear about turning away from sin and choosing the path of life and about how sinners can enter the Kingdom of God. The Prayer over the Offerings reminds us that the offering we make is "the wellspring of all blessing." The Prayer after Communion highlights our union with Christ through the Eucharist: we are united in his suffering when we proclaim his Death, so we ask to be "coheirs in glory with Christ."

In choosing the Preface for today, you might consider Preface II of the Sundays in Ordinary Time, with its mention of Christ responding with compassion to "the waywardness that is ours"; or Preface IV, with its emphasis on Christ bringing renewal, on his cancelling out our sins, and on his opening the way to eternal life; or Preface VII, as it mentions our disobedience, which has been overturned by Christ's obedience. Consider also Eucharistic Prayer for Reconciliation I, with its Preface, as another possibility; all of these would echo the theme of the return of the sinner.

Other Ideas

In our readings today we hear about those who do work in God's name. How do you empower members of your congregation? Does the staff delegate and use volunteers well? Do you show your gratitude for those with other skills? Consider offering a ministry fair, or a ministry appreciation day or evening. Recognize those with outstanding contributions, or do a feature story on a long-term volunteer in the parish newsletter or website. Have an experienced minister mentor someone who is new to the parish or a committee. How do you acknowledge those who retire from a ministry? These people can be your angels if you just let them do so.

Later this week we celebrate the feast of the Archangels, Guardian Angels, and Saint Thérèse. Ironically, Thérèse had a beautiful poem prayer titled "To my angel guardian." Introduce it to the community to tie the week together.

MON 28 (#455) green
Weekday

Optional Memorials of St. Wenceslaus, Martyr / red; St. Lawrence Ruiz and Companions, Martyrs / red

The Lectionary for Mass

◆ FIRST READING: We may be inclined to focus on the word "jealous" here, but the meaning of the word is more akin to passion or concern. The oracle speaks to the abundance of what comes with God's presence: generations of people that make up a "faithful city" and a "holy mountain."

◆ RESPONSORIAL PSALM 102: These stanzas describing God's goodness come at the end of a psalm expressing fury toward God. In the midst of the railing, there is a statement of faith in God's fidelity. Although the full sense of the psalm is absent, this selection is an ideal complement to the selection from Zechariah.

◆ GOSPEL: In the Gospel, we see Jesus address questions of status and inclusion. The apostles are more comfortable talking about their individual rank and the behavior of others than they have been with discussing the true nature of Jesus. His choice of the child demonstrates that anyone can represent Jesus, even the most lowly or invisible. Despite this demonstration, they still do not understand what following him will require.

Today's Saints

Most people are familiar with Wenceslaus (903 – 935), due to the popular Christmas carol "Good King Wenceslaus." Although this ancient carol is not based on historical events, it illustrates the fame King Wenceslaus received because of his heroic life. As a Christian king in Bohemia, a primarily pagan country, he worked fervently to Christianize his people. His attempt to evangelize the Bohemians was not received well by some, including his brother who eventually murdered him. As he was dying, he prayed that God would forgive his brother. Shortly following his death, people proclaimed him a martyr.

St. Lawrence Ruiz (1600–1637), a married man with three children, fled to Japan from Manila to escape an unjust charge. Upon arrival he was greeted with hostility, due to a recent edict that banned Christianity. When he and fifteen other companions would not adhere to the state religion and trample on religious images associated with the Catholic faith, they were executed. St. Lawrence and his companions join 231 other Catholics martyred in Japan between the sixteenth and seventeenth centuries.

(#647) white
T U E 29 Feast of Sts. Michael, Gabriel, and Raphael, Archangels

About this Feast

We celebrate the feast of three archangels, Sts. Michael, Gabriel, and Raphael, the great heralds of salvation and defenders against the power of evil. St. Michael is guardian and protector of the Church, from its roots in Israel to the Church of today and beyond. In Hebrew, his name means "who is like God." St. Gabriel, whose name means "hero of God," announces that John the Baptist will be born to Elizabeth and Zechariah. He is entrusted with the most important task of revealing to Mary that she will bear the Son of God. Then, there is St. Raphael, whose name is Hebrew for "God has healed." He is named in Tobit 12 as the one standing in the presence of God, and in 1 Enoch (early Jewish writing) as the healer of the earth (10:7).

Lectionary for Mass

◆ FIRST READING: The Book of Daniel and the Book of Revelation are the only two apocalypses in the Bible. Here, Daniel presents a vivid description of God enthroned, those that surround him, and the coming of "One like a son of

man"—a human being. Note that God's kingdom is represented by the human.

◆ RESPONSORIAL PSALM 138: The psalmist gives thanks, noting that God acted not because somehow the psalmist was deserving, but because God keeps his promises. This inspires nothing less than praise in the presence of God's angels.

◆ GOSPEL: On this feast day of the great Archangels of God, we hear Jesus promise Nathanael that he will see "heaven opened." This faithful and forthright man who has been called by Phillip is the first to proclaim, in Johannine faith, Jesus as the Son of God. Jesus cautions that it is one thing to be driven to faith by wonder at the small action of Jesus recognizing him; more significant acts are to come.

The Roman Missal

The texts for this Mass, all proper for the feast day, are located in the Proper of Saints section of the Missal at September 29. The Gloria is sung or said today, since it is a feast.

The Collect speaks of the "marvelous order" of creation, which includes the ministry of the angels who both watch over us and defend us on earth, and who minister to God in heaven. The Prayer over the Offerings describes that it is the ministry of angels who bear the gifts we offer into the presence of God's majesty; it is a beautiful reference to how not only these gifts are lifted up, but how our hearts can be lifted up, as we will proclaim shortly in the Preface dialogue. The text for the Preface proper for today is given right there along with the other texts for this Mass; musical notation is provided. The Preface reminds us that when we pay honor to the angels, in fact we are praising God, since their great dignity and splendor shows how great God is. The Prayer after Communion begs that we might "advance boldly along

the way of salvation" through both the nourishment of the Eucharist and the protection of the angels.

(#457) white
W E D 30 Memorial of St. Jerome, Priest and Doctor of the Church

The Lectionary for Mass

◆ FIRST READING: The work of Nehemiah begins humbly: He is serving wine to the king and queen of Persia. His sadness and plight are addressed as the king sends him out empowered to return to Judah to rebuild the city. Here, a small conversation between people of unequal power produces an extraordinary result.

◆ RESPONSORIAL PSALM 137: This soulful lament is the song of captivity sung in Babylon as the community grieves for all that it has lost. This act of remembering affirms a defiant hope in the face of despair and the mocking of those who seek to remember Jerusalem.

◆ GOSPEL: The journey of Jesus to Jerusalem begins at this point in the Gospel according to Luke. Many of the short teachings of this section are instructions to the disciples regarding what it will take to follow him. This is not a geographically focused journey (he has no place to lay his head); rather, it is a journey of relationship and learning, and the severing of conventional ties.

The Roman Missal

All the orations are proper for today, and are located in the Proper of Saints at September 30. The Collect acclaims St. Jerome for his "living and tender love for Sacred Scripture," asking that we "may be ever more fruitfully nourished by your Word." The prayer offers a fitting introduction to the Liturgy of the Word. The Prayer over the Offerings goes on to remind us of how the Word leads to Eucharist:

it notes how now that we have meditated on God's Word, we can ask to "more eagerly draw near to offer your majesty the sacrifice of salvation." The Prayer after Communion prays that, having received the holy gifts of the Eucharist, our hearts may be stirred up to be more attentive to sacred teachings (namely, the Scriptures) and so better understand the path we are to follow, thus obtaining everlasting life. How wonderful it is to note how the orations for this day provide a mystagogy on the unity between Word and sacrament! Either the Preface of Holy Pastors or Preface I or Preface II of Saints would be appropriate choices today.

Today's Saint

St. Jerome (345–420) is the patron saint of scholars and librarians. With a great love of learning and books, as a monk and priest he developed a passion for the interpretation of Sacred Scripture. With a comprehensive knowledge of classical languages, St. Jerome produced a Latin text of the entire Bible eventually known as the Vulgate. He wrote numerous commentaries on several books of the Bible, including a highly reputable work on the Gospel according to Matthew. Along with writing, he provided spiritual guidance to wealthy widows and mentored young monks in monastic discipline. St. Jerome joins three other saints (Ambrose, Augustine, and Gregory the Great) as the first Doctors of the Church.

October
Month of the Holy Rosary

(#458)   white

THU 1

Memorial of St. Thérèse of the Child Jesus, Virgin and Doctor of the Church

The Lectionary for Mass

◆ FIRST READING: The people are finally liberated to fully embrace the teachings of the Torah, and Ezra proclaims it before all assembled. Some grieve as they hear the law, perhaps because the community has strayed so far from their religious practices. Still, they are to rejoice and celebrate, because they will be restored as a great people.

◆ RESPONSORIAL PSALM 19: This uplifting prayer reminds us that following the law of God is not a burden. It is the source of wisdom, enlightenment, refreshment, and more. Like the precepts of the Wisdom literature, the verses here inspire listeners to learn and live the law joyfully.

◆ GOSPEL: Jesus sends out not only the Twelve, as earlier in the Gospel, but seventy-two disciples — an echo of Moses's choice of seventy elders. Jesus instructs them in the humility and openness they are to bring to this mission. Consistent with earlier passages, he notes that they are to receive hospitality as given and not be separated from those with whom they speak due to custom. Jesus requires witnesses for his message that are flexible and filled with a sense of purpose. Do we demonstrate those qualities in our evangelization?

The Roman Missal

All the orations are proper for today, as found in the Proper of Saints at October 1. The Collect explicitly mentions the "Little Way" of St. Thérèse, noting how God's kingdom is open "to those

who are humble and to little ones." The Prayer over the Offerings asks that "our dutiful service may find favor" in the sight of God — and by "dutiful service" we can hear both the work of doing the ritual of worship and the work of doing acts of love in the Christian life, which we bring to offer at this Eucharist. The Prayer after Communion prays that the Sacrament we receive will "kindle in us the force of that love with which St. Thérèse dedicated herself" to God; we can be reminded that reception of the Eucharist is never a mere passive reception, but an active pledge to be renewed and revived in living the Christian life. The Preface of Holy Virgins and Religious would seem to be the most appropriate choice for a Preface today, although certainly Preface I or II of Saints could also be used.

Today's Saint

St. Thérèse of Lisieux of the Child Jesus (1873–1897), known as the "Little Flower," was a spiritual athlete, but not in the same way as her contemporaries. Contrary to the spirituality of her time, which favored self-mortification and miraculous phenomena, she approached God through the ordinary experiences of everyday life.

As a Carmelite nun, she coined the phrase "the Little Way," referring to her belief that every act, no matter how small, is an opportunity to meet and praise God. While struggling with the debilitating disease of tuberculosis, she wrote her spiritual autobiography, *The Story of a Soul*. Her autobiography, translated into over fifty languages, has inspired faith in the skeptic and strengthened the soul of the believer. She is patron saint of the missions and a Doctor of the Church.

F R I 2 (#459, Gospel #650) white
Memorial of the Holy Guardian Angels

About this Memorial

Today we honor the countless unnamed angels assigned to guide, guard, and protect us throughout our lives. The belief in angels is supported by their mention in the Book of Psalms and other books of the Old Testament, as well as the Gospel, as in today's passage from Matthew 18:10.

The Lectionary for Mass

◆ FIRST READING: This confession of the people of Israel is both poignant and responsible. They do not cast blame elsewhere; they look to their own actions and repent. Baruch was Jeremiah's assistant. This prayer to God has echoes in the Confiteor, in which we recognize that we have sinned through no one's fault but our own.

◆ RESPONSORIAL PSALM 79: Like the reading from Baruch, this psalm of lament speaks of repentance and recognition of culpability. The psalm recounts the horror of the defiling of the temple and is a cry to God for forgiveness and restitution.

◆ GOSPEL: On the memorial of the Holy Guardian Angels, we hear the beautiful passage of Jesus inviting his followers to bcome as innocent and as vulnerable as a child. The notion of heaven having angels who guard children sourced the teaching about "guardian" angels. This is a strong exhortation given the posturing and climbing the disciples continue to demonstrate. This notion that the least will be first is an overturning of their conventional understanding of God's plan.

The Roman Missal

Like yesterday, all the orations are proper again for today, and these are found at October 2. The Collect pleads that God will always have

the holy angels guard and defend us. The Prayer over the Offerings also asks for the protection of our guardian angels, so that "we may be delivered from present dangers / and brought happily to life eternal." The proper Preface, "God glorified through the Angels," is given right there along with the other texts for this memorial; it is the same text used for the Feast of Sts. Michael, Gabriel, and Raphael the Archangels on September 29 (refer to the text for that day if you wish to have the musical notation to sing the Preface). This Preface describes how the honor we pay to angels results in God being glorified; to venerate the angels is to praise God. The Prayer after Communion reminds us that the nourishment we receive in the Eucharist is nourishment for eternal life; we therefore ask this day that the angels guide us into that life.

S A T 3 (#460) green
Weekday

Optional Memorial of the Blessed Virgin Mary / white

The Lectionary for Mass

◆ FIRST READING: The people strayed from God and his law, and yet redemption is still possible. They have been in exile and have suffered, but this can empower them "ten times the more to seek him." Note that the city of Jerusalem is personified in a lamenting voice.

◆ RESPONSORIAL PSALM 69: The suffering in this long psalm includes recognition of the loss of the holy Temple. Truly Israel is among the poorest of the poor, having been stripped of all that has meaning. Still, despite being truly those bereft of resources, faith that God is listening is affirmed.

◆ GOSPEL: Although Jesus has prepared the disciples for moments of failure, and in fact has decried those places that are not receiving

his message, the seventy-two return "rejoicing." They have been truly empowered to bring the Good News of healing and restoration to all. Jesus is inspired to praise and thank God, modeling for his listeners that the power comes from God. Nothing less than the fall of Satan is possible.

4 (#140) green
Twenty-Seventh Sunday in Ordinary Time

The Lectionary for Mass

◆ FIRST READING: Genesis presents us with the image of a person alone and helpless. To resolve the problem, God puts the man into a sleep so deep that he cannot watch what is going to happen. Then, having created the woman, God presents her to the man, almost like the father of the bride escorting a daughter to her groom. The man expresses his delight as he repeats: this one, this one, this one! The point is that it is not good for a person to be alone. Human beings are social by nature. We are created to be partners and helpers one for another.

◆ RESPONSORIAL PSALM 128: Praying this psalm leads us to recapture the joy of that garden where God created humanity.

◆ SECOND READING: The author admits that Jesus was, for a time, less than the angels, and immediately explains why that was so. Jesus chose inferiority to the angels precisely so that he could be one with humanity in all things, including death. Adding an exceptional development to the teaching of Genesis, Hebrews asserts that in the person of Jesus, God became one with humanity to consecrate us, to be brother and helper to us.

◆ GOSPEL: In this scene, we find the Pharisees trying to put Jesus in danger or trap him in legalities. The danger came from the fact that John the Baptist had been beheaded over the question of divorce (Mark 6:17–29). While that lurked in the background, rabbis of that day debated the legitimacy of divorce. As so often happened, rather than answer the Pharisees' question, Jesus asked one of his own and, as usual, caught them in their own trap.

The Roman Missal

The Mass texts for today are found in the "Ordinary Time" section of the Proper of Time. The Gloria is sung or said today.

The Collect recalls that God's love and grace are super-abundant and overflowing; that is the basis for our asking God "to pardon what conscience dreads / and to give what prayer does not dare to ask." God will always surpass our expectations and fill us with life and love, despite our unworthiness. The Prayer over the Offerings recalls that the sacrifice we celebrate today was instituted by divine command, and its purpose is to continue the sanctifying work by which we are redeemed (in the liturgy, the work of our redemption is actually being accomplished). The Prayer after Communion speaks of the important action of transformation: we are to "be transformed into what we consume." (Shades of St. Augustine!)

Any one of the eight Prefaces of the Sundays in Ordinary Time is equally appropriate today.

The Blessing of Animals

Many parishes prepare the blessing of the animals on this Sunday. If you will be inviting animals and their caregivers don't forget to place the invitation in the Sunday bulletin in advance and draw attention to it in the announcements. Invite people to donate food, blankets, towels, toys, and money to local no-kill animal shelters. Ten thousand animals are needlessly euthanized every day in the United States because of the lack of space and funding. We are called to help even the smallest of God's creatures.

If parishioners are not able to bring their animals to the blessing of pets, encourage families to bless their beloved pets at home. Here is a prayer they can use from the *Book of Blessings,* chapter 25:

O God,
you have done all things wisely;
in your goodness you have made us
in your image
and given us care over other
living things.
Reach out with your right hand and
grant that these animals may
serve our needs
and that your bounty in
the resources of this life
may move us to seek more
confidently
the goal of eternal life.
We ask this through Christ
our Lord.
Amen.

Other Ideas

The readings today speak much of Marriage. Include an intercession for all married and engaged couples. October has many options for prayer services and additional parish observances. It is the Month of the Holy Rosary so you may wish to pray as a community at special times, or encourage families to pray the Rosary before dinner. Wednesday of this week is the celebration of Our Lady of the Rosary. It is also Respect Life Month. There are many wonderful resources

available from the United States Bishops. Encourage the congregation to participate in life chains, a baby shower for life, or peaceful protests of a prisoner on death row. Invite parishioners to visit a nursing home. The idea is to respect life in all its stages and forms. Be careful that you are not too zealous in these actions. If you have screens in your church, this is not the place to display larger-than-life pictures of aborted fetuses or similar images, to post these pictures on the parish website or Facebook page or in the bulletin. Don't use the shock-value approaches. We know the atrocities of abortion. Please also be respectful to those who have had abortions. You know not of their pain or repentance. Be welcoming to them and show a spirit of reconciliation. As such, it probably isn't the best practice to display fifty-one crosses in front of the church to symbolize the fifty-one million plus children who have been aborted. Find another appropriate place for this memorial, such as the parish cemetery.

MON 5 (#461) green **Weekday**

The Lectionary for Mass

◆ FIRST READING: This long and colorful story reminds us of the lengths to which this prophet went in his attempts to avoid God's will. First he flees in the opposite direction from which he was sent; then he volunteers himself for execution. But God does not relent, and in a symbolic three days spent in the belly of the great fish, he spends time in prayer.

The Canticle allows us to enter into the prayer that Jonah offered to God. Even from the depths of the sea, from being cast into the "pit," Jonah's voice is heard. From within the great fish—a symbol of chaos in the ancient world—comes Jonah's clarity about obeying God.

◆ GOSPEL: Here we see Jesus affirm the answer offered by a scholar of the law. The Torah has revealed a path that is life giving. But following the law is not the end of the story. Love and mercy are also important. The parable calls us to ask about the "Samaritans" in our lives. Is our response legalism or mercy? Judgment or love?

T U E 6 (#462) green
Weekday

Optional Memorials of St. Bruno, Priest / white; Bl. Marie-Rose Durocher, Virgin / white

The Lectionary for Mass

◆ FIRST READING: Here, God makes a second call to Jonah, and this time Jonah listens. In parallel to the three days he has spent in the belly of the great fish, Jonah will need three days to get through this "great" city. As the people respond with conversion, so too is the King inspired. This profound alteration of heart and penitential response results in God's mercy.

◆ RESPONSORIAL PSALM 130: The psalm speaks of powerful repentance and God's generous response. Although it speaks of Israel, the Assyrians of the book of Jonah truly embody this relationship of trust and action. What do we make of a story that elevates the hated enemy as an exemplar?

◆ GOSPEL: Jesus is welcomed into the home of Mary and Martha, the sisters of Lazarus. We know from other texts of the intimacy he felt with this family — also reflected in Martha's willingness to try to hook him into a domestic spat! What is significant here is the question of what true hospitality is. Is it providing food, per custom, or is it paying profound attention to the guest? Mary here is also claiming the dignity that is hers as a disciple, despite the social expectations that come with being a woman.

Today's Saints

St. Bruno (1035–1101) longed for a deeper relationship with God, nourished by solitude and austerity; thus, he and six companions built an oratory surrounded by several small hermitages, or cells, in a remote area in the French Alps known as *La Chartreuse*. This marks the beginning of the Carthusian order whose motto is *Stat crux dum volvitur orbis*, Latin for "The cross is steady while the world is turning." Following the *Rule of St. Benedict* in a strict manner, Carthusian monks live an eremitical (reclusive) life, solely seeking the will of God through prayer and manual labor.

Blessed Marie-Rose Durocher (1811–1894) was raised in a large family just outside of Montreal, Quebec. From a young age she expressed the desire to join a religious order, but her poor health stood in the way of this dream. With the approval of the bishop, she founded the Congregation of the Sisters of the Most Holy Names of Jesus and Mary dedicated to the education of the young and poor. Little did she know, the ministry of the sisters would stem beyond Canada to the United States and some developing countries.

W E D 7 (#463) white
Memorial of Our Lady of the Rosary

Today's Memorial

Pope John Paul II called the Rosary "the school of Mary," a special devotion that teaches us about the profoundly close relationship Mary shared with her Son, Jesus Christ. More than this, praying the Rosary invites us into this relationship, nurturing our faith and deepening our understanding of who Jesus Christ was for the world. The Church celebrates Our Lady of the Rosary in order to honor Mary's example and guidance to her Son. May we learn in her school how to open our lives to her Son Jesus, and how to imitate his example of sharing God's love with the world.

The Lectionary for Mass

◆ FIRST READING: Here we see that Jonah, although prophetic, does not really trust God. He is infuriated that the enemy has been spared. Jonah's fit, his petty reaction about the gourd plant, and God's effort to exhort him to some sense of perspective are powerful comments on human frailty. Note that the story does not tell us whether or not Jonah's heart was changed.

◆ RESPONSORIAL PSALM 86: The psalm today perfectly affirms the God of Jonah — if in fact it does not sound like something we'd hear from Jonah's lips. Mercy is a primary characteristic of God, and must be a quality expressed by his followers.

◆ GOSPEL: Jesus clearly was a man of prayer, as so many narratives reflect. No wonder his disciples ask for his instructions on how to pray. Notice how the themes of the Lord's Prayer — building God's kingdom and who disciples need to be — are the themes of the Gospel according to Luke as a whole. To follow Jesus is to know and be in relationship with his God.

The Roman Missal

All the orations are proper for today and can be found in the Proper of Saints at October 7. All who pray the Angelus will recognize the text of today's Collect. The prayer recaps the mysteries of faith — the Annunciation, the Incarnation, and the Paschal Mystery — and it asks for the intercession of the Blessed Virgin Mary in bringing us to the glory of sharing in her Son's Resurrection. The Prayer over the Offerings reminds us that we are to be conformed to the offerings we bring — in other words, we are to offer ourselves with Christ and so die and rise with him in this celebration. It is only in that way that we can, in the words of this prayer, "honor the mysteries . . . / as to be made worthy of his promises." Either Preface I or Preface II of the Blessed Virgin Mary is the Preface assigned for today; if Preface I is chosen, use the phrase "on the feast day" where the various options are given in the Preface. The Prayer after Communion again speaks about the way our lives share in the Paschal Mystery through our participation in this liturgy; liturgy and life intersect.

THU 8 (#464) green
Weekday

The Lectionary for Mass

◆ FIRST READING: Malachi writes in the period just before Nehemiah comes to Jerusalem to govern. As his name says, he is a "messenger" reminding people of their misplaced priorities. God, however, will bring about justice.

◆ RESPONSORIAL PSALM 1: This first in the Book of Psalms is considered a "wisdom psalm," offering practical direction on living a blessed life similar to the wisdom literature. Action is central to the moral life, and those who act rightly will be rewarded.

◆ GOSPEL: Luke, known for the stories that so vividly describe the real lives of Jesus's listeners, offers here the perfect illustration of part of the Lord's Prayer. We pray that we will receive our daily bread. It will come to us from each other, and also from God who will be with us and provide for our needs. Jesus reminds us not to be shy about letting God know that for which we long: we must ask, seek, and knock.

FRI 9 (#465) green
Weekday

Optional Memorials of St. Denis, Bishop, and Companions, Martyrs / red; St. John Leonardi, Priest / white

The Lectionary for Mass

◆ FIRST READING: The community of Judah gathers to lament after a decimating plague of locusts has destroyed everything in its path. Joel fears that the people will not realize that this natural disaster is a judgment by God. A liturgical gathering is convened in which people can repent and ask for God's favor.

◆ RESPONSORIAL PSALM 9, which affirms the right action people should take toward God—thanks, affirmation, joy, and praise—seems like the response that the people might have made to Joel's exhortation regarding the natural disaster they have experienced. What is our response when disaster strikes?

◆ GOSPEL: Jesus responds to the suspicions of the crowd, who think he is using the power of demons, with an affirmation of his power as coming from "the finger of God," a phrase that ties him to Moses as it appears only in the Book of Exodus. In the story, reliance on personal power and focusing on possessions is a failed strategy. Reliance on God's power is essential.

Today's Saints

In Paris there stands one of the world's oldest churches still in continuous use, the Royal Abbey of St. Denis. Its first stones were laid in the third century. Renowned as the major burial place of the French monarchy, it owes its establishment and subsequent prestige to the presence of the relics of St. Denis, first Bishop of Paris, martyred during the third century. The legend surrounding the saint's life is complex, as three historical figures appear to have been conflated into one legendary figure. He is portrayed as Dionysius, the evangelizer of Gaul; Dionysius the Areopagite, a disciple of Paul; and later as Pseudo-Dionysius the Areopagite, the author of mystical works. Who was the real St. Denis?

Historians have not reached a consensus, partly because the stories are too good not to be told. The favorite of the French is about the beheading of Bishop Denis on the hill of Montmartre; he did not lose his head, however, for he picked it up and walked two miles, his lips chanting the psalms, until he reached his chosen burial spot. There his relics have remained ever since. This miracle of cephalophore (picking up your head after being decapitated and walking away) is well attested to in hagiographical accounts and in medieval iconography. Besides being the patron saint of those with headaches, he is the patron of France and of the city of Paris.

St. John Leonardi, founder of Clerks Regular of the Mother of God of Lucca, was born in Tuscany and ordained in 1572. He founded the Confraternity of Christian Doctrine and the College for the Propagation of the Faith, an important part of the Counter-Reformation.

SAT 10 (#466) green
Weekday

Optional Memorial of the Blessed Virgin Mary / white

The Lectionary for Mass

◆ FIRST READING: The Valley of Jehoshaphat, which some place as the Kidron Valley, was believed to be the place in which the last judgment would occur. The images are those of the harvest, appropriate for a people who have just had their crops destroyed by locusts. But nature will overflow due to the Lord's goodness.

◆ RESPONSORIAL PSALM 27: Those who are just do not have to fear the final judgment. God's light will dawn, and the upright will be glad. The Lord, who is King of all, will reward his people.

◆ GOSPEL: On its surface, the woman in the crowd offers a positive affirmation of Jesus. He is so great that he is the source of blessing to the woman that bore him. But he offers a correction. He is much more than a human man doing good; he is God's prophet and, as will be revealed, God's Son come to preach a new path. The most important affirmation of him that can be made is not verbal praise but hearing God's word through him and following it.

(#143) green

11 Twenty-Eighth Sunday in Ordinary Time

The Lectionary for Mass

◆ FIRST READING: The selection we read today recalls Solomon's prayer for wisdom (1 Kings 3:6–9). Wisdom is more important than power, wealth, health, or beauty. The speaker would choose wisdom even over sight, knowing that with wisdom one can assign everything else its true and lasting value.

◆ RESPONSORIAL PSALM 90: The verses we pray are an apt response to the First Reading's proclamation about wisdom. We ask not only to know how to value the days of our lives, but also to learn to appreciate the lessons of times of trial. Our refrain recapitulates the message as we implore God to give us the only thing necessary: the love that gives meaning to life.

◆ SECOND READING: Just as the First Reading encourages us to seek true wisdom, this selection from Hebrews calls us to meditate on our appreciation of the word of God. Do we believe in its power? Do we consciously seek an encounter with the living God in Scripture? Do we allow that word to judge and guide our daily activities and attitudes? Do we seek the wisdom of the word beyond other values?

◆ GOSPEL: Jesus reminds the man in the passage of the Commandments that refer to human relationships, and the man claims to have lived without transgressing them. Then, Jesus looks at him with the discerning gaze that tenderly lays bare the heart. Having searched the man's soul, Jesus invites him to follow him in truly fulfilling the Commandments by giving his very self for others. With that, the wealthy man's enthusiasm disappears and he who had run to kneel before Jesus turns away, utterly disenchanted. As the man left, Jesus addressed his followers to underscore the fact that the invitation he had issued applied to them as well as to the retreating rich man.

The Roman Missal

The Mass texts for today are found in the "Ordinary Time" section of the Proper of Time. The Gloria is sung or said today.

The Collect reminds us that it is only with the help of God's grace that we are able to carry out good works. The Prayer over the Offerings points to the ultimate goal both of the liturgical celebration of the Eucharist and our life as a whole: we pray that as a result of both, "we may pass over to the glory of heaven." The Prayer after Communion asks that we might have some share in that eschatological fullness now by sharing in the divine nature of the Son through our feeding on his Body and Blood at this celebration.

Any one of the eight Prefaces of the Sundays in Ordinary Time could be considered equally appropriate today, although perhaps Preface VI, with its mention that "even now [we] possess the pledge of life eternal," could be understood as connecting with the imagery of the kingdom, which, although it is a promise of fullness yet to come, is also something that has begun in our midst ("For in you we live and move and have our being, and . . . experience the daily effects of your care").

Other Ideas

The Scripture readings today provide us with many tools for right living, and yet, our lives are never on a straight line. There are always the obstacles of sin, human weakness, and our own limitations. Mark's account of the Gospel tells us, "It is easier for a camel to pass through the eye of a needle than for one who is rich to enter the kingdom of God" (Mark 19:24). The reality is difficult things will be asked of all of us throughout our lives. The *Rule of Saint Benedict* has a chapter called "The Assignment of Impossible Tasks." When a monk was asked to do something, he should accept the order; but, if the burden was too much for the monk, he could explain gently to the superior why he couldn't do the job. The superior might relent, or may say "do it anyway" and then the monk, "trusting in God's help . . . must in love obey." That isn't just a story for those who live in monasteries, but a story for all of us. Sometimes we may not know how we will finish a task at work; get through a crying baby's illness; pay all the bills for our household, company, or parish; or overcome an addiction. Pray about it and tell God—then entrust it to God.

Thursday is the Memorial of Saint Teresa of Avila, and Saturday is that of Saint Ignatius of Antioch.

Teresa said "I grew certain the work was God's and so I threw myself into difficult tasks, although always with advice and under obedience." Ignatius once said, "It is dangerous to imagine that one could offer God suitable service on one's own. . . . The person who does not come to the assembly shows arrogance, having already separated himself."

MON 12 (#467) green
Weekday

The Lectionary for Mass

◆ FIRST READING: Paul greets the community in Rome in his customary manner, offering them grace and peace. He outlines for them who he is and his mission, affirming the Good News that he, and they, have received. The formal greetings are stylistically in keeping with the times and offer us a snapshot of Paul's self-understanding and intent in writing.

◆ RESPONSORIAL PSALM 98: In this psalm extolling the kingship of the Lord, we hear messages of salvation. God has done great things for Israel, and this is to be shouted joyfully to the entire earth. This uplifting hymn affirms our relationship with this saving God.

◆ GOSPEL: Jesus evokes the story of Jonah as he chastises his listeners. Unlike the people of Nineveh, who although they were not Jews listened to the preaching of a Jewish prophet, the people he is encountering demand a sign. The theme of having to see something in order to believe is embedded here. The Queen Bathsheba, who went to great length to sit and learn from Solomon, is also evoked. Jesus's wisdom far exceeds that of Jonah or Solomon, and still the people resist listening.

TUE 13 (#468) green
Weekday

The Lectionary for Mass

◆ FIRST READING: Paul writes to the community of Christians in Rome, which includes both Jews and Gentiles. He is eager to uphold the holy path to which Christians are called. God, revealing himself from creation, asks that we worship him, not the false Gods of pagans.

◆ RESPONSORIAL PSALM 19: The psalm reinforces the excerpt from Paul's letter to the Roman by affirming that God's presence can be found in creation. God has drawn order from the chaos through creation, and his imprint is upon it all. Gospel: The Pharisaic movement of the Judaism of Jesus's day had incorporated many Temple practices into the home. Jesus had clearly forgotten what would have been expected by his host, not a major washing but a ritual hand dipping. Jesus is quick to castigate those that are gathered. As in other passages of Luke, what matters most to Jesus is not the outward appearance or gesture, but the alignment of the interior with the exterior. Where do we find the superficial sort of judgment of the Pharisee?

WED 14 (#469) green
Weekday

Optional Memorial of St. Callistus I, Pope and Martyr / red

The Lectionary for Mass

◆ FIRST READING: The community of Jews and Gentiles in Rome is experiencing the challenge of a blended community. The Jews were often upset by the practices of the "Greeks," and vice versa. Here, Paul reminds both groups of the risks of judgment and both the judgment and impartiality of God.

◆ RESPONSORIAL PSALM 62 reminds us today of the steadfast, reliable stronghold that is God. True confidence can be ours in relying on him. At the same time, the refrain reminds us of the responsibility we have toward God and the works to which we are called.

◆ GOSPEL: The harsh critique Jesus makes of his host and those gathered is a continuation of yesterday's Gospel. Jesus has no tolerance for the self-aggrandizement he sees around him, and for the ways in which the holy law of God is used to oppress and abuse. Jesus has no tolerance, here or elsewhere in the Gospels, for hypocrisy. Remembering that Jesus is criticizing the very tradition from which he springs — Pharisaism — we may be called to examine our own inclinations toward self-righteousness, arrogance, superiority, or oppressiveness.

Today's Saint

Following a life of slavery and hard labor, St. Callistus I († 222) was appointed deacon in charge of the Christian cemetery on the Appian Way, now called the catacomb of San Callisto. Recognized for his abounding wisdom and natural bent for leadership, he was eventually elected pope. He had many critics, due to his liberal stance regarding the forgiveness of those who had apostatized during times of persecution. St. Callistus, heeding the commands of Christ, believed the repentant should be forgiven and welcomed back into the Church. Tradition maintains that he began the Ember Days, periods of fasting and abstinence, which are no longer observed among Catholics. He is commemorated as a martyr; he was probably killed during a public disturbance.

T H U (#470) white

15 Memorial of St. Teresa of Jesus, Virgin and Doctor of the Church

The Lectionary for Mass

◆ FIRST READING: Continuing this week's theme of the place of the law, Paul recognizes that while all are sinners, Christians—Jew and Greek alike—are justified through their "faith in Jesus." Faith is the heart of the matter for all. Through faith, all are redeemed, but our response is humility, not boasting.

◆ RESPONSORIAL PSALM 130 is the perfect complement to Paul's reassurance of the community in Rome. While we are sinful, the Lord is ready to forgive us provided we are attentive to our relationship with him. We need only ask.

◆ GOSPEL: The reading today continues the story of Jesus's harsh assessment of his host and those gathered. He will not toleate religious hypocrisy. Although this group was extremely knowledgeable about the law, he accuses them of being obstructive of others. Although they elevate themselves and obtain status, he sees them as phony. It is insufficient to build monuments to the prophets; what matters is receiving their message and acting. This passage marks the turning point in Luke's account of the Gospel where the Scribes and Pharisees start looking to snare Jesus and condemn him.

The Roman Missal

All the orations are proper for this obligatory memorial, and they can be found in the Proper of Saints at October 15. The Collect recognizes St. Teresa's work as a reformer by noting that God raised her up "to show the Church the way to seek perfection." Thus, we pray that we may be nourished by her teaching and be "fired with longing for true holiness." We bring that hunger and longing for holiness and perfection to this and every celebration of the Eucharist. The Prayer over the Offerings asks that our offerings at this celebration will be as pleasing to God as was the "devoted service of St. Teresa." Pointing out that we have been fed with the Bread of Heaven, the Prayer after Communion asks that we "may follow the example of St. Teresa / and rejoice to sing of your mercies for all eternity." It would seem that the Preface of Holy Virgins and Religious would be the most logical choice for the Preface today.

Today's Saint

St. Teresa of Jesus (1515–1582), more commonly known as St. Teresa of Avila, joined the Carmelite Convent of the Incarnation at the age of 21. Disheartened by convent life, in particular, its spiritual laxity, opulent nature, and overly social atmosphere, she began a reform movement that provided the framework for the Discalced Carmelites. Members of this new branch of Carmelites modeled themselves on the poor and crucified Christ, adopting a life of poverty and abstinence. In collaboration with St. John of the Cross, Teresa helped bring this new way of life to the male Carmelite communities. Their reforms met with great resistance, but they moved forward with faith and persistence.

F R I (#471) green

16 Weekday

Optional Memorials of St. Hedwig, Religious / white; St. Margaret Mary Alacoque, Virgin / white

The Lectionary for Mass

◆ FIRST READING: Paul holds out the example of Abraham to the community. Although God justified Abraham, and showered him with blessing, he never boasted about these riches. Abraham, who lived before God gave Moses the Torah, was justified in his faith not by his actions. Note that two of the blessings from Psalm 32 end this passage.

◆ RESPONSORIAL PSALM 32: The psalm opens with the verses we just heard proclaimed in the First Reading. God forgives our sins, and so we offer ourselves in total honesty to God, asking for forgiveness. The response is to be filled with joy. If only we could all bring this confidence to our practice of the Sacrament of Reconciliation!

◆ GOSPEL: On the heels of the harsh interaction in the home of the Pharisee, we hear Jesus reassuring his rattled disciples. They are warned of the "leaven" of "hypocrisy" that characterizes the Pharisees. Leaven cannot be seen, but it nevertheless makes things grow and inflate. They are to be confident; nothing in Jesus's teaching is hidden. Notice that he tells them, in effect, "fear not," the message of God's angels and the prophets. They are God's, and they can be transparent about their convictions.

Today's Saints

St. Hedwig married the Duke of greater Poland, with whom she lived a pious life. Together they founded a Cistercian convent, which Hedwig entered when she was widowed.

St. Margaret Mary Alacoque was a French Visitation nun and mystic who promoted devotion to the Sacred Heart of Jesus. In a series of visions, the form of this devotion was revealed: Holy Communion on the first Friday of each month, and the institution of the Solemnity of the Sacred Heart. Margaret Mary was criticized by the other nuns but had the support of the community's confessor, Blessed Claude de la Colombière.

S A T
17 Memorial of St. Ignatius of Antioch, Bishop and Martyr
(#472) red

The Lectionary for Mass

◆ FIRST READING: Paul evokes here the great father of the faith of Israel, and our faith, Abraham. Faith is the heart of the matter, but it comes to us as a gift. Despite the evidence of Sarah's barren womb, Abraham believed in God's promise. Paul speaks to his descendants — then and now.

◆ RESPONSORIAL PSALM 105: The psalmist invites the followers in faith of Abraham and Jacob to praise their God. Reminded of God's great covenant with Abraham and his oath to Isaac, we are also reminded of God's faithfulness to his covenants. This principle underscores the Catholic teaching on the unique relationship between God and the Jews found in *Nostra aetate*.

◆ GOSPEL: Having reassured the disciples that they need not fear, Jesus now recognizes that they may face persecution. They don't have to have prepared responses; they can trust that the Spirit will be with them in their moment of need. Luke will go on to write a second volume, the Acts of the Apostles, where the persecution of the disciples is writ large. The emphasis on blaspheming against the Holy Spirit, versus the Son of Man, may reflect Luke's knowledge of where this story leads.

The Roman Missal

All the orations, found at October 17, are proper for today. The Collect highlights the "glorious passion of St. Ignatius of Antioch." The Prayer over the Offerings contains a wonderful reference to the saint's proclamation before his martyrdom that he was the wheat of Christ, to be ground by the teeth of beasts (a statement that is used as today's Communion Antiphon); the prayer asks that just as St. Ignatius was accepted as the wheat of Christ, so may our oblation be pleasing to God — in other words, may we too be wheat and bread, transformed into an offering acceptable to God as this gift of bread will be transformed. The Prayer after Communion connects with this thought in asking that the heavenly bread we receive this day renew us "and make us Christians in name and in deed" — the deed perhaps including martyrdom, following the example of St. Ignatius. Given the emphasis on martyrdom in the orations, the most likely choice for the Preface would be one of the Prefaces of Holy Martyrs, although the Preface of Holy Pastors or even one of the two Prefaces of Saints could not be excluded as possibilities.

Today's Saint

St. Ignatius was born in the year 50 and died somewhere between 98 and 117 in Rome. An Apostolic Father and possible disciple of John the Evangelist, he served the community of Antioch as bishop. Living during the anti-Christian reign of the Roman emperor Trajan, he was sentenced to be fed to animals in the Roman Colosseum because he refused to engage in idol worship. His journey to Rome was marked by extensive writing in which he composed seven letters. These letters, directed to various churches, emphasized the humanity and divinity of Christ, the centrality of Eucharist, and the importance of Church unity.

18 Twenty-Ninth Sunday in Ordinary Time
(#146) green

The Lectionary for Mass

◆ FIRST READING: Although the opening line of today's selection sounds exceptionally harsh, the point is not that God is pleased with pain; rather, God is pleased with the faithfulness of the servant in spite of and through the course of the servant's suffering.

◆ RESPONSORIAL Psalm 33: The refrain we chant sums up and deepens our appreciation of the prayer as we beg for God's mercy and proclaim and promise our trust.

◆ SECOND READING: The author designates Jesus as Son of God, and his emphasis is on divine compassion. The Son of God, far from being aloof, sympathizes with each human creature and, as we proclaimed in the psalm, offers mercy and grace whenever we are in need.

◆ GOSPEL: Not unlike the rich man of last week's Gospel, the disciples had not yet understood that the only real security and power come from trust in God. Neither wealth nor power can prevent or survive death.

The Roman Missal

The Mass texts for today are found in the "Ordinary Time" section of the Proper of Time. The Gloria is sung or said today.

The Collect prays that we might always conform our will to God's will, and serve him in sincerity of heart. This petition might in some way be seen as connecting with the Gospel for today, in that discernment of God's will is important in figuring out how we are to live as both citizens of heaven and citizens of the civil society in which we find ourselves. That kind of discernment demands that we constantly seek to purify our actions and our motives, to be focused on the values of the kingdom, and so the Prayer over the Offerings appropriately prays for that purification through our participation in this celebration: that "we may be cleansed by the very mysteries we serve." We need to look at everything through the lens of the Paschal Mystery, celebrated in the Eucharist, in order to properly discern. The Prayer after Communion also assists us in this discernment as it describes how, from our participation in heavenly things (that is, this Eucharist), "we may be helped by what you give in this present age and prepared for the gifts that are eternal."

In choosing a Preface for today, consider how Preface I of the Sundays in Ordinary Time describes for us how we are to live in the world, namely, as a chosen race, a holy nation, and a people belonging to God who proclaim everywhere his mighty works. Also consider using Eucharistic Prayer IV this week, with its own proper Preface; the sweeping résumé of salvation history it gives sets our notions of civil society in its proper perspective before God's majesty.

Other Ideas

Today is World Mission Sunday. Take up a special collection, invite a missionary to speak at Mass, or find other ways to bring attention to this day. The USCCB provides a good deal of information about this day (www.usccb.org/about/evangelization-and-catechesis/world-missions/).

(#473) red

Memorial of Sts. John de Brébeuf and Isaac Jogues, Priests, and Companions, Martyrs

MON 19

The Lectionary for Mass

◆ FIRST READING: Paul continues to extol the faith of Abraham, who did not doubt but believed. Speaking to believers who have not seen Jesus and yet believe in him, Paul affirms their belief both in the risen Christ and the one who raised him.

◆ CANTICLE: Today in lieu of a psalm we hear the prophecy of Zechariah, who upon the birth of his son John speaks of the blessing God has showered upon Israel. John's birth, like Isaac's, is miraculous — a child who has come to someone beyond childbearing age.

◆ GOSPEL: There is no place for greed in the Kingdom of God. First, we hear the greed of a brother who demands his inheritance. In the parable, Jesus points to the misplaced attention on storing up possessions and wealth. The man is rich, and still he would rather tear his barns down and build bigger ones than disperse his excess. He will, in fact, not live into the future for which he is hoarding. This parable invites all of us to analyze how we use our wealth and our gifts.

The Roman Missal

The Collect for the memorial is found in the Proper of Saints, with the remaining prayers drawn from the Common of Martyrs: For Missionary Martyrs.

Today's Saints

We celebrate the Martyrs of North America (1642–1649), six Jesuit priests and two lay missionaries, who were killed for evangelizing New France, known today as Canada. Their missionary endeavors were successful on many levels, especially with the Huron tribe, but they were despised by the Iroquois and Mohawks, the enemies of the Hurons. The anti-Christian sentiment of the Iroquois and Mohawks led to the killing of seven priests and laypeople over an eight-year period of time. Two of the more notable figures, Saint John de Brébeuf (1593–1649) and Saint Isaac Jogues (1607–1646), both priests, formed the backbone of the mission. Three of these martyrs were killed in what is now New York state.

TUE 20

(#474) green

Weekday

Optional Memorial of St. Paul of the Cross, Priest / white

The Lectionary for Mass

◆ FIRST READING: This passage from Romans was the source of centuries of debate tied to the concept of Original Sin. Just as humanity fell from grace through Adam's defiance of God, it is restored to right relationship with God in grace through Christ Jesus. Sin and death are forces that impact the "flesh" — unredeemed, weak humanity. This text is the source for the English translation of the word "many" in the Institution Narrative.

◆ RESPONSORIAL PSALM 40: This psalm emphasizes the priority of obedience in following God over the obligations of Temple piety. While the law is external and calls for observation, a higher law written in the heart is the source of salvation and praise.

◆ GOSPEL: The narrative begins with phrases that echo the book of Exodus and the preparation for Passover by the Israelites. Reminiscent of the parable about the ten virgins, Jesus reminds his listeners — then and now — of the importance of readiness. Notice that while the master may be delayed, those who are worthy remain vigilant. The total reversal of rank here will be emodied in Jesus himself, who will wash the feet of the disciples in the manner of a servant.

Today's Saint

After having a vision of himself clothed in a black habit, St. Paul of the Cross (1694–1775) established the Congregation of the Passion (the Passionists, or Congregation of the Discalced Clerks of the Most Holy Cross and Passion of Our Lord Jesus Christ). The Passionists, a community of priests, were to live a strict monastic life while fostering an intense devotion to the Passion of Christ through preaching and missions. Along with the traditional vows of other religious communities, they took a fourth vow to spread the memory of Christ's Passion. Unique to their habit was a large badge in the shape of a heart, bearing a cross and the words *Jesu XPI Passio*. As they grew in numbers, they engaged in ministry to the sick and dying. Toward the end of his life, St. Paul founded a community of Passionist nuns.

WED 21 (#475) green Weekday

The Lectionary for Mass

◆ FIRST READING: The letter of Paul to the Romans includes many passages that clarify, through concrete direction, how the followers of Jesus should behave. Here, listeners are called to resist unhealthy desires. In this age where addictions of many kinds are prominent, this passage has particular resonance.

◆ RESPONSORIAL PSALM 124 extols God's saving action. The very existence of Israel is due to God's goodness. Thanksgiving is the response, not unlike the litany of thanksgiving for God's saving works found in the Passover prayer, *Dayenu*.

◆ GOSPEL: Jesus's call for staying alert and prepared continues today. Peter, the sometimes clueless and always inquisitive disciple, asks for clarification. The good and wise servant is resourceful and ready, and is rewarded. The servant who is unready is punished. This metaphor of the servant is apt given that the life of discipleship is a life of service to others. The closing verse well sums up the demands of the gift of following the Lord.

THU 22 (#476) green Weekday

Optional Memorial of St. John Paul II, Pope / white

The Lectionary for Mass

◆ FIRST READING: Paul continues his effort to persuade the community that they are now free of the forces that had once enslaved them. The freedom of the children of God leads to holiness, and so to give oneself to God—fully, in the manner of a slave—is to truly live in grace and not in "death."

◆ RESPONSORIAL PSALM 1: To live the life that has just been described in the letter to Romans requires a profound hope in the promise of God. Here, Psalm 1 offers us the contrast between those who live in sin versus those who follow the ways of the Lord. They are perfect complements.

◆ GOSPEL: The reading today presents us with a vivid picture of conflict and upheaval. The Jews of Jesus's day are expecting a Messiah who would conquer the oppressor. Here he speaks of the disruption his ministry will bring, proposing a scandalous division of family relationships. This passage stands in contrast with the softer passages that precede it.

Today's Saint

In the early years, Catholics and non-Catholics alike were attracted to the athletic man who sneaked out of his villa to ski and reached out to the young at World Youth Days. People of many faiths prayed for him when he was shot in St. Peter's Square and were awed with the mercy he granted his assailant. And none escaped the poignancy of a feeble John Paul II praying at the Western Wall in Israel, leaving a prayer inside the wall. Even a scant follower of the pope knew that the man who forgave his assailant, traveled the world to evangelize, and sought healing in relations with the Jewish people looked to the Blessed Virgin as a model of faith. To John Paul II, the woman who carried the Savior in her womb, who first gazed on him at birth, and stayed with him by the Cross is the person who can bring followers closest to Christ. In the apostolic exhortation *Ecclesia in America*, he called Mary "the sure path to our meeting with Christ." The pope noted that Our Lady of Guadalupe's meeting with Juan Diego evangelized beyond Mexico and voiced hope that the Mother and Evangelizer of America would guide the Church in America, "so that the new evangelization may yield a splendid flowering of Christian life." John Paul II was canonized along with Pope John XXIII, by Pope Francis on Divine Mercy Sunday, the Second Sunday of Easter in 2014, a day that John Paul II established for the Church. Saint John Paul II . . . pray for us! For Mass, use the texts from the Common of Pastors: For a Pope.

FRI 23 (#477) green Weekday

Optional Memorial of St. John of Capistrano, Priest / white

The Lectionary for Mass

◆ FIRST READING: Paul shares his struggles with his readers — and us—in this passage. Even those who are deeply pious will fail in perfectly following the Lord. We can take heart in hearing this, recognize our flaws, and with Paul ask God to deliver us from the weaknesses that keep us from following him completely.

◆ RESPONSORIAL PSALM 119: This psalm is the longest of all the psalms, and it offers eight different words that stand for "law," such as precept, statutes, and more. These verses speak to the desire that we might deeply know God's ways and delight in them, so that we might follow more fully.

◆ GOSPEL: Luke presents Jesus challenging his listeners. There are those who are not willing to see who he is, and what his ministry represents fully. The analogy of taking matters in hand and not waiting—akin to working out an issue with an opponent—is apt. It is time for those who are listening to make a decision about whether they will truly hear and accept his message. Are we willing to hear and accept in the same way?

The Roman Missal

The Collect for this optional memorial, the only prayer proper for today, is found at October 23. The prayer recognizes St. John for the way he brought comfort to the faithful in turbulent times. The Prayer over the Offerings and the Prayer after Communion are taken either from the Common of Pastors: For Missionaries, or from the Common of Holy Men and Women: For Religious. The Preface of Holy Pastors would be a good choice for the Preface today, as would one of the two Prefaces of Saints

Today's Saint

St. John of Capistrano was born in Italy and entered the Franciscans in 1416. He was drawn to the ascetic life and became a follower of St. Bernardine of Siena. After his ordination, John traveled throughout Italy, Germany, Bohemia,

Austria, Hungary, Poland, and Russia, preaching penance and establishing numerous communities of Franciscan renewal. When Mohammed II threatened Vienna and Rome, John, then seventy, was commissioned by Pope Callistus III to lead a crusade against the invading Turks. Marching at the head of an army of 70,000 Christians, he was victorious in the battle of Belgrade in 1456.

SAT 24 (#478) green Weekday

Optional Memorials of St. Anthony Mary Claret, Bishop / white; Blessed Virgin Mary / white

The Lectionary for Mass

◆ FIRST READING: Paul continues to unfold the contrast between the flesh and the spirit. The Spirit of God is the liberator, freeing all who believe to live in righteousness. This Spirit is the same spirit that raised Jesus. Subject to the Spirit, we are given life.

◆ RESPONSORIAL PSALM 24: This psalm was sung in the Temple liturgy, asking for admittance during solemnities. In speaking to the Lord, it affirms both God's greatness and our need for God, calling out for God's blessing in both humility and hope.

◆ GOSPEL: The response of Jesus to the stories of the Galileans and those crushed in Siloam is to disconnect behavior from sudden disaster. They did not bring these tragedies upon themselves. But the question is, were they ready for life to end? Were they prepared to go before God exactly as they were? Note that this version of the fig tree story leaves open the possibility that the tree will not be cut down for lack of fruit, but will grow and bear fruit in the future. Now is the moment to cultivate change, to be prepared for judgment.

Today's Saint

St. Anthony Mary Claret, the son of a Spanish weaver, wanted to be a Jesuit, but ill health prevented him from entering that religious order. Instead, he became a secular priest, overseeing a parish in Spain before heading to Catalonia and the Canary Islands as a missionary. He established the Congregation of the Immaculate Heart of Mary (the Claretians), a group of priests and brothers dedicated to seeing the world through the eyes of the poor.

They operate a diverse number of ministries throughout the world. St. Anthony was instrumental in spreading the devotion to the Immaculate Heart of Mary and the Rosary.

☀ 25 (#149) green Thirtieth Sunday in Ordinary Time

The Lectionary for Mass

◆ FIRST READING: Addressed to a people in exile, refugees scattered "to the ends of the world," Jeremiah underlines the great contrast between the weakness of the people and God's strength and faithfulness. Their restoration has nothing to do with their merit and everything to do with God's great love. Jeremiah offers us an image of God as a consoler, a shepherd who leads the people to refreshing streams, a road-building Father who is careful to see that no one stumbles along the way.

308 ORDINARY TIME (DURING SUMMER AND FALL): OCTOBER

◆ RESPONSORIAL PSALM 126: This psalm reflects both the remembrance of God's saving actions and the hope that the same will happen in the future.

◆ SECOND READING: Hebrews indicates that Melchizedek ranked over even Abraham, and because no one knew his ancestry, his priesthood was forever (7:3). The point the author makes over and again is that Christ's priesthood is superior to any other; it is eternal and it is God the Father who has given him his glory.

◆ GOSPEL: Bartimaeus hears that Jesus is nearby and begins to call to him for help. By using the title "Son of David," he acknowledges Jesus as a successor to Israel's most important king. Although the crowds attempted to silence him, Bartimaeus's hope in Jesus proved more powerful than their objections. The very people who tried to suppress his shouts were sent to tell him to take courage because Jesus was calling him. Bartimaeus modeled the faith that the disciples had been failing to attain. Asking for healing rather than money, he responded to Jesus with the insight and courage to become a disciple and join him on the fateful road to Jerusalem.

The Roman Missal

The Mass texts for today are found in the "Ordinary Time" section of the Proper of Time. The Gloria is sung or said today.

Today's Collect asks that we may be made to love what God commands. The Prayer over the Offerings bids that what we do in service to God — presumably both within the liturgy (the immediate context for this prayer) and outside of the liturgy (the wider connection with everyday life with which liturgical celebration must always be situated) — may be directed to his glory. The prayer can remind

us that we enter into worship not for our own sake, and not to our own ends, but to glorify God and thank God for what he has done. Liturgy ultimately is always about what God has done and is doing, not about what we do. The Prayer after Communion makes an identification between the sacrament and us: it asks that what is within them (that is, the mystery and grace of salvation) may be perfected in us, so "that what we now celebrate in signs / we may one day possess in truth." Thus, are we reminded that the sacramental significations in our liturgies communicate to us the heavenly realities they signify, which one day we will experience in all their fullness. The liturgical signs participate in the reality and truth of what they signify.

Of the eight Prefaces of the Sundays in Ordinary Time that can possibly be used today, perhaps.

Finally, in view of the call to love one's neighbor, perhaps the dismissal formula "Go in peace, glorifying the Lord by your life" would be apropos for today.

Other Ideas

Include an intercession for those with eye problems and for all eye-care professionals. Many times local service organizations such as the Lions Club or Boy Scouts collect eye glasses which are refurbished and given to those in need. Perhaps you can partner with them to have a collection at the parish this weekend.

Saturday evening is All Hallows' Eve. The Thirty-First Sunday in Ordinary Time is superceded by the Solemnity of All Saints. All Souls' Day, the Commemoration of All the Faithful Departed, is the following Monday. Explain and announce the liturgy times for All Saints and All Souls' Day this weekend so people are prepared. Also remind people to turn back their clocks next Sunday for Daylight Savings Time, where appropriate.

MON 26 (#479) green
Weekday

The Lectionary for Mass

◆ FIRST READING: To be filled with God's Spirit is to become his child. Just as Jesus called out to his "*Abba*, Father," we too are truly able to embrace God as his children. This profound relationship invites us to an even deeper connection to Christ, in his suffering and his glorification.

◆ RESPONSORIAL PSALM 68: Like Psalm 24, this psalm was most likely used in Temple liturgies. It is a proclamation of the qualities of God, and the relationship that those who believe in him have with him. This is a God of great strength and power, blessing and salvation.

◆ GOSPEL: Here, Jesus defies the prohibitions of working on the Sabbath to heal the woman who is crippled. He challenges those who criticize him. They let their animals loose to meet their physical needs on the Sabbath, but he cannot set loose this woman from her bondage? Notice that Jesus calls her "daughter of Abraham," a term of dignity that recognizes her faith and her stature. She does not ask that Jesus heal her; she simply is in his path. Her response is to glorify God.

TUE 27 (#480) green
Weekday

The Lectionary for Mass

◆ FIRST READING: While this life is full of suffering, the community can hope for the glory that awaits them. Paul points to creation as an example. Although it struggles, it remains an example. Although we struggle, groaning, we also testify to the promise of God that awaits us.

◆ RESPONSORIAL PSALM 126: This psalm may have been sung upon the return of the Israelites from Babylon. Affirming all that God has done, it also implores God for the restoration of his people. Suffering is not the final word; though they have lived through weeping, they hope for rejoicing.

◆ GOSPEL: These simple parables actually remind listeners that the Kingdom of God will come in unexpected forms. Mustard as a plant could be an unruly pest in the garden, hard to restrain and prone to overtaking other plants. Yeast, in the time of Jesus, was a gooey slop left open to the air to collect oxygen from the atmosphere. And yet both of these unlikely sources produce extraordinary results. Here, images of transformation remind us that the kingdom will enter small and expand into something of significance.

W
E **28** (#666) red
D **Feast of Sts. Simon and Jude, Apostles**

About the Feast/Saints

Today we honor two Apostles about whom we know very little. Tradition maintains that St. Simon the Zealot preached missions throughout Persia and Egypt. St. Jude, not to be confused with Judas Iscariot, is the patron of hopeless causes and is called Thaddeus in the Gospel according to Matthew and the Gospel according to Mark. It is believed that he engaged in missionary work in Mesopotamia and Persia. Both Apostles are thought to have been martyred in Persia, and their relics were transferred to St. Peter's Basilica in Rome sometime during the seventh or eighth century.

The Lectionary for Mass

◆ FIRST READING: As Christianity reaches out beyond the boundaries of the Jewish community into the Gentile world, Paul offers reassurance that all those who receive the message of Jesus are part of the household of God. The new temple is built on the foundation of what has gone before, a new household in which God dwells.

◆ RESPONSORIAL PSALM 19 takes the form of a poem, a prayer to God affirming that God's law can enlighten those who follow it. Here the verses speak to the ways in which God's law is proclaimed by the entirety of creation, made by the one who governs it.

◆ GOSPEL: Jesus calls the Twelve from among his followers, a symbolic number echoing the number of the tribes of Israel. Luke calls them "apostles," from the Greek *apostolos*, one who is sent on a mission. These envoys have been chosen after a night of prayer. Note the difference in the names: Judas son of James takes the place of Thaddeus, who is mentioned in Mark and Matthew. Luke's account of the Gospel is the root of an Eastern tradition of naming seventy original Apostles.

The Roman Missal

The texts for this Mass, all proper for the feast, are in the Proper of Saints at October 28. The Gloria is sung or said today, since it is a feast.

The Collect asks for the intercession of these two saints so that the Church may constantly grow. The Prayer over the Offerings prays that our veneration of the Apostles Simon and Jude may "lead us to worthy celebration of the sacred mysteries." The Prayer after Communion includes a mention of the Holy Spirit, through which we make our prayer that we may remain in God's love in honoring "the glorious passion / of the Apostles Simon and Jude."

Today's Saints

Two of the Twelve we remember today: Simon, who was called a Zealot, and Judas, also called Thaddeus. That is the end of the historical record. But the memory of the Church, which might not meet all the requirements of modern historians, does have a deeper record of these two saints.

Sometime after Pentecost the two of them went off to spread the Gospel in Persia. There they freed people from the oppression that comes with worshipping idols and confronting magicians and pagan priests. The magicians of the false gods demanded a showdown with the holy Apostles, challenging them like the Egyptian priests challenged Moses and Aaron in the courts of Pharaoh. Many were amazed and came to know the truth of Christ, but the magicians and pagan priests rushed upon the Apostles and killed them.

T
H **29** (#482) green
U **Weekday**

The Lectionary for Mass

◆ FIRST READING: This beautiful passages offers two themes. First, we encounter the image of God as a court judge, the ultimate arbiter, who acquits us. Then, we are reminded that nothing in life, no matter how dire, will separate us from the love of Christ. Incorporated into him through faith and Baptism, we can stand in confidence. This hymn-like passage is a celebration of what has been achieved for us in Christ.

◆ RESPONSORIAL PSALM 109: In Psalm 109, the psalmist cries out in distress over the ways in which he has been slandered. This long psalm of lamentation speaks of the pain that the faithful one feels when maligned, and of God's ability to stand with him and save him.

◆ GOSPEL: This interaction appears only in the Gospel according to Luke. Jesus is leaving Galilee, Herod's territory. The Pharisees are not being kind in imparting this information. Rather, they point to the reality that going to Jerusalem means that Jesus will be confronted about his prophetic claims and face death. Effectively, to turn from Jerusalem would be to admit to being a false prophet. Jesus's final statement is drawn from Psalm 117, an image that will be fulfilled shortly in his triumphant entrance into the city.

F R I 30 (#483) green
Weekday

The Lectionary for Mass

◆ FIRST READING: In this passage we are reminded that Paul was a devout Jew. He has not lost his love for the people of Israel. In a litany of affirmation, he reminds the community of Rome of the gifts that his community has received. These blessings remain—then and now.

◆ RESPONSORIAL PSALM 147: There are three parts to this psalm, and here we hear the closing third. It is from the holy city that offers praise to God who acts on behalf of the people. This is the place in which the divine is revealed and from which God sends his people forth.

◆ GOSPEL: Again we hear a story unique to the Gospel according to Luke, another story of healing on the Sabbath. This one, however, ends with quiet, rather than contention. Who was this person with dropsy? A guest? Someone in the household? The story of the pit ties to a familiar debate among the rabbis regarding helping an ox on the Sabbath. The ox can be helped provided it is immediately slaughtered, they concluded. What is urgent where help and healing are concerned, and what is not?

S A T 31 (#484) green
Weekday

Optional Memorial of the Blessed Virgin Mary / white

The Lectionary for Mass

◆ FIRST READING: Paul continues to deal with the complexity of the blended community of Jews and Gentiles. They have not been rejected by God; they remain beloved.

At the same time, Paul affirms that salvation has come through Jesus. This is the contemporary teaching of the Church regarding the Jews, as well.

◆ RESPONSORIAL PSALM 94 is the ideal complement to the reading from the letter to the Romans. God does not abandon his people. Once God has entered into a covenant, it will not be severed. This is true despite human frailty and failure.

◆ GOSPEL: Jesus's words echo Proverbs 25:6–7, where the listener is reminded to act with humility in the presence of the king: "Claim no honor in the king's presence, / nor occupy the place of superiors; / For it is better to be told, 'Come up closer!' / than to be humbled before the prince." This obvious advice takes on an even greater meaning when considered in light of the kingdom of God, where self-aggrandizement has no place.

November
Month of All Souls

☀ 1 (#667) white
Solemnity of All Saints

About this Solemnity

Today we celebrate the Solemnity of All Saints, remembering all the saints known and unknown to us who enjoy the glory of heaven. In today's Gospel account we hear the Beatitudes, which are guidelines for true joy and the attainment of sanctity in our Christian lives. We hear how to live lives of holiness so that we may attain happiness in this life, but even more happiness in the next life as we strive to likewise be numbered among all the saints in heaven.

The Lectionary for Mass

◆ FIRST READING: John recounts a vision of those who will be delivered in the end times. The group is described as a great multitude representing every people and nation on the earth. In response to the question of who these people are, the answer is the cryptic "they have washed their robes and made them white in the Blood of the Lamb." Because their clothing is symbolic of who one is, the author wants us to know that while sharing in the sufferings of Christ, these are the ones who remained faithful, even to the shedding of their own blood. They now rejoice in the presence of God.

◆ RESPONSORIAL PSALM 24: This psalm is considered a processional psalm. It begins by declaring that all creation belongs to the creator. In order to truly enter into the presence of God, one must have pure hands and heart. In other words, one's actions and attitudes must be rooted in love of God and neighbor, not in the vanities of the world. Like the multitudes described in Revelation, these people who long to see the face of God will have a blessed ending to their search.

◆ SECOND READING: Our passage opens with an exclamation: "See what love . . . " The greatness of God's love is not just an esoteric idea. It becomes palpable in its effects. It actually makes us children of God. Those who believe in Jesus's name are children begotten by God (John 1:12–13), reborn from above (John 3:3). This is more than simply being God's creatures, or even a Chosen People. According to John, this is the most profound relation to God possible in this life. And yet, there is more.

John goes on to say that what we will be has not been revealed. Now, as believers, we submit our lives to him, imitating the earthly Jesus to the best of our ability. But, the day is coming when we will not simply remember Jesus, nor merely experience what it means to be children of God. In the future, when we see Christ as he is in the glory of the Father, that vision will transform us. Now we strive to imitate him, then we will "be like him." Now, as Paul says, we see dimly, as in a mirror. Then, when we see the glorified Christ face to face, we will be transformed in ways we cannot imagine (see 1 Corinthians 13:12 and 2 Corinthians 3:18).

◆ GOSPEL: The people who are the objects of divine favor, the blessed, are those who recognize that they have nothing to bring to God but are dependent on grace for everything. Injustice causes them to mourn, while their desire for right is as strong as hunger and thirst. Hearts fully devoted to God lead them to act with mercy and to sow peace. Their way of living, like that of Jesus himself, will be an affront to powers of domination and thus, like the Master, they, too, will suffer. But even as they have grown in his image, they cannot imagine what awaits them in the end.

The Roman Missal

The Gloria is sung or said today.

The Collect reminds us of the great cloud of witnesses by which we are surrounded as it tells of how in this one celebration we venerate the merits of all the saints. Thus, we can take comfort in asking for the reconciliation with God "for which we earnestly long" because we can count on the intercession of so many saints.

Remember that the Creed is said or sung at this Mass.

The Prayer over the Offerings reiterates that we live our lives, and offer this Eucharist, in the Communion of Saints, and therefore they celebrate with us. We can experience their solidarity with and concern for us because they are assured of immortality in the Lord.

The Preface, titled "The glory of Jerusalem, our mother," is given, with and without musical notation, right there among the pages for all the other texts for this Mass. The Preface points to Jerusalem as our mother and the heavenly city where our brothers and sisters who have gone before us give God eternal praise. The key point to be emphasized is that we as pilgrims seek to advance to the heavenly Jerusalem as well, and our hope of arriving there is not unfounded since we have the strength and good example of the saints to assist us. This reminds us that the liturgical celebration of All Saints is not only about those faithful upon whom the Church has designated the title of sanctity, but it is also about our call to that same sanctity.

Eucharistic Prayer I, the Roman Canon, with its two listing of saints' names, might be considered an appropriate choice for use at this solemnity.

The Prayer after Communion reminds us that the holiness of the saints is only possible because it is rooted in God's holiness, God who alone is holy. In addition, although not explicitly so, the image of the heavenly Jerusalem — the eschatological aspect inherent in every Eucharist — is again invoked as the prayer asks that "we may pass from this pilgrim table to the banquet of our heavenly homeland."

The Solemn Blessing formula for All Saints, found in the section of the Missal "Blessings at the End of Mass and Prayers over the People," is suggested for today, and would

be well used. Also, in light of the call to sanctity that is given to us all as we strive to imitate and be in communion with the saints, perhaps the dismissal formula "Go in peace, glorifying the Lord by your life" would be the most appropriate form of dismissal for today.

Other Ideas

It would be fun to have a family "All Hallows' Eve" potluck after your Saturday evening liturgy. Clocks change today, so make sure the staff and congregation all remember to make the necessary adjustments.

Include a Litany of the Saints in the liturgy this week and, if you have access to relics, icons, or other images of the saints, incoporate them into the liturgy. Or invite people to bring forth their own images to display in a "Saint Corner" of the narthex or gathering space. Perhaps this could be combined with the *Book of the Names of the Dead*, which should be made available throughout the month of November. Consider printing up holy cards with the parish patron saint.

Make sure the congregation is aware of times for All Souls' Day Masses and any particular event like a candle-lit service for the deceased of the parish, or anything in conjunction with *Día de Muertos, Araw ng mga Patay*, or other ethnic celebrations which may fit your parish. Masses this week are from the Thirty-First Week in Ordinary Time, even though the Sunday was not used.

(#668 or #1011–1016)
white / violet / black

MON 2 The Commemoration of All the Faithful Departed (All Souls' Day)

About this Commemoration

All Souls' Day is unique on the liturgical calendar. Neither a solemnity nor a feast, this *commemoration* outranks other feasts and even takes the place of a Sunday in Ordinary Time (should this commemoration fall on a Sunday). Prayer for the dead reaches deep into our human history, and it has been our custom from the earliest days of the Church. The belief that our prayers can be of assistance to the dead is a treasured tenet of our Catholic faith. We profess it every time we recite the Nicene Creed: "I look forward to the resurrection of the dead / and the life of the world to come."

The Lectionary for Mass

Please note that the Lectionary provides many options for today's Mass. The commentary below pertains to Lectionary #668.

◆ FIRST READING: On this day we commemorate those who have died but who have not yet been fully purified from sin. The Wisdom reading speaks of the refinement of the just who will share in God's grace and mercy. The image of sparks through stubble reflects the agrarian practice of burning spent fields.

◆ RESPONSORIAL PSALM 23: The great psalm of God's fidelity and comfort is offered on this feast. The travails and challenges of life are not to be feared, because God is unfailing in his care. This beloved psalm is affirmation for all, and particularly for those who grieve.

◆ GOSPEL: This passage from the "bread of life" discourse affirms the generosity of the Father, and in turn the unlimited generosity of Christ Jesus. All who come to him will be welcome, and those who do will participate in the eternal life he offers. On this feast, it is useful to both pray for those who have gone before us but also to reflect on how deeply we have embraced this promise of Jesus ourselves.

The Roman Missal

Because this Commemoration replaces the Sunday in Ordinary Time, all the texts are taken from November 2 in the Proper of Saints. Any one of the three sets of formularies may be chosen, at the discretion of the priest celebrant or, as appropriate, the parish's liturgy preparation/worship team. All the texts proclaim the centrality of the Paschal Mystery in understanding the meaning of Christian death: because of Jesus's Death and Resurrection, death leads to new life for all those united to Christ. Therefore, because of our faith in the risen Christ, we can find hope in death. Some of the Mass prayers (the Prayer over the Offerings in formulary set 2; the Prayer after Communion in formulary set 3) explicitly mention Baptism; thus, calling to mind the baptismal symbols used in the funeral Mass (sprinkling with holy water, Paschal candle, white garment). Any one of the five Prefaces for the Dead may be used today, again at the discretion of the priest celebrant or according to the preparations made by a parish committee. Also, the Solemn Blessing formula "In Celebration for the Dead" (number 20 under "Blessings at the End of Mass and Prayers over the People") is suggested and should be used for all Masses today.

TUE 3 (#486)   green
Weekday (Thirty-First Week in Ordinary Time)

Optional Memorial of St. Martin de Porres, Religious / white

The Lectionary for Mass

◆ FIRST READING: Paul offers us here a description of the true nature of the Christian community and a roadmap for living its values. The metaphor of the body with its many parts is offered, and each is recognized for its intrinsic value. All are able to fulfill the imperatives of the mutual love required (see verses 9–16).

◆ RESPONSORIAL PSALM 131: The profound image of peace offered here is that of a child who, no longer clamoring for maternal feeding, is mature enough to be well fed, content, and still. So is the soul of the one who has learned how to rest in the Lord.

◆ GOSPEL: In this parable, the servant is dispatched three times. In the first instance, he is dismissed with three reasons, all grounded in the teachings of Deuteronomy. The infuriated king sends his servant out a second and third time, now to gather to the banquet all who are encountered, even those who are not the conventional or appropriate guests. This parable calls us to examine what we consider more important than our relationship with God and how we relate to the invitations that place us in his presence.

Today's Saint

St. Martin de Porres (1579–1639) had a special love for the marginalized in society; he knew what it was like to feel unaccepted. As the son of an unwed couple (a Spanish knight and a freed slave from Panama), he hardly fit the norm. His father essentially disowned him because he inherited his mother's features, primarily her skin color. Instead of wallowing in his own pain, he chose to become a Dominican brother, focusing on ministry to the "forgotten" in society. St. Martin, called the "father of charity," cared for sick people in the monastery, fed the needy with food from the monastery, and began a home for abandoned children. He had a close friendship with St. Rose of Lima and is considered the patron saint of racial justice. Include a petition in the Prayer of the Faithful for an end to racial tension and violence.

W E D 4 (#487) white
Memorial of St. Charles Borromeo, Bishop

The Lectionary for Mass

◆ FIRST READING: Paul pulls from the Ten Commandments those that have to do with direct human interaction. We are reminded that the greatest injunction of all is that we love each other as we love ourselves. This is the true fulfillment of God's law, particularly for the followers of Jesus, who must expand the traditional understanding of "neighbor" beyond the kinship circles of Judaism.

◆ RESPONSORIAL PSALM 112: The one who fears the Lord — who stands in awe and wonder at God's greatness — is the blessed one. To stand fully aware of God's amazing love and gifts is to be drawn into a life of generosity and graciousness. Justice is his way.

◆ GOSPEL: To follow Jesus is not going to be an easy path. He is quite upfront about this. To choose the Kingdom may be the most divisive act ever taken, severing the filial bonds which were precious and critical to survival in the time of Jesus. The cost of following Jesus should be considered and counted no less than one would consider the cost of any great undertaking, such as a building project or going to battle. God's call will press in and demand that all other claims of life be examined and perhaps rejected. Nothing less than the scandal of the Cross will be involved.

The Roman Missal

All the orations are proper for this obligatory memorial and are found in the Proper of Saints at November 4. The Collect asks that the Church in our time might be constantly renewed with the same spirit that filled bishop St. Charles Borromeo, thus, identifying the saint as someone noted for reforming the Church in his time. The prayer articulates

that the Church is ever in need of being more deeply conformed to the likeness of Christ. The Prayer over the Offerings prays for the specific fruits and good works we are requesting to result from this offering, namely, good fruit and works that embody the same virtues as St. Charles that made him such an attentive pastor. We pray for today's Eucharist to have concrete effect in our lives in the Prayer after Communion also, this time praying for the same determination, "which made St. Charles faithful in ministry / and fervent in charity." The Preface of Holy Pastors could be considered the preferred choice for a Preface today, although Preface I or II of Saints could be used as well.

Today's Saint

St. Charles Borromeo (1538–1584), a doctor of civil and canon law, was a great champion of the Church redefining itself in light of the Protestant Reformation. As Archbishop of Milan, he promulgated the reforms of the Council of Trent, giving special attention to liturgical and clerical renewal. Other significant contributions he made to the Church include the establishment of new seminaries for the education of the clergy, defining a code of moral conduct for clergy, and founding the Oblates of St. Ambrose, a society of diocesan priests, to enforce the reforms of Trent. St. Charles adopted a simple life in which he responded to the needs of the poor and sick by providing monetary and spiritual support.

T H U 5 (#488) green
Weekday

The Lectionary for Mass

◆ FIRST READING: After reminding us what it means to be the Lord's community and to care for one another, we are asked to remember who it is that we live and die for: the Lord. We need not judge

one another; that is for God alone. Ultimately, the one to whom we must answer is God.

◆ RESPONSORIAL PSALM 27: That God's goodness will be seen both in this life and in the life to come echoes the reading from Romans. Life is not to be feared, because as people of promise, we trust not only God's presence to be with us in our trials but ultimately to be one with God.

◆ GOSPEL: These two parables of what is lost and what is found illuminate Jesus's interest in those who are often missed, disregarded, or in the margins. Those who seek him out are those who are despised by the authorities, and he is criticized for engaging with tax collectors and sinners. The parable of the Good Shepherd is shared with Matthew, but the parable of the lost coin (and the Prodigal Son, which follows) are unique to Luke. Both drive home the unreasonable, unrelenting longing of God to save his people.

F R I 6 (#489) green
Weekday

The Lectionary for Mass

◆ FIRST READING: Paul brings his letter to a close with this passage. He has spoken boldly to this growing community, challenging and exhorting them to the practices of their faith. Now he explains his motivations and intent. He has done this simply to be an agent of Christ and to proclaim his Gospel.

◆ RESPONSORIAL PSALM 98: This psalm almost describes the actions that Paul has taken in singing the new song he has heard through Jesus Christ, as described at the close of his letter. God's saving power is revealed now to all the nations, inspiring joy and praise.

◆ GOSPEL: This parable has been among the most debated. Note that his crime is wastefulness, not dishonesty. Why is the steward at first castigated and then applauded? While it appears that he is cleverly "cooking the books" by changing the notes, it is possible that he is gathering what is owed by foregoing his commission. He gives the master what is owed by giving up his self-interest. This parable calls into question our own relationship with possessions and sacrifice.

S A T 7 (#490) green
Weekday

Optional Memorial of the Blessed Virgin Mary / white

The Lectionary for Mass

◆ FIRST READING: Here Paul adds a second close, which mentions all those he considers partners in the ministry in Rome. Some verses mention those in Ephesus (see verses 21–23) and may be a later addition. Here we see that the community was male and female, free person and slave, all of whom are instructed to greet each other as equals with a "holy kiss."

◆ RESPONSORIAL PSALM 145: The phrase that is noteworthy here is "generation after generation." Just as the many workers for the ministry are witnessing to their faith, those that have gone before them have proclaimed the Lord's goodness and works. This praise will go on forever.

◆ GOSPEL: This passage completes the teaching of Jesus in which money is used as a metaphor. What is the right relationship to money? Certainly, it is to be honest. Still, if it is hard to be honest around earthly wealth, how much harder is it to be honest in relationship to what is genuine, good, and God-given? How we use our possessions becomes a measure by which we can think about how we use the gifts God has given us as individual persons.

(#155) green
8 Thirty-Second Sunday in Ordinary Time

◆ FIRST READING: God speaks through the prophet and brings his words to fulfillment, bestowing blessing. The prophet is the spokesman, but it is God who acts. We see the dawning of a universalism in which God extends a hand of compassion and mercy to draw in all people, demonstrating the love of the one who is Creator of all.

◆ RESPONSORIAL PSALM 146 acknowledges and repeats the teaching of the preceding passage: our Creator and God cares for all, the work of divine hands. This psalm expresses so well God's care for the oppressed, the hungry, prisoners, the blind, the stranger, and the widow and orphan. This is understood as divine justice, affirming the right relationship that underlies authentic righteous behavior.

◆ SECOND READING: This passage in Hebrews tells us that Jesus, our perfect and blameless High Priest, has now taken his own blood and entered the heavenly sanctuary to bring about our forgiveness and reconciliation. He has become the mercy seat of the new law, from which has come our eternal redemption. Another important allusion to the Old Testament is found in the final verse of this passage where it reads, "offered once to take away the sins of many." In the fourth song of the servant in Second Isaiah (read on Good Friday), we find reference to the redemptive death of the servant, which brings about the forgiveness of sins (cf. Isaiah 53:11–12). The author of Hebrews saw Jesus as the fulfillment of both these Old Testament images (the High Priest and the Servant). The author of Hebrews makes the point that this one perfect sacrifice of Jesus need never be repeated, for it has surpassed and completed what the Old Law never envisioned could be accomplished. When Christ appears again, this time it will be to bestow salvation at the end of time.

◆ GOSPEL: Throughout the Scriptures, the biblical authors portray God as caring for the poor. The widow, the orphan, the foreigner, and all who are in need are the concern of God and his people. The Gospel shows Jesus in this same light, having a heart open to the needs of the poor, bringing them healing of body and consolation of spirit. The religious leaders fail to show or appreciate the kind of compassion expected of God's ambassadors to the poor. Rather, their religious practice is for show and self-aggrandizement. They understand neither their calling nor their deepest responsibility.

The Roman Missal

We ask God to "keep from us all adversity," not so that we may carry out our own plans, but so that "we may pursue in freedom of heart / the things that are" God's (Collect). In the Mass, we celebrate "in mystery" the Passion of Christ. We pray that we may always honor this great mystery with "loving devotion" (Prayer over the Offerings). We ask "the grace of integrity" for all those who have received God's "heavenly power" through sharing in the "sacred gift" of the Eucharist (Prayer after Communion).

Other Ideas

"Poor widows" are mentiond in the Scriptures today. Many of these widows and widowers are people of deep prayer. They are the folks who come early on Saturday night Mass to socialize and pray, or are regular attendees at daily Mass. Think about ways you can engage the power of their prayer and lived experience. They are strong and have survived much. Use that wisdom and prayerful spirit for the parish. Get them on a prayer chain, or offer special things just for them. Perhaps a small faith group on a weekday morning would do well.

(#671) white

MON 9 Feast of the Dedication of the Lateran Basilica

About this Feast

St. John Lateran is one of the four major basilicas in Rome, with St. Peter, St. Mary Major, and St. Paul Outside the Walls. It is unique among the four since it (not St. Peter's) is the cathedral church of the Bishop of Rome, the pope. "Lateran" was the name of a Roman family whose lands were seized for the Church by the Emperor Constantine, and which then became the site of a great basilica dedicated in honor of John the Baptist. For centuries, the old Lateran palace was the residence of the popes. It was only when the popes returned from the Avignon exile in the fourteenth century that they took up residence at the Vatican. The basilica now has a triple dedication in honor of St. John the Baptist, St. John the Evangelist, and our Lord. Across the front of the basilica is a Latin inscription that says, "This is the mother and head of all churches in the whole world." It is a reminder of why the dedication of this one church is celebrated by the universal Church: we are one family, one flock, and we are led by one shepherd, the successor of St. Peter.

The Lectionary for Mass

◆ FIRST READING: The Lateran Basilica, consecrated in Rome in the time of Constantine, is celebrated today with readings that speak to the place of the temple. Ezekiel's vision of the restoration of the temple places it at the center of abundance. It's water flowing to feed all creation around it.

◆ RESPONSORIAL PSALM 46: This song extoling Zion praises God who is always ready to help in distress. The image of the stream running through God's holy city is reminiscent of the images from the vision of Ezekiel. The waters of God are the source of life, not the unruly destructive force that they can be in nature.

◆ GOSPEL: The passage of the cleansing of the Temple is very significant in the ministry of Jesus, for it very well may have been his threat of its destruction that instigated action against him. The sale of animals for ritual sacrifice, particularly to pilgrims, was a critical service. It was probably the abuse of this power—the dishonest use of money and the exorbitant charges to those unable to shoulder them—that infuriated Jesus. His symbolic speech about rebuilding the Temple in three days foreshadows the Resurrection.

The Roman Missal

The Gloria is sung or said today, since it is a feast.

There is a choice between two options for the Collect today. The first option uses the imagery of living stones to refer to the dwelling place of God, and thus asks for an increase of the spirit of grace in the Church. When the prayer goes on to ask that God's faithful people build up the heavenly Jerusalem by "new growth," it is presumably by a growth in holiness and grace, although certainly growth by the incorporation of new living stones

(new members) could also be understood as well. The second option for the Collect uses the imagery of the Church as the Bride of Christ and has a little more of an eschatological focus as it specifically asks that the people of God may be led to attain God's promises in heaven.

Since this feast falls on a Monday, the Creed is not said or sung.

The Prayer over the Offerings, in asking God to accept the offering being made, also asks that those who make that offering may receive "in this place / the power of the Sacraments / and the answer to their prayers." We can note an emphasis intended by inclusion of the phrase "in this place," thus, highlighting the Church both as the living stones and as a people who gather in a sacred space to enact the divine liturgy.

The text for today's proper Preface is given right along with the other texts for this Mass, and it is given both with and without musical notation. The Preface, titled "The mystery of the Church, the Bride of Christ and the Temple of the Spirit," reiterates the imagery of the people as the temple of the Spirit who make the Church resplendent through their living lives acceptable to God. The visible buildings that make up the Church are foreshadows of her heavenly glory.

The Prayer after Communion continues this eschatological theme of foreshadowing by addressing God as the one "who chose to foreshadow for us / the heavenly Jerusalem / through the sign of your Church on earth." Thus, the prayer goes on to ask that by our partaking of the Eucharist, "we may be made the temple of your grace / and may enter the dwelling place of your glory." Indeed, we can be reminded that it is only by celebrating the Eucharist that the Church can be the Church; without Eucharist, the Church does not exist.

A Solemn Blessing formula, "For the Dedication of a Church," is suggested as the final blessing, and it would be good to use it today. Given the emphasis in the prayers on the people of God as the living stones of the Church, perhaps the dismissal formula, "Go in peace, glorifying the Lord by your life" should be used today.

(#492) white

T U E 10 Memorial of St. Leo the Great, Pope and Doctor of the Church

The Lectionary for Mass

◆ FIRST READING: We hear a fuller offering of the reading proclaimed earlier this month on All Souls' Day. Used often at funerals, this passage powerfully reminds us that the suffering in death is the suffering experienced by the grieving living. Those who have gone before us in faith are in "the hand of God."

◆ RESPONSORIAL PSALM 34, like the reading from the Book of Wisdom, reminds us that God sees and protects the just. He listens to the cries of those who call out to him, including those who are distressed and brokenhearted. To bless God at all times — even times such as these — is the challenge.

◆ GOSPEL: The teaching of Jesus draws upon what masters might expect from their slaves. His rhetorical questions would be answered "no." In the same way, those who would serve this Master — Jesus — should not somehow expect that they will be thanked for doing that which is expected of them. This is a sort of radical humility. We are invited to ask what the difference is between being a profitable versus an unprofitable servant ourselves.

The Roman Missal

All the orations are proper for today, as found in the Proper of Saints at November 10. The Collect communicates to us the place of greatness among the successors to the Apostles that Pope St. Leo holds in the life of the Church as the prayer asks the intercession of St. Leo to stand firm in the truth and to "know the protection of lasting peace." Such firmness and protection is assured because God is addressed as the one who never allows the gates of hell to prevail against the Church, founded firmly as it is on apostolic rock. The Prayer over the Offerings prays particularly for those who shepherd the Church, asking that they may be pleasing to God, and also prays that the flock everywhere may prosper. The Prayer after Communion also speaks of governance, noting that it is God who governs the Church he nourishes with the Eucharist; the prayer also asks that under God's direction, "she may enjoy ever greater freedom / and persevere in integrity of religion." Although the Prayer over the Offerings and the Prayer after Communion do not specifically mention Pope St. Leo by name, they certainly reflect the virtues that he lived as pope, and the concerns he faced and addressed in his ministry. Certainly the Preface of Holy Pastors would be perhaps the most appropriate choice for today, although Preface I or II of Saints could also be used.

Today's Saint

As pope and Doctor of the Church, St. Leo the Great († 461) strongly supported the teachings of the Council of Chalcedon, especially on the humanity and divinity of Christ. He advocated papal authority by moving from the traditional approach that the pope is a successor to St. Peter's chair to the pope as St. Peter's heir. Under his leadership, uniformity of pastoral practice was encouraged, liturgical and clerical abuses were corrected, and priests were sent on a mission to extinguish Priscillianism, a heresy that claimed the human body was evil. St. Leo is recognized as a "protector of the people" because he persuaded Attila the Hun to not invade the city of Rome and later prevented the Vandals (East German invaders) from torching the city of Rome and massacring its people.

(#493) white

W E D 11 Memorial of St. Martin of Tours, Bishop

The Lectionary for Mass

◆ FIRST READING: The author of the Book of Wisdom speaks in the voice of the great and wise king, Solomon. Here, rulers are warned that authority is a gift. God expects those who are given power to be just; abuse of power shall be judged harshly. Those with the most receive the greatest scrutiny.

◆ RESPONSORIAL PSALM 82: The image of God as judge is evoked here. Those who have abused the lowly, the fatherless and the poor will be called to account. No one is beyond reckoning with God.

◆ GOSPEL: Why is it that Jesus appears to be irritated when the lepers, in fact, do exactly as he has told them in going to the priests? We can be sympathetic to their urgency; in doing so, they would have restored themselves to the community and the worship of the Temple. However, it is the outsider, the Samaritan, who returns in gratitude to thank the one who was the source of his healing. In his recognition and gratitude comes not only his physical cure, but his salvation. How do gratitude and self-interest interfere with each other?

The Roman Missal

All the orations, found at November 11, are once again proper for the day. The Collect asks that the wonders of God's grace will be renewed in our hearts. The Prayer over the Offerings prays that the spiritual offering of our lives, expressed through the spiritual offering we make through the Eucharistic offerings, will always be the guiding force in our lives, "whether in tribulation or in prosperity." (Commitment to the Eucharistic life is similar to commitment to the nuptial life—in good times and in bad.) The Prayer after Communion expresses how the Eucharist, the "Sacrament of unity," restores us, and, so restored, we ask for perfect harmony with God's will, just as St. Martin submitted himself entirely to God. Use either the Preface of Holy Pastors or Preface I or II of Saints as the Preface today.

Today's Saint

St. Martin of Tours (316–397) was forced by his father, a pagan officer in the Roman army, to join the military. While serving in the military, he had a life-changing event in which he cut his cloak in half to clothe a freezing beggar. Following this encounter he had a vision of Christ wrapped in the cloak. As a result of this experience, St. Martin chose to be baptized and declared himself a soldier of peace for Christ, refusing to participate in any act of violence. He took up the life of a hermit, thereby introducing monasticism into Gaul. Following his election as bishop of Tours he continued living as a monk, but made numerous trips to visit his people and establish new monasteries. The people of Gaul converted to Christianity due to his example.

(#494) red

T H U 12 Memorial of St. Josaphat, Bishop and Martyr

The Lectionary for Mass

◆ FIRST READING: The Book of Wisdom personifies the wisdom of God in the figure of the "Wisdom Woman." Her twenty-one characteristics are all reflections of God's might and glory; to live a life

dwelling in these qualities invites God's love. The "Wisdom Woman," a poetic female figure, also appears in Proverbs 31:1–31, the Song of Songs, and Sirach 24. Her primary mode of being is relational.

◆ RESPONSORIAL PSALM 119: Once again we receive sections of the rather long Psalm 119. These verses underscore the value of God's teaching. As with the one who lives in Wisdom, the one who understands and lives according to God's word is worthy of God's love.

◆ GOSPEL: The Pharisees continue to test and challenge Jesus. When will the Kingdom come? Jesus says that it is already happening; it is opening up before them in his life and ministry. Turning to the disciples, he warns them the fullness of the kingdom will not be hidden. It will be visible and break through to all creation.

The Roman Missal

All the orations are proper today, and are taken from November 12. The Collect focuses on the martyrdom of the saint as it asks that "the Spirit that filled St. Josaphat / as he laid down his life for the sheep" be given to the Church and particularly to all of us, so that we will not be afraid to lay down our lives for others. The Prayer over the Offerings continues the recognition of Josaphat as martyr as it asks that the offerings made at this Mass will "confirm us in the faith / that St. Josaphat professed by the shedding of his blood." The Prayer after Communion asks for the gift of "a spirit of fortitude and peace" as a result of our participation in the Eucharist this day. Strengthened by the Eucharist that way, we pray that we will be able to follow the saint's example, particularly in the way he worked for the unity of the Church. Given the emphasis in the orations today, one of the two Prefaces of Holy Martyrs would seem to be the

most logical choice for a Preface; the Preface of Holy Pastors or one of the two Prefaces of Saints could also be considered.

Today's Saint

As a young man, St. Josaphat (1580–1623) was excited about the possibility of the Orthodox metropolitan city of Kiev, comprising Belarussians and Ukrainians, reuniting with the Church of Rome. When he was elected Archbishop of Polotsk, Lithuania, he worked tirelessly to continue the efforts to bring the Orthodox communities of Kiev into full communion with the Catholic Church. Many people were strongly opposed to this reunion; therefore, they established a rival hierarchy and set up groups to defame his name. While preaching in a particularly hostile city, he was murdered. His commitment to ecumenical relations was eventually realized in the Byzantine Rite of Catholicism. St. Josaphat the martyr is the first Eastern saint to be formally canonized.

(#495) white

F R I 13 Memorial of St. Frances Xavier Cabrini, Virgin

The Lectionary for Mass

◆ FIRST READING: The thirteenth chapter of the Book of Wisdom offers cautions against the worship of nature and the worship of idols. Here, the glory of nature is held up as something through which God's glory is revealed. By analogy, looking at the spectacular works of God's hand, we get a glimpse of God.

◆ RESPONSORIAL PSALM 19: The psalm choice underscores the thoughts from the Book of Wisdom. While we see God in creation, we don't declare that creation is God. Instead, all creation is made to reflect and glorify God.

◆ GOSPEL: Jesus draws on two of the great stories of the Torah to disclose what it will be like when the Kingdom comes upon them. Just as people were living their daily lives and caught up in everyday concerns in the times of Noah and Lot, so too will life be occurring normally as the fullness of God's Kingdom comes. Lot's wife made the mistake of looking back longingly at the place and possessions she left behind, and she was turned into a pillar of salt. So too the disciples cannot be caught up in nostalgia and material longing. These themes are worthy of our reflection, as well.

The Roman Missal

The Collect is the only proper for today, and it is found at November 13. The prayer describes how the saint was called from Italy to serve the immigrants of America, and then goes on to ask that we might be taught to have the same concern for the stranger and all those in need. The Prayer over the Offerings and the Prayer after Communion are taken from either the Common of Virgins: For One Virgin, or from the Common of Holy Men and Women: For Those Who Practiced Works of Mercy. An appropriate Preface for this celebration would be either the Preface of Holy Virgins and Religious or Preface I or II of Saints.

Today's Saint

Frances Xavier Cabrini was the first American citizen to be canonized. Born in Italy, she studied to be a teacher and wanted to join a religious community but was rejected because of ill health. When the orphanage she managed closed in 1880, Frances and six others took religious vows and founded the institute of the Missionary Sisters of the Sacred Heart of Jesus. Her work brought her to the attention of Leo XIII, who sent her to New York in 1889 to minister to Italian immigrants. St. Frances founded

institutions all over the United States of America, as well as in South America and Europe. She died in Chicago in 1917. Visit her shrine in Chicago: http://www.cabrinishrinechicago.com/.

SAT 14 (#496) green
Weekday

Optional Memorial of the Blessed Virgin Mary / white

The Lectionary for Mass

◆ FIRST READING: In the final chapters of the Book of Wisdom, Israel and Egypt are presented as representations of wisdom and folly. The exodus and wilderness experience (as well as a few events not mentioned in the biblical record) are described with wisdom as a central character. Jewish sources speculate that this is a fragment of an Alexandrian Haggadah.

◆ RESPONSORIAL PSALM 105: The verses of this psalm speak to how God remembered and saved Israel during their captivity in Egypt. This story, which is the heart of the Passover, is the great affirmation of God's faithfulness to Israel.

◆ GOSPEL: The parable of the persistent widow is found only in the Gospel according to Luke. The disciples will need to persevere as they await the coming of the Kingdom, calling out in prayer with comparable persistence. The judge is unjust because he is not responding to a woman who, in fact, should receive priority in treatment (see Deuteronomy 24:17–22). His inaction may have to do with fear of her opponent or another factor. Finally he acts. If such a character can do the right thing, would not God do even more?

15 (#158) green
Thirty-Third Sunday in Ordinary Time

The Lectionary for Mass

◆ FIRST READING: Daniel, who earlier interpreted dreams and advised the Babylonian king, is here warning the people to live uprightly, for there will come a day of severe reckoning. Wisdom and prudence tell us to live in a manner that acknowledges a day of judgment, when our lives shall be evaluated and a sentence passed. A key point of this passage is its reference to the notion of resurrection. While earlier Jewish thought told only of Sheol, the abode of the dead, here we find one of the earliest references to the resurrection of the just, to be later developed in the New Testament.

◆ RESPONSORIAL PSALM 16: There are several lines of connection between the previous reading and this psalm. In verse 8, "I set the LORD ever before me" is a poetic way of expressing the will and desire to follow God's law; on the day of judgment, God, who knows the human heart, will reward the upright. In verses 9–11, the psalmist refers to both *Sheol* (death) and the "path to life." Though this psalm is not expressing a belief in resurrection, to experience the "abounding joy in [God's] presence" is a way of living uprightly, and righteously coming before God in the Temple.

◆ SECOND READING: This week, the author of Hebrews brings another dimension to the fruitless efforts of sacrifice according to the Old Law. The priests offer sacrifice daily, but it failed to bring about its hoped-for results. Again, it is Christ whose sacrifice has accomplished the reconciliation that had never been done before; he thus eliminates the levitical priesthood. Christ's once-for-all and single sacrifice, perfected by his total offering, has opened the way for our eternal salvation.

◆ GOSPEL: Watching for the signs has given rise to predictions of the final and awesome day; yet Jesus clearly says of that day, "no one knows," but the Father. With all the upheaval that will take place, the one thing that will remain is God's Word: "my words will not pass away." Mark is encouraging the early Christians to hold fast to their faith, for in the end it brings them a share in the heavenly and eternal kingdom. Most importantly, they must remain firm and faithful.

The Roman Missal

The Mass texts for today are found in the "Ordinary Time" section of the Proper of Time. The Gloria is sung or said today.

The Collect identifies for us where the source of "constant gladness" and "full and lasting happiness" is to be found: it is to be found in serving "with constancy / the author of all that is good." This Collect asks that we make sure we are using all our gifts and resources to serve God well; it is only by doing so that we can hope to share in the fullness of the joy of the kingdom. We must also stay alert and sober so we can serve with constancy. The Prayer over the Offerings has an eschatological focus, appropriate for this penultimate Sunday of the liturgical year, as it asks that what we offer at this Eucharist may "gain us the prize of everlasting happiness." The Prayer after Communion, however,

is focused more on the present as it implores that, having partaken of "the gifts of this sacred mystery," we may be given "a growth in charity."

Any one of the eight Prefaces of the Sundays in Ordinary Time are appropriate options for today, but perhaps Preface V might be considered the best choice with its emphasis on God setting humanity "over the whole world in all its wonder"; the text could serve to reinforce the theme of taking responsibility for using the gifts God has given us and building the Kingdom of God.

Other Ideas

The end is near, the end is near! The Scripture readings have a dark, apocryphal tone as we continue to hear of "the Son of Man" and end times. "The End of the World" is something we hear about in songs from Skeeter Davis to R.E.M. (or the failed Mayan calendar of a few years back!). A YouTube search can show a scary selection of dooms-day preachers predicting the end of times. Perhaps this would be something good to talk about with the congregation. Explain the term "Son of Man" and its Old Testament origins; explain and reiterate the teachings of the second coming from the Catholic perspective. Refer to articles 668–679 in the *Catechism of the Catholic Church* for guidance.

Begin to announce times for Thanksgiving Masses, collections for the poor or food pantries, and any other Thanksgiving or holiday events in the parish.

MON 16 (#497) green
Weekday

Optional Memorials of St. Margaret of Scotland / white; St. Gertrude, Virgin / white

The Lectionary for Mass

◆ FIRST READING: The first Book of Macabees recounts the evil that overtakes Israel as the Seleucid king

Antiochus attempts to unify the kingdom by universally imposing the practices of Greek culture. In submitting, many Jews are defying the law, and those who remain observant are being killed.

◆ RESPONSORIAL PSALM 119: The verses that evoke the persecution experienced by Israel from the oppressors in Psalm 119 are now offered. The author cries out to God to sustain him and promises that he will keep the Lord's commands — even in the midst of apostates and sinners.

◆ GOSPEL: In the time of Jesus, a beggar might well have cried out for mercy as a way of asking for alms. This beggar is asking for much more; recognizing Jesus's power, he asks that his sight be restored. Consistent with the other healing stories in Luke, the man's faith in God through Jesus is the source of his salvation. Those up front try to stop his entreaties. But the lowly are heard by Jesus and he responds to them.

Today's Saints

St. Margaret of Scotland (1045/46 –1093), the wife of King Malcolm III of Scotland, managed to raise eight children while promoting Church reform, especially in the area of liturgical practice. As a woman of great faith, she founded and restored monasteries, provided hospitality to pilgrims, spoke out on behalf of the falsely accused, and fed the poor from her own dining table. All of her charitable activity was grounded in a strong prayer life.

St. Gertrude the Great (1256 –1302) was a nun at the Benedictine monastery of Helfta, the abbey where two other great female spiritual writers lived: Mechtild of Magdeburg and St. Mechtild (Matilda von Hackeborn-Wippra). Through prayer she was graced with many mystical and ecstatic experiences, which are recorded in a five-volume work entitled *Legatus divinae pietatis*, commonly called *The Life and Revelations of Saint Gertrude the Great*. Her spirituality focused on the humanity of Christ and was characterized by a strong devotion to the Sacred Heart of Jesus. According to many scholars, Saint Gertrude's writings should be "shelved" with other influential mystics, such as Saint Teresa of Avila.

(#498) white
TUE 17 Memorial of St. Elizabeth of Hungary, Religious

The Lectionary for Mass

◆ FIRST READING: The poignant and powerful story of Eleazar, the elder who goes willingly to his death rather than abrogate God's law, reminds us of the power of a life of witness. He will die rather than compromise his exemplary life. His death is a lesson to the young and to us: Where are our lines of compromise regarding our faith?

◆ RESPONSORIAL PSALM 3 seems to offer us the inner life of Eleazar from the First Reading. The moral person, the person who fights for faith, may find him—or herself facing terrible adversaries. But the Lord's promise is that we will be sustained and upheld, as the psalmist affirms.

◆ GOSPEL: The description of Zacchaeus's stature contrast with the importance and wealth that accrue to the chief tax collector. A pariah among his own people and openly hated, he is nevertheless a figure of spontaneity and humility — after all, he is willing to scale a tree to get a glimpse of Jesus. Zacchaeus, while not a Jew in the manner of the Pharisees, is still a son of Abraham in Jesus's eyes, and Jesus takes the initiative in achieving his conversion. How do we judge who is "in" and who is "out" in our times?

The Roman Missal

The Collect, found at November 17 in the Proper of Saints, is the prayer that is proper for today. The Collect recognizes St. Elizabeth's ministry to the poor and therefore asks "that we may serve with unfailing charity / the needy and those afflicted." Ministry to the poor is not something that is optional in the Christian life; it is part-and-parcel of what it means to follow Christ. The Prayer over the Offerings and the Prayer after Communion come from the Common of Holy Men and Women: For Those Who Practiced Works of Mercy. For the Preface, use either Preface I of Saints or Preface II of Saints.

Today's Saint

St. Elizabeth of Hungary (1207–1231), the Queen of Hungary and mother of four children, had a special love for the downtrodden. She built a hospital in the basement of her castle, nursed the sick, fed the hungry, and provided life-giving work for the poor. After the death of her husband, she took the habit of a Franciscan tertiary (Third Order Franciscan), devoting herself to a life of simplicity and almsgiving. Along with her selfless service to those in need, she actively pursued God through prayer and spiritual discipline. St. Elizabeth is the patron saint of Franciscan tertiaries, bakers, beggars, brides, the homeless, and charities (among others).

(#499) green
WED 18 Weekday

Optional Memorials of the Dedication of the Basilicas of Sts. Peter and Paul, Apostles / white; St. Rose Philippine Duchesne, Virgin / white

The Lectionary for Mass

◆ FIRST READING: The courageous mother of this story stands firm even as her sons are slaughtered. Gripped by courage, she speaks of the mystery of life forming in the womb, and affirms God's place in the creation. No bribe can persuade her or her son to turn their back on their God.

◆ RESPONSORIAL PSALM 17 is an outcry that God bring justice to the suffering. The witness of the woman and her sons are exemplars of lives that have been steadfast in the paths of God. While there is no joy in the moment of trial, when the fullness of God's glory arrives so too will joy.

◆ GOSPEL: The Kingship parable of Luke, as this is often called, is heard on the road to Jerusalem as Jesus is preaching the kingdom of God. We hear the stories of three of the ten servants commissioned to a task. Two were enterprising, producing results. One, in fear, hoarded the money he was given. He is reprimanded and the money is given to the most productive servant. Note that people grumble, akin to the parable in Matthew about the workers in the vineyard.

Optional Memorial of the Basilicas

There are four major basilicas in Rome, and each of them has an observance on the Church's universal calendar: St. Mary Major on August 5, St. John Lateran on November 9, and now the Basilicas of St. Peter and St. Paul. It is not so much the church buildings we are honoring, of course, as the saints to whom they are dedicated.

The proper readings for today's memorial focus our attention on the special grace God gave all believers through two imperfect, impetuous, but exceptional men: Peter and Paul.

Today's Saint

Beginning her life as a nun in the Order of the Visitation in France, St. Rose Philippine Duchesne (1769–1852) eventually joined the Society of the Sacred Heart, founded by St. Madeleine Sophie Barat. Due to her missionary zeal, she was sent, along with five other sisters, to St. Louis, Missouri, to care for the poor and educate Native Americans. Under her leadership, the sisters established numerous schools and orphanages. She is remembered for her remarkable work, including evangelization and catechesis with Native Americans, particularly the Potawatomi people. Recognizing her extraordinary ministry, amazing ability to navigate difficulties, and profound spirituality, a contemporary said, "She was the Saint Francis of Assisi of the Society."

T H U 19 (#500) green
Weekday

The Lectionary for Mass

◆ FIRST READING: The oppression of the Jews reaches a breaking point. Mattathias, the head of the family of the Maccabees, is being seduced into apostasy. He resists, and then, seeing a Jew who has compromised his faith, takes action, killing the man, the messenger of the king, and tearing down the altar. On the heels of this violence, he and his family are forced to flee to the mountains. Following the Lord will require complete sacrifice and defiance of the dominating culture.

◆ RESPONSORIAL PSALM 50 recounts how God gathers his people into a community and judges their faithfulness. Once in the covenant he has made, they are called to fulfill their vows and offer praise in the same manner of Mattathias. What does it mean in our age to be the upright follower of God?

◆ GOSPEL: The mourning of Jesus over the future destruction of Jerusalem is unique to the Gospel according to Luke. His lament is reminiscent of the words of Jeremiah who decried the blindness of Jerusalem surrounding him. The destruction that looms will come from blindness that keeps them

from recognizing the Messiah who is among them.

F R I 20 (#501) green
Weekday

The Lectionary for Mass

◆ FIRST READING: The temple is purified by Judas and his brothers, and the celebration that ensues goes on for eight days. Careful restoration by upright people is needed, and once it is achieved, there is joy and celebration. This dedication is still celebrated in the festival of Hannukah.

◆ CANTICLE: This selection from the Book of Chronicles is the prayer of King David from the Book of Samuel that is inserted at the end of the book. Here he praises God upon the completion of the Temple, and the refrain offers us an opportunity to proclaim this praise, as well.

◆ GOSPEL: Jesus has arrived in Jerusalem and he immediately takes on the ultimate tasks of his ministry. Driving out the dishonest moneylenders and sellers who are gouging the poor, he begins teaching in the Temple area. New opponents are present: the chief priests, scribes, and leaders, who see him as a threat. The people, in contrast, are captivated by his message. The contrast between the "leaders" and the "people" is an ongoing theme in Luke's account.

S A T 21 (#502) white
Memorial of the Presentation of the Blessed Virgin Mary

Today's Memorial

According to tradition, Mary spent her life at the Temple from the time she was a little girl. Her parents, Joachim and Anne, presented their young daughter to the Temple for service and study, in thanksgiving for the great gift God had given them through her. Today's memorial celebrates this occasion. It also

calls us to think about the ways we prepare and ready ourselves for Jesus Christ in our lives. Mary, conceived in grace, was prepared to carry the Son of God, but her time at the Temple helped form her mind and heart. Likewise, intentionally nurturing our relationship with God builds on the grace God offers each of us. What are some ways you can ready yourself to encounter Jesus Christ today?

The Lectionary for Mass

◆ FIRST READING: The practice of the Seleucids was to raid and plunder temples. Here, Antiochus is unsuccessful in his robbery. Hearing that his forces have been thwarted, he falls into grief and fear. The evil he has perpetrated against the Jews is returned to him in punishment and death.

◆ RESPONSORISAL PSALM 9 affirms that God will save Israel from her enemies. Like the oppressor Antiochus, enemies will be overthrown — caught in their own snares. Hope in God will never die.

◆ GOSPEL: This is the only place in the Gospel of Luke in which the Sadducees, a wealthy "philosophical school" of Jews, is mentioned. Unlike the Pharisees, they rejected oral tradition and adhered to the written word of the Torah. They did not believe in resurrection or in angels. They are intentionally preposterous in the scenario they present to Jesus. His creative answer, including the use of the passage from Exodus, puts them off and they leave him alone. He has met them on their own terms.

The Roman Missal

The proper Collect is found at November 21 in the Proper of Saints. The prayer asks for the intercession of the Blessed Virgin Mary as we venerate her on this day. The Prayer over the Offerings and the Prayer after Communion are to be taken from the Common of the Blessed

Virgin Mary, with the Preface being either Preface I or Preface II of the Blessed Virgin Mary; use "on the feast day" as the choice of phrasing in Preface I.

(#161)   white

22 Solemnity of Our Lord Jesus Christ, King of the Universe

About this Solemnity

Today is the Thirty-Fourth or Last Sunday in Ordinary Time. Its official name is the Solemnity of Our Lord Jesus Christ, King of the Universe. This solemnity was established by Pope Pius XI in 1925, an observance celebrating an aspect of Jesus's identity rather than of his life. Conventional understandings of kingship and power are transformed. Rather than calling up images of Jesus Christ dressed in kingly robes, the Gospel proclaims him as king by the sign over his head on the throne of a wooden cross (I.N.R.I.— *Iesus nazarenus rex iudaeorum*—Jesus of Nazareth, King of the Jews). Paradoxically, it is the thief who recognized in Christ the Lord and Messiah.

The Lectionary for Mass

◆ FIRST READING: The Son of Man will come on the clouds of heaven. He will receive dominion over all. All nations shall serve him. His dominion shall never be taken away. All this is foreseen by the prophet Daniel.

◆ RESPONSORIAL PSALM 93: The Lord, the Creator, the one who entered into a covenant with Moses — that Lord is king. He wears majestic robes. He is armed. He established the firmament. His throne has been around from time immemorial, and it will continue to last for ages to come. Furthermore, the decrees of this Lord are trustworthy. They are a sign of the eternity of God's power. This psalm links the images of God the Father and God the Son. God the Father created the world and established the covenant; God the Son is Lord of all, the one whose Gospel is trustworthy, and whose kingdom shall last forever.

◆ SECOND READING: To Jesus Christ belongs all glory and power forever and ever. The Book of Revelation assigns the vision of clouds (see First Reading) to Jesus as well. In this one passage we meet prophecy and fulfillment as we are reminded of the words Jesus used to speak of himself.

◆ GOSPEL: This passage helps us understand what we mean by the title "King" as applied to Jesus. To a contemporary society in which kings are held in low esteem, the word carries a sense of entitlement and caste. But the kingship of Jesus is not of this world. We all yearn for a ruler who will take responsibility for society, whose own goodness will influence the goodness of others, who will contain evildoers and rescue the poor. Jesus Christ is the ideal ruler, and we have given to him the throne of our hearts.

The Roman Missal

The texts for this Mass are found at the very end of the "Ordinary Time" section of the Missal, immediately following the Mass for the Most Sacred Heart of Jesus, and immediately before the "Order of Mass" section of the Missal.

You might want to consider using the Rite for the Blessing and Sprinkling of Water today. The rite could serve as a reminder of the kingdom to which we belong, a kingdom into which we have been baptized; we are subjects of the crucified-risen one whose Death and Resurrection we participate in through our Baptism. The rite is found at Appendix II at the back of the Missal.

The Gloria is sung or said today.

The Collect names God as the one whose will it is to restore all things in Christ, the king of the universe; it is therefore the whole of creation that is set free from slavery. The universal sovereignty of Christ as King is thus proclaimed.

The Creed is, of course, said at this Mass, as it is every Sunday.

The Prayer over the Offerings defines the Eucharistic sacrifice we are offering as "the sacrifice / by which the human race is reconciled" to God; because of that, we can pray that the Son "may bestow on all nations / the gifts of unity and peace." To proclaim Christ as King means by definition to participate in the unity and peace his one kingdom will establish.

The Preface is proper for today.

The Prayer after Communion uses the phrase "food of immortality" to describe the Eucharistic food we have just received, a fitting phrase insofar as that heavenly food nourishes us in the ways of Christ's eternal kingdom. Thus do we ask in the prayer that "we may live with him eternally in his heavenly Kingdom," a fitting eschatological focus on this last Sunday of the liturgical year.

Other Ideas

This week can be especially taxing on church musicians and liturgical environment volunteers. Chances are, the rehearsal they had last week had included Christ the King, Thanksgiving, and the First Sunday of Advent. The environment will be changing a few times this week. Be sure and thank those ministers for their time and commitment.

MON 23 (#503) green
Weekday (Thirty-Fourth or Last Week in Ordinary Time)

Optional Memorials of St. Clement I, Pope and Martyr / red; St. Columban, Abbot / white; Bl. Miguel Agustín Pro, Priest and Martyr / red

The Lectionary for Mass

◆ FIRST READING: Yet again we hear of some of the "children of Israel" who prioritize God's law and see their reward. Daniel and his companions will not eat the impure food and wine they are offered. Instead, they live on vegetables. Not only are they more robust than the others, they are rewarded by God for their obedience.

◆ CANTICLE: The song of Shadrach, Meshach, and Abednego, who are miraculously untouched in the furnace of Nebuchadnezzar, is featured here. Despite their dire circumstances, they praise God fully in the midst of the fire. Their witness changes the heart of the king.

◆ GOSPEL: The story of the widow who gives so generously from her meager means draws our attention to what it means to be a Christian giver. It is one thing to give from excess; it has little meaning because it represents little sacrifice. On the other hand, to give from that which sustains us is an act of remarkable generosity — and Jesus applauds it. This text offers us a moment to pause and reflect on the place of giving — and sacrifice — in our own lives.

TUE 24 (#504) red
Memorial of St. Andrew Dũng-Lạc, Priest, and Companions, Martyrs

The Lectionary for Mass

◆ FIRST READING: Daniel becomes indispensable to Nebuchadnezzar because of his ability to interpret dreams. The Babylonian king is told of the destruction of successive empires. Interestingly, the concluding verses, in which Nebuchadnezzar extols Daniel's God, are omitted.

◆ CANTICLE: More verses from the song of praise in the fiery furnace are offered. God's wisdom is to be blessed, and all are called to join in the song — his works on earth and his works in heaven, the Angels.

◆ GOSPEL: Although the Temple is sacred and beautifully adorned, Jesus tells of a day in which it will be destroyed. Disasters will prevail — including war and natural calamities. Here, Jesus the prophet is predicting the dire destruction that is not far away. To find meaning when the very house of God would be no more is a grave task. He exhorts them not to fear; these things must occur before the end times are reached. This is his last appearance in the Temple precincts.

The Roman Missal

All the orations are proper for today, and are found in the Proper of Saints at November 24. The Collect recognizes the martyrs St. Andrew Dũng-Lạc and his companions as being faithful to the Cross of Christ, "even to the shedding of their blood," and so asks their intercession that we may be God's children "both in name and in truth." The Prayer over the Offerings asks that in accepting the offerings we bring, God will make us faithful "amid the trials of this life." The Prayer

after Communion focuses on unity: having been "renewed by the one Bread," we pray that "we may merit by endurance an eternal prize" by abiding as one in God's love. It is the strength that we draw from our unity in the Eucharist and in the Church that gives us the endurance to face the trials of life. It would seem that one of the two Prefaces of Holy Martyrs would be the most appropriate choice of Preface for today, although certainly Preface I or II of Saints could also be chosen.

Today's Saints

St. Andrew Dũng-Lạc (1785–1839), a Vietnamese priest, is one of one hundred seventeen martyrs canonized in 1988 who died trying to establish and spread the Catholic faith in Vietnam. This effort, which began in 1533 and continued well into the nineteenth century, was fraught with periods of persecution. Although St. Andrew was born into a Buddhist family, he was raised Catholic. His priestly ministry involved evangelization, parish catechesis, and service to the persecuted. Living under a particularly oppressive edict, St. Andrew was killed because he would not renounce his Christian apostolate and succumb to idolatrous ritual.

WED 25 (#505) green
Weekday

Optional Memorial of St. Catherine of Alexandria, Virgin and Martyr / red

The Lectionary for Mass

◆ FIRST READING: The arrogant King Belshazzar calls for the vessels stolen from the temple to be brought to a banquet and used by those attending. Suddenly, a hand appears, and Daniel reads the sign as a condemnation of Babylon and by association its gods. This story gives us the familiar phrase of "reading the writing on the wall."

◆ CANTICLE: The Canticle of Daniel continues here. All things are invited to bless the Lord; including fire and heat, the destructive forces surrounding the three in the furnace! Note the similarities of this passage to some of the verses of the Canticle of St. Francis, which this text may have influenced.

◆ GOSPEL: Again, Jesus as prophet predicts the future his followers will face. They will be seized and persecuted, but those acts will lead to witness. They are not to worry about what to say, because he will be with them. The lives that they are securing are not their earthly lives, but their eternal lives in his company and the Fathers. The testimony given by Jesus will be irresistible. To let the Spirit of God work through us in this manner is the challenge.

Today's Saint

St. Catherine of Alexandria (fourth century) lived in Alexandria, Egypt, during the reign of the Roman emperor Maxentius. Legend says that Catherine bravely confronted the emperor about his pagan beliefs.

Maxentius gathered fifty pagan philosophers and challenged her to a debate. Her arguments were so convincing that many of the philosophers converted to Christianity. He then threatened to kill her unless she married him and renounced her faith. She refused and was condemned to death on a spiked wheel, but the wheel fell apart when she touched it. She was then beheaded, and legend says that angels carried her to Mount Sinai. She has been venerated since the tenth century.

T H U 26 (#506) green
Weekday

Optional Mass for Thanksgiving (U.S.A.) / white

The Lectionary for Mass

◆ FIRST READING: Daniel is set up by his enemies. When he refuses to worship King Darius, Daniel is sentenced to death and cast into the lion's den. Like the three in the furnace, he is unscathed. Darius pulls him to freedom, and then casts his persecutors into the den where they are destroyed. Daniel's faith becomes the turning point for the king, who converts and decrees that the realm will reverence his God.

◆ CANTICLE: The Canticle continues, here offering us the beautiful images of nature in all its grandeur and glory blessing the Lord. The Litany draws from the seasons and the elements that it characterizes. Each stands as a short prayer that can be prayed when God's creation is encountered.

◆ GOSPEL: This apocalyptic vision of Jerusalem prophesies what the end of time will look like. This judgment will come to the entire world, not just the people of Israel, Rome, or Greece. Note that there is no prediction of the timing of these occurrences, simply a description. Again, people are encouraged not to fear. The signs for those who believe are providential because they harken redemption.

F R I 27 (#507) green
Weekday

The Lectionary for Mass

◆ FIRST READING: The apocalyptic vision of Daniel is one of dreadful beasts. These however, are defeated. The image of God here, the "Ancient One," is evocative of wisdom and awe, a God who holds court and who destroys the evil beast. One "like a son of man" comes to him, a human form which Christians believe is the foreshadowing of the birth of Jesus Christ, the King whose dominion is everlasting.

◆ CANTICLE: The descriptive praises of the Canticle of Daniel continue here. All things bless the Lord, including the beasts of the earth, the birds of the air, and the creatures of the sea, echoing the outputs of the days of creation. As we complete the Church year, the canticle refrain reminds us that this praise is eternal.

◆ GOSPEL: After speaking in frightening terms, Jesus now offers his disciples a softer image of the coming of the Kingdom. Nature, in its cycle, offers signals that the seasons are changing. His example is the bursting buds of the trees, including the fig, which foreshadow the coming of the summer's warmth. The phrase "this generation" points more to a posture of resistance by people rather than to a time frame. Jesus's words will endure until all has come into fulfillment.

S A T 28 (#508) green
Weekday

Optional Memorial of the Blessed Virgin Mary / white

Morning Mass: The Lectionary for Mass

◆ FIRST READING: The liturgical year concludes with Daniel's interpretation of his remarkable vision. Those who are being persecuted will be destroyed. The oppressions of Antiochus IV against the Temple cult are referenced in verse 25. But God's holy ones will prevail, despite the attacks and subjugation to which they have been submitted.

◆ CANTICLE: Just as all corners of the creation are called to bless the Lord and give him glory, humanity is also called to eternal praise. The canticle now speaks of the human participation in these acts of praise—sons of men, Israel, priests, servants, spirits and souls of the just, holy men of humble heart.

◆ GOSPEL: The apocalyptic predictions of Jesus end on a powerful note. Stay awake, and don't allow life to distract you. Be vigilant and pray. The lack of temporal horizons in this long chapter points to the fact that the followers of Jesus may be called to endure the passage of time before he comes again. These practices of prayer and vigilance are liberative, enabling his followers to stand firm and stay prepared to meet him.

The Roman Missal

If you are celebrating the Mass for the weekday in Ordinary Time, remember that you do not go back to use the texts from the previous Sunday which was the Solemnity of Our Lord Jesus Christ, King of the Universe. Instead, use the orations given for the Thirty-Fourth Week in Ordinary Time, which are found on the next page following the Thirty-Third Sunday in Ordinary Time.